Book 12

A Careers Advice Guide

Choosing and Applying for Higher Education Courses at UK Universities

- **Find out about universities, higher education colleges and specialist institutions in the UK**
- **Choose a higher education course which is right for you**
- **Find out about entry requirements and subject requirements for higher education courses**
- **Find out about 'A' level and equivalent subject requirements for undergraduate courses**
- **Find out about professional qualifications**
- **Apply for a higher education course**
- **Apply for higher education as an international student**
- **Apply for student accommodation**
- **Apply to take admissions tests for specified courses**
- **Find out about student funding**
- **Study abroad**

Janice Eglin

www.janiceeglincareers.co.uk

First edition 2019

ISBN: 9781793164896

Imprint: Independently published

Acknowledgements

I would like to thank everyone who provided support in the production of this book, including professional contacts, my husband Greg, daughters Sophia and Rhiannon, family and friends in providing professional support and advice.

A Careers Advice Guide: Series written by Janice Eglin
Career Options and Qualification Requirements in the UK: Choosing a career, working in the:

Book 1: Animals, Plants, Environment, Healthcare Science and Science Sectors
Agriculture and Horticulture
Animals
Environmental Science and Studies
Healthcare Science
Science

Book 2: Art, Media and Performing Arts: Dance, Drama and Music Sectors
Art and Design
Media: Advertising, Editing, Journalism, Marketing, Public Relations, Publishing and Writing
Media: Film, Radio, Television and Theatre
Dance, Drama, Music

Book 3: Building, Property, Engineering and Computer Technology Sectors
Architecture, Planning, Surveying and Construction
Property and Housing Management
Electrician; Gas Installation / Plumbing; Heating, Ventilation and Air Conditioning
Engineering; Computer Technology

Book 4: Business, Finance, Retail, Hospitality, Leisure, Sport and Tourism Sectors
Business Finance
Business Management and Administration
Retail
Hospitality and Events Management
Leisure Activities;
Leisure: Travel and Tourism

Book 5: Education: Teaching, Lecturing and Support Sectors
Primary and Secondary Teaching and Support
Further and Higher Education Teaching
Teaching English as a Foreign, Second / Other Language; Training and Tutoring

Book 6: Healthcare: Allied, Alternative, Complementary, Nursing and Medicine Sectors
Allied Health Professions
Alternative and Complementary Health
Chiropractic and Osteopathy
Nursing and Midwifery
Public, Environmental and Occupational Health;
Dentistry; Medicine; Pharmacy; Vision Science

Book 7: History, Library, Languages and Working Abroad Sectors
History, Anthropology and Archaeology
Information and Library
Languages
Work Abroad; Work for the European Union Institutions and Bodies; Work for the United Nations

Book 8: Law Enforcement: Armed Forces, Public Protection and Security Sectors
Armed Forces: British Army; Royal Air Force; Royal Navy
Law Enforcement: Public Protection
Law Enforcement: Security
National Security / Secret Service: GCHQ; MI5; MI6

Book 9: Law, Politics, Political Organisations and Social Science Sectors
Law, Politics and Social Sciences
Political Organisations: UK Parliament; Government Civil Service; and Local Government

Book 10: Psychology, Counselling, Religion and Social Care Sectors
Psychology, Counselling and Psychotherapy
Religion and Theology
Social Care

Book 11: Transport: Aviation, Marine, Rail, Road and Logistics Sectors
Logistics; Aviation Industry; Marine Industry; Rail Industry; Road Industry

Book 12: Choosing and Applying for Higher Education Courses at UK Universities

About the Author

Janice Eglin (BA, MA, DipCG, PGCert Teaching and Learning in HE) is a careers adviser with over 30 years' experience. She has provided careers advice and guidance for young people and adults considering career and education options as well as for people who want a change in career or to get back into employment. The majority of Janice's experience has been in the higher education sector providing careers advice to students, graduates and postgraduates, providing advice on undergraduate and postgraduate courses and lecturing on higher education courses. She has also worked in schools and colleges. Janice gained a BA hons in Sociology, an MA in Education, a Diploma in Careers Guidance as well as a Postgraduate Certificate in Teaching and Learning in Higher Education and a Careers Guidance Assessment qualification. Janice is currently a member of the Career Development Institute (CDI) and a previous member of the Association of Graduate Careers Advisory Services (AGCAS). After retiring, Janice wanted to share her careers knowledge to help people who are considering their career options or a change in career direction. Janice has written extensively on careers information for university students, graduates and postgraduates.

Information and Website Disclaimer

The information contained in this book is for general information purposes only. Regulations and policies may change quickly. The information is provided by the author, Janice Eglin, and whilst I have endeavoured to carefully check and keep the information up to date and correct, I make no representations or warranties of any kind, expressed or implied about the completeness, accuracy, reliability, suitability or availability with respect to websites listed or information contained in the book. Any reliance you place on such information is therefore strictly at your own risk.

I cannot accept responsibility for any errors or omissions. In no event will I be responsible for the content or reliability of websites or information listed in this book and will not be liable for any loss or damage including without limitation, indirect or consequential loss or damage in connection with the use of the websites and information. Through this book you are able to link on to other websites which are not under control of Janice Eglin. I have no control over the nature, content and availability of those websites and I do not recommend or endorse the views expressed within any websites or organisations listed.

I have endeavoured to keep the careers information in this book up to date and correct, however changes may occur and you are advised to confirm information with professional organisations.

Contents

Applying for Undergraduate Higher Education Courses at Universities in the UK

Chapter 6:
Higher Education Course Modes of Study, Teaching and Assessment   279

Chapter 7: Universities, Higher Education Colleges and Specialist Institutions   289

Chapter 8:
Applying For Higher Education Courses   353

Chapter 1:
Preparing for your Future

1.1 Introduction to Preparing for your Future

Preparing for your future and considering whether to study in higher education is a very important decision. You will need to think through your options very carefully and spend enough time researching and planning in order to make the right choice for you. Studying in higher education will give you the opportunity to gain new experiences and develop a range of valuable skills.

Higher education (HE) in the United Kingdom (UK) consists of academic courses at undergraduate level which include those up to degree level, as well as graduate entry courses, postgraduate courses. Some academic and professional courses at undergraduate and postgraduate level also lead to professional qualifications which are required for some professional careers. Higher education courses are available in universities; higher education colleges (some also combine further and higher education); and specialist institutions such as art schools, conservatoires that specialise in music, dance and drama courses, agriculture and horticulture colleges, theology or nautical colleges.

There are over 300 universities and colleges offering higher education in the United Kingdom (UK) spread across the four countries; England, Wales, Northern Ireland and Scotland. With so many higher education institutions and thousands of courses to choose from, this book aims to help you make informed decisions. You may still be considering which subject to study but if you have already decided on a course you will also need to spend time deciding the right type of course, the right university, college or specialist institution for you and where you want to live while you are studying.

Give yourself enough time to plan ahead in order to meet the deadlines for applications. To help you make

appropriate decisions, read information on the higher education institution (HEI) websites and talk to staff and students to find out more about the universities, colleges and specialist institutions at higher education fairs and open days.

You will also need to give yourself plenty of time to carry out your research, complete your application, write a personal statement, register and apply for admissions tests where required for some courses. In addition you will need to find out about financial aspects, including higher education costs and accommodation, as well as spending time completing forms to apply for finance support, grants or bursaries which may be available for some courses.

You may be a younger student studying in school or college or a mature student considering going back into study. However, if you aren't sure if higher education is right for you at this stage, you should consider all your options before making a decision. You may wish to gain further experience in the type of work you are interested in before entering higher education and decide to look for an internship or relevant work experience.

If you are undecided, you can apply for a higher education course and if you decide at a later date that you either want a gap year or you don't want to study in higher education at this stage, then you can decline any offers you are made. In some cases, universities may allow you to defer the course you have applied to for the following year to allow you to take a gap year. During your gap year you may choose to find work and / or travel, but you should check with individual institutions as you may need to put in a fresh application the following year.

Although the job market can be unpredictable, there may be more job options available for people with higher education qualifications. Salaries are also generally higher in a range of graduate and professional careers. However, employers will also be looking for people with the right skills and abilities, as well as the appropriate qualifications. Studying in higher education will also give you the opportunity to develop valuable skills and abilities, as well as learning more about a subject that you enjoy. You will also gain new friendships and have new experiences.

The cost of studying in higher education is also important to consider and you may want to enter work with the skills and qualifications you already have and to study for a higher education course part-time whilst working. However, if you decide that higher education isn't for you at this stage, there are other options. You may wish to apply for a job or an apprenticeship, which will provide training whilst working. With so many decisions to make, the content in this book will provide useful information which will help you make the right choice for you.

There are many positive reasons to study for an undergraduate or postgraduate course in higher education, as well as subject enjoyment, greater job opportunities and higher earning potential, studying will provide you with a range of valuable transferable skills. However, you may be weighing up the financial implications of higher education, especially if you are a mature student or have dependent children, although studying part-time or by distance learning may be another option. Check the chapters on modes of study and student finance.

Enjoyment and job opportunities

You may really enjoy studying for a particular subject from your current or previous studies and wish to continue to study this subject at a higher level, or you may wish to study for a related or new subject that you find interesting. Higher education provides the opportunity to study subjects in more detail and enable you to expand your knowledge at undergraduate or postgraduate level.

Although having a higher education qualification doesn't guarantee a job, graduates are more likely to have a wider range of career choice than non-graduates and are less likely to be unemployed. Graduates may have the competitive edge when applying for jobs that don't necessarily require a degree or other undergraduate qualification to enter. Senior positions are more likely to require people with a degree or postgraduate qualification. Graduates are not only employed by large organisations but may also work for small and medium sized employers (SMEs).

Some careers are graduate or postgraduate entry only and, without a degree and sometimes a postgraduate qualification, you won't be able to enter certain careers. Some careers require a specialist higher education subject and some require you to have a higher education qualification that includes a professional qualification, or you may need a higher education qualification before you can study for a professional qualification.

Graduates with a 'vocational' subject may find a 'graduate' job more quickly after graduation as you may have a clearer idea of what career you want to do. It may be the case that you don't have a definite career in mind when you start your higher education course and there are many 'graduate' jobs that accept any discipline, or you may find that you need to specialise in a different graduate or postgraduate subject.

For some competitive graduate jobs, employers also take into consideration 'A' level subjects and grades / equivalent qualifications or the Universities and Colleges Admission Service (UCAS) Tariff points. Further information about UCAS Tariff points may be found at UCAS https://www.ucas.com/ucas/ucas-Tariff-points

Many higher education courses aren't professionally accredited but for some career subjects, employers may require you to undertake a specialist subject such as art, drama, dance, music, sport, history or languages. A postgraduate qualification may also be useful for some job roles providing you with more career opportunities or if you decide to specialise further.

Many graduate careers will accept graduates in any discipline although additional professional qualifications may be required whilst you are in relevant work such as accountancy and finance or human resources. It may also be possible to work in a specialist area such as accounting and finance without a higher education qualification and gain the professional qualifications whilst in work, although for more senior job roles most people will be required to have an honours degree and often a postgraduate qualification.

Some undergraduate courses also lead to a master's level qualification, providing a professional qualification, such as medicine, dentistry or pharmacy courses. Other subjects, such as some engineering courses may also be offered as integrated master's degrees, allowing you to graduate with a master's qualification as well as a bachelor's honours degree.

In some cases, it may be a requirement to achieve Chartered status, such as for some engineering or psychology job roles, or having chartered status for other professions may provide more job opportunities. To obtain Chartered status you would need to register with a relevant professional body and have accredited qualifications of a certain level as well as meeting the work experience requirements.

Postgraduate study
If you decide to undertake postgraduate study, you will need to be very interested in the subject and need to remain motivated. Studying for a postgraduate qualification will provide you with intellectual reward and may allow you to pursue an area of interest that you have developed during your previous studies or your career.

A postgraduate course may give you the opportunity to develop more specialist knowledge and expertise and you may also want to study a subject that you enjoy to a higher level. Having a postgraduate qualification may also provide you with greater career opportunities, especially in a competitive job market and some professional careers will require you to have a postgraduate qualification. Some accredited undergraduate and postgraduate courses may also provide some exemptions for professional qualifications. For many senior job roles in any career subject, having a postgraduate qualification may be a requirement.

For some careers, if your honours degree is in another subject you will need a graduate or postgraduate 'conversion' course before you can continue to study for professional postgraduate

qualifications, such as law or psychology. Some professional careers such as nursing, some allied health subjects, social work, surveying or engineering require you to have the option of gaining either a professionally accredited honours degree or a professionally accredited postgraduate qualification, if your honours degree is in another subject.

For some subjects, there may be fewer professional honours degree courses compared with professional postgraduate courses, such as town planning, teacher training or librarianship courses, therefore many people working in these fields will have a postgraduate qualification. A professionally accredited undergraduate and postgraduate qualification may be essential for some professional level careers, including architecture, medicine, dentistry, pharmacy, engineering, law (solicitor or barrister), some science specialisms or psychology specialisms.

If you want an academic career teaching in higher education, a master's degree and a doctorate degree is essential. Many job roles that involve research will usually require you to have a master's degree and usually a doctorate degree such as science, technology or engineering research, whereas social policy or research job roles often require a minimum of a master's degree. A master's degree will also give you the chance to prepare for PhD research although if you choose to study for a postgraduate research degree, this will be a big commitment therefore you will need to be highly motivated and interested in your chosen subject.

Changing your career direction
You may need to undertake a graduate or postgraduate qualification to progress in your chosen career, change your career or you may wish to specialise and study for a subject that interests you.

If your first degree is in a different subject to the one you want to specialise in, a postgraduate qualification may also give you the opportunity to change your career direction.

A graduate or postgraduate course may be a professional requirement if you want to convert to a different career. Graduate or postgraduate level conversion courses are available for some professions if your honours degree is in another subject and where you need an accredited honours degree before you can continue to study for additional professional qualifications such as law or psychology.

Graduate level or postgraduate qualifications are also available for some professions if your honours degree is in another subject and you need an accredited higher education and professional qualification such as medicine, dentistry, nursing, social work or an allied health profession. For engineering specialisms, if your honours degree is in a non-accredited related subject, it may be possible to undertake an accredited master's degree.

Before you make a decision, you should research your options carefully and check out job profiles on the relevant careers websites. Check on the qualifications and training required for the career you are interested in by looking at professional body websites and if you will need a professionally accredited higher education qualification. It is also helpful to check vacancy details to find out the qualifications required. Attending postgraduate fairs, higher education open days and careers events are also useful to discuss what type of course you want to study.

Skills gained in postgraduate study
With a competitive job market, a postgraduate qualification may provide you with the competitive edge when making job applications and attending interviews. You may also be better placed for future job promotion. Employers may value the enhanced skills you have gained through postgraduate study as the additional qualification you have acquired will prove you have the determination, tenacity and ability to develop high level knowledge.

The combination of taught modules, course work and research projects or dissertations will help you improve your organisation and time management, with the ability to meet deadlines. You will also further develop your transferable skills in communication, project management, data analysis, IT, independent thinking, self-discipline, self-motivation, analytical skills, critical thinking and problem solving.

Time commitments
Many undergraduate and postgraduate courses are available to study part-time or distance learning, although some specific higher education qualifications are only available to study on a full time basis, therefore for many courses this provides you with the opportunity to decide what mode of study would better suit you.

You may want to study for a shorter period of time therefore a full-time course would be most suitable. Some professional careers involve studying for professional qualifications over a longer time period, with some requiring you to be in relevant work therefore it may be more practical to study for previous undergraduate or postgraduate qualifications full-time giving you a quicker route to fully qualify. If finance is an issue or if you have personal commitments, you may wish to study part time, whilst working.

Earning potential and graduate salaries
Earning levels for graduates in a life-time are likely to be considerably higher on average than for most non-graduates. Graduate salaries may also differ depending on which degree subject is studied as well as varying according to the type of industry and the geographical location of where you work.

The Higher Education Statistics Agency (HESA) https://www.hesa.ac.uk/ is the official agency for the collection, analysis and dissemination of statistics about higher education. HESA publishes useful data, which includes the percentages of graduates and postgraduates entering employment by work sector as well as graduate salaries.

The publication produced by Prospects (the graduate careers website) https://www.prospects.ac.uk/ and the Association of Graduate Careers Advisory Service (AGCAS) https://www.agcas.org.uk/ on behalf of the Higher Education Careers Service Unit (HECSU) 'What do graduates do?' https://www.hecsu.ac.uk/current_projects_what_do_graduates_do.htm examined first degree graduate destinations six months after graduation and showed the average annual graduate salary after six months stood at £22,399 (2018).

The Office of National Statistics (ONS) lists the top ten highest paying UK jobs as the following however there will be variation in salaries. Further information may be found at ONS: Average Weekly Earnings https://www.ons.gov.uk/employmentandlabourmarket/peopleinwork/employmentandemployeetypes/bulletins/uklabourmarket/latest#average-weekly-earnings

Financial Brokers
Chief Executive Officers (CEOs)
Marketing Directors
Aircraft Pilots
Financial Managers and Directors
In-house Lawyers
Air Traffic Controllers
Medical Practitioners
IT and Telecommunications Directors
Financial Institution Managers and Directors

National minimum wage, national living wage, graduate wage and apprenticeship wage

National minimum wage and national living wage
The national minimum wage and national living wage is set by the UK government and is usually updated every April. Further information may be found at:
UK Government:
National Minimum Wage Rates
https://www.gov.uk/national-minimum-wage-rates

National minimum wage and national living wage rates from April 2018

Apprentice:	= £3.70 per hour
Aged under 18 years:	= £4.20 per hour
Aged 18-20 years:	= £5.90 per hour
Aged 21-24 years:	= £7.38 per hour
Aged 25 and over is:	= £7.83

National minimum wage and national living wage rates from April 2019

Apprentice:	= £3.90 per hour
Aged under 18 years:	= £4.35 per hour
Aged 18-20 years:	= £6.15 per hour
Aged 21-24 years:	= £7.70 per hour
Aged 25 and over is:	= £8.21

Apprenticeships wage rate
Apprentices are entitled to the apprentice rate if aged below 19 years of age; or aged over 19 years in the first year of their apprenticeship.

Apprentices are entitled to the minimum wage for their age if they are aged 19 years or over or have completed the first year of their apprenticeship. Apprenticeships wage rate further information may be found at:
UK Government: apprenticeships https://www.gov.uk/apprenticeships-guide/pay-and-conditions

Living wage
The 'living wage' is promoted by the Living Wage Foundation http://www.livingwage.org.uk/ and is based on the amount an individual needs to earn to cover the basic costs of living. Although it has received widespread political support, it has had limited endorsement by employers.

The minimum wage and national living wage is a legal requirement, whereas the living wage is optional. If you don't think you are being paid the minimum wage, there is a government help line to contact on the following web site: UK government: pay and work rights helpline https://www.gov.uk/pay-and-work-rights-helpline

Salary ranges for graduate careers
The following websites provide information on the range of salaries for the different job roles:

- Central Careers Hub: Longtiudinal Education Outcomes Data https://www.centralcareershub.co.uk/longitudinal-education-outcomes-data/
- Glass Door: Salaries https://www.glassdoor.co.uk/Salaries/
- Prospects: Graduate Careers: Job Profileshttps://www.prospects.ac.uk/
- Target Jobs: Choosing an Employer https://targetjobs.co.uk/careers-advice/choosing-an-employer
- UK Government: Graduate Employment and Earnings https://www.gov.uk/government/collections/statistics-higher-education-graduate-employment-and-earnings
- UK Government: Office for National Statistics https://www.ons.gov.uk/employmentandlabourmarket/peopleinwork/earningsandworkinghours
- Unistats https://unistats.ac.uk/
- Which? University https://university.which.co.uk/courses

Transferable skills
Studying in higher education will enable you to gain valuable transferable skills which are those qualities and competencies that employers seek in addition to academic knowledge which will benefit you in your future employment. These skills enable you to learn for yourself throughout life, communicate effectively, negotiate with others, solve problems, work with others in a team, assess risks and take decisions, reflect and plan on your own development; as well as presenting your strengths to potential employers when applying for jobs.

Some professional or vocational higher education courses will provide you with essential skills needed to work in a particular job role. However, all higher education courses will provide you with the opportunity to gain transferable skills valued by all employers and the most required skills include:

Communication skills
Good interpersonal skills
Listening and empathy skills
Negotiation and logical persuasion skills
Speaking confidently to individuals and groups skills
Visual presentation / public speaking skills
Written communication skills

Working with others skills
Assertiveness skills
Counselling skills
Influencing and making a good impact on others skills
Leadership and instruction skills
Managing people skills
Teamwork skills: establishing effective working relationships with others; having the ability to appreciate the skills and needs of others; understanding the dynamics of the team

Information technology skills
Administration skills
Computer skills
Microsoft packages skills
Typing ability skills
Programming ability skills (if relevant)

Planning skills
Ability to take appropriate action skills
Flexible approach skills
Good time management skills
Motivation skills
Organisation skills
Working to deadlines skills

Problem solving skills
Adaptability skills
Analytical skills
Conceptual skills
Critical thinking skills
Independence skills
Initiative skills
Research skills

Career Planning

When considering what type of job you might be interested in or if you are considering a career change, you will need to explore and research the options and opportunities available to you. Career planning can take place at any time whilst as a student, school or college leaver, new graduate, if wanting to move into a new area of expertise, as an experienced professional looking for a change of direction or as a returner to the workforce.

You will need to research what qualifications will be required as a number of jobs will require vocational, professional or academic qualifications which may need to be undertaken before making job applications although some jobs will enable you to train and gain qualifications whilst working. Qualifications may be run as courses provided by training centres, further or higher education colleges, specialist institutions or universities, and may be studied part time, full time or by distance learning. Give some thought as to how long you want to study for, as some professional jobs will require an undergraduate course, with some also requiring a postgraduate qualification. Some people may choose to study for an honours degree and move straight into postgraduate study, whereas others may decide to have a break in between.

You need to consider what you are looking for in a job. Everyone is different and will have different ideas as to what satisfaction they will gain from a job. Consider what is important to you, what you like doing, enjoy and what interests you have. This will help you to identify your skills and personal qualities when considering what career you may be interested in. Specific skills, qualities and attributes are referred to in a job description or person specification when a job is advertised.

Consider the career options you are interested in and check out vacancies for the type of work that interest you. Completing the career questionnaire in

this book should help you to determine the skills that you already possess, those you may need to develop, what interests you have and match these with the type/s of work you are interested in. Work experience in your chosen career is helpful to gain experience and to find out more about training opportunities.

It is a good idea to draw up a personal pan or action plan of how you will achieve your chosen job, setting realistic objectives to help you get there. There may be a number of actions you need to take to reach your end goal, so set yourself realistic timescales to achieve your aim. It is also important to prepare for job changes, especially in times of recession, so building your skills and gaining as much experience as possible will help for the future.

When you are in work it is useful to undertake regular professional development and keep a record to add to your CV. The skills and knowledge that you gain will need to be updated and developed over time. Having the skills that will be required in other jobs will show any future prospective employers that you have a commitment to update your professionalism and allows for 'A' level of job security should your current role end. Planning your career should be an ongoing process, helping you with career progression and shaping your professional development requirements.

If you are unsure what job you would like to do or what education and training your will need, it is always helpful to discuss your career plans with and experienced and qualified careers adviser.

However there are official careers websites as well as many other careers websites and professional organisation websites that provide useful careers information on careers and jobs; apprenticeships; courses; information on writing CVs, job applications, covering

letters and interview advice, as well as relevant links to other sources.
University websites will also provide information about making applications for courses, what to write in a personal statement and how to impress at an interview (if required), as well as careers information. Check the university websites in the links to universities section.

Applications for full time undergraduate and some postgraduate courses in the UK are usually made through the University and College Admissions Service (UCAS) https://www.ucas.com/ . Applications for undergraduate courses in Ireland are usually made through the Central Applications Office (CAO) in Ireland https://www.cao.ie/ . Further information may be found at:

Chapter 8
Applying for Higher Education Courses

Professional bodies for specific professions also often provide careers information, as well identifying accredited or recommended professional qualifications you may need.

You may find the information you want on the websites but it may also be useful to speak to a careers adviser to help you explore your options further.

Further information on undergraduate and postgraduate courses may be found at:

Chapter 5.1
Choosing a Higher Education Subject
Choosing a Higher Education Course
Choosing a University, College of Higher Education or Specialist Institution

Chapter 5.4
Professional Organisations: Accredited Undergraduate and Postgraduate Courses

Chapter 7
Universities, Higher Education Colleges and Specialist Institutions

General Careers Information and Vacancy Sources

National careers websites in the UK and Ireland

England National Careers Service — https://nationalcareersservice.direct.gov.uk/

Wales Careers Wales — http://www.careerswales.com/en/

Northern Ireland
Northern Ireland Direct Careers — https://www.nidirect.gov.uk/campaigns/careers

Ireland Careers Portal — https://careersportal.ie/

Scotland Skills Development Scotland:
Careers — https://www.skillsdevelopmentscotland.co.uk/
Scotland Skills Development Scotland:
My World of Work — https://www.myworldofwork.co.uk/

Graduate careers

Graduate Prospects: graduate careers website http://www.prospects.ac.uk

Apprenticeships websites

Apprenticeships: England
UK Government:
Find Apprenticeships: https://www.findapprenticeship.service.gov.uk/apprenticeshipsearch
UK Government: Find a Traineeship — https://www.gov.uk/find-traineeship

Apprenticeships: Wales
Careers Wales Apprenticeships — https://ams.careerswales.com

Apprenticeships: Northern Ireland
NI Direct: Apprenticeship — http://www.nidirect.gov.uk/apprenticeshipsni

Apprenticeships: Scotland
Apprenticeships in Scotland — http://www.apprenticeshipsinscotland.com/

Additional websites with apprenticeship information
Babcock — http://www.babcock.co.uk
EEF the Manufacturers Organisation — http://www.apprentices.co.uk/
Fish4Jobs — http://www.fish4.co.uk/Jobs/apprenticeships/
Learn Direct — http://www.learndirect.com/
The Apprenticeship Guide — http://www.apprenticeshipguide.co.uk/about/

Additional general careers websites

Active Informatics — https://www.activeinformatics.com/
Adviza — http://www.adviza.org.uk/
Big Dog — http://www.bigdog.co.uk
Careers Box — http://www.careersbox.co.uk
Career Camel — http://www.careercamel.com/
Career Kickstart: Royal Bank of Scotland:
General Life and Skills Information — https://www.careerkickstart.rbs.com/
Career Player — http://www.careerplayer.com/
Career Pilot — http://www.careerpilot.org.uk/
Careers Gateway — http://www.careers-gateway.co.uk/
Careers World — http://www.careersworld.co.uk
City and Guilds:
Career Ideas — https://www.cityandguilds.com/what-we-offer/learners/career-ideas
I could: Career videos; Job information; Apprenticeships;
Resources; Parents' information — http://icould.com/
Input Youth — http://www.inputyouth.co.uk/index.php
Learn Direct — http://www.learndirect.com
Not going to Uni — http://www.notgoingtouni.co.uk
Parent Adviser — http://www.parentadviser.co.uk/
Success at School — https://successatschool.org/
Total Professions — http://www.totalprofessions.com

Business, mentoring and work experience support websites

London Ambitions — https://londonambitionsportal.london.gov.uk/
Inspiring the Future — https://www.inspiringthefuture.org/
Founders for Schools — https://www.founders4schools.org.uk/
Mencap: work placements
https://www.mencap.org.uk/about-us/our-projects/right-place-work-placements-send-learners

Careers education and guidance websites

Careers and Enterprise Company in partnership with the GATSBY foundation:
COMPASS careers benchmark tool: a self-evaluation tool for all secondary schools and 6th forms in England
Careers and Enterprise Company
https://www.careersandenterprise.co.uk/news/new-careers-guidance-tool
GATSBY charitable foundation: science and engineering http://www.gatsby.org.uk/
Cegnet — http://www.cegnet.co.uk/
Central Careers Hub — http://www.centralcareershub.co.uk/
Education Association — https://www.pshe-association.org.uk/
Guidance (CEIAG) award primarily for England   http://www.qualityincareers.org.uk/
How 2 Become — https://www.how2become.com/about-us/
JCA Global — https://www.jcaglobal.com/
National Careers Education Information Advice and
Personal, Social, Health and Economic (PSHE)
PLOTR incorporated in start.profile.com — https://www.startprofile.com/
PLOTR: Careers resources for teachers and advisers https://www.plotr.co.uk/educator-zone/
PLOTR: careers website for 12-24 year olds — https://www.plotr.co.uk/
Quality in Careers Standard (QiCS):
Scotland's Enterprising Schools — http://enterprisingschools.scot/

Careers information which charge a license fee websites (usually available in schools, colleges and Universities

Job Explorer Database (JED) http://www.careersoft.co.uk/Products/Job_Explorer_Database/
Cascaid: Kudos and Adult Directions   https://www.cascaid.co.uk/
Cascaid: Launchpad   https://launchpad.cascaid.co.uk/

Health careers
NHS Health Careers   https://www.healthcareers.nhs.uk/

School and college leavers' careers and job information websites
All About Careers   http://www.allaboutcareers.com/
All About School Leavers   http://www.allaboutschoolleavers.co.uk/
Fast Tomato   https://www.fasttomato.com/
MeTycoon   http://playgen.com/play/me-tycoon/
My Career Springboard   http://www.mycareerspringboard.org/
PlanITPlus   https://www.planitplus.net/
Rate my Apprenticeship   https://www.ratemyapprenticeship.co.uk/
School leavers: Milkround   http://schoolleavers.milkround.com/jobs/
Talking Jobs   http://www.talkingjobs.net/
The Big Choice   http://www.thebigchoice.com/
UCAS 16-18 choices   https://www.ucas.com/ucas/after-gcses
UCAS: Career Ideas   https://www.ucas.com/ucas/16-18-choices/find-career-ideas
Up to Work   https://uptowork.com/

Students with disabilities websites
Ability Housing Association   http://www.ability-housing.co.uk/
Disability Rights UK
http://www.disabilityrightsuk.org/how-we-can-help/helplines/disabled-students-helpline
Equality Advisory and Support Services   http://www.equalityadvisoryservice.com/

Teaching young people about money websites
Personal Finance Education Group   https://www.pfeg.org/

University information websites
Applications for undergraduate and some postgraduate courses in the UK
Universities and Colleges Admissions Service (UCAS)   https://www.ucas.com/

Applications for undergraduate courses in Ireland
Central Applications Office (CAO) in Ireland   https://www.cao.ie/

University careers websites
Most university and college websites have a dedicated section on careers. Check Section: Universities, Colleges of Higher Education and Specialist Institutions for website links. The following are a selection.
Cambridge University Careers Information   http://www.careers.cam.ac.uk/
Oxford University Careers Information   https://www.careers.ox.ac.uk/
The Russell Group:
Informed Choices HE Advice   http://www.russellgroup.ac.uk/informed-choices/
University of Edinburgh Careers Information   http://www.ed.ac.uk/careers
University of Kent Careers Information   https://www.kent.ac.uk/careers/

Higher education websites

There are many websites with information about higher education including:

Access to HE	http://www.accesshe.ac.uk/
Apply to Uni	http://www.applytouni.com/
Bright Knowledge	https://www.brightknowledge.org/
HE in London	https://www.heinlondon.ac.uk/
Open Days: University and College Directory	http://www.opendays.com/
Pure Potential	http://purepotential.org/
Push: Independent Guide to HE	http://www.push.co.uk/
Quality Assurance Agency (QAA)	http://www.qaa.ac.uk/en
Rate my Placement	https://www.ratemyplacement.co.uk/
Studential	http://www.studential.com/
The Complete University Guide	http://www.thecompleteuniversityguide.co.uk/
The Student Room	http://www.thestudentroom.co.uk/
Top Universities	http://www.topuniversities.com/
Unistats	https://unistats.ac.uk/
Which University Guide	http://university.which.co.uk

Recruitment agencies: general job search websites

Agency Central	https://www.agencycentral.co.uk/
All Jobs in the UK	http://alljobsintheuk.co.uk/
Adzuna	https://www.adzuna.co.uk/
Badenoch and Clark	https://www.badenochandclark.com/
Capita	http://www.capita.com/careers/
Career Builder	http://www.careerbuilder.co.uk/
Career Jet	http://www.careerjet.co.uk/
Change Work Now	http://www.changeworknow.co.uk/partners/
City Jobs	http://www.cityjobs.com/
Fish 4	http://www.fish4.co.uk/
Gumtree	http://www.gumtree.com/
Indeed	http://www.indeed.co.uk/
Inside Careers	http://www.insidecareers.co.uk/
Jobs go public	http://www.jobsgopublic.com/
Jobs Word	http://www.jobsword.co.uk/
Jobserve	http://www.jobserve.com/gb/en/Job-Search/
Jobsite	http://www.jobsite.co.uk/
Local Recruit	http://www.localrecruit.co.uk/Jobs-by-industry/
Monster	http://www.monster.co.uk/
My Job Search	http://www.myjobsearch.com/
Red Goldfish	http://www.redgoldfish.co.uk/
Reed	http://www.reed.co.uk/
Tip Top Job	http://www.tiptopjob.com/
Total Jobs	http://www.totaljobs.com/
Trovit	https://jobs.trovit.co.uk/
UK Government Universal Job Match Information	https://www.gov.uk/jobsearch
UK Government Universal Job Match Vacancies	https://jobsearch.direct.gov.uk/
Wiki Job	https://www.wikijob.co.uk/
Work Circle	http://www.workcircle.com/
WSP Group	http://www.wspgroup.com/

Links to recruitment agencies
Recruitment and Employment Confederation   https://www.rec.uk.com/
The Recruitment and Employment Confederation (REC) is the professional body for the recruitment industry. You can search on the member's list for recruitment consultancies that specialise in particular job sectors if you know what type of work you want and the region where you wish to travel to. Go to membership and members' directory; search with a job title for a list of relevant recruitment agencies
CV Library   http://www.cv-library.co.uk/
The CV Library has links to recruitment agencies by sector and region.

Movement to work scheme
Movement to Work Scheme (for young people) http://www.movementtowork.com/

Companies in the UK: links to employing organisations
Best Companies Guide   http://bestcompaniesguide.co.uk/
First Directory: Links to sector businesses   https://1stdirectory.co.uk/
Glass Door Best Places to Work
http://www.glassdoor.co.uk/Best-Places-to-Work-UK-LST_KQ0,22.htm
GTI published in partnership with Guardian News and Media:
Kompass: Global Business Database   http://gb.kompass.com/
Milkround   https://www.milkround.com/

Top employers in the UK
Guardian Top Employers   http://www.theguardian.com/careers/top-employers-uk
Times Top 100 graduate employers   http://www.top100graduateemployers.com/
(Should be available free in universities and colleges)
The Sunday Times:
Best 100 Companies   http://features.thesundaytimes.co.uk/public/best100companies/
Top 300 Graduate Employers
in the UK   http://gtimedia.co.uk/work/products/guardian-uk-300
Top Employers Publishing   http://topemployers.co.uk/

Companies in the world: links to employing organisations
Forbes: The World's Biggest Public Companies   http://www.forbes.com/global2000/list/
Statista: The Largest Companies in the World by Revenue
http://www.statista.com/statistics/263265/top-companies-in-the-world-by-revenue/
The Telegraph: The World's Biggest Public Companies
http://www.telegraph.co.uk/finance/globalbusiness/10002790/The-worlds-biggest-companies.html
Top Employers Institute   http://www.top-employers.com/Certified-Top-Employers/

National newspaper job vacancy sources
Financial Times Jobs   http://www.newsnow.co.uk/classifieds/Jobs/financial-times-Jobs.html
Independent: iJobs   http://iJobs.independent.co.uk/
Independent:
Career Planning   http://www.independent.co.uk/student/career-planning/getting-job/
Sunday Times Appointments   http://appointments.thesundaytimes.co.uk/
The Economist   http://jobs.economist.com/
The Guardian Careers Information   http://Jobs.theguardian.com/careers/
The Guardian: Jobs   http://Jobs.theguardian.com/
The Telegraph: Jobs   http://www.telegraph.co.uk/finance/Jobs/
Times Educational Supplement   https://www.tes.co.uk/Jobs/
Times Higher Education Jobs   http://Jobs.timeshighereducation.co.uk/
London
Evening Standard Jobs   https://www.standard.co.uk/topic/jobs

British library industry guides: information and business directories
British Library: Business and
IP Centre Industry Guides   http://www.bl.uk/bipc/dbandpubs/industry-guides/industry.html

Networking online organisations
Facebook   https://www.facebook.com/login
Hiive: Creative Network for Professional People   https://app.hiive.co.uk/
Linkedin: Professional network   https://uk.linkedin.com
Twitter   https://twitter.com/

Volunteering
Volunteering UK
England
Volunteering England part of NVCO   http://www.volunteering.org.uk
National Council for Voluntary Youth Services http://www.ncvys.org.uk
Wales
Volunteer Wales   http://www.volunteering-wales.net
Wales Council for Voluntary Action   http://www.wcva.org.uk
Northern Ireland
Volunteer Now Northern Ireland   http://www.volunteernow.co.uk
Northern Ireland Council for Voluntary Action   http://www.nicva.org
Scotland
Volunteer Scotland   http://www.volunteerscotland.net
Scottish Council for Volunteer Organisations   http://www.scvo.org.uk
Project Scotland   http://www.projectscotland.co.uk/

Volunteering UK general websites
Association of Chief Executives of
Voluntary Organisations   https://www.acevo.org.uk/about-us
Charity Choice: Database of Charities in England and Wales http://www.charitychoice.co.uk/
Charity Choice: Volunteering   http://www.charitychoice.co.uk/volunteering
Charity Job   http://www.charityjob.co.uk/
Community Service Volunteers   http://www.csv.org.uk/
Do It: Volunteering Opportunities   https://Do-It.Org
Guide Star UK: database of charities in England and Wales http://www.guidestar.org.uk/
National Council for Voluntary Organisations NVCO http://www.ncvo.org.uk
Project Scotland   http://www.projectscotland.co.uk/
Reach Skilled Volunteers   http://www.reachskills.org.uk
St John Ambulance   http://www.sja.org.uk/
The Conservation Volunteers   http://www.tcv.org.uk/
Third Sector: http://www.thirdsector.co.uk/
Timebank UK: voluntary and not-for-profit sector http://timebank.org.uk/
Vinspired   https://vinspired.com/
Voluntary Sector Jobs   http://voluntarysectorJobs.co.uk/
Volunteering Matters   http://volunteeringmatters.org.uk/
Youthnet   http://www.youthnet.org/

Volunteering overseas

Gap Medics	http://www.gapmedics.co.uk/
Global Vision International GVI	http://www.gvi.co.uk/
Go Abroad	http://www.goabroad.com/volunteer-abroad
Kaya Volunteer	http://www.kayavolunteer.com/
Latitude Global Volunteering	https://lattitude.org.uk/
One World: International NGO	http://www.oneworld.net/
Pod Volunteer	https://www.podvolunteer.org/
Raleigh International	http://www.raleighinternational.org/
Voluntary Service Overseas	http://www.vso.org.uk
Voluntary Service Overseas	http://www.vso.org.uk/
Volunteering Australia	http://www.volunteeringaustralia.org/
World-wide volunteering	http://www.wwv.org.uk
Youth Action	http://www.youthactionnet.org/

Graduate jobs, graduate training schemes, internships websites and recruitment agencies

Adopt an Intern	http://www.adoptanintern.org.uk
Bright Network	https://www.brightnetwork.co.uk/
Career player Graduate Jobs	http://www.careerplayer.com
E4S	http://www.e4s.co.uk/
Employment 4 Students	http://www.e4s.co.uk/
Fish4Jobs	http://www.fish4.co.uk/graduate/
Grad Cornwall: Graduate Jobs in Cornwall	http://www.gradcornwall.co.uk/
Grad Plus	http://www.gradplus.com/

Grads South West: Graduate Jobs in the South West http://www.gradsouthwest.com/

Graduate Jobs	http://www.graduate-jobs.com/
Graduate Opportunities Wales (GO Wales)	http://www.gowales.co.uk
Graduate Recruitment Bureau	http://www.grb.uk.com/
Graduate Talent Pool: Graduate internships	http://graduatetalentpool.direct.gov.uk

Graduate Talent Pool is run by the government department for Innovation and Business. It is designed to help new and recent graduates match with internship opportunities and gain relevant work experience.

GTI Media	http://gtimedia.co.uk/
Hays Salary Guide	http://salaryguide.hays.co.uk/
Hays: Recruiting Experts Worldwide	http://www.hays.co.uk/

Inside Careers Specialists in Graduate Careers http://www.insidecareers.co.uk

Intern Jobs	http://www.internjobs.com

Jobs.ac.uk: Academic Jobs; Education, Research and Administrative http://www.Jobs.ac.uk/

Milkround: Student and Graduate Job Website https://www.milkround.com

Morgan Hunt: Recruitment Services in the Public,

Not for Profit and Commercial Sectors	http://www.morganhunt.com
Prospects: Graduate Jobs	https://www.prospects.ac.uk/graduate-Jobs

Prospects: Graduate Jobs:
Alphabetical list of graduate employers http://www.prospects.ac.uk/graduate_employers.htm

Rate my Placement	http://www.ratemyplacement.co.uk/internships

Save the Student:
Graduate Training Schemes and Money Information http://www.savethestudent.org/

Step Enterprise:
Student and Graduate Placements and Internships http://www.step.org.uk/

Student Job	https://www.studentjob.co.uk/internship
Target Jobs Series	https://targetjobs.co.uk/
Target Jobs Internships	https://targetjobs.co.uk/internships

Target publishes graduate Jobs, schemes and training opportunities. Target also publishes careers publications which are available in university careers departments as well as online.

The Big Choice	http://www.thebigchoice.com/
UK Jobs Net	http://www.ukjobsnet.com/graduate-jobs
United Nations Careers: Internships	https://careers.un.org/
Work and Volunteer	http://www.workandvolunteer.com/internships

Assessment centres

Psychometric tests information and practice

British Psychological Society:
Information about Psychometric Testing   http://www.psychtesting.org.uk/

Practice online psychometric tests:

Assessmentday	http://www.assessmentday.co.uk/
Cubiksonline	http://www.cubiksonline.com/cubiks/practicetests/
Jobtestprep	http://www.jobtestprep.co.uk/
Morrisby	http://www.morrisby.com/Practice-Questions
Psychometricinstitute	http://www.psychometricinstitute.co.uk/

Psychtesting
http://www.psychtesting.org.uk/directories/companies-that-offer-practice-tests.cfm

SHLdirect   http://www.shldirect.com/en

Research council websites

| Research Councils UK | http://www.rcuk.ac.uk/ |
| UK Research and Innovation | https://www.ukri.org/ |

Arts and Humanities Research Council (AHRC) http://www.ahrc.ac.uk
Arts and Humanities Research Council (AHRC):
Funding   http://www.ahrc.ac.uk/Funding-Opportunities/
Biotechnology and Biological science Research Council (BBSRC) http://www.bbsrc.ac.uk/
Biotechnology and Biological science Research Council (BBSRC):
Funding   http://www.bbsrc.ac.uk/funding/funding-index.aspx
Economic and Social Research Council (ESRC) http://www.esrc.ac.uk
Economic and Social Research Council (ESRC):
Funding   http://www.esrc.ac.uk/funding-and-guidance/
Engineering and Physical Sciences Research Council (EPSRC) http://www.epsrc.ac.uk
Engineering and Physical Sciences Research Council (EPSRC):
Funding   http://www.epsrc.ac.uk/funding/
Medical Research Council (MRC)   http://www.mrc.ac.uk
Medical Research Council (MRC): Funding   http://www.mrc.ac.uk/funding/
National Environment Research Council (NERC) http://www.nerc.ac.uk
National Environment Research Council (NERC): Funding http://www.nerc.ac.uk/funding/
NERC Careers   http://www.nerc.ac.uk/skills/careers
Research Centres Supported by NERC
- British Antarctic Survey   http://www.antarctica.ac.uk
- British Geological Survey   http://www.bgs.ac.uk
- Centre for Ecology and Hydrology   http://www.ceh.ac.uk
- National Centre for Atmospheric Science https://www.ncas.ac.uk
- National Centre for Earth Observation http://www.nceo.ac.uk
- National Oceanography Centre   http://noc.ac.uk

Science and Technology Facilities Council (STFC) http://www.stfc.ac.uk/
Science and Technology Facilities Council (STFC): Funding http://www.stfc.ac.uk/funding

Research councils' jobs vacancy sources

Jobs.ac.uk:
Academic Jobs; Research Councils   http://www.jobs.ac.uk/employers/research-councils
Jobs, training vacancies, apprenticeships and careers information may also be found on the relevant professional bodies and organisations websites.

Careers Activity 1: Choosing Which Higher Education Courses and Higher Education Institutions to Apply For

When making your choice about which higher education courses and higher education institutions to apply to, it may be helpful to undertake personal planning which is a process that helps you to understand more about your abilities and preferences. Highlight:

- What skills you have
- What skills you need to develop
- What motivates you
- What you want from study
- What you want from your career
- What you need to do to achieve your goals and aims

Using the SMART acronym:
Specific:
Is your goal well-defined, clear and precise?

Measurable:
Be clear on how you will meet your achieved objectives

Attainable:
Make sure your goals are realistic

Relevant:
Get an overview of the different areas in your life such as academic, personal and career, considering how relevant your objective is to the overall picture

Time-bound:
Set a realistic time-scale to complete each goal, reviewing as you progress.

Consider the following questions and check out the relevant chapters in this book to find out more information.

1.   If you know what career you are interested in, what qualifications do you need and do you need to undertake relevant work experience?
Go to:
Chapter 5.2
Undergraduate Courses and University Entry Requirements

Chapter 5.4
Professional Organisations: Accredited Undergraduate and Postgraduate Courses

2.   What higher education institutions (HEIs) offer the course/s you want to study?
Go to:
Chapter 1.3
Careers Advice and Useful Websites
Chapter 5.1
Choosing a higher education subject
Choosing a university, college of higher education or specialist institution
Chapter 7.1
Types and Groups of Universities, Colleges of Higher Education and Specialist Institutions

3.   What are the entry requirements for your chosen course/s?
Go to:
Chapter 5:
Higher Education Qualification Subjects and Courses   137

4.   What type of higher education institution you want to study at?
Are you considering applying to an older traditional university, which may be a collegiate university; a new university; or a specialist institution offering specialist subjects such as a conservatoire or art college?

Universities, colleges and specialist institutions are all unique and offer different student experiences so it is difficult to generalise. However, 'old traditional' universities may be more competitive to apply to as they are considered 'prestigious', offering traditional academic courses, hence entry requirement grades or UCAS Tariff points are likely to be high. Some of these university buildings are older, being steeped in history.

Some older universities are Collegiate, composed of various colleges which are all equal standing. As a student, you will live as a member of one college which is part of a larger collegiate university.

Collegiate universities include the University of Oxford (with 38Colleges); University of Cambridge (with 31 Colleges); Lancaster University; University of Kent; Durham University and the University of York. Teaching may be in other university buildings outside of the college where you are living. Other universities have colleges that are nearly or completely separate, awarding their own degrees such as the University of London and the University of Wales. Some colleges of higher education are linked with universities however these are not to be confused with the old traditional collegiate universities.

'New' universities are likely to offer a range of academic and vocational courses, with entry requirements sometimes lower for some courses. Some 'new' university and accommodation buildings may be more modern in design. Colleges of higher education, and those that have been given university status, may be smaller and more personal with entry requirements that may be less competitive.

Conservatoires will require applicants to be of a high standard in the relevant specialist music, drama or dance subject that you want to study, alongside the qualification entry requirements. For further information, check the higher education institution websites.
Go to:
7.1   Types and Groups of Universities, Colleges of Higher Education and Specialist Institutions

5.   Would you prefer to study at a higher education institution with large numbers of students?

The number of students enrolled at universities and colleges vary considerably. You may want to attend a university with a larger body of students enrolled or you may feel more comfortable with a smaller institution. Some HEIs have in excess of 30,000 enrolled students whilst smaller and some specialist institutions may have less than 2,000 enrolled students.

A smaller HEI may be more personal whereas a larger HEI may provide more social activities. Larger universities that have a collegiate system with smaller colleges may create the feeling of a smaller university. Some larger HEIs may be located on smaller sites in a city location, giving the feeling of a smaller institution but possessing the advantages of a big university.

If you want to find out the numbers of students enrolled at universities and higher education colleges, the Higher Education Statistical Agency http://www.hesa.ac.uk/ publishes information on its website and go to 'The Students and Qualifiers' data tables.

6.   Do you want to study at a higher education institution with a campus?

A university with a campus usually means that the main facilities are situated on the one site, with teaching and research facilities, leisure activities and some shops all reachable within walking distance. Some campuses also have student accommodation on site, whilst other institutions may have student accommodation outside of the campus.

A number of universities fit into this campus description but others are part campus. Some universities have more than one main site. Non-campus universities may have building/s for teaching but no other facilities at that location and any student accommodation will be situated off campus. For further information, check the higher education institution websites.

7. What region of the UK do you want to study and do you want to stay at your home address or move away?

If you are considering living at your family home during your higher education, you will save money on rent and other living costs, so your student finance loan may be lower when you have graduated. Some students won't have a choice to move away but if you do live away, you will develop a range of skills in independent living, such as managing your finances, making decisions, being responsible for how you manage your time and finding out about living in another part of the UK. If you aren't living at home whilst studying for your higher education course, you will need to give some thought where you would like to live.

You might want to live within easy access to your home or you might want to further away. Consider if you want to study in England, Wales, Northern Ireland or Scotland. Check out the student funding options as this may influence where you study. If you want to study in England, consider if you want to study in the South West, South East, London, Midlands, North West or North East.

Universities and colleges usually provide student entertainment and leisure activities on site but you may be interested in what else is available outside of the institution. Cities will have lots of leisure facilities such as theatres, cinemas, sports facilities, clubs, music venues, restaurants and culture centres. Towns may also have a good selection of leisure facilities, but not so many as in a city. Universities in rural places might provide more student entertainment and leisure activities on site or you might be more interested in the tranquil setting. Institutions by the sea may also be near to towns, so there is the added bonus of a sea-side setting.

It may cost more money to live in a city. London is a more expensive place to live and the student finance loan options take this into account. Maps of where universities and colleges are located in the UK can be found on the internet using your preferred search engine.

Go to:
Chapter 7.2
Universities, Higher Education Colleges and Specialist Institutions by Region in the UK
Chapter 9
Studying Abroad
Chapter 12
Student Finance

Some work experience or study periods may be available overseas. The Erasmus programme is for higher education students, studying any subject, in the UK who would like to study, undertake a work placement, or be a language assistant for between three months and one academic year as part of a degree in another European country.
Go to:
Chapter 9.3
Erasmus: Study and Work Experience Programme in another European Country
Chapter 12.6
Erasmus Funding Support for Undergraduate and Postgraduate Students

8. Do you want to study in a UK higher education institution which offers work experience?

Some courses include work experience for periods of time usually up to one year. University and college careers services may also provide opportunities to undertake work experience or internships. If you are studying for a professional degree course, you may be required to undertake placements which will be assessed. Some professional higher education courses include work experience as an essential part of the course. Opportunities to undertake work experience or internships should be available on individual university or college websites.

9. What type of student accommodation is available, if living away from home?

If you choose to live away from your regular or permanent address, you will need to consider where you will live as a student.

Student accommodation costs private rental costs will vary depending on what part of the UK you are studying.

Student accommodation may be owned and managed by a university or college; owned and managed in partnership with a private company; or solely owned and managed by a private company.

Student accommodation is commonly known as 'halls'. Some halls may be self-catering, with access to a shared kitchen and others have the option of being half-board or full-board with breakfast, lunch and dinner being provided in the cost of the accommodation. Costs will vary according to the type of accommodation provided and it is important to consider what would be most suitable for you depending on your preferences. It is more expensive to live in London compared to other parts of the country.

For accommodation in student halls, in many cases, priority is given to students in the first year of their studies, international students meeting specified conditions and to students with disabilities, although it may also be possible for students in other years to rent rooms in halls if there is availability. It is important to check out information on accommodation on the HEI website as there may be deadlines for accommodation applications that you need to be aware of. Check with the relevant HEI student accommodation department to ensure they are reliable. Go to:
Chapter 11
Student Accommodation

10. What student support facilities are there?

Student support facilities will vary at each university and college and it is useful to consider what is important to you. On the HEI websites, you may wish to check out the following:

Computing facilities and IT support

As a student you will most likely have your own computer but you may need to use the university or college computers at times. IT support should also be available to help you with your computer enquiries or problems.

Library

Check where the library is situated. You should get briefed at induction on how to use the library catalogue systems.

Study support

You may need some extra support to help you with your studies and some universities and colleges will provide additional facilities with specialist tutors to help you.

Careers and employability

You will need to consider your future career options as a student and you may wish to find part time employment whilst studying for your course. The career and employability centres should be able to help and advise you with your career options as well as helping you prepare a CV, write job applications and interview techniques. There may be presentations from graduate recruiters, careers fairs and job seminars available during your time as a student.

Counselling services

Universities and colleges may have counsellors should you need to talk through any problems during your time as a student.

Language support

Your English skills will need to be of a high enough standard before you are offered a place on a course but if English isn't your first language, there may be additional support for you to help you improve your written and spoken English.

Disability and dyslexia support

Universities and colleges will usually have a specialist department to support students if you have a disability, medical condition or specific learning difficulty, including dyslexia, as well as supporting and advising other university departments and staff to ensure the needs of disabled students are met.

The support you can have may include implementing special arrangements for lectures, exams and field trips; arranging for note takers, support tutors, library assistance, interpreters and transcribers; and applying for the Disabled Students Allowance (DSA) which helps to fund these types of support in higher education.

Sports facilities
Some Universities and colleges will have their own sports facilities on the campus. Others may have links with local leisure centres. If you have a particular sport you enjoy, check out the facilities available at the university or college.

Student Union activities
The Students Union consists of paid elected members, available to all students and there will be clubs or societies that you can join and take part in. Usually in the induction week, also known as freshers' week, there will be stalls and information about what is running. You may also be able to start up your own club or society if you have enough students interested in joining but check the requirements with your Student Union. Events such as music, films and other entertainment may also be organised by your Student Union. There may be Student Union run bars which also employ students.

Dining
Some halls will provide meals and some eating facilities may be situated within the student living accommodation. There will also be access to restaurants and cafes so check out what is available on campus and in the local area.

11.　How much the tuition fees will be?
The higher education tuition fees system means that there is a maximum amount per academic year that can be charged to students who meet the residence requirements in the UK including for EU students, although changes may occur when the UK leaves the EU. Many higher education institutions (HEIs) charge different fees for different courses so check out the information on the HEI websites.

Tuition fees and funding support is dependent on where you will study and what your country of residence is. England, Wales, Northern Ireland and Scotland all have different tuition fee schemes. International student tuition fees are usually higher than for UK and EU students.

Postgraduate tuition fees for UK and EU resident students will vary depending on the course and HEI. It may be possible to obtain funding from the relevant Student Finance Company, bursary funding organisation, from one of the UK research councils or through the university, although funding is competitive to obtain and there are application deadlines to be aware of. Postgraduate tuition fees for international students will also vary but are usually higher than for UK and EU students.

12.　How much money you will need to spend in living costs?
You will need to consider the cost of your accommodation and other living costs such as utility bills, food, household goods, insurance, personal items, travel and leisure. Living in London is more expensive compared with the rest of the UK.

Depending on your choice of accommodation and your lifestyle, your living costs will vary. Halls of residence rents usually include utility costs (gas, electricity, water) and in catered halls your food will also be included in your rent for your accommodation. Students in shared student housing may have a lower rent but you will need to buy your own food. In privately rented accommodation, you will need to pay utility bills in addition to your rent.

The National Union of Students has further information about student living costs:
National Union of Students
http://www.nus.org.uk/

13. What are the destinations of graduates after completing higher education?

You may want to find out the types of jobs that graduates do who study your chosen course/s. This information may be useful in opening up career options as well as checking average salaries. The Destinations of Leavers from Higher Education survey (DELHE) asks all leavers from higher education what they are doing six months after graduation.

This information may also be used in the league tables. It is organised through the Higher Education Statistics Agency (HESA) https://www.hesa.ac.uk/stats-dlhe See published data on universities, higher education colleges and courses, go to: Chapter 5.1
Choosing a higher education subject
Choosing a higher education course
Choosing a university, college of higher education or specialist institution
Information about courses and universities colleges of higher education or specialist institutions

This careers questionnaire has been designed to help you consider what you like doing, enjoy and what interests you have, in order to help identify your skills and personal qualities when considering what career you may be interested in.

Completing this careers questionnaire should help you to build up a personal profile which you can match with the requirements of the types of jobs you may be interested in. This should help you when you are researching to find out about the qualifications you may need, especially what you will need to study in higher education.

Specific skills, qualities and attributes are referred to in the job description or person specification when a job is advertised. When you make a job application, you should refer to your skills, interests and personal qualities, as well as giving examples of your experience where these have been gained or developed. You will be assessed on these at the application and interview stage, as well as through psychometric tests (if required).

Highlight the skills, qualities and attributes which are important to you to build up a personal profile and use this to help you identify your strengths, what you enjoy and any skills that you feel you will need to develop for the type of job you are interested in. This should help you when researching job roles and making job applications.

The official careers websites for the UK countries should have useful information about what qualifications may be needed for the jobs you are considering. There are also many additional careers sites you may check out. Professional bodies for specific professions often also provide careers information, as well identifying accredited or recommended professional qualifications you may need.
See the chapters
Chapter 1.3
Careers Advice and Useful Websites and
Chapter 5.4
Professional Organisations: Accredited Undergraduate and Postgraduate Courses

There are no right or wrong answers in the following careers questionnaire, circle as many skills, qualities and attributes which are important to you. Some job groups will overlap with others, with skills and interests being similar requirements for a range of jobs. Everyone has different skills, interests and personal qualities so consider what is most appropriate for you.

SKILLS

A. Communication Skills

A1 Speaking skills
1. Talking to other people
2. Speaking to individuals
3. Speaking to groups of people
4. Speaking on a phone
5. Having conversations with people I don't know

A2 Effective speaking
1. Speaking with confidence to others
2. Explaining information to other people
3. Interviewing people
4. Influencing other people
5. Speaking clearly

A3 Listening skills
1. Listening to other people
2. Being open minded about other people
3. Counselling people
4. Listening carefully to what other people say
5. Collecting information by asking questions

A4 Reading skills
1. Reading instructions
2. Reading factual information
3. Reading fiction
4. Reading articles
5. Scanning text quickly to understand key points

A5 Writing skills
1. Writing letters to people
2. Writing fiction stories
3. Writing factual information
4. Summarising information (ability to identify a brief statement of the main points)
5. Writing about new ideas

A6 Researching skills
1. Researching information
2. Clarifying information (making information more understandable)
3. Reflecting on what has been said to you (thinking and understanding)
4. Generating new knowledge
5. Doing experiments

A7 Negotiating skills
1. Persuading other people to your point of view
2. Persuading other people to accept new ideas
3. Negotiating with others to reach agreements
4. Influencing other people
5. Helping others to reach agreements

B. People Skills

B1 Interpersonal skills
1. Meeting new people
2. Supporting other people
3. Socialising with friends
4. Sharing ideas, decisions and responsibility with other people
5. Providing encouragement to other people

B2 Teamwork skills
1. Working as part of a team
2. Working with small groups of people
3. Working with large groups of people
4. Putting other peoples' ideas into practice
5. Helping people to achieve their goals

B3 Caring skills
1. Helping other people
2. Providing advice to other people
3. Sympathising with other people
4. Being aware of the needs of others
5. Respecting other people

B4 Empathy
1. Understanding other peoples' emotions
2. Responding to the needs of others
3. Considering other peoples' opinions without making judgements
4. Being patient with other people
5. Assessing the behaviour of other people

B5 Compassion
1. Helping people who are unwell
2. Helping people who are disadvantaged
3. Supporting other people
4. Working with people with a disability
5. Respecting how other people are treated

B6 Working with types of people
1. Working with children
2. Working with adolescents
3. Working with adults
4. Working with families
5. Working with people with a disability or health condition

B7 Teaching skills
1. Giving information to other people
2. Giving a presentation to small groups of people
3. Giving a presentation to large groups of people
4. Teaching other people
5. Advising and guiding people

B8 Managing skills
1. Managing / supervising individuals
2. Delegating work fairly to other people
3. Managing / supervising / leading small teams of people
4. Managing / supervising / leading large groups of people
5. Chairing meetings

C. Organisation Skills

C1 Organisation skills
1. Organising events or activities
2. Making preparations in advance
3. Being organised
4. Being methodical
5. Attention to detail

C2 Time management skills
1. Managing your time
2. Arriving on time for your appointments
3. Completing one task before starting a new one
4. Preparing activities in advance
5. Finishing activities within a set time

C3 Planning
1. Planning events or activities
2. Planning my own work
3. Planning to complete tasks within set times
4. Thinking through a problem before acting
5. Planning the work of others

D. Problem Solving Skills

D1 Problem solving skills
1. Solving problems
2. Critical analysis
3. Finding out how things work
4. Critically evaluate information
5. Dealing with difficult situations

D2 Decision making skills
1. Making important decisions
2. Deciding what is right or wrong
3. Dealing with emotionally difficult problems
4. Asking for help when needed
5. Reflecting on how you can improve

D3 Making appropriate judgements
1. Confronting or challenging the attitudes of others
2. Challenging other peoples' opinions
3. Challenging the behaviour of other people
4. Dealing appropriately with stressful situations
5. Being assertive

D4 Creative thinking skills
1. Thinking strategically (long term planning)
2. Thinking how your ideas will happen
3. Taking risks
4. Working out how to overcome a difficult problem
5. Multi-tasking

E. Independence Skills

E1 Initiative skills
1. Thinking things through
2. Working on your own
3. Planning your work
4. Controlling your own work load
5. Keeping busy

E2 Motivation
1. Motivating yourself
2. Motivating other people
3. Being determined to succeed
4. Taking action
5. Taking responsibility

F.G.H.I.J. Specialist Skills

F1. Sales skills
1. Selling a product
2. Selling your ideas to others
3. Helping other people to make decisions
4. Knowing if a product or idea is good value
5. Working to targets

G1 Other language ability
1. Speaking another language other than English
2. Writing in another language other than English
3. Reading another language other than English

H. Computer skills

H1. General computer skills
1. Typing / keyboard accuracy skills
2. Typing/keyboard speed skills
3. Using the internet to research information
4. Sending emails
5. Responding to emails efficiently

H2. Using information on a computer
1. Presenting data using a computer
2. Presenting information using a computer
3. Collating information on a computer
4. Storing information on a computer
5. Programming skills

E3 Adaptability skills
1. Taking on new challenges
2. Adapting to change
3. Following complex instructions
4. Changing plans at short notice
5. Keeping calm in difficult situations

H3. Computer packages
Microsoft Office
1. Microsoft Word
2. Microsoft Excel
3. Microsoft PowerPoint
4. Microsoft Access
5. Microsoft Outlook

H4. Other computer packages
1. Animation computer package
2. Computer Aided Design software
3. Financial computer package
4. Geographical Information Systems
5. Graphics computer package
6. Mathematics computer package
7. Scientific computer package
8. Statistical computer package
9. Any additional computer packages

I1. Mathematics skills
1. Using numbers
2. Solving mathematical problems
3. Keeping accurate finance records
4. Attention to detail
5. Ability to estimate

J1. Creative ability
1. Drawing or painting
2. Designing things
3. Making things
4. Playing a musical instrument
5. Dancing
6. Acting
7. Performing in front of an audience
8. Thinking up new ideas
9. Practical activities

K. Work Environment

Work environments often require a certain amount of flexibility, however if you could choose your ideal work conditions, hours of work, salary, career development and type of work environment, consider what is important to you.

K1. Work values

1. Having secure and stable employment
2. Being resilient, able to stay focused and positive with any job changes that may happen
3. Recognition, acknowledgement and praise for your work
4. Having a wide variety of work tasks
5. Having autonomy over your work (having control with what you do)
6. Being creative and inventive
7. Having a good work / life balance

K2. Hours of work

1. Working regular hours (usually Monday to Friday 9.00 a.m. – 5.00 p.m.)
2. Working evenings
3. Working nights
4. Working weekends
5. Working part-time
6. Working in short or long term contracts

K3. Salary

1. Job satisfaction is more important than your salary
2. Having a higher than average salary
3. Having a salary linked to your work performance
4. Having enough salary to live on

K4. Career development

1. Work that provides opportunities for training and development / gaining qualifications
2. Work that provides opportunities to learn or develop new skills
3. Work that provides opportunities to learn or develop new ideas
4. Work that provides opportunities for job / career progression
5. Work that provides opportunities to move into management positions

K5. Work and qualification levels

1. Working in a job requiring qualifications up to level 3 (RQF) E,W, NI or 6 (SCQF) S
2. Working in a job requiring a degree or other undergraduate course
3. Working in a job requiring a postgraduate qualification
4. Working in a job requiring a vocational qualification
5. Working in a job requiring a professional qualification
6. Working in a job requiring specific skills

K7. Working practice

1. Working in one place
2. Working in different places
3. Work that involves travel
4. Working in an office
5. Working inside
6. Working outdoors
7. Working with technology
8. Working with machinery

K6. Working environment

1. Working in an environment that generates profit
2. Working in a not-for-profit environment
3. Working in a competitive work environment e.g. meeting targets
4. Working in a non-competitive work environment
5. Working in a fast-paced, busy organisation
6. Working in a quiet, non-pressured organisation
7. Working in an organisation dealing with global issues
8. Working for an ethical organisation
9. Persuading people to buy goods or services
10. Using commercial skills to generate profit or success
11. Being aware of consumer requirements

L. Job Satisfaction
Work Sector, Type of Work, Work Environment, Work Values
The following questions should help you understand the type of work sector, type of job, work environment and work values you feel are important to you.

L1. Work sector
What type of work are you interested in?
1. Working in the public sector
2. Working in the private sector
3. Working for a charity or voluntary organisation
4. Working as self-employed / freelance
5. Volunteering

L2. Type of work
What work sector you are interested in?
1. Accounting and finance
2. Banking or business finance
3. Economics, mathematics or statistics
4. Administration or business management
5. Business: human resources or recruitment
6. Agriculture or plants
7. Animals
8. Building design, surveying or construction
9. Building property management or estate agency
10. Creative: fine art, illustration, ceramics or sculpture
11. Creative: art and design, crafts or product design
12. Creative: computer design, graphic design or printing
13. Creative: fashion design, visual merchandising or interior / theatre design
14. Creative: make-up artistry, hair or beauty industry
15. Creative: photography or filming
16. Education and training
17. Engineering
18. Environment
19. Events organising
20. Healthcare
21. History
22. Hospitality
23. Housing management
24. Information / computer technology
25. Information or library
26. Languages (using)
27. Law enforcement: armed forces
28. Law enforcement: protection or security service
29. Legal
30. Leisure or tourism
31. Media: advertising, marketing, public relations
32. Media: journalism or publishing
33. Media: film, TV, radio, theatre
34. Performing arts: dance
35. Performing arts: drama
36. Performing arts: music, music technology
37. Religion
38. Retail: sales or customer service
39. Science
40. Social care
41. Social science / arts or politics
42. Sport
43. Transport and Logistics
44. Transport: air industry
45. Transport: marine industry
46. Transport: rail industry
47. Transport: road industry
48. Transport: motor industry

INTERESTS

M. Work Interests

M1. Working with people

1. Working as part of a large organisation
2. Working as part of a medium sized organisation
3. Working as part of a small sized organisation
4. Working on your own
5. Dealing with people in difficult situations

M2. Working with animals

1. Working with small animals
2. Working with large animals
3. Studying the behaviour of animals
4. Treating sick animals
5. Protecting animals

M3. Working with plants

1. Digging and planting in the garden
2. Growing flowers and shrubs
3. Growing and harvesting vegetables / crops
4. Growing and harvesting fruit
5. Arranging flowers

M4. Working with technology

1. Using a computer all the time
2. Using a computer some of the time
3. Using a computer to design something
4. Using a computer to present information to other people
5. Learning new computer skills

M5. Working with machinery or equipment

1. Using machinery or equipment all the time
2. Using machinery or equipment some of the time
3. Understanding how things work
4. Understanding of health and safety issues when operating machinery or equipment
5. Understanding of selecting the appropriate machine or equipment suited for the task

N. Personal Interests
Circle the following interests that you like. Add any additional interests or hobbies that you enjoy doing. Put your interests in order of how much you like them with number 1 being what you like the most.

Animals	Making things	Selling
Art	Mathematics	Singing
Being creative	Performing acting	Social media
Competitions	Performing dance	Socialising with people
Cooking	Playing a musical instrument	Solving puzzles
Debating	Playing computer games	Technology
Designing	Playing mind or board	Travelling
Drama	games e.g. chess,	Using a computer
Environmental activities	scrabble	Using another language
Finding out how things work	Playing quizzes	Watching dance
Gardening	Playing sport	Watching films
Helping others	Politics	Watching plays
Keeping fit	Reading	Watching opera
Listening to music	Researching	Writing
Making money	Science	

O. Personal Qualities
Read through the following adjectives that describe positive personal qualities. Circle those that you believe applies to your personality.

Accurate	Efficient	Organised
Active	Empathic	Patient
Adaptable	Energetic	Perceptive
Adventurous	Enterprising	Persistent
Ambitious	Entertaining	Persuasive
Analytical	Enthusiastic	Polite
Appreciative	Ethical	Practical
Articulate	Experienced	Productive
Assertive	Fair	Punctual
Broad minded	Friendly	Reasonable
Calm	Hard working	Reliable
Careful	Helpful	Respectful
Cheerful	Honest	Responsible
Committed	Imaginative	Self- motivated
Competent	Independent	Self-confident
Competitive	Industrious	Self-disciplined
Confident	Innovative	Self-reliant
Conscientious	Inquisitive	Sensible
Considerate	Intellectual	Sociable
Constructive	Interesting	Studious
Cooperative	Kind	Sympathetic
Creative	Knowledgeable	Systematic
Curious	Logical	Tactful
Decisive	Loyal	Tidy
Dedicated	Mathematical	Tolerant
Dependable	Methodical	Trustworthy
Determined	Meticulous	Understand
Diligent	Observant	
Diplomatic	Open minded	
Effective	Optimistic	

Chapter 2
Qualification Regulation and Accreditation

2.1 Organisations that Maintain Standards for Qualifications in the UK

For a qualification to be recognised in the UK, it must be accredited through one of the qualification awarding bodies. These awarding bodies are regulated by official regulation organisations. In the UK there are many different types of regulated qualifications which may be academic, professional or vocational, which you can study at different levels. See the chapter Qualification Frameworks.

The purpose of accreditation is to ensure that a programme of study meets essential criteria in the training and education of students in particular subject areas. Registration means that a qualified individual is licensed to work as a specialist professional in a particular career. To register to work in a specialist career, an individual must successfully complete an accredited course, receive a recognised award and demonstrate relevant competencies.

All approved qualifications are accredited by recognised awarding bodies, meaning they are officially recognised. There are different systems and organisations that regulate academic and vocational qualifications in all four countries of the UK in England, Wales, Northern Ireland and Scotland. England, Wales and Northern Ireland has a similar qualification system whereas Scotland has a slightly different qualification system. There are numerous recognised awarding bodies that also include professional bodies, which are recognised as awarding and regulating bodies. See the chapter:
Chapter 5.4
Professional Organisations: Accredited Undergraduate and Postgraduate Courses

The following information highlights organisations which are responsible for maintaining qualification standards.

2.2 Higher Education Policy

Higher education is a devolved area which means that most decisions and policies about higher education are taken by the relevant Government departments in the UK:

England
- UK Government: Department for Education
  https://www.gov.uk/government/organis ations/department-for-education

Wales
- Welsh Government:
  Department for Education and Skills
  http://gov.wales/topics/educationandskil ls/

Northern Ireland
Department for the Economy: Higher Education
https://www.economy-ni.gov.uk/topics/higher-education

Scotland
- Scottish Government
  http://www.gov.scot/

Regulation of Public Sector Higher Education Qualifications

Public sector higher education qualifications in England, Wales and Northern Ireland are regulated by the:

- Quality Assurance Agency for Higher Education (QAA) http://www.qaa.ac.uk

The QAA monitors and advises on standards and quality in UK higher education, ensuring that students get the expected standard of higher education experience. The QAA has responsibility for securing the academic standards of UK higher education. QAA: Right to Award Degrees http://www.qaa.ac.uk/en/Publications/ .

The QAA also owns and maintains the Access to HE website which provides information about the Access to Higher Education Diploma, a qualification at level 3 (RQF) delivered by colleges in England and Wales, preparing people without traditional qualifications to study in higher education.

Higher education qualifications in Scotland are regulated by the:

- Scottish Office of the Quality Assurance Agency for Higher Education (QAA Scotland) http://www.qaa.ac.uk/about-us/scotland

Works in partnership with other higher education organisations:

- Scottish Qualifications Authority (SQA) http://www.sqa.org.uk , the
- Scottish Credit and Qualifications Framework (SCQF) http://www.scqf.org.uk
- Colleges Scotland http://www.collegesscotland.ac.uk/
- Universities Scotland http://www.universities-scotland.ac.uk/ .

Publicly Funded Higher Education Awarding Bodies

A UK degree can be awarded only by an authorising degree-awarding body, typically a university, which has the overall responsibility for the standard and quality of the qualification. This applies even if all or part of the course is provided by a separate college or organisation. The

- Privy Council https://privycouncil.independent.gov.uk/

is a formal body of advisors to the Queen, and is responsible for decisions about organisations with Awarding Powers (DAP) and university title (UT) with further information at the

- Quality Assurance Agency for Higher Education (QAA) http://www.qaa.ac.uk .

From August 2019, the authority to grant degree awarding powers in England will transfer from the Privy Council to the

- The Office for Students https://www.officeforstudents.org.uk/advice-and-guidance/the-register/

All genuine UK degree courses are approved by a university or other legally recognised degree awarding body which will award the final qualification.

All publicly funded UK universities and some additional higher education institutions are approved listed bodies, recognised as awarding bodies with the official power to award UK degrees. They are known by the UK government as 'recognised bodies' with powers to award undergraduate and postgraduate higher education qualifications. Other colleges that are approved to provide full higher education programmes on behalf of recognised bodies are known as 'listed bodies'. They don't have the right to award degrees but will be linked to a recognised university which does award the degrees. It is also possible for other organisations approved by the QAA to deliver learning opportunities on behalf of a degree awarding body.

These may be higher education providers without degree-awarding powers; a degree awarding body other than that granting the award; an employer or another organisation approved by the degree awarding body. Organisations that only offer part of a degree course do not have listed body status and it is advisable to confirm with the degree awarding body that the course was originally set up by them, if you are unsure, information about which university or college accredits or validates courses should be available on the higher education institution websites, therefore check with the relevant university or college before applying.

There are three different types of degree awarding powers that a university recognised body can have:

Foundation degree awarding powers (FDAP): in England and Wales at level 5 Framework for Higher Education Qualifications (FHEQ).

Taught degree awarding powers for undergraduate courses, up to bachelor's and taught master's degrees at level 4 - 7 (FHEQ).

Research degree awarding powers (RDAP) with the additional right to award research master's and doctorate degrees at level 7 – 8 (FHEQ).

Recognised higher education institutions with degree awarding powers and listed bodies without degree awarding powers, can be found on the QAA website.

To find recognised universities go to the:
- UK Government: Check a university is officially recognised https://www.gov.uk/check-a-university-is-officially-recognised/overview .

Further information may also be found at:
- UK Government: recognised degrees and bodies https://www.gov.uk/guidance/recognised-uk-degrees#recognised-bodies
and
- UK Government: recognised UK degrees https://www.gov.uk/recognised-uk-degrees

Some professional organisations may also accredit professional higher education qualifications in collaboration with universities which are required in order to work in that profession. These professional organisations should also list accredited undergraduate and postgraduate courses on their websites; see the chapter See the chapter on Professional Organisations which Officially Accredit Undergraduate and Postgraduate Courses.

Higher national certificates and higher national diplomas awarding bodies
Higher national certificates (HNCs) and higher national diplomas (HNDs) in England, Wales and Northern Ireland are awarded by

- Pearson qualifications http://qualifications.pearson.com/ and in
- Scotland, awarded by the Scottish Qualifications Authority (SQA) http://www.sqa.org.uk/ .

Regulation of Private Sector Further and Higher Education Qualifications

Private sector further and higher education qualifications in the UK that are officially recognised are regulated by the:
- British Accreditation Council (BAC) http://www.the-bac.org/

BAC is a registered UK charity established in 1984 and responsible for maintaining standards, providing a system of accreditation in private further and higher education providers. .

Privately Funded Higher Education Awarding Bodies

There are a number of privately funded higher education institutions (HEIs) that are officially recognised in the UK. Some privately funded universities have degree awarding powers and accredit their own courses.

Recognised privately funded HEIs that don't have degree awarding powers have formed partnerships with universities and colleges that do have degree awarding powers which accredit their degree courses. Information about such partnerships should be available on the higher education institution (HEI) website.

The British Council https://www.britishcouncil.org/education/accreditation/centres accredits UK centres which may be English centres, privately funded colleges and universities. Links to accredited institutions may be found on the website.

The British Accreditation Council http://www.the-bac.org/ provides a quality assurance scheme for independent further and higher education in the UK and oversees the inspection of private post-16 education.

English Language Centres in the UK

English UK https://www.englishuk.com/ is the national association of accredited English language centres in the UK with members ranging from small private English language school to universities.

2.4 Higher and Further Education Funding Bodies

The higher education funding bodies are responsible for funding higher education and there are separate organisations for England, Wales, Northern Ireland and Scotland.

They are the lead regulators for higher education in the UK and assess the quality of the education that they fund with advice from the Quality Assurance Agency for Higher Education (QAA) http://www.qaa.ac.uk

Further and higher education funding bodies
England
- The Office for Students https://www.officeforstudents.org.uk/
- Research England https://re.ukri.org/

Links to universities and colleges may be found at:
- The Office for Students: the Register https://www.officeforstudents.org.uk/advice-and-guidance/the-register/

The Office for Students https://www.officeforstudents.org.uk/ from March 2018 has replaced the Higher Education Funding Council for England http://www.hefce.ac.uk/ and provides funding for teaching in higher education.in England.

Research England https://re.ukri.org/ is the new council within the UK Research and Innovation https://www.ukri.org/ and provides funding for research in higher education in England.

Wales
- Higher Education Funding Council for Wales http://www.hefcw.org.uk/

Northern Ireland
- Department for the Economy: Higher Education https://www.economy-ni.gov.uk/topics/higher-education

Scotland
- Scottish Funding Council: Further and Higher Education http://www.sfc.ac.uk/)

2.5 National Union of Students (NUS)

Whilst the NUS for England, Wales, Northern Ireland or Scotland aren't directly involved with higher education policy, useful information about higher education issues may be found on the websites.

National Union of Students NUS
http://www.nus.org.uk/
National Union of Students NUS Scotland
http://www.nus.org.uk/en/nus-scotland/

2.6 Regulation of Academic and Vocational Qualifications below Higher Education Level and Awarding Bodies in the UK

Non-higher academic and vocational qualifications are regulated by different organisations depending on which country the qualifications are delivered in England, Wales, Northern Ireland or Scotland. There are numerous recognised awarding bodies which award mostly non-higher education qualifications and many professional bodies may also be recognised as awarding and regulating bodies. See the chapter on Secondary and Further Education Qualification Subjects and Courses

England and Northern Ireland Non-Higher Education Academic and Vocational Qualifications Regulation

In England and Northern Ireland the
- Office of Qualifications and Examinations Regulation (Ofqual) https://www.gov.uk/government/organis ations/ofqual

is the official body that regulates non-higher education academic General Certificate of Secondary Education (GCSEs), General Certificate of Education (GCE) Advanced Subsidiary (AS) levels and Advanced (A) Levels; vocational qualifications, examinations and assessments in England and just vocational qualifications in Northern Ireland.

Ofqual is not involved with higher education, although there are qualifications on Ofqual's Register of

Regulated Qualifications at level 4 to level 8 (RQF) which are broadly comparable with higher education qualifications.

Ofqual works in partnership with the:
- Council for the Curriculum Examinations and Assessment (CCEA) in Northern Ireland http://ccea.org.uk/
and the
- Welsh Government http://wales.gov.uk

Regulated qualifications and courses that are found in the Regulated Qualification Framework (RQF) may be found at:
- UK Government: Ofqual https://www.gov.uk/government/news/o fqual-to-introduce-new-regulated-qualifications-framework

Northern Ireland Non-Higher Education Academic and Vocational Qualifications Regulation

In Northern Ireland,
- Northern Ireland Council for the Curriculum Examinations and Assessment (CCEA) http://ccea.org.uk/

is a non-departmental public body reporting to the Department of Education in Northern Ireland. The CCEA regulates GCSEs, GCE 'AS' levels and 'A' levels, as well as essential and key skills in Northern Ireland.

Wales Non-Higher Education Academic and Vocational Qualifications Regulation

In Wales
- Qualification Wales
  http://qualificationswales.org/

is the regulator of non-degree qualifications and the qualification system in Wales. It is a Welsh Government Sponsored Body, independent of government and accountable to the National Assembly for Wales.

Qualification Wales regulates GCSEs, GCE AS, 'A' levels, the Welsh Baccalaureate (Welsh Bacc), vocational qualifications, entry level, and essential skills as well as credit based higher education that are recognised within the Credit and Qualification Framework for Wales (CQFW). The CQFW is managed by a strategic operational partnership comprising of the Welsh Government, the Higher Education Funding Council for Wales (HEWCW) http://www.hefcw.ac.uk/ and Qualifications Wales http://qualificationswales.org/.

Ofqual Register of Non-Higher Education Academic and Vocational Qualifications Regulated Qualifications

You can search for recognised non-higher education academic and vocational qualifications and awarding organisations in England, Wales and Northern Ireland that are regulated by Ofqual, including GCSEs and 'A' levels, on the Ofqual Register http://register.ofqual.gov.uk/

Scotland Non-Higher Education Academic and Vocational Qualifications Regulation

In Scotland, the
- Scottish Qualifications Authority (SQA)
  http://www.sqa.org.uk/

accredits academic qualifications which include Nationals, Highers, Advance Highers, Higher National Certificates, Higher National Diplomas and Scottish Vocational Qualifications (SVQs) offered across Scotland, and approves awarding bodies that award these qualifications, working with schools, colleges, universities, industry and the Scottish government.

Chapter 3
Qualifications Frameworks

3.1 About Qualification Frameworks

In the UK, regulated qualifications are accredited to qualification 'frameworks' known as the Regulated Qualifications Framework (RQF) which consist of qualifications placed at levels, showing the value of their difficulty and complexity of knowledge and skills. Most qualifications are assigned a single level, although some qualifications such as GCSEs may span more than one level. The Register of Regulated Qualifications includes GCSEs, 'A' levels, 'AS' levels and vocational qualifications in England and Northern Ireland. Qualifications are accredited differently in Wales and Scotland. Further information may be found at UK Government: Find a Regulated Qualification https://www.gov.uk/find-a-regulated-qualification

The levels provide an indication of the level of demand of the different qualifications, comparing and providing clear progression routes from one level to the next, helping you to make informed decisions about which type and level of qualification you want to study and need for your career. The levels are based on the standard of knowledge, skill and competence required for each qualification although qualifications at the same level may be different in terms of content and how long they take to complete.

The frameworks in the UK differ by country and the type of qualifications. Some approved qualifications may not be on the Regulated Qualifications Framework (RQF) although these qualifications are recognised within the particular professional fields and accredited by the relevant professional organisations. England, Wales and Northern Ireland use the Regulated Qualifications Framework (RQF); Wales also uses the Credit and Qualifications Framework for Wales (CQFW) which follows the same format as the RQF.

In Scotland, the regulated qualification framework is known as the Scottish Credit and Qualifications Framework (SCQF). Higher education qualifications may be placed in the Framework for Higher Education Qualifications (FHEQ) for England, Wales and Northern Ireland; and the Scottish Credit and Qualifications Framework (SCQF) for Scotland. In Europe, the framework is known as the European Qualifications Framework (EQF). The RQF replaced the Qualification Credit Framework (QCF) and the National Qualifications Framework (NQF) in October 2015.

Regulated Qualifications Framework (RQF) for England, Wales and Northern Ireland

The Regulated Qualifications Framework (RQF) for England, Wales and Northern Ireland places qualifications at entry level, level 1 and going up to level 8 being the highest level of qualifications. Entry levels are the lowest level available as 3 sub levels 1- 3, with entry 1 being the lowest level and entry 3 being the most difficult.

Credit and Qualifications Framework for Wales (CQFW)

The Credit and Qualifications Framework for Wales (CQFW) is referred to in Wales and follows the same format as the RQF with levels starting at entry level and going up to level 8. The CQFW recognises full and partially completed general and vocational courses and qualifications.

Scottish Credit and Qualifications Framework (SCQF)

In Scotland, the regulated qualification framework is known as the Scottish Credit and Qualifications Framework (SCQF) with qualification levels starting at level 1 going up to level 12 being the highest level of qualifications. The SCQF recognises all full and partially completed general, vocational and higher education courses and qualifications in Scotland.

European Qualifications Framework (EQF)

In Europe, the framework is known as the European Qualifications Framework (EQF) with qualifications starting at level 1 going up to level 8 being the highest level of qualifications, which ensures that there is an easy way to compare the level of qualifications throughout the European countries and systems.

The European Credit Transfer Systems (ECTS) provides a method for European qualifications which are credit based to be compared across Europe, especially when students study in other parts of Europe.

Framework for Higher Education Qualifications (FHEQ)

The Framework for Higher Education Qualifications (FHEQ) for England, Wales and Northern Ireland is for higher education courses which start at level 4 and go up to level 8, being the highest level of qualifications, in the FHEQ framework. Some courses available in higher education (HE) are also available 'AS' level 3 (RQF) as higher education (HE) preparation qualifications.

In Scotland, the qualification levels are slightly different with all regulated qualifications, including higher education qualifications, placed in the Scottish Credit and Qualifications Framework (SCQF) which have levels from 1 – 12, with higher education qualifications starting at level 7 - 12 (which equate with level 4-8 FHEQ).

3.2 Regulated Qualifications and Framework Levels

Secondary and Further Education Qualifications

Entry level (RQF) ; level 1-3 (SCQF) courses

Entry level and some BTEC award, certificate and diploma qualifications including essential and functional skills and English for speakers of other languages (ESOL) are available as entry levels 1- 3 (with 3 being the most difficult) (RQF) in England, Wales and Northern Ireland; and equate to Scottish Nationals at level 1-3 in Scotland (SCQF).

Level 1 (RQF); level 4 (SCQF) courses

GCSEs grades D-G / 3 - 1 and some BTEC award, certificate and diploma qualifications including essential and functional skills and English for speakers of other languages (ESOL), national vocational qualifications (NVQs), and music grades 1,2 and 3 are available at level 1 (RQF) in England, Wales and Northern Ireland; and equate to Scottish Nationals at level 4 (SCQF) in Scotland.

Level 2 (RQF); level 5 (SCQF) courses

GCSEs grades A*-C / 9 – 4 and some BTEC award, certificate and diploma, national certificate and diploma

qualifications including essential and functional skills and English for speakers of other languages (ESOL), national vocational qualifications (NVQs), and music grades 4 and 5 are available at level 2 (RQF) in England, Wales and Northern Ireland; and equate to Scottish Nationals at level 5 (SCQF) in Scotland.

Level 3 (RQF); level 6 (SCQF) courses

'AS' levels, 'A' levels grades A*-E, Access to Higher Education Diplomas, Foundation Diplomas in Art and equivalent qualifications, some BTEC award, certificate and diploma, national certificate and diploma qualifications including essential and functional skills and English for speakers of other languages (ESOL), national vocational qualifications (NVQs), music grades 6,7 and 8, are available at level 3 (RQF) in England, Wales and Northern Ireland; and equate to Scottish Nationals and Highers at level 6 (SCQF) in Scotland; and Advance Highers and Scottish Baccalaureates available at level 7(SCQF) in Scotland

Higher Education Level Qualifications

Level 4 - 8 (FHEQ); level 7 – 12 (SCQF)
Higher education qualifications are available from 4-8 (FHEQ) in England, Wales and Northern Ireland; and equate to level 7-10 (SCQF) in Scotland.

Undergraduate higher education qualifications are available from 4-6 (FHEQ) in England, Wales and Northern Ireland and from level 7-10 (SCQF) in Scotland. Postgraduate higher education qualifications are available from 7-8 (FHEQ) in England, Wales and Northern Ireland and from level 10-12 (SCQF) in Scotland.

Level 4 (FHEQ); level 7 (SCQF): undergraduate courses
Certificates of Higher Education, Undergraduate Certificates, Higher National Certificates (BTEC), some Foundation Diplomas in Art are at level 4 (FHEQ) in England, Wales and Northern Ireland; and equate to level 7 (SCQF) in Scotland.

Level 5 (FHEQ); level 8 (SCQF): undergraduate courses
Diplomas of Higher Education, Undergraduate Diplomas, Higher National Diplomas (BTEC) and Foundation Degrees are at level 5 (FHEQ) in England, Wales and Northern Ireland; and equate to level 8 (SCQF) in Scotland.

Level 6 (FHEQ); level 9 /10 (SCQF): undergraduate courses
Bachelor ordinary degrees and bachelor honours degrees are at level 6 (FHEQ) in England, Wales and Northern Ireland; and equate to Bachelor's Ordinary Degrees at level 9 and Bachelor's Honours Degrees at level 10 (SCQF) in Scotland.

Level 6 (FHEQ); level 10 (SCQF): graduate courses
Graduate certificates and graduate diplomas (which require a bachelor's degree to enter) are at undergraduate levels of level 6 (FHEQ) in England, Wales and Northern Ireland; and equate to level 10 (SCQF) in Scotland

Level 7 (FHEQ); level 11 (SCQF): postgraduate courses
Postgraduate certificates, postgraduate diplomas and master's degrees are at level 7 (FHEQ) in England, Wales and Northern Ireland; and equate to level 11 (SCQF) in Scotland.

Level 8 (FHEQ); level 12 (SCQF): postgraduate courses
Doctorate degrees are at level 8 (FHEQ) in England, Wales and Northern Ireland; and equate to level 12 (SCQF) in Scotland.

Professional Qualifications

Level 1 - 8 (RQF); level 1 – 12 (SCQF)
Professional qualifications are available from 1-8 (RQF) in England, Wales and Northern Ireland; and equate to level 1-12 (SCQF) in Scotland.

National Vocational Qualifications (NVQs); and Scottish Vocational Qualifications (SVQs)

Level 1 – 5 NVQs: level 1 - 8 (RQF); level 4 – 12 (SCQF)

National vocational qualifications (NVQs) and Scottish vocational qualifications (SVQs) are available from level 1 and go up to level 5, with level 4 and 5 being broadly equivalent to higher education qualifications.

In England, Wales and Northern Ireland, the levels of NVQs are placed in the Regulated Qualification Framework (RQF) with NVQ level 1 equal to level 1 (RQF); NVQ level 2 equal to level 2 (RQF); NVQ level 3 equal to level 3 (RQF); NVQ level 4 equal to level 4-6 (RQF); NVQ level 5 equal to level 7-8 (RQF).

In Scotland the level of SVQs are placed in the Scottish Credit and Qualifications Framework (SCQF) with SVQ level 1 equal to level 4 (SCQF); SVQ level 2 equal to level 5 (SCQF); SVQ level 3 equal to level 6 (SCQF); SVQ level 4 equal to level 7-10 (SCQF); SVQ level 5 equal to level 11-12 (SCQF).

Intermediate apprenticeships are at level 2 (RQF); advanced apprenticeships are at level 3 (RQF); higher apprenticeships are at level 4 (RQF); and degree apprenticeships are at level 6 (RQF) and (FHEQ)

Where you can Study

Qualifications may be studied with a range of education and training providers. Academic and vocational qualifications up to level 3 Regulated Qualifications Framework (RQF) / level 6 Scottish Credit and Qualifications Framework (SCQF) may be studied in schools, sixth form colleges, further education colleges or training centres. Some vocational and professional qualifications at level 4 (RQF) / level 7 (SCQF) and above may also be studied in further education colleges.

Academic, vocational and professional qualifications at levels 4 to 8 Framework for Higher Education Qualifications (FHEQ) (RQF)in England, Wales and Northern Ireland / levels 7 – 12 (SCQF) in Scotland, as well as some level 3 (RQF) HE preparation qualifications may be studied in universities, higher education colleges and specialist institutions. Vocational and professional qualifications at all levels 1-8 (RQF/SCQF) may be studied in workplaces, community centres or training centres. Some academic, vocational and professional qualifications can also be studied by distance learning organisations.

Qualification Framework Tables

The following qualification framework tables show qualifications at certain levels in England, Wales, Northern Ireland and Scotland.

Abbreviations for qualifications framework tables

Regulated Qualifications Framework (RQF)
European Qualification Framework (EQF)
Framework for Higher Education Qualifications (FHEQ)
Scottish Credit and Qualification Framework (SCQF)

National Vocational Qualifications (NVQs) Scottish Vocational Qualifications (SVQs)
England (E)
Wales (W)
Northern Ireland (NI)
Scotland (S)
Certificate of higher education (Cert HE)
Diploma of higher education (Dip HE)
Higher National Certificate (HNC)
Higher National Diploma (HND)
Undergraduate Certificate (UG Certificates)
Undergraduate Diploma (UG Diplomas)

Table 1: Entry levels (1-3) and 1-3 (RQF); levels 1-6 (SCQF)

RQF levels	RQF levels	FHE level	Types of Quals (E;W;NI)	BTEC Quals	NVQ / SVQ levels	SCQF levels	Types of Quals (S)
Level 3	Level 3		'A' levels 'AS' levels Access to HE Diplomas Foundation Diplomas in Art: level 3 HE Preparation Courses: Extended degree year Foundation Certificates	BTEC Nationals BTEC Specialist Quals BTEC Foundation Diplomas in Art and Design L 3	NVQ/ SVQ level 3	Level 6	Nationals level 6: Highers
Level 2	Level 2		GCSEs g A*-C / 9 - 4	BTEC Firsts BTEC Specialist Quals	NVQ/ SVQ level 2	Level 5	Nationals Level 5 Intermediate 2
Level 1	Level 1		GCSEs g D-G / 3 - 1 Key Skills Skills for Life	BTEC Introductory	NVQ/ SVQ level 1	Level 4	Nationals Level 4 Intermediate 1
Entry level 3			Entry level awards, certificates diplomas Skills for Life	BTEC Entry		Level 3	Nationals Level 3 Advance 3
Entry level 2			Entry level awards, certificates diplomas Skills for Life	BTEC Entry		Level 2	Nationals Level 2 Advance 2
Entry level 1			Entry level awards, certificates, diplomas Skills for Life	BTEC Entry		Level 1	Nationals Level 1 Advance 1

Table 2: Levels 4-8 (RQF); levels 7-12 (RQF)

RQF levels	EQF levels	FHEQ levels	Types of Quals (E;W;NI)	BTEC Quals	NVQ / SVQ levels	SCQF levels	Types of Quals (S)
Level 8	Level 8	Level 8	Doctorate Degrees		NVQ /SVQ level 5	Level 12	Doctorate Degrees
Level 7	Level 7	Level 7	Master's Degrees Postgrad Diplomas Postgrad Certificates	BTEC Professional Quals	NVQ /SVQ level 5	Level 11	Master's Degrees Postgraduate Diplomas Postgraduate Certificates
Level 6	Level 6	Level 6	Bachelor's Honours Degrees Bachelor's Ordinary Degrees	BTEC Professional Quals	NVQ /SVQ level 4	Level 10 / Level 9	Bachelor's Honours Degrees / Bachelor's Ordinary Degrees
Level 5	Level 5	Level 5	Dip HEs UG Diplomas Foundation Degrees	BTEC HND BTEC Professional Quals	NVQ /SVQ level 4	Level 8	National Highers: SQA Higher National Diplomas
Level 4	Level 4	Level 4	Cert HEs UG Certificates Foundation Diplomas in Art: level 4	BTEC HNC BTEC Professional Quals BTEC Foundation Diplomas in Art and Design L 4	NVQ/ SVQ level 4	Level 7	National Highers: SQA Higher National Certificates Advanced Highers Scottish Baccalaureates

Table 3: Framework for higher education qualifications: levels 3 (RQF) and 4 – 8 (FHEQ); levels 6 – 12 (SCQF)

FHEQ Levels England Wales Northern Ireland	SCQF Levels Scotland	HE Level or HE Year	Typical Higher Education Qualifications
8	12	5	Doctoral Degrees: PhD/DPhil, Professional Doctorates: EdD, DBA, DClinPsy etc.
7	11	4	Master's Degrees / Integrated Master's Degrees: MPhil, MRes, MA, MSc, MEng, MChem, MPhys, MPharm etc. Postgraduate Diplomas; Postgraduate Certificates Post Graduate Certificate in Education: (PGCE)
6	9 / 10	3	Bachelor's Degrees with Honours: BA, BSc, BEng, BMus etc. Bachelor's Ordinary Degrees Professional Graduate Certificate/ Diploma in Education:(PGCE/PGDE) Graduate Diplomas; Graduate Certificates
5	8	2	Foundation Degrees: FdA, FdSc etc Diplomas of Higher Education: DipHE Higher National Diplomas: HND
4	7	1	Higher National Certificates: HNC Certificates of Higher Education: CertHE
3	6	0	Foundation year; Extended degree foundation year

Table 4: Undergraduate higher education courses and credits awarded: level 3 (RQF) 4 - 6 (FHEQ) levels 6 - 12 (SCQF)

FHEQ Level E,W,NI	SCQF level (S)	Title of Qualification	Single subject Credits	Joint subject Credits	Major/Minor subject Credits
Level 6 HE level 3	Level 10	Bachelor's Honours Degree	360 credits in total	360 credits in total with 180 and 180 in each subject	360 credits in total with 240 in Major subject and 120 in Minor subject
Level 6 HE level 3	Level 9	Bachelor's Ordinary Degree	300 credits		
Level 5 HE level 2	Level 8	Diploma of Higher Education (DipHE) Undergrad Diploma (UGDip)	240 credits		
Level 4 HE level 1	Level 7	Certificate Higher Education (CertHE) Undergrad Certificate (UG Cert)	120 credits		
Level 3 HE level 0	Level 6	Foundation Certificate Extended year of Degree course	120 credits (not usually counted towards the degree course but will need to pass before progressing)		

Table 5: Postgraduate higher education courses and credits awarded: levels 6 – 8 (FHEQ) levels 9 – 12 (SCQF)

There may be some variation with courses and HEIs with credit values, the following is a general guide.

FHEQ (E, W, NI)	SCQF levels (S)	Title of Qualification	Single subjects Credits	Full-time period	Part-time period
8	12	Doctor of Philosophy (PhD) (DPhil) Professional Doctorates (D subject) Doctor of Medicine (DM)	540 credits (where awarded)	3-4 years	4-8 years
7	11	Master of Philosophy (MPhil)	360 credits (where awarded)	2 years	4-6 years
7	11	Master's by Research	180 credits at Level 7	1 year	2+ years
7	11	Taught Master's Degree	180 credits at Level 7 Usually: 120 credits for taught stage; and 60 credits for Dissertation	1 – 2 years	2-4 years
7	11	Postgraduate Diploma (PGDip)	120 credits at Level 7	1 year	2 years
7	11	Postgraduate Certificate (PGCert)	60 credits with at least 50 credits at Level 7	6 months	1 year
7	11	Integrated Master's (Honours degree also awarded)	480 credits with 120 at Level 7 120 at Level 6 120 at Level 5 120 at Level 4	2 or 3 years	5 years
6	9/10	Graduate Diploma (GDip)	120 credits at Level 6 Some credits may be at Level 5	9 months to 1 year	18 months – 2 years
6	9/10	Graduate Certificate (GCert)	60 credits at Level 6 Some credits may be at level 5	6 months	1 year

46

Chapter 4
Secondary and Further Education Qualification Subjects and Courses

4.1 Secondary and Further Education Courses; Universities and Colleges Admissions Service (UCAS) Tariff Points

Secondary and Further Education (FE) Qualifications

Secondary and further education (FE) academic courses are placed at entry level and levels level 1 - 3 in the Regulated Qualification Framework (RQF) or levels 1 - 6/7 in the Scottish Credit and Qualification Framework (SCQF). They may be studied by young people up to the age of 18 / 19 years in secondary schools, sixth form centres, further education colleges and some training centres, usually full time.

These qualifications are also available to be studied by older students usually in further education colleges or by distance learning with options to study part time, flexible learning and distance / e-learning (online). England, Wales and Northern Ireland have similar secondary and further education qualification systems whereas Scotland has a slightly different secondary and further education qualifications system.

Some students may decide to study work related / vocational qualifications known as National Vocational Qualifications (NVQs) or Scottish National Vocational Qualifications (SNVQs) at levels 1-5 in the Regulated Qualification Framework (RQF) and Scottish Credit and Qualification

Framework (SCQF) which are accredited by industry led approved awarding organisations. Professional qualifications available from level 1- 8 (RQF) and 1-12 (SCQF) are usually studied post-secondary or further education (FE) and accredited by professional organisations.

Recognised secondary and further education (FE) academic courses are accredited by approved awarding organisations which are regulated by Ofqual in England, Wales and Northern Ireland and can be searched for on the: Ofqual Register http://register.ofqual.gov.uk/ ; or for Scotland, the Scottish Qualifications Authority (SQA) http://www.sqa.org.uk/

On successful completion of a qualification all recognised awarding bodies will issue a qualification certificate which is required as evidence of attainment. If you need to obtain replacement certificates, information may be found at UK Government: Replacement Exam Certificate https://www.gov.uk/replacement-exam-certificate

Funding for Secondary and Further Education Courses

Eligible students studying for qualifications in the public education sector between the ages of 16 – 18/19 years in the academic year of studying don't need to pay for these courses. Some private colleges also offer GCSEs, AS and 'A' levels and will usually charge tuition fees. Further education colleges are for students usually over the age of 16 years.

If you are aged over 19 years you may study for academic or vocational courses in a college of further education but tuition fees are usually charged, so contact the relevant college for details. Costs vary depending on the learning provider.

If you are aged 24 years and over and considering studying for 'A' level 3 or level 4 (RQF) course you may be eligible for funding.

In England you may be eligible for a 24+ Advanced Learning Loan check:

- UK Government: Advanced Learning Loans https://www.gov.uk/advanced-learning-loans/overview .

In Wales, you may be eligible for a learning grant, check:
- Student Finance Wales http://www.studentfinancewales.co.uk/fe/

In Northern Ireland you may be eligible for a bursary, scholarship or award, check:
- Northern Ireland Direct https://www.nidirect.gov.uk/information-and-services/adult-learning/financial-help-adult-learners

In Scotland you may be eligible for a bursary check:
- Scotland Government http://www.gov.scot/Topics/Education/UniversitiesColleges/16640/learnerfunding

For further details, Go to::
Chapter 12
Student Finance

Secondary and Further Education Qualifications in England, Wales and Northern Ireland

In England, Wales or Northern Ireland, students will usually study academic subjects known as General Certificate of Secondary Education (GCSEs) at level 1 or 2 (RQF) depending on the grade achieved, up to the age of 16 years in secondary school.

Students may then continue on to study level 3 (RQF) academic Advanced Subsidiary (AS) levels and Advanced (A) levels, or vocational subjects such as BTEC qualifications, between the ages of 16 to 18 / 19 years in schools, 6th form centres or colleges of further education.

There are also other qualifications that can be studied to level 3 (RQF) such as Baccalaureates, Cambridge Pre-U, Foundation Diploma in Art (with some courses also available at level 4 (RQF) and Access courses for mature students. Some students may decide to study work related qualifications known as National Vocational Qualifications (NVQs).

Secondary and Further Education Qualifications in Scotland

In Scotland, students will usually study academic subjects known as Scottish National Courses at level 4 and 5 (SCQF) up to the age of 16 years and then level 6 (SCQF) Scottish Highers up to the age of 17 years or level 7 (SCQF) Advanced Highers or a Scottish Baccalaureate up to the age of 18 years.

Some students may decide to undertake work related Scottish National Vocational Qualifications (SNVQs) at levels 1-5 (SCQF), Scottish National Certificates (NCs) or National Progression Awards (NPAs) at levels 2-6 (SCQF).

Vocational Qualifications

Vocational qualifications are work related qualifications available in a wide range of subjects which emphasise the knowledge and skills sought after by industry and employers. Qualifications may be available as National Vocational Qualifications (NVQs) in England, Wales and Northern Ireland or as Scottish Vocational Qualifications (SVQs) in Scotland at levels or 1-5 which equates across levels 1- 8 Regulated Qualification Framework (RQF) and level 1-12 Scottish Credit and Qualification Framework (SCQF).

Other vocational courses include BTEC Nationals at levels 1- 3 (RQF), BTEC Higher Nationals at levels 4 and 5 (RQF), Scottish National Certificates (NCs) or National Progression Awards (NPAs) at levels 2-6 (SCQF). Vocational qualifications are made up of subject units, each with a credit value that allows you to predict approximately how long you will need to achieve the qualification, with 1 credit usually equalling 10 hours of learning.

Professional qualifications provided by industry professional bodies are available at levels 1 - 8 (RQF) or 1 - 12 (SCQF).

Vocational qualifications are regulated:
In England and Northern Ireland by the:
- Office of Qualifications and Examinations Regulation (Qfqual) https://www.gov.uk/government/organis ations/ofqual

In Wales, by the:
- Qualification Wales http://qualificationswales.org/;

In Scotland by the
- Scottish Qualifications Authority (SQA) http://www.sqa.org.uk/ .

European Qualifications

There are many European qualifications outside of the UK that are considered suitable to study in higher education in the UK. The European Commission has information about learning opportunities and qualifications in Europe that fall in the European Qualifications Framework at:
- Europa: Ploteus https://ec.europa.eu/ploteus/en

International Qualifications

There are many international qualifications which have been studied outside of Europe that are considered suitable to study in higher education in the UK. Further information for EU and international students applying to UK universities may be found on the universities and higher education colleges' websites where you can find accepted qualifications and on the UCAS website:
- UCAS: EU and International Guides https://www.ucas.com/ucas/undergradu ate/getting-started/international-and-eu-students/international-guides

Overseas qualifications may be compared with equivalent UK qualifications through the organisation:

- National Academic Recognition Information Centre (NARIC) http://www.ecctis.co.uk/naric/
NARIC is the National Agency working on behalf of the UK Government. See the: Chapter 5.2
Undergraduate Courses and University Entry Requirements
National Academic Recognition Information Centre (NARIC)

- National Occupational Standards (NOS) http://www.ukstandards.org.uk/ are developed for employers through the relevant Sector Skills Council or Standards Setting Organisation. National Occupational Standards describe what a person needs to be able to do, know and understand in order to perform a particular job role or function and form the basis of work based qualifications and designing and training development programmes. An accredited vocational qualification provides the evidence that you are adequately trained and have the necessary knowledge and skills which are required by the National Occupational Standards (NOS) to ensure you are able to perform a particular job role as well as allowing for progression on to higher level qualifications.

The National Occupational Standards (NOS) are defined by the relevant Sector Skills Councils (SSCs) and Standard Setting Organisations (SSOs). SSCs and SSOs with links found at the:
- Federation for Industry Sector Skills Standards http://fisss.org/sector-skills-council-body/directory-of-sscs/

SSCs and SSOs are independent employer led UK wide organisations designed to guide a skills system that is driven by employer demand and ensure that the qualifications meet employer needs.

Further information about National Occupational Standards (NOS) may be found at
- UK Government Commission for Employment and Skills (UKCES): National Occupational Standards (NOS): https://www.gov.uk/government/publications/national-occupational-standards

- NOS UK Standards http://www.ukstandards.org.uk/

- NOS UK Standards: Links to Sector Skills Councils http://www.ukstandards.org.uk/Pages/Contacts.aspx

4.2 General Certificates of Secondary Education (GCSEs) level 1 and 2 (RQF)

In England, Wales and Northern Ireland, General Certificates of Secondary Education (GCSEs) are mapped at level 1 and 2 in the Regulated Qualification Framework (RQF). GCSEs are usually studied between the ages of 14 – 16 years (years 10 and 11) as two year full-time courses in secondary schools or colleges of further education (FE) being available in over 40 subjects. It may be possible to study some subjects as shorter courses as well as part-time options in further education or through distance learning, usually for older students.

There are no formal entry requirements. Each GCSE qualification is at level 1 or 2 on the Regulated Qualification Framework (RQF), depending on the grade achieved, with GCSEs at level 2 (RQF) being the

first step towards studying for 'A' levels or other level 3 (RQF) qualifications. Students will usually take up to 8 GCSE subjects, although some will undertake more.

GCSE changes 2015-18
Between August 2015 to 2018, GCSEs have undergone changes with different systems in place in England, Wales and Northern Ireland. The awarding organisations AQA, Pearson Qualifications, Oxford and Cambridge and RSA (OCR) used in England and Northern Ireland will have a new grading scale of 9 to 1 to be used with 9 being the top grade which distinguishes new GCSEs from the previous ones which are graded A* - E. The awarding organisations the Welsh Joint Education Committee (WJEC) and

the Council for Curriculum Examinations and Assessment (Northern Ireland), will retain the grades of A* - E.

The Welsh Joint Education Committee (WJEC) subsidiary company, Eduqas will offer GCSE grades 9 – 1. In the summer of 2019, the Council for Curriculum Examinations and Assessment (Northern Ireland) will change the way in which GCSEs are graded and the C* will appear in the grading for the first time. By summer 2020 the remaining 9 – 1 graded GCSE subjects will be introduced.

GCSE grades
Grades 9, 8 and 7 are equal to:
Grades A* to A;
Grades 6, 5 and 4 are equal to:
Grades B to C;
Grades 3, 2 and 1 are equal to:
Grades D, E, F and G

The new GCSEs in English language, English literature and mathematics have been taught in schools in England since September 2015, with the first results and new grades issued in August 2017.
Further new GCSEs were introduced in 2017. Assessment will be mainly by exam with other types of assessment used only where needed to test essential skills. The GCSE subjects will no longer be divided into different modules and students will take their exams in one period at the end of the course.
Exams are only split into foundation tier and higher tier if one exam paper does not

give all students the opportunity to show their knowledge. Resit opportunities will only be available each November for English language and mathematics. Further information about secondary and further education qualifications may be found at:

England
UK Government: GCSE, AS and 'A' level reform
https://www.gov.uk/government/publications/get-the-facts-gcse-and-a-level-reform

Wales
Qualifications Wales
http://qualificationswales.org/

Northern Ireland
Northern Ireland Direct
http://www.nidirect.gov.uk/guide-to-qualifications

GCSE level 1 and 2 (RQF) grades
GCSE Level 2 (RQF):
Grades A*; A;   B;   C
Grades 9; 8; 7; 6; 5; 4

GCSE Level 1 (RQF):
Grades D; E; F; G
Grades 3;   2;   1

The Awarding Organisations offering GCSEs may be used across England, Wales and Northern Ireland for some subjects.

England GCSE Grades

In England GCSEs will have a new grading scale of 9 to 1 to be used with 9 being the top grade which distinguishes new GCSEs from the previous ones (which were graded A*-G). GCSEs will be graded 9-4, mapped at level 2 in the Regulated Qualification Framework (RQF) level 2, and grades 3-1 mapped at level 1 (RQF). The awarding organisations are AQA; Pearson Edexcel; and Oxford and Cambridge and RSA (OCR).

GCSE grades
GCSE Level 1 (RQF):
Grades 3;   2;   1
GCSE Level 2 (RQF):
Grades 9; 8; 7; 6; 5; 4

Awarding Organisations: GCSEs England: Awarding Organisations: GCSEs (grades 9 - 1)
AQA http://www.aqa.org.uk/
Pearson Qualifications
https://qualifications.pearson.com/
Oxford and Cambridge and RSA (OCR)
http://www.ocr.org.uk/

Northern Ireland GCSE Grades

In Northern Ireland GCSEs will retain the present GCSE system of grades A*-G. GCSEs will be graded A*-C, mapped at level 2 in the Regulated Qualification Framework (RQF), and grades D-G mapped at level 1 (RQF). However by summer 2020 the new grading system 9 – 1 will be used for all GCSEs by the awarding organisation, the Council for Curriculum Examinations and Assessment (CCEA) which is the main awarding organisation.

Some GCSEs are also offered by additional awarding bodies which will be changing to the grading system of 9-1 and discussions are taking place to confirm how they can be supported to make the necessary arrangements to continue to offer GCSEs in Northern Ireland, these are AQA , Pearson Edexcel, and Oxford, Cambridge and RSA (OCR).

GCSE grades
GCSE Level 2 (RQF):
Grades A*; A; B; C
Grades 9; 8; 7; 6; 5; 4
GCSE Level 1 (RQF):
Grades D; E; F; G
Grades 3; 2; 1

Northern Ireland Awarding Organisation; GCSEs (grades A*-G; by summer 2020 the remaining 9 - 1 graded GCSE subjects will be introduced).
The Council for Curriculum Examinations and
Assessment (CCEA) (Northern Ireland)
http://www.ccea.org.uk/

Wales GCSE Grades

In Wales GCSEs will retain the present GCSE system virtually intact with GCSEs graded A* - G. GCSEs will be graded A*-C, mapped at level 2 in the Regulated Qualification Framework (RQF) and grades D-G mapped at level 1 (RQF).

The awarding organisation is the Welsh Joint Education Committee (WJEC). However, the Welsh Joint Education Committee (WJEC) subsidiary company, Eduqas will offer GCSE grades 9 – 1.

GCSE grades
Welsh Joint Education Committee (WJEC)
GCSE Level 2 (RQF):
Grades A*; A; B; C

GCSE Level 1 (RQF):
Grades D; E; F; G

Welsh Joint Education Committee (WJEC) subsidiary company, Eduqas
GCSE Level 2 (RQF):
Grades 9; 8; 7; 6; 5; 4

GCSE Level 1 (RQF):
Grades 3; 2; 1

Wales: Awarding Organisation: GCSEs (grades A* - G)
Welsh Joint Education Committee (WJEC)
http://www.wjec.co.uk/

Wales: Awarding Organisation: GCSEs (grades 9 - 1)
Welsh Joint Education Committee (WJEC) subsidiary company:
Eduqas http://www.eduqas.co.uk/

In Scotland, Scottish National Courses level 4 and 5 Scottish Credit and Qualification Framework (SCQF) are studied usually between the ages of 14 - 16 years as two year full-time courses in secondary schools or colleges of further education (FE). It may be possible to study some subjects as shorter courses as well as part-time options in further education or through distance learning, usually for older students. There are no formal entry requirements for Scottish National Courses level 4 and 5.

Each Scottish National qualification is at level 4 or 5 Scottish Credit and Qualification Framework (SCQF) with Scottish National qualification is at level 5 being the first step towards studying for Scottish Highers or Scottish Advanced Highers. Students will usually take up to 8 Scottish National Course level 4 and 5 subjects, although some may undertake more.

Scottish Nationals level 1-4 (SCQF) are not graded but assessed as pass or fail. Scottish Nationals level 5 (SCQF) are graded A to D based on the student's performance and course assessment and carry 24 SCQF points reflecting the level of demand and challenge involved.

Scottish National Courses 4 and 5 (SCQF) Grades
Sottish Nationals level 5 (SCQF):
Grades A; B; C; D

Scottish Nationals level 4 (SCQF)):
awarded pass but ungraded

Awarding Organisation: Scottish National Courses 4 and 5 (SCQF)
Scottish Qualifications Authority (SQA)
http://www.sqa.org.uk/scqf

'A' Levels and 'AS' Levels at Level 3 (RQF)

In England, Wales and Northern Ireland, General Certificate of Education (GCE) Advanced levels are commonly known as 'A' levels, GCE Advanced Subsidiary levels are commonly known as 'AS' levels and are mapped at level 3 in the Regulated Qualification Framework (RQF)

'A' levels and 'AS' levels are for students usually between the ages of 16 years to 18/19 years who are in school or college in years 12 and 13.

'A' levels are usually studied as a two year full-time course and 'AS' levels as a one year full time course in secondary schools' 6th forms, 6th form colleges or colleges of further education (FE) and are available in over 100 subjects.

It may be possible to study some 'A' level subjects as accelerated one year full time courses as well as part-time options in further education or through distance learning, usually for older students.

Depending on the awarding organisation and the UK country, 'AS' levels and 'A' levels are studied as either linear stand-alone (separate) courses or as modular courses with an 'AS' level being the first year of an 'A' level course.

The second year of an 'A' level course may also be referred to as A2. Students will usually take up to 4 'AS' level subjects and up to 3 'A' level subjects, although some will undertake more. Entry requirements for 'A' level courses are usually a minimum of 4 or 5 GCSE passes grades A*-C / 9-4.

'A' and 'AS' level changes 2015-18
Between August 2015 to 2018, 'A' levels and 'AS' levels have undergone changes with different systems in place in England, Wales and Northern Ireland.
The awarding organisations AQA, Pearson Edexcel and Oxford, Cambridge and RSA (OCR) used in England and Northern Ireland will provide linear 'A' level and 'AS' level courses with exams taken at the end of the course.

'A' levels became modular after 2008, being composed of AS and A2 modules and the awarding organisations, the Welsh Joint Education Committee (WJEC) and the Council for Curriculum Examinations and Assessment (Northern Ireland) will retain the AS qualification.

The AS is now set at 40% (previously 50%) of the overall 'A' level grade. The timescales for the change of the new AS and 'A' levels were introduced over a three year period beginning in September 2015 to 2018.

'A' level subjects
The UK Government is undertaking reform on GCSEs, AS and 'A' levels, with some subjects being amended; further information may be found on the following websites:
UK Government: GCSE, AS and 'A' level reform
https://www.gov.uk/government/publicatio ns/get-the-facts-gcse-and-a-level-reform

Further information about secondary and further education qualifications may be found at:

England
UK Government: GCSE, AS and 'A' level reform
https://www.gov.uk/government/publicatio ns/get-the-facts-gcse-and-a-level-reform

Wales
Qualifications Wales
http://qualificationswales.org/

Northern Ireland
Northern Ireland Direct
http://www.nidirect.gov.uk/guide-to-qualifications

England: 'AS' levels and 'A' levels

In England, 'AS' levels and 'A' levels are mostly studied as linear stand-alone (separate) qualifications, although some may still be modular courses with an 'AS' level being the first year of an 'A' level course.

'A' levels and 'AS' levels taught from 2015 in England are fully linear, being assessed mainly by an exam at the end of the course, with other types of assessment used only when needed to test essential skills. 'AS' level assessments will take place after one year of study, and 'A' levels after two years of study. The courses will no longer be divided into modules. AS results will no longer count towards an 'A' level. 'A' levels will be taught as one course, although 'AS' levels, contributing to 40% of the 'A' level grade (rather than the previous 50%), can be taught alongside the first year of 'A' levels.

Wales 'AS' levels and 'A' levels

In Wales 'AS' levels and 'A' levels are studied as modular courses with an 'AS' level being the first year of an 'A' level course. 'A' levels and 'AS' levels taught from 2015 in Wales are remaining modular and involve a subject studied at 'AS' level contributing to 40% of the 'A' level grade (rather than the previous 50%).

Students will have the opportunity if necessary to improve their grades at AS by retaking AS modules at the end of year 13. Students can still use their AS grades as part of their UCAS application, with 'A' level grade predictions based largely on AS grades.

Northern Ireland 'AS' levels and 'A' levels

In Northern Ireland 'AS' levels and 'A' levels are studied as either linear stand-alone (separate) qualifications or as modular courses with an 'AS' level being the first year of an 'A' level course.

'A' levels and 'AS' levels taught from 2015 in Northern Ireland are a mix with some being of fully linear, being assessed mainly by an exam at the end of the course, and others will offer modular options, depending on which awarding organisation is used for the subject concerned.

Linear 'AS' level assessments will take place after one year of study and 'A' levels after two years of study with AS results will no longer counting towards an 'A' level. Modular 'A' levels will involve a subject studied at 'AS' level contributing to 40% of the 'A' level grade (rather than the previous 50%).

'A' Levels and 'AS' Levels UCAS Grades and UCAS Tariff Points

Confirm UCAS Tariff points at UCAS: Tariff Calculator
https://www.ucas.com/ucas/Tariff-calculator

'A' level UCAS Grades and UCAS Tariff points from 2017
'A' level grades:
A*, A, B, C, D, E being pass grades and U (unclassified) a fail

UCAS Tariff points for 'A' level grades from 2017:
A* = 56
A   = 48
B   = 40
C   = 32
D   = 24
E   = 16

'AS' level Grades and UCAS Tariff points from 2017
'AS' level grades
A*, A, B, C, D, E being pass grades and U (unclassified) a fail

UCAS Tariff points for 'AS' level grades from 2017 (worth 40% of an 'A' level grade):
A = 20
B = 16
C = 12
D = 10
E =   6

The following examination bodies provide 'A' level qualifications (as well as GCSEs and 'AS' levels), although each one won't offer all subjects. To find 'A' level subjects and other regulated qualifications you can check the:

Office of Qualifications and Examinations Regulation (Ofqual): register of qualifications
http://register.ofqual.gov.uk/Qualification

Awarding organisations for GCSEs, 'AS' levels and 'A' levels in England, Wales and Northern Ireland
AQA http://www.aqa.org.uk/
Oxford and Cambridge and RSA (OCR)
http://www.ocr.org.uk/
Pearson qualifications
http://qualifications.pearson.com/
The Council for Curriculum Examinations and Assessment (Northern Ireland)
http://www.ccea.org.uk/
Welsh Joint Education Committee (WJEC)
http://www.wjec.co.uk/
Welsh Joint Education Committee (WJEC) subsidiary company:
Eduqas   http://www.eduqas.co.uk/

England: Awarding organisation: 'AS' levels and 'A' levels
AQA http://www.aqa.org.uk/
Pearson Edexcel http://www.edexcel.com/
Oxford and Cambridge and RSA (OCR)
http://www.ocr.org.uk/

Wales: Awarding organisation: 'AS' levels and 'A' levels
Welsh Joint Education Committee (WJEC)
http://www.wjec.co.uk/
Welsh Joint Education Committee (WJEC) subsidiary company: Eduqas
http://www.eduqas.co.uk/

Northern Ireland: Awarding organisation: 'AS' levels and 'A' levels
The Council for Curriculum Examinations and Assessment (Northern Ireland)
http://www.ccea.org.uk/

Northern Ireland: Additional Awarding Organisation: 'AS' levels and 'A' levels
AQA http://www.aqa.org.uk/
Pearson qualifications
http://qualifications.pearson.com/
Oxford and Cambridge and RSA (OCR)
http://www.ocr.org.uk/

In England and Wales the Access to Higher Education (HE) Diploma http://www.accesstohe.ac.uk/ is a qualification mapped at level 3 in the Regulated Qualification Framework (RQF), there is one course available in Northern Ireland with further information at Northern Ireland Direct: Routes to Higher Education https://www.nidirect.gov.uk/articles/routes-higher-education . A different scheme operates in Scotland through the Scottish Wider Access Programme http://www.scottishwideraccess.org/ .

The Access to Higher Education (HE) Diploma course provides higher education preparation for mature students who are aged over 19 years of age, without traditional qualifications, or for those who have been out of education for some time. The Access to HE Diploma is available as a one year full time or two year part time course, usually in colleges of further education but there may be options to study by distance learning.

There are more than 1,000 Access to HE Diploma courses available in a range of subject specialist areas with a named subject, using a common title e.g. Access to HE Diploma (Nursing) or Access to HE Diploma (Law); Access to HE Diploma (Social Studies); Access to HE Diploma (Art and Design) so you need to consider what higher education subject you are interested in studying first.

Access to HE validating agencies are licensed by the Quality Assurance Agency for Higher Education (QAA) http://www.qaa.ac.uk/en . A database of all providers and recognised Access courses are listed at Access to Higher Education (HE) Diploma: How Diplomas are Regulated; Access Validating Agencies http://www.accesstohe.ac.uk/

Entry requirements for Access to HE Diploma courses may vary but many don't have formal entry requirements. Applicants may be required to take a test to demonstrate English language and mathematics ability and some colleges offer pre-Access courses for students who need additional support. Check with the relevant learning provider about entry requirements. Applications are made directly to the Learning Provider.

Costs vary depending on the Learning Provider. If you are aged 24 years and over, and considering studying 'A' level 3 course, you may be eligible for a 24+ Advanced Learning Loan in England, with further information at UK Government: Advanced Learner Loan https://www.gov.uk/advanced-learner-loan or a Learning Grant in Wales, with further information at Student Finance Wales: FE; Learning Grant FE https://www.studentfinancewales.co.uk/fe . Further information about Access to HE Diplomas may be found at Access to HE http://www.accesstohe.ac.uk/ .

Access to higher education (HE) Diploma grades and UCAS Tariff points
Access to Higher Education Diploma courses will be awarded UCAS Tariff points from 2017 for entry to higher education courses based on a pass of 60 credits with 45 credits at level 3 (RQF) awarded as Distinctions, Merits and Passes.

Access to HE Diploma UCAS Tariff Points:
Confirm UCAS Tariff points at UCAS: Tariff Calculator https://www.ucas.com/ucas/Tariff-calculator

45 credits at level 3 (RQF) with Distinction =145 UCAS Tariff points

45 credits at level 3 (RQF) with Merit   = 96 UCAS Tariff points

45 credits at level 3 (RQF) with Pass   = 48 UCAS Tariff points
Combinations of credits with Distinctions, Merits and Passes will be awarded UCAS Tariff points accordingly

The Access to HE Diploma course consists of a particular approved set of subject unit titles, with units specifying a set of particular learning outcomes and assessment criteria as well as grade descriptors awarded as a grade of Pass, Merit or Distinction. The set of grades achieved across the course is known as the grade profile. Subject units may be worth 3, 6 or 9 credits depending on the amount of study required for that unit.

To successfully pass the Access to HE Diploma, the total number of credits required is 60, some credits may be at level 2 (RQF) but a minimum of 45 credits at level 3 (RQF) are required for the award of the Access to HE Diploma. The final result will be a grade profile recorded on the achievement transcript, showing titles and grades achieved, issued with the Access to HE Diploma.

Access to HE Certificates and Diplomas started before September 2014 aren't allocated UCAS Tariff points; Access to HE Certificates and Diplomas started after September 2014 are allocated UCAS Tariff points relating to the grade, volume and level of study which have been used for entry to higher education since September 2017.

Awarding Organisation: Access to HE Diploma

The Quality Assurance Agency for Higher Education (QAA) manages the scheme for the recognition and quality assurance of Access to HE courses. QAA licenses Access Validation Agencies (AVAs) to validate Access to HE Diploma courses and award Access to HE Diplomas to students.

There are 13 AVAs across England and Wales that are responsible for overseeing Access to HE Diploma courses, most of which are delivered in colleges of further education. Information on the Validation Agencies (AVAs) may be found at Access to HE: AVA Profiles http://www.accesstohe.ac.uk/HowCourses/AVA-profiles/Pages/Default.aspx

Baccalaureates

Baccalaureates are broad-based coursed that combine academic subjects with additional components which are designed to develop skills. The AQA, Welsh and Scottish Baccalaureates are available throughout the UK. The International Baccalaureate is a qualification available throughout the world. The European Baccalaureate is available throughout Europe in some schools.

AQA Baccalaureate

The AQA Baccalaureate comprises of three 'A' level subjects awarded by any awarding body; independent learning through the Extended Project Qualification (EPQ); skills development through Enrichment activities such as work-related learning, community participation and personal development; breadth through one 'AS' level, 'A' level or level 3 (RQF) Core Mathematics qualification provided this differs from the main programme of study.

AQA Baccalaureate Grades
The grading of the AQA Baccalaureate involves achieving an overall grade of: Pass, Merit or Distinction in addition to your 'A/''AS' level grades

Awarding Organisation: AQA Baccalaureate
AQA https://www.aqa.org.uk/

European Baccalaureate Diploma (EB)

In Europe, the European Baccalaureate Diploma (EB) is the school leaving examination for students who attend one of the European Schools, of which 14 European Schools are in the UK and mapped at level 3 in the Regulated Qualification Framework (RQF). The European Baccalaureate Diploma (EB) is usually studied between the ages of 16 - 18 /19 years as a two year full-time course in one of the European Schools.

Students study 10 or 11 subjects and are required to study their own language, at least one foreign language to a high level, history and geography, mathematics, at least one science subject, philosophy, physical education and religion/moral education.

Elective courses must be added to these subjects. Further information may be found at
UK Government: European Baccalaureate https://www.gov.uk/government/publications/information-on-the-european-baccalaureate

European Baccalaureate Diploma (EB) Grades
The grading of European Baccalaureate Diploma (EB):
10 or 11 subjects: each marked out of 10, with 6 required to pass.

The EB Diploma is based on performance in the final year and to pass, a student must obtain a minimum of 60% overall. A mark out of 10 is also awarded for each individual subject with 6 required to pass. Currently there are no UCAS Tariff points allocated.

Awarding Organisation: European Baccalaureate Diploma (EB)
European Schools http://www.eursc.eu/
European Schools: European Baccalaureate
https://www.eursc.eu/en/European-Schools/studies-certificates/European-Baccalaureate

Internationally, the International Baccalaureate (IB) Diploma Programme (DP) is an international qualification offered by IB schools worldwide as well as some of the private schools and a few state schools in the UK. It is overseen by the International Baccalaureate Organisation (IBO) in Switzerland http://www.ibo.org/. The International Baccalaureate (IB) Diploma Programme (DP) is for students usually aged 16 to 19 years of age as a two year full-time course in secondary school.

All students take six subjects to include one subject from each of the five groups; your own language, a foreign language, social science, experimental science, mathematics and a sixth from either an arts based subject or another subject from one of the five groups.

Students also undertake the DP core which comprises of theory of knowledge (TOK), creativity, and activity service (CAS) as well as the extended essay.

Three or four subjects are studied to Higher Level (HL) which is equivalent to 'A' level and the others to Standard Level (SL), which is the equivalent to 'AS' level. HL and SL courses differ in scope but are assessed against the same grade descriptors, with HL courses consisting of a greater body of knowledge, understanding and skills. Further information may be found at the International Baccalaureate Organisation (IBO) in Switzerland http://www.ibo.org/ .

International Baccalaureate (IB) Diploma Programme Grades and UCAS Tariff points from 2017
Confirm UCAS Tariff points at UCAS: Tariff Calculator
https://www.ucas.com/ucas/Tariff-calculator

The Diploma Programme (DP) grades awarded for each course range from 7 (highest) to 1 (lowest). The final Diploma result score is made up of the combined scores for each subject.

The Diploma is awarded to students who gain at least 24 points subject to certain minimum levels of performance which includes successful completion of the three DP core elements, theory of knowledge (TOK), creativity, activity service (CAS) and the extended essay.

The theory of knowledge (TOK) and the extended essay are awarded individual grades and can collectively contribute up to 3 additional points towards the overall Diploma score. Creativity, activity service (CAS) doesn't contribute to the points total score but successful participation is a requirement for the award of the Diploma. The same number of points is awarded for the higher level (HL) and standard level (SL).

A bilingual Diploma is awarded to candidates who complete and receive a grade 3 or higher in two languages selected from the DP course in language and literature. Students who gain a grade 3 or higher in studies in language and literature and a grade 3 or higher in an individuals and societies or science subject completed in a different language will also receive the bilingual Diploma.

International Baccalaureate (IBO) Diploma Programme grades:
Six subjects at Higher Level (HL) or Standard Level (SL), each subject: Graded 7 (highest) to 1 (lowest)
Extended Essay graded A-E and Theory of Knowledge: graded A-E

Approximately at Higher Level,
Grade 6 = grade A at 'A' level and
Grade 7 = grade A* at 'A' level.
A minimum of 24 points is required to obtain a Diploma.

The grading of the International Baccalaureate (IB) Diploma Programme: Six subjects plus Extended Essay and Theory of Knowledge Grades

IB Higher Level Grades and UCAS Tariff points
H7 = 56
H6 = 48
H5 = 32
H4 = 24
H3 = 12

IB Standard Level Grades and UCAS Tariff points
S7 = 28
S6 = 24
S5 = 16
S4 = 12
S3 = 6

IB Extended Essay Grades and UCAS Tariff points
A = 12
B = 10
C = 8
D = 6
E = 4

IB Theory of Knowledge Grades and UCAS Tariff points
A = 12
B = 10
C = 8
D = 6
E = 4

Awarding and Overseeing Organisation: International Baccalaureate (IB) Diploma Programme
International Baccalaureate Organisation (IBO) in Switzerland http://www.ibo.org/

Welsh Baccalaureate Advanced Diploma

In Wales, the Welsh Baccalaureate (WBQ) is delivered at Foundation level 1 in the Regulated Qualification Framework (RQF); National level 2 (RQF); and Advanced level 3 (RQF). The Welsh Baccalaureate Advanced Diplom'A' level 3 (RQF) is for students usually between the ages of 16 years – 18 /19 years and studied as a two year full-time course in secondary school 6th forms, 6th form colleges, colleges of further education (FE) or training centres across Wales.

To gain a Welsh Baccalaureate Advanced Diploma at level 3 (RQF), students must achieve the Advanced Skills Challenge Certificate which is also known as the Core Certificate involving challenges consisting of one individual project worth 50% and three challenges based on themes of enterprise and employability, global citizenship and community worth 50%; as well as optional qualifications at level 3 (RQF) which includes 'A' levels, 'AS' levels or BTEC National qualifications.

Together, the Core and Options make up the Welsh Baccalaureate Qualification. You must achieve GCSE English Language or Welsh grades A*-C, mathematics and two or three 'A' levels or equivalent.

The Welsh Baccalaureate Advanced Diploma can be studied in English or Welsh or a combination of the two languages. Students who meet the requirements of the Core and Options are awarded the full Diploma at the appropriate level. Further information may be found at Welsh Baccalaureate http://www.welshbaccalaureate.org.uk/

Welsh Baccalaureate Advanced Diploma grades and UCAS Tariff points from 2017
The grading of the Welsh Baccalaureate Advanced Diploma: Skills Challenge Certificate grades for first teaching from 2015:
Grades A*; A ; B; C; D; E
UCAS Tariff points for the Welsh Baccalaureate Advanced Diploma Grades:
A* = 56
A = 48
B = 40
C = 32
D = 24
E = 16

Optional qualifications at level 3 (RQF) are awarded separate UCAS Tariff points depending on the qualification and grade. 'A' levels will be graded A* - E and attract

UCAS Tariff points:
Grades:
A* = 56
A   = 48
B   = 40
C   = 32
D   = 24
E   = 16

Awarding Organisation: Welsh Baccalaureate
WJEC   http://www.wjec.co.uk/

BTEC Nationals Level 3 (RQF)

In England, Wales and Northern Ireland, Business and Technology Education Council (BTEC) qualifications lead to vocational qualifications (work related) and have been available for over 25 years. The design of the qualifications have undergone different formats over this time and are currently available from entry level through to level 7 (RQF).

BTEC National courses are mapped at level 3 (RQF), available as BTEC National: Certificate, Extended Certificate, Foundation Diploma, Diploma and Extended Diploma, and are for students usually between the ages of 16 years – 18 /19 years (years 12 and 13) as one or two year full-time courses, although in some cases, they may take up to three years to complete, depending on the qualification.

They may be studied in secondary school 6th forms, 6th form colleges or colleges of further education (FE), and are available in a range of vocationally related subjects.

As they are built up of units, the qualifications are designed to be studied flexibly. BTEC Nationals are considered acceptable for entry into work or to study a higher education course.

Entry requirements to enter a BTEC National qualification are usually a minimum of 4 GCSEs at grade C or above / grade 4 or above, including English and mathematics or a BTEC Intermediate Level 2 qualification (grades may be specified).

BTEC National qualifications up to 2016
BTEC National qualifications level 3 (RQF) courses from 2013 to 2016 were available as a: National Certificate; National Subsidiary Diploma; National 90-credit Diploma; National Diploma; or National Extended Diploma.

The number of credits completed determined the qualification awarded, therefore it is usual, for example, for students to have completed the National Subsidiary Diploma before going on to complete the National Diploma or Extended National Diploma. A BTEC National Diploma or Extended National Diploma developed from 2007 to 2012 was available as an Award, Certificate or Diploma.

BTEC National qualifications from 2016
BTEC National qualifications level 3 (RQF) courses have changed since 2016 and are available to study as a BTEC National Certificate, National Extended Certificate, National Foundation Diploma, National Diploma and National Extended Diploma. The number of credits completed determines the qualification awarded, therefore it is usual, for example, for students to complete the National Certificate or National Extended Certificate before going on to complete the National Diploma or National Extended Diploma. A BTEC National Diploma or Extended Diploma will usually take two years to complete in full, although in some cases, they may take up to three years to complete.

BTEC National Qualification Grades and UCAS Tariff Points

Confirm UCAS Tariff points at UCAS: Tariff Calculator
https://www.ucas.com/ucas/Tariff-calculator

BTEC National level 3 (RQF) qualifications are made up of units with credits obtained for each unit. Qualifications are designed by combining units together with the required number of credits which need to be passed differing depending on which BTEC National qualification is achieved. BTEC Nationals grades:
Distinction* (D*); Distinction (D); Merit (M); and Pass (P).

BTEC National qualification UCAS Tariff points from 2017

UCAS Tariff points for BTEC National qualifications depend on which qualification is taken, the number of credits achieved and the grade/s (see chart at the end of this chapter).

BTEC National Extended Diploma (3 grades; 180 credits)

The BTEC National: Extended Diploma is awarded 3 grades which may be a combination of:
Distinction*, Distinction, Merit or Pass with UCAS Tariff points set accordingly;

D*D*D*	= 168
DDD	= 144
MMM	= 96
PPP	= 48

Subject grade
Distinction* (D*)	=	56
Distinction (D)	=	48
Merit (M)	=	32
Pass (P)	=	16

Combinations of D*, D, M and Passes are awarded UCAS Tariff points accordingly.

BTEC National Diploma (2 grades; 120 credits)

The BTEC National Diploma is awarded 2 grades, which may be a combination of:
Distinction*, Distinction, Merit or Pass with UCAS Tariff points set accordingly;

D*D*	= 112
DD	= 96
MM	= 64
PP	= 32

Each subject:
D*	=	56
D	=	48
M	=	32
P	=	16

Combinations of Distinction*, Distinction, Merit and Pass are awarded UCAS Tariff points accordingly.

BTEC National Foundation Diploma (1 grade; 90 credits)

The BTEC National Foundation Diploma is worth one grade with UCAS Tariff points set to take account of the different number of credits for each qualification.

Distinction* (D*)	=	84
Distinction (D)	=	72
Merit (M)	=	48
Pass (P)	=	24

BTEC National Extended Certificate (1 grade; 60 credits)

The BTEC National Extended Certificate is worth one grade with UCAS Tariff points set to take account of the different number of credits for each qualification.

Distinction* (D*)	=	56
Distinction (D)	=	48
Merit (M)	=	32
Pass (P)	=	16

BTEC National certificate (1 grade; 30 credits)

The BTEC National Certificate is worth one grade with UCAS Tariff points set to take account of the different number of credits for each qualification.

Distinction* (D*)	=	28
Distinction (D)	=	24
Merit (M)	=	16
Pass (P)	=	8

Awarding Organisation: BTEC National

Pearson qualifications
http://qualifications.pearson.com/

In England, the Cambridge International Exams http://www.cie.org.uk/ provide a range of international education programmes and qualifications, including Cambridge International AS and 'A' level as well as Cambridge International Pre-U certificate. The Cambridge International Pre-U is a new post-16 qualification mapped at level 3 in the Regulated Qualification Framework (RQF)and for students usually between the ages of 16 years - 18 /19 years (years 12 and 13) as a two year full-time course in mostly independent but some public secondary school 6th forms, 6th form colleges.

The Cambridge International Pre-U prepares students with the skills and knowledge needed to succeed at university. It promotes independent and self-directed learning in preparation for undergraduate study. The Cambridge International Pre-U is available in 25 Principal Subjects which are two year programmes of study with exams at the end. Short courses, lasting one year, are also available in some subjects. Each Pre-U subject has a bigger syllabus compared to an 'A' level subject.

Many universities in the UK, including the Russell Group, as well as universities around the world have accepted Cambridge Pre-U as equivalent to other pre-university qualifications. Students can take Cambridge Pre-U syllabuses separately and receive a grade for each one or they can take the full Cambridge Pre-U Diploma.

To achieve the Diploma, students must take at least three Cambridge Pre-U principal subjects or a combination of Cambridge Pre-U principal subjects and up to two 'A' levels, plus Cambridge Pre-U Global Perspectives and Research. Further information may be found at: Cambridge International Exams http://www.cie.org.uk/

Cambridge International Pre-U principal Subjects Grades and UCAS Tariff Points from 2017

Confirm UCAS Tariff points at UCAS: Tariff Calculator
https://www.ucas.com/ucas/Tariff-calculator

The grading of the Cambridge Pre-U: The Cambridge Pre-U reports achievement on a scale of nine grades for each subject:
Distinction: 1, 2 and 3 (D1, D2, D3)
Merit: 1, 2 and 3 (M1, M2, M3)
Pass: 1, 2 and 3 (P1, P2, P3)

Distinction 1 (D1) is the top grade and reports achievement above Grade A* at 'A' level.

Cambridge International Pre-U principal subjects
UCAS Tariff points from 2017
D1 = 56;   D2 = 56;   D3 = 52
M1 = 44;   M2 = 40;   M3 = 36
P1 = 28;   P2 = 24;   P3 = 20

Cambridge International Pre-U global perspectives and research grades
UCAS Tariff points from 2017
D1 = 56;   D2 = 56;   D3 = 52
M1 = 44;   M2 = 40;   M3 = 36
P1 = 28;   P2 = 24;   P3 = 20

Cambridge International Pre-U principal subject grade and 'A' level equivalent:
D1 = A*;   D2 = A*;   D3 = A
M1 = B;   M2 = B;   M3 = C
P1 = D;   P2 = D;   P3 = E

Awarding Organisation: Cambridge International Pre-U
Cambridge International Exams
http://www.cie.org.uk/

Foundation Diploma in Art (FDA) (Level 3 and Level 4 (RQF)

In England, Wales, Northern Ireland and Scotland, the foundation Diploma in art (FDA)is mapped with most courses at level 3 in the Regulated Qualification Framework (RQF) although some courses may be at level 4 (RQF) and are for students usually aged over 18 years of age.

The foundation Diploma in art will take one academic year full time to complete with part time courses usually taking two years to complete and may be available in some secondary school 6th forms, 6th form colleges, colleges of further education (FE), some universities or art schools. Although the foundation Diploma in art course title varies according to which awarding Organisation accredits the course, it is usually referred to as a foundation Diploma in art (FDA) and may include art, design and media.

The FDA provides the opportunity to develop a wide range of project based art, design and media based activities. This helps to prepare for the move on to study a degree in a range of specialist art subjects in higher education. The FDA also supports you with building up your portfolio to provide a stronger application for relevant degree courses.

Many higher education institutions (HEIs) require the FDA as part of the entry requirements in addition to 'A' levels /or equivalent qualifications for Art subject degrees. The foundation Diplomas in art may vary in content, therefore it is important to consider what art subject area/s you are interested in and read the information on the relevant websites or prospectus before you make an application.

Students that meet the residency requirements, who are under 19 years of age on 31st August in the year they are enrolled for the course, don't usually have to pay tuition fees for the course, although some institutions may charge a small amount.

Some institutions offer tuition fee concessions for level 3 RQF courses to students over the age of 19 so you may not have to pay full costs. For FDA courses in higher education institutions (HEIs), if eligible you may be able to obtain student finance and the tuition fees may be lower than for an honours degree year tuition fees, but check information with the relevant HEIs.

Entry requirements may vary between courses and education providers but generally 'A' levels or equivalent qualifications will be required and you will need to be able to demonstrate a good ability in an art subject. Applications are usually made directly to the education institution where you want to study and although there may be no advised deadlines, it may be advisable to apply early for competitive courses.

If applying directly to a 6th form, university or college, there is no limit on the number of applications you can make, however, some education institutions provide more than one FDA and usually you can only apply for one FDA per institution. Some courses may require an application through UCAS http://www.ucas.com/ and you can select up to five courses to apply for. If applying through UCAS you will need to meet advised deadlines. Application information will be on the relevant education institution website.

Foundation Diploma in Art Grades and UCAS Tariff Points from 2017

Confirm UCAS Tariff points at UCAS: Tariff Calculator
https://www.ucas.com/ucas/Tariff-calculator
The level 3 (RQF) Foundation Diploma in Art and Design is awarded as a Pass, Merit or Distinction and has the following overall UCAS points:
Distinction = 112; Merit = 96; Pass = 80

Awarding Organisations: Foundation Diploma in Art

The following are the Awarding Bodies that offer the Foundation Diploma / Studies in Art and Design (FDA). Universities may also be awarding bodies for higher education studied FDAs For further details, check on the relevant website.
ABC Level 3 and level 4 Diploma in Foundation Studies in Art and Design
ABC level 3 Foundation Diploma in Art, Design and Media
ABC Awards

http://www.abcawards.co.uk/
Pearson Edexcel Level 3 BTEC Foundation Diploma in Art and Design
Pearson Qualifications
http://qualifications.pearson.com/
University of the Arts (UAL): Foundation Diploma in
Art and Design
http://www.arts.ac.uk/about-ual/awarding-Organisation/qualifications/
WJEC Diploma in Foundation Studies in Art, Design and Media
WJEChttp://www.wjec.co.uk/

Scottish Qualifications: National Certificates Level 6; Highers; Advanced Highers and Baccalaureate Levels 6/7 SCQF

Scottish Highers (H) Level 6 (SCQF)

In Scotland, Scottish Highers, also known as Highers (may be abbreviated to H) are mapped at level 6 Scottish Credit and Qualification Framework (SCQF) and are for students usually between the ages of 16 years - 17years. Scottish Highers are usually studied as a one year full time course in secondary school or a college of further education in the fifth year of secondary schooling (S5) being available in a range of subjects and provide students with a broad general education.

Scottish highers are the main route for students aiming to enter higher education and are National Courses, with students usually expected to take 3-5 Highers. Each Higher is achieved by gaining credit points with 24 credits at level 6 Scottish Credit and Qualification Framework (SCQF) required for the qualification to be awarded and takes around 240 learning hours.

Entry requirements for Scottish Higher courses are usually a minimum of National Qualifications level 5 (SCQF) which have replaced the Standard Grade Credit level or Intermediate 2 although in some cases mature students may not need previous qualifications in order to study Scottish Highers. Applications should be made direct to the secondary school or college you wish to attend. Further information

may be found at Scottish Qualifications Authority (SQA)
http://www.sqa.org.uk/scqf

Scottish Highers Grades and UCAS Tariff Points from 2017

Confirm UCAS Tariff points at UCAS: Tariff Calculator
https://www.ucas.com/ucas/Tariff-calculator

The grading of Scottish Highers:
Grades: A; B; C; D; or No Award
UCAS Tariff points for Scottish Highers from 2017
Grades
A   =   33
B   =   27
C   =   21
D   =   15

Awarding Organisation: Scottish Highers

Scottish Qualifications Authority (SQA)
http://www.sqa.org.uk/scqf

In Scotland, Scottish Advanced Highers, also known as Advanced Highers (which may be abbreviated to AH) are mapped at level 7 Scottish Credit and Qualification Framework (SCQF) and are for students usually between the ages of 17 years – 18years. Scottish Advanced Highers are usually studied as a one year full time course in secondary school or a college of further education in the sixth year of secondary schooling (S6) being available in a range of subjects and help students develop higher level skills such as research and analysis, extended essay writing and investigation techniques.

They are another route for students aiming to enter higher education and are National Courses, with students usually expected to take expected to take three (although some students take two) National Units as well as an external assessment. National Units may be achieved by passing an assessment marked in the school or college where you are studying which may be coursework, tests or practical work.

Marking is checked by the SQA and there is also an external assessment which may be an exam or project marked by professionals appointed by SQA. To study for Advanced Highers, you would usually be required to have passed Highers. Entry requirements for mature students may be flexible. Further information may be found at Scottish Qualifications Authority (SQA) http://www.sqa.org.uk/scqf

Scottish Advanced Highers Grades and UCAS Tariff Points from 2017
Confirm UCAS Tariff points at UCAS: Tariff Calculator
https://www.ucas.com/ucas/Tariff-calculator

The grading of Scottish Advanced Highers:
Grades: A; B; C; D; or No Award

UCAS Tariff points for Scottish Advanced Highers from 2017
Grades:
A = 56
B = 48
C = 40
D = 32

Awarding Organisation: Scottish Advanced Highers
Scottish Qualifications Authority (SQA)
http://www.sqa.org.uk/scqf

In Scotland, the Scottish Baccalaureate (may be abbreviated to Scot Bacc) is mapped at level 7 Scottish Credit and Qualification Framework (SCQF) and are for students usually between the ages of 16 years – 18years.

The Scottish Baccalaureate is usually studied as a one year full time course in secondary school or a college of further education in the fifth or sixth year (S5 or S6) of secondary schooling (S6) being available in four subjects: Expressive Arts, Languages, Science and Social Sciences, consisting of a coherent group of current Higher and Advanced Higher qualifications including an Interdisciplinary Project..

To achieve a Scottish Baccalaureate, you will need to achieve 2 Advanced Higher Courses and 1 Higher Course from an approved list of subjects within the relevant curriculum area. However, the Scottish Baccalaureate in addition includes the Interdisciplinary Project which involves applying the subject knowledge in realistic contexts which usually takes place outside of your school or college.

The Interdisciplinary Project is an Advanced Higher Unit in which you apply your subject knowledge in realistic contexts and helps you to develop and show evidence of initiative, responsibility and independent working.

To study for the Scottish Baccalaureate, you would usually be required to have passed Scottish Highers. Further information may be found at the Scottish Qualifications Authority (SQA): Baccalaureates
http://www.sqa.org.uk/baccalaureates

Scottish Baccalaureate Grades and UCAS Tariff Points

The Scottish Baccalaureate is marked at Pass or Distinction. A Distinction will require a grade A in one eligible Advanced Higher Course, one other grade A in any other component, and at least a grade B in all other components.

A pass will be awarded to those who achieve at least a grade C in all mandatory components and who don't meet the criteria for Distinction. The grades and UCAS Tariff points are the same as the Advanced Higher and Higher Courses. The Interdisciplinary Project part of the Scottish Baccalaureate is graded A – C and has been recommended as Tariff rated to receive half the points of an Advanced Higher at the same grade.

Scottish Baccalaureate Grades and UCAS Tariff Points from 2017

Confirm UCAS Tariff points at UCAS: Tariff Calculator
https://www.ucas.com/ucas/Tariff-calculator

Scottish Baccalaureate: 2 Advanced Higher Courses; 1 Higher Course; and Interdisciplinary Project grades:

Distinction: grade A in one eligible Advanced Higher Course with one other A grade in any other component, and at least a grade B in all other components. Pass: grade C or above in all mandatory components and who don't meet the criteria for Distinction.

The grading of Scottish Highers:
Grades: A; B; C; D; or No Award
UCAS Tariff points for Scottish Highers from 2017
Grades:

A	=	33
B	=	27
C	=	21
D	=	15

The grading of Scottish Advanced Highers:
Grades: A; B; C; D; or No Award

UCAS Tariff points for Scottish Advanced Highers from 2017
Grades:

A	=	56
B	=	48
C	=	40
D	=	32

UCAS Tariff points for the Interdisciplinary Project are:

Grades:

A = 28
B = 24
C = 20

Awarding organisation

Scottish Qualifications Authority (SQA)
http://www.sqa.org.uk/

Advanced Highers are at the same level as an HNC level 7 (SCQF) or level 4 (RQF) in England, Wales and Northern Ireland) and may enable credit transfer for part of that qualification.

It may be possible to get subject exemptions or enter directly into the 2nd year of a Scottish 4 year degree course, although individual higher education institutions (HEIs) would make a decision on how many credit points can be transferred to the appropriate course.

Grade or UCAS Tariff point requirements will vary across courses and between HEIs, so check entry requirements with the relevant HEI and course details.

Awarding Organisation: Scottish Baccalaureate

Scottish Qualifications Authority (SQA)
http://www.sqa.org.uk/scqf

Qualification Tables: Grades and University and College Admission Service (UCAS) Tariff Points

Confirm UCAS Tariff points at UCAS: Tariff Calculator
https://www.ucas.com/ucas/Tariff-calculator

Table 1: GCSE Grading Structure Awarded from September 2017

GCSE original grading structure	GCSE (some awarding bodies) new grading structure 2017	
A*	9	
	8	
A	7	
B	6	
	5	Awarding: 5 and above = top of C and above good pass (DfE)
C	4	Awarding: 4 and above = bottom of C and above
D	3	
E		
	2	
F		
G	1	
U	U	

Table 2: 'A' Levels: Size Band 4: Grade Bands 4-14 Grading Structure and UCAS Tariff Points Awarded from September 2017

Qualification and Grade	UCAS Tariff from 2017
'A' level grade A*	56
'A' level grade A	48
'A' level grade B	40
'A' level grade C	32
'A' level grade D	24
'A' level grade E	16

Table 3: 'AS' levels: Size band 2; Grade Bands 3-10 Grading Structure and UCAS Tariff Points Awarded from September 2017

Qualification and Grade	UCAS Tariff from 2017
'A' level grade A	20
'A' level grade B	16
'A' level grade C	12
'A' level grade D	10
'A' level grade E	6

Table 4: Scottish Advanced Highers Grading Structure and UCAS Tariff Points Awarded from September 2017

Qualification and Grade	UCAS Tariff from 2017
Scottish Advanced Higher grade A	56
Scottish Advanced Higher grade B	48
Scottish Advanced Higher grade C	40
Scottish Advanced Higher grade D	32

Table 5: Scottish Highers Grading Structure and UCAS Tariff Points Awarded from September 2017

Qualification and Grade	UCAS Tariff from 2017
Scottish Higher grade A	33
Scottish Higher grade B	27
Scottish Higher grade C	21
Scottish Higher grade D	15

Table 6: Scottish Interdisciplinary Project (Scottish Baccalaureate) Grading Structure and UCAS Tariff Points Awarded from September 2017

Qualification and Grade	UCAS Tariff from 2017
Scottish Interdisciplinary Project grade A	28
Scottish Interdisciplinary Project Scottish grade B	24
Scottish Interdisciplinary Project grade C	20

Table 7: BTEC National Certificate: Size Band 2 Grade Bands 4-14 Grading Structure and UCAS Tariff Points Awarded from September 2017

Qualification and Grade	UCAS Tariff from 2017
BTEC National Distinction*	28
BTEC National Distinction	24
BTEC National Merit	16
BTEC National Pass	8

Table 8: BTEC National Subsidiary Diploma: Size Band 4; Grade Bands 4-14 Grading Structure and UCAS Tariff Points Awarded from September 2017

Qualification and Grade	UCAS Tariff from 2017
BTEC National Distinction*	56
BTEC National Distinction	48
BTEC National Merit	32
BTEC National Pass	16

Table 9: BTEC National 90 Credit Diploma: Size Band = 3+3 (6); Grade Band 4-14 Grading Structure and UCAS Tariff Points Awarded from September 2017

Qualification and Grade	UCAS Tariff from 2017
BTEC National D*D*	84
BTEC National D*D	78
BTEC National DD	72
BTEC National DM	60
BTEC National MM	48
BTEC National MP	36
BTEC National PP	24

Table 10: BTEC National Diploma: Size Band =4+4 (8); Grade Band 4-14 Grading Structure and UCAS Tariff Points Awarded from September 2017

Qualification and Grade	UCAS Tariff from 2017
BTEC National D*D*	112
BTEC National D*D	104
BTEC National DD	96
BTEC National DM	80
BTEC National MM	64
BTEC National MP	48
BTEC National PP	32

Table 11: BTEC National Extended Diploma: Size Band =4+4+4 (12); Grade Band 4-14 Grading Structure and UCAS Tariff Points Awarded from September 2017

Qualification and Grade	UCAS Tariff from 2017
BTEC National D*D*D*	168
BTEC National D*D*D	160
BTEC National D*DD	152
BTEC National DDD	144
BTEC National DDM	128
BTEC National DMM	112
BTEC National MMM	96
BTEC National MMP	80
BTEC National MPP	64
BTEC National PPP	48

A
Accounting
Anthropology
Applied Art and Design
Applied Business
Applied ICT
Applied science
Arabic
Archaeology
Art and Design
B
Bengali
Biblical Hebrew
Biology
Biology B (Advancing Biology)
Business
Business (applied)
Business Studies
C
Chemistry
Chemistry B (Salters)
Chinese
Chinese (Mandarin)
Citizenship studies
Classical Civilisation
Classical Greek
Classics
Classics: Ancient History
Classics: Classical Civilisation
Classics: Classical Greek
Classics: Latin
Communication and Culture
Communications
Computer Science
Computing
Counselling
Creative Writing
Critical Thinking
Critical Thinking
D
Dance
Dance, Drama and Performing Arts
Design and Technology
Design and Technology: Food Technology
Design and Technology: Product Design

Design and Technology: Product design (3D design)
Design and Technology: Product design (textiles)
Design and Technology: systems and control
Drama and Performing Arts
Drama and Theatre
Drama and Theatre Studies
Dutch
E
Economics
Economics and Business
Economics and Culture
Electronics
Engineering
English
English Language
English Language and Literature
English Literature
Environmental studies
Environmental Technology
Expressive Arts
F
Film studies
Food Preparation and Nutrition
French
Further mathematics
G
General Studies
Geography
Geology
German
Global Development
Government and Politics
Greek
Gujarati
H
Health and Social Care
Health and Social Care (applied)
Health and social care single award
History
History of Art
Home Economics (Food, Nutrition and Health)

Home economics (food, nutrition and health)
Home Economics: Food
Human Biology
Humanities
I
ICT
ICT (applied)
ICT and Computer Science
International development
Irish
Italian
J
Japanese
Journalism
L
Latin
Law
Leisure and Tourism
Leisure Studies
Leisure Studies (applied)
M
Mathematics
Media
Media Studies
Media: Communication and Production
Modern Hebrew
Modern Languages
Moving Image Arts
Music
Music Technology
P
Panjabi
Performance Studies
Performing Arts
Performing Arts (applied)
Persian
Philosophy
Physical Education
Physics
Physics B (Advancing Physics)
Polish
Portuguese
Psychology
Pure Mathematics
Q
Quantitative Methods
Quantitative Methods (AS only)

R
Religious Studies
Russian
S
Science (applied)
Science (AS only)
Science in society
Sociology

Software Systems
Development
Spanish
Sports Science ant the
Active leisure Industry
Statistics
Statistics (AS only)
T
Technology and Design

Travel and Tourism
Travel and Tourism
(applied)
Turkish
U
Urdu
W
World/Global
Development

How to Choose 'A' level or Equivalent Qualification Subjects

The following information refers to 'A' level subjects, however if you are taking other recognised level 3 (RQF) or level 6/7 (SCQF) qualifications, the subjects will still be relevant.

Entry requirements for undergraduate courses will vary depending on the course and university, however, honours degree courses may require 3 'A' levels, although some will accept 2 subjects; 4 Scottish Highers, although some competitive entry courses may require 5 subjects or 3 Advanced Scottish Highers although some may require 2 Advanced Highers and 1 Scottish Higher; however the number of 'A' level subjects studied is usually 3 and Scottish Highers is usually 4.

When you choose which subjects you want to study at 'A' level (or equivalent qualification) you should consider those subjects you enjoy and are confident with so as to aim for the best marks for your ability. However it is also important to think about what career you might want to do in the future and to consider which subjects will be the best combination to choose, especially as certain higher education subjects may require specific 'A' level or equivalent subjects.

If you don't have a higher education course or career in mind yet, you may want to choose subjects that will help you to keep your options open. It is a good idea to discuss your options with a careers adviser, as well as teachers, lecturers and family, but it is important that it is you who makes the final decision about which subjects to choose.

If you are intending to study for a course in higher education it is important to check on the course entry requirements on the university or college websites as there may be variations for the same subject at the different universities or colleges and it is always a good idea to contact a university or college if you are unsure.

Whilst many universities and colleges will usually require three 'A' level subjects, four Scottish Highers or equivalent qualifications, especially for those degree courses that are competitive to enter, some may accept fewer and may take into account other qualifications. There may also be more flexibility for mature applicants who can provide evidence of relevant work experience.

Entry requirements for higher national certificates, higher national diplomas, certificates or diplomas of higher education and foundation degrees may be lower than those required for the same subject at degree level. Specified grades or a set number of UCAS Tariff points may also be a requirement, especially with competitive entry courses requiring higher grades.

Entry requirements listed on the higher education institution (HEI) websites are often a typical offer and should be used as a general guide. Often an HEI will operate a flexible admissions policy for some courses, which means you could receive a lower conditional offer than the typical offer, made on the basis of the university assessment of your complimentary non-academic achievements and experiences.

For any courses that require an interview or a portfolio review, if your application is successful, this may also be considered in the level of any conditional offer that follows.

Some universities and colleges may require essential subjects at 'A' level or equivalent for some specific courses and a few may require specified subject/s to be studied up to 'AS' level if not at 'A' level.

Other higher education institutions (HEIs) may have preferred subjects for certain courses but will also consider other subjects as well, although relevant subjects at 'A' level or equivalent may also be helpful in support of your degree application.

However many HEIs may accept any subjects for a large number of higher education courses and will accept a wide range of subjects, as well as taking into account relevant experience.

There may also be variation of entry requirements for the same subjects at different HEIs. Some HEIs won't consider certain subjects at 'A' level to be included as part of an offer, such as General Studies or Critical Thinking, whilst other HEIs will accept one or both of these subjects. Some HEIs won't accept subjects with overlapping content for some degree courses, whilst others will accept such subjects, and especially for some subjects such as mathematics degrees, mathematics and further mathematics may be preferred.

Some degree subjects such as medicine, dentistry, pharmacy, veterinary, sciences, health sciences and engineering will require science and mathematics subjects, with some HEIs specifying certain subjects and grades or UCAS Tariff points.

Dance, drama and music degree course entry requirements will also vary and

whilst some HEIs either specify an essential or preferred relevant subject, others may accept a wide range of subjects and qualifications, with in some cases essay-based 'A' level subjects being acceptable for some drama degree courses. HEIs may also take account of other performance or music theory related qualifications.

If you want to study for an art related degree subject you may be required to have an art portfolio which is often developed whilst undertaking a foundation diploma course in art, or a BTEC national diploma course in art. As well as an art foundation diploma you may be required to have one or more additional 'A' level subjects (or equivalent qualifications).

Some universities are generally more competitive to enter, such as those who are members of the Russell Group http://www.russellgroup.org/ and may set higher grades or UCAS Tariff points as entry requirements for their courses, as well as being more likely to set essential 'A' level, or equivalent, subjects.

The Russell Group have published a guide called 'Informed Choices', informing the most common subject requirements for different degree courses at Russell Group universities. If you haven't made up your mind as to what you may want to study in the future, there is a list of "facilitating subjects" which advises on choosing a combination to include two of these subjects which may keep open more degree and professional course options.

The Russell Group facilitating subjects include: mathematics, further mathematics, English literature, physics, biology chemistry, geography, history, languages (classical and modern).
Russell Group Informed Choices
http://www.russellgroup.org/InformedChoic es-latest.pdf

Undergraduate Course Entry Requirements: Relevant 'A' level Subjects and Professional Body Accreditation Listed In Job Sectors

As entry requirements will vary between universities and colleges, even for the same course, the following 'A' level / equivalent qualification subjects highlighted as being required as either essential, preferred or relevant for specific honours degree subjects is a general guide only and therefore it is important to check specific entry requirements on the individual university and college websites for up-to-date information. A number of other 'A' level subjects will be accepted as entry for a range of degree courses and as there are many other degree course subjects, the following are main subjects only. Higher education subjects that are accredited by professional organisations, which are needed to enter a specific profession, have been highlighted as being 'required' for professional accreditation. Also see the chapter on Professional Organisations and Accredited Undergraduate and Postgraduate Courses.

Essential, Preferred and Relevant 'A' level Subjects for Main Higher Education Course Subjects and Professional Body Accreditation

1. Agriculture and Plants Sector

Landscape Architecture see Building Design, Planning, Surveying and Construction sector
Agricultural Engineering see Engineering sector

Degree Subject	Essential or Preferred 'A' level / equivalent subject/s	Relevant 'A' level / equivalent subject/s
Agriculture	Usually two Science subjects preferred from Chemistry, Physics, Biology or Mathematics	Business Studies, Economics, Geography, Mathematics, Psychology
Agronomy	Usually at least one Science subject is usually preferred	Chemistry, Mathematics, Biology, Physics, Business Studies, Law, Accountancy
Farm Management	Usually a Science subject is preferred	Biology, Physics, Mathematics Business Studies, Economics, Accounting
Forestry Some courses professionally accredited with: Institute of Chartered Foresters http://www.charteredforesters.org Chartered Forester Chartered Arboriculturist	Usually at least one Science subject	Chemistry, Mathematics, Biology, Physics, Environmental Studies, Geology, Computer Science, Statistics
Garden Design	Some may require Art	Art and Design, Graphic

Some courses professionally accredited with: The Landscape Institute http://www.landscapeinstitute.org International Federation of Landscape Architects http://iflaonline.org/	and Design and / or Art Foundation Diploma course with an Art Portfolio	Design, Chemistry, Mathematics, Biology, Physics, Environmental Studies, Computing / Computer Science
Horticulture Courses recognised with: Chartered Institute of Horticulture https://www.horticulture.org.uk/ List of courses on website Grow Careers http://www.growcareers.info/	Usually at least one Science subject	Chemistry, Mathematics, Biology, Physics, Environmental Studies, Geology, Computer Science, Statistics
Land Management Some courses professionally accredited with: Royal Institution of Chartered Surveyors http://www.rics.org/uk/	Usually at least one Science subject	Chemistry, Mathematics, Biology, Physics, Environmental Studies, Geology, Computer Science, Statistics, Business Studies, Economics
Plant Science	Usually two Science subjects from Biology, Chemistry, Physics or Mathematics	Biology, Chemistry, Physics or Mathematics, Geography, Environmental Studies, Psychology

2. Animals and Conservation Sector		
Biology see Science sector Environmental Science see Environmental sector		
Degree Subject	**Essential or Preferred 'A' level / equivalent subject/s**	**Relevant 'A' level / equivalent subject/s**
Animal Husbandry	Usually prefer a Science subject	Biology, Chemistry, Physics, Mathematics
Animal Science, Biology and Conservation Some courses professionally accredited with: Royal Society of Biology https://www.rsb.org.uk/ Courses recognised enable registration with: British Society of Animal Science http://bsas.org.uk/accreditation	Usually at least two science based subjects, Biology and Chemistry may be preferred; other subjects may include Physics, Mathematics, Psychology, Geography	Biology, Chemistry, Physics, Mathematics, Environmental Studies
Animal Science: Nutrition Some courses professionally accredited	Usually at least two science based subjects,	Physics, Mathematics, Psychology, Geography

with: Association for Nutrition: Nutrition http://www.associationfornutrition.org	Biology and Chemistry may be preferred; other subjects may include Physics, Mathematics, Psychology, Geography	
Biological Science: Animal Behaviour and Welfare Some courses professionally accredited with: Royal Society of Biology https://www.rsb.org.uk/	Usually Biology or Human Biology and some may require an additional Science subject	Chemistry, Physics, Mathematics, Psychology
Conservation and Environment Some courses professionally accredited with: Chartered Institute of Ecology and Environmental Management (CIEEM) http://www.cieem.net Some courses professionally accredited with: Royal Society of Biology https://www.rsb.org.uk/	Usually at least one Science subject, some may prefer two Science subjects.	Biology, Chemistry, Environmental Science, Geography, Physics, Geology, Mathematics, Computing, Statistics
Ecology and Environmental Conservation Some courses professionally accredited with: Chartered Institute of Ecology and Environmental Management (CIEEM) http://www.cieem.net Some courses professionally accredited with: Royal Society of Biology https://www.rsb.org.uk/	Usually at least one Science subject: Biology, Geography, Chemistry, Physics, Mathematics	Biology, Geography, Chemistry, Physics, Mathematics, Geology
Equine Management	Any subjects usually considered.	Business Studies, Economics, Mathematics
Equine Science	Usually Biology/Human Biology and some require an additional Science subject	Biology, Chemistry, Physics, Mathematics
Equine Therapy	Usually at least one Science subject	Biology, Physics, Mathematics
Marine Biology Some courses professionally accredited with: Royal Society of Biology https://www.rsb.org.uk/	Usually Biology/Human Biology and some require an additional Science subject	Biology, Physics, Mathematics
Veterinary Medicine / Science Professional accreditation is a	Chemistry and two usually from Biology/	Biology, Physics, Mathematics

	Human Biology, Physics, Mathematics	
requirement with: Royal College of Veterinary Surgeons http://www.rcvs.org.uk/	Human Biology, Physics, Mathematics	
Zoology Some courses professionally accredited with: Royal Society of Biology https://www.rsb.org.uk/	Usually Biology/Human Biology and an additional Science subject	Biology, Physics, Mathematics

3. Art and Design Sector		
Beauty Therapy see Leisure and Tourism sector		
Degree Subject	**Essential or Preferred 'A' level / equivalent subject/s**	**Relevant 'A' level / equivalent subject/s**
3D Design	Usually Art and Design and / or Art Foundation Diploma course with an Art Portfolio	Design and Technology: 3D Design, Computing / Computer Science, Drama and Theatre Studies; Film Studies; Media Studies, Business Studies
Animation	Usually Art and Design and / or Art Foundation Diploma course with an Art Portfolio	Computing / Computer Science, Design and Technology
Art and Design	Usually Art and Design and / or Art Foundation Diploma course with an Art Portfolio	Design and Technology, Computing / Computer Science, Business Studies
Art History	Any subjects usually considered.	Art and Design, History, English, Classics
Ceramics / Glass	Usually Art and Design and / or Art Foundation Diploma course with an Art Portfolio	Design and Technology, Business Studies
Computer Games	Any subjects usually considered, some may prefer Computing / Computing Science	Design and Technology, Art and Design, Mathematics, Computing / Computer Science, Physics, Further Mathematics
Costume Design	Usually Art and Design; an art portfolio may be required	Art and Design, Design and Technology, English, Drama, Film Studies, Business Studies
Costume for Performance	Usually prefer at least one from Art and Design, English	Art and Design, English Language, English Literature, Drama, Film

	Language, English Literature, Drama, Film Studies. An art portfolio is usually required.	Studies
Fashion Buying and Merchandising	Any subjects usually considered.	Design and Technology: Textiles, Mathematics, Economics, Business Studies, Biology, Chemistry, Physics, Computing, Geography, Psychology, English Language / Literature, Foreign Language
Fashion / Textile Design Some courses professionally accredited with:: Chartered Society of Designers http://www.csd.org.uk	Usually Art and Design and / or Art Foundation Diploma course with an Art Portfolio	Design and Technology, Business Studies
Fashion Journalism	May require Art and Design or Art Foundation Diploma course. Some may require a written or visual Portfolio	Art and Design, Design and Technology: Textiles, English Language, English Literature, Business Studies
Fashion Management and Marketing	May require Art and Design or Art Foundation Diploma course	Art and Design, Design and Technology: Textiles, English Language, English Literature, Business Studies, Economics, Accounting
Fine Art	Usually Art and Design and / or Art Foundation Diploma course with an Art Portfolio	Design and Technology, Computing / Computer Science, Business Studies
Furniture Design	Usually Art and Design and / or Art Foundation Diploma course with an Art Portfolio	Design and Technology, Mathematics, Computing / Computer Science, Business Studies
Graphic Design Some courses professionally accredited with:: Chartered Society of Designers http://www.csd.org.uk	Usually Art and Design and / or Art Foundation Diploma course with an Art Portfolio	Computing / Computer Science, Design and Technology, Business Studies
Illustration	Usually Art and Design and / or Art Foundation Diploma	Design and Technology, Computing / Computer Science, Business

	course with an Art Portfolio	Studies
Interior Design / Spatial Design Some courses professionally accredited with: Chartered Society of Designers http://www.csd.org.uk	Usually Art and Design and / or Art Foundation Diploma course with an Art Portfolio	Design and Technology, Business Studies, Computing / Computer Science
Jewellery; Gemmology and Jewellery Studies One course professionally accredited with: The Gemmological Association of Great Britain http://www.gem-a.com	Usually Art and Design and / or Art Foundation Diploma course with an Art Portfolio	Design and Technology, Computing / Computer Science, Business Studies
Make-up Artistry	Usually Art and Design and / or Art Foundation Diploma course with an Art Portfolio	Art and Design, Media Studies, Film Studies Design and Technology: Textiles, Business Studies
Photography	Usually Art and Design and / or Art Foundation Diploma course with an Art Portfolio	Design and Technology, Computing / Computer Science, Film Studies, Computing / Computer Science, Business Studies
Product Design Some courses professionally accredited with: Chartered Society of Designers http://www.csd.org.uk	Some may require Art and Design	English, Mathematics, Art and Design, Design and Technology: Product Design, Chemistry, Biology, Physics, Computing / Computer Science, Business Studies
Sculpture	Usually Art and Design and / or Art Foundation Diploma course with an Art Portfolio	Design and Technology, Business Studies
Theatre Design Some courses professionally accredited with:: Chartered Society of Designers http://www.csd.org.uk Some courses professionally accredited with: Drama UK http://www.dramauk.co.uk	Usually Art and Design and / or Art Foundation Diploma course with an Art Portfolio	Design and Technology, Film Studies, Media Studies, Computing / Computer Science, Business Studies

4. Building Design, Planning, Surveying and Construction Sector
Architectural Engineering see Engineering sector
Building Services Engineering see Engineering sector

Degree Subject	Essential or Preferred 'A' level / equivalent subject/s	Relevant 'A' level / equivalent subject/s
Architectural / Building Technology Professional accreditation is a requirement with: Chartered Institute of Architectural Technologists http://www.ciat.org.uk Some courses also professionally accredited with: Chartered Institute of Building http://www.ciob.org/	Some require Mathematics; some usually require subjects from Art and Design, Science, Mathematics, Design and Technology; some may require an Art and /or Design portfolio; and some may also require an Art and Design Foundation Diploma.	Mathematics, Physics, Chemistry, Design and Technology, Further Mathematics, Statistics
Architecture ARB / RIBA part 1 Professional accreditation is a requirement with: Architects Registration Board (ARB) http://www.arb.org.uk Royal Institute of British Architecture http://www.architecture.com see postgraduate courses for RIBA part 2	Some require Art and Design; some require Art and Design combined with Sciences: Mathematics, Physics or Design Technology preferred; some look favourably on a Foundation Diploma in Art and Design, although this isn't the case for all	Art and Design, Design and Technology, Mathematics, Chemistry, Physics, Design and Technology, Computing / Computer Science, History, Geography, English, Sociology, Philosophy, Psychology
Construction / Management Some courses professionally accredited with: Chartered Institute of Building http://www.ciob.org/ Association for Project Management APM http://www.apm.org.uk Royal Institution of Chartered Surveyors (RICS) http://www.rics.org Project Management Institute http://www.pmi.org/	Usually a Science and /or Design and Technology subject	Mathematics, Physics, Chemistry, Biology, Design and Technology, Computing / Computer Science
Landscape Architecture Professional accreditation is a requirement with: Landscape Institute http://www.landscapeinstitute.co.uk/ International Federation of Landscape Architects http://iflaonline.org/	Some require Art and Design, with an Art Portfolio; some require Art combined with Sciences; some look favourably on a Foundation Diploma in Art and Design	Art and Design, Design and Technology, Geography, Biology, English, Chemistry, Mathematics, Physics, Design and Technology, Computing / Computer Science, History. Environmental Studies
Surveying: Construction / Building / Quantity Land	Any subjects usually considered.	Art and Design, Mathematics, Physics, Design Technology, Computing / Computer

Degree Subject	Essential or Preferred 'A' level / equivalent subject/s	Relevant 'A' level / equivalent subject/s
Property Professional accreditation is a requirement with: Royal Institution of Chartered Surveyors (RICS) http://www.ricscourses.org/Course/ Some courses also with: Chartered Institution of Civil Engineering Surveyors https://www.cices.org/		Science, English Business Studies, Languages Economics, Law, Geography, Geology
Town Planning Professional accreditation is a requirement with: Royal Town Planning Institute (RTPI) http://www.rtpi.org.uk	Any subjects usually considered.	Art and Design, Mathematics, Physics, Geography, Design and Technology, Computing / Computer Science

5. Building Property Management and Housing Sector		
Degree Subject	**Essential or Preferred 'A' level / equivalent subject/s**	**Relevant 'A' level / equivalent subject/s**
Facilities Management	Any subjects usually considered.	Accounting, Business Studies, Economics, Mathematics, Law, English
Housing Undergraduate approved qualification may provide exemption from some of the training courses with: Chartered Institute of Housing (CIH) http://www.cih.org	Any subjects usually considered.	Sociology, Psychology, Business Studies, Geography, English, History
Property Development and Management	Any subjects usually considered.	Accountancy, Business Studies, Economics, Mathematics, Geography, Chemistry, Physics, English
Property Finance and Investment	Any subjects usually considered.	Accounting, Business Studies, Economics, Mathematics
Real Estate (also see Surveying) Professional accreditation is a requirement with: Royal Institution of Chartered Surveyors (RICS) http://www.rics.org	Any subjects usually considered.	Accountancy, Business Studies, Economics, Mathematics, Geography, Chemistry, Physics, English

6. Business Finance; Economics; Mathematics; Statistics Sector		
Degree Subject	**Essential or Preferred 'A' level / equivalent subject/s**	**Relevant 'A' level / equivalent subject/s**
Accounting and Finance	Some require	Accounting, Business

Approved undergraduate qualification may provide exemption from some of the professional training courses with: Institute of Chartered Accountants England and Wales ICAEW http://www.icaew.com Institute of Chartered Accountants Scotland ICAS http://icas.org.uk Chartered Accountants Ireland CAI http://www.charteredaccountants.ie Association of Chartered Certified Accountants ACCA http://www.accaglobal.com Chartered Institute of Management Accountants CIMA http://www.cimaglobal.com Chartered Institute of Public Finance Accountancy CIPFA http://www.cipfa.org/ Chartered Institute of Taxation http://www.tax.org.uk	Mathematics	Studies, Economics, Mathematics
Actuarial Science Approved undergraduate qualification may provide exemption from some of the professional training courses with: Institute of Faculty of Actuaries http://www.actuaries.org.uk	Usually Mathematics; Further Mathematics may be highly desirable	Accounting, Statistics, Business Studies, Economics
Banking and Business Finance	Any subjects usually considered.	Accounting, Business Studies, Economics, Mathematics
Economics / Econometrics	Some require Mathematics, Further Mathematics may be desirable	Economics, Mathematics, Statistics, Further Mathematics Accounting, Business Studies
Mathematics Some courses professionally accredited with: Institute of Mathematics and its Applications http://www.ima.org.uk	Mathematics, some require Further Mathematics	Further Mathematics, Statistics, Physics Economics, Computing
Statistics Some courses professionally accredited with: Royal Statistical Society (RSS) http://www.rss.org.uk	Mathematics, some require Further Mathematics, a Science may be recommended by some	Statistics, Further Mathematics Physics Economics, Computing
Operational research	Mathematics	Further Mathematics, Statistics, Physics, Economics, Computing

7. Business Management and Administration; Human Resources and Recruitment Sector		
Degree Subject	**Essential or Preferred 'A' level / equivalent subject/s**	**Relevant 'A' level / equivalent subject/s**
Business Administration	Any subjects usually	Combination of

	considered.	Mathematics / Sciences with Arts / Humanities may be useful, Business Studies, Economics, Accounting, Further Mathematics, English
Business Management Some courses offered in some universities, colleges and training centres professionally accredited with: Chartered Management Institute http://www.managers.org.uk/	Any subjects usually considered.	Mathematics, Business Studies, Economics, Accounting, Further Mathematics, English
Business Studies	Any subjects usually considered.	Mathematics, Business Studies, Economics, Accounting, Further Mathematics, English
Human Resource Management Some accredited undergraduate courses with some in universities and others in training centres. Professional accreditation is a requirement with: Chartered Institute of Personnel and Development http://www.cipd.co.uk	Any subjects usually considered.	Business Studies, Economics, Mathematics, English Language English Literature, Law, Psychology, Sociology
Public Administration	Any subjects usually considered.	Mathematics, Business Studies, Economics, Accounting, Further Mathematics, English, Law, Sociology, Psychology
Project management Some courses professionally accredited with: Association for Project Management APM http://www.apm.org.uk	Any subjects usually considered	Mathematics, Business Studies, Economics, Accounting, Further Mathematics, English, Law, Sociology, Psychology

8. Education and Teacher Training Sector

Education Support

Degree Subject	Essential or Preferred 'A' level / equivalent subject/s	Relevant 'A' level / equivalent subject/s
Community Education	Any subjects usually considered.	English, Sociology, Psychology, Biology, Art and Design, Drama / Performing Arts, Music, Language
Early Years Education	Any subjects usually considered.	English, Sociology, Psychology, Biology, Art and Design, Music, Language Drama / Performing Arts
Education	Any subjects usually considered.	English, Sociology, Psychology, Biology, Art and Design, Music, Language, Drama / Performing Arts
Special Educational Needs	Any subjects usually considered.	English, Sociology, Psychology, Biology, Art and Design, Music, Language Drama / Performing Arts
Sports Coaching	Science courses will usually require at least one Science subject; Arts courses, any subjects usually considered.	Physical Education, English, Sociology, Psychology, Biology, Chemistry, Physics, Mathematics

Teacher Training

Degree Subject	Essential or Preferred 'A' level / equivalent subject/s	Relevant 'A' level / equivalent subject/s
Teaching English as a Foreign Language (TEFL) Teaching English as a Second or Other Language (TESOL) Professional accreditation is a requirement with: Cambridge English Language Assessment http://www.cambridgeenglish.org Trinity College London http://www.trinitycollege.co.uk/ Or a pre-registration teacher training course leading to a Teacher Training qualification	Usually require English	English Language, English Literature, History, Foreign Language, Sociology, Psychology
Undergraduate course:	Any subjects usually	English, Sociology,

	considered.	Psychology, Biology, Art and Design, Music, Language Drama / Performing Arts, Mathematics, Science, History, Geography
Primary Teaching with QTS Professional accreditation is a requirement with: UK Teaching Registration Councils **England:** Department for Education and Teaching Regulation Agency https://www.gov.uk/government/organis ations/department-for-education **Wales:** General Teaching Council Wales http://www.gtcw.org.uk **Northern Ireland:** General Teaching Council Northern Ireland http://www.gtcni.org.uk **Scotland:** General Teaching Council Scotland http://www.gtcs.org.uk	GCSEs/ equivalent to include: English Language, Mathematics and Science	
Undergraduate course: Secondary Teaching with QTS Professional accreditation is a requirement with: the UK Teaching Registration Councils **England:** Department for Education and Teaching Regulation Agency https://www.gov.uk/government/organis ations/department-for-education **Wales:** General Teaching Council Wales http://www.gtcw.org.uk **Northern Ireland:** General Teaching Council Northern Ireland http://www.gtcni.org.uk **Scotland:** General Teaching Council Scotland http://www.gtcs.org.uk	A subject related to the teaching subject GCSEs/ equivalent to include: English Language and Mathematics	English, Mathematics, Science, Art, Computing, Design and Technology, Geography, History, Foreign Languages, Music, Physical Education, Sociology, Psychology
Teacher Training: Further and Adult Education Level 3, 4 and 5 Diploma Professional accreditation is a requirement with a range of awarding organisations. Check FE Advice https://www.feadvice.org.uk/	Professional, vocational or academic training and experience in the subject you wish to teach usually to at least level 3. An honours degree in a relevant subject usually required for academic teaching. GCSEs/ equivalent to include: English Language and Mathematics; IT may also be required.	

9. Engineering and Technology Sector

Architectural Technology see Building Design, Planning, Surveying and Construction

Degree Subject	Essential or Preferred 'A' level / equivalent subject/s	Relevant 'A' level / equivalent subject/s
Agricultural Engineering Professional accreditation is a requirement with: Engineering Council http://www.engc.org.uk/ Institution of Agricultural Engineers IAgrE http://www.iagre.org	Usually Mathematics and / or Physics	Environmental Science, Biology, Chemistry
Architectural Engineering Professional accreditation is a requirement with: The Engineering Council http://www.engc.org.uk Some courses professionally accredited with: Institution of Civil Engineers http://www.ice.org.uk Institution of Structural Engineers ISTRUCTE http://www.istructe.org Institution of Mechanical Engineers IMECHE http://www.imeche.org Energy Institute EI https://www.energyinst.org/	Usually Mathematics, some also require a Science subject	Mathematics, Physics, Chemistry, Design and Technology, Further Mathematics, Statistics, Art and Design
Biomedical (Clinical) / Medical / Engineering Professional accreditation is a requirement with: Engineering Council http://www.engc.org.uk/ Some courses professionally accredited with: Institute of Physics and Engineering in Medicine IPEM http://www.ipem.ac.uk/	Usually one or two subjects from Mathematics and / or Physics with other sciences preferred such as Biology or Chemistry.	Mathematics, Physics, Chemistry, Biology, Design and Technology, Computer Science, Electronics, Engineering, Further Mathematics
Building / Services Engineering Professional accreditation is a requirement with: The Engineering Council http://www.engc.org.uk Some courses professionally accredited with: Energy Institute EI https://www.energyinst.org/ Chartered Association of Building Engineers CBUILDE http://www.cbuilde.com	Usually Mathematics and Physics or at least one other Science or Technology subject	Physics, Chemistry, Design and Technology, Computer Science, Electronics, Engineering, Further Mathematics
Chemical Engineering Professional accreditation is a	Usually Mathematics and Chemistry; Physics	Physics, Design and Technology, Computer

requirement with: Engineering Council http://www.engc.org.uk/ Some courses professionally accredited with: Institution of Chemical Engineers IChmeE http://www.icheme.org/ Energy Institute https://www.energyinst.org	also required by some.	Science, Electronics, Engineering, Further Mathematics, Statistics
Civil / Structural Engineering Professional accreditation is a requirement with: Engineering Council http://www.engc.org.uk/ Institution of Civil Engineers https://www.ice.org.uk/ Institution of Structural Engineers https://www.istructe.org/	Usually Mathematics and Physics or at least one other Science or Technology subject	Physics, Chemistry, Design and Technology, Computer Science, Electronics, Engineering, Further Mathematics
Computer Systems Engineering; Communications Systems Engineering Professional accreditation is a requirement with: Engineering Council http://www.engc.org.uk/	Usually Mathematics and Physics or at least one other Science or Technology subject, desirably Electronics, Engineering or Further Mathematics	Physics, Chemistry, Design and Technology, Computer Science, Electronics, Engineering, Further Mathematics
Control Engineering Professional accreditation is a requirement with: Engineering Council http://www.engc.org.uk/	Usually Mathematics and Physics	Physics, Chemistry, Design and Technology, Computer Science, Electronics, Engineering, Further Mathematics
Design / Manufacturing Engineering / Product Design Professional accreditation is a requirement with: Engineering Council http://www.engc.org.uk/ Some courses professionally accredited with:: Institution of Engineering Designers IED http://www.ied.org.uk	Usually Mathematics and Physics or Further Mathematics, Design and Technology, Engineering or Electronics	Physics, Chemistry, Design and Technology, Computer Science, Electronics, Engineering, Further Mathematics
Electrical and Electronic Engineering; Electrical Power Engineering Professional accreditation is a requirement with: Engineering Council http://www.engc.org.uk/ Some courses professionally accredited with: Energy Institute https://www.energyinst.org	Usually Mathematics and at least one other Science or Technology subject desirably Physics or Electronics	Physics, Chemistry, Design and Technology, Computer Science, Electronics, Engineering, Further Mathematics
Engineering Science Professional accreditation is a	Usually Mathematics and Physics.	Chemistry, Design and Technology, Computer

requirement with: Engineering Council http://www.engc.org.uk/		Science, Electronics, Engineering
Environment / Water Engineering Professional accreditation is a requirement with: Engineering Council http://www.engc.org.uk/ Some courses professionally accredited with:: Chartered Institution of Water and Environmental Management CIWEM http://www.ciwem.org.uk	Mathematics and usually Physics or at least one other Science	Physics, Chemistry, Computer Science, Environmental Science, Engineering, Further Mathematics
Fire Engineering Professional accreditation is a requirement with: Engineering Council http://www.engc.org.uk/ Some courses professionally accredited with: Energy Institute EI https://www.energyinst.org/	Usually at least one from Mathematics, Physics, Chemistry or Environmental Science	Mathematics, Physics, Chemistry or Environmental Science
Materials / Minerals / Mining Engineering Professional accreditation is a requirement with: Engineering Council http://www.engc.org.uk/ Institute of Materials, Minerals and Mining IOM3 http://www.iom3.org/ Some courses professionally accredited with:: Energy Institute EI https://www.energyinst.org/	Usually Mathematics and usually one from Physics, Chemistry or Design and Technology	Physics, Chemistry, Design and Technology, Computer Science, Electronics, Engineering, Further Mathematics, Biology, further Mathematics, Statistics, Geography, Geology
Mechanical Engineering Professional accreditation is a requirement with: Engineering Council http://www.engc.org.uk/ Some courses professionally accredited with: Energy Institute https://www.energyinst.org Institution of Mechanical Engineers IMECHE http://www.imeche.org	Usually Mathematics and Physics	Physics, Chemistry, Design and Technology, Computer Science, Electronics, Engineering
Metallurgy Engineering Professional accreditation is a	Usually Mathematics and usually one from	Physics, Chemistry, Design and Technology,

	Physics or Chemistry, some may accept Design and Technology	Computer Science, Electronics, Engineering, Further Mathematics, Biology, further Mathematics, Electronics, Statistics, Geography, Geology
requirement with: Engineering Council http://www.engc.org.uk/		
Nuclear Engineering Professional accreditation is a requirement with: Engineering Council http://www.engc.org.uk/	Usually Mathematics and Physics	Chemistry, Design and Technology, Computer Science, Electronics, Engineering
Petroleum /Oil and Gas Engineering Professional accreditation is a requirement with: Engineering Council http://www.engc.org.uk/ Some courses professionally accredited with: Energy Institute https://www.energyinst.org	Usually Mathematics and Chemistry	Physics, Chemistry, Design and Technology, Computer Science, Engineering, Further Mathematics, Biology, Geography, Geology
Product Engineering Design Professional accreditation is a requirement with: Engineering Council http://www.engc.org.uk/ Some courses professionally accredited with: Institution of Engineering Designers IED http://www.ied.org.uk	Usually Mathematics and Physics	Physics, Chemistry, Design and Technology, Computer Science, Engineering, Further Mathematics, Biology

Transport Engineering: Automotive; Aviation; Marine; Railway; Road		
Degree Subject	**Essential or Preferred 'A' level / equivalent subject/s**	**Relevant 'A' level / equivalent subject/s**
Transport Engineering		
Transport and Mechanical Engineering Professional accreditation is a requirement with: Engineering Council http://www.engc.org.uk/	Usually Mathematics and Physics	Chemistry, Design and Technology, Computer Science, Electronics, Engineering, Further Mathematics
Air Industry Engineering		
Aeronautical Engineering /	Usually Mathematics	Computer Science,

Aerospace Engineering / Astronautics Professional accreditation is a requirement with: Engineering Council http://www.engc.org.uk/ Some courses professionally accredited with: Royal Aeronautical Society AEROSOCIETY http://www.aerosociety.com Some courses professionally accredited with: Institution of Mechanical Engineers IMECHE http://www.imeche.org	and Physics; some may prefer a third subject in Further Mathematics or Design and Technology	Design and Technology, Further Mathematics, Chemistry
Aircraft Engineering with Pilot Studies Professional accreditation is a requirement with: Engineering Council http://www.engc.org.uk/	Usually require Mathematics and Physics	Computer Science, Design and Technology, Further Mathematics, Chemistry
Marine Industry Engineering		
Marine Engineering / Technology / Naval Architecture Professional accreditation is a requirement with: Engineering Council http://www.engc.org.uk/ Institute of Marine Engineering, Science and Technology IMarEST http://www.imarest.org/ Some HE courses provide a full engineer officer cadet programme leading to the award of a UK Maritime and Coastguard Agency (MCA) Standards of Training, Certification and Watchkeeping (STCW) Engineer Certificate of Competency (CoC)	Usually require Mathematics and preferably Physics and / or Chemistry	Physics, Chemistry, Design and Technology, Computer Science, Electronics, Engineering, Further Mathematics
Railway Industry Engineering		
Civil and Railway Engineering Professional accreditation is a requirement with: Engineering Council http://www.engc.org.uk/	Usually require Mathematics and preferably Physics	Physics, Chemistry, Design and Technology, Computer Science, Electronics, Engineering
Road Industry Engineering		
Automotive and Motorsports Engineering Professional accreditation is a requirement with: Engineering Council http://www.engc.org.uk/	Some usually require Mathematics and Physics	Physics, Chemistry, Design and Technology, Computer Science, Electronics, Engineering

10. Environment Sector
Ecology see Animal and Plant sector

Environmental Health see Healthcare Public Health sector		
Degree Subject	**Essential or Preferred 'A' level / equivalent subject/s**	**Relevant 'A' level / equivalent subject/s**
Astronomy	Mathematics and Physics	Biology, Chemistry, Geology, Computer Science
Environmental Science Some courses professionally accredited with: Institution of Environmental Science https://www.the-ies.org Chartered Institution of Water and Environmental Management CIWEM http://www.ciwem.org Some courses professionally accredited with: Royal Society of Biology https://www.rsb.org.uk/	Usually Chemistry, and additional Science subject such as Biology/Human Biology, Physics, Mathematics, Environmental Studies	Biology, Chemistry, Physics, Mathematics, Environmental Studies Geography, Psychology
Geographical Information Science / Systems / Mapping Science Some courses professionally accredited with: by Royal Institution of Chartered Surveyors http://www.rics.org/uk/ Chartered Institution of Civil Engineering Surveyors https://www.cices.org/	Usually require two subjects from Mathematics, Science or Geography	Mathematics, Physics, Chemistry and Biology, Computer Science, Environmental Studies, Geology, Geography
Geography Courses recognised with: Royal Geographical Society http://www.rgs.org/	Most require Geography	Biology, Chemistry, Mathematics, Physics, Geology, Computer Science, Environmental Studies
Geology Some courses professionally accredited with: The Geological Society http://www.geolsoc.org.uk	Some may require Mathematics plus Physics and / or Chemistry; some may require two subjects from Mathematics, Physics, Chemistry and Biology	Mathematics, Physics, Chemistry and Biology, Computer Science, Environmental Studies
Meteorology Courses recognised with: Royal Meteorological Society https://www.rmets.org/	Usually Mathematics and Physics	Physics, Mathematics, Chemistry, Biology, Geography, Geology, Computer Science, Environmental Studies
Oceanography and Hydrography Some courses professionally accredited with:	Usually to include two science subjects	Physics, Mathematics, Chemistry, Biology, Geography, Geology,

		Computer Science, Environmental Studies
Institute of Marine Engineering, Science and Technology http://www.imarest.org/ Royal Institution of Chartered Surveyors http://www.rics.org/uk/ Chartered Institute of Civil Engineering Surveyors https://www.cices.org/		

11. Healthcare Sector		
Allied Healthcare		
Art Therapy; Dance Movement Psychotherapy; Dramatherapy; Music Therapy see Postgraduate Courses.		
Degree Subject	**Essential or Preferred 'A' level / equivalent subject/s**	**Relevant 'A' level / equivalent subject/s**
Dietetics Professional accreditation is a requirement with: Allied Health Profession Federation http://www.ahpf.org.uk Association of UK Dieticians https://www.bda.uk.com Registration is a requirement with Health and Care Professions Council http://www.hcpc-uk.org	Usually Biology and some also require Chemistry	Mathematics, Physics, Psychology, Sociology
Occupational Therapy Professional accreditation is a requirement with: Allied Health Profession Federation http://www.ahpf.org.uk British Association and College of Occupational Therapists http://www.cot.co.uk Registration is a requirement with Health and Care Professions Council http://www.hcpc-uk.org	Some require Biology	Psychology, Sociology, Art and Design, Physical Education, Health and Social Care
Orthoptics Professional accreditation is a requirement with: Allied Health Profession Federation http://www.ahpf.org.uk British and Irish Orthoptic society http://www.orthoptics.org.uk Registration is a requirement with Health and Care Professions Council http://www.hcpc-uk.org	Usually at least one Science subject	Biology, Chemistry, Mathematics, Physics, Psychology
Paramedic Science Professional accreditation is a requirement with: Allied Health Profession Federation	Usually at least one Science subject	Biology, Chemistry, Mathematics, Physics, Physical Education, Psychology, Sociology

http://www.ahpf.org.uk College of Paramedics https://www.collegeofparamedics.co.uk Registration is a requirement with Health and Care Professions Council http://www.hcpc-uk.org		
Physiotherapy Professional accreditation is a requirement with: Allied Health Profession Federation http://www.ahpf.org.uk Chartered Society of Physiotherapy http://www.csp.org.uk/ Registration is a requirement with Health and Care Professions Council http://www.hcpc-uk.org	Usually Biology or Human Biology, some may accept Physical Education	Chemistry, Mathematics, Physics, Physical Education
Podiatry / Chiropody Professional accreditation is a requirement with: Allied Health Profession Federation http://www.ahpf.org.uk College of Podiatry http://www.scpod.org Registration is a requirement with Health and Care Professions Council http://www.hcpc-uk.org	Usually at least one Science subject preferably Biology, Human Biology or Chemistry	Biology, Chemistry, Mathematics, Physics, Psychology
Prosthetics/ Orthotics Professional accreditation is a requirement with: Allied Health Profession Federation http://www.ahpf.org.uk British Association of Prosthetists and Orthotists http://www.bapo.com Registration is a requirement with Health and Care Professions Council http://www.hcpc-uk.org	Usually at least one subject from Mathematics, Physics or Engineering	Biology, Chemistry, Mathematics, Physics, Psychology
Radiography Professional accreditation and registration is a requirement with: Allied Health Profession Federation http://www.ahpf.org.uk Society and College of Radiographers Diagnostic and Therapeutic https://www.sor.org/ Registration is a requirement with Health and Care Professions Council http://www.hcpc-uk.orgps://www.sor.org	Usually Biology or Physics	Biology, Chemistry, Mathematics, Physics, Psychology
Speech and Language Therapy Professional accreditation is a requirement with: Allied Health Profession Federation	Some require Biology, some accept Chemistry or Physics, some will accept other subjects	Biology Chemistry, Physics, English Language, English Literature, French,

http://www.ahpf.org.uk Royal College of Speech and Language Therapists http://www.rcslt.org Registration is a requirement with Health and Care Professions Council http://www.hcpc-uk.org		German, Spanish, Italian, Psychology

Alternative Health, Complementary and Creative Therapy

Degree Subject	Essential or Preferred 'A' level / equivalent subject/s	Relevant 'A' level / equivalent subject/s
Acupuncture Professional accreditation is a requirement with: British Acupuncture Accreditation Board (BAAB) http://www.baab.co.uk	At least one Science subject	Biology, Chemistry, Mathematics, Physics, Psychology
Complementary Therapies May need to register with a holistic therapy accredited body such as: Complementary and Natural Healthcare Council (CNHC) http://www.cnhc.org.uk/	Any subjects usually considered.	Biology, Chemistry, Mathematics, Physics, Psychology, Sociology
Creative Therapy	Any subjects usually considered.	Dance, Drama, Drama and Performing Arts, Drama and Theatre, Music, English language
Nutrition / Therapy Some courses professionally accredited with: Association for Nutrition http://www.associationfornutrition.org	At least one science from Biology or Chemistry	Biology, Chemistry, Food Technology, Psychology, Mathematics, Physics, Home Economics

Complementary Medicine

Degree Subject	Essential or Preferred 'A' level / equivalent subject/s	Relevant 'A' level / equivalent subject/s
Chiropractor (some lead to an integrated master's degree) Professional accreditation is a requirement with: General Chiropractic Council http://www.gcc-uk.org	Usually Biology and one other Science subject	Biology, Chemistry, Mathematics, Physics, Psychology
Osteopathic Medicine (some lead to an integrated master's degree) Professional accreditation is a requirement with: General Osteopathic Council http://www.osteopathy.org.uk	Usually at least two Science subjects	Biology, Chemistry, Mathematics, Physics, Psychology

Health, Social Care and Management

Degree Subject	Essential or Preferred 'A' level / equivalent subject/s	Relevant 'A' level / equivalent subject/s

Health Management	Any subjects usually considered.	English, Business Studies, Economics, Biology, Mathematics, Chemistry, Physics
Social Policy: Health and Social Care	Any subjects usually considered.	English, Business Studies, Economics, Biology, Mathematics, Chemistry, Physics

Medicine; Dentistry; Nursing and Midwifery; Operating Department; Optometry; Pharmacy

Degree Subject	Essential or Preferred 'A' level / equivalent subject/s	Relevant 'A' level / equivalent subject/s
Dentistry Professional accreditation is a requirement with: British Dental Association https://www.bda.org	Most require Chemistry, Biology, and either Mathematics or Physics; Some require Chemistry and Biology and will accept a third subject A few may accept Chemistry and Mathematics or Physics A few may accept Chemistry AS with three additional 'A' level Science subjects	Mathematics, Physics, Further Mathematics, Computer Science
Dentistry Graduate entry Professional accreditation is a requirement with: British Dental Association https://www.bda.org	Usually a minimum of 2:1 in a Biomedical / Health related degree subject; Science 'A' levels usually required	Chemistry, Biology, Physics, Mathematics
Dentistry with a Pre-Dental year For students without the 'A' level / equivalent subjects requirements for the standard Medicine course Professional accreditation is a requirement with: British Dental Association https://www.bda.org	Usually one Science from Biology Chemistry or Physics and two Arts subjects; or three Arts subjects Course entry requirements may vary so confirm	Usually one Science from Biology Chemistry or Physics and two Arts subjects; or three Arts subjects
Dental Hygiene and Therapy Professional accreditation is a requirement with: British Dental Association https://www.bda.org	Usually Biology or Human Biology	Mathematics, Biology, Chemistry, Physics, English, Psychology
Dental Nursing (Cert HE / Fd Degree) Professional accreditation is a requirement with: British Dental Association	Usually one Science subject: Biology, Chemistry or Physics	Mathematics, Biology, Chemistry, Physics, English, Psychology

https://www.bda.org		
Dental Technology Professional accreditation is a requirement with: British Dental Association https://www.bda.org	Usually at least one Science subject	Mathematics, Biology, Chemistry, Physics, English
Medicine Professional accreditation is a requirement with: General Medical Council (GMC) http://www.gmc-uk.org	Most require Chemistry, Biology, and either Mathematics or Physics; Some require Chemistry and Biology and will accept a third subject A few may accept Chemistry and Mathematics or Physics and a third subject A few may accept Chemistry AS with three additional 'A' level Science subjects	Mathematics, Physics, Further Mathematics, Computer Science
Medicine Graduate entry Professional accreditation is a requirement with: General Medical Council (GMC) http://www.gmc-uk.org	Usually a minimum of 2:1 in an approved Biomedical science / health related degree subject; Most require 'A' levels / equivalent to include Chemistry and some usually require Biology	Chemistry, Biology, Physics, Mathematics
Medicine with a Foundation / Pre- Clinical / Preliminary year For students without the 'A' level / equivalent subjects requirements for the standard Medicine course Professional accreditation is a requirement with: General Medical Council (GMC) http://www.gmc-uk.org	Usually one in Chemistry and two Arts subjects or three Arts subjects. Course entry requirements may vary so confirm	Usually one in Chemistry and two Arts subjects or three Arts subjects.
Nursing and Midwifery: Adult Nursing Learning Disabilities Nursing Mental Health Nursing Paediatrics / Children's Nursing Midwifery Professional accreditation is a requirement with: Nursing and Midwifery Council http://www.nmc-uk.org	Usually require Biology or another Science	Sociology, Psychology, Chemistry
Operating Department Practice Professional accreditation is a requirement with: Health Care Professions Council	Usually prefer Biology or another Science	Sociology, Psychology, Chemistry

http://www.hcpc-uk.org		
Optometry Ophthalmic Dispensing Optician Professional accreditation is a requirement with: General Optical Council (GOC) https://www.optical.org	Some require Biology or two from Biology, Chemistry, Mathematics or Physics	Biology, Chemistry, Mathematics, Physics
Pharmacy (leads to a master's degree) Professional accreditation is a requirement with: General Pharmaceutical Council (GPhC) http://www.pharmacyregulation.org	Usually Chemistry and two from Biology, Mathematics and Physics, although a few may accept a third other subject	Biology, Mathematics, Physics

Public Health; Environmental Health; Health Promotion; Occupational Health

Environmental Science see Environment sector

Degree Subject	Essential or Preferred 'A' level / equivalent subject/s	Relevant 'A' level / equivalent subject/s
Environmental Health Professional accreditation is a requirement with: Chartered Institute of Environmental Health (CIEH) http://www.cieh.org	Usually at least one Science or Technology subject	Biology, Chemistry, Physics, Mathematics, Computing / Computer Science Design and Technology, Environmental Studies
Health Promotion	Any subjects usually considered.	Biology, Chemistry, Mathematics, English, Sociology, Psychology, Health and Social Care
Public Health	Any subjects usually considered.	Biology, Chemistry, Mathematics, English, Sociology, Psychology, Health and Social Care, Business Studies
Occupational Health and Safety Professional accreditation is a requirement with: Chartered Institution of Occupational Safety and Health (IOSH) https://www.iosh.co.uk/	Any subjects usually considered; at least one Science or Technology subject may be preferred

May be required to have the NEBOSH https://www.nebosh.org.uk/ General Certificate in Health and Safety | Biology, Chemistry, Physics, Mathematics, Computing / Computer Science Design and Technology, Environmental Studies |

12. History, Anthropology and Archaeology Sector		
Forensic Anthropology see Science sector		
Degree Subject	Essential or Preferred 'A' level / equivalent	Relevant 'A' level / equivalent subject/s

	subject/s	
Anthropology	Any subjects usually considered.	Biology, Chemistry, Sociology, English Language, English Literature, History, combination of Arts and Sciences may be helpful
Archaeology	Arts based: Any subjects usually considered. Science based: usually require at least one Science subject	Archaeology, Classics: Classical Civilisations, Geography, Geology, History, Biology, Chemistry, Physics, English Language, English Literature; combination of Arts and Sciences may be helpful.
Archaeology / Ancient History	Usually require History	Classics: Language, Classics: Classical Civilisation, History, Archaeology, Biology, Chemistry, English Language, English Literature
Art History	Any subjects usually considered.	Art and Design, History, English Language, English Literature
Classics	Usually require Latin and / or Greek	History, English Language, English Literature, Philosophy
Conservation Studies Not professionally accredited but courses confirmed that meet the professional standards in conservation with: Institute of Conservation http://www.icon.org.uk	Usually Chemistry preferred	Biology, Physics, Mathematics, History, English Language, English Literature, Environmental Studies
Egyptology	Any subjects usually considered.	History, English Language, English Literature, Classics
Historic Building Conservation Some recognised courses can be found at: Institute of Historic Building Conservation (IHBC) http://www.ihbc.org.uk	Any subjects usually considered.	Art and Design, History, English Language, English Literature, Design and Technology, Mathematics
History	Usually require History	Government and Politics, Sociology, English Language, English Literature, Classics
History and Heritage Studies	Usually require History	Government and Politics,

		Sociology, English Language, English Literature, Classics
Humanities	Any subjects usually considered.	History, English Language, English Literature, Classics, Philosophy, Sociology
Museum Studies Course list with information on courses can be found at: Museums Association http://www.museumsassociation.org/	Any subjects usually considered	History, English Language, English Literature , Classics, Philosophy, Sociology

13. Hospitality, Culinary and Events Management Sector		
Degree Subject	**Essential or Preferred 'A' level / equivalent subject/s**	**Relevant 'A' level / equivalent subject/s**
Culinary Arts	Any subjects usually considered.	English Language, English Literature, Business Studies, Art and Design, Sociology, Psychology, Home Economics
Events Management Some courses recognised with: Institute of Hospitality https://www.instituteofhospitality.org/	Any subjects usually considered.	English Language, English Literature, Business Studies, Art and Design, Design and Technology, Sociology, Psychology
Food and Consumer Science	Usually prefer two Science subjects	Biology, Chemistry, Physics, Mathematics, Home Economics, Business Studies
Food Marketing Management	Any subjects usually considered.	English Language, English Literature, Business Studies, Art and Design, Design and Technology, Sociology, Psychology, Languages, Home Economics
Hospitality and Hotel Management Some courses recognised with: Institute of Hospitality https://www.instituteofhospitality.org/	Any subjects usually considered.	English Language, English Literature, Business Studies, Art and Design, Design and Technology, Sociology, Psychology, Languages, Home Economics
Hotel Management Some courses recognised with: Institute of Hospitality https://www.instituteofhospitality.org/	Any subjects usually considered.	English Language, English Literature, Business Studies, Art and Design, Design and Technology, Sociology, Psychology, Languages,

		Home Economics

14. Information and Library Studies Sector

Archived Administration (see Postgraduate Courses)

Degree Subject	Essential or Preferred 'A' level / equivalent subject/s	Relevant 'A' level / equivalent subject/s
Business Information Systems	Any subjects usually considered.	Computing / Computer Science, Mathematics, Physics, Design and Technology, English, Engineering
Library and Information Management (very few undergraduate courses) Professional accreditation is a requirement with: Chartered Institute of Library and Information Professionals CILIP http://www.cilip.org.uk	Any subjects usually considered.	History, English Language, English Literature, Computing / Computer Science

15. Information / Computer Technology Sector

Degree Subject	Essential or Preferred 'A' level / equivalent subject/s	Relevant 'A' level / equivalent subject/s
Artificial Intelligence / Cybernetics Some courses accredited with the Chartered Institute of IT (BCS) http://www.bcs.org/	Usually Mathematics and some require Physics / Electronics	Design and Technology, Art and Design, Computing / Computer Science, Physics, Engineering, Electronics, Further Mathematics
Business Computing Some courses accredited with the Chartered Institute of IT (BCS) http://www.bcs.org/	Usually Mathematics or Computing	Design and Technology, Computing / Computer Science, Engineering, Electronics, Mathematics, Physics, Business Studies, Further Mathematics
Computer Engineering Professional accreditation is a requirement with: Engineering Council http://www.engc.org.uk/ Some courses accredited with the Chartered Institute of IT (BCS) http://www.bcs.org/	Usually Mathematics and Physics	Design and Technology, Computing / Computer Science, Engineering, Electronics, Further Mathematics
Computer Forensics / Ethical Hacking / Computer Security Some courses accredited with the Chartered Institute of IT (BCS) http://www.bcs.org/	Usually Mathematics	Design and Technology, Computing / Computer Science, Engineering, Electronics, Mathematics, Physics, Further Mathematics
Computer Games Some courses accredited with the	Any subjects usually considered; some may	Design and Technology, Art and Design,

Chartered Institute of IT (BCS) http://www.bcs.org/	prefer Computing / Computing Science	Mathematics, Computing / Computer Science, Physics, Further Mathematics, Further Mathematics
Computer Information Systems Some courses accredited with the Chartered Institute of IT (BCS) http://www.bcs.org/	Usually Mathematics; Further Mathematics, Computing / Computer Science, Physics may be advantageous	Physics, Chemistry, Computing/ Computer Science, Electronics, Engineering, Statistics, Design and Technology (Systems and Control), Further Mathematics
Computer Networks Some courses accredited with the Chartered Institute of IT (BCS) http://www.bcs.org/	Usually at least one subject from Computing, Mathematics or Physics	Design and Technology, Computing / Computer Science, Engineering, Electronics, Mathematics, Physics, Further Mathematics
Computer Science Some courses accredited with the Chartered Institute of IT (BCS) http://www.bcs.org/	Usually Mathematics; Further Mathematics or Computing / Computer Science may be preferred	Physics, Chemistry, Computing/ Computer Science, Electronics, Engineering, Statistics, Design and Technology (Systems and Control), Further Mathematics
Computing Some courses accredited with the Chartered Institute of IT (BCS) http://www.bcs.org/	Usually Mathematics or Computing	Design and Technology, Computing / Computer Science, Engineering, Electronics, Mathematics, Physics, Business Studies, Further Mathematics
Data Science Some courses professionally accredited with: Chartered Institute of IT (BCS) http://www.bcs.org/	Usually Mathematics and some may also require Further Mathematics; Computing / Computer Science may be advantageous	Physics, Chemistry, Computing/ Computer Science, Electronics, Engineering, Statistics, Design and Technology (Systems and Control), Further Mathematics
Digital / Web Design Some courses accredited with the Chartered Institute of IT (BCS) http://www.bcs.org/	Usually prefer one creative subject and one technical subject; some may accept a Foundation Diploma in Art	Creative subjects include: Art and Design, Music, Design and Technology (Product Design). Technical subjects include: Mathematics, Chemistry, Computing, Electronics,

		Statistics, Design and Technology (Systems and Control), Physics.
Informatics Some courses accredited with the Chartered Institute of IT (BCS) http://www.bcs.org/	Usually Mathematics	Design and Technology, Computing / Computer Science, Engineering, Electronics, Mathematics, Physics,
Information Technology Some courses accredited with the Chartered Institute of IT (BCS) http://www.bcs.org/	Any subjects usually considered; some may prefer Computing / Computing Science	Design and Technology, Computing / Computer Science, Engineering, Electronics, Mathematics, Physics
Software Engineering Professional accreditation is a requirement with: Engineering Council http://www.engc.org.uk/ Some courses accredited with the Chartered Institute of IT (BCS) http://www.bcs.org/	Usually at least one Science or Technology subject	Design and Technology, Computing / Computer Science, Engineering, Electronics, Mathematics, Physics
Sound Engineering and Production Some courses professionally accredited with: Engineering Council http://www.engc.org.uk/	Any subjects usually considered, some may prefer Computing / Computing Science	Design and Technology, Computing / Computer Science, Engineering, Electronics, Mathematics, Physics Music, Music Technology
Telecommunications Professional accreditation is a requirement with: Engineering Council http://www.engc.org.uk/ Some courses accredited with the Chartered Institute of IT (BCS) http://www.bcs.org/	Usually Mathematics and Physics or Electronics	Design and Technology, Computing / Computer Science

16. Languages Sector

Speech and Language Therapy see Allied Health sector
Teaching English as a Foreign / Second Language or Other language (TEFL / TESOL) see Education sector

English, Linguistics, Classics and Related Subjects

Degree Subject	Essential or Preferred 'A' level / equivalent subject/s	Relevant 'A' level / equivalent subject/s
Anglo-Saxon, Norse and Celtic	Any subjects usually considered.	English Language, English Literature, History, Foreign Language, Philosophy, Classics: Classical Civilisation, Classics: Language
Classics	Usually Latin	English Language, English Literature, History, Foreign Language, Philosophy
Creative Writing	Usually prefer English Literature or English Language and English Literature	English Language, English Literature, History, Foreign Language, Sociology
English Language	Usually prefer English Language or English Language and English Literature	English Language, English Literature, History, Foreign Language, Sociology
English Literature	Usually prefer English Literature or English Language and English Literature	English Language, English Literature, History, Foreign Language, Sociology
Linguistics	Any subjects usually considered.	English Language, English Literature, History, Foreign Language, Sociology

European Languages and Literature

Degree Subject	Essential or Preferred 'A' level / equivalent subject/s	Relevant 'A' level / equivalent subject/s
French	French With a two language degree, a second relevant language subject usually required, except when the second language is to be studied from beginners' level	English Language, English Literature, History, any other Modern Language.
German	German	English Language,

	With a two language degree, a second relevant language subject usually required, except when the second language is to be studied from beginners' level	English Literature, History, any other Modern Language
Spanish	Spanish With a two language degree, a second relevant language subject usually required, except when the second language is to be studied from beginners' level	English Language, English Literature, History, any other Modern Language
Italian	Italian With a two language degree, a second relevant language subject usually required, except when the second language is to be studied from beginners' level	English Language, English Literature, History, any other Modern Language
Russian	Russian With a two language degree, a second relevant language subject usually required, except when the second language is to be studied from beginners' level	English Language, English Literature, History, any other Modern Language
Portuguese	Portuguese With a two language degree, a second relevant language subject usually required, except when the second language is to be studied from beginners' level	English Language, English Literature, History, any other Modern Language
European Studies	Any subjects usually considered.	English Language, English Literature, History, Foreign Language, Government and Politics, Sociology
Russian Studies	Any subjects usually	English Language,

		English Literature, History, Foreign Language, Government and Politics
Scandinavian Studies	Preferably a language other than English	English Language, English Literature, History, Foreign Language, Government and Politics, Sociology

British Sign Language; Translation and Interpreting

Degree Subject	Essential or Preferred 'A' level / equivalent subject/s	Relevant 'A' level / equivalent subject/s
British Sign Language undergraduate courses Professional accreditation is a requirement with: National Registers of Communication Professionals working with Deaf and Deafblind People (NRCPD) http://www.nrcpd.org.uk	Any subjects usually considered.	English, Sociology, Psychology, Biology, Art and Design, Music, Language Drama / Performing Arts
Translation and Interpreting Some courses professionally accredited with: Chartered Institute for Linguistics https://www.ciol.org.uk/ Some courses professionally accredited with: Institute of Translating and Interpreting http://www.iti.org.uk/	Relevant Foreign Language	English Language, English Literature, History, additional Foreign Language, Sociology, Psychology, Drama / Performing Arts

Country and Language Studies outside the European Union: Eastern, Asiatic, African, American Languages and Literature

Degree Subject	Essential or Preferred 'A' level / equivalent subject/s	Relevant 'A' level / equivalent subject/s
African studies	Any subjects usually considered.	Geography, History, English Language, English Literature, Foreign Language, Sociology, Archaeology
American studies	Some may prefer English Literature and / or History	Geography, History, English Language, English Literature, Foreign Language, Sociology
Arabic and Islamic Studies	Foreign language may be preferred	Geography, History, English Language, English Literature, Foreign Language Sociology
Burmese and Linguistics	Foreign language may	History, English

	be preferred	Language, English Literature, Foreign Language, Geography, Sociology
Chinese Studies	Foreign language may be preferred	History, English Language, English Literature, Foreign Language, Geography
Hebrew and Israeli Studies	Foreign language may be preferred	History, English Language, English Literature, Foreign Language, Geography
Japanese Studies	Foreign language may be preferred	History, English Language, English Literature, Foreign Language, Geography
Middle Eastern Studies	Any subjects usually considered.	Foreign language; History, English Language, English Literature, Geography
South Asian Studies	Any subjects usually considered.	Foreign language; History, English Language, English Literature, Geography

17. Law Enforcement: Armed Forces Sector		
Degree Subject	Essential or Preferred 'A' level / equivalent subject/s	Relevant 'A' level / equivalent subject/s
Armed Forces Additional professional and Leadership qualifications Courses accredited and approved with: Armed Forces: Education and Training http://www.army.mod.uk/	Any subjects usually considered. Subjects dependent on the specialist subject	Physical Education / Sports Science, History, English Language, English Literature, Geography, Science subject

18. Law Enforcement: Protection and Security Services Sector

Environmental Health see Healthcare: Public Health sector
Fire Engineering see Engineering sector
Forensic Science see Science sector
Probation Service see Social Care sector

Degree Subject	Essential or Preferred 'A' level / equivalent subject/s	Relevant 'A' level / equivalent subject/s
Fire and Leadership	Any subjects usually considered	Physical Education / Sports Science, Law, English Language, English Literature, Mathematics, Business Studies
Police Studies List of approved Certificate in Knowledge of Policing (CKP) course with some offered in universities Professional accreditation is a requirement with: College of Policing http://www.college.police.uk/	Any subjects usually considered. May be a requirement that you also become a special Police Constable of Police Volunteer during your studies	Physical Education / Sports Science, Law, English Language, English Literature, History, Mathematics, Government and Politics
Public Services	Any subjects usually considered.	Business Studies, Law, English Language, English Literature, History, Mathematics, Government and Politics
War Studies	Usually History	History, English Language, English Literature, Classics, Philosophy, Sociology

19. Law

Environmental Health see Public Health sector; Fire Engineering see Engineering sector
Forensic Science see Science sector

Degree Subject	Essential or Preferred 'A' level / equivalent subject/s	Relevant 'A' level / equivalent subject/s
Criminology	Any subjects usually considered.	Law, English Language, English Literature, Foreign Language, History, Mathematics, Government and Politics, Philosophy, Sociology
Human Rights	Any subjects usually considered.	Sociology, Psychology, Media Studies, English Language / Literature, History, Government and Politics, Mathematics, Statistics, European Language
Law LLB Professional accreditation as a solicitor	Any subjects usually considered.	Law, English Language, English Literature,

is a requirement with: Solicitors Regulation Authority (SRA) http://www.sra.org.uk		History, Foreign Language, Mathematics, Government and Politics, Philosophy, Sociology
Paralegal Studies	Any subjects usually considered.	Law, English Language, English Literature, History, Foreign Language, Mathematics, Government and Politics, Philosophy, Sociology
Legal Executive level 3 and level 6; Graduate Fast-Track Diploma Professional accreditation is a requirement with: Chartered Institute of Legal Executives (CILEx) http://www.cilexcareers.org.uk/	Entry requirements for stage one: CILEx level 3, you will usually need a minimum of four GCSEs or equivalent qualification with grades C or above to include English. Employers may have additional academic requirements. Entry requirements for stage two: CILEx level 6, you will need to successfully complete the CILEx level 3 diploma qualification. Entry requirements for stage two: CILEx level 6 Graduate Fast-track diploma, if you already hold a Solicitor's Regulation Authority qualifying law degree or Graduate Diploma in law awarded within the last seven years, you may be eligible to enter the graduate fast-track diploma.	Law, English Language, English Literature, History, Foreign Language, Mathematics, Government and Politics, Philosophy, Sociology

20. Leisure and Tourism Sector

Degree Subject	Essential or Preferred 'A' level / equivalent subject/s	Relevant 'A' level / equivalent subject/s
Beauty Therapy Management	Any subjects usually considered.	English, Business Studies, Art and Design, Sociology, Psychology, Languages
Tourism Management Some recognised with: Institute of Hospitality https://www.instituteofhospitality.org/ Some recognised with: Institute of Travel and Tourism http://www.itt.co.uk/	Any subjects usually considered.	English, Business Studies, Art and Design, Design and Technology, Sociology, Psychology, Languages, Home Economics

21. Media: Advertising, Communications, Marketing and Public Relations Sector

Advertising, Media Communications, Marketing, Public Relations

Degree Subject	Essential or Preferred 'A' level / equivalent subject/s	Relevant 'A' level / equivalent subject/s
Advertising	Any subjects usually considered.	English Language, English Literature, History, Media, Business, Art and Design, Sociology, Psychology
Media Communications	Any subjects usually considered.	English Language, English Literature, History, Media, Business, Art and Design, Sociology, Psychology
Digital Communication Design	May require either Art and Design with a portfolio or Information Technology with evidence of an aptitude for creative coding	Computing / Computer Science, Physics, Mathematics, Media, Art and Design, English Language, English Literature
Fashion Marketing	May require Art and Design or Art Foundation Diploma course. .	Art and Design, Design and Technology: Textiles, English Language, English Literature, Business Studies, Economics, Accounting
Marketing Certificate and Diploma training	Any subjects usually considered.	English Language, English Literature,

		History, Media, Business, Art and Design, Sociology, Psychology
courses with some in universities and training centres Some courses professionally accredited with: Chartered Institute of Marketing http://www.cim.co.uk		
Multimedia Computing	Usually prefer Mathematics or Computing/ Computer Science	Computing / Computer Science, Physics, Mathematics, Media, Art and Design, English Language, English Literature
Public Relations Some courses professionally recognised with: Chartered Institute of Public Relations http://www.cipr.co.uk	Any subjects usually considered.	English Language, English Literature, History, Media, Business, Art and Design, Sociology, Psychology

Journalism and Publishing		
Degree Subject	**Essential or Preferred 'A' level / equivalent subject/s**	**Relevant 'A' level / equivalent subject/s**
Creative Writing	Some may require English Language, English Literature or Creative Writing	English Language, English Literature, History, Media, Art and Design, Sociology, Psychology, Philosophy
Journalism Some courses professionally accredited with: British Journalism Training Council BJTC http://www.bjtc.org.uk Professional Publishers Association: Journalism and Publishing http://www.ppa.co.uk	Some may require at least one Humanities subject	English language, English Literature, History, Sociology, Psychology, Philosophy, Media
Fashion Journalism	May require Art and Design or Art Foundation Diploma course. Some may require a written or visual Portfolio	Art and Design, Design and Technology: Textiles, English Language, English Literature, Business Studies, Media
Music Journalism	Some may require at least one Humanities subject	Music, Music Technology, English language, English Literature, History, Sociology, Psychology, Philosophy
Photojournalism	Some require Art and Design: Photography	English Language, English Literature,

	and / or Art Foundation Diploma course with an Art Portfolio	History, Media, Sociology, Psychology, Computing / Computer Science, Film Studies, Computing / Computer Science, Business Studies
Publishing	Any subjects usually considered.	English Language, English Literature, History, Media Sociology, Psychology, Philosophy

22. Media: Film, Radio, Television and Theatre Sector		
Theatre Set and Stage Design see Art and Design sector		
Film, Television, Production and Technology		
Degree Subject	**Essential or Preferred 'A' level / equivalent subject/s**	**Relevant 'A' level / equivalent subject/s**
Design Communication: Digital Media Production Some courses accredited with: BKSTS: Craft Skills and Technology: Film Industry https://www.bksts.com/	Some may prefer Media, Film, Art, Photography or English; Foundation Diploma in Art may also be required by some	English Language / Literature, History, Film Studies, Media Studies, Art and Design, Sociology, Psychology
Film Production, Digital Film and Cinematography Some courses accredited with: BKSTS: Craft Skills and Technology: Film Industry https://www.bksts.com/	Some may prefer Media, Film, Art, Photography or English; Technology may also be preferred by some; Foundation Diploma in Art may also be accepted by some	Music, Dance, Drama, Media, Music Technology, Art and Design, Design and Technology, Film Studies, English Language / Literature
Media and Culture	Any subjects usually considered.	English Language / Literature, History, Film Studies, Media Studies, Art and Design, Sociology, Psychology
Media Studies / Film and Television Studies	Some may prefer Humanities subjects including English Language English Literature, Media, Film Studies, History	English Language / Literature, Media Studies, Film Studies, Drama / Theatre / Performance, Music, Sociology, Psychology, Technology, Art & Design
Multimedia, Interactive, Games and Web Design Some courses accredited with:	Some may prefer Media, Film, Art, Photography or	Music, Dance, Drama, Media, Music Technology, Art and

BKSTS: Craft Skills and Technology: Film Industry https://www.bksts.com/	English; Technology may also be preferred by some; Foundation Diploma in Art may also be required by some	Design, Design and Technology, Film Studies, English Language, English Literature
Sound Design for Film and Television Some courses accredited with: BKSTS: Craft Skills and Technology: Film Industry https://www.bksts.com/ Some courses accredited with: Joint Audio Media Educational Support (James) http://www.jamesonline.org.uk/	Some may prefer Media or Music Technology / evidence of relevant experience	Media, Music Technology, Design and Technology, Film Studies, Mathematics, Music
Video, Television and Broadcasting Some courses accredited with: BKSTS: Craft Skills and Technology: Film Industry https://www.bksts.com/	Some may prefer Media, Film, Art, Photography or English; Technology may also be preferred by some; Foundation Diploma in Art may also be required by some	Music, Dance, Drama, Media, Music Technology, Art and Design, Design and Technology, Film Studies, English Language, English Literature

23. Performing Arts Sector		
Dance, Drama and Music Therapy see Postgraduate Healthcare sector		
Dance		
Degree Subject	**Essential or Preferred 'A' level / equivalent subject/s**	**Relevant 'A' level / equivalent subject/s**
Dance Performance Dance Teaching in specialist institutions Some courses professionally accredited with: Council for Dance Education and Training http://www.cdet.org.uk	Some may prefer Dance or evidence of dance ability	Dance, Drama, Music Performance, English, English Literature, Media Studies

Drama

Degree Subject	Essential or Preferred 'A' level / equivalent subject/s	Relevant 'A' level / equivalent subject/s
Acting / Drama Some courses professionally accredited with: Drama UK http://www.dramauk.co.uk Grade and Certificate Examinations professionally accredited with: Trinity College London http://www.trinitycollege.com	Some require English, English Literature or Theatre Studies	Drama, English, English Literature, Media Studies Performance, Dance
Stage Management / Production Some courses professionally accredited with: Drama UK http://www.dramauk.co.uk	Usually prefer Drama, Dance, Performance or related subject	Drama, Dance, Music Performance, English, English Literature, Media Studies
Theatre Practice Some courses professionally accredited with: Drama UK http://www.dramauk.co.uk	Some may prefer a relevant subject such as Drama, Dance, Music Performance, English	Drama, Dance, Music Performance, English, English Literature, Media Studies, History

Music

Degree Subject	Essential or Preferred 'A' level / equivalent subject/s	Relevant 'A' level / equivalent subject/s
Music Music performance examinations awarded by Associated Board of the Royal Schools of Music http://gb.abrsm.org/en/ Royal Academy of Music https://www.ram.ac.uk/ Trinity College London http://www.trinitycollege.com	Usually Music; some require grade 7 or 8 for your main instrument; some require at least a grade 5 ABRSM in theory	Music Technology, Mathematics, English Language, English Literature, History, Biology, Chemistry, Philosophy
Music Technology Music performance examinations awarded by Associated Board of the Royal Schools of Music http://gb.abrsm.org/en/ Royal Academy of Music https://www.ram.ac.uk/ Trinity College London http://www.trinitycollege.com	Usually require Music or Music Technology; or some may require ABRSM in theory at a designated grade	Music Technology, Music, Mathematics, Media, Film Studies, Design and Technology
Music Production Music performance examinations awarded by Associated Board of the Royal Schools of Music http://gb.abrsm.org/en/ Royal Academy of Music https://www.ram.ac.uk/ Trinity College London http://www.trinitycollege.com	Usually require Music or Music Technology; or some may require ABRSM in theory at a designated grade	Music Technology, Music, Mathematics, Media, Film Studies, Design and Technology

24. Psychology, Counselling and Psychotherapy Sector		
Counselling		
Degree Subject	**Essential or Preferred 'A' level / equivalent subject/s**	**Relevant 'A' level / equivalent subject/s**
Counselling Professional accreditation is a requirement with a relevant professional body listed in: Professional Standards Authority https://www.professionalstandards.org.uk/what-we-do/accredited-registers/find-a-register Such as: British Association of Counselling and Psychotherapy http://www.bacp.co.uk Counselling and Psychotherapy in Scotland http://www.cosca.org.uk/ Irish Association for Counselling and Psychotherapy http://www.irish-counselling.ie	Any subjects usually considered.	Sociology, Psychology, English Language, English Literature, Art and Design, Drama, Music

Psychology		
Degree Subject	**Essential or Preferred 'A' level / equivalent subject/s**	**Relevant 'A' level / equivalent subject/s**
Psychology Professional accreditation is a requirement with: The British Psychological Society (BPS) http://www.bps.org.uk Practitioner and Registered Psychologist Registration is a requirement with Health and Care Professions Council http://www.hcpc-uk.org	Some require at least one Science subject from Biology, Chemistry, Physics or Mathematics	Psychology, Biology, Chemistry, Physics, Mathematics, English Language English Literature, History, Economics, Sociology, Statistics, Government and Politics, Philosophy, Further Mathematics

25. Religion and Theology Sector

Arabic and Islamic Studies see Languages sector
Hebrew and Israeli Studies see Languages sector

Degree Subject	Essential or Preferred 'A' level / equivalent subject/s	Relevant 'A' level / equivalent subject/s
Chaplaincy Studies Hospital Chaplaincy Studies Professional accreditation is a requirement with: Hospital Chaplaincies Council http://www.nhs-chaplaincy-spiritualcare.org.uk/	You may be required to be employed in a paid or voluntary position as a chaplain; have a letter of recommendation from your religious sponsor or chaplaincy team leader. You would need to be accredited or approved in a recognised faith community. Each religious organisation will have individual requirements on training. Usually any 'A' level subjects considered although Religious Studies may be preferred.	Religious Studies, Sociology, Psychology, English Language, English Literature, History, Philosophy
Christian Ordination Training: Baptist Church Church of England Church of Scotland Church of Wales Evangelical Church Baptist Church Recognised professional courses approved with: Baptist colleges http://www.baptist.org.uk/Groups/220658/Colleges.aspx Church of England Recognised professional courses approved with: Church of England: recognised Theological training institutions https://www.churchofengland.org/ Church of Scotland Recognised professional courses approved with: Church of Scotland: Ministries http://www.churchofscotland.org.uk/serve/ministries_council/ministries_in_the_church	You will need to be practicing and committed to the relevant faith and put forward by a Sponsoring Bishop or senior Minister. For undergraduate study you would usually need 'A' levels or equivalent in any subjects, although Religious Studies may be preferred.	Religious Studies, Sociology, Psychology, English Language, English Literature, History, Philosophy
Christian Ordination Training:	You will need to be	Religious Studies,

Church of Wales Recognised professional courses approved with: St Michaels College http://stmichaels.ac.uk/ Evangelical Church Recognised professional courses approved with: Fellowship of Independent Evangelical Churches https://fiec.org.uk/what-we-do/article/equipping-individuals	practicing and committed to the relevant faith and put forward by a Sponsoring Bishop or senior Minister. For undergraduate study you would usually need 'A' levels or equivalent in any subjects, although Religious Studies may be preferred.	Sociology, Psychology, English Language, English Literature, History, Philosophy
Catholic Priest Formation Training Approved Catholic Training courses for Priests and Religious Brothers (Monks) may be found at: National Office for Vocation http://www.ukvocation.org/	You will need to be practicing and committed to the Catholic faith. You would firstly need to contact your Diocesan Vocation Director. Any subjects usually considered; Religious Studies may be advantageous.	Religious Studies, Sociology, Psychology, English Language, English Literature, History, Philosophy
Salvation Army Officer Training Diploma of higher education validated by the University of Gloucestershire Recognised professional courses approved with: Salvation Army http://www.salvationarmy.org.uk/	You will need to be practicing and committed to the Salvation Army. You will need to be put forward by your corps officer and divisional leaders. You will need the academic ability to complete the course; 'A' level subjects may be advantageous though not essential.	Religious Studies, Sociology, Psychology, English Language, English Literature, History, Philosophy
Religion and Theology	Any subjects usually considered; Religious Studies or Philosophy may be preferred	Religious Studies, Sociology, Psychology, English Language, English Literature, History, Philosophy

26. Retail Sector

Marketing see Media: Advertising, Communications, Marketing and Public Relations Sector

Degree Subject	Essential or Preferred 'A' level / equivalent subject/s	Relevant 'A' level / equivalent subject/s
Business Purchasing and Supply chain Management Some courses professionally accredited with: Chartered Institute of Purchasing and Supply CIPS http://www.cips.org	Any subjects usually considered	Mathematics, Economics, Business Studies, Computing, Psychology, Sociology, English Language, English Literature, Foreign Language
Fashion Buying and Merchandising	Any subjects usually considered	Design and Technology: Textiles, Mathematics, Economics, Business Studies, Biology, Chemistry, Physics, Computing, Geography, Psychology, English Language, English Literature, Foreign Language
Fashion Management	Any subjects usually considered	Design and Technology: Textiles, Business Studies, Sociology, Economics, Mathematics, Geography, Biology, Chemistry, Physics
Retail Management	Any subjects usually considered	Mathematics, Economics, Business Studies, Design and Technology: Textiles, Biology, Chemistry, Physics, Computing, Psychology, Sociology, English Language, English Literature, Foreign Language
Visual Merchandising	Any subjects usually considered Some may require an Art portfolio	English Language English Literature, Mathematics, Art and Design, Design and Technology: Textiles, Business Studies, Foreign Language

119

27. Science Sector		

Ecology see Environment sector
Environmental Science see Environment sector
Marine Engineering / Technology/ Naval architecture see Engineering sector
Marine Biology see Animals sector
Medicine, Dentistry, Pharmacy, Nursing and Midwifery, Allied Health see Healthcare sector
Naval Architecture / Maritime Engineering / Ship Science see Engineering sector
Psychology see Psychology and Counselling sector
Sport Science see Sports sector
Veterinary Science see Animals sector

To become a Registered Science Technician (RSciTech), Registered Scientist (RSci), Chartered Scientist (CSci) or Chartered Science Teacher (CSciTeach) awarded under license from the Science Council: Professional registration http://www.sciencecouncil.org you would need to need to meet the qualification and work experience requirements of the relevant member professional organisation. Links to professional organisations may be found at: http://www.charteredscientist.org/licensed-bodies/links

Biology, Chemistry and Healthcare Science (also see Healthcare sector and NHS Healthcare training scheme below)

Degree Subject	Essential or Preferred 'A' level / equivalent subject/s	Relevant 'A' level / equivalent subject/s
Biochemistry Some courses professionally accredited with: Royal Society of Biology https://www.rsb.org.uk/	Usually require Chemistry plus at least one other Science or Mathematics	Biology, Human Biology, Mathematics, Physics, Geography, Psychology, Further Mathematics, Environmental Science, Electronics, Geology, Applied Science
Biology Some courses professionally accredited with: Royal Society of Biology https://www.rsb.org.uk/	Usually Biology/Human Biology and some require an additional Science subject	Chemistry, Mathematics, Physics, Geography, Geology, Psychology, Further Mathematics, Environmental Science, Statistics, Human Biology, Applied Science
Biology: Plant Science Some courses professionally accredited with: Royal Society of Biology https://www.rsb.org.uk/	Usually Biology and one other science	Chemistry, Mathematics, Physics, Geography, Geology, Psychology, Further Mathematics, Environmental Science, Statistics, Applied Science
Biomedical Science	Usually Biology and	Chemistry, Mathematics,

Professional accreditation is a requirement with: Institute of Biomedical Science IBMS https://www.ibms.org/go/qualifications/ibms-courses Non-accredited degree required to have degree assessed by IBMS Some courses professionally accredited with: Royal Society of Biology https://www.rsb.org.uk/	one other science	Physics, Psychology, Further Mathematics, Environmental Science, Statistics, Human Biology, Applied Science
Brewing and Distilling Professional accreditation is a requirement with: Institute of Brewing and Distilling https://www.ibd.org.uk/	Usually require one science subject from Biology, Chemistry, Mathematics or Physics; Biology, Human Biology may be required.	Biology, Chemistry, Mathematics, Physics, Applied Science
Chemistry Some courses professionally accredited with: Royal Society of Chemistry RSC http://www.rsc.org/	Usually require Chemistry, and many require at least one other from Mathematics, Physics, Biology	Mathematics, Physics, Biology, Applied Science
Food / Nutrition Science /Technology Some courses professionally accredited with: Institute of Food Science and Technology IFST http://www.ifst.org/ Nutrition Some courses professionally accredited with: Association for Nutrition: Nutrition http://www.associationfornutrition.org Some courses endorsed with: National Skills Academy: Food and Drink http://foodanddrink.nsacademy.co.uk/	Usually at least one from Home Economics or Sciences	Biology, Physics, Mathematics, Human Biology, Applied Science
Forensic Biology Some courses professionally accredited with: Royal Society of Biology https://www.rsb.org.uk/	Usually at least one Science, to include Biology, Chemistry, Human Biology, Applied Science or Mathematics	Biology, Physics, Mathematics, Computing / Computer Science, Human Biology, Applied Science
Forensic Science Some courses professionally accredited with: The Chartered Society for Forensic Sciences http://www.charteredsocietyofforensicsciences.org/	Usually at least one Science, preferably Chemistry	Biology, Physics, Mathematics, Computing / Computer Science, Human Biology, Applied Science, Enviornmental Technology
Genetics / Genomics	Usually Biology/Human	Biology, Chemistry,

Some courses professionally accredited with: Royal Society of Biology https://www.rsb.org.uk/	Biology and some require an additional Science subject	Physics, Mathematics, Human Biology, Applied Science
Hearing Aid Audiology Foundation degree / Diploma of Higher Education Some universities offer the Hearing Aid Dispensing aptitude test	Usually one 'A' level in any subject, although a relevant science subject may be advantageous and 3 or more GCSE passes including English and Mathematics You would need to be working as a trainee in the right healthcare context. Employers may set their own entry requirements.	Biology, Human Biology, Chemistry, Physics, Mathematics, Applied Science
Human Bioscience Some courses professionally accredited with: Royal Society of Biology https://www.rsb.org.uk/	Usually Biology and one other science	Chemistry, Mathematics, Physics, Psychology, Further Mathematics, Environmental Science, Statistics, Human Biology, Applied Science
Human Nutrition Some courses professionally accredited with: Royal Society of Biology https://www.rsb.org.uk/	Usually Biology and one other science	Chemistry, Mathematics, Physics, Psychology, Further Mathematics, Environmental Science, Statistics, Human Biology, Applied Science
Immunology Some courses professionally accredited with: Royal Society of Biology https://www.rsb.org.uk/	Usually Biology and one other science	Chemistry, Mathematics, Physics, Psychology, Further Mathematics, Environmental Science, Statistics, Human Biology, Applied Science
Microbiology Some courses professionally accredited with: Institute of Biomedical Science IBMS https://www.ibms.org/	Usually Biology/Human Biology and some require an additional Science subject	Chemistry, Mathematics, Physics, Psychology, Further Mathematics, Environmental Science, Statistics, Human Biology, Applied Science
Molecular and Cellular Biology Some courses professionally accredited with: Institute of Biomedical Science IBMS https://www.ibms.org/	Usually require Chemistry and Biology / Human Biology	Chemistry, Mathematics, Physics, Psychology, Further Mathematics, Environmental Science, Statistics, Human Biology, Applied Science
Neuroscience	Usually require at least	Chemistry, Mathematics,

Some courses professionally accredited with: Royal Society of Biology https://www.rsb.org.uk/ Links to courses available at the British Neuroscience Association https://www.bna.org.uk/careers/courses	one science from Biology or Chemistry	Physics, Psychology, Further Mathematics, Environmental Science, Statistics, Human Biology, Applied Science
Pharmacology Some courses professionally accredited with: Royal Society of Biology https://www.rsb.org.uk/ Core curricula guidelines for courses with: British Pharmacology Society https://www.bps.ac.uk/education-careers/teaching-pharmacology/core-curricula	Usually one from Chemistry, Biology or Human Biology plus preferably one other Science or Mathematics.	Biology, Mathematics, Physics, additional third subject also may be accepted.
Physiology Clinical Physiology (see Healthcare Science below) Some courses professionally accredited with: Registration Council for Clinical Physiologists https://www.rccp.co.uk Some courses professionally accredited with: Royal Society of Biology https://www.rsb.org.uk/	Usually two science subjects to include Biology and / or Chemistry, some accept Physics or Mathematics	Biology, Chemistry, Mathematics, Physics, Physical Education/ Sports Science, Geography, Psychology, Environmental Science
Sports Science Some courses endorsed by British Association of Sport and Exercise Science http://www.bases.org.uk/Courses	Usually at least one subject from Mathematics, Biology, Chemistry, Physics, Design and Technology, Physical Education/ Sports Science	Mathematics, Biology, Chemistry, Physics, Design and Technology, Physical Education/ Sports Science
Zoology Some courses professionally accredited with: Royal Society of Biology https://www.rsb.org.uk/	Usually Biology/Human Biology and an additional Science subject	Biology, Physics, Mathematics, Chemistry
Bio-veterinary Science Some courses professionally accredited with: Royal Society of Biology https://www.rsb.org.uk/	Usually Biology/Human Biology or Chemistry and an additional Science subject	Biology, Physics, Mathematics, Chemistry, Human Biology

Physical Science

Biomedical Engineering see Engineering sector and NHS Healthcare Science (below)
Computer Science see Information / Computer Technology sector
Environmental Science, Hydrology and Water Science see Environment sector
Geology see Environmental sector
Informatics see Information / Computer Technology sector
Mathematics see Business Finance; Economics; Mathematics; Statistics Sector
Metallurgy / Materials Science see Engineering sector
Meteorology see Environment sector
Oceanography and Hydrography see Environment sector

Degree Subject	Essential or Preferred 'A' level / equivalent subject/s	Relevant 'A' level / equivalent subject/s
Astronomy	Usually Mathematics and Physics	Biology, Chemistry, Geology, Computing / Computer Science
Astrophysics	Usually Mathematics and Physics	Chemistry, Biology, Computing / Computer Science, Electronics, Engineering, Statistics, Design and Technology
Biological Modelling	Usually Mathematics and either Biology or Further Mathematics	Physics, Chemistry, Computing/ Computer Science, Electronics, Engineering, Statistics, Design and Technology: Systems and Control
Biotechnology / Applied Molecular Biology Some courses professionally accredited with: Institute of Biomedical Science IBMS https://www.ibms.org/	Usually Biology and Chemistry	Physics, Mathematics, Computing / Computer Science, Electronics, Engineering, Design and Technology
Materials Science Some courses professionally accredited with: Engineering Council http://www.engc.org.uk/ Some courses professionally accredited with: Institute of Materials, Minerals and Mining http://www.iom3.org/	Usually two subjects from Mathematics, Physics or Chemistry	Mathematics, Physics or Chemistry, Computing / Computer Science, Engineering, Design and Technology
Medical Physics Some courses professionally accredited with: Engineering Council http://www.engc.org.uk/ Institute for Physics and Engineering in Medicine http://www.ipem.ac.uk/	Usually require Mathematics and Physics	Further Mathematics, Statistics, Chemistry, Biology, Computing / Computer Science; Engineering; Electronics

Natural Science	Usually require Mathematics and Chemistry, additional subject preferably from Biology, Physics	Biology, Physics, Computing / Computer Science
Nuclear Science Some courses accredited with: Institute of Physics https://www.iop.org/	Usually Mathematics and Physics	Chemistry, Design and Technology, Computer Science, Electronics, Engineering
Physics Some courses accredited with: Institute of Physics https://www.iop.org/	Usually require Mathematics and Physics	Further Mathematics, Statistics, Physics, Chemistry, Biology, Computing / Computer Science; Engineering; Electronics

Healthcare Science Undergraduate NHS Practitioner Training Programme (PTP)
Academy for Healthcare Science: Overarching body for the whole of healthcare science http://www.ahcs.ac.uk Registration as a Clinical Scientist, Biomedical Scientist and Hearing Aid Dispenser is with: Health and Care Professions Council HCPC http://www.hcpc-uk.org Registration as a Medical Physiologist, Medical Physical Scientist and Biomedical Engineer is with: Academy for Healthcare Science: http://www.ahcs.ac.uk There are separate healthcare science training schemes which accredit courses in England, Wales, Northern Ireland and Scotland **England and Wales** National School for Healthcare Science http://www.nshcs.hee.nhs.uk/ **Wales** NHS Wales   http://www.wales.nhs.uk/nhswalesaboutus **Northern Ireland** Northern Ireland Government   http://www.nidirect.gov.uk/healthcare-scientist **Scotland** NHS Education for Scotland   http://www.nes.scot.nhs.uk/education-and-training/

Life Sciences / Biomedical Sciences NHS Practitioner Training Programme (PTP)		
Degree Subject	**Essential or Preferred 'A' level / equivalent subject/s**	**Relevant 'A' level / equivalent subject/s**
Blood Science Professional accreditation is a requirement with: Institute of Biomedical Science IBMS https://www.ibms.org/ Registration as a Biomedical Scientist is with: Health and Care Professions Council HCPC http://www.hcpc-uk.org	Usually Biology and Chemistry; some may accept Mathematics or Physics as a second subject	Biology, Chemistry, Mathematics, Physics, Geography, Psychology, Further Mathematics, Environmental Science, Psychology

Cellular Science Professional accreditation is a requirement with: Institute of Biomedical Science IBMS https://www.ibms.org/ Registration as a Biomedical Scientist is with: Health and Care Professions Council HCPC http://www.hcpc-uk.org	Usually Biology and Chemistry; some may accept Mathematics or Physics as a second subject	Biology, Chemistry, Mathematics, Physics, Geography, Psychology, Further Mathematics, Environmental Science, Psychology
Genomics /Genetics Science / Technology Professional accreditation is a requirement with: Institute of Biomedical Science IBMS https://www.ibms.org/ Registration as a Biomedical Scientist is with: Health and Care Professions Council HCPC http://www.hcpc-uk.org	Usually Biology and Chemistry; some may accept Mathematics or Physics as a second subject	Biology, Chemistry, Mathematics, Physics, Geography, Psychology, Further Mathematics, Environmental Science, Psychology
Infection Science Professional accreditation is a requirement with: Institute of Biomedical Science IBMS https://www.ibms.org/ Registration as a Biomedical Scientist is with: Health and Care Professions Council HCPC http://www.hcpc-uk.org	Usually Biology and Chemistry; some may accept Mathematics or Physics as a second subject	Biology, Chemistry, Mathematics, Physics, Geography, Psychology, Further Mathematics, Environmental Science, Psychology
Life science (provides a broad base before specialising in one of the above areas Professional accreditation is a requirement with: Institute of Biomedical Science IBMS https://www.ibms.org/ Registration as a Biomedical Scientist is with:Health and Care Professions Council HCPC http://www.hcpc-uk.org	Usually Biology and Chemistry; some may accept Mathematics or Physics as a second subject	Biology, Chemistry, Mathematics, Physics, Geography, Psychology, Further Mathematics,

Medical Physics Technology and Biomedical (Clinical) Engineering NHS Practitioner Training Programme (PTP)		
Biomedical (Clinical) Engineering NHS Practitioner Training Programme (PTP)		
Degree Subject	**Essential or Preferred 'A' level / equivalent subject/s**	**Relevant 'A' level / equivalent subject/s**
Biomedical / Clinical / Medical / Engineering Professional accreditation is a requirement with: Engineering Council http://www.engc.org.uk/ Some courses professionally accredited with: Institute of Physics and Engineering in Medicine IPEM http://www.ipem.ac.uk/ Registration as a Medical Physical Scientist / Biomedical Engineer is with: Academy for Healthcare Science (AHCS) http://www.ahcs.ac.uk/	Usually at least one or two subjects from Mathematics and / or Physics with other sciences preferred such as Biology or Chemistry. Some may also accept Human Biology	Biology, Chemistry, Mathematics, Physics, , Further Mathematics, Environmental Science, Electronics, Psychology
Radiation Engineering Professional accreditation is a requirement with: Engineering Council http://www.engc.org.uk/ Some courses professionally accredited with: Institute of Physics and Engineering in Medicine IPEM http://www.ipem.ac.uk/ Registration as a Medical Physical Scientist / Biomedical Engineer is with: Academy for Healthcare Science (AHCS) http://www.ahcs.ac.uk/	Usually one or two subjects from Mathematics and / or Physics with other sciences preferred such as Biology or Chemistry. Some may also accept Human Biology	Biology, Chemistry, Mathematics, Physics, , Further Mathematics, Environmental Science, Electronics, Psychology
Rehabilitation Engineering Professional accreditation is a requirement with: Engineering Council http://www.engc.org.uk/ Some courses professionally accredited with: Institute of Physics and Engineering in Medicine IPEM http://www.ipem.ac.uk/ Registration as a Medical Physical Scientist / Biomedical Engineer is with: Academy for Healthcare Science (AHCS) http://www.ahcs.ac.uk/	Usually one or two subjects from Mathematics and / or Physics with other sciences preferred such as Biology or Chemistry. Some may also accept Human Biology	Biology, Chemistry, Mathematics, Physics, , Further Mathematics, Environmental Science, Electronics, Psychology

| Renal Technology Professional accreditation is a requirement with: Engineering Council http://www.engc.org.uk/ Some courses professionally accredited with: Institute of Physics and Engineering in Medicine IPEM http://www.ipem.ac.uk/ Registration as a Medical Physical Scientist / Biomedical Engineer is with: Academy for Healthcare Science (AHCS) http://www.ahcs.ac.uk/ | Usually one or two subjects from Mathematics and / or Physics with other sciences preferred such as Biology or Chemistry. Some may also accept Human Biology | Biology, Chemistry, Mathematics, Physics, , Further Mathematics, Environmental Science, Electronics, Psychology |

Medical Physics Technology NHS Practitioner Training Programme (PTP)

Degree Subject	Essential or Preferred 'A' level / equivalent subject/s	Relevant 'A' level / equivalent subject/s
Radiation Physics Professional accreditation is a requirement with: Engineering Council http://www.engc.org.uk/ Some courses professionally accredited with: Institute of Physics and Engineering in Medicine IPEM http://www.ipem.ac.uk/ Registration as a Medical Physical Scientist / Biomedical Engineer is with: Academy for Healthcare Science	Usually one or two subjects from Mathematics and / or Physics with other sciences preferred such as Biology or Chemistry. Some may also accept Human Biology	Biology, Chemistry, Mathematics, Physics, Further Mathematics, Environmental Science, Electronics, Psychology
Radiotherapy Physics Professional accreditation is a requirement with: Engineering Council http://www.engc.org.uk/ Some courses professionally accredited with: Institute of Physics and Engineering in Medicine IPEM http://www.ipem.ac.uk/ Registration as a Medical Physical Scientist / Biomedical Engineer is with: Academy for Healthcare Science (AHCS) http://www.ahcs.ac.uk/	Usually one or two subjects from Mathematics and / or Physics with other sciences preferred such as Biology or Chemistry. Some may also accept Human Biology	Biology, Chemistry, Mathematics, Physics, Further Mathematics, Environmental Science, Electronics, Psychology

Nuclear Medicine Professional accreditation is a requirement with: Engineering Council http://www.engc.org.uk/ Some courses professionally accredited with: Institute of Physics and Engineering in Medicine IPEM http://www.ipem.ac.uk/ Registration as a Medical Physical Scientist / Biomedical Engineer is with: Academy for Healthcare Science (AHCS) http://www.ahcs.ac.uk/	Usually one or two subjects from Mathematics and / or Physics with other sciences preferred such as Biology or Chemistry. Some may also accept Human Biology	Biology, Chemistry, Mathematics, Physics, , Further Mathematics, Environmental Science, Electronics, Psychology

Physiological Sciences (Clinical) NHS Practitioner Training Programme (PTP)

Degree Subject	Essential or Preferred 'A' level / equivalent subject/s	Relevant 'A' level / equivalent subject/s
Audiology Professional accreditation is a requirement with: Registration Council for Clinical Physiologists https://www.rccp.co.uk Registration as a Hearing Aid Dispenser is with: Health and Care Professions Council HCPC http://www.hcpc-uk.org	Usually at least one science subject with Biology and or Chemistry preferred. Some may also accept Physics, Human Biology or Mathematics	Biology, Human Biology, Chemistry, Physics, Mathematics Further Mathematics, Human Biology, Sports Science, Psychology
Cardiac physiology Professional accreditation is a requirement with: Registration Council for Clinical Physiologists https://www.rccp.co.uk Registration as a Medical Physiologist, is with: Academy for Healthcare Science: http://www.ahcs.ac.uk	Usually at least one science subject with Biology and or Chemistry preferred. Some may also accept Physics, Human Biology or Mathematics	Biology, Human Biology, Chemistry, Physics, Mathematics Further Mathematics, Human Biology, Sports Science, Psychology
Neurophysiology Professional accreditation is a requirement with: Registration Council for Clinical Physiologists https://www.rccp.co.uk Registration as a Medical Physiologist, is with: Academy for Healthcare Science: http://www.ahcs.ac.uk	Usually at least one science subject with Biology and or Chemistry preferred. Some may also accept Physics, Human Biology or Mathematics	Biology, Human Biology, Chemistry, Physics, Mathematics Further Mathematics, Human Biology, Sports Science, Psychology

Respiratory and sleep physiology Professional accreditation is a requirement with: Registration Council for Clinical Physiologists https://www.rccp.co.uk Registration as a Medical Physiologist, is with: Academy for Healthcare Science: http://www.ahcs.ac.uk	Usually at least one science subject with Biology and or Chemistry preferred. Some may also accept Physics, Human Biology or Mathematics	Biology, Human Biology, Chemistry, Physics, Mathematics Further Mathematics, Human Biology, Sports Science, Psychology

28. Social Care

Housing see Building Management sector;
Human Resources see Business Management sector;
Money advice see Business Finance sector
Psychology and Counselling see Psychology and Counselling sector;

Degree Subject	Essential or Preferred 'A' level / equivalent subject/s	Relevant 'A' level / equivalent subject/s
Charity / International Development	Any subjects usually considered	Sociology, Psychology, English Language / Literature, History, Government and Politics
Child and Youth Studies	Any subjects usually considered	Sociology, Psychology, English Language / Literature, Art and Design, Drama, Music
Coaching and Mentoring	Any subjects usually considered	Sociology, Psychology, English Language / Literature
Criminology	Any subjects usually considered	Law, English Language, English Literature, Foreign Language, History, Mathematics, Government and Politics, Philosophy, Sociology
Early Childhood Studies	Any subjects usually considered	Sociology, Psychology, English Language / Literature, Art and Design, Drama / Performing Arts, Music
Health and Social Care	Any subjects usually considered	Sociology, Psychology, English Language / Literature, Biology Chemistry
Health Promotion	Any subjects usually considered	Biology, Chemistry, Mathematics, English, Sociology, Psychology, Health and Social Care
Human Rights	Any subjects usually	Sociology, Psychology,

	considered	Media Studies, English Language / Literature, History, Government and Politics, Mathematics, Statistics, European Language
Public Services	Any subjects usually considered	Business Studies, Law, English Language, English Literature, History, Mathematics, Government and Politics
Probation Service Professional Qualification in Probation (PQiP) programme (England and Wales): which is 'A' level 6 academic programme equivalent to the last part of an honours degree, alongside 'A' level 5 vocational qualification. Undergraduate and Graduate entry Professional accreditation is a requirement with: **England and Wales** National Probation Service http://www.traintobeaprobationofficer.com/ **England and Wales** National Probation Service England and Wales https://www.gov.uk/government/organisations/national-probation-service	**England and Wales** You will need a level 5 vocational qualification, higher apprenticeship, diploma of higher education (Dip HE), foundation degree or honours degree: in a subject which includes the following four required modules: the criminal justice system; understanding crime and criminal behaviour; penal policy and the punishment of offenders; rehabilitation of offenders: relevant subjects may include criminology, police studies, community justice or criminal justice Or you may study for the following four required modules studied in a contracted university: the criminal justice system; understanding crime and criminal behaviour; penal policy and the punishment of offenders; rehabilitation of offenders Train to be a Probation Officer: University Providers http://www.traintobeaprobationofficer.com/	Relevant degree subjects: Criminology, Police Studies, Community Justice or Criminal Justice.

Probation Service **Northern Ireland** Social Work qualification Northern Ireland Social Care Council http://www.niscc.info/index.php/educati on-for-our-training-providers/degree-in- social-work-education **Scotland** Social Work qualification Scottish Social Services Council: Social workhttp://www.sssc.uk.com	**Northern Ireland and Scotland** In Northern Ireland and Scotland you will need a professional Social Work qualification which may be a bachelor's degree or postgraduate qualification.	Relevant degree subjects: Criminology, Police Studies, Community Justice or Criminal Justice.
Social Work Professional accreditation is a requirement with: **England** Health and Care Professions Council regulates Social Workers in England: register of courses http://www.hcpc- uk.org/education/programmes/register/ **Wales** Care Council for Wales: Social Work courses http://www.ccwales.org.uk/social-work- degree/ **Northern Ireland** Northern Ireland Social Care Council http://www.niscc.info/index.php/educati on-for-our-training-providers/degree-in- social-work-education **Scotland** Scottish Social Services Council (SSSC)Social Workers http://www.sssc.uk.com	Any subjects usually considered	Sociology, Psychology, Media Studies, English Language, English Literature, History, Government and Politics
Youth and Community Work Professional accreditation is a requirement with: **England** National Youth Agency England http://www.nya.org.uk Recognised by the Joint Negotiating Committee for youth and community workers **Wales** Education and Training Standards Wales: Youth Work http://www.etswales.org.uk **Northern Ireland** Youth Council Northern Ireland http://www.ycni.org **Scotland** The Standards Council: Community Learning and Development for Scotland http://www.cldstandardscouncil.org.uk	Any subjects usually considered; most usually require specified relevant work experience in youth and community work. **Additional Requirements:** You would need relevant paid or voluntary work experience working with young people between 13 and 19 years of age.	Sociology, Psychology, English Language / Literature, Art and Design, Drama, Music

29. Social Science, Social Arts, Social Policy, Philosophy and Politics Sector

Operational Research see Business Management and Administration; Human Resources and Recruitment Sector

Degree Subject	Essential or Preferred 'A' level / equivalent subject/s	Relevant 'A' level / equivalent subject/s
Anthropology	Any subjects usually considered	Sociology, Psychology, Biology, Chemistry, English Language, English Literature, History, Mathematics, Statistics
Digital Culture	Any subjects usually considered	Art and Design, English Language, English Literature History, media Studies, Philosophy, Communication and Culture
European Studies	Any subjects usually considered	Sociology, Psychology, Media Studies, English Language, English Literature, History, Government and Politics, Mathematics, Statistics, European Language
Human Rights	Any subjects usually considered	Sociology, Psychology, Media Studies, English Language, English Literature, History, Government and Politics, Mathematics, Statistics, European Language
International Relations	Any subjects usually considered	Sociology, Psychology, Media Studies, English Language, English Literature, History, Government and Politics, Mathematics, Statistics, European Language
Philosophy Links to some Philosophy courses British Philosophy Association http://www.bpa.ac.uk/	Any subjects usually considered	Mathematics, History, Philosophy, English Language, English Literature, Religious Studies/Theology, Government and Politics
Politics	Any subjects usually considered	History, Law, English Language, English Literature, Sociology, Economics, Government and Politics
Social Policy	Any subjects usually	Sociology, Psychology,

		considered	Media Studies, English Language, English Literature, History, Government and Politics
Social Science		Any subjects usually considered	Sociology, Psychology, media Studies, English Language English Literature, History, Government and Politics, Mathematics, Statistics
Sociology Links to some Sociology courses British Sociological Association https://www.britsoc.co.uk/		Any subjects usually considered	Sociology, Psychology, Media Studies, English Language English Literature, History

30. Sport Sector		
Degree Subject	**Essential or Preferred 'A' level / equivalent subject/s**	**Relevant 'A' level / equivalent subject/s**
Equine Sports Management	Most prefer one Science subject	Physical Education or Sports Science, Business Studies, Economics, Mathematics, Biology, Chemistry, Physics, Psychology
Golf Management Studies	Usually require at least two of the following Physical Education or Sports Science, Business Studies or Economics, Design and Technology or Mathematics, Science subject: Physics, Biology or Psychology. Applicants may also need to meet a golf handicap as stipulated by the PGA	Physical Education or Sports Science, Business Studies, Economics, Design and Technology, Mathematics, Biology, Chemistry Physics, Psychology
Marine Sports Science	Any subjects usually considered	Physical Education or Sports Science, Business Studies, Economics, Mathematics, Biology, Chemistry, Physics, Psychology
Sport and Social Science	Any subjects usually considered	Physical Education, Sociology, Psychology, Biology, Chemistry, Mathematics. Physics
Sport Business Management	Any subjects usually considered	Physical Education or Sports Science,

		Business Studies, Economics, Mathematics, Physics, Biology, Psychology
Sport and Exercise Psychology Professional accreditation is a requirement with: British Psychology Society http://www.bps.org.uk/	Any subjects may be considered	Biology / Human Biology, Physics, Mathematics. Psychology, Physical Education, Chemistry, Sports Science
Sports and Exercise Science Some courses professionally endorsed with: British Association of Sport and Exercise Sciences BASES http://www.bases.org.uk/	Usually at least one Science from Biology / Human Biology, Physics, Mathematics. Psychology may also be accepted as a Science if combined with Sports subject such as Physical Education or Sports Science	Biology / Human Biology, Physics, Mathematics. Psychology, Physical Education, Chemistry, Sports Science
Sports Coaching Some courses endorsed with: Chartered Institute for the Management of Sport and Physical Activity (CIMSPA): Endorsed degrees http://www.cimspa.co.uk British Association of Sport and Exercise Sciences: http://www.bases.org.uk/Courses Formal recognition of some training courses with: Sports Coach UK http://www.sportscoachuk.org	Usually a minimum of one subject from Physical Education, Sports Science, Psychology or a Science subject	Physical Education, Sports Science, Psychology, Biology, Chemistry, Physics, Mathematics.
Sports Development Some courses endorsed with: Chartered Institute for the Management of Sport and Physical Activity (CIMSPA) http://www.cimspa.co.uk	Some may require a relevant subject from Physical Education, Sports Science, Psychology or a Science subject	Physical Education, Sports Science, Psychology, Biology, Chemistry, Physics, Mathematics, Sociology
Sports Performance	Any subjects usually considered Performance of a high standard in a chosen sport.	Physical Education, Sociology, Psychology, Biology, Chemistry, Mathematics. Physics
Sports Therapy Professional accreditation is a requirement with: The Society of Sports Therapists http://www.society-of-sports-therapists.org	Usually one or more relevant subjects from Physical Education or Sports Science, Mathematics, Biology / Human Biology, Chemistry, Physics, Psychology.	Physical Education or Sports Science, Mathematics, Biology / Human Biology, Chemistry, Physics, Psychology
31. Transport and Logistics Sector		
Air industry engineering see Engineering sector		

Marine industry engineering see Engineering sector
Rail industry engineering see Engineering sector
Road industry engineering see Engineering sector

Degree Subject	Essential or Preferred 'A' level / equivalent subject/s	Relevant 'A' level / equivalent subject/s
Aviation Transport Management Some courses professionally accredited with: (provides some exemption from the academic requirements for membership) Chartered Institute of Logistics and Transport http://www.ciltuk.org.uk/	Any subjects usually considered	Business Studies, Economics, Mathematics
Marine Operations / Management / Nautical Science Leading to the award of a UK Maritime and Coastguard Agency (MCA) Standards for Training Certification and Watch keeping (STCW) Deck Officer Certificate of Competency Professional accreditation is a requirement with: Maritime and Coastguard Agency (MCA) https://www.gov.uk/government/organis ations/maritime-and-coastguard-agency and approved by the Merchant Navy Training Board (MNTB) http://mntb.org.uk/ Some courses are supported by the Honourable Company of Master Mariners http://www.hcmm.org.uk/	Any subjects usually considered Some courses are offered through a sponsored cadetship Entry to the top up BSc: Usually aimed at those who have already completed a foundation degree in marine operations or HND in nautical science.	Mathematics, English, Engineering
Logistics / Transport Management Some courses professionally accredited with: (provides some exemption from the academic requirements for membership) Chartered Institute of Logistics and Transport http://www.ciltuk.org.uk/	Science courses: Some may prefer a numerate or science based subject Arts courses: Any subjects usually considered	Business, Economics, Mathematics, Chemistry, Physics, Biology, English Language, English Literature
Logistics and Supply Chain Management Courses in universities, colleges and training centres Some courses professionally accredited with: Chartered Institute of Logistics and Transport CILT http://www.ciltuk.org.uk Some courses professionally accredited with: Chartered Institute of Purchasing and Supply CIPS: http://www.cips.org	Usually prefer numerate subjects Business, Economics, Mathematics	Business, Economics, Mathematics, Computer Science, Chemistry, Physics, Biology, English Language, English Literature

Chapter 5
Higher Education Qualification Subjects and Courses

5.1 Choosing a Higher Education Subject, Course and Higher Education Institution

Choosing and Higher Education Subject

Choosing which higher education subject to study may be easy if you know exactly what career you want to enter, however with thousands of undergraduate and postgraduate course subjects available, making a choice may be a difficult decision.

When choosing subject/s to study, you will need to focus on those you enjoy as you will need to remain motivated for the duration of the course. At 'A' level or equivalent qualification, you will be studying each subject as a key subject such as art, biology, chemistry, English, geography, mathematics, music, physics, sociology etc. However at higher education level, these core subjects may be undertaken as a range of specialist and varied courses. For example if you have enjoyed studying art at 'A' level or equivalent, you may choose to study one of the many art courses which includes art and crafts; jewellery and metal design; product design; animation and games design; graphic design; fashion design; interior design; fine art; illustration; make-up artistry or photography, as well as many more.

If you have studied mathematics, there are many mathematics degrees and other courses which require or prefer mathematics at 'A' level or equivalent such as specialist engineering subjects, specialist science subjects, surveying, architecture, astronomy, computer science, environmental science, accounting and finance or operational research as well as many more.

However, there are also many higher education courses which accept any 'A' level or equivalent subjects. You will also need to consider the course entry requirements, which may differ between courses and universities. Subjects with the same course title may differ at each university or college and the course content, structure, teaching and assessment may also vary. For further information see the chapter on 'A' level or Equivalent Qualification Requirements for Entry to Undergraduate Course Subjects

Undergraduate and postgraduate courses may be available as purely academic courses or combining academic study with a professional qualification accredited by a professional organisation, which may be required if you want a career in that particular subject. Some professions require you to possess a professional qualification accredited by a work related relevant professional body in order to practice.

Professional qualifications may be integrated with undergraduate or postgraduate courses, or you may need a bachelor degree or postgraduate qualification before being able to undertake additional professional qualifications. Professional organisations will provide information about recognised training, the modes of study and approved institutions providing accredited qualifications on the relevant professional body website. Check the chapter on Professional Organisations and Accredited Undergraduate and Postgraduate Courses. Some courses include work experience and may be known as 'sandwich' courses or may include a shorter period of work experience such as a placement or internship. A number of courses, especially those that include a professional qualification, will include integral work experience which may be assessed. Other courses, especially some language degrees, may include the option to study or work abroad.

Types of courses available at undergraduate level include:

- Preparation courses as Extended and Foundation Courses
- Certificates of Higher Education (CertHE)
- Higher National Certificates (HNC)
- Diplomas of Higher Education (DipHE)
- Higher National Diplomas (HND)
- Foundation Degrees (Fd)
- Bachelor Honours Degrees and Ordinary Degrees (in Scotland) (BA / BSc etc.)

Types of courses available at postgraduate level include:

- Postgraduate level Graduate Certificates (GradCert)
- Graduate Diplomas (GradDip) Postgraduate Certificates (PGCert)
- Postgraduate Diplomas (PGDip)
- Master's Degrees (MA/MSc etc.)
- Doctorate Degrees (PhD/DPhil)

Higher education courses are available at over 300 universities, colleges and specialist institutions in the UK. There may be options to study full time, part time, flexible learning and distance / e-learning (online). Higher education academic subjects may also include vocational or professional qualifications which are required to work in specified professional careers.

Higher education course levels start at level 4 and go up to level 8 in the Framework for Higher Education Qualifications (FHEQ) in England, Wales and Northern Ireland; and start at level 7 and go up to level 12 in the Scottish Credit and Qualifications Framework (SCQF) in Scotland.

Each higher education course will be taught as a selection of modules which are separate subject components. You can study an ordinary or honours degree as a single subject or if you want to combine two subjects, you may be able to study for a combined degree course either as joint course, where each subject is studied as half of all the modules studied, or major minor course, with the major subject being studied as two thirds and the minor subject as one third of all the modules studied, although combined subject courses may only be available for some subjects and not offered by all universities.

There are a number of different degree titles, with first degrees conferred as Bachelor of Arts (BA) or Bachelor of Science (BSc) being the most usual, however there are other titles which include Bachelor of Engineering (BEng), Bachelor of Music (BMus) or Bachelor or Laws (LLB) amongst others. Master's degrees may be conferred as Master of Arts (MA) and Master of Science (MSc) being the most usual but other titles include Master of Engineering (MEng), Master of Music (MMus) or Master of Laws (LLM) amongst others.

It may also be possible to study some undergraduate subjects as an integrated master's which allows you to gain an honours degree and master's degree. Most honours degrees in England, Wales and Northern Ireland last for three years full-time or four years full-time in Scotland, however some honours degree courses are available as accelerated courses, allowing you to complete in less time.

There are also a small number of honours degree professional courses which are available as graduate entry which are for graduates in a different subject, such as medicine, nursing or dentistry. To practice in some professional careers, you will be required to take a conversion course if your first degree is in a different subject before you can continue to study for the professional qualifications, such as law or psychology.

You may also want a course that includes work experience or you may choose to study or work abroad. The duration of the course may be another factor to consider and the majority of honours degrees studied full time in England, Wales and Northern Ireland last for three years, with full-time honours degree courses in Scotland, usually lasting for four years (although there are variations). Integrated master's courses will add another year if studying full-time. If you decide to study part time or through distance learning, it will take you longer to complete a degree course.

If you are applying for an undergraduate course through UCAS, you may choose up to five courses therefore although you may consider similar courses, they may differ slightly. Entry requirements will also be listed on the relevant university or college website and you should consider courses that you are likely to meet the entry requirements for, however you may choose to opt for one course that has lower entry requirements you are predicted, as an insurance option.

If you want to undertake work experience overseas as part of your course you may check out the Erasmus Programme http://www.erasmusprogramme.com/ or the British Council https://www.britishcouncil.org/ , which is the UK's national agency for Erasmus also check the
Chapter 9.3
Erasmus: Study and Work Experience Programme in another European Country
Chapter 12.6
Erasmus Funding Support for Undergraduate and Postgraduate Students

Choosing a University, College of Higher Education or Specialist Institution

When you are making a decision about which university, college of higher education or specialist institution that you want to attend, you should consider what is most important to you.

There will be a number of factors to consider but firstly, you will need to check which higher education institutions (HEIs) offer the course/s you are interested in studying. General subjects may be offered at many HEIs whereas specialist subjects are available at a smaller number of HEIs.

Before you make a decision about which course or university to study, you will need to carry out some research about the universities and colleges you are interested in to find out how suitable they are for you and how relevant the content of your chosen course is.

There are a number of websites you can use to search for higher education courses at undergraduate and postgraduate level as well as websites with information about universities and course guides.

However, you should always check on the university or college websites for up to date information as course titles may change. If you want to study a professionally accredited higher education course, approved universities and courses will also be listed on the relevant professional body website. You will need to consider what type of HEI suits you and where you want to live. You may decide to live at home with your family or you may want to move away.

You may prefer to study in a particular geographical location and will need to check what courses are offered at the universities in that area. If you decide to move away from home, you will need to consider what type of student accommodation is available at the universities offering your chosen course, as well as the costs, and it will generally cost more in London than elsewhere in the country. In addition, you may want to research what student support facilities there are, such as study support, sports activities or careers and job support.

Other factors you will need to consider are the type of student accommodation available. For further information see the chapter on Student Accommodation. Financial considerations are also important such as the cost of the tuition fees and living costs. Tuition fees charged may also vary depending where your home region is in England, Wales, Northern Ireland, Scotland, EU or International and which UK country you are studying.

Financial information will also be found on the higher education institutions' websites. Postgraduate tuition fees will also vary considerably between courses and universities. Studying part time may also provide you with the option to spread the costs further and at some universities, may cost less than studying the same course full time.
For further information see the chapters on Student Finance.

Information about Courses and Universities Colleges of Higher Education or Specialist Institutions

Officially Recognised Universities Colleges of Higher Education or Specialist Institutions

To find recognised universities in England, Wales, Northern Ireland or Scotland go to the UK Government:
- UK Government: Check a University is Officially Recognised
  https://www.gov.uk/check-a-university-is-officially-recognised/overview

Information about higher education degrees and recognised awarding bodies:
- UK Government: recognised degrees and bodies
  https://www.gov.uk/guidance/recognised-uk-degrees#recognised-bodies

Information about recognised bodies and listed bodies:
- UK Government: recognised UK degrees
  https://www.gov.uk/recognised-uk-degrees

A list of universities, higher education colleges and specialist institutions can be found on each of the higher education funding bodies' websites for England, Wales, Northern Ireland and Scotland

Higher Education Funding Bodies: **England**
- The Office for Students
  https://www.officeforstudents.org.uk/
Register of English higher education providers:
- The Office for Students
  https://www.officeforstudents.org.uk/advice-and-guidance/the-register/

Wales
- Higher Education Funding Council for Wales
  http://www.hefcw.org.uk/

Northern Ireland
- Department for the Economy: Higher Education
  https://www.economy-ni.gov.uk/topics/higher-education

Scotland
- Scottish Funding Council
  http://www.sfc.ac.uk/

Groups, Associations and Affiliations of Higher Education Institutions

Some universities and colleges are members of a mission group or association. The following groups may change members at times, so check on the given websites for up to date information. (The 1994 group disbanded in November 2013).

- Universities UK
  http://www.universitiesuk.ac.uk
- The Cathedrals Group
  http://www.cathedralsgroup.ac.uk/
- Million Plus Group
  http://www.millionplus.ac.uk/
- The Russell Group
  http://www.russellgroup.ac.uk/
- University Alliance
  http://www.unialliance.ac.uk/
- GuildHE
  http://guildhe.ac.uk/

Associate and Sub Associate groups of Guild HE:
- Consortium for Research Excellence, Support and Training (CREST)
  http://crest.ac.uk/
- United Kingdom Arts and Design Institutions Association (UKADIA)
  http://ukadia.ac.uk/

Professional organisations
Professional organisations may also have links to undergraduate and postgraduate courses. See the chapter on Professional Organisations and Accredited Undergraduate and Postgraduate Courses.

Undergraduate and Postgraduate Course Search

You can search for courses on the following websites but should also confirm up to date information on the relevant university and college websites.

Undergraduate course and subject search in the UK
- University and College Admission Service UCAS
  http://www.ucas.com
- UCAS Conservatoires
  https://www.ucas.com/
- UK Course Finder
  http://www.ukcoursefinder.com/
- Hot Courses
  http://www.hotcourses.com/
- HEAP University Degree Course Offers
  http://www.heaponline.co.uk/

Your school or college will need to buy a licence for you to access this online; alternatively it is published as a book and may be found in education or public libraries.

Undergraduate course and subject search in Ireland
- Central Applications Office (CAO) in Ireland https://www.cao.ie/

Higher National Certificate / Diploma courses and subject search
Check availability with the relevant university or college.
- Pearson Edexcel
  http://qualifications.pearson.com/en/qualifications.html
- Scottish Qualification Authority
  http://www.sqa.org.uk/

Postgraduate course and subject search
- Find a master's
  http://www.findamaster's.com/
- Find a PhD
  http://www.findaphd.com/
- Master's portal
  http://www.master'sportal.eu/
- Postgrad.com
  http://www.postgrad.com/
- Prospects: Postgraduate Study
  http://www.prospects.ac.uk/postgraduate_study.htm
- Target postgrad
  http://targetpostgrad.com/
- UCAS postgraduate
  http://www.ucas.com
- UCAS Teacher Training
  http://www.ucas.com

Further Education Colleges Links

Links to publicly funded further education colleges in the UK can be found on the higher education funding bodies for the relevant country websites. You can search for further education courses on the following websites but should also confirm up to date information on the relevant further education college websites.

England
- Association of Colleges England
  https://www.aoc.co.uk/

Wales
- College Wales
  http://www.collegeswales.ac.uk/

Northern Ireland
- Colleges Northern Ireland
  http://www.anic.ac.uk/

Scotland
- Colleges Scotland
  http://www.collegesscotland.ac.uk/

Additional Further Education College links
- Association of Employment and Learning Providers
  http://www.aelp.org.uk
- Access to Higher Education
  https://www.accesstohe.ac.uk/
- University Technical Colleges (UTCs)
  http://www.utcolleges.org/

Published Data on Universities, Higher Education Colleges and Courses

Published data relating to universities, higher education colleges and courses is available from the following organisations, as well as the various higher education league tables which make use of national data.

Higher Education Statistics Agency

Higher Education Statistics Agency (HESA) http://www.hesa.ac.uk/ is the official source of data about UK universities and higher education colleges.

The National Student Survey (NSS) is a census of students' opinions and satisfaction about their experience of their courses conducted annually. You can compare data and useful information which should help you make informed decisions when you are considering which universities or higher education colleges to apply to. The NSS is commissioned by the Higher Education Funding bodies for the four UK countries and

- Health Education England
https://hee.nhs.uk/ .

The NSS is conducted independently by Ipsos MORI and the data is published annually at:

- Unistats website
https://unistats.direct.gov.uk/

The information provided on Unistats is designed to give an indication about what it might be like on your selected course as the experience of each course will be different for each person. However, not all students will respond to the survey and not all courses will be represented. The information should be helpful when you are considering your options but it is also important to be aware that the student satisfaction score will be for students who have studied before you will have started your course.

The tuition fee information and accommodation cost information will be for the next academic year. To find out more about the NSS and for current eligible students completing the NSS, the survey is available at

- The Student Survey
http://www.thestudentsurvey.com/

The Unistats website https://unistats.direct.gov.uk/ provides the following information for a large number of courses, universities and higher education colleges:

Student satisfaction
- Overall satisfaction of the course
- Teaching on the course

- Assessment and course feedback
- Academic support
- Organisation and management
- Learning resources
- Personal development
- Satisfaction with the Students Union

Study information
- The time spent in lectures, seminars and similar, independent study and placements (if part of the course)
- Class of degree
- Continuation after one year of starting

Cost and accommodation
- The average annual fee for students
- The typical cost for university/college accommodation
- The typical cost for private accommodation

Employment and accreditation
- If the course is accredited by a professional body
- The percentage of graduates who go on to work or study
- Employment 6 months after graduating
- Average salary 6 months after graduating

Entry information
- Entry qualifications
- UCAS Tariff point scores

National Student Survey website references
- Higher Education Statistics Agency (HESA)
https://www.hesa.ac.uk/
- National Student Survey (NSS)
http://www.thestudentsurvey.com/
- Unistats website
https://unistats.direct.gov.uk/
- Ipsos MORI
https://www.ipsos-mori.com/
- Quality Assurance Agency for Higher Education (QAA) http://www.qaa.ac.uk
- Scottish Qualifications Authority (SQA)
http://www.sqa.org.uk/
- Health Education England
https://hee.nhs.uk/

Universities and colleges may be placed into annual league tables which can provide information on the reputation and quality of the education provided at that institution, however there are a range of factors that need to be considered when you look at the league tables. Information is also available on the destinations of graduates which may help you consider what type of job you want to at the end of the course.

There are different league tables and an issue with these is the different methodology used in the rankings, therefore it may be difficult to identify what might be most important. In addition, not all universities or colleges will be considered in some league tables.

League tables may help you to understand the reputation of the university or college but it is important not to make decisions on your education and career based just on statistics alone. Talking to university and college staff and students at higher education fairs and events will help you to make a more informed decision.

There are lots of rankings of universities and colleges internally to the UK and also worldwide, each with their own measures of success. You can compare data on a range of topics, including:

- The ranking of the Higher Education Institution or department
- Average UCAS tariff points for entry
- Number of Firsts and 2:1s awarded
- Completion rate
- Student satisfaction rating
- Research quality
- The ratio of the numbers of staff to numbers of students

- What the academic excellence is, student drop-out rates and pass rates
- Information about Graduate employment
- The amount of money spent on university or college facilities

The following are a selection of league tables.

UK Universities League Tables
- The Times and Sunday Times Good University Guide http://www.thesundaytimes.co.uk/sto/University_Guide/

- The Complete University Guide http://www.thecompleteuniversityguide.co.uk/

- The Guardian University Guide http://www.theguardian.com/education/universityguide

The Main Three Worldwide Universities League Tables:
- The Times Higher Education World Rankings (THE) http://www.timeshighereducation.co.uk/world-university-rankings/

- The Academic Ranking of World Universities (ARWU) http://www.shanghairanking.com/

- The Q5 World University Ranking (QS) http://www.topuniversities.com/university-rankings

If you wish to study overseas, each country will have individual league tables as well. For information on these, go to your preferred search engine and type in university rankings and the country you are interested in.

The best way to find out more about the university or college is to visit in person, so check out when the higher education open days are as dates should be advertised on institutions' websites as well as on the UCAS website. This will give you a chance to look at the teaching environment, student accommodation, the surrounding environment and speak to the staff.

To choose which universities or colleges to consider before you visit, you will need to carry out some research about the courses, geographical location and student facilities. Higher education fairs are also another opportunity to talk to staff from the institution, although it is always a good idea to visit the HEIs you are interested in as well.

Dates for open days and events can be found advertised on the university websites as well as with UCAS http://www.ucas.com/how-it-all-works/explore-your-options/events-and-open-days .

If you can't attend an open day in person, UCAS has virtual tours for a number universities and colleges.
UCAS: Virtual Tours
https://www.ucas.com/events/exploring-university/virtual-tours
It may also be possible to attend a university taster course where you can meet lecturers and students, finding out more about the university and course. Taster courses may last for one day or over a weekend. Some universities offer summer courses and you may get the opportunity to stay overnight on the campus.

Check out careers and information websites listed in the:
Chapter 1.3
Careers Advice and Useful Websites

5.2   Undergraduate Courses and University Entry Requirements

Undergraduate Course Entry Requirements

If you want to study for an honours degree or other undergraduate course the qualification entry requirements will vary between higher education institutions (HEIs) and courses however you will usually need 'A' levels or equivalent qualifications at level 3 Regulated Qualification Framework (RQF) or Scottish Highers, Scottish Advanced Highers or equivalent qualifications at level 6/7 Scottish Qualification and Credit Framework (SCQF). You will also need in addition, GCSEs at level 2 (RQF) or Scottish Nationals at level 5 (SCQF) or equivalent qualifications, to usually include English and mathematics as well as science for science based undergraduate courses.

There are additional qualifications available in the UK as well as international equivalent qualifications at this level that may be considered suitable for entry to

higher education. The Access to Higher Education diploma courses at level 3 (RQF) have been especially designed for mature students who want to study in higher education.

Universities and colleges may require specific qualifications, subjects, grades or UCAS tariff points, with higher requirements especially for competitive entry or professional courses. Some universities or colleges may exclude qualifications if the content is duplicated with other qualifications and will generally only count the highest level of achievement, such as 'AS' levels being superseded by 'A' levels. You should also check on the course entry requirements for the relevant university or college. A list of qualifications for entry to university or college may be found at UCAS https://www.ucas.com/

Universities and Colleges Admission Service (UCAS) Tariff Points

The Universities and Colleges Admission Service (UCAS) tariff points system was developed by universities and colleges to allow for broad comparisons to be made about a wide range of qualifications which is used to represent a value for the different grades for entry to higher education courses in the UK.

However, some universities and colleges don't use the tariff points system and not all qualifications attract UCAS Tariff points with only around one third of all qualifications at level 3 Regulated Qualification Framework (RQF) including 'A' levels and BTEC Nationals or level 6/7 Scottish Qualification and Credit Framework (SCQF) including Scottish Highers and Scottish Advanced Highers being on the Tariff system.

Many universities and colleges express their entry requirements and make offers on the basis of qualification subjects and

grades instead of UCAS Tariff points and may accept a range of qualifications studied around the world providing they are at the required level of ability.

Other universities and colleges may require specific qualifications and a set number of Tariff points; or may link the Tariff points required to specific qualification subjects and grades; or just use Tariff points with no reference to specific qualifications or grades.

Tariff points are usually counted for the highest level of achievement in a subject therefore if you have an AS and 'A' level in the same subject you would count the 'A' level and not the 'AS' level Tariff points. Some universities or colleges may limit the qualifications required such as only Tariff points from the best three 'A' levels.

146

Qualifications change over time, therefore the Tariff calculator is updated annually to reflect these changes or to add new qualifications. Universities or colleges will provide entry requirement information in terms of qualifications, subjects, grades, and UCAS Tariff points published on the entry requirements on their websites. A list of qualifications that are awarded UCAS Tariff Points may be found at

- UCAS: entry requirements
  https://www.ucas.com/ucas/undergradu
  ate/getting-started/entry-requirements

UCAS tariff points 2017 entry to higher education

The UCAS Tariff points system will be changing for entry to higher education in September 2017 and are lower than the old UCAS Tariff due to the way in which they are calculated, allowing for more qualifications to be added. The new Tariff is based on a finite scale and it is not possible to get more than a certain number of points for a single award qualification, although in some instances top grades of different qualifications will receive the same number of points.

The new UCAS Tariff operates by allocating qualifications at level 3 (RQF) / 6 and 7 (SCQF) a size band of 1 to 4 based on their guided learning hours (GLH); and across a grade band of 3 to 14. The size band and grade are then multiplied to form the overall Tariff score. This methodology is different to the version developed in 2001 and means the two systems are not comparable. You can check your qualifications and the new Tariff points by going to

- UCAS: Tariff Calculator
  https://www.ucas.com/ucas/undergradu
  ate/getting-started/entry-
  requirements/tariff/calculator

English Language Requirements

Your English language skills will need to be of the required level to cope with the demands of a higher education course and universities and colleges will specify the English requirements on their websites. You will usually be required to have GCSEs grade C / 4 or above or Scottish Nationals level 5 (SCQF) to include English.

Generally if you are an overseas student with English as a second language, you will need one of the following:

- IELTS: 6.5 (minimum 5.5 in all areas)
- Pearson: 58 (51 in all sub scores)

Universities may also have their own English language tests and some will have a range of pre-sessional English language courses for students who don't meet these requirements or who want to improve their English. Some universities have international pathways and language centres that offer foundation and pre-master's' courses to provide you with the academic skills required for your chosen course (also Go to: on International Students).

Further information may be found at English language requirements:

- UK Government tier 4 general visa
  https://www.gov.uk/tier-4-general-
  visa/knowledge-of-english

European Network of Information Centres (ENIC)

Information about European and some non-European countries' education systems including links to recognised higher education institutions, university education and qualification frameworks

may be found at European Network of Information Centres (ENIC) and the National Academic Recognition Information Centres (NARIC) ENIC-NARIC http://www.enic-naric.net/ .

National Academic Recognition Information Centre (NARIC)

The National Academic Recognition Information Centre (NARIC) is the designated United Kingdom National Agency and is responsible for providing information, advice and expert opinion on qualifications worldwide. NARIC can provide information about European and international qualifications, making a comparison with the equivalent UK qualifications.

There may be a charge for this service and NARIC usually charge a fee for the service of sending you an official documentation with equivalency statements, however many universities and colleges subscribe to NARIC and may be able to provide information on international qualifications free of charge, therefore check with the university or college first. Further information may be found at the National Academic Recognition Information Centre (NARIC) http://www.ecctis.co.uk/naric/

Higher Education Courses and Levels

Undergraduate courses in England, Wales and Northern Ireland are at:
- Level 4, 5 and 6 in the Framework for Higher Education Qualifications (FHEQ)

Undergraduate courses in Scotland are at:
- Level 7, 8, 9 and 10 in the Scottish Credit and Qualification Framework (SCQF

Although some higher education preparation courses are available at:
- Level 3 Regulated Qualification Framework (RQF) or level 6 (SCQF);

Some graduate certificates, diplomas or degrees are available for those who have graduated in another subject at:
- Level 6 (FEHQ) or level 10 (SCQF).

Most undergraduate higher education courses are available to study as a:
- Bachelor's Honours Degree at: Level 6 (FHEQ) or 10 (SCQF) also often referred to as higher education level 3 (HE level 3),

Although some courses may be available as a:
- Higher National Certificate (HNC); Certificate of Higher Education (CertHE) at: Level 4 (FHEQ) level 7 (SCQF) also often referred to as higher education level 1 (HE level 1);

- Higher National Diploma (HND); Diploma of Higher Education level (DipHE) or Foundation Degree at: Level 5 (FHEQ) level 8 (SCQF) also often referred to as higher education level 2 (HE level 2).

Some courses are also available as an:
- Integrated Master's Degree at: Level 7 (FHEQ) level 11 (SCQF), whereby you gain a Bachelor's Honours Degree and a Master's Degree in a limited number of subjects.

Some higher education institutions provide preparation for undergraduate courses such as:

- Extended year or Foundation year at: Level 3 Regulated Qualification Framework (RQF) or level 6 (SCQF) and often referred to as higher education level 0 (HE level 0).

These courses are for those who don't have the necessary entry requirements to enter an Honours Degree or other undergraduate course.

Some undergraduate courses also have professional accreditation, which may be required if you want a career in that particular subject. Some professional courses may be graduate entry but not placed at postgraduate level.

These courses may be:

- Graduate Certificates, Diplomas or Degrees include Graduate 'Conversion' courses, which are accredited courses at the same level for an Honours Degree at:
  Level 6 (FHEQ) level 10 (SCQF)

Although some 'conversion' courses may also be available at:

- Postgraduate Certificate, Diploma and Master's Degree at:
  Level 7 (FHEQ) level 11 (SCQF)

These courses provide the opportunity for graduates of other subjects to graduate with competence in a required accredited professional course subject.
Teacher training courses which include the Post / Professional Graduate Certificate of Education (PGCE) in England, Wales and Northern Ireland or Postgraduate Diploma of Education (PGDE) in Scotland, are at:
- Honours Degree:
  Level 6 (FHEQ) level 10 (SCQF),

Although some courses may have postgraduate credit levels included which can be used towards gaining a Master's Degree. Professional organisations should also list accredited undergraduate and postgraduate courses on their websites.
See the chapter:
Chapter 5.4
Professional Organisations: Accredited Undergraduate and Postgraduate Courses

5 Higher Education Modes of Study, Teaching and Assessment
Higher education courses and levels
Level 3 (RQF) level 6 (SCQF): FE / HE
- HE preparation courses: Foundation or Extended year (HE 0)

Level 4 (FHEQ) level 7 (SCQF): HE
- Bachelor's Degree first year level (HE1)
- Higher National Certificate (HE1)
- Certificate of Higher Education (HE1)

Level 5 (FHEQ) level 8 (SCQF): HE
- Bachelor's Degree second year level (HE2)
- Higher National Diploma (HE2)
- Diploma of Higher Education (HE2)

Level 6 (FHEQ) level 9 / 10 (SCQF): HE
- Bachelor's Degree third year level (HE3) (and additional levels if relevant), most are Honours Degrees, some may be Ordinary Degrees;
- Graduate Certificates; Graduate Diplomas; Graduate entry Degrees

Level 7 (FHEQ) / level 11 (SCQF): HE
- Postgraduate Certificate; Postgraduate Diploma; Master's Degree

Level 8 (FHEQ) / level 12 (SCQF): HE
- Doctorate Degree

Extended / Foundation year courses may be offered by some higher education institutions (HEIs) as entry to some honours degree courses in the UK. The extended / foundation year is an additional year, added on to the total duration of the Honours Degree course which is usually a one year full-time preparatory course for students to gain a successful transition to continue on through to the first level of a degree course.

These courses are for students who don't have the set entry requirements to enter directly into the first level of the degree course of their choice. Extended / Foundation year courses may be suitable if you haven't the specified subjects or grades to enter the degree; are a mature student who lacks formal qualifications; have experienced interruptions in your education; or if you prefer not to return to further education to retake 'A' levels or equivalent qualifications. Many Foundation year courses have also been designed especially for international students and may include additional English language teaching.

The Extended / Foundation course usually lasts for one academic year full-time. Most are full-time courses, including those for International students, although there may be options to study part-time of a longer duration for UK or EU students, but you would need to confirm this with relevant HEIs.

If studying full-time, an Extended / Foundation Course continuing onto a full-time degree course will take in total at least four years to complete.

You can usually apply for an Extended / Foundation course through UCAS if you think you won't meet the entry requirements for the degree.

However if you apply for the degree course of your choice and don't obtain the entry requirements needed, you may be offered an Extended / Foundation year during clearing after the 'A' level / equivalent qualifications results come out, providing this as an option.

Entry Requirements for Extended / Foundation Year Courses level 3 (RQF) 6 (SCQF) (HE level 0)

Typical entry requirements for Extended / Foundation year courses

- 1/2 'A' levels grades D/E or equivalent with some courses specifying specific subjects
- Minimum of four GCSEs or equivalent grade C /4 or above

Typical entry requirements for Extended / Foundation year medicine / dentistry courses

- 3 'A' levels grades AAA / AAB in Arts and Humanities, may accept one science in addition
- Minimum of seven GCSEs or equivalent grades A/B / 4/5 or above including English, mathematics, biology, chemistry, physics or double science

Entry requirements for Extended / Foundation year courses will vary depending on the course subject and higher education institution (HEI), but these courses are for students who don't have the qualifications required to enter directly into the first level of the degree course of their choice.

Generally, however, you may be required to have studied relevant courses such as 'A' levels at level 3 (RQF) or Scottish Highers / Advanced Highers at level 6/7 (SCQF) or equivalent qualifications and you may be required to have specified grades or UCAS Tariff points.

Qualification entry requirements for Foundation / Extended year courses may vary such as a minimum of 1 / 2 'A' level grades D / E or above, although competitive entry courses may require 2 or 3 'A' level subjects; minimum of 1 Scottish Highers / Advanced Highers grade C or above although competitive entry courses may require 2 or more subjects; BTEC National Diploma (2 unit grades) or National Extended Diploma (3 unit grades) with individual units as Passes although competitive entry courses may require 1 or more Merit/s; Access to Higher Education diploma pass with 45 credits at level 3 (RQF) as Passes although competitive entry courses may require credits as Merits; International Baccalaureate with an overall score of 24, although competitive entry courses may require 30 or more points, and may specify a minimum number of credits at Higher Level; or any other equivalent qualification.

You will also usually need in addition a minimum of between 3 - 5 GCSEs at level 2 (RQF) / Scottish Nationals at level 5 (SCQF) or equivalent qualifications including English language and mathematics. Other qualifications and relevant work experience may be also considered and you should contact the relevant HEI for further information.

Universities will have flexibility on entry and may accept applicants with lower or no formal education qualifications but you will usually need to complete an aptitude test to demonstrate your ability complete the course. You may also need to attend an interview.

The exception are the Extended / Foundation / Pre-Clinical Year Medical / Dentistry Degree courses, which are for students who don't have the required subjects at 'A' level or Scottish Highers / Advanced Highers, but will be required to have 3 subjects at 'A' levels or 4 subjects at Highers / Advanced Highers with high grades of As and Bs. For further information see book 8 in the series: **A Careers Advice Guide: Healthcare Sector (2)**

If you don't meet the entry requirements for the degree course of your choice, you may be offered entry on the Extended / Foundation Year course, which may be soon after you submit your application or during clearing when the exam results are known. International students may be offered a Foundation course if your English language skills need to improve. Check course information with relevant HEIs.

Providing you meet the requirements for passing the modules on the Extended / Foundation year, set by the HEI, you should be able to continue onto the relevant degree subject within the same HEI. If you wish to change HEIs on successful completion, you would need to check with the relevant HEI that they would accept the Extended / Foundation year for entry and confirm that the content meets with the standards required. You may need to put in an additional application through UCAS http://www.ucas.com/ so check with the relevant HEIs well in advance to meet the application deadlines.

Certificate of Higher Education (Cert HE) Level 4 (FHEQ), Level 7 (SCQF) (HE Level 1) Courses

Certificate of Higher Education courses are usually abbreviated to Cert HE and may be studied as a stand-alone qualification at some universities for some courses or as the first level of an Honours Degree course (HE level 1). If you study for a degree course and decide to leave early, you may be awarded a Cert HE providing you successfully complete this level.

A Cert HE is made up elements of subjects called modules. Some modules may be mandatory or compulsory, which means you will have to study these subjects, and others are optional enabling you to have a choice as to which to take. The length of time to complete a full-time Cert HE is usually one year in England, Wales, Northern Ireland and Scotland.

If studying for a part-time degree or by distance / e-learning, it will take you longer to complete.

If studying part time, depending on the course and HEI, you may be able to choose how many modules you study for each year depending on what suits your own personal circumstances. Some modules may be available to study during the evening as well as during the day time. The duration of your Cert HE course will be dependent on the number of modules you choose to complete each year.

If you are studying for a stand-alone Cert HE and decide to continue on to a full-time degree course there may be provision for you to transfer within your university of college, providing you pass the required modules, or you may need to apply for the course through UCAS http://www.ucas.com/. If you have previously been awarded a Cert HE, or if you have left a degree course early with a Cert HE award, you will need to check the HEI requirements regarding time limits for credit transfer for studying an Honours Degree course.

If you wish to apply for a degree course in a similar subject to your Cert HE, you may be eligible to enter onto the 2nd level of a Degree course. Check information with relevant HEIs before applying.

Higher National Certificate (HNC) 4 (FHEQ), Level 7 (SCQF) (HE Level 1)

The Business and Technology Education Council (BTEC) Higher National Certificate (HNC) is awarded by Pearson Qualifications https://qualifications.pearson.com/ in England, Wales and Northern Ireland; and the Scottish Qualification Agency (SQA) http://www.sqa.org.uk/ in Scotland.

It is usually abbreviated to BTEC HNC and SQA HNC respectively although commonly known as HNC. Although awarded by different awarding bodies, the HNCs have many similarities. The main difference, however, is how they are both assessed.

HNCs are higher education qualifications at level 4 (FHEQ) and level 7 (SCQF) and are available in England, Wales, Northern Ireland and Scotland mainly in colleges of further / higher education and some universities.

In Scotland, HNCs are also available in some training centres.

An HNC usually lasts for one academic year as a full time course or if studying part time, flexible learning or distance / e-learning, available at some HEIs, will usually take two academic years or longer to complete.

HNCs are vocational qualifications (work related) and are available in a wide range of vocational subjects.

They have been developed in partnership with industry and commerce, and are designed to provide the skills related to a particular job, meeting the needs of employers, reflecting the requirement of professional organisations and meeting the National Occupational Standards http://www.ukstandards.org.uk/ for each sector or industry (see Qualification Regulation and Accreditation). HNCs provide a more technical route into higher education.

You can study for an HNC as a stand-alone qualification or, on successful completion, the first level towards a Higher National Diploma (HND) and potentially onto a degree course in a similar subject. You can usually be awarded an HNC if you leave an HND course early after successful completion of one year for full-time courses or if part-time, longer duration. Some HNCs may provide exemptions if you want to move onto a degree course in a similar subject.

On successful completion of your HNC it may be possible to enter onto the first level (HE level 1) of a degree course and in some situations the may occasionally allow for direct entry into the 2nd level (HE level 2) of a degree course in a similar subject, but this is dependent on the type of degree and is up to the discretion of the higher education institution.
If you want to continue onto an HND course at the same HEI where you are currently studying, you may be able to complete and internal transfer form. If you want to attend a different HEI you may need to apply through UCAS http://www.ucas.ac.uk . Check with relevant HEIs.

Some HNC qualifications may count towards membership of professional bodies. HNCs are for school leavers, adults who want to return to education or for people in employment who want to enhance their career prospects.

Entry requirements for stand-alone Certificate of Higher Education Courses (Cert HE); Higher National Certificates (HNCs)
Typical entry requirements for Certificate of Higher Education (CertHE); Higher National Certificate (HNC) courses

- 1/2 'A' levels grades D/E or above or equivalent with some courses specifying specific subjects
- Minimum of four GCSEs or equivalent grade C /4 or above

As part of the entry requirements for stand-alone Certificate of Higher Education courses (Cert HE) or Higher National Certificate (HNC) courses requirements will vary depending on the course subject and higher education institution (HEI).

Generally, however, you may be required to have studied relevant courses such as 'A' levels at level 3 (RQF) or Scottish Highers / Advanced Highers at level 6/7 (SCQF) or equivalent qualifications and you may be required to have specified grades or UCAS Tariff points, which will usually be lower than those required for entry to an Honours Degree course.

Qualification entry requirements may vary such as a minimum of 1 'A' level grade D / E or above, although competitive entry courses may require 2 'A' level subjects and higher grades; minimum of 1 Scottish Highers / Advanced Highers grade C or above. Other accepted qualifications are BTEC National Diploma (2 unit grades) or National Extended Diploma (3 unit grades) with individual units as Passes and some courses may require 1 or more Merit/s; Access to Higher Education diploma pass with 45 credits at level 3 (RQF) as Passes although competitive entry courses may require credits as Merits; International Baccalaureate with an overall score of 24 points, although competitive entry courses may require more points, and may specify a minimum number of credits at Higher Level; or any other equivalent qualification.

You will also usually need in addition a minimum of between 3 - 5 GCSEs level 2 (RQF), Scottish Nationals level 5 (SCQF) or equivalent qualifications including English language and mathematics. Other qualifications and relevant work experience may be also considered and you should contact the relevant HEI for further information.

Universities will have flexibility on entry and may accept applicants with lower or no formal education qualifications but you will usually need to complete an aptitude test to demonstrate your ability complete the course. You may also need to attend an interview.

Providing you meet the requirements for passing the modules on the Certificate of Higher Education (Cert HE) or Higher National Certificate (HNC), set by the HEI, you should be able to continue onto a Diploma of Higher Education (Dip HE) in a relevant subject within the same HEI. If you wish to change HEIs on successful completion, you would need to check with the relevant HEI that they would accept the Certificate of Higher Education (Cert HE) or Higher National Certificate (HNC) for entry and confirm that the content meets with the standards required.

You may need to put in an additional application through UCAS http://www.ucas.com/ so check with the relevant HEIs well in advance to meet the application deadlines.

Higher National Diploma (HND) Level 5 (FHEQ), Level 8 (SCQF) (HE Level 2)

The Business and Technology Education Council (BTEC) Higher National Diploma (HND) is awarded by Pearson Qualifications https://qualifications.pearson.com/ in England, Wales and Northern Ireland; and the Scottish Qualification Agency (SQA) http://www.sqa.org.uk/ in Scotland. It is usually abbreviated to BTEC HND and SQA HND respectively although commonly known as HND. Although awarded by different awarding bodies, the HNDs have many similarities.

The main difference, however, is how they are both assessed. HNDs are higher education qualifications at level 5 (FHEQ) or level 8 (SCQF) and are available in England, Wales, Northern Ireland and Scotland mainly in colleges of higher education and some universities. In Scotland, HNDs are also available in some training centres.

An HND usually lasts for two academic years as a full time course or if studying part time, flexible learning or distance / e-learning, available at some HEIs, will usually take three or more academic years or longer to complete. HNDs are vocational qualifications (work related) and are available in a wide range of vocational subjects. They have been developed in partnership with industry and commerce, and are designed to provide the skills related to a particular job, meeting the needs of employers, reflecting the requirement of professional organisations and meeting the National Occupational Standards http://www.ukstandards.org.uk/ for each sector or industry (see Qualification Regulation and Accreditation). HNDs provide a more technical route into higher education.

You can study for an HND as a stand-alone qualification or, on successful completion, may potentially lead onto a degree course in a similar subject. Some HNDs may provide exemptions if you want to move onto a degree course in a similar subject. On successful completion of your HND it may be possible to enter onto the second level (HE level 2) of a degree course and in some situations the may occasionally allow for direct entry into the 3rd level (HE level 3) of a degree course in a similar subject, but this is dependent on the type of degree and is up to the discretion of the higher education institution.

If you leave your HND course early before completion, you may be awarded an HNC if you have reached the required standard.

If you want to continue onto a degree course at the same HEI where you are currently studying, you may be able to complete an internal transfer form. If you want to attend a different HEI you may need to apply through UCAS http://www.ucas.ac.uk . Check with relevant HEIs

Some HND qualifications may count towards membership of professional bodies. HNDs are for school leavers, adults who want to return to education or for people in employment who want to enhance their career prospects.

Professional Accreditation for HNDs
Many UK professional bodies recognise HND qualifications and have entered into agreements with the awarding body to give exemptions (partial or full) for professional body exams and HNDs may be accepted as a membership entry requirement, check the professional body websites for information.

The Scottish Qualification Authority (SQA) has links to Professional Bodies with SQA HND agreements in Scotland. These are reviewed but always check to make sure the information is current with the relevant Professional Organisation). SQA: HNCs and HNDs http://www.sqa.org.uk/sqa/168.2432.html

Assessment of HNCs and HNDs in England, Wales and Northern Ireland
Each higher national unit for an HNC is at level 4 RQF/FHEQ and has a credit value which is normally 15 credits. Units can vary in size and can be worth more than 15 credits, depending on the HNC subject and learning provider. To achieve a full HNC qualification, you must gain a minimum of 120 credits at level 4 (RQF / FHEQ). The amount of Guided Learning Hours (GLH) of teacher supervised or directed study time required for the teaching of an HNC is 480 hours. To achieve a full HND qualification, you must gain a minimum of 120 credits at

level 4 and 120 credits at level 5 (QCF / FHEQ), with a total of 240 credits. The amount of Guided Learning Hours (GLH) of teacher supervised or directed study time required for the teaching of an HND is 960 hours. The majority of BTEC units are assessed through internal assessment.

Each HEI determines the overall qualification grade in line with that used for other awards made by the HEI. Typically, individual Higher National units are graded at Pass, Merit or Distinction. HNC / HND awards will have a subject specific title and will also have an overall grade:

HNC / HND with Distinction =70% +
HNC / HND with Merit =55% - 69%
HNC / HND (Pass) =40% - 54%

Assessment of HNCs and HNDs in Scotland
Each higher national unit for an HNC is at level 7 SCQF and has a credit value which is normally 8 credit points. Units can vary in size and can be worth more than 8 credit points, depending on the HNC subject and learning provider.

To achieve a full HNC qualification, you must gain a minimum of 12 higher national unit credits at level 7 SCQF which is worth 96 Credit Points. The amount of Guided Learning Hours (GLH) of teacher supervised or directed study time required for the teaching of an HNC is 480 hours.

Each higher national unit for the second level of an HND is at level 9 SCQF and has a credit value which is normally 8 credit points. Units can vary in size and can be worth more than 8 credit points, depending on the HND subject and learning provider.

To achieve a full HND qualification, you must gain a total number of 30 higher national unit credits at level 7 and level 8 SCQF which is worth 240 Credit Points.

The amount of Guided Learning Hours (GLH) of teacher supervised or directed study time required for the teaching of an HNC 960 hours.

SQA HNC / HND higher national unit credits are assessed on a pass or fail basis. There is also a Graded Unit assessment which assesses the knowledge and/ or skills from all of the units that make up the HNC / HND.

The Graded Unit assessment will be an examination, a case study, an investigation or a practical assignment (depending on the HNC / HND subject).

The result will be an A, B, C or Fail.
HNC / HND grade A =70%+
HNC / HND grade B =60%-69%
HNC / HND grade C =50%-59%
HNC / HND grade Fail =less than 50%

Awarding Bodies for HNCs and HNDs
In England, Wales and Northern Ireland, BTEC HNCs are awarded by Pearson Qualifications
http://qualifications.pearson.com/
In Scotland, HNCs are awarded by the Scottish Qualifications Authority (SQA)
http://www.sqa.org.uk/

Diploma of Higher Education (Dip HE) Level 5 (FHEQ), Level 8 (SCQF) (HE Level 2)

Diploma of Higher Education courses, usually abbreviated to Dip HE, may be studied as a stand-alone qualification or as the second level of an Honours Degree course (HE level 2). If you study for a degree course and decide to leave early, you may be awarded a Dip HE providing you successfully complete this level. The length of time to complete a full-time Dip HE is usually two years in England, Wales, Northern Ireland and Scotland. If studying for a part-time Dip HE or by distance / e-learning, it will take you longer to complete.

A Dip HE is made of elements of subjects called modules. Some modules may be mandatory or compulsory, which means you will have to study these subjects, and others are optional, meaning you will have a choice as to which to take. If studying part-time, depending on the Dip HE and HEI, you may be able to choose how many modules you study for each year, depending on what suits your own personal circumstances. The duration of your Dip HE course will be dependent on the number of modules you choose to

complete each year. Some Dip HEs may include professional qualifications, usually involving relevant work experience as part of the course.

If studying for a stand-alone Dip HE and decide to continue onto an Honours Degree at the same HEI, you may be able to transfer, providing you pass the modules at the level required, or you may need to put in a new application though UCAS. If you have left a degree course early being awarded a Dip HE, and decide to apply for a full-time degree course starting at the beginning of the academic year in September/October, you will need to apply through UCAS http://www.ucas.com/.

There are advised deadlines to submit your application. If you wish to apply for a Degree course in a similar subject to your Dip HE, you may be eligible to enter at HE level 3 of a Degree course. HEIs will consider the amount of time between finishing your Dip HE and the start of the degree as there may be time limits.

Foundation Degree (Fd) Level 5 (FHEQ), Level 8 (SCQF) (HE Level 2)

Foundation Degree courses are available in some higher education institutions and there may be options to study full-time, part-time, flexible learning and distance /e-learning. A Foundation Degree is at level 5 (FHEQ), and is the equivalent of two thirds of a full Honours Degree (HE level 2) and, on successful completion, you may continue onto level 3 of an Honours Degree in a related subject. A full-time Foundation Degree will take two academic years to complete and if you study part time, it will take longer to achieve. They are only available in England, Wales and Northern Ireland.

A Foundation Degree, which may be abbreviated to Fd together with the subject initials, is a degree level qualification which combines academic study

integrated with relevant work-based learning undertaken with an employer. Foundation Degrees have been designed in association with employers and are qualifications which develop relevant skills, knowledge and understanding of academic subjects as well as work related skills. Foundation Degrees focus on a particular job or profession and are intended to increase the professional and technical skills for people who are intending to work in, or are currently working in, a particular profession. They are made up elements of subjects called modules. Some modules may be mandatory or compulsory, which means you will have to study these subjects, and others are optional, meaning you will have a choice as to which to study.

If studying part time, depending on the Foundation Degree course and HEI, you may be able to choose how many modules you study for each year, depending on what suits your own personal circumstances. The duration of your Foundation Degree course will be dependent on the number of modules you choose to complete each year.

There are a range of different subjects and titles of Foundation Degrees and they are usually abbreviated to Fd with the name of the subject:

Foundation Degree titles (selection):
Foundation Degree, Arts = FdA
Foundation Degree, Science = FdSc
Foundation Degree, Engineering = FdEng
Foundation Degree, Education= FdEd
Foundation Degree, Music = FdMus

Successful completion of a Foundation Degree usually allows you to progress on to HE level 3 of a degree course in a similar subject. If you want to continue onto a degree course at the same HEI where you are currently studying, you may be able to complete an internal transfer form. If you want to attend a different HEI you may need to apply through UCAS http://www.ucas.ac.uk . Check with relevant HEIs. Alternatively, you may wish to enter or continue with your employment, either changing or furthering your current career.

1. Entry Requirements for Stand-Alone Diploma of Higher Education Courses (Dip HE); Higher National Diplomas (HND); or Foundation Degrees (Fd)

Typical entry requirements for Diploma of Higher Education (Dip HE); Higher National Diplomas (HND); Foundation Degree courses
- 1/2 'A' levels or equivalent with some courses specifying specific subjects, especially sciences.
- Minimum of four GCSEs or equivalent grade C /4 or above

As part of the entry requirements for stand-alone Diploma of Higher Education Courses (Dip HE); Higher National Diplomas (HND); or Foundation Degrees (Fd) requirements will vary depending on the course subject and higher education institution (HEI).

Generally, however, you may be required to have studied relevant courses such as 'A' levels at level 3 (RQF) or Scottish Highers / Advanced Highers at level 6/7 (SCQF) or equivalent qualifications and you may be required to have specified grades or UCAS Tariff points, which will usually be lower than those required for entry to an Honours Degree course.

Qualification entry requirements may vary such as a minimum of 2 'A' level grades D / E or above, although competitive entry courses may require 3 'A' level subjects and higher grades; minimum of 2 or 3 Scottish Highers / Advanced Highers grade C or above although competitive entry courses may require 3 or 4 subjects and higher grades.

Equivalent qualifications include BTEC National Diploma (2 unit grades) or National Extended Diploma (3 unit grades) with individual units as Passes although competitive entry courses may require 1 or more Merit/s; Access to Higher Education diploma pass with 45 credits at level 3 (RQF) as Passes although competitive entry courses may require credits as Merits; International Baccalaureate with an overall score of 30 points with some flexibility for less, although competitive entry courses may require more points, and may specify a minimum number of credits at Higher Level; or any other equivalent qualification.

You will also usually need in addition a minimum of between 3 - 5 GCSEs level 2 (RQF), Scottish Nationals level 5 (SCQF) or equivalent qualifications including English language and mathematics. Other qualifications and relevant work experience may be also considered and you should contact the relevant HEI for further information.

Universities will have flexibility on entry and may accept applicants with lower or no formal education qualifications but you will usually need to complete an aptitude test to demonstrate your ability complete the course. You may also need to attend an interview.

Providing you meet the requirements for passing the modules on the Diploma of Higher Education, Higher National Diploma (HND); or Foundation Degree (Fd) set by the HEI, you should be able to continue onto an Honours Degree in a relevant subject within the same HEI. If you wish to change HEIs on successful completion, you would need to check with the relevant HEI that they would accept the Diploma of Higher Education Courses (Dip HE); Higher National Diplomas (HND); or Foundation Degrees (Fd) for entry and confirm that the content meets with the standards required.

You may need to put in an additional application through UCAS http://www.ucas.com/ so check with the relevant HEIs well in advance to meet the application deadlines.

Bachelor Degree Level 6 (FHEQ), Level 9/10 (SCQF) (HE Level 3)

Bachelor degree courses are available in higher education institutions (HEIs) and there may be options to study full time, part time, flexible learning and distance / e-learning. A Bachelor Degree may also be referred to as a first degree.

Most bachelor's degree courses are 'Honours' Degrees although if you don't achieve the required credits, you may be awarded an 'Ordinary' Degree. A degree with honours involves more study and achievement than an Ordinary Degree.

Most degrees are studied as Honours Degrees in England, Wales and Northern Ireland. In Scotland you can also apply to study for an Ordinary, also known as a 'General' Degree, which when studied full time, usually lasts for one year less than the duration of an Honours Degree. Graduate entry jobs will usually require you to have an Honours Degree.

If you want to study for a postgraduate course, the usual entry requirements will be an Honours Degree, although an Ordinary Degree may be accepted along with relevant work experience or professional qualifications.

A full-time Honours Degree course will usually last for a minimum of three years in England, Wales and Northern Ireland and usually four years in Scotland, although it may be possible to complete in three years as some students with Advanced Highers may be able to enter the second year of a degree course.

It may also be possible to gain an ordinary or general degree in Scotland in three years. In Scotland, it is possible to start university a year younger than in the rest of the UK as the Scottish Highers (university entrance qualifications) are usually taken at the age of 17, although Advanced Highers and the Scottish Baccalaureate are usually completed at the age of 18.

In England, Wales and Northern Ireland, students are usually aged 18 when they have completed their 'A' levels or equivalent qualifications and can then start studying for a degree course.

Some full time degree courses last longer than three years, such as Medicine, Dentistry and Veterinary Science degrees or degree courses which involve extended periods of work experience.
Integrated full time Master's Degree courses, which include an Honours Degree and a Master's Degree, usually last for an additional year which is four

years in England, Wales and Northern Ireland or five years in Scotland.

If you are studying full time for the Extended year or Foundation year, this will also add an additional year to your higher education study.

Some degree courses are available as accelerated courses and last for a shorter time to complete although these courses will usually involve study through the summer term. Some degrees may include professional qualifications and these courses may take longer to complete, usually involving relevant work experience as part of the course.

If studying part time, it will take longer for you to complete your degree course. Depending on the degree course and HEI, you may be able to choose how many modules you study for each year with what suits your own personal circumstances. The duration of your degree course will be dependent on the number of modules you choose to complete each year.

Generally a part time, flexible or distance learning honours degree course usually

lasts for between four - six academic years although some may be gained within eight years, depending on the university regulations, in England, Wales and Northern Ireland; in Scotland, depending on the university regulations, you may have a maximum of eight years to gain a general or ordinary degree and 10 years to gain an honours degree. However, the Open University allows for a qualification to be gained up to a maximum of 16 years.

Additional courses

In addition to bachelor's degree courses, some HEIs may provide additional courses such as foreign language lessons or the European Computer Driving Licence (ECDL) courses. There may also be courses to support you with your career such as support with starting your own business and graduate internship schemes. There may also be opportunities to study or work overseas, see Study Abroad and Working in Europe chapters.

2.   Entry requirements for Bachelor Degrees

Typical entry requirements for bachelor's honours degree courses
- 2/3 'A' levels or equivalent with some courses specifying specific subjects, especially sciences.
- Minimum of five GCSEs or equivalent grade C / 4or above

As part of the entry requirements for Bachelor degrees qualification requirements will vary depending on the course subject and higher education institution (HEI). Generally, however, you may be required to have studied relevant courses such as 'A' levels at level 3 (RQF) or Scottish Highers / Advanced Highers at level 6/7 (SCQF) or equivalent qualifications and you may be required to have specified grades or UCAS Tariff points.

GCSE level 2 (RQF) university entry requirements

As part of the entry requirements for undergraduate courses, you will usually need to have a minimum of 3, 4 or 5 GCSE or equivalent level 2 (RQF) grades 9 - 4 or A* - C passes to include English and mathematics, with science based degrees usually requiring one or more passes in GCSE science subjects in addition to 'A' level or equivalent level 3 (RQF) qualifications. Some universities may provide admissions tests in English and mathematics for students who don't possess GCSE certificates.

Scottish nationals level 5 (SCQF) university entry requirements

As part of the entry requirements for undergraduate courses, you will usually need to have a minimum of 4 or 5 Scottish National Courses level 5 (SCQF) grades

A-C passes to include English, mathematics, and for science based courses, one or more science subjects in addition to the Scottish Highers or Advanced Highers at level 6/7 (SCQF). Some universities may accept level 4 (SCQF) pass in English, mathematics or other numerate subject for some courses. Other qualifications and relevant work experience may be also considered and you should contact the relevant HEI for further information.

'A' levels university entry requirement

Typical and minimum entry qualification requirements are usually 2 or 3 'A' level subjects although more competitive courses will require 3 'A' level subjects. For many degree programmes you will need specific subjects and pass grades being A*- E, although for some courses you may be required to have specified grades or UCAS Tariff points which are awarded for each grade.

Competitive entry courses, especially those universities which are part of the Russel group, will usually require high grades of AAA, AAB or ABB although for less competitive entry courses requirements will be lower.

If you are taking more than 3 'A' levels, additional 'A' levels are not usually included within the offer. Some courses may consider 'AS' levels or require a specific subject at 'AS' level if not studied to 'A' level, with 'AS' level UCAS Tariff points equal to around 40% of an 'A' level grade, as part of the admissions process along with additional 'A' level subjects, however more competitive courses may not consider 'AS' level results except for some Dentistry or Medicine courses where a high grade at 'AS' level may be required in addition to 3 'A' levels.

General studies, although welcomed, may not be considered by many universities as part of a standard offer, and will no longer be offered, with the last exams for students ending in June 2018. 'A' levels combined with other level 3 (RQF) will also usually be considered unless there are specific entry requirements.

If you have resat 'A' levels to improve your grades, universities will consider your application but may require further information

International 'A' levels university entry requirements

International 'A' levels will usually be seen as equivalent to GCE 'A' levels and grades awarded.

Access to Higher Education Diploma university entry requirements

Typical and minimum entry qualification requirements are usually an Access to Higher Education Diploma pass of 60 credits with a minimum of 45 credits at level 3 (RQF) in certain unit subjects awarded at certain grades, Pass, Merit or Distinction.

More competitive entry courses may require a set number of credits with merits and / or distinctions. Regarding GCSE equivalents, some higher education institutions (HEIs) will accept the Access to HE Diploma equivalent subject units usually to include English and mathematics as well as science where relevant however, however for some selective higher education courses you may also be required to have a GCSE subject qualification in these subjects.

The Access to Higher Education Diploma is widely recognised by higher education institutions as entry onto a higher education course in the UK. However some selective higher education courses may require traditional qualifications, such as 'A' levels/equivalent.

It is important to check with relevant higher education institutions that the Access to HE Diploma is an appropriate subject area and recognised as an entry requirement. Access to HE Diplomas may be taught in subject specialist areas and will have a named subject, using a common title e.g. Access to HE Diploma (Nursing) or Access to HE Diploma (Law) so you need to consider what higher education subject you are interested in studying first.

AQA Baccalaureate university entry requirements

Typical and minimum entry qualification requirements are usually based on the three 'A' level grades. However, the grading of the AQA Baccalaureate involves achieving an overall grade of: Pass, Merit or Distinction in addition to your A/'AS' level grades and the experience of the units of broader study, enrichment activities and the Extended Project are considered to be valuable elements of the AQA Baccalaureate which may be drawn upon when writing your personal statement.

European Baccalaureate Diploma (EB) level 3 (RQF) university entry requirements

Typical and minimum entry qualification requirements usually involve higher education institutions making offers by specifying an overall European Baccalaureate Diploma (EB) score as a percentage or specifying an overall EB score as a percentage combined with marks out of 10 in specific subjects.

For competitive entry courses you would usually be required to have between 77% - 88% pass with a minimum of 7, 8 or 8.5 out of 10 in specified subjects. For less competitive honours degree courses may accept 60 - 70% with a minimum score of 6 out of 10. The EB is officially recognised as an entry qualification for Higher Education in all the countries of the European Union, as well as many countries worldwide

International Baccalaureate (IB) Diploma Programme (DP) level 3 (RQF) university entry requirements

Typical and minimum entry qualification requirements for more competitive honours degree courses the standard minimum requirements for the International Baccalaureate (IB) Diploma Programme may be the full International Baccalaureate Diploma with at least three subjects studied at Higher Level and 32 - 37 points overall including core points with grades 5, 6 or 7. Highly competitive courses may require 38 – 40 points including core points with 6s and 7s for at least 3 subjects at HL. If 2 Higher Level subjects are required a grade 6 or higher may be specified. A grade 6 may be seen as equivalent to grade A; a grade 7 may be seen as equivalent to A* at 'A' level by some universities.

Less competitive honours degree courses may generally accept between 26 and 30 points including core points with a minimum of 15 points for HL subjects, although requirements will vary.

For many degree programmes you will need specific subjects studied at Higher level (HL). For general courses, English language may be required with a minimum of 4 points at Standard Level. Universities in the UK, including the Russell Group, as well as universities around the world have accepted the International Baccalaureate as equivalent to other pre-university qualifications.

Welsh Baccalaureate Advanced Diploma university entry requirements

Typical and minimum entry qualification requirements will usually be a Welsh Baccalaureate Advanced Diploma at level 3 (RQF), including the Advanced Skills Challenge Certificate which is also known as the core certificate as well as optional qualifications at level 3 (RQF) which includes 'A' levels, 'AS' levels or BTEC National qualifications.

You would usually need a minimum of Welsh Baccalaureate Advanced Diploma at level 3 (RQF) and minimum of 1 or 2 'A' levels for entry onto a bachelor's degree, with Welsh Baccalaureate Advanced Diploma and 2 'A' levels required with high grades As and Bs for competitive entry honours degree courses.

Some courses may accept 'AS' levels or require a specific subject at 'AS' level if not studied to 'A' level. For many degree programmes you will need specific subjects and pass grades with the Advanced Skills Challenge Certificate first teaching from 2015 awarded grades A*-E.

Optional qualifications at level 3 (RQF) are awarded separate UCAS Tariff points depending on the qualification and grade. The Welsh Baccalaureate Advanced Diploma is widely accepted by higher education institutions.

BTEC National Qualifications university entry requirements

Typical and minimum entry qualification requirements will usually be a BTEC National Extended Diploma which is awarded 3 grades or the National Diploma which is awarded 2 grades with a combination of Distinction*, Distinction, Merit or Pass, required to study for an honours degree course. A BTEC National Foundation Diploma, which is worth one grade combined with one or two 'A' level subjects may also be considered. Some higher education institutions (HEIs) will specify grades required and the type of BTEC National qualification, whilst other HEIs may just specify the number of UCAS Tariff points required.

For entry onto highly competitive degree courses, 3 grades of Distinctions may be required; for entry onto competitive degree courses, grades of Distinctions and Merits may be required, however, many other degree courses will accept lower grades. A combination of 'A' levels and BTEC level 3 diplomas may also be accepted although you should avoid combinations of similar subjects. Many HEIs accept BTEC National qualifications, although there are some selective courses such as Dentistry, Medicine and some Life Sciences which don't accept BTEC qualifications for entry and will only accept 'A' levels or Scottish Highers/ Advanced Highers.

BTEC HNC or HND courses may be considered for entry onto a bachelor degree and may allow entry directly to year 2 of a degree course, depending on the courses and university.

Cambridge International Pre-U Certificate / Diploma university entry requirements

Typical and minimum entry qualification requirements will usually be a Cambridge International Pre-U Certificate / Diploma with 3 pre-U Principal subjects or a combination of the Pre-U subject/s at grades Distinction, Merit or Pass and 'A' levels. For entry onto competitive degree courses, grades of Distinctions and Merits may be required.

Foundation Diploma in Art (Level 3 and Level 4 QCF) university entry requirements

Typical and minimum entry qualification requirements for some undergraduate Art courses may require a Foundation Studies Diploma in Art and Design at level 3 (RQF) which includes a portfolio, with a pass or above, in addition to a minimum of one 'A' level pass and 3 / 4 GCSE passes grades C / 4 or above. Universities will usually accept a BTEC National Extended Diploma or National Diploma in Art which includes an art portfolio.

Some universities may consider 'A' levels / equivalent subjects. You may be required to submit a digital mini-portfolio. For many degree programmes you will need specific subjects and specified grades or UCAS Tariff points.

Scottish Highers (H) Level 6 (SCQF) / Scottish Advanced Highers (AH) university entry requirements

Typical and minimum entry qualification requirements usually require Scottish Higher passes grades A – D with a minimum of 3 or 4 subjects to study for an ordinary (Scotland) or honours degree course; for competitive entry honours degree courses you may be required to have 4 Highers with high grades As and Bs although for more selective courses and those with specific subject requirements you may be required to have a minimum of 3 or more Highers combined with Advanced Highers.

Competitive entry courses, especially those universities which are part of the Russel group, will usually require Highers with high grades of AAAA through to ABBB, however for less competitive entry courses requirements will be lower. For many degree programmes you will need specific subjects and specified grades or UCAS Tariff points.

Requirements for Medicine, Dentistry and Veterinary Medicine degree courses will usually be higher with 5 Highers at the required grades or a combination of Highers and an additional 2 Advanced Highers required with high grades of As and Bs.

Advanced Highers are not required for entry for most degree courses although may be advantageous but universities will only usually count the same subject at both Higher and Advanced Higher as one subject. Achievement of 3 specific Advanced Highers subject/s may allow students to enter certain bachelor degree course subjects directly on to the second year of a bachelor's' degree available in Scotland.

Scottish Baccalaureate university entry requirements

The Scottish Baccalaureate is the same level as Advanced Highers which includes at least 4 subjects at Higher level and is at level 7 (SCQF) or level 4 (RQF) in England, Wales and Northern Ireland) and may enable credit transfer for part of that qualification. It may be possible to get subject exemptions or enter directly into the 2nd year of a Scottish 4 year degree course, although individual HEIs would make a decision on how many credit points can be transferred to the appropriate course.

Grade or UCAS tariff point requirements will vary across courses and between HEIs, so check entry requirements with the relevant HEI and course details. The Scottish Baccalaureate is considered as excellent preparation for entry to a bachelor's' Honours Degree. For further information see the chapter:
Chapter 4
Secondary and Further Education Qualification Subjects and Courses

.

Types of Degree Courses

Single subject degrees
Degree courses are available to study as single subject courses, giving you the opportunity to study all modules related to the single subject, enabling you to study in greater depth the subject you are especially interested in.

Combined subject degrees
Degree courses, in some cases, may also be available to study combining two subjects. Combined degrees may be available to study as two subjects equally, involving the study of 50% of all modules in each subject, known as 'joint' degrees, with the final award listing 'and' between the two subjects.

Combined degree courses may also be available as Major / Minor degree courses with the Major subject usually consisting of 2/3rds of the total number of modules and the Minor subject, usually consisting of 1/3 of the total number of modules.

Major/Minor degree courses have the final award listing 'with' between the two subjects. Very occasionally there are triple subject degrees available to study.

Sandwich degrees
Sandwich degree courses will last longer, usually four years, if studying full time, and involve a period of time undertaking a work placement, giving you relevant industry experience related to the type of work you are interested in.

A 'thick' sandwich degree course involves one longer period of time in a work placement, usually up to one year and usually in the third year of a full-time four year degree course.

A 'thin' sandwich degree usually involves shorter periods of work experience, and there may be options to have more than one placement.

Professional degrees

These types of degrees provide professional accreditation as well as academic undergraduate, graduate or postgraduate qualifications which are required to enter a specific professional career. Undergraduate and postgraduate courses follow a set curriculum to meet the requirements of the relevant professional organisation so that you are prepared to enter you chosen profession after graduating.

You will also need to work for a probationary period after graduating before being fully qualified. There are some subjects where professional accreditation is provided for some courses and may not be a necessary requirement to enter the profession. Some professions allow for exemptions from the professional qualifications if you have an approved degree or postgraduate subject. Go to: on Professionally Accredited Undergraduate and Postgraduate Courses.

Ordinary degrees

In England, Wales and Northern Ireland, you would usually register for an Honours Degree however, if you don't obtain the required number of credits for assessed work and you pass fewer modules required for an Honours Degree, you may be awarded Pass or Ordinary degree, also known as a General or Designated degree in Scotland, which is without honours, provided you meet the HEI requirements for this qualification.

The regulations in which students are unable to progress at Honours Degree level are individual to each HEI and course. In order to progress to a higher HE level, you will be required to gain a minimum number of credits to pass at the preceding HE level, and this varies between courses and HEIs. Some HEIs allow flexibility allowing students to resume an Honours Degree pathway course if they make enough improvement to meet the required number of credits for a set number of modules.

In Scotland, some HEIs in Scotland offer three year degree courses which lead to the award of an Ordinary or General degree also known as a Designated degree. A Scottish Ordinary Degree may be sufficient to study a postgraduate course in Scotland, but elsewhere you may need relevant work experience or professional qualifications in addition. Students can usually decide at the end of the 2nd or 3rd year if they want to complete a fourth honours year in the same subject.

Integrated master's degrees

Integrated master's degree courses include a bachelor's honours degree qualification and lead on to a master's degree. Full-time integrated master's courses will vary in duration but typically last for an additional year compared with an honours degree which is at least four academic years, in England, wales and Northern Ireland and five academic years in Scotland. Some courses include relevant work experience and these courses may last longer.

Conferred master's degree from the University of Oxford and University of Cambridge

In most UK universities, the Master of Arts (MA) is a free standing graduate degree awarded by examination. However in the University of Oxford and University of Cambridge reaching the status of Master of Arts is a mark of seniority within the University which may be conferred by right on holders of the Bachelor of Arts (BA) degree, twenty one terms after matriculation.

It is not an upgrade of a BA or an additional postgraduate qualification and doesn't have a subject or class, therefore the nominals MA is represented in place of, not in addition to the BA, on documents such as CVs. If you have successfully completed a BA or Bachelor of Fine Arts (BFA) at the university of Oxford, you will be eligible to take an MA within or after the 21st term (7 years) since matriculating by applying to graduate at a degree ceremony either in person or absentia.

If you have successful completed a BA at the university of Cambridge, you will be eligible to take an MA not less than six years from the end of your first term of residence providing you have held your BA degree for at least two years.

You must have your BA or BFA conferred in order to take your MA but they can be conferred at the same ceremony provided sufficient time as elapsed since you matriculated. This doesn't relate to integrated Master's' degree courses as you will be awarded a Master's Degree as well as a Bachelor's degree on successful completion.

These universities also provide postgraduate Master's' degree courses that require further study and examination but with different titles including Master of Letters (MLitt), Master of Philosophy (MPhil), Master of Studies (MSt), Master of Engineering (MEng) and Master of Science (MSc), Master of Philosophy (MPhil), Master of Business Administration (MBA)

Further information may be found at the individual Colleges:
- University of Oxford: Colleges http://www.ox.ac.uk/about/colleges
- University of Cambridge: Colleges http://map.cam.ac.uk/colleges
- University of Cambridge http://www.cambridgestudents.cam.ac.uk/your-course/graduation-and-what-next/cambridge-ma

Accelerated degrees
Accelerated degrees follow a faster route which allows you to complete your degree in less time than is usual (normally a reduction of one year).

These options in England, Wales and Northern Ireland, enable a three year Honours Degree to be completed in two years; in Scotland, enable a standard Honours Degree of four years to be completed in three years and a standard Honours Degree of five years, to be completed in four years.

A small number of accelerated courses are also offered as integrated Master's Degrees, so you could graduate with a Master's Degree in less time.

You will usually start the course at the beginning of the academic year, have shorter vacations and the course may involve study through the summer vacation.

This means that you will be able to save on living costs during your studies and enter employment more quickly than your peers. This type of study is quite intensive so it doesn't suit everyone. This option is only available for some courses at some HEIs.

Advance entry degrees
In Scotland, if you have exceptional 'A' level or Advanced Highers grades or equivalent qualifications, it may be possible to gain exemption from Year 1 study of a degree course and enter through an Advanced entry route directly into Year 2.

If you have professional qualifications, you may get exemption from some modules for some degree courses as some HEIs may consider accreditation of prior learning (APEL). You would need to confirm entry requirements with individual HEIs as this option isn't available for all courses.

Graduate entry professional certificates, diplomas and degrees
Graduate entry professional certificates, diplomas and degrees are for students who have usually already obtained a degree in one subject but wish to retrain in another subject to gain a professional qualification, at graduate level.

Graduate entry courses may be accelerated or advanced entry courses, lasting for less time than the undergraduate degree and may be more intensive. Some professional undergraduate Honours Degree courses may accept graduates along with non-graduates.

However, student finance should be checked as you may need to be self-funding for some or all of the duration of the course.

Some professional postgraduate courses are also available for graduates to retrain and gain a professional qualification. Graduate entry professional courses include law, medicine, dentistry, nursing, other allied health courses, teaching, engineering, surveying and information technology.

Graduate conversion courses

Some careers that require a professional degree to enter before continuing on with further professional qualifications may have the option of studying for a conversion course which is for graduates of other subjects.

These courses are usually for one year and are at the same level as a degree, and include subjects such as psychology and law.

Extended / foundation year degrees

Extended / Foundation year degree courses incorporate an additional introductory year to provide relevant knowledge, skills and learning to prepare you for your chosen degree course before continuing on to the first year of an Honours Degree. See section on Extended / Foundation Degrees.

Aegrotat degree

If you are unable to take exams, or other types of assessment, because of serious illness, you can sometimes be awarded an Aegrotat degree. This is an Honours Degree without classification, which is awarded in specific situations on the understanding you would have passed if you had not been unwell.

Classification of bachelor's degrees

A degree may be awarded with or without honours. In the UK there is a classification system, which is a grading structure for Honours Degrees which have the suffix (Hons) designated to the title of the degree e.g. BA (Hons) or BSc (Hons).

Universities award a class of degree based on the average mark of the assessed work a candidate has completed. The class of an Honours Degree is based on a weighted average mark of the assessed work you have completed. The weighted average mark is determined by some assessments having a higher contribution to add to the overall mark.

Many HEIs allow for some flexibility so that if the total numbers of weighted marks are close to a higher class, and you have attained a selection of assessed work at higher levels, you may be awarded a higher class of degree.

However, if some assessments are not passed, or if deadlines aren't met, you may be 'capped' at a set mark and this may result in you being awarded a lower class, even if your other assessed work is of a higher level, as this will affect the overall percentage.

Universities and colleges may have different weighted marks for different courses and may vary the percentage awarded for each class, but the following is an indication of how many honours classification for degree courses are awarded.

Degree Classifications:

An Honours Degree is awarded as a class, with the highest class, being a first class, second class is divided into an upper second class and lower second class, then third class, and finally a pass, usually known as 1st; 2.1; 2.2; 3rd and pass without honours. An Ordinary Degree is also without honours.

If you wish to continue into higher study at postgraduate level, or if you want to work in a competitive job field, you would usually be required to have an Honours Degree and you may be required to gain a higher class, but this will vary depending on the higher education institution and employer. Some degrees aren't awarded an honours classification, such as Medicine and Dentistry. Medical graduates hold a conjoined degree of Bachelor of Medicine and Bachelor of Surgery which entitles graduates to have one of the following, depending where the medical degree was studied, MBBS, BM BCh or MB ChB. Individual medicine degrees are marked pass or fail, although some may pass with merit.

Honours Degree Classifications

Degree with honours: First class
= 1st class = 70% +
Degree with honours: Second class, upper division
= 2:1 class = 60% to 69%
Degree with honours: Second class, lower division
= 2:2 class = 50% to 59%
Degree with honours: Third class
= 3rd class = 40% to 49%

Degree without Honours: Ordinary Degree (Pass): Awarded with usually 300 credits, including a set number at level 6 (FHEQ)

Unclassified: Some degrees aren't classified e.g. medicine, dentistry

A small number of universities also award an Honours Degree as First class honours with Distinction, or starred first. A Double First may also refer to a First class honours in a combined subject in a small number of universities.

Slang terms for classification of degrees

(This question was asked on University Challenge!)
First: Geoff / Damien (rhymes with Geoff Hurst / Damien Hirst)
2:1: Attila the Hun (rhymes with the Hun)
2:2: Desmond (rhymes with Desmond Tutu)
3rd: Thora / Douglas (rhymes with Thora Hird / Douglas Hurd)

List of Bachelor degrees and abbreviations

Bachelor degrees are usually known as an abbreviation depending on the subject studied:

Bachelor of Accountancy (Scotland)	= BAcc
Bachelor of Arts	= BA
Bachelor of Architecture	= BArch
Bachelor Science	= BSc
Bachelor of Engineering	= BEng
Bachelor of Fine Art	= BFA
Bachelor of Music	= BMus
Bachelor of Education	= BEd
Bachelor of Science: Economics	= BScEcom
Bachelor of Laws	= LLB
Bachelor of Medical Sciences	= BMedSci
Bachelor of Medicine and Bachelor of Surgery	= BMBS
Bachelor of Midwifery	= BMid
Bachelor of Theology	= BTh
Bachelor of Veterinary Medical Sciences	= BVMedSci
Bachelor of Veterinary Medicine and Bachelor of Veterinary Surgery	= BVM BVS

Where two subjects are studied as a joint degree from different subject areas:

Bachelor of Arts and Bachelor of Science	= BA BSc

The title of the subject/s studied is placed after the Bachelor and Honours abbreviation. Honours Degrees are usually abbreviated to Hons and placed in brackets after the bachelor degree abbreviation, e.g. BA (Hons)

Single subject:
Title naming one subject:
BA (Hons) Business Studies

Joint subjects:
Title naming two distinct subjects studied equally as x and y:
BSc (Hons) Chemistry and Mathematics
BA BSc (Hons) English and Computer Science

Major/Minor subjects:
Title naming two distinct subjects as x with y:
BA (Hons) English with History
BA BSc (Hons) English with Computer Science

Multidisciplinary subjects:
Title listing three distinct subjects:
BA (Hons) French, Spanish and Italian

There are thousands of different higher education course subjects (also known as disciplines) to choose from but the following is a list of some of the main undergraduate subjects. A selection of postgraduate subjects are also listed where these may be a requirement to enter a specific professional job role or where there is a postgraduate route to qualify if your honours degree is in a different subject.

The list of courses has been placed in similar subject groups, although the course titles may differ slightly depending which university or college you choose to study at. Some courses may be relevant to jobs in more than one sector, such as some healthcare and science job roles. Not every undergraduate course will be listed, however you can check the range of undergraduate and some postgraduate courses available to study full time with the University and College Admissions Service UCAS http://www.ucas.com/ as well as checking up to date information on university and college websites.

A selection of higher education search engines is listed in the chapter above. It may be a good idea to make a list of similar courses and consider subjects in related groups before researching individual subjects.

Universities and colleges group similar subjects together and may have 'Schools' or 'Academic Departments' where related subjects are taught. Although some jobs will require specific or accredited higher education subjects and /or professional qualifications, there are many types of jobs that can be entered with an honours degree or other undergraduate qualification in any subject.

A conversion graduate or postgraduate course may be another option for some job roles if you are required to have a specific or accredited subject and your honours degree is in a different or non-accredited subject. You can research which subjects are relevant for which careers in the chapter on Professional Organisations and Accredited Undergraduate and Postgraduate Courses. Also check the range of careers websites listed in the chapter on Careers Advice and Useful Websites.

The following courses are a selection of main subjects arranged within the course sectors. The majority of courses are undergraduate courses leading to a degree, although some subjects can also be studied at higher national certificate / certificate of higher education; higher national diploma /diploma of higher education or foundation degree level. Some graduate and postgraduate courses have been added if this level is required for a specific job role, or if a conversion course is an option.

The subjects listed show the variety of options available, however course titles may vary so confirm on university and college websites.

Agriculture and Plants Sector

Agricultural Engineering and Technology
Undergraduate

Agricultural engineering
Agricultural machinery
engineering

Agricultural technology

Agriculture and
mechanisation
management

Agricultural Science
Undergraduate

Agricultural bioscience
Agricultural crop science
Agricultural livestock
science
Agricultural resource
management

Agricultural science
Agriculture
Agriculture and fisheries
science
Agriculture and food
Agronomy

Food and nutrition
Food science
International agriculture
Plant and soil science

Agriculture, Farm Management
Undergraduate

Agriculture and
countryside management
Agriculture and farm
management
Agriculture and rural
studies
Agriculture management
Agriculture with dairy
heard management
Agriculture with land
management

Agriculture, conservation
and sustainable
management
Applied farm
management
Countryside conservation
Countryside management
Environmental
management
Farm management
Food production and
supply management

International equine and
agricultural management
Land management
Landscape management
Rural studies
Sustainability and
environmental
management
Sustainable agriculture
and food security

Forestry and Horticulture

Floristry, Garden and Landscape Design
Undergraduate

Architecture and
landscape
Floristry design
Garden and greenspace
design
Garden and landscape
design
Garden design
Garden design
restoration and
management

Green-space design and
management
Horticulture - garden
design
Horticulture (garden and
landscape design)
Horticulture and garden
design
Landscape and garden
design
Landscape and garden
management

Landscape architecture
Landscape architecture
and design
Landscape construction
and garden design
Landscape design
Landscape design and
management
Landscape management
Landscape studies

Forestry
Undergraduate

Arboriculture and tree management
Arboriculture and urban forestry
Conservation with forestry

Forest management
Forest sciences
Forestry
Forestry and woodland management

Sustainable forest management
Woodland conservation management
Woodland ecology and conservation

Horticulture and Plant Science
Undergraduate

Applied horticulture
Biological sciences (plant biology)
Conservation
Countryside management
Floristry design
Forest sciences
Forestry

Garden and greenspace design
Garden and landscape design
Garden design
Green space management
Horticulture
Horticulture – commercial

Horticulture gardens
Horticulture-landscape construction
International horticulture
Land management
Natural history
Plant science
Production horticulture
Rural land management

Animals and Conservation Sector

Animal and Plant Conservation
Undergraduate

Animal behaviour and wildlife conservation
Animal biology and wildlife conservation
Animal conservation
Animal conservation and biodiversity
Animal conservation science
Animal conservation science
Animal management – wildlife conservation
Animal management and conservation

Animal management: companion and zoo animals
Animal production science
Applied zoology and conservation
Conservation and ecology
Conservation biology
Conservation biology and ecology
Ecology and environment
Environmental biology
Environmental conservation

Environmental science
Marine ecology
Marine science
Palaentology
Palaeobiology
Wildlife and plant biology
Wildlife conservation
Wildlife conservation with natural resource management
Wildlife education and media
Wildlife management and conservation
Zoological conservation

Animal Studies
Animal Behaviour, Management and Welfare
Undergraduate

Animal behaviour
Animal behaviour and training
Animal behaviour and welfare
Animal husbandry
Animal husbandry and welfare
Animal management
Animal science with animal behaviour

Animal welfare
Applied animal behaviour and training
Applied animal studies
Management of animal collections with conservation
Animal behaviour and psychology
Wildlife education and media

Zoological conservation
Animal management and zoology
Animal conservation and biodiversity
Animal behaviour, science and welfare
Zoo management
Marine zoology

Animal Science
Undergraduate

Agricultural livestock science
Agriculture with animal science
Animal biology
Animal health and welfare
Animal management
Animal management and science

Animal production science
Animal science
Animal science and welfare
Applied animal science
Applied marine zoology
Applied zoology
Biological sciences

Biology
Environmental science
Zoology
Conservation and ecology
Animal conservation

Animal Veterinary and Health
Undergraduate

Animal health
Bio veterinary science
Veterinary bioscience
Veterinary biosciences
Veterinary medicine

Veterinary medicine
Veterinary nursing
Veterinary nursing and practice management

Veterinary nursing science
Veterinary nursing science
Veterinary science

Postgraduate

Graduate accelerated Veterinary medicine

Graduate diploma / MSc Animal manipulation

Equine
Undergraduate

Equestrian practice and technology
Equestrian psychology and sports science
Equestrian sports science
Equine and veterinary bioscience
Equine behaviour
Equine management
Equine nutrition

Equine performance management
Equine science
Equine science and welfare management
Equine science with rehabilitation therapies
Equine science with rehabilitation therapies
Equine sports coaching
Equine sports science

Equine sports therapy and rehabilitation
Equine studies
Equine therapies
Equine training and management
Equitation and coaching
Equitation science
International equine and agricultural management

Aquatics, Fish Farming; Marine and Freshwater Science
Aquatics and Fish Farming
Undergraduate

Agriculture and fisheries science

Aquaculture

Aquaculture and fisheries management

Aquaculture and fisheries science

Aquatic science

Aquatic zoology

Fisheries management

Marine and Freshwater Science
Undergraduate

Applied marine biology

Applied marine zoology

Coastal marine biology

Marine and freshwater biology

Marine and freshwater conservation

Marine biology

Marine biology with oceanography

Marine biology, biodiversity and conservation

Marine conservation

Marine ecology and conservation

Marine environmental studies

Marine science

Marine zoology

Art and Design Sector

Art and Design, Crafts, Jewellery and Product Design
Art and Design; Crafts
Undergraduate

Applied architectural stonework and conservation

Applied arts

Art and crafts

Art and design

Art and design in the creative industries

Art enterprise

Artist designer: maker

Contemporary arts practice

Crafts

Creative arts and design practice

Creative arts therapies studies

Design for art direction

Design management

Floristry design

Media and culture

Media design

Jewellery, Horology/ Watch Design
Undergraduate

3d design crafts

3d design: contemporary jewellery and fashion accessories

Arts and crafts

Contemporary crafts

Contemporary creative practice

Contemporary design crafts

Contemporary design crafts: jewellery

Contemporary jewellery

Crafts, jewellery and horology

Design: textiles.

Jewellery, product and furniture

Fashion jewellery

Fashion jewellery

Gemmology and jewellery studies

Glass, ceramics, jewellery, metalwork

Horology

Jewellery and Fashion

Jewellery and metal design

Jewellery and metal design

Jewellery and metalwork

Jewellery and silversmithing

Jewellery and silversmithing for industry

Jewellery design

Jewellery design and related products

Silversmithing and jewellery design

Silversmithing, goldsmithing and jewellery

Professional floristry and floral design

174

Product and Furniture Design

Undergraduate

3D design
Art and design: 3D spatial design and interior design
Artist blacksmithing
Creative 3D design for decorative arts
Design engineering
Design for product and interiors
Design: applied arts

furniture
Furniture and fine product
Furniture and lifestyle products
Furniture and product design
Furniture design
Furniture design and make
Industrial / product design

Model design
Product and furniture design
Product design
Product design: furniture
Sustainable product design
Three dimensional design
Visual effects design and production

Postgraduate

Ergonomics

Computer Design; Graphic Design and Printing
Animation, Digital, Computer Games Design / Development

Undergraduate

2D Animation and character for digital media
3D Animation and games
3D Animation and modelling
3D Computer animation
3D Computer generated imagery (architectural visualisation)
3D Computer generated imagery (modelling and animation)
3D Design
3D Design craft
3D Digital design and animation
Animation
Animation (2D and stop motion)
Animation and games design
Animation and illustration
Animation and moving image
Animation and visual effects
Animation production
Animation visual effects and game art
Computer and video games
Computer animation
Computer animation and visual effects
Computer animation arts

Computer animation with digital art
Computer arts
Computer character animation
Computer character animation
Computer games
Computer games (indie)
Computer games applications development
Computer games art
Computer games design
Computer games development
Computer games modelling and animation
Computer games programming
Computer games technology
Computer generated imagery
Computer graphics technology
Computer graphics, imaging and multimedia
Computer graphics, vision and games
Computer science (game engineering)
Computer visualisation and animation
Computing and gaming

Computing games programming
Creative computing
Creative media (games development)
Creative media production (computer games animation)
Creative media production (computer games design)
Creative multimedia design
Creativity for the interactive industries
Design
Design (illustration and animation)
Digital advertising
Digital animation
Digital design
Digital design (3D animation and visualisation)
Digital film and 3D animation technology
Digital film and visual effects production
Digital illustration
Digital media design
Digital media development
Digital media technologies

Animation, Digital, Computer Games Design / Development continued
Undergraduate

Digital SFX (Special Effects) animation
Digital video and computer animation
Film technology and visual effects
Film, radio and television studies (animation)
Game art design
Game design and product management
Games and digital design
Games and multimedia technology
Games animation and screen design
Games art design
Games assets development
Games design
Games design and development
Games design for industry
Games design for industry
Games development
Games modelling, animation and effects
Games programming
Games technology
Graphics for games
Illustration animation
Illustration for screen arts
Independent game development
Independent games production
Interactive and visual design
Interactive animation
Interactive digital media
Interactive media
Interactive media and games development
Interactive media: games art and animation
Interactive systems and video games design
Interface design
Media arts
Media production games animation
Model design: character and technical effects
Motion graphics design and production
Multimedia and mobile development
Multimedia design
Stop-motion animation and puppet making
VFX (Visual Effects)
Visual communication
Visual effects
Visual effects and model making
Visual effects design and production
Web design

Graphic Design and Printing
Undergraduate

Communication design
Computer aided design
Computer graphics, imaging and multimedia
Creative digital media
Creative enterprise (digital media)
Creative media production
Design for exhibitions and museums
Graphic and digital design
Graphic branding and identity
Graphic communication with typography
Graphic communications
Graphic design
Graphic design and illustration
Graphic design and visual communication
Graphic design for digital media
Print journalism
Printing

Fashion Design, Visual Merchandising, Interior and Theatre Design

Fashion and Textile Design
Undergraduate

3D effects for performance and fashion
Beauty promotion
Bespoke tailoring
Contemporary textile products
Costume and textiles
Creative enterprise fashion and textiles
Design and fashion technology
Design and technology
Design for textiles
Fashion (apparel design and constructions)
Fashion advertising
Fashion and clothing technology
Fashion and costume for performance
Fashion and costume for performance
Fashion and dress history
Fashion and textiles
Fashion bags and accessories

Fashion brand management
Fashion business and promotion
Fashion contour
Fashion design
Fashion design and technology
Fashion designer with garment technology
Fashion illustration
Fashion management
Fashion marketing
Fashion media practice and criticism
Fashion pattern cutting
Fashion photography
Fashion print
Fashion production management
Fashion promotion
Fashion promotion and imaging
Fashion textiles
Fashion textiles: print

Fashion: media and promotion
Footwear: product design and innovation
Hand embroidery for fashion, interiors textile art
International fashion branding
International fashion management
International fashion production management
International fashion promotion
Leather technology
Printed and constructed textiles
Printed textiles and surface design
Textile design
Textile practice
Textiles: knit, weave and mixed media

Interior, Spatial, Film, Television, Theatre Set and Stage Design; Visual Design
Undergraduate

Advertising design
Architectural design
Costume and set design
Costume construction
Costume design and construction
Costume production and associated crafts
Creative Advertising Technologies
Creative arts for theatre and film
Design for performance
Design for the stage
Design studies
Design: film and photography
Events and festival technology

Fashion visual merchandising and branding
Film and television set design
Interior architecture
Interior and spatial design
Interior design
Production design for stage and screen
Scenic arts (construction, props and painting)
Scenic construction
Scenography and theatre design
Spatial design
Special effects
Technical theatre

Theatre and Performance Technology
Theatre arts
Theatre and screen: costume interpretation
Theatre design
Visual art
Visual design
Visual merchandising
Visual merchandising and promotional design
Production design for stage and screen
Retail design
Visual arts
Visual communication
Visual effects and concept design

Ceramics, Glass and Sculpture
Undergraduate

Architectural glass arts
Architectural technology and glass
Art and ceramics
Artist blacksmithing
Ceramics
Ceramics and glass
Fine art (3D and sculptural practice)

Fine art fine art sculpture
Fine art with sculpture (digital media, drawing and painting, printmaking, sculpture)
Fine art: environmental art/sculpture
Glass
Glass and ceramics

Glass, ceramics, jewellery, metalwork
Sculpture
Sculpture: casting, carving and construction

Fine Art and Illustration
Undergraduate

Contemporary fine art practice
Drawing
Drawing and print
Fine art
Fine art for design

Fine art installation
Fine art painting
Fine art painting and drawing
Fine art practice
Fine art print making

Fine art printmaking
Fine art with textiles
Illustration
Illustration and animation
Illustration for screen arts
Painting and drawing

Medical Illustration
Postgraduate

Forensic Art
Graphic design for health

Medical Art

Medical visualisation and human anatomy

Make-up Artistry and Hair
Undergraduate

Advanced beauty technology
Artistic make-up and special effects
Beauty promotion
Cosmetic science
Design in media make-up
Fashion styling
Fashion, theatrical and media hair and make-up
Hair and beauty management
Hair and make-up for fashion

Hair, make-up and prosthetics for performance
Make up artistry
Make-up and prosthetics for performance
Make-up for media and performance
Media make up with special effects
Media make-up
Media make-up and character design

Media make-up for fashion
Media make-up with special effects
Media special effects and theatrical make-up design
Specialist hair and media make-up
Specialist make-up
Theatre arts: make-up and hair for theatre and media
Theatrical, media and special effects make-up

Photography and Filming
Undergraduate
Commercial photography
Commercial photography for fashion, advertising and editorial
Creative and editorial photography
Digital imaging and photography
Digital photography
Fashion photography
Film and photography
Film and television production
Film production
Film, photography and media
Graphic design and photography
Marine and natural history photography
Media and communication: media photography
Moving image
Photographic journalism
Photographic media
Photographic practice
Photography
Photography and video
Photography and video art
Photography for digital media
Photography: editorial and advertising
Practical filmmaking
Press and editorial photography
Professional photography
Visual effects and motion graphics

Medical Photography
Postgraduate
Clinical photography

Building Design, Planning, Surveying and Construction Sector

Building Design, Planning and Surveying

Architecture
Undergraduate
3D computer generated imagery (architectural visualisation)
Applied architectural stonework and conservation
Architectural design
Architectural design technology
Architectural engineering
Architectural engineering design
Architectural glass arts
Architectural history
Architectural studies
Architectural technology
Architectural technology and glass
Architecture
Architecture and environmental engineering
Architecture and planning
Architecture studies
Architecture: spaces and objects
Civil and architectural engineering
History of art and architectural history
Interior architecture and design
Naval architecture

Graduate / postgraduate: an accredited postgraduate qualification is also required for professional architecture practice
Architecture
Environmental design in architecture
Advanced architectural studies
Advanced architectural design
Practice and management in architecture

Landscape Architecture

Undergraduate

Garden design
Landscape architecture
Architecture and landscape
Environmental science

Landscape and garden design
Landscape architecture with ecology

Landscape architecture with planning
Landscape management
Diploma landscape architecture

Graduate / postgraduate: an accredited postgraduate qualification is an option for graduates in other subjects

Landscape design
Landscape architecture

Landscape management
Landscape ecology

Land reclamation and restoration

Surveying

Building / Construction Surveying

Undergraduate

Building and valuation surveying
Building control
Building information management
Building services engineering project management
Building surveying
Building surveying and the environment

Built environment
Civil engineering
Commercial building surveying
Commercial management and quantity surveying
Construction and commercial management
Construction management

Construction management and surveying
Construction project management
Quantity surveying
Quantity surveying and commercial management
Quantity surveying consultancy

Land Surveying

Undergraduate

City and regional planning
City and regional planning / diploma in planning
Environmental management
Environmental planning
Geographic information science

Geomatics: land/engineering surveying
Geomatics: hydrographic surveying
Historic conservation
Integrated maintenance and facilities services
Land economy
Land use and environmental management

Marine geography
Rural business management
Rural enterprise and land management
Rural land management
Surveying
Surveying and mapping sciences

Property Surveying
Undergraduate

Asset management and development

Conservation of historic buildings

Estate management

Investment and finance in property

Planning and development

Planning and property development

Planning and real estate

Planning and real estate development

Project management (surveying)

Project management for construction

Property and planning

Property development

Property development and management

Property finance and investment

Property investment and management

Property investment appraisal and development

Property management and valuation

Real estate

Real estate and asset management

Real estate management

Real estate surveying

Residential property

Rural property management

Urban planning design and management

Postgraduate: an accredited postgraduate qualification is an option for graduates in other subjects

Range of accredited Graduate Diploma; Postgraduate Diploma; and Master's courses similar to undergraduate in Land; Property; and Construction / Building / Quantity Surveying for graduates in other subjects

Mining
Undergraduate

Mining engineering

Marine geography

Marine sciences and oceanography;

Petroleum geology

Physical geography

Town Planning
Undergraduate (some undergraduate courses provide the option of a postgraduate qualification)

Architecture and planning

City and regional planning

Environmental planning

European planning

Geography, planning and environmental policy

Master in geography with planning

Master in planning (Mplan)

Master of town and country planning

Planning

Planning and development

Planning and geography

Planning and property development

Planning and sustainable development

Planning, environment and development

Real estate with urban planning and development

Town and country planning

Town and regional planning

Urban and environmental planning

Urban planning

Urban planning and property development

Urban studies and planning

Town Planning continued
Postgraduate: an accredited postgraduate qualification is an option for graduates in other subjects

City and regional planning

City planning and real estate development

City planning and regeneration

Conservation of the historic environment

Diploma Spatial planning

Environmental assessment and management

Environmental impact assessment and management

Environmental planning

Environmental policy

Global urban development planning

Historic conservation

International development and planning

International housing development and management

International planning

International planning and sustainable development

International planning and sustainable urban management

International planning studies

International spatial planning

Marine planning and management

Planning

Planning and environment research

Planning and real estate

Planning and regeneration

Planning and sustainability

Planning for sustainability and climate change

Spatial planning and development

Spatial planning and research

Tourism, environment and development

Town and country planning

Town and regional planning

Town planning

Transport planning

Urban and regional planning

Urban and regional planning

Urban and rural design

Urban and rural planning

Urban design

Urban design and international planning

Urban design and planning

Urban planning

Urban planning design

Urban regeneration

Urban regeneration and development

Building Services and Construction
Undergraduate

Building and valuation surveying
Building design management
Building services
Building services engineering
Building surveying
Building surveying and environment
Building surveying and property management
Built environment
Civil engineering
Commercial management and quantity surveying
Construction
Construction and commercial management
Construction and project management
Construction and property development
Construction and surveying
Construction and the built environment
Construction commercial management
Construction engineering
Construction engineering and management
Construction management
Construction management and environment
Construction management and property development
Construction management and surveying
Construction operations management
Construction project management
Construction project management
Environmental hazards
Estate and farm enterprise management
Land economics
Land studies
Landscape construction
Landscape design
Landscape management
Planning and development
Planning, environment and development
Property development
Quantity surveying
Real estate
Real estate management
Real estate surveying
Rural business management
Rural property management
Surveying
Surveying and mapping science
Sustainable building technology
Sustainable construction
Sustainable construction and the built environment
Urban planning

Postgraduate: an accredited postgraduate qualification is an option for graduates in other subjects

Range of accredited courses similar to undergraduate: Graduate Diploma, Postgraduate Diploma, Master's

Building Property Management and Housing Sector
Housing
Undergraduate

Community and social care
Community development and leadership
Health and social care
Housing
Housing and communities
Housing and sustainable communities
Housing management
Housing policy and practice
Housing practice
Housing studies
Housing, communities and regeneration
Housing: supported housing
Management of social and affordable housing
Personal and professional development: housing
Regeneration and sustainability
Residential property
Social policy
Social policy: housing and communities
Social policy, health and housing
Support housing
Sustainable communities
Urban planning

Property Management and Estate Agencies
Building and Property Auctioneering and Valuation
Undergraduate

Building and valuation surveying

Property finance and investment

Property investment and management

Property investment appraisal and development

Property investment appraisal and development

Property management and valuation

Facilities and Property Management
Undergraduate

Building surveying and property management

Construction and property

Construction management and property development

Estate and farm enterprise management

Facilities management

Real estate and asset management

Real estate management

Rural business management

Rural enterprise and land management

Rural land management

Rural property management

Property and Estate Agencies
Undergraduate

Building services engineering project management

Building surveying

City and regional planning

Commercial management and quantity surveying

Estate management

Investment and finance in property

Land economy

Planning and real estate

Property development

Property development and management

Quantity surveying and commercial management

Real estate

Residential property

Postgraduate

Various accredited postgraduate Diplomas and Master's' degree courses

Business Finance; Economics; Mathematics; Statistics Sector

Accountancy and Finance, Actuarial Science, Auditing and Risk Management
Undergraduate

Accountancy
Accounting
Accounting for management
Actuarial mathematics
Actuarial science

Applied accounting
Auditing
Business accounting
Financial risk management
Forensic accounting

International accountancy
Management accounting
Risk management

Banking and Business Finance
Undergraduate

Banking
Business finance
Commerce
E-commerce
Finance
Financial economics

Financial management
Financial mathematics
Financial services
International finance
International financial services

Investment
Managerial finance
Money, banking and finance

Economics
Undergraduate

Applied economics
Business economics
Econometrics
Econometrics and mathematical economies

Economic history
Economics
Economics and econometrics
Financial economics

International economics
International political economy
Land economy
Political economy

Mathematics and Statistics
Undergraduate

Actuarial mathematics
Applied mathematics
Business statistics
Computational mathematics
Discrete mathematics
Education and training: numeracy
Engineering mathematics
Financial mathematics

Mathematical and theoretical physics
Mathematical computation
Mathematical physics
Mathematical sciences
Mathematics
Mathematics applications
Mathematics, operational research and statistics

Physical, mathematical and applied sciences
Statistics
Statistics and operational research
Teaching: primary education: mathematics
Teaching: secondary Education: Mathematics

Postgraduate
Subjects similar to undergraduate subjects

Administration and Business Management

Undergraduate

Administration and management

Aerospace technology with management

Agri-business

Airline, airport and aviation management

Applied golf management studies

British sign language and business management

Business administration

Business analysis and technology

Business analytics

Business and globalisation

Business and healthcare management

Business and supply chain management

Business economics

Business enterprise

Business entrepreneurship

Business information systems

Business innovation

Business innovation and enterprise

Business intelligence

Business law

Business management

Business management and information systems

Business operations management

Business psychology

Business statistics

Business studies

Business studies-operations and project management

Business technology

Business, accountancy and human resource management

Care and administrative practice

Coastal safety management

Computer systems management

Countryside management

Design management

Disaster management and emergency planning

E-commerce

Education, human resource development and training

Entrepreneurship

Facilities management

Global business

Global industries

Global management

Health service management

Informatics

Information technology management for business

International business

International business law

International business management

International business strategy

International fashion branding

International football business

International hotel management

International management

International spa management

International studies

It management for business

Leadership and management

Management

Management and organisation with human resource management

Management science

Management with a language

Managing business resources

Maritime business

Marketing management and web technologies

Oil and gas management

Outdoor leisure management

Project and risk management

Public administration

Public policy

Public relations

Public services

Small business enterprise

Supply chain management

Sustainable business

Sustainable environment management and technologies

Waste management

Human Resources and Recruitment
Undergraduate
Business and human resource management

Business and management studies with human resource management

Business management and human resource management

Business with human resource management

Business, human resource management and business law

Business, human resource management and public relations

Human resource management

Human resource management with development

International business and human resource management

Management and organisation with human resource management

Postgraduate
Master of business administration (MBA)

Human resource management

Education, Teacher and Training Sector

Education Support

Education and Early Childhood Studies
Undergraduate
Advanced practice in work with children and families

Advanced studies in early years

Applied languages and translating

Applied studies (early childhood)

Applied studies (learning support)

Applied studies in education

Care and education

Childhood and learning support studies

Childhood studies

Children and families

Children and young people

Children and young people's workforce

Children, schools and families

Children, young people and their services

Children's care learning and development

Community education

Community learning and development

Community music

Computing for education

Conductive education

Contemporary education

Drama, applied theatre and education

Early childhood education and care

Early childhood education studies

Early childhood policy and practice

Early childhood professional studies

Early education and childcare

Early years

Early years and practice

Early years care and education

Early years' education

Early years' education and practice

Early years' educator

Early years' play-work and education

Early years, childcare and education

Education

Education administrative management

Education and early childhood

Education and European studies

Education and learning

Education and learning

Education and professional practice

Education and professional studies

Education and training

Education and training: literacy

Education and training: numeracy

Education studies

Education studies and early years

Education studies with early childhood studies

Education, culture and society

Education, human resource development and training

Educational psychology

English as a foreign language

English in education

English language and education

English studies for teaching

Environmental geography and outdoor education
Families and childhood studies
Integrated education and care of children and young people
Learning and teaching (schools)
Learning support
Music education
Outdoor education
Outside adventure and environment
Performance and pedagogy

Primary education early years and key stage 1
Primary education studies
Primary teaching and learning
Professional development in early years
Professional development in teaching assistants
Psychology (education)
Public services with adventurous activity leadership
Social inclusion
Supporting teaching and learning

Teacher and learning support
Teaching and learning support
Teaching dance in the private sector
Teaching in the lifelong learning sector
Technological education
Wildlife education and media
Working with children, young people and families
Young children's learning and development

Special Educational Needs
Undergraduate

British sign language
British sign language and business management
British sign language and deaf studies
British sign language and English language

British sign language and English literature
Education and special educational needs
Education, special needs and disability
Interpreting (British sign language/English)

Special education
Special educational needs and inclusive practice
Theatre arts education and deaf studies

Teacher Training

Undergraduate Teacher Training Courses: Early Years and Primary Education
Undergraduate
Primary General / Early Years / Upper Primary / Some Specialist Subjects

Degree QTS
General primary
Early years / lower primary 3-7/8
Later years / upper primary 5-11

Some offer a specialist subject:
Art
Citizenship
Computing
English;
Environment
Gaelic
History
Humanities

Mathematics;
Modern foreign languages
Music;
Physical education
Religious studies
Science
Special educational needs

Undergraduate Teacher Training Courses: Secondary Education
Undergraduate
Secondary Specialist Subjects

Degree QTS secondary
Specialist subject:
Biology
Chemistry

Computer science
English
Mathematics;
Modern Foreign language

Music
Physical education
Religious education

Postgraduate Teacher Training Courses: Early Years and Primary

Postgraduate

Post / Professional Graduate Certificate of Education (PGCE) qualified teacher status (QTS)
Professional Graduate Diploma of Education (PGDE) qualified teacher status (QTS)

Primary General / Early Years / Upper Primary / Some Specialist Subjects

PGCE QTS: England, Wales, Northern Ireland: PGDE QTS: Scotland School Direct QTS (England) Teach First QTS: England and Wales Graduate Teaching Programme (GTP) QTS: Wales

School Centered Initial Teacher Training (SCITT) QTS: England

Some Specialist Subjects
Art
Computing
English;
Geography and History
Humanities

Mathematics;
Modern foreign languages
Music;
Physical education
Religious studies
Science
Special educational needs

Postgraduate Teacher Training Courses: Secondary

Postgraduate

Post / Professional Graduate Certificate of Education (PGCE) qualified teacher status (QTS)
Professional Graduate Diploma of Education (PGDE) qualified teacher status (QTS)

Secondary Specialist Subjects

PGCE QTS: England, Wales, Northern Ireland: PGDE QTS: Scotland School Direct QTS (England)

Teach First QTS: England and Wales Graduate Teaching Programme QTS: Wales

School Centered Initial Teacher Training (SCITT) QTS: England

Secondary Teaching Specialist Subjects

Arabic
Art and design
Biology
Business studies
Chemistry
Citizenship
Classics / Latin
Communication and media studies
Computer studies
Dance
Design and technology (Food; Product Design; Systems and Control; Textiles)

Drama and theatre studies
Economics
English
Geography
Health and social care
History
Languages: Chinese (mandarin)
Languages: Modern foreign languages:
French, German; Italian Spanish
Languages: modern foreign languages with

Japanese; Mandarin; Urdu; Latin; Russian
Leisure and Tourism
Mathematics
Music
Physical education
Physics
Psychology
Religious education
Religious education / philosophy
Social science
Special education needs
Welsh

Further and Adult Education / Post-compulsory Teacher Training

Further Education

Level 3 Award in
Education and Training

Undergraduate (some subjects may also require a degree)

Level 4 Certificate in
Education and Training
Level 5 Diploma in
Education and Training

Level 5 Diploma in
Education and Training:
including a specialist
pathway

Level 5 Integrated
Specialist Diploma
Level 5 Stand Alone
Specialist Diploma

Postgraduate

Level 6 Post-compulsory
PGCE (PCET)

Level 7 Post-compulsory
PGCE (PCET)

Teaching English as a Foreign / Other / Second Language (TEFL/ TESOL)

Further Education

Certificate of English
Language Teaching to
Adults (CELTA)

Certificate in Teaching
English to Speakers of

Other Languages (Cert
TESOL)

Undergraduate

Level 5 Diploma in
Education and Training
with specialist pathway
English and English
language teaching
English and TEFL
English as a foreign
language (EFL)
English as a foreign
language (EFL) combined

English language and
TEFL
English literature and
TEFL
English studies for
teaching (EFL)
Languages and TEFL
Linguistics and TESOL
Teaching English as a
foreign language (TEFL)

Teaching English as a
second or other language
(TESOL) combined
Teaching English to
speakers of other
languages (TESOL)
TESOL and educational
studies
TESOL and language
TESOL and modern
languages

Postgraduate

Level 6 Post-compulsory
PGCE (PCET): Education
and training: Teaching

English to speakers of
other languages (TESOL)
Level 7 Post-compulsory
PGCE (PCET)

Teaching English as a
second or other language
(TESOL) master's degree

Higher Education Lecturing Courses

Postgraduate

Certificate, Diploma,
Master's (in-house):

Teaching and Learning in
Higher Education

Engineering and Technology Sector
Transport Engineering (see Transport sector)

Chemical and Process Engineering
Undergraduate

Applied chemistry and chemical engineering
Biochemical engineering
Biological and bioprocessing engineering
Biomedical electronics engineering
Biomedical engineering
Ceramic science and engineering
Chemical and biomolecular engineering
Chemical and bioprocessing engineering

Chemical and energy engineering
Chemical and process engineering
Chemical engineering
Chemical engineering with brewing and distilling technology
Chemical offshore engineering
Food engineering

Technology:
Bakery and confectionery technology
Biochemistry with biotechnology

Ceramics and glass
Chemical engineering with industrial study
Chemistry with green nanotechnology
Food technology
Food technology and development
Food technology with bio processing
Polymers and textiles

Computing, Communication and Telecommunication Engineering
Undergraduate

Acoustics engineering
Animation and visual effects programming
Animation technology and special effects
Applied computing
Applied electronic engineering and cybernetics
Applied nanotechnology
Applied physics
Artificial intelligence
Audio acoustics
Audio and music technology
Audio and recording technology
Audio and recording technology
Audio and video engineering
Audio electronics
Audio engineering
Audio media engineering
Audio production
Audio systems engineering
Audio technology
Audio technology
Audio technology and audio engineering

Audio technology with electronics
Audio technology with multimedia
Audio Technology/Audio Engineering
Broadband telecommunications networks
Broadcast audio technology
Broadcast systems technology
Business analysis and technology
Business computing systems
Business information technology
Business information technology
Business systems analysis and design
Business technology
Cloud computing
Commercial music technology
Communication engineering
Communication systems

Communications and control engineering
Communications and electronics engineering
Communications and signal processing
Communications engineering
Communications network engineering
Communications networks
Communications systems engineering
Communications technology
Component engineering
Computational engineering
Computations
Computer aided design engineering
Computer aided engineering
Computer and communication systems
Computer and control engineering
Computer and electrical / electronic engineering

Undergraduate

Computer and electronic systems engineering

Computer and information engineering

Computer and information security

Computer and microprocessor systems

Computer and network technology

Computer and robotic systems

Computer and robotic systems

Computer animation and graphical technology applications

Computer engineering

Computer engineering

Computer forensics

Computer games engineering

Computer games technology

Computer graphics

Computer hardware and software engineering

Computer intelligence and robotics

Computer modelling and simulation

Computer networks

Computer programming

Computer science

Computer science with artificial intelligence

Computer systems engineering

Computer systems engineering

Computer technology

Data communication systems

Data processing

Database systems

Digital broadcast technology

Digital broadcasting

Digital communications

Digital electronics

Digital film and 3d animation technology

Digital forensics and cybercrime analysis

Digital forensics and system security

Digital media

Digital media technology

Digital music processing

Digital photography

Digital signal processing

Digital systems design

Digital technology

E-commerce engineering

Electronic, telecommunications and internet engineering

Engineering design

Engineering Mathematics

Film and television production technology

Film production technology

Games technology

Healthcare computing systems

Informatics

Information and communication technology

Information and computer engineering

Information engineering

Information security

Information systems

Information technology networking and security

Infrastructure engineering

Integrated engineering

Intelligent robotics

Interactive computing

Interactive digital technologies

Internet computing

Internet engineering

Maintenance engineering

Manufacturing engineering

Manufacturing systems engineer

Manufacturing technology

Marketing management and web technologies

Marketing, innovation and technology

Microcomputer systems engineering

Music production and technology

Music technology

Nano-electronics

Nanoscience

Network engineering

Network systems

Network technology

Networking and mobile technologies

Operations engineering

Outside broadcast technology

Physics with planetary and space physics

Physics with satellite technology

Popular music technology

Production technology and management

Radio engineering

Robotic engineering

Robotics engineering

Satellite communications

Security technology

Software engineering

Sound engineering

Sound engineering and design

Systems engineering

Teaching secondary education: design and technology QTS

Technical informatics

Technological education

Technology and e-commerce

Telecommunication engineering

Telecommunication systems engineering

Telecommunications and network engineering

Telecommunications and networks

Computing, Communication and Telecommunication Engineering continued

Undergraduate

User experience design
VFX (visual effects)
Video and audio engineering
Virtual design in engineering
Web design
Web technologies
Web technology
Wireless communication
Wireless networking

Software and Hardware Engineering: Designing, Building, Developing and Testing

Undergraduate

Application development
Applied computing
Computer aided design
Computer aided draughting and design
Computer aided mechanical engineering
Computer aided product design
Computer programming
Computer software
Computing and information systems
Computing and systems design
Computing and systems development
Computing application development
Computing software development
Computing with database development
Design and coding
Software development
Software engineering

Electrical and Electronic Engineering (also see Computing Engineering)

Undergraduate

Applied instrumentation and control
Control and instrumentation engineering
Control engineering
Creative lighting control
Creative music technology
Creative sound technology
Creative technologies
Design and technology engineering
Design engineering
Electrical and electronic engineering
Electrical and information systems
Electrical and mechanical engineering
Electrical energy systems
Electrical engineering
Electrical field engineer
Electrical mechanical engineering
Electrical power engineering
Electrical systems engineering
Electro-acoustics
Electromechanical engineering
Electronic and broadcast engineering
Electronic and communications engineering
Electronic design
Electronic engineering
Electronic engineering and cybernetics
Electronic engineering and telecommunications
Electronic engineering with space science technology
Electronic physics for new technology
Electronic systems engineering
Electro-technical industries
Engineering with music technology
Magnetics
Mathematical engineering
Physics with energy science and technology
Physics with satellite technology
Plant engineering
Power engineering
Process engineering
Process systems engineering

Energy, Power and Utilities Engineering / Offshore Engineering
Undergraduate

Chemical and energy engineering
Chemical and nuclear engineering
Electrical engineering
Electrical engineering and renewable energy
Energy and building services engineering
Energy and environmental engineering
Energy and industrial sustainability
Energy and power engineering
Energy engineering
Energy systems
Energy technology
Engineering: mechanical with oil and gas
Green technology
Material science with nuclear engineering
Nuclear engineering
Nuclear engineering: project management
Nuclear reactor technology
Nuclear science
Nuclear science and technology
Oil, gas and energy management
Petroleum engineering
Petroleum geoscience
Petroleum production engineering
Petroleum products engineering
Petroleum technology
Physics
Physics with nuclear science
Pipeline engineering

Environmental, Building and Civil Engineering
Undergraduate

Agricultural and environmental engineering
Agricultural engineering
Architectural design and technology
Architectural engineering
Architectural engineering and design management
Architectural glass arts
Architectural technology
Architectural technology and glass
Aviation technology and management
Bridge engineering
Building design engineering
Building engineering
Building engineering: civil and structural
Building engineering: structural
Building environment and services engineering
Building services engineering
Civil and architectural engineering
Civil and coastal engineering
Civil and construction engineering
Civil and environmental engineering
Civil and geological engineering
Civil and infrastructure engineering
Civil and maritime engineering
Civil and railway engineering
Civil and structural engineering
Civil and timber engineering
Civil and transport engineering
Civil engineering
Civil engineering design
Civil engineering technology
Civil, structural and environmental engineering
Clean technology with diploma in professional practice
Construction and building engineering
Construction engineering
Construction engineering management
Construction project management
Electrical engineering
Energy and building services engineering
Energy and environmental engineering
Environment and sustainable technology
Environmental and architectural acoustics
Environmental and civil engineering
Environmental and ecological engineering
Environmental and energy engineering
Environmental biogeochemistry
Environmental biotechnology
Environmental civil engineering
Environmental design and engineering
Environmental engineering
Environmental engineering with land and water

Environmental, Building and Civil Engineering continued

Environmental forensics
Environmental geology
Environmental management and technology
Environmental science and technology
Environmental technology

Fire engineering
Fire engineering
Fire and rescue service management
Fire risk engineering
Fire and leadership studies
Fire and safety and risk management

Fire safety engineering
Fire investigation
Fire safety engineering
Structural and fire safety engineering
Mechanical engineering
Renewable energy and the built environment
Safety engineering
Soil mechanics
Structural and architectural engineering
Structural design
Structural engineering
Structural engineering and mechanics
Surveying engineering

Sustainability and engineering
Sustainable building technology
Sustainable energy
Sustainable environment management and technologies
Sustainable environment management and technologies
Sustainable systems engineering
Welding engineering

Manufacturing and Design Engineering

Undergraduate

Biotechnology
Chemical engineering
Design and engineering materials
Design and manufacture
Design and technology
Design engineering
Design technology
Design technology for cyberspace
Design technology for e-commerce
Design technology for film production
Design technology for mobile communications
Design technology for multimedia
Design technology for music
Design technology for robotics

Design technology for security
Design technology for sports
Design technology for transport
Design technology with animatronics
Design technology with music
Design with manufacturing systems
Design with product development
Glass science and engineering
Guided weapon systems
Industrial design
Industrial engineering
Maintenance engineering
Manufacturing and mechanical engineering

Manufacturing and production engineering
Manufacturing consultancy
Manufacturing engineering
Manufacturing engineering and technology
Manufacturing metallurgy
Manufacturing systems
Operations Engineering
Quality and reliability engineering
Sports technology
Technology and management
Technology with design
Turbomachinery

Materials, Metals and Mining Engineering

Undergraduate

Asphalt and pavement technology
Asphalt technology
Ceramics and glass
Chemical engineering
Civil and geological engineering
Civil engineering
Composites materials engineering
Earth science
Engineering geology and geotechnics
Immersive technology
Material, design and manufacture
Materials design and engineering
Materials engineering

Materials in manufacture
Materials process engineering
Materials science and engineering
Materials science and engineering: biomaterials
Materials science and engineering: ceramics
Materials science and engineering: polymers
Materials science and materials engineering
Materials science and metallurgy
Materials science and technology
Materials technology
Materials with physics

Mathematics
Mechanical engineering
Metallurgical engineering
Metallurgy
Minerals technology
Mining and petroleum engineering
Mining and quarry engineering
Mining and quarry engineering
Mining engineering
Mining geology
Natural gas engineering
Petroleum engineering
Physics
Polymers and textiles

Mechanical Engineering

Undergraduate

Mechanical and production engineering
Mechanical design
Mechanical design and manufacturing engineering
Mechanical engineering
Mechanical engineering design
Mechanical engineering manufacturing
Mechanical engineering technology

Mechanical engineering, materials and manufacture
Mechanical engineering: biomedical
Mechanical engineering: building services
Mechanical engineering: metallurgy / materials
Mechanical engineering: modelling
Mechanical engineering: nuclear power

Mechanical power engineering
Mechanical systems
Mechanical technology
Mechatronics
Mechatronics and robotics
Mechatronics systems engineering

Medical / Clinical / Bioengineering and Medical Physics (also see Science sector)

Healthcare Science: Clinical / Biomedical Engineering

Undergraduate

Bioengineering
Biomaterials and tissue engineering
Biomedical engineering

Biomedical materials science
Biometrics
Bioprocess engineering

Biotechnology
Mechanical and materials engineering
Industrial biotechnology

Healthcare Science: Medical Physics

Undergraduate

Clinical technology
Physics with nuclear technology
Physics with nuclear science
Biomedical materials science

Dental materials
Dental technology
Diagnostic imaging
Medical and healthcare product design
Medical electronics
Medical engineering

Medical imaging
Medical product design
Medical systems engineering
Physics with nuclear technology

Environment Sector

Earth Sciences
Astronomy
Undergraduate

Astronomy
Astronomy and mathematics
Astronomy and physics
Astronomy, space science and astrophysics
Astrophysics
Cosmology
Geology with planetary science
Mathematics with astronomy

Nuclear astrophysics
Observational astronomy
Particle physics
Physics
Physics with astronomy
Physics with astrophysics
Physics with nuclear astrophysics
Physics with nuclear technology
Physics with space science

Physics with space science and technology
Physics with theoretical astrophysics
Physics, astrophysics and cosmology
Planetary science
Planetary science with astronomy
Space science
Theoretical astrophysics
Theoretical physics

Geology
Undergraduate

Applied and environmental geology
Applied geology
Earth and environmental science
Earth and ocean science
Earth sciences
Engineering geology and geotechnics
Environmental earth sciences

Environmental geology
Environmental geophysics
Environmental geoscience
Exploration and resource geology
Geochemistry
Geography and geology
Geo-informatics
Geological hazards

Geological oceanography
Geology
Geology and geophysics
Geology and petroleum geology
Geology with palaeobiology
Geophysics and geology
Geoscience
Palaeontology
Petroleum engineering

Meteorology Meteorology; Climate and Atmospheric Science
Undergraduate

Climate change
Environmental geophysics

Geophysics and meteorology
Mathematics and meteorology

Meteorology and climate
Meteorology and oceanography
Physics with meteorology

Oceanography
Undergraduate

Earth and ocean science
Geography and oceanography
Geological oceanography
Marine biology with oceanography
Mathematics with ocean and climate sciences

Meteorology and oceanography
Naval architecture with ocean engineering
Navigation and maritime science
Ocean exploration and surveying

Ocean science and marine conservation
Ocean sciences
Oceanography
Oceanography and coastal processes
Physical oceanography
Physical science

Earth Studies and Additional Sciences

Geography: Physical and Human
Undergraduate

Coastal geography
Earth sciences
Ecology and conservation
Environment and sustainability
Environmental conservation
Environmental earth science
Environmental geography
Environmental geography and climate change
Environmental geophysics
Environmental geoscience
Environmental hazards and disaster management
Environmental science

Environmental stewardship
Geographic information science
Geography
Geography and oceanography
Geography and planning
Geography and society
Geography with environmental studies
Geography with geo-informatics
Geography with quantitative research methods
Geography, ecology and environment
Geography, society and environment

Geography, urban environments and climate change
Geography: human and physical
Human and social geography
Human geography
Human geography and environment
Marine geography
Physical geography
Population and geography
Surveying and mapping science
Town planning
Urban studies

Cartography / Mapping; Geographical Information Systems (GIS), Geomatics
Undergraduate

Civil engineering
Geographic information systems
Geography
Geography with geomatics

Informatics
Ocean exploration and surveying
Quantity surveying
Surveying and mapping science

Town planning
Geographic Information Science

Hydrography / Hydrographic Surveying

Undergraduate

Earth and ocean science
Geographical information systems
Geography
Geography and oceanography
Geological oceanography
Geomatics

Marine biology with oceanography
Mathematics with ocean and climate sciences
Meteorology and oceanography
Naval architecture with ocean engineering
Ocean exploration

Ocean exploration and surveying
Ocean sciences
Oceanography
Oceanography and coastal processes
Physical oceanography
Surveying

Postgraduate

Hydrographic surveying

Hydrology Science, Flood Defense and Water Resource Management

Undergraduate

There are no undergraduate courses in hydrology however the following subjects may include Hydrology elements.

Civil engineering
Ecology

Environmental science
Geology

Physical geography
Plant and soil sciences

Postgraduate: may include Hydrology elements

Various Master's courses including:

Catchment Hydrology and Management
Civil engineering
Geography
Hydrogeology

Hydrology and climate change
Hydrology for water resource management
Physical geography
River environments

River system dynamics and management
Water engineering
Water management
Wetland science

Environmental Science and Studies

Undergraduate

Agriculture
Applied zoology and conservation
Aquaculture and fisheries science
Biochemistry
Biological sciences
Biotechnology
Business environment
Chemical engineering
Chemical physics
Coastal marine biology
Coastal safety management
Conservation and environment
Conservation biology
Countryside conservation
Countryside management
Earth and environmental science

Earth sciences
Ecology
Ecology and wildlife conservation
Energy engineering with environmental management
Environment earth science
Environmental and resource geology
Environmental archaeology
Environmental biology
Environmental chemistry
Environmental conservation
Environmental geography and outdoor education
Environmental geology
Environmental geology

Environmental geophysics
Environmental geoscience
Environmental hazards and biology
Environmental hazards and disaster management
Environmental hazards and geology
Environmental health
Environmental management
Environmental management and technology
Environmental management and technology

Environmental Science and Studies continued
Undergraduate
Environmental resource management

Environmental science

Environmental science and technology

Environmental science: clean technology

Environmental social sciences

Environmental sustainability

Forest management

Geography

Geography and natural hazards

Geography, ecology and environment

Geoscience

Global development and sustainability

Marine and freshwater biology

Marine biology

Marine science

Palaeontology and evolution

Physical geography

Public health

Renewable energy and sustainable technologies

Sustainable product design

Wildlife management and conservation

Healthcare Sector

Allied Healthcare Professional Practice

Art Therapy
Postgraduate: Master's degree
Art therapy

Art psychotherapy

Dietetics
Undergraduate: Honours degree
Dietetics

Human nutrition and dietetics

Nutrition and dietetics

Postgraduate
Dietetics

Dietetics and nutrition

Human nutrition and dietetics

Nutrition

Nutrition

Nutrition and dietetics

Drama Therapy
Postgraduate: Master's degree
Drama therapy / drama movement therapy

Music Therapy
Postgraduate: Master's degree
Music therapy

Occupational Therapy
Undergraduate: Honours degree
Occupational therapy

Postgraduate: PgDip; Master's degree
Occupational therapy

Orthoptics
Undergraduate: Honours degree
Orthoptics

Paramedic Science
Undergraduate: DipHE; Foundation degree; Honours degree
Paramedic science

Physiotherapy
Undergraduate: Honours degree
Physiotherapy

Postgraduate: Master's degree
Physiotherapy

Podiatry / Chiropody
Undergraduate

Podiatry   Podiatric medicine

Prosthetics/ Orthotics
Undergraduate: Honours degree
Prosthetics and Orthotics

Postgraduate: PgCert; PgDip; Master's degree
Prosthetics / Orthotics Rehabilitation

Radiography
Undergraduate: Honours degree

Diagnostic imaging	Radiography (Diagnostic	Radiotherapy and
Diagnostic radiography	imaging)	oncology
Medical imaging	Radiotherapy	Therapeutic radiography
(diagnostic radiography)		

Postgraduate: Diploma / Master's

Diagnostic radiography	Radiotherapy and oncology	Therapeutic radiography

Speech and Language Therapy
Undergraduate: Honours degree

Human communication: speech and language therapy	Psychology and speech pathology	Speech and language therapy
	Speech and language sciences	Speech pathology and therapy

Postgraduate: PgDip; Master's degree
Speech and language
therapy

Alternative and Complementary Health; Food and Nutrition

Alternative Health, Complementary and Creative Therapy
Undergraduate

Acupuncture
Art and design and
psychology
Chinese medicine:
acupuncture
Complementary
healthcare
Complementary medicine
Complementary therapies
Creative and therapeutic
arts

Creative arts therapies
studies
Creative expressive
therapies
Creative therapy
Fine art and professional
practice
Health and
complementary therapies
Herbal medicine

Holistic health therapies
and spa management
Physical and
psychological therapies
Professional practice in
complimentary health
Professional studies:
complementary health

Postgraduate

Dance movement
psychotherapy

Nutrition and Food Science (also see Dietetics)
Undergraduate

Applied food and nutrition
Dance and nutrition
Food and culinary arts
Food and human nutrition
Food and nutrition
Food bioscience
Food design and nutrition
Food marketing and
nutrition
Food, nutrition and health
Health and nutrition

Health, nutrition and
exercise
Human nutrition
Nutrition
Nutrition and exercise for
health
Nutrition and exercise
sciences
Nutrition and food
science
Nutrition and health

Nutrition and human
health
Nutrition, diet and
lifestyles
Nutritional sciences
Professional culinary arts
Public health nutrition
Social nutrition and health
Sport and nutrition for h

Complimentary Medicine Professional Practice

Osteopathy
Undergraduate: Honours degree
Osteopathic medicine

Postgraduate: Integrated Master's degree
Osteopathic medicine

Chiropractoric
Undergraduate and Postgraduate: Integrated Master's degree
Chiropractic

Health Administration, Information and Management
Undergraduate

Business and healthcare management

Business management and health and wellbeing

Community and health management

Health and community development

Health and social care

Health and social care management

Health and social care: administration and management

Health and wellbeing

Health care practice

Health management

Health practice management

Health promotion

Health services management

Health, wellbeing and social care

Social policy (health and social care)

Medicine and Dentistry
Dentistry
Undergraduate

Dental surgery / dentistry 5 years BDS or BChD

Dentistry with a preliminary / foundation year 6 years BDS or BChD

Dental surgery / dentistry intercalated 6 years BDS or BChD with science BSc

Dentistry graduate entry: accelerated: BDS or BChD: 4 years

Dentistry entry programme for medical graduates: 3 years

Postgraduate

Intercalated Master's / some PhDs: science subjects (optional additional 1 year or

longer as part of Dentistry degree)

Dentistry specialist training requirement

Maxillofacial / craniofacial technology

Foundation postgraduate course

Dental Hygiene / Therapy; Technology; Nursing; Equine Dentistry
Undergraduate

Dental hygiene DipHE

Dental hygiene and therapy BSc

Oral and dental health sciences BSc

Dental materials

Dental technology

Equine dentistry

Dental nursing FdSc

Dental nursing CertHE

Orthodontic therapy

Postgraduate
Dental technology

Medicine
Undergraduate: leads to a postgraduate qualification

Medicine and Surgery 5 years MB: MBBS; MBBS/BSc; MBChB; MBBCh; BMBS

Medicine and Surgery with pre-medical / foundation year: 6 years

MB: MBBS; MBBS/BSc; MBChB; MBBCh; BMBS

Medicine and Surgery intercalated 6 years MB: MBBS; MBBS/BSc; MBChB; MBBCh; BMBS with science BSc or MSc

Graduate entry

Medicine and Surgery accelerated 4 years MB: MBBS; MBBS/BSc; MBChB; MBBCh; BMBS

Postgraduate

Intercalated Master's / some PhDs: science subjects (optional additional 1 year or

longer as part of Medicine degree)

Foundation training postgraduate course (in house)

Specialist postgraduate training (in house)

Nursing and Midwifery; Operating Department Practice

Undergraduate

Nursing: Adult
Nursing: Child Health
Nursing: Children's
Nursing and Social Work
Nursing: Learning
Disability

Nursing: Learning
Disability and Social
Work
Nursing: Mental Health
Nursing: Midwifery
Operating department
practice

Graduate entry
Accelerated nursing
degree: for graduates in a
health related subject
Health visitor: for qualified
nurses

Postgraduate

Specialist degree
specialisms for registered
nurses and midwives
including:

Public health practice:
Specialist community
public health nursing
Various nursing
postgraduate specialisms
in advance practice

High intensity therapy:
Cognitive
Analytical/Behaviour
Therapy (CBT /CAT)

Optometry and Ophthalmic Dispensing Opticians

Undergraduate

Ophthalmic dispensing
Optometry BOpto 3 years

Optometry with
preliminary year 4 years

Rehabilitation work
(visual impairment) FdSc
(from Sept 2017

Postgraduate
Optometry MOptom 4 years

Pharmacy

Undergraduate: leads to a postgraduate qualification

Pharmacy MPharm

Pharmacy foundation
degree (may lead onto
year 2 of the MPharm)

Public Health; Environmental Health; Environmental Science; Occupational Health (also see Environment sector)

Undergraduate

Environmental and public
health
Environmental health
Environmental science
Health promotion

Medicinal sciences:
environment and public
health
Occupational safety,
health and environment
Public and environmental
health

Public health
Public health and health
promotion
Safety, health and
environmental
management

Ergonomics

Undergraduate
User centred design

Postgraduate

Applied ergonomics
Ergonomics and
organisational behaviour
Ergonomics: human
factors
Health ergonomics

Human computer
interaction with
ergonomics
Human factors and
ergonomics

Human factors for
inclusive design
Human factors in
transport

History; Anthropology and Archaeology Sector

Anthropology
Undergraduate

Anthropology
Anthropology and African Studies
Anthropology and geography
Anthropology and history
Anthropology with native American studies
Applied anthropology
Archaeological, anthropological and forensic Science
Biological anthropology
Cultural Studies
Evolutionary anthropology
Forensic anthropology
Forensic archaeology and anthropology
Social anthropology

Postgraduate
Various archaeology specialist subjects

Archaeology
Undergraduate

Archaeological practice
Archaeological studies
Archaeology
Archaeology and anthropology
Archaeology and forensic investigation
Archaeology and heritage
Archaeology and historic landscape conservation
Archaeology and history
Archaeology and landscape history
Archaeology and paleoecology
Archaeology of ancient civilisations
Archaeology of Egypt and the near east
Archaeology sciences
Archaeology with forensic science
Bioarchaeology
Classical archaeology
Egyptian archaeology
Environmental archaeology
Forensic archaeology and anthropology
Forensic investigation
Heritage, history and archaeology
Historical archaeology
Nautical archaeology
Prehistoric archaeology

Postgraduate
Various archaeology specialist subjects

History, Heritage, Conservation and Museum Studies

Art History
Undergraduate

Archaeology and landscape history
Art history
Art history and heritage management
Fashion and dress history
Fashion communication: fashion history and theory
History and philosophy of art
History of art
History of art / art history
History of art and architectural history
History of art and architectural history
History of art and design
History of art with curating
History of decorative arts and crafts
History of decorative arts and crafts
History of design

Conservation
Undergraduate
Historic Building Conservation, subjects include:

Architectural conservation
Historic building conservation

Applied architectural stonework and conservation

Archaeology and historic landscape conservation

Arts, Textiles and Furniture Conservation, subjects include:

Conservation and restoration
Conservation studies

Conservation of cultural heritage

Postgraduate
Historic Building Conservation, subjects include:

Architectural conservation
Building conservation
Building conservation and regeneration
Conservation and regeneration
Conservation of buildings
Conservation of historic buildings

Conservation of the historic environment
European urban conservation
Historic Building Conservation
Historic conservation
Historic environment conservation

Sustainable building conservation
Architectural design for the conservation of built heritage
Conservation studies

Arts, Textiles and Furniture Conservation, subjects include:

Conservation for archaeology and museums

Conservation of archaeological and museum objects
Conservation science
Conservation studies

Furniture conservation
Paper science
Stained glass conservation
Textile conservation

History, Classics, Heritage and Museum Studies
Undergraduate

American history
American studies
Ancient and medieval history
Ancient history
Ancient history and history
Ancient, classical and medieval studies
Ancient, medieval and modern history
Anthropology and history
Art history and heritage management
Art history and heritage management
Chinese civilisation and history
Classical civilisation
Classical studies

Classics
Contemporary history
Contemporary history and politics
Economic and social history
Economic history
Egyptology
Egyptology and ancient near eastern studies
English and history
European history
Fashion and dress history
Fashion communication: fashion history and theory
Global history and politics
Heritage management
Heritage studies
Heritage studies with nautical heritage

Heritage, history and archaeology
Historic conservation
History
History and archaeology
History and heritage
History and politics
History with professional development
History, ancient and medieval
History, civilisations and beliefs
History, heritage and archaeology
History, literature and culture
History, literature and cultures of the Americas

History, Classics, Heritage and Museum Studies continued

History: medieval and modern
History: medieval, modern and Scottish
Humanities
Irish history and society
Law: history
Liberal arts
Medieval and early modern history
Medieval and renaissance studies
Medieval history

Medieval studies
Modern and contemporary history
Modern and international history
Modern history
Museum and heritage studies
Museum studies
Natural history
Politics and contemporary history

Politics and contemporary history
Scottish historical studies
Scottish history
Social history
Social sciences: history
Sports business and sports history
Sports history and culture
Teaching secondary education: history
Welsh history

Hospitality and Events Management Sector

Events Management
Undergraduate

Arts and festival management
Creative events management
Events and festival technology

Events management
Events planning
Festival and event and hospitality management
International events management

Live events and television
Venues, events and hospitality management

Hospitality
Undergraduate

Bakery and patisserie technology
Baking technology management
Culinary arts
Culinary arts management
Food and beverage enterprise management
Food and consumer sciences
Food and consumer studies
Food and culinary arts
Food and professional cookery
Food consumer management

Food marketing and nutrition
Food marketing management
Hospitality
Hospitality and event management
Hospitality and licensed retail management
Hospitality and service management
Hospitality and travel management
Hospitality business management
Hospitality management
Hospitality, tourism and event management

Hotel and catering
Hotel and food services management
Hotel and resort management
Hotel management
International hospitality management
International spa management
Leisure and hospitality
Management of culinary arts
Professional cookery
Professional culinary arts
Service sector management

Information and Library Studies Sector

Archives, Information and Records Management
Postgraduate courses include:

Archive administration
Archives and records
management
Digital curation
Digital information
services

Information management
and leadership
International archives,
records and information
management

Records and information
management
Records Management

Library
Undergraduate

Information and library
studies
Information management

Business information
management

Library and information
management

Postgraduate courses include

Digital asset and media
management
Digital library
management
Digital media and
information studies
Health informatics
Information and library
studies

Information and records
management
Information capability
management
Information governance
and assurance
Information management
Information management
and preservation

Information science
Information studies
Information systems
Librarianship
Library and information
management
Library science
Records and information
management

Information Technology (IT) Information Systems
Undergraduate

Business information
systems
Business information
technology

Business management
and information systems
Computer information
systems
Computing

Computing for business
Informatics
Information systems
Information technology
management

Information / Computer Technology Sector

Computer Science, Artificial Intelligence, Robotics and Nanotechnology
Undergraduate
Artificial intelligence

    Artificial intelligence
    Artificial intelligence
    and robotics
    Intelligent
    computing
    Intelligent systems
    and robotics
    Mechatronics /
    robotics

Nanotechnology
Applied computer science
Computation in biology
and medicine
Computational physics
Computer science
Computer science (bio-
computing)
Computer science
innovation

Data science
Geographical information
systems
Mathematics
Theoretical and
computational physics
Data science and
analytics

Computer Security
Undergraduate
Computer and digital forensics

Computer forensic investigation

Computer forensics

Computer forensics and it security

Computer forensics and security

Computer network security with ethical hacking

Computer networks and security

Computer science with mobile and secure systems

Computer science: security and resilience

Computer security

Computer security and forensics

Computer security and networks

Computing forensics

Computing: networking, security and forensics

Cyber security

Cyber security and networks

Cybernetics

Digital security, forensics and ethical hacking

Ethical hacking

Ethical hacking and network security

Forensic computing

Forensic computing and security

Information technology networking and security

Mathematics, cryptography and network security

Network engineering, security and systems administration

Network infrastructure and security

Network security with penetration testing

Networking and security

Postgraduate
Cryptography

Cyber security

Mathematics of cryptography and communications

E-Commerce; Business Computing /Technology Management; Information/Data Management
Undergraduate
Applied business computing

Business computer systems

Business computing

Business computing solutions

Business information systems

Business information systems with multimedia

Business information technology

Business management and information systems

Computational management

Computer information systems

Computing

Computing for business

Computing for education

Computing innovations

Data science for health

E-commerce

Enterprise computing

Informatics

Information systems

Information technology management

IT management for business

IT support

Multimedia applications development

Multimedia computing

Operational research

Multimedia Computing
Undergraduate
Audio production

Broadcast computing

Creative music technology

Design for digital media

Digital culture

Digital film making

Digital illustration

Digital interaction design

Digital marketing

Multimedia applications development

Multimedia computing

Music production and sound recording

Websites, IT Content and Systems Network Management

Undergraduate

Cloud computing
Communication and computer networks
Computer and information technology
Computer and network technology
Computer communication and networks
Computer information systems
Computer network management and design
Computer networking
Computer networks and security
Computer networks and systems support
Computer systems and networks
Computer technology
Computing
Computing and education
Computing and internet technologies
Computing and IT
Computing and systems development
Computing networking and software development
Computing with networking
ICT and computing
Informatics
Information systems
Information technology
Internet computer science
Internet computing
Internet computing and systems administration
IT systems and applications
Network computing
Network engineering, security and systems
Network infrastructure and security
Network management
Web design
Web design and development
Web design and social media
Web development
Web systems
Web technologies

Languages Sector

English Language and Language Support

Classics

Undergraduate

Ancient languages
Anglo-saxon, Norse and Celtic
Celtic studies
Classical Greek studies
Classical studies
Classics
Classics and comparative literature
Latin studies

English Language, Literature, Creative Writing, Linguistics, Performance

Undergraduate

Actor / drama performance
Creative writing
Creative writing led community practices
English language
English language and communication
English language and English literature
English language and linguistics
English language studies
English language, linguistics and English literature
English literature
English, language and communication
English: communication at work
Foreign language and linguistics
International English language
Language and linguistics
Language and society
Languages
Linguistics
Linguistics and the English language
Literary studies

Postgraduate

Similar to undergraduate courses
Interpreting; translating

Foreign Languages

British Sign Language
Undergraduate

British Sign Language
British Sign Language and business management

British Sign Language and deaf studies
British Sign Language and English language

British Sign Language and interpreting (British Sign Language/English)

Postgraduate British sign language Interpreting and Translating
Graduate diploma British Sign Language
Postgraduate diploma in BSL / English interpreting and translation
MA BSL interpreting, translating and applied language studies; languages (interpreting and translating); translation studies

European Languages and Studies
Undergraduate

Applied languages
French
French and Spanish linguistic studies
French linguistic studies
French studies
German

German and Spanish linguistics studies
German studies
Italian
Italian studies
Modern languages
Portuguese
Portuguese studies

Russian
Russian and East European studies
Scandinavian studies
Spanish
Spanish studies
Translation studies: specific languages

Interpreting and Translating
Undergraduate

Applied languages and translating
Bilingualism
Chinese studies with translation studies
Interpreting and translation
Italian with translation studies
Languages interpreting and translating

Modern languages and translation
Modern languages: translation studies
Spanish with translation studies
Translation
Translation and interpreting
Translation studies: French

Translation studies: French and German
Translation studies: French and Spanish
Translation studies: German
Translation studies: German and Spanish
Translation, media and modern languages

Non-European Country Language Studies
Undergraduate

African studies
American studies
Arabic studies
Burmese and linguistics

Chinese studies
Hebrew
Japanese studies
Middle Eastern studies

Modern Middle Eastern studies
South Asian studies

Law Enforcement: Armed Forces Sector

Armed Forces
Undergraduate

Armed forces — Relevant academic qualification required for a specific job role

Check the academic and professional qualifications required for the relevant job roles at undergraduate and postgraduate level (some higher education qualifications may be sponsored and some may be studied whilst serving in the armed forces).

British Army — https://www.army.mod.uk/
Royal Airforce — https://www.raf.mod.uk/
Royal Navy — https://www.royalnavy.mod.uk/

Law Enforcement: Protection and Security Services Sector

Fire Studies
Undergraduate

Fire and leadership
Fire and rescue

Fire and rescue service management
Fire engineering

Fire risk engineering
Fire safety engineering
Fire safety management

Police Studies, Crime and Security
Undergraduate

Applied criminal justice studies
Applied criminology
Community policing
Community policing and justice management
Forensic and investigative science
Forensic science
International politics and intelligence studies
International politics and intelligence studies
International relations and security studies
Occupational safety

Police and community studies
Police and criminology
Police and forensic studies
Police studies
Police studies
Police studies and forensic science
Police studies with criminal investigation
Police studies with criminology psychology
Policing
Policing, investigation and criminology

Policing, law and investigation
Policing, politics and governance
Professional policing
Public and emergency services
Public services
Public services and public sector management
Public services: policing
Public services: security
War and security studies
War studies
War, peace and international relations

Law Sector

Criminology and Paralegal
Undergraduate

Applied criminal justice studies
Applied criminology
Crime and investigation
Crime, terrorism and deviance
Criminal justice

Criminal justice practice: policing
Criminal law
Criminology
Criminology and criminal justice
Criminology and law

Criminology and policing
Forensic science with criminology
Human rights
Paralegal studies

Law
Undergraduate
Business law LLB
Commercial law LLB
Criminal law LLB
English and European law LLB
English and French laws LLB
English law with German law LLB
Entertainment and media law
European and international law LLB
European business law
European law LLB
European legal studies LLB
International business law
International law LLB

International commercial law LLB
Law LLB
Law and criminology LLB
Law and criminal justice LLB
Law and European legal studies LLB
Law and French law LLB
Law and German law LLB
Law: business law LLB
Law: criminology LLB
Law: European and international LLB
Law: European studies LLB
Law: European legal studies LLB
Law: history LLB

Law, human rights and social justice LLB
Law: international legal studies LLB
Law: philosophy LLB
Law: politics LLB
Law: Scots LLB
Law with business LLB
Law with European legal systems LLB
Law with French law LLB
Law with German law LLB
Law with legal studies in Europe LLB
Law with management LLB
Law with Hispanic law LLB
Legal studies

Postgraduate
Graduate Diploma in Law GDL / Common Professional Exam CPE (Law conversion course)

Legal Practice Course LPC
Bar Professional Training Course BPTC

Various Law Master's' courses: MA / LLM

Leisure and Tourism Sector

Leisure Activities Sector

Beauty Therapy and Spa Management
Undergraduate
Advanced beauty technology
Beauty therapies management
Beauty therapies management
Beauty therapy

Beauty therapy and spa management
Hair and beauty management
Hair and beauty therapy management

International spa management
Spa hair and beauty management
Spa management
Spa management and advanced therapies

Entertainment and Leisure
Undergraduate
Entertainment and leisure marketing
Entertainment and media law LLB
Entertainment management

Entertainment technology
Events management with arts and entertainment
Leisure and Hospitality
Music business and live entertainment

Music, theatre and entertainment management
Marine leisure

Tourism
Undergraduate

Cruise management
Entertainment and leisure marketing
Event and tourism management
Hospitality and tourism management
Hospitality in the visitor economy
Hospitality, tourism and event management
International tourism business management

International tourism management
International travel and tourism management
Leisure and hospitality
Leisure and tourism
Marine and coastal tourism
Service sector management: travel and tourism
Strategic tourism and hospitality management

Tourism and enterprise management
Tourism and hospitality management
Tourism and leisure studies
Tourism management
Travel and tourism management
Travel operations management

Media: Advertising, Communications, Marketing and Public Relations Sector

Advertising, Communications, Marketing and Public Relations

Advertising
Undergraduate

Advertising
Advertising and brand management
Advertising and business
Advertising and design
Advertising and digital marketing
Advertising and marketing communications
Advertising and public relations
Advertising design
Advertising management and digital communication

Advertising, marketing and public relations
Advertising, public relations and media
Advertising: creative
Brand management
Business, advertising and public relations
Creative advertising
Creative advertising and brand
Creative advertising technologies
Creative advertising technologies

Design for advertising and digital media
Design for art direction
Digital advertising and design
Fashion brand management
Graphic branding and identity
Graphic design and visual communication
Media communication and advertising

Communications
Undergraduate

Communication and media studies
Communication Studies
Communication, advertising and public relations
Communications: marketing communications and public relations

English language
English language and communication
English literature
English studies
English: communication at work
Graphic communication
Mass communication

Mass communication and promotion
Media and communication
Media and communication
Media communications
Visual communication

Marketing
Undergraduate
Business and marketing management
Business management: marketing
Business management: sales and marketing
Business: marketing
Consumer behaviour and marketing
Digital marketing
Events management and marketing
Fashion business and promotion
Fashion buying and brand management
Fashion management and marketing
Fashion marketing
Fashion marketing and journalism
Fashion marketing and retailing
Fashion media and marketing
Fashion promotion and imaging
Fashion: media and promotion
Food marketing and business economics
Football business and marketing
Global marketing
International fashion promotion
International marketing
Leather technology: marketing
Marketing
Marketing and advertising
Marketing and advertising management
Marketing and business
Marketing and consumer psychology
Marketing communications
Marketing communications and advertising
Marketing communications and advertising
Marketing management
Marketing with advertising management
Marketing with digital communications
Marketing, advertising and branding
Marketing, advertising and branding
Marketing, PR and advertising
Publicity studies
Retail marketing
Sport marketing
Tourism management and marketing

Public Relations
Undergraduate
Business, advertising and public relations
Business, human resource management and public relations
Journalism and public relations
Media and public relations
Public Relations
Public relations and advertising
Public relations and communications
Public relations and marketing
Public relations and media
Public relations in practice
Public relations, marketing and events
Public relations, media and marketing

Journalism and Publishing

Journalism and Writing
Undergraduate
Broadcast journalism
Creative media production: journalism
Creative writing
Creative writing and journalism
English language
English and creative writing
Fashion journalism
Fashion marketing and journalism
Imaginative writing
International journalism
International journalism
Journalism
Journalism and communication
Journalism and creative writing
Journalism and digital media
Journalism and media
Journalism studies
Journalism: broadcast
Journalism: investigative
Journalism: multimedia
Magazine journalism
Mass communications
Media and communication studies
Media production: journalism
Media studies
Media, communication and journalism

Media, culture and journalism
Media, journalism and culture
Multimedia broadcast journalism
Multimedia journalism

Multi-platform journalism
Music journalism
Photojournalism
Photojournalism and documentary photography
Print journalism

Professional writing
Scriptwriting
Sports journalism
Wildlife media

Publishing and Editing
Undergraduate
Design for publishing
Editing and post production
English with publishing

Graphic communication with typography
Magazine publishing
Publishing

Publishing and English
Publishing media

Media: Film, Radio, Television and Theatre

Film, Radio Television, Theatre, Music Production and Technology
Undergraduate
Audio production
Broadcast audio technology
Broadcast media
Broadcast systems technology
Broadcast technology
Broadcasting
Creative lighting control
Creative media production (film making)
Creative media production (moving image)
Creative sound production
Design for digital media
Digital broadcast technology
Digital film and television production
Digital film making
Digital film production
Digital film production and screenwriting
Digital media
Digital media production

Digital media production and 3D techniques
Digital media technology
Digital production and filmmaking
Digital television
Drama and technical theatre
Electronic engineering
European arts (film)
Film and music video production
Film and television
Film and television production
Film and television production
Film and television production technology
Film and television studies
Film music and soundtrack production
Film practice
Film production
Film production technology
Film studies

Film, photography and media
Film, radio and television studies (broadcasting)
Global cinemas and screen arts
Independent film making
Interactive media
Interactive media development
Media production
Media production (radio)
Multimedia computing
Musical theatre
Outside broadcast technology
Practical filmmaking
Production design for stage and screen
Sound technology
Television production
Time based art and digital film
TV production technology
Web and interactive media
Photographic media

Media Studies
Undergraduate
Broadcast media
Costume for performance
Creative media production
Creative studies
Creative writing
Fashion media practice and criticism
Film and media
Film and television studies
Film studies
Global cinemas and screen arts
Global media
Media
Media and communication
Media and communication studies
Media and communication: journalism
Media and cultural studies
Media and culture
Media communications
Media design
Media marketing
Media performance
Media practice
Media studies
Media, journalism and culture
Media, writing and production
Multimedia journalism
Performing arts production
Screenwriting/scriptwriting
Social media development
Theatre media performance
TV production and media studies

Performing Arts Sector

Dance

Dance Performance and Dance Theatre
Undergraduate
Applied performance
Ballet education
Choreography and dance
Contemporary dance
Dance
Dance and choreography
Dance and community practice
Dance and drama
Dance and fitness
Dance and performance
Dance and professional practice
Dance and theatre arts
Dance education
Dance led community practices
Dance performance and teaching
Dance practice
Dance studies
Dance theatre
Dance theatre performance
Dance: urban practice
Modern ballet
Musical arts
Musical theatre
Performing arts
Physical education and dance
Professional and commercial dance
Sports and dance therapy
Teaching dance in the private sector
Technical theatre
Theatre arts

Dance Therapy
Postgraduate
Dance movement psychotherapy

Drama Performance and Theatre Studies
Undergraduate

Acting
Acting and community theatre
Acting and performance practice
Acting and screen performance
Acting and stage combat
Acting and theatre
Acting and theatre arts
Acting for stage and media
Acting for stage and screen
Acting for stage screen and radio
Acting performance
Acting with theatre practice
Actor musician
Actor training for theatre and media performance
American theatre arts
Applied drama
Applied performance
Community drama
Contemporary screen acting
Contemporary theatre and performance
Creative enterprise
Creative expressive therapies (drama)
Creative industries
Creative performance
Creative studies

Dance and drama
Dance and theatre arts
Drama
Drama and applied theatre
Drama and contemporary media
Drama and performance
Drama and technical theatre
Drama and theatre
Drama and theatre arts
Drama and theatre practice
Drama and theatre studies
Drama in the community
Drama led community practice
Drama practitioners
Drama studies
Drama, applied theatre and education
Drama, applied theatre and performance
European theatre arts
Film and theatre
Media and communication
Musical theatre
Opera studies
Performance and events production
Performance and media
Performance and professional practice

Performance and theatre arts
Performance for stage and screen
Performance: drama and theatre
Performance: media performance
Performing arts
Small scale theatre
Theatre
Theatre and drama
Theatre and performance
Theatre and performance practice
Theatre and performance technology
Theatre and professional practice
Theatre and screen: costume interpretation
Theatre and screen: technical arts and special effects
Theatre arts
Theatre arts education and deaf studies
Theatre media performance
Theatre studies
Theatre, performance and event design
Theatre, television and performance
Theatre: writing, directing and performance

Stage / Production Management

Broadcast media
Broadcast production and presenting
Costume and set design
Creative media production
Creative media production
Film and television production

Live events and television
Media production
Music, theatre and entertainment management
Practical film making
Production arts for stage managers
Stage and production management

Stage management
Stage management and technical services
Television production
Theatre production
Theatre technology

Postgraduate
Various subjects similar to undergraduate
Dramaturgy
Creative writing
European theatre and
dramaturgy

Playwriting and
dramaturgy
Shakespeare studies
Text and performance
studies

Theatre, criticism and
dramaturgy
Writing for performance
Voice
Voice studies

Drama Therapy
Postgraduate
Drama therapy

Music and Music Technology
Music Composition, Performance and Support
Undergraduate

Acting-musical theatre
Actor musician
Advanced diploma
(performance)
Advanced studies in
composition
Advertising, film and
music video production
Applied music
Applied music practice
Bmus
Bmus composition
Bmus jazz
Bmus music
Commercial music
Community music
Contemporary and
popular music
Contemporary music
performance
Contemporary popular
music
Contemporary song-
writing and artist
development
Creative expressive
therapies
Creative music
Creative musicianship
Creative musicianship
bass
Creative musicianship
drums
Creative musicianship
guitar
Creative musicianship
vocals
Drama, theatre and
performance studies
Folk and traditional music
Global popular music

Independent musician
Instrumental performance
/ composition /music
technology / musicology
International foundation
music
Jazz and popular music
Jazz performance
Jazz, popular and
commercial music
Media and
communication
Media, film and television
Music
Music (classical)
Music (jazz)
Music (performance and
production)
Music (performance)
Music (popular)
Music (production)
Music and communities
Music and popular music
studies
Music business
Music business and
creative industries
Music business and live
entertainment
Music composition
Music education
Music Gaelic medium
Music industry
management
Music industry studies
Music led community
practices
Music performance
Music performance
(heavy metal)

Music performance
(popular)
Music performance and
artist development
Music performance and
production
Music performance in
jazz
Music practice and
production
Music practitioners
Music with enterprise
Music with humanities
Music, theatre and
entertainment
management
Musical theatre
Musical theatre and
performance
Performance jazz studies
Performing arts
Performing arts: music
theatre
Popular music
Popular music
performance
Popular music practice
Popular music studies
Professional dance and
music theatre
Scottish music
Scottish music: piping
Song-writing
Teaching primary
education: music
Teaching secondary
education: music
Theatre and performance
Theatre arts – musical
theatre

Music Therapy
Postgraduate
Music therapy

Music Instrument Repair and Making
Undergraduate
Foundation degree in historic craft practices: musical instruments

Music Management
Undergraduate

Arts and festival management
Arts management
Event and festival management

Events and festivals sustainability management
Music and live events management
Music and media management

Music industry management
Music management
Music management and studio production

Music Media
Undergraduate

Music for media
Music journalism

Music journalism and broadcasting

Popular music journalism

Music Sound Production and Technology (also see Media sector)
Undergraduate

Advertising, film and music video production
Audio acoustics
Audio and music production
Audio and music technology
Audio and recording technology
Audio engineering and music production
Audio post production
Audio production
Audio recording and production
Audio technology with electronics
Broadcast audio and music technology
Broadcast television and radio
Commercial music technology
Contemporary music production

Creative audio technology
Creative media production (moving image)
Creative music production
Creative music technology
Creative sound and music
Creative sound design
Creative sound production
Creative sound technology
Digital design
Digital film making
Digital music
Digital music and sound arts
Digital post production
DJ and electronic music production
Electronic engineering with music technology

Electronic music and DJ practice
Electronic music: production and composition
Electronics with music and audio systems
Event and festivals technology
Film and television production
Film music and soundtrack production
Live sound production
Media production: radio
Music and audio technology
Music and creative music technology
Music and sound production
Music and sound recording
Music and sound technology

Music Sound Production and Technology (also see Media sector) continued

Music composition and technology for film and games
Music for film and television
Music production
Music production and business
Music production and creative recording
Music production and sound design
Music production and sound recording
Music production and technology
Music technology
Music technology and artist development
Music technology and production
Music technology and sonic arts
Music technology systems
Music technology with humanities
Music, multimedia and electronics
Popular music technology
Radio
Sonic arts
Sound and music technology
Sound arts and design
Sound design
Sound production
Sound technology
Sound, light and live event technology
Theatre sound
Urban and electronic music

Psychology, Counselling and Psychotherapy Sector

Counselling and Psychotherapy
Undergraduate

Addictions counselling
Counselling
Counselling and psychology in community settings
Counselling and psychotherapy studies
Counselling integrative-relational
Counselling skills and psychology
Counselling skills and sociology
Counselling skills and theology and religious studies
Counselling studies
Counselling: cognitive behavioural
Counselling: person centred
Forensic psychology
Humanistic and integrative counselling
Humanistic counselling practice
Integrative counselling
Person centred counselling
Person centred counselling
Psychodynamic counselling
Psychosocial analysis of offending behaviour
Psychotherapy
Sports therapy
Theory and practice of counselling
Therapeutic communication and counselling studies
Therapeutic counselling
Transactional analysis counselling

Postgraduate

Accredited Postgraduate Certificate / Diploma / Master's Counselling /
Therapy / Psychotherapy specialism

Psychology
Undergraduate

Advanced psychology
Applied psychology
Consumer psychology
Educational psychology
Experimental psychology
Forensic psychology
Philosophy, religion and
applied psychology
Psychology
Psychology and
counselling
Psychology and
criminology

Psychology and society
Psychology: experimental
Psychology with
behaviour analysis
Psychology with
counselling
Psychology with
counselling and
psychotherapy
Psychology with
counselling theory
Psychology, counselling
and therapies

Psychology: clinical
Psychology: counselling
skills
Psychosocial studies
Religion, ethics and
applied psychology
Social psychology
Therapeutic psychology
Sport psychology

Postgraduate
Graduate psychology conversion course

Graduate Certificate in
Psychology (introductory
course for graduates with
insufficient study of
psychology at degree

level leading to Graduate
Psychology Conversion
course)

Graduate Diploma;
Postgraduate Diploma;
Master's: Graduate
psychology conversion
course

Postgraduate specialisms
Postgraduate diploma:
Clinical Neuropsychology

Master's degree:

Educational psychology
plus the BPS award in
educational psychology
(Scotland)

Clinical neuropsychology
Forensic psychology
Health psychology
Occupational psychology

Sports psychology

Doctoral degree:

Clinical Psychology
Counselling Psychology
Educational Psychology

Forensic Psychology
Health Psychology
Occupational Psychology

PhD in a relevant
psychology specialist
subject

Religion and Theology Sector
Religion / Theology
Undergraduate

Biblical studies
Biblical studies and theology
Children and family work and theology
Christian theology
Church community and theology
Development studies and the study of religion
Divinity
Hebrew and New Testament
Ministerial theology
Muslim cultures and civilisation
Philosophy
Philosophy, ethics and religion
Philosophy, religion and applied psychology
Philosophy, religion and ethics
Politics, religion and philosophy
Practical theology
Religion and education
Religion and theology
Religion, culture and ethics
Religion, culture and society
Religion, ethics and applied psychology
Religion, philosophy and ethics
Religion, philosophy and ethics with theology
Religion, politics and society
Religion, theology and ethics
Religion, theology and the bible
Religious and theological studies
Religious studies
School, youth and community work and practical theology
School, youth and community work and practical theology
Teaching secondary education: religious education
Theological studies
Theology
Theology and religion
Theology and religion, philosophy and ethics
Theology and religious studies
Youth work and theology

Retail Sector
Retail Management
Undergraduate

Advertising and marketing communications
Business and supply chain management
Business finance
Business management (retail)
Business purchasing and supply chain management
Creative enterprise (fashion and textiles)
Digital retail management
Fashion and textile buying management
Fashion brand management
Fashion business
Fashion business and promotion
Fashion buying and merchandising
Fashion design
Fashion management
Fashion marketing and retail design
Fashion marketing and retailing
Fashion media and marketing
Fashion retail and enterprise
Fashion retail management
Fashion visual merchandising and branding
Hospitality and licensed retail management
Interior design
International fashion branding
International retail management
International supply chain and procurement management
International supply chain and shipping management
Logistics and supply chain management
Retail management
Retail management and distribution
Retail management and innovation
Retail marketing management
Retailing
Retailing, marketing and management
Service sector management: retail management
Spatial design
Sports business, retailing and merchandising
Supply chain management
Textile design: retail management
Visual merchandising
Visual merchandising and promotional design

Retail Management
Postgraduate
Procurement and supply chain management | Logistics

Science Sector

Biology, Pharmacology and Pharmaceutical Sciences
Undergraduate
Biology General

Agricultural science
Anatomy
Applied biology
Biochemistry
Biological and medicinal chemistry
Biological chemistry
Biological sciences for industry
Biology
Cellular and molecular medicine
Clinical science
Clinical technology
Combined Sciences
Conservation biology
Environmental science
Food sciences
Forensic psychobiology
Forensic science

Genetics
Genetics and evolution
Global health
Global health and social medicine
Health and human sciences
Human biology
Human bioscience
Immunology
Life science
Medical biochemistry
Medical genetics
Medical microbiology
Medical sciences
Medical sciences: health research clinical trials management
Medicinal and pharmaceutical chemistry

Medicinal chemistry
Medicinal sciences
Microbiology
Molecular biology
Paramedics
Parasitology
Pathology
Pharmaceutical and medicinal chemistry
Pharmaceutical science
Pharmacology
Pre-medical studies
Psychology
Quality assurance
Sport and exercise science
Sports Science
Stratified medicine

Animal Biology (also see Animals Sector)

Agricultural science
Animal behaviour
Animal biology
Aquaculture
Biology

Conservation
Ecology
Environmental science
Equine science
Marine biology

Marine science
Veterinary medicine
Veterinary nursing
Wildlife conservation
Zoology

Conservation and Sustainability Biology (also see Environment Sector)

Biochemistry
Biology
Conservation

Ecology
Environmental health
Environmental science

Forestry
Microbiology
Oceanography

Plant Biology (also see Plants Sector)

Agricultural science
Biology
Botany
Farm management
Food science

Nutrition
Environmental science
Forestry
Horticulture
Microbiology

Plant and soil science
Plant biology
Plant science

224

Biology, Pharmacology and Pharmaceutical Sciences continued

Sport and Exercise Biology (also see Sports Sector)

Exercise, nutrition and health

Physiotherapy

Sport and exercise

Sport and exercise psychology

Sports science

Postgraduate: Various postgraduate science specialist subjects relating to undergraduate subjects

Chemistry and Biochemistry

Undergraduate

Analytical chemistry

Applied chemistry

Biochemical / bioprocess engineer

Biochemistry

Biological and medicinal chemistry

Biological chemistry

Brewing and distilling

Chemical and process engineering

Chemical engineering

Chemical physics

Chemical science for industry

Chemistry

Chemistry for drug discovery

Chemistry with drug discovery

Chemistry with green nanotechnology

Chemistry with industrial experience

Chemistry with medicinal chemistry

Chemistry with molecular medicine

Chemistry, biological and medicinal chemistry

Cosmetic science

Data science

Forensic science

Materials science

Medicinal sciences

Metallurgy

Microbiology

Paleontology

Paramedics

Pharmaceutical science

Pharmacology

Process chemist

Product design

Radiography

Sports science

Textile science and technology

Waste resource management

Postgraduate: Various postgraduate science specialist subjects relating to degree subjects

Physical Science and Mathematics (also see Accounting and Finance; Engineering sectors)

Undergraduate

Aeronautics

Aeronautics engineering

Aerospace engineering

Applied physics

Archaeology

Architecture

Artificial intelligence

Artificial intelligence and robotics

Astronautics

Astrophysics

Biotechnology

Chemical engineering

Chemical physics

Civil engineering

Computational mathematics

Computer science

Data modelling and analytics

Data science

Earth sciences

Astronomy

    Astronomy, space science and astrophysics

Geology

Meteorology

Oceanography

Engineering

Engineering technology

Environment science

Environmental geography

Explosives engineer/scientist

Forensic Science

Geographical information systems

Geographical science

Geography

Geography and geo-informatics

Geology

Geophysics

Materials science

Materials science and engineering

Mathematical and theoretical physics

Mathematical sciences

Mathematics

Mathematics and theoretical physics

Mathematics, operational research and statistics

Metallurgy

Minerals engineering

Mining engineering

Nanoscience

Natural sciences

Physical Science and Mathematics (also see Accounting and Finance; Engineering sectors) continued
Undergraduate
Naval architecture
Neuro-engineering
Nuclear engineering
Operational yacht science
Physical sciences
Physical, mathematical and applied sciences
Physics
Physics for new technology

Physics with energy science and technology
Physics with planetary and space physics
Physics with satellite technology
Product design
Ship science (engineering)
Sonar engineer

Space science and robotics
Statistics
Theoretical and computational physics
Theoretical physics

Postgraduate: Various postgraduate science specialist subjects relating to degree subjects
Specialist postgraduate subjects include:
Radiation and environmental protection
Nuclear science

Food Science and Technology (also see Healthcare Sector)
Undergraduate
Agricultural science
Bakery and confectionary technology
Bakery and patisserie technology
Baking technology management
Biotechnology
Brewing
Brewing and distilling
Dietetics
Food and consumer studies

Food design and technology
Food manufacturing
Food process engineering
Food production and supply management
Food quality, safety and nutrition
Food science
Food science and nutrition

Food science and technology
Food technology
Food technology and development
Food technology and development
Food technology with bio processing
Food technology with bio processing
Nutrition
Plant science

Postgraduate:
Various postgraduate science specialist subjects relating to degree subjects

Forensic Medicine
Postgraduate: Medical, Dentistry, or Podiatry degree required plus a postgraduate specialism:
Forensic odontology

Forensic pathology

Forensic podiatry

Forensic Science
Undergraduate
Forensic analysis
Forensic anthropology
Forensic archaeology and anthropology
Forensic biology

Forensic biology
Forensic chemistry
Forensic crime scene
Forensic computing
Forensic investigations

Forensic IT: digital, e-crime, cyber crime
Forensic psychobiology
Forensic psychology
Forensic science

Postgraduate
Various forensic specialist subjects including:
Forensic analysis
Forensic anthropology

Forensic engineering and science
Forensic psychology

Forensic radiography
Forensic science
Forensic toxicology

Radiation Protection Advice
Undergraduate

Radiation protection
physics
Medical physics
Radiography

Nuclear engineering
mathematics or medical
engineering
Biology
Biomedical science
biochemistry

Chemistry
Environmental science
environmental health
physiology

Postgraduate
Radiation protection

Healthcare Science
Healthcare Science: NHS Practitioner Training Programme (PTP)
Undergraduate
Healthcare Science: NHS Scientific Training Programme (STP)
Postgraduate
Graduate entry courses: Employed by the NHS, leading to an accredited Master's degree
Healthcare Science: NHS Higher Specialist Scientific Training Programme (HSST)
Postgraduate
Postgraduate entry: Employed by the NHS, leading to an accredited Doctorate degree

Healthcare Science: Clinical Bioinformatics / Health Information (also see Information Technology and Library Sector)
Undergraduate

Business information
systems
Business information
technology
Business management
and information systems

Computer information
systems
Computing
Computing for business
Data science for health
Informatics

Information systems
Information technology
management

Postgraduate

Similar to undergraduate
Bioinformatics

Genomics
Health informatics

Healthcare Science Scientific Training Programme (STP):
Postgraduate

Clinical bioinformatics:
genomics

Clinical bioinformatics:
health informatics

Clinical bioinformatics:
physical sciences

Healthcare Science: Life Sciences / Biomedical Sciences
Undergraduate

Biomedical materials
science
Biomedical science
Biomedicine
Clinical science
Clinical technology
Genetics
Health and human
sciences
Immunology

Medical biochemistry
Medical genetics
Medical microbiology
Medical sciences
Medical sciences: health
research clinical trials
management
Medicinal and
pharmaceutical chemistry
Medicinal chemistry

Medicinal sciences
Microbiology
Molecular biology
(postgrad)
Parasitology
Pathology
Pharmacology
Pre-medical studies
Stratified medicine

Healthcare Science / Biomedical Science: NHS Practitioner Training Programme (PTP):
Undergraduate

Healthcare science: blood sciences

Healthcare science: cellular sciences

Healthcare science: genomic / genetic science

Healthcare science: genomic / genetics technology

Healthcare science: infection science

Healthcare science: life science

Healthcare Science: Life Sciences / Biomedical Sciences
Postgraduate:
Various specialisms including:

Blood sciences
Clinical biochemistry
Haematology / transfusion science
Clinical immunology
Cellular science
Cytopathology
Histopathology
Reproductive science
Genetics
Bioinformatic genomics
Genetic science
Immunogenetics
Life sciences general
Clinical biochemistry

Clinical immunology
Epidemiology
Genetics
Haematology
Herpetology
Histocompatibility and immunogenetics
Histology
Histopathology
Imaging biology
Immunology
Infection science
Microbiology
Molecular pathology of acquired disease

Molecular pathology of infection
Mycology
Neurobiology
Paleaobiology
Pathology
Reproductive science
Microbiology
Bacteriology
Infection control and epidemiology
Mycology
Parasitology
Analytical toxicology
Virology

Healthcare Science / Biomedical Science: NHS Scientific Training Programme (STP)
Postgraduate

Clinical biochemistry
Clinical immunology
Clinical microbiology
Cytopathology

Genomic counselling (formerly genetic counselling)
Genomics Science (formerly genetics)

Haematology and transfusion science
Histocompatibility and immunogenetics
Histopathology
Reproductive science

Healthcare Science: Medical Physics and Biomedical / Clinical Engineering
Undergraduate

Bioengineering
Biomaterials and tissue engineering
Biomedical engineering
Biomedical materials science
Biometrics
Bioprocess engineering
Biotechnology
Clinical engineering
Clinical technology
Dental materials
Dental technology
Diagnostic imaging

Engineering
Industrial biotechnology
Mathematics
Mechanical and materials engineering
Medical and healthcare product design
Medical electronics
Medical engineering
Medical imaging
Medical physics
Medical product design
Medical systems engineering

Medical technology
Nuclear medicine
Pharmaceutical science, technology and business
Physics
Physics with nuclear science
Physics with nuclear technology
Radiation engineering
Radiotherapy physics
Rehabilitation engineering

Healthcare Science: Medical Physics and Biomedical / Clinical Engineering continued

Undergraduate

Healthcare Science / Clinical Engineer: NHS Practitioner Training Programme (PTP)

Clinical engineering
Medical engineering
Nuclear medicine
Radiation engineering
Radiation physics

Rehabilitation
engineering
Renal technology
Clinical photography

Graduate diploma:
healthcare science with
pathways in radiotherapy
or nuclear medicine

Postgraduate
Various specialisms similar to undergraduate subjects
Postgraduate

Healthcare Science / Clinical Engineer: NHS Scientific Training Programme (STP)

Postgraduate
Clinical Engineering

Rehabilitation
engineering
Clinical measurement
and development and

device risk management
and governance
Clinical pharmaceutical
science

Medical physics

Critical care science
Imaging with ionising
radiation

Imaging non ionising
radiation
Radiation safety physics
Radiotherapy physics

Reconstructive science
Clinical science:
maxillofacial technology

Medical Illustration and Photography

Undergraduate

Graphic design

Illustration

Photography

Postgraduate

Clinical photography
Forensic art
Graphic design for
healthcare

Medical and biological
illustration
Medical art
Medical illustration

Medical visualisation and
human anatomy

Healthcare Science: Physiological Sciences

Undergraduate

Cardiovascular Science
Cardiac physiology
Healthcare science:
Respiratory and sleep
physiology
Neurosensory Science
Audiology
Neurophysiology
Neuroscience

Physiology General
Biological science,
neuroscience
Biomedical science
Biomedical science,
physiology
Health physiology
Human physiology
Medical biology
Medical physiology
Medical physiology and
therapeutics

Natural sciences,
physiology, development
and neuroscience
Neuroscience
Physiology
Physiology and sports
science
Physiology science
Sport and exercise
science

Healthcare Science: NHS Practitioner Training Programme (PTP)
Undergraduate

Audiology/ Hearing Aid
Cardiac physiology
Neurophysiology

Respiratory and sleep
physiology

Clinical Perfusion NHS
Trainee: clinical perfusion
science

Healthcare Science: NHS Scientific Training Programme (STP)
Postgraduate

Audiology science
Neurophysiology
Ophthalmic and vision
science

Cardiac science
Gastrointestinal
physiology

Respiratory and sleep
science
Urodynamic science
Vascular science

Social Care Sector

Advice and Guidance
Undergraduate

Childhood studies and
guidance and counselling
Coaching and mentoring
Combined professional
studies

Counselling, coaching
and mentoring
Disability studies and
guidance and counselling
Guidance and counselling
and early years

Health in contemporary
society and guidance
counselling
Investment advice
Social welfare, law, policy
and advice practice

Postgraduate
Postgraduate Diploma; Master's degree in Career Guidance / Development / Education/
Coaching

Charity, Voluntary and International Development
Undergraduate

Business and
international development
Charity development
Development and
Globalisation
Development and Peace
Studies
Economics and
development studies
Education and
international development
Geography with
international development

Global Poverty and
Development
Human rights
International and
development economics
International development
International development
with economics
International development
with NGO management
International politics
International politics with
professional development

International relations
International relations and
global development
International Studies
Peace studies
Politics and charity
development
Politics and international
relations
Public services
Public services and public
sector management

Children and Youth Work
Youth Work
Undergraduate

Child and adolescent mental health

Child and adolescent studies

Child and youth studies

Childhood and youth studies

Childhood and youth: theory and practice

Childhood, youth and education studies

Children and young people's workforce

Children, young people and their services

Community and youth work studies

Community youth work

Criminology: youth justice

Physical education and youth sport

School, youth and community work and practical theology

Supporting young people

Working with children, young people and families

Working with young people and communities

Working with Young People and Communities

Young People, Communities and Society

Youth and community studies

Youth and community work

Youth justice studies

Youth work

Youth work and community development

Youth work and theology

Youth, Community and Families

Children
Undergraduate

Applied studies: children and youth work

Child and family studies

Childhood and youth studies

Childhood studies

Childhood studies and early years

Children and families

Children and family work and practical theology

Children and family work and theology

Children and integrated professional care

Children and young people

Children and young people in social care practitioner

Children and young people's services

Children and young people's workforce

Children, schools and families

Children, young people and their services

Children's care, learning and development

Early childhood studies

Early years

Early years care and education

Early years' play-work and education

Education and childhood studies

Family support and wellbeing

Positive practice with children and young people

School, youth and community work and practical theology

Working with children, young people and families

Community Justice
Undergraduate

Community policing and criminal investigation

Criminal investigations with policing studies

Criminology

Criminology and criminal justice studies

Criminology and sociology

Police and criminal justice studies

Policing studies

Youth and community work

Youth and community work: youth justice

Youth justice

Community Support
Undergraduate

Abuse studies
Adult health and social care
Adult social care
Advance practice work with children and families
Applied health and social care
Applied health and social science
Applied performance (community and education)
Care studies
Church community and theology
Community
Community and neighbourhood studies
Community and society
Community development

Community development and social care
Disability studies
Drama in the community
Family support and wellbeing
Global health and social medicine
Health and community studies
Health and social care
Health and social care management
Health and social care of adults
Health and social care studies
Health and social care supervision
Health and social care: rehabilitation
Health and social welfare

Health promotion
Health, community and social care studies
Health, wellbeing and community
Healthcare practice
Public and community services
Public health and social care
Social care
Social care practice
Social care studies
Social enterprise leadership
Social inclusion
Social policy
Social studies
Social work
Social work and applied social studies
Substance misuse

Social Arts, Social Science, Social Policy, Philosophy, Politics Sector

Philosophy
Undergraduate

Ethics
Humanities
Philosophy

Philosophy, politics and economics

Philosophy, politics and ethics
Theology

Politics
Undergraduate

American studies
American studies and politics
British politics
British politics and legislative studies
Business and globalisation
Business, management and public policy
Development and peace studies
Education and politics
Education and social policy
Education and social science
Elections, public opinion and parties

European politics
European social and political studies
European studies
Geopolitics
Global history and politics
Global politics
Government and economies
Government and European Union studies
Government and politics
Human rights
Human, social and political sciences
Humanities
International development
International political economy

International politics
International politics and intelligence studies
International politics and policy
International politics with professional development
International relations
International relations and history
International relations and law
International relations and politics
International relations and security studies

Politics continued
Undergraduate
Law with politics
Law, human rights and social justice
Middle Eastern studies
Peace studies
Policy, politics and economics
Political communication
Political economy
Political science
Politics
Politics and charity development
Politics and contemporary history

Politics and global studies
Politics and international relations with a language
Politics and philosophy
Politics with international relations
Politics with professional development
Politics with quantitative research methods
Politics, international studies and quantitative methods
Public service management

Public services
Public services and social justice
Public services and social justice
Russian studies: politics, economics, culture and society
War and security studies
War studies
War, peace and international relations

Sociology, Social Science, Social Policy and Social Research
Undergraduate
Applied health and social science
Applied social science
Applied social science and social policy
Applied social science: children and young people
Applied social science: crime and criminal justice
Applied social studies
Crime scene and investigative studies
Criminological studies with social care
Criminological studies with social science
Criminology
Criminology and criminal justice
Criminology with applied social science

Cultural studies
Economic and social history
Health and social care policy
Human, social and political sciences
Humanities
Language and society
Liberal arts
Public and social policy
Social and political studies
Social anthropology
Social history
Social media development
Social policy
Social policy (crime, policing and community justice)
Social policy (housing and communities)

Social policy and practice
Social policy with quantitative methods
Social policy with quantitative research methods
Social policy, health and housing
Social psychology
Social sciences
Social sciences: politics
Social studies
Social work
Sociology
Sociology with social policy
Statistical social research

Operational Research
Undergraduate
Business analysis and technology
Business technology
Data science
Life / medical science

Logistics and transport management
Mathematics and statistics

Mathematics operational research and statistics
Statistics

Sport Sector

Equestrian Sport
Undergraduate

Equestrian psychology and sports science
Equestrian sports science
Equine performance coaching
Equine science and sports performance
Equine sports coaching
Equine sports management
Equine sports performance
Equine sports therapy
Equine sports therapy and rehabilitation
Equine studies
Equitation and coaching
Equitation coaching
Sport horse management and coaching

Sport Coaching, Education, Psychology, Rehabilitation, Science and Therapy

Sport Coaching, Education, Psychology and Science
Undergraduate

Adventure leadership
Applied outdoor adventure
Ballet education
Children's physical education
Coach education
Community sports coaching
Dance education
Exercise, health and fitness
Exercise, health and wellbeing
Exercise, nutrition and health
Health and fitness
Health and personal training
Health related exercise and fitness
Health, exercise and physical activity
Outdoor activities
Outdoor and adventure education
Outdoor education
Physical activity, health and wellbeing
Physical education
Physical education and school sport
Physical education and sport
Physical education and youth sport
Primary education, physical education and sport
Sport and exercise
Sport and exercise psychology
Sport and exercise sciences
Sport and fitness studies
Sport and physical development
Sport and physical education
Sport coaching
Sport coaching and sports development
Sport fitness and personal training
Sport psychology
Sport psychology and coaching science
Sport, health and exercise sciences
Sport, health and physical education
Sport, physical education and development
Sports coaching and physical education
Sports coaching, education and development
Sports development and coaching science
Sports science
Sports studies
Teaching secondary education: physical education

Sport Therapy and Rehabilitation
Undergraduate

Physiotherapy
Rehabilitation work: visual impairment
Rehabilitation; sport therapy
Sport and dance therapy
Sport and exercise therapy
Sport and recreation management
Sport physiology
Sport rehabilitation
Sport therapy
Sports massage therapy
Sports therapy and rehabilitation
Sports therapy, health and fitness

Sports Development, Management, Media and Professional Specialist Sport

Sports Administration, Development, Management and Media
Undergraduate

Adventure media
Applied sports studies
Outdoor leisure
management
Sport

Sport and leisure
management
Sport journalism
Sport leisure surface
management
Sport management

Sports development
Sports history and culture
Sports management
Sports surface
management

Golf
Undergraduate

Applied golf management
studies
Golf club management
Golf coaching and
performance

Golf course management
Golf management
Golf performance
Professional golf

Sport coaching science
and tournament golf
Sports management
(golf)
Tournament golf

Football
Undergraduate

Applied football coaching
and performance
Business management:
sport and football
Coaching and
performance in football
Community football
coaching and
development
Football business
Football business and
finance

Football business and
marketing
Football business and
media
Football business
management and
coaching
Football coaching
Football coaching and
development
Football coaching and
performance
Football studies

International football
business management
Physical education and
football coaching with
Arsenal in the community
sports coaching
Science and football
Sport science with
professional football
coaching
Sports coaching practice:
football

Water Sports
Undergraduate

Coastal safety
management

Marine sports science
Operational yacht science

Transport and Logistics Sector

Logistics, Transport Planning and Management
Undergraduate

Air transport
management
Airline and aviation
management
Aviation and airport
management
Business and supply
chain management

Business logistics and
transport management
Business management
Business purchasing and
supply chain
management
Express logistics
Food logistics

International logistics and
trade finance
International supply chain
and procurement
management

Logistics, Transport Planning and Management continued
Undergraduate

International supply chain and shipping management
International trade and operations management
Logistics
Maritime transport and logistics
Supply chain management
Supply chain management with logistics

Transport
Transport and business management
Transport and infrastructure engineering
Transport and logistics management
Transport and sustainable development
Transport design
Transport engineering and planning
Transport management

Transport planning
Transport planning and engineering
Transport radio equipment maintenance
Transportation
Transportation engineering
Transportation planning and engineering
Transportation planning and policy

Air Industry; Air Industry Engineering and Technology
Undergraduate

Aeronautical and mechanical engineering
Aeronautical and mechanical manufacturing
Aeronautical engineering
Aeronautical systems
Aeronautical technology
Aeronautics and astronautics
Aeronautics and astronautics / computational engineering
Aeronautics and astronautics /aerodynamics
Aerospace engineering
Aerospace engineering manufacturing

Aerospace engineering with space technology
Aerospace systems
Aerospace systems engineering
Aerospace technology
Aerospace technology with management
Air transport engineering
Aircraft engineering
Aircraft engineering and air transport operations
Aircraft maintenance engineering
Aircraft maintenance, repair and overhaul
Astronautics
Aviation technology and management
Avionic systems

Avionics and aerospace systems
Avionics and space systems
Avionics systems engineering
Avionics technology
Electronic engineering with space systems
Mechanical engineering: aerospace
Mechanical engineering with aeronautics
Space systems engineering
Mechanical engineering: aerospace

Air Industry Management
Undergraduate

Air transport management
Airline and aviation management

Airline, airport and aviation management
Aviation and airport management
Aviation management

Aviation management and operations
Air safety management
Airline and airport management

Aircraft Pilot
Undergraduate

Air transport with commercial pilot training
Air transport with pilot training
Air transport with private pilot training

Aircraft engineering with pilot studies
Aviation engineering with pilot studies
Aviation technology with pilot studies

Professional aviation pilot practice: helicopter
Avionics systems with pilot studies
Professional aviation pilot practice

236

Marine Industry Engineering and Technology
Undergraduate

Applied geology
Applied geotechnics
Civil engineering
Coastal engineering
Data mining
Drilling and well engineering
Earthquake and offshore engineering
Energy engineering
Environment and sustainable technology
Environmental and civil engineering
Environmental and ecological engineering
Environmental and energy engineering
Environmental biogeochemistry
Environmental biotechnology
Environmental civil engineering
Environmental coastal engineering
Environmental engineering
Environmental engineering with land and water
Environmental forensics
Environmental geology
Environmental Management
Environmental technology
Flood risk
Geodetic surveying
Geo-environmental engineering
Geographical information systems
Geological engineering
Geology and exploration of mineral sources
Geotechnical engineering
Hydro-environment engineering
Hydroinformatics

Hydrology and water resources management
Infrastructure: wind farm development
Marine and offshore engineering
Marine and offshore power systems
Marine and offshore technology
Marine engineering
Marine engineering with naval architecture
Marine power plant
Marine renewable energy
Marine systems engineering
Marine systems technology
Marine technology
Marine technology with naval architecture
Maritime civil engineering
Maritime technology
Mechanical engineering with subsea technologies
Mechanical engineering: automotive
Mechanical engineering: marine technology
Naval architecture
Naval architecture and marine engineering
Naval architecture and small craft engineering
Naval architecture with high performance marine vehicles
Naval architecture with high performance marine vehicles
Naval architecture with marine engineering
Naval architecture with ocean engineering
Naval architecture with ocean engineering
Naval architecture with offshore engineering

Naval architecture: shipbuilding
Naval engineering
Navigation and maritime science
Navigation technology
Nuclear engineering
Nuclear technology
Ocean exploration and surveying
Ocean science
Ocean science and marine conservation
Off road vehicle design
Offshore engineering
Oil and gas engineering
Oilfield corrosion engineering
Operational yacht science
Packaging technology
Performance car technology
Petroleum engineering
Petroleum products engineering
Pharmaceutical engineering
Physical geography
Physics
Pipeline engineering
Polymer engineering
Process engineering
Product design engineering
Production engineering
Propulsion and engine systems engineering
Quarrying
Racing engine design
Renewable energy
Renewable energy and sustainability
Renewable energy engineering
Renewable energy systems technology
Reservoir engineering
Ship science
Ship science / naval architecture

Marine Industry Engineering and Technology continued
Undergraduate

Ship science/ naval engineering

Shipping and port management

Subsea engineering

Sustainable energy

Sustainable engineering

Thermal power

Thermal power and fluids engineering

Thermal power: aerospace propulsion

Thermal power: gas turbine technology

Thermal power: power propulsion and the environment

Vehicle operations management

Warship naval architecture

Water and environmental engineering

Water engineering

Water sanitation and health engineering

Water supply and water disposal

Water supply and water waste

Water technology and management

Water, energy and the environment

Water, energy and waste

Yacht and power-craft design and production

Yacht design

Marine Industry Management
Undergraduate

International supply chain and shipping management

Marine operations / management / Nautical science:

Leading to the award of a UK Maritime and coastguard Agency (MCA) Deck Officer Certificate of Competency (CoC) Standards for

Training Certification and Watch keeping (STCW) II/1 Officer of the Watch (OOW)

Rail Industry
Rail Industry Engineering and Technology
Undergraduate

Civil and railway engineering

Civil engineering

Construction

Electrical engineering

Electronic engineering

Mechanical and railway engineering

Mechanical engineering

Railway engineering

Railway systems engineering

Signal processing

Road Industry
Road Industry Engineering and Technology
Undergraduate

Automatic control

Automation

Automation systems engineering

Automobile engineering

Automobile roads and airfields

Automotive and motorsports engineering

Automotive and transport design

Automotive calibration and control

Automotive design

Automotive diagnostics and management principles

Automotive electronic engineering

Automotive electronic technology

Automotive electronics

Automotive engineering

Automotive engineering and technology

Automotive engineering design

Automotive manufacturing

Automotive materials

Automotive systems engineering

Automotive technology

Autosport engineering and technology

Control and automation engineering

Mechanical and automotive engineering

Mechanical and vehicle protection

Motorcycle engineering

Motorsport engineering

Motorsports technology

5.4 Professional Organisations: Accredited Undergraduate and Postgraduate Courses

Higher Education Course Professional Recognition

All approved higher education qualifications will be accredited by a recognised university or college. However, some professions require you to have a professional qualification before you can work in a specific job role and these may be a higher education qualification accredited by a university and / or a qualification accredited by a professional body.

Some accredited professional qualifications may be at higher education level as an undergraduate level 4, 5 or 6 (FHEQ); graduate level 6 (FHEQ) (for graduates in other subjects who are required to undertake a degree) and / or postgraduate level 7 or 8 (FHEQ). Professionally accredited courses are available in universities and colleges of higher education as well as some being available in training centres or by distance learning providers.

Other accredited qualifications may be at further education level 1, 2 or 3 (RQF) or level 6/7 (SCQF). Professionally accredited courses at this level are available in colleges of further education, training centres or by distance learning providers.

Some professional organisations provide accredited training courses that aren't linked to higher education courses, although having a higher education qualification may be advantageous and you may be able to undertake higher level professional qualifications if you possess a bachelor's degree or postgraduate qualification.

Membership or registration with a professional organisation may be a requirement to practice in a particular career, whereas other membership may be optional or advantageous. Membership may be at varying levels dependent on your qualifications and experience, with

some offering Chartered status and others also having Fellowship, Associateship, Incorporated, Registered or Technician status. Many professional organisations also have student membership options.

The following highlights the different professional requirements which are essential or optional with the relevant professional bodies and websites.

Essential Higher Education Courses Which are also Accredited by Professional Bodies

All specific higher education qualifications at undergraduate, graduate and / or postgraduate level are also accredited by a relevant professional body and the qualification is an essential requirement to work in a specified career. Careers include architecture, surveying, town planning, medicine, dentistry, pharmacy, nursing, veterinary science and primary or secondary teaching.

Sometimes more than one professional organisation may accredit the same higher education subject. Some professions require membership or registration with the relevant professional organisation/s to enable you to practice. The relevant professional body will have information about accredited higher education courses listed on the website in addition the professional accreditation will be highlighted on the university website.

Essential Graduate or Postgraduate Courses Accredited by Professional Bodies Which are Required Before Undertaking Additional Professional Qualifications

You may need an accredited bachelor's degree or if you have a non-accredited degree, you will need a graduate or postgraduate 'conversion' qualification before you can undertake professional postgraduate qualifications such as for careers in law or psychology.

If you have a non-accredited bachelor's degree, you may be able to take a 'conversion' course at graduate certificate or diploma; or postgraduate certificate, diploma or master's level. The relevant professional body will have information about accredited higher education courses listed on the website.

Optional Higher Education Courses With Some Courses Accredited by Professional Bodies

Some higher education qualifications at undergraduate and / or postgraduate level may be accredited by a relevant professional body and undertaking a professionally accredited course is an option to work in a specific career, undertaking a non-accredited higher education qualification will still allow you to work in that career, such as for careers involving information technology, art, business management or project management. The relevant professional body will have information about accredited higher education courses listed on the website.

Some Higher Education Courses Accredited by Some Professional Bodies Allowing for Exemptions From the Professional Qualifications

Some higher education qualifications at undergraduate or postgraduate level may be accredited with a professional body and will also provide exemptions from some professional training. You may still enter the career with a non-accredited professional higher education qualification but may not get exemptions from the professional body examinations, such as for careers involving accountancy or actuarial science. The relevant professional body will have information about accredited higher education courses listed on the website.

Some Higher Education Courses Which are Recognised or Endorsed by Some Professional Bodies

all higher education qualifications at undergraduate and / or postgraduate level may be recognised or endorsed but not accredited by a relevant professional body and undertaking a professionally recognised course is an option to work in a specific career, although such courses that aren't endorsed may still be valued by employers, such as for careers involving geography or biology. The relevant professional body will have information about recognised higher education courses listed on the website.

Listed Higher Education Subjects are Highlighted by Some Professional Bodies

Some or all higher education qualifications at undergraduate and / or postgraduate level may be highlighted by a professional body. These courses are not accredited by the professional body and undertaking a non-listed course will also give you an option to work in a specific career. The relevant professional body will have information about listed higher education courses on the website and there may be additional courses not included in the list that are appropriate. Further information may be found in part 2, the Jobs and Professional Qualifications section.

The following highlights higher education courses at undergraduate, graduate and postgraduate level which are also accredited or endorsed by professional bodies.

1. Agriculture and Plants Sector

Forestry: Undergraduate and Postgraduate
Some courses professionally accredited with:
Institute of Chartered Foresters   http://www.charteredforesters.org
Chartered Forester
Chartered Arboriculturist

Garden Design: Undergraduate and Postgraduate
Some courses professionally accredited with:
The Landscape Institute   http://www.landscapeinstitute.org
Chartered Landscape Architect
International Federation of Landscape Architects   http://iflaonline.org/

Horticulture
Courses recognised with:
Chartered Institute of Horticulture   https://www.horticulture.org.uk/
Chartered Horticulturalist

Land Management: Undergraduate and Postgraduate
Some courses professionally accredited with:
Royal Institution of Chartered Surveyors   http://www.rics.org/uk/
Chartered Surveyor

Land Management: Postgraduate
Some courses professionally accredited with: with:
Institute of Agricultural Engineers   http://www.iagre.org/

2. Animals and Conservation Sector

Animal Biology and Conservation: Undergraduate
Some courses professionally accredited with:
Royal Society of Biology   https://www.rsb.org.uk/

Animal Nutrition: Undergraduate and Postgraduate
Some courses professionally accredited with:
Association for Nutrition: Nutrition   http://www.associationfornutrition.org

Biological Science: Animal Behaviour and Welfare: Undergraduate
Some courses professionally accredited with:
Royal Society of Biology   https://www.rsb.org.uk/

Ecology and Environmental Conservation: Undergraduate and Postgraduate
Some courses professionally accredited with:
Chartered Institute of Ecology and Environmental
Management (CIEEM)   http://www.cieem.net
Chartered Environmentalist
Chartered Ecologist

Ecology: Undergraduate
Some courses professionally accredited with:
Royal Society of Biology   https://www.rsb.org.uk/

Marine Biology: Undergraduate
Some courses professionally accredited with:
Royal Society of Biology   https://www.rsb.org.uk/

Zoology: Undergraduate
Some courses professionally accredited with:
Royal Society of Biology   https://www.rsb.org.uk/

Veterinary Medicine / Science: Undergraduate and Graduate
Professional accreditation is a requirement with:
Royal College of Veterinary Surgeons   http://www.rcvs.org.uk/
Registered Veterinary Surgeon

3.   Art and Design Sector
Fashion / Textile Design: Undergraduate
Some courses professionally accredited with:
Chartered Society of Designers   http://www.csd.org.uk
Chartered Designer

Graphic Design: Undergraduate
Some courses professionally accredited with:
Chartered Society of Designers   http://www.csd.org.uk
Chartered Designer

Interior Design / Spatial Design: Undergraduate
Some courses professionally accredited with:
Chartered Society of Designers   http://www.csd.org.uk
Chartered Designer

Jewellery: Undergraduate
Gemmology and Jewellery Studies
One course professionally accredited with:
The Gemmological Association of Great Britain   http://www.gem-a.com

Medical Illustration: Postgraduate
Registration with
Academy for Healthcare Science   https://www.ahcs.ac.uk/
Registered Medical Illustrator

Medical Photography: Postgraduate
Registration with
Academy for Healthcare Science   https://www.ahcs.ac.uk/
Registered Medical Photographer

Product Design: Undergraduate
Some courses professionally accredited with:
Chartered Society of Designers   http://www.csd.org.uk
Chartered Designer

Theatre Design: Undergraduate
Some courses professionally accredited with:
Chartered Society of Designers   http://www.csd.org.uk
Chartered Designer
Some courses professionally accredited with:
Drama UK   http://www.dramauk.co.uk

4.   Building Design, Planning, Surveying and Construction Sector
Architectural / Building Technology: Undergraduate and Postgraduate
Professional accreditation is a requirement with:
Chartered Institute of Architectural Technologists   http://www.ciat.org.uk
Chartered Architectural Technologist
Some courses professionally accredited with:
Chartered Institute of Building   http://www.ciob.org/
Chartered Builder
Chartered Construction Manager

Architecture ARB / RIBA part 1: Undergraduate
Professional accreditation is a requirement with:
Architects Registration Board (ARB)   http://www.arb.org.uk
Royal Institute of British Architecture   http://www.architecture.com

Architecture ARB / RIBA part 2: Postgraduate
Professional accreditation is a requirement with:
Architects Registration Board (ARB)   http://www.arb.org.uk
Royal Institute of British Architecture   http://www.architecture.com
Chartered Architect

Construction / Management: Undergraduate and Postgraduate
Some courses professionally accredited with:
Association for Project Management APM   http://www.apm.org.uk
Registered Project Manager
Chartered Project Manager
Chartered Institute of Building   http://www.ciob.org/
Chartered Builder
Chartered Construction Manager
Royal Institution of Chartered Surveyors (RICS)   http://www.rics.org
Chartered Surveyor
Project Management Institute   http://www.pmi.org/

Landscape Architecture: Undergraduate and Postgraduate
Professional accreditation is a requirement with:
Landscape Institute   http://www.landscapeinstitute.co.uk/
Chartered Landscape Architect
International Federation of Landscape Architects   http://iflaonline.org/

Surveying: Undergraduate and Postgraduate
Construction / Building /Quantity; Land; Property (including Art and Antiques)
Professional accreditation is a requirement with:
Royal Institution of Chartered Surveyors (RICS)   http://www.ricscourses.org/Course/
Chartered Surveyor
Some courses professionally accredited with:
Chartered Institution of Civil Engineering Surveyors   https://www.cices.org/
Chartered Civil Engineer

Town Planning: Undergraduate and Postgraduate
Professional accreditation is a requirement with:
Royal Town Planning Institute (RTPI)   http://www.rtpi.org.uk
Chartered Town Planner

5.   Building Property Management and Housing Sector
Housing: Undergraduate and Postgraduate
Undergraduate approved qualification may provide exemption from some of the
professionally accredited training courses
Chartered Institute of Housing (CIH)   http://www.cih.org
Chartered Housing Member

Real Estate (also see Surveying): Undergraduate and Postgraduate
Professional accreditation is a requirement with:
Royal Institution of Chartered Surveyors (RICS)   http://www.rics.org
Chartered Surveyor

6.   Business Finance; Economics; Mathematics; Statistics Sector
Accounting and Finance: Undergraduate and Postgraduate
Approved undergraduate or postgraduate qualification may provide exemption from some of
the professionally accredited training courses
Institute of Chartered Accountants England and Wales ICAEW http://www.icaew.com
Institute of Chartered Accountants Scotland ICAS   http://icas.org.uk
Chartered Accountants Ireland CAI   http://www.charteredaccountants.ie
Association of Chartered Certified Accountants ACCA http://www.accaglobal.com
Chartered Institute of Management Accountants CIMA http://www.cimaglobal.com
Chartered Institute of Public Finance Accountancy CIPFAhttp://www.cipfa.org/
Chartered Institute of Taxation   http://www.tax.org.uk
Chartered Accountant

Actuarial Science: Undergraduate and Postgraduate
Approved undergraduate or postgraduate qualification may provide exemption from some of
the professionally accredited training courses
Institute of Faculty of Actuaries   http://www.actuaries.org.uk
Chartered Enterprise Risk Actuary
Certified Actuarial Analyst

Banking and Finance: Postgraduate
Some postgraduate courses are professionally accredited and may provide exemption from
some of the professionally accredited training courses
Chartered Banker Institute   http://www.charteredbanker.com
Chartered Banker

Mathematics: Undergraduate and Postgraduate
Some courses professionally accredited with:
Institute of Mathematics and its Applications   http://www.ima.org.uk
Chartered Mathematician

Statistics: Undergraduate and Postgraduate
Some courses professionally accredited with: courses
Royal Statistical Society (RSS)   http://www.rss.org.uk
Chartered Statistician

7. Business Management and Administration; Human Resources and Recruitment Sector

Human Resource Management: Undergraduate and Postgraduate

Some accredited undergraduate and postgraduate courses with some in universities and others in training centres.

Professional accreditation is a requirement with:

Chartered Institute of Personnel and Development   http://www.cipd.co.uk
Chartered Member

Management: Undergraduate and Postgraduate

Some courses offered in some universities, colleges and training centres professionally accredited with:

Chartered Management Institute   http://www.managers.org.uk/
Chartered Manager

Master's of Business Management (some specialist subjects available): Postgraduate

Some are professionally accredited
Association of MBAs   http://www.mbaworld.com

Project management: Undergraduate and Postgraduate

Some courses professionally accredited with:
Association for Project Management APM   http://www.apm.org.uk
Registered Project Manager
Chartered Project Manager

8. Education and Teacher Training Sector

Teaching English as a Foreign Language (TEFL) /Teaching English as a Second or Other Language (TESOL): Undergraduate and Postgraduate

Professional accreditation is a requirement with:
Cambridge English Language Assessment   http://www.cambridgeenglish.org
Trinity College London   http://www.trinitycollege.co.uk/
Or a teacher training course leading to a Teacher Training qualification with QTS

Primary Teaching QTS: Undergraduate and Postgraduate

Professional accreditation is a requirement with:
UK Teaching Registration Councils
England: Department for Education and Teaching Regulation Agency
https://www.gov.uk/government/organisations/department-for-education
Wales: General Teaching Council Wales   http://www.gtcw.org.uk
Northern Ireland: General Teaching Council Northern Ireland   http://www.gtcni.org.uk
Scotland: General Teaching Council Scotland   http://www.gtcs.org.uk
Registered Teacher

Secondary Teaching QTS: Undergraduate and Postgraduate

Professional accreditation is a requirement with:
UK Teaching Registration Councils
England: Department for Education and Teaching Regulation Agency
https://www.gov.uk/government/organisations/department-for-education
Wales: General Teaching Council Wales   http://www.gtcw.org.uk
Northern Ireland: General Teaching Council Northern Ireland   http://www.gtcni.org.uk
Scotland: General Teaching Council Scotland   http://www.gtcs.org.uk
Registered Primary or Secondary Teacher

Teacher Training: Further and Adult Education: Undergraduate
Level 3, 4 and 5 Diploma
Professional accreditation is a requirement with a range of awarding organisations.
Postgraduate course: Professional Graduate Certificate / Diploma of Education PGCE /
PGDE (1 year) / Post Compulsory Education and Training Teaching (PCET)
Professional accreditation is a requirement with higher education institutions:
Check with:
FE Advice   https://www.feadvice.org.uk/

Teacher Training: Further and Adult Education: Undergraduate and Postgraduate
Qualifications approved by:
England
Society for Education and Training (SET)   https://set.et-foundation.co.uk/
Wales
Education Workforce Council (EWC): Wales   http://www.ewc.wales/
Northern Ireland
Government, Northern Ireland: Department for the Economy
https://www.economy-ni.gov.uk/topics/further-education/qualifications-required-teach-further-education
Scotland
Scotland: General Teaching Council Scotland   http://www.gtcs.org.uk

Higher Education Lecturing; Further Education Lecturing: Postgraduate
Teaching and Learning in Higher Education postgraduate Certificate; Diploma; Master's
Professional accreditation is a requirement with:
The Higher Education Academy   https://www.heacademy.ac.uk/
Lecturers are usually required to have a doctorate degree or working towards. Not all
lecturers will be required to undertake the Teaching and Learning in Higher Education
postgraduate course.

9.   Engineering and Technology Sector
To qualify and practice as a registered engineer you would need to undertake a qualification
professionally accredited and approved by the Engineering Council and the relevant
engineering professional body licensed or affiliated with the Engineering Council.
Engineering Council   http://www.engc.org.uk/
Chartered Engineer (CEng)
Incorporated Engineer (IEng),
Engineering Technician (Eng Tech)
Information and Communication Technology Technician (ICTTech)

The following professional bodies accredit or approve higher education qualifications and
some approve additional qualifications

Environment Sector
Agricultural Engineering: Undergraduate and Postgraduate
Professional accreditation is a requirement with:
Engineering Council   http://www.engc.org.uk/
Institution of Agricultural Engineers IAgrE   http://www.iagre.org

Architectural Engineering: Undergraduate and Postgraduate
Professional accreditation is a requirement with:
The Engineering Council   http://www.engc.org.uk
Some courses professionally accredited with:
Institution of Civil Engineers   http://www.ice.org.uk
Some courses professionally accredited with:
Institution of Structural Engineers ISTRUCTE   http://www.istructe.org
Some courses professionally accredited with:
Institution of Mechanical Engineers IMECHE   http://www.imeche.org
Some courses professionally accredited with:
Energy Institute EI   https://www.energyinst.org/

Biomedical (Clinical) / Medical / Engineering / Medical Physics: Undergraduate and Postgraduate
Professional accreditation is a requirement with:
Engineering Council   http://www.engc.org.uk/
Institute of Physics and Engineering in Medicine IPEM http://www.ipem.ac.uk/

Building / Services Engineering: Undergraduate and Postgraduate
Professional accreditation is a requirement with:
The Engineering Council   http://www.engc.org.uk
Some courses professionally accredited with:
Energy Institute EI   https://www.energyinst.org/
Chartered Association of Building Engineers CBUILDE http://www.cbuilde.com

Chemical Engineering: Undergraduate and Postgraduate
Professional accreditation is a requirement with:
Engineering Council   http://www.engc.org.uk/
Some courses professionally accredited with:
Institution of Chemical Engineers IChemE   http://www.icheme.org/
Some courses professionally accredited with:
Energy Institute   https://www.energyinst.org

Civil / Structural Engineering: Undergraduate and Postgraduate
Requirement of
Professionally accredited
Engineering Council   http://www.engc.org.uk/
Institution of Civil Engineers   https://www.ice.org.uk/
Institution of Structural Engineers   https://www.istructe.org/

Computer Systems Engineering; Communications Systems Engineering: Undergraduate and Postgraduate
Professional accreditation is a requirement with:
Engineering Council   http://www.engc.org.uk/

Control Engineering: Undergraduate and Postgraduate
Professional accreditation is a requirement with:
Engineering Council   http://www.engc.org.uk/

Design / Manufacturing Engineering: Undergraduate and Postgraduate
Professional accreditation is a requirement with:
Engineering Council   http://www.engc.org.uk/
Some courses professionally accredited with:
Institution of Engineering Designers IED   http://www.ied.org.uk

Electrical and Electronic Engineering; Electrical Power Engineering: Undergraduate and Postgraduate
Professional accreditation is a requirement with:
Engineering Council   http://www.engc.org.uk/
Some
Energy Institute   https://www.energyinst.org

Engineering Project Management: Postgraduate
Professional accreditation is a requirement with:
Engineering Council   http://www.engc.org.uk/
Some courses professionally accredited with:
Association for Project Management APM   http://www.apm.org.uk
Royal Institution of Chartered Surveyors (RICS)   http://www.rics.org
Project Management Institute   http://www.pmi.org/

Engineering Science: Undergraduate and Postgraduate
Professional accreditation is a requirement with:
Engineering Council   http://www.engc.org.uk/

Environment / Water Engineering: Undergraduate and Postgraduate
Professional accreditation is a requirement with:
Engineering Council   http://www.engc.org.uk/
Some courses professionally accredited with:
Chartered Institution of Water and
Environmental Management CIWEM   http://www.ciwem.org.uk

Fire Engineering: Undergraduate and Postgraduate
Professional accreditation is a requirement with:
Engineering Council   http://www.engc.org.uk/
Some courses professionally accredited with:
Energy Institute EI   https://www.energyinst.org/

Materials / Minerals / Mining Engineering: Undergraduate and Postgraduate
Professional accreditation is a requirement with:
Engineering Council   http://www.engc.org.uk/
Some courses professionally accredited with:
Institute of Materials, Minerals and Mining IOM3   http://www.iom3.org/
Some courses professionally accredited with:
Energy Institute EI   https://www.energyinst.org/

Mechanical Engineering: Undergraduate and Postgraduate
Professional accreditation is a requirement with:
Engineering Council   http://www.engc.org.uk/
Some courses professionally accredited with:
Energy Institute   https://www.energyinst.org
Institution of Mechanical Engineers IMECHE   http://www.imeche.org

Metallurgy Engineering: Undergraduate and Postgraduate
Professional accreditation is a requirement with:
Engineering Council   http://www.engc.org.uk/
Some courses accredited with
Institute of Materials, Minerals and Mining   http://www.iom3.org/accreditation

Nuclear Engineering: Undergraduate and Postgraduate
Professional accreditation is a requirement with:
Engineering Council   http://www.engc.org.uk/
Some courses links
Nuclear Institute   http://www.nuclearinst.com

Petroleum /Oil and Gas Engineering: Undergraduate and Postgraduate
Professional accreditation is a requirement with:
Engineering Council   http://www.engc.org.uk/
Some courses professionally accredited with:
Energy Institute   https://www.energyinst.org

Product Engineering Design: Undergraduate and Postgraduate
Professional accreditation is a requirement with:
Engineering Council   http://www.engc.org.uk/
Some courses professionally accredited with:
Institution of Engineering Designers IED   http://www.ied.org.uk

Transport Engineering: Automotive; Aviation; Marine; Railway; Road Transport and Mechanical Engineering: Undergraduate and Postgraduate
Professional accreditation is a requirement with:
Engineering Council   http://www.engc.org.uk/

Aeronautical Engineering / Aerospace Engineering / Astronautics: Undergraduate and Postgraduate
Professional accreditation is a requirement with:
Engineering Council   http://www.engc.org.uk/
Some courses professionally accredited with:
Royal Aeronautical Society AEROSOCIETY   http://www.aerosociety.com
Some courses professionally accredited with:
Institution of Mechanical Engineers IMECHE   http://www.imeche.org

Aircraft Engineering with Pilot Studies: Undergraduate
Professional accreditation is a requirement with:
Engineering Council   http://www.engc.org.uk/

Marine Engineering / Technology/ Naval Architecture: Undergraduate and Postgraduate
Professional accreditation is a requirement with:
Engineering Council   http://www.engc.org.uk/
Institute of Marine Engineering, Science and Technology IMarEST http://www.imarest.org/

Civil and Railway Engineering: Undergraduate and Postgraduate
Professional accreditation is a requirement with:
Engineering Council   http://www.engc.org.uk/

Automotive and Motorsports Engineering: Undergraduate and Postgraduate
Professional accreditation is a requirement with:
Engineering Council   http://www.engc.org.uk/

10. Environment Sector

Environmental Science: Undergraduate and Postgraduate
Some courses professionally accredited with:
Institution of Environmental Science   https://www.the-ies.org
Chartered Institution of Water and
Environmental Management CIWEM   http://www.ciwem.org
Chartered Environmental Scientist
Environmental Science: Undergraduate
Some courses professionally accredited with:
Royal Society of Biology   https://www.rsb.org.uk/

Geographical Information Science / Systems / Mapping Science: Undergraduate and Postgraduate
Some courses professionally accredited with: by
Royal Institution of Chartered Surveyors   http://www.rics.org/uk/
Chartered Surveyor
Chartered Institution of Civil Engineering Surveyors https://www.cices.org/
Chartered Civil Engineer

Geography: Undergraduate and Postgraduate
Courses recognised with:
Royal Geographical Society   http://www.rgs.org/
Chartered Geographer

Geology: Undergraduate and Postgraduate
Some courses professionally accredited with:
The Geological Society   http://www.geolsoc.org.uk
Chartered Geologist
Chartered Scientist

Hydrology: Postgraduate
Some courses professionally accredited with: accepted
Chartered Institution of Water and Environmental Management http://www.ciwem.org/
Chartered Water and Environmental Manager
Engineering Council   http://www.engc.org.uk/
Chartered Engineer
Society for the Environment   http://socenv.org.uk/
Chartered Environmentalist
Science Council   https://sciencecouncil.org/
Chartered Scientist
Royal Meteorological Society   https://www.rmets.org/
Chartered Meteorologist
Royal Geographical Society   http://www.rgs.org/
Chartered Geographer

Meteorology: Undergraduate and Postgraduate
Courses recognised with:
Royal Meteorological Society   https://www.rmets.org/

Oceanography and Hydrography: Undergraduate and Postgraduate
Some courses professionally accredited with:
Institute of Marine Engineering, Science and Technology http://www.imarest.org/
Royal Institution of Chartered Surveyors   http://www.rics.org/uk/
Chartered Institute of Civil Engineering Surveyors https://www.cices.org/

11.   Healthcare Sector
Allied Healthcare

Art Psychotherapy / Art Therapy MA: Postgraduate
Professional accreditation and registration is a requirement with:
Allied Health Profession Federation   http://www.ahpf.org.uk
Health and Care Professions Council   http://www.hcpc-uk.org
British Association of Art Therapists   http://www.baat.org
Registered Art Therapist / Art Psychotherapist

Dramatherapy MA: Postgraduate
Professional accreditation and registration is a requirement with:
Allied Health Profession Federation   http://www.ahpf.org.uk
Health and Care Professions Council   http://www.hcpc-uk.org
British Association of Drama Therapists   https://badth.org.uk
Registered Drama-therapist

Dietetics: Undergraduate and Postgraduate
Professional accreditation and registration is a requirement with:
Allied Health Profession Federation   http://www.ahpf.org.uk
Health and Care Professions Council   http://www.hcpc-uk.org
Association of UK Dieticians   https://www.bda.uk.com
Registered Dietician

Occupational Therapy: Undergraduate and Postgraduate
Professional accreditation and registration is a requirement with:
Allied Health Profession Federation   http://www.ahpf.org.uk
Health and Care Professions Council   http://www.hcpc-uk.org
British Association and College of Occupational Therapists http://www.cot.co.uk
Registered Occupational Therapist

Orthoptics: Undergraduate
Professional accreditation and registration is a requirement with:
Allied Health Profession Federation   http://www.ahpf.org.uk
Health and Care Professions Council   http://www.hcpc-uk.org
British and Irish Orthoptic society   http://www.orthoptics.org.uk
Registered Orthoptist

Paramedic Science: Undergraduate
Professional accreditation and registration is a requirement with:
Allied Health Profession Federation   http://www.ahpf.org.uk
Health and Care Professions Council   http://www.hcpc-uk.org
College of Paramedics   https://www.collegeofparamedics.co.uk
Registered Paramedic

Physiotherapy: Undergraduate and Postgraduate
Professional accreditation and registration is a requirement with:
Allied Health Profession Federation   http://www.ahpf.org.uk
Health and Care Professions Council   http://www.hcpc-uk.org
Chartered Society of Physiotherapy   http://www.csp.org.uk/
Registered Chartered Physiotherapist

Podiatry / Chiropody: Undergraduate
Professional accreditation and registration is a requirement with:
Allied Health Profession Federation http://www.ahpf.org.uk
Health and Care Professions Council http://www.hcpc-uk.org
College of Podiatry http://www.scpod.org
Registered Podiatrist

Prosthetics/ Orthotics: Undergraduate
Professional accreditation and registration is a requirement with:
Allied Health Profession Federation http://www.ahpf.org.uk
Health and Care Professions Council http://www.hcpc-uk.org
British Association of Prosthetists and Orthotists http://www.bapo.com
Registered Prosthetist / Orthotist

Radiography: Undergraduate and Postgraduate
Professional accreditation and registration is a requirement with:
Allied Health Profession Federation http://www.ahpf.org.uk
Health and Care Professions Council http://www.hcpc-uk.org
Society and College of Radiographers Diagnostic and Therapeutichttps://www.sor.org
Registered Radiographer

Speech and Language Therapy: Undergraduate and Postgraduate
Professional accreditation and registration is a requirement with:
Allied Health Profession Federation http://www.ahpf.org.uk
Health and Care Professions Council http://www.hcpc-uk.org
Royal College of Speech and Language Therapists http://www.rcslt.org
Registered Speech and Language Therapist

Alternative Health, Complementary and Creative Therapy
Acupuncture: Undergraduate and Postgraduate
Requirement of professional accreditation
British Acupuncture Accreditation Board (BAAB) http://www.baab.co.uk
Registered acupuncturist

Complementary Therapies: Undergraduate
May need to register with a holistic therapy accredited body such as:
Complementary and Natural Healthcare Council (CNHC) http://www.cnhc.org.uk/

Dance Movement Therapy: Postgraduate
Professional accreditation is a requirement with:
Association for Dance Movement Psychotherapy UKhttp://www.admt.org.uk
Registered Dance Movement Therapist

Nutrition / Therapy: Undergraduate and Postgraduate
Some courses professionally accredited with:
Association for Nutrition http://www.associationfornutrition.org

Complementary Medicine
Chiropractor (some lead to an integrated master's degree): Undergraduate
Professional accreditation is a requirement with:
General Chiropractic Council http://www.gcc-uk.org
Chiropractor specialism: Postgraduate
Professional accreditation is a requirement with:
General Chiropractic Council http://www.gcc-uk.org
Registered Chiropractor

252

Osteopathic Medicine (some lead to an integrated master's degree): Undergraduate and Graduate
Professional accreditation is a requirement with:
General Osteopathic Council http://www.osteopathy.org.uk
Registered Osteopath

Dentistry; Medicine; Nursing and Midwifery; Operating Department; Optometry; Pharmacy

Dentistry: Undergraduate and Graduate
Professional accreditation is a requirement with:
British Dental Association https://www.bda.org
Registered Dentist

Dental Hygiene and Therapy: Undergraduate
Professional accreditation is a requirement with:
British Dental Association https://www.bda.org
Registered Dental Hygienist

Dental Nursing (Cert HE / Fd Degree): Undergraduate
Professional accreditation is a requirement with:
British Dental Association https://www.bda.org
Registered Dental Nurse

Dental Technology: Undergraduate
Professional accreditation is a requirement with:
British Dental Association https://www.bda.org
Registered Dentist al Technologist

Medicine: Undergraduate and Graduate
Professional accreditation is a requirement with:
General Medical Council (GMC) http://www.gmc-uk.org
Registered Doctor of Medicine

Physician Associate: Postgraduate
Professional accreditation is a requirement with:
Faculty of Physician Associates: Royal College of Physicians http://www.fparcp.co.uk/

Nursing and Midwifery: Undergraduate and Postgraduate
Adult Nursing; Learning Disabilities Nursing; Mental Health Nursing; Paediatrics / Children's Nursing; Midwifery
Professional accreditation is a requirement with:
Nursing and Midwifery Council http://www.nmc-uk.org
Registered Nurse
Registered Midwife
Specialist Nurse Training: Postgraduate
Professional accreditation is a requirement with:
Nursing and Midwifery Council http://www.nmc-uk.org
Registered Nurse

Operating Department Practice: Undergraduate
Professional accreditation is a requirement with:
Health Care Professions Council http://www.hcpc-uk.org
Registered Operating Department Practitioner

Optometry; Ophthalmic Dispensing Optician: Undergraduate
Requirement of professional accreditation
General Optical Council (GOC)   https://www.optical.org
Registered Optometrist

Pharmacy (leads to a master's degree): Undergraduate
Professional accreditation is a requirement with:
General Pharmaceutical Council (GPhC)   http://www.pharmacyregulation.org
Registered Pharmacist

Sonography: Postgraduate
Professional accreditation is a requirement with:
Consortium for the Accreditation of Sonographic Education http://www.case-uk.org/
Registered Sonographer

Public Health; Environmental Health; Health Promotion;
Environmental Health: Undergraduate and Postgraduate
Professional accreditation is a requirement with:
Chartered Institute of Environmental Health (CIEH)   http://www.cieh.org
Chartered Environmental Health Practitioner

Ergonomics: Undergraduate (from 2017) Postgraduate
Professional accreditation is a requirement with:
Chartered Institute of Ergonomics and Human Factors http://www.ergonomics.org.uk
Registered Chartered Ergonomist

Occupational Health: Undergraduate and Postgraduate
Professional accreditation is a requirement with:
Institution of Occupational Safety and Health (IOSH) https://www.iosh.co.uk/
Registered Occupational Health Practitioner

12.   History, Anthropology and Archaeology Sector
Conservation Studies: Undergraduate and Postgraduate
Not professionally accredited but courses confirmed that meet the professional standards in conservation
Institute of Conservation   http://www.icon.org.uk

Historic Building Conservation: Undergraduate and Postgraduate
Some recognised courses
Institute of Historic Building Conservation (IHBC)   http://www.ihbc.org.uk

Museum Studies: Undergraduate and Postgraduate
Course list with information on courses
Museums Association   http://www.museumsassociation.org/

13.   Hospitality, Culinary and Events Management Sector
Events Management: Undergraduate and Postgraduate
Some courses recognised by
Institute of Hospitality   https://www.instituteofhospitality.org/

Hospitality and Hotel Management: Undergraduate and Postgraduate
Some courses recognised by
Institute of Hospitality   https://www.instituteofhospitality.org/

Hotel Management: Undergraduate and Postgraduate
Some courses recognised by
Institute of Hospitality   https://www.instituteofhospitality.org/

14.   Information and Library Studies Sector
Archives Administration postgraduate diploma/ master's degree: Postgraduate
Professional accreditation is a requirement with:
Archives and Records Association (ARA)   http://www.archives.org.uk

Library and Information Management: Undergraduate (very few undergraduate courses) and Postgraduate
Professional accreditation is a requirement with:
Chartered Institute of Library and Information Professionals CILIP http://www.cilip.org.uk

15.   Information / Computer Technology Sector
Computing; Computer Science; Computer Engineering; Health Informatics
Chartered Engineer
Registered IT Technician

Artificial Intelligence / Cybernetics: Undergraduate and Postgraduate
Some accredited with the Chartered Institute of IT (BCS) http://www.bcs.org/

Business Computing: Undergraduate and Postgraduate
Some courses accredited with the Chartered Institute of IT (BCS) http://www.bcs.org/

Computer Engineering: Undergraduate and Postgraduate
Professional accreditation is a requirement with:
Engineering Council   http://www.engc.org.uk/
Chartered Engineer

Computer Forensics / Ethical Hacking / Computer Security: Undergraduate and Postgraduate
Some courses professionally accredited with:
Chartered Institute of IT (BCS)   http://www.bcs.org/
                                                        http://wam.bcs.org/wam/coursesearch.aspx

Computer Games: Undergraduate and Postgraduate
Some courses accredited with the Chartered Institute of IT (BCS) http://www.bcs.org/

Computer Information Systems: Undergraduate and Postgraduate
Some courses accredited with the Chartered Institute of IT (BCS) http://www.bcs.org/

Computer Networks: Undergraduate and Postgraduate
Some courses accredited with the Chartered Institute of IT (BCS) http://www.bcs.org/

Computer Science: Undergraduate and Postgraduate
Some courses accredited with the Chartered Institute of IT (BCS) http://www.bcs.org/

Computing: Undergraduate and Postgraduate
Some courses accredited with the Chartered Institute of IT (BCS) http://www.bcs.org/

Data Science: Undergraduate and Postgraduate
Some courses professionally accredited with:
Chartered Institute of IT (BCS)   http://www.bcs.org/

Digital / Web Design: Undergraduate and Postgraduate
Some courses accredited with the Chartered Institute of IT (BCS) http://www.bcs.org/

Informatics: Undergraduate and Postgraduate
Some courses accredited with the Chartered Institute of IT (BCS) http://www.bcs.org/

Information Technology: Undergraduate and Postgraduate
Some courses accredited with the Chartered Institute of IT (BCS) http://www.bcs.org/

Software Engineering: Undergraduate and Postgraduate
Professional accreditation is a requirement with:
Engineering Council   http://www.engc.org.uk/
Chartered Engineer
Some courses accredited with the Chartered Institute of IT (BCS) http://www.bcs.org/

Sound Engineering and Production: Undergraduate and Postgraduate
Some courses professionally accredited with:
Engineering Council   http://www.engc.org.uk/
Chartered Engineer

Technical Writing; Science Communication: Postgraduate
Links to optional postgraduate and accredited short courses with:
Institute of Scientific and Technical communications http://www.istc.org.uk/

Telecommunications: Undergraduate and Postgraduate
Professional accreditation is a requirement with:
Engineering Council   http://www.engc.org.uk/
Chartered Engineer
Some courses accredited with the Chartered Institute of IT (BCS) http://www.bcs.org/

16. Languages Sector
British Sign Language: Undergraduate and Postgraduate
Professional accreditation is a requirement with:
National Registers of Communication Professionals
working with Deaf and Deafblind People (NRCPD) http://www.nrcpd.org.uk
Registered British Sign Language Practitioner

Conference Interpreting: Postgraduate
Some courses professionally accredited with:
Chartered Institute for Linguistics   https://www.ciol.org.uk/

Translation and Interpreting: Undergraduate and Postgraduate
Some courses professionally accredited with:
Chartered Institute for Linguistics	https://www.ciol.org.uk/
Some courses professionally accredited with:
Institute of Translating and Interpreting	http://www.iti.org.uk/

17.   Law Enforcement: Armed Forces Sector
Armed Forces: Undergraduate and Postgraduate
Additional professional and Leadership qualifications
Courses accredited and approved with:
Armed Forces: Education and Training	http://www.army.mod.uk/

18.   Law Enforcement: Protection and Security Services Sector
Probation Officer see Social Care Sector

Police Studies: Undergraduate and Postgraduate
Certificate in Knowledge of Policing (CKP) course (requirement for some)
Professional accreditation is a requirement with:
College of Policing	http://www.college.police.uk/
List of approved Certificate in Knowledge of Policing (CKP) courses with some at universities

19.   Law Sector
Law LLB: Undergraduate
Professional accreditation is a requirement with:
Solicitors Regulation Authority (SRA)	http://www.sra.org.uk

Law LLB accelerated Degree (2 years) for Graduates: Graduate Conversion course
Professional accreditation is a requirement with:
Solicitors Regulation Authority (SRA)	http://www.sra.org.uk

Graduate Diploma in Law: Graduate Conversion course
Professional accreditation is a requirement with:
Lawcabs: Central applications Board	http://www.lawcabs.ac.uk/

Legal Practice Course: Postgraduate
Solicitor
Professional accreditation is a requirement with:
Law Cabs	http://www.lawcabs.ac.uk/
Registered Solicitor

Bar Professional Training Course: Postgraduate
Barrister (England, Wales and Northern Ireland) / Advocate (Scotland)
Professional accreditation is a requirement with:
England and Wales
Bar Standards Board	https://www.barstandardsboard.org.uk
The Bar of Northern Ireland	http://www.barofni.com
The Faculty of Advocates Scotland	http://www.advocates.org.uk
Registered Barrister

Legal Executive level 3 and level 6; Graduate Fast-rack Diploma: Undergraduate and Graduate
Professional accreditation is a requirement with:
Chartered Institute of Legal Executives (CILEx) http://www.cilexcareers.org.uk/
Registered Legal Executive

20.   Leisure and Tourism Sector
Tourism Management: Undergraduate and Postgraduate
Some courses recognised by
Institute of Hospitality https://www.instituteofhospitality.org/
Some courses recognised by
Institute of Travel and Tourism http://www.itt.co.uk/

21.   Media: Advertising, Communications, Marketing and Public Relations Sector
Advertising, Media Communications, Marketing, Public Relations
Marketing: Undergraduate and Postgraduate
Some courses professionally recognised with:
Chartered Institute of Marketing http://www.cim.co.uk
Chartered Marketer

Public Relations: Undergraduate and Postgraduate
Some courses professionally recognised with:
Chartered Institute of Public Relations http://www.cipr.co.uk
Chartered Public Relations Practitioner

Journalism and Publishing
Journalism: Undergraduate and Postgraduate
Some courses professionally accredited with:
British Journalism Training Council BJTC http://www.bjtc.org.uk
Professional Publishers Association: Journalism and Publishing http://www.ppa.co.uk

22.   Media: Film, Radio, Television and Theatre Sector
Film, Television, Production and Technology
Design Communication: Digital Media Production: Undergraduate and Postgraduate
Some courses professionally accredited with:
BKSTS: Craft Skills and Technology: Film Industry https://www.bksts.com/

Film Production, Digital Film and Cinematography: Undergraduate and Postgraduate
Some courses professionally accredited with:
BKSTS: Craft Skills and Technology: Film Industry https://www.bksts.com/

Multimedia, Interactive, Games and Web: Undergraduate and Postgraduate
Some courses professionally accredited with:
BKSTS: Craft Skills and Technology: Film Industry https://www.bksts.com/

Sound Design / Recording for film and Television: Undergraduate and Postgraduate
Some courses professionally accredited with:
BKSTS: Craft Skills and Technology: Film Industry https://www.bksts.com/
Some courses professionally accredited with:
Joint Audio Media Educational Support (James) http://www.jamesonline.org.uk/

Video, Television and Broadcasting: Undergraduate and Postgraduate
Some courses professionally accredited with:
BKSTS: Craft Skills and Technology: Film Industry   https://www.bksts.com/

23.   Performing Arts Sector
Dance
Dance Performance: Undergraduate and Postgraduate
Professionally accredited dance teaching in specialist institutions
Some courses professionally accredited with:
Council for Dance Education and Training   http://www.cdet.org.uk

Dance Choreography: Postgraduate
Professionally accredited dance teaching in specialist institutions
Some courses professionally accredited with:
Council for Dance Education and Training   http://www.cdet.org.uk

Drama
Acting / Drama: Undergraduate and Postgraduate
Some courses professionally accredited with:
Drama UK   http://www.dramauk.co.uk
Grade and Certificate Examinations professionally accredited with:
Trinity College London   http://www.trinitycollege.com

Actor Training and Coaching: Postgraduate
Some courses professionally accredited with:
Drama UK   http://www.dramauk.co.uk

Stage Management / Production: Undergraduate and Postgraduate
Some courses professionally accredited with:
Drama UK   http://www.dramauk.co.uk

Theatre Practice: Undergraduate and Postgraduate
Some courses professionally accredited with:
Drama UK   http://www.dramauk.co.uk

Music
Music / Music Technology /Music Production: Undergraduate and Postgraduate
Music performance examinations awarded by
Associated Board of the Royal Schools of Music   http://gb.abrsm.org/en/
Royal Academy of Music   https://www.ram.ac.uk/
Trinity College London   http://www.trinitycollege.com

Teaching Music postgraduate certificate and diploma: Postgraduate
Music performance examinations awarded by
Associated Board of the Royal Schools of Music   http://gb.abrsm.org/en/
Royal Academy of Music   https://www.ram.ac.uk/
Trinity College London   http://www.trinitycollege.com

24. Psychology, Counselling and Psychotherapy Sector

Counselling and Psychotherapy

Counselling and Psychotherapy: Some Undergraduate mostly Postgraduate

Professional accreditation is a requirement with an organisation registered with:
Professional Standards Authority
https://www.professionalstandards.org.uk/what-we-do/accredited-registers/find-a-register

Behavioural and Cognitive Psychotherapy

British Association for Behavioural and Cognitive Psychotherapies http://www.babcp.com

British Association for Behavioural and Cognitive Psychotherapies (BABCP)

British Association for Behavioural and
Cognitive Psychotherapies (BABCP)   http://www.babcp.com

British Association of Counselling and Psychotherapy

British Association of Counselling and Psychotherapy http://www.bacp.co.uk

British Psychoanalytic Council

British Psychoanalytic Council (Training Centres)   http://www.bpc.org.uk

British Psychological Society (BPS)

British Psychological Society (BPS)   http://beta.bps.org.uk/

Child Psychotherapy

Association of Child Psychotherapists   http://www.childpsychotherapy.org.uk/

Christian Counselling

Association of Christian Counsellors   https://www.acc-uk.org/

Cognitive Analytic Therapy

Association for Cognitive Analytic Therapy (CAT)   http://www.acat.me.uk/

Counselling and Psychotherapy in Scotland

Counselling and Psychotherapy in Scotland   http://www.cosca.org.uk/

Counselling and Psychotherapy Central Awarding Body (CPCAB)

Counselling and Psychotherapy Central Awarding Body (CPCAB) http://www.cpcab.co.uk/

Federation of Drug and Alcohol Professionals

Federation of Drug and Alcohol Professionals   http://www.fdap.org.uk

Human Givens

Human Givens Institute   http://www.hgi.org.uk/

Humanistic Psychology Practitioners

UK Association for Humanistic Psychology Practitioners http://www.ahpp.org

Irish Association for Counselling and Psychotherapy

Irish Association for Counselling and Psychotherapy http://www.irish-counselling.ie

National Counselling Society

National Counselling Society   http://www.nationalcounsellingsociety.org

Play Therapy
British Association of Play Therapists (BAPT)   http://www.bapt.info/
British Council for Therapeutic Interventions with Children http://www.bctiwc.org/
Play Therapy UK   http://www.playtherapy.org.uk/
Register of Play and Creative Arts Therapists   http://www.playtherapyregister.org.uk/

Psychoanalysis
Institute of Psychoanalysis   http://www.psychoanalysis.org.uk

Sexual and Relationship Therapy
College of Sexual and Relationship Therapists (COSRT) http://www.cosrt.org.uk/

UK Council for Psychotherapy
UK Council for Psychotherapy   http://www.psychotherapy.org.uk
Registered Counsellor
Registered Psychotherapist

Genomic / Genetic Counselling: Postgraduate
Professional accreditation is a requirement with:
Professional registration with:
Genetic Counselling Registration Board (GCRB)   http://www.gcrb.org.uk/
Registered Genomic / Genetic Counsellor

High Intensity Therapy
Professional accreditation is a requirement with:
British Association of Behavioural and Cognitive Psychotherapies
(BABCP)   http://www.babcp.com/
Registered High Intensity Therapist

Psychology
Psychology: Undergraduate
Professional accreditation is a requirement with:
The British Psychological Society (BPS)   http://www.bps.org.uk
Registration is a requirement with
Health and Care Professions Council   http://www.hcpc-uk.org
Chartered Psychologist

Psychology Conversion Course: Graduate and Postgraduate
Graduate diploma; Postgraduate Diploma; Master's degree
Professional accreditation is a requirement with:
The British Psychological Society (BPS)   http://www.bps.org.uk
Registration is a requirement with
Health and Care Professions Council   http://www.hcpc-uk.org
Chartered Psychologist

Clinical Psychology Doctorate; Professional Doctorate: Postgraduate
Professional accreditation is a requirement with: courses
The British Psychological Society (BPS)   http://www.bps.org.uk
Registered Chartered Clinical Psychologist
Counselling Psychology Doctorate: Postgraduate
Professional accreditation is a requirement with: courses
The British Psychological Society (BPS)   http://www.bps.org.uk
Registration is a requirement with
Health and Care Professions Council   http://www.hcpc-uk.org
Registered Chartered Counselling Psychologist

Educational / and Child Psychology Doctorate: Postgraduate
Professional accreditation is a requirement with: courses
The British Psychological Society (BPS)   http://www.bps.org.uk
Association of Educational Psychologists   http://www.aep.org.uk/
Registration is a requirement with
Health and Care Professions Council   http://www.hcpc-uk.org
Registered Chartered Educational Psychologist

Educational / and Child Psychology Master's degree plus the BPS Award in Educational Psychology (Scotland only): Postgraduate
Professional accreditation is a requirement with: courses
The British Psychological Society (BPS)   http://www.bps.org.uk
Registration is a requirement with
Health and Care Professions Council   http://www.hcpc-uk.org
Registered Chartered Educational Psychologist

Forensic Psychology Doctorate Master's or Doctorate: Postgraduate
Professional accreditation is a requirement with: courses
The British Psychological Society (BPS)   http://www.bps.org.uk
Registration is a requirement with
Health and Care Professions Council   http://www.hcpc-uk.org
Registered Chartered Forensic Psychologist

Health Psychology Master's; Doctorate; Professional Doctorate: Postgraduate
Professional accreditation is a requirement with: courses
The British Psychological Society (BPS)   http://www.bps.org.uk
Registration is a requirement with
Health and Care Professions Council   http://www.hcpc-uk.org
Registered Chartered Health Psychologist

Neuropsychology Post-Doctorate: Postgraduate
Professional accreditation is a requirement with:
The British Psychological Society (BPS)   http://www.bps.org.uk
Registration is a requirement with
Health and Care Professions Council   http://www.hcpc-uk.org
Registered Chartered Neuropsychologist

Occupational Psychology Master's: Postgraduate
Professional accreditation is a requirement with:
The British Psychological Society (BPS)   http://www.bps.org.uk
Registration is a requirement with
Health and Care Professions Council   http://www.hcpc-uk.org
Registered Chartered Occupational Psychologist

Sport and Exercise Psychology Master's: Postgraduate
Professional accreditation is a requirement with: courses
The British Psychological Society (BPS)   http://www.bps.org.uk
Registration is a requirement with
Health and Care Professions Council   http://www.hcpc-uk.org
Registered Chartered Sport and Exercise Psychologist

25. Religion and Theology Sector

Chaplaincy Studies: Undergraduate and Postgraduate
Professional accreditation is a requirement with:
Hospital Chaplaincies Council   http://www.nhs-chaplaincy-spiritualcare.org.uk/
Registered Chaplain

Christian Ordination Training: Undergraduate and Postgraduate
Baptist Church
Recognised professional courses approved with:
Baptist colleges   http://www.baptist.org.uk/Groups/220658/Colleges.aspx

Church of England
Recognised professional courses approved with:
Church of England:
Recognised Theological training institutions   https://www.churchofengland.org/

Church of Scotland
Recognised professional courses approved with:
Church of Scotland: Ministries
http://www.churchofscotland.org.uk/serve/ministries_council/ministries_in_the_church

Church of Wales
Recognised professional courses approved with:
St Michaels College   http://stmichaels.ac.uk/

Evangelical Churches
Recognised professional courses approved with:
Fellowship of Independent
Evangelical Churches   https://fiec.org.uk/what-we-do/article/equipping-individuals

Rabbinical Training: Jewish Education: Postgraduate
Recognised Rabbi Semicha (authorised) programmes may be found at
Leo Baeck College   http://www.lbc.ac.uk/
Montefiore College   https://www.montefioreendowment.org.uk/
run in partnership with the
London School of Jewish Studies   http://www.lsjs.ac.uk/

Catholic Priest Formation Training: Undergraduate and Postgraduate
Approved Catholic Training courses for Priests and Religious Brothers (Monks) may be found at:
National Office for Vocation   http://www.ukvocation.org/

Salvation Army Officer Training: Undergraduate
Diploma of higher education validated by the University of Gloucestershire
Recognised professional courses approved with:
Salvation Army   http://www.salvationarmy.org.uk/

26. Retail Sector

Business Purchasing and Supply Chain Management: Undergraduate and Postgraduate
Some courses professionally accredited with:
Chartered Institute of Purchasing and Supply CIPS   http://www.cips.org
Chartered Institute of Purchasing and Supply Professional

Procurement and Supply MBA: Postgraduate
Some courses professionally accredited with:
Chartered Institute of Purchasing and Supply CIPS   http://www.cips.org
Chartered Institute of Purchasing and Supply Professional

Management with Operations / Supply Chain Management: Postgraduate
Some courses professionally accredited with:
Chartered Institute of Purchasing and Supply CIPS   http://www.cips.org
Chartered Institute of Purchasing and Supply Professional

27. Science Sector

To qualify and practice as a registered scientist you would need to undertake a course approved by the Science Council and the relevant science professional body which is a member of the Science Council. Links to professional organisations may be found at:
http://www.charteredscientist.org/licensed-bodies/links
Science Council   http://www.sciencecouncil.org
Chartered Scientist (CSci)
Chartered Science Teacher (CSciTeach)
Registered Scientist (RSci),
Registered Science Technician (RSciTech), or

Biology and Chemistry

Biochemistry: Undergraduate
Some courses professionally accredited with:
Royal Society of Biology   https://www.rsb.org.uk/
Chartered Scientist

Biology: Undergraduate
Some courses professionally accredited with:
Royal Society of Biology   https://www.rsb.org.uk/
Chartered Scientist

Biology: Plant Biology: Undergraduate
Some courses professionally accredited with:
Royal Society of Biology   https://www.rsb.org.uk/
Chartered Scientist

Biomedical Science: Undergraduate and Postgraduate
Professional accreditation is a requirement with:
Institute of Biomedical Science IBMS   https://www.ibms.org/go/qualifications/ibms-courses
Chartered Scientist

Biomedical Science: Undergraduate
Some courses also professionally accredited with:
Royal Society of Biology   https://www.rsb.org.uk/
Chartered Scientist

Blood Transfusion Science: Postgraduate
Some courses run in partnership the universities and the
British Blood Transfusion Society   https://www.bbts.org.uk

Brewing and Distilling: Undergraduate
Professional accreditation is a requirement with:
Institute of Brewing and Distilling   https://www.ibd.org.uk/
International Centre for Brewing and Distilling   http://www.icbd.hw.ac.uk/courses.html

Chemistry: Undergraduate and Postgraduate
Some courses professionally accredited with:
Royal Society of Chemistry RSC   http://www.rsc.org/
http://www.rsc.org/Education/courses-and-careers/accredited-courses/index.asp
Chartered Scientist

Food / Nutrition Science /Technology: Undergraduate and Postgraduate
Some courses professionally accredited with:
Institute of Food Science and Technology IFST   http://www.ifst.org/
Chartered Scientist
Some courses endorsed with:
National Skills Academy: Food and Drink   http://foodanddrink.nsacademy.co.uk/
Chartered Scientist

Nutrition: Undergraduate and Postgraduate
Some courses professionally accredited with:
Association for Nutrition: Nutrition   http://www.associationfornutrition.org

Forensic Anthropology: Postgraduate
Some courses professionally accredited with:
The Chartered Society for
Forensic Sciences   http://www.charteredsocietyofforensicsciences.org/
The Royal Anthropological Institute of
Great Britain and Ireland   https://www.therai.org.uk/forensic-anthropology/
Registered Forensic Anthropologist

Forensic Biology: Undergraduate
Some courses professionally accredited with:
Royal Society of Biology   https://www.rsb.org.uk/
Chartered Scientist

Forensic Science: Undergraduate and Postgraduate
Some courses professionally accredited with:
The Chartered Society for
Forensic Sciences   http://www.charteredsocietyofforensicsciences.org/
Chartered Scientist

Genetics / Genomics: Undergraduate
Some courses professionally accredited with:
Royal Society of Biology   https://www.rsb.org.uk/
Chartered Scientist

Genomic Medicine: Postgraduate
England
Professional accreditation is a requirement with:
Health Education England: Genomic Medicine
https://www.genomicseducation.hee.nhs.uk/taught-courses/courses/master's-in-genomic-medicine/

Human Bioscience: Undergraduate
Some courses professionally accredited with:
Royal Society of Biology   https://www.rsb.org.uk/
Chartered Scientist

Human Nutrition: Undergraduate
Some courses professionally accredited with:
Royal Society of Biology   https://www.rsb.org.uk/
Chartered Scientist

Immunology: Undergraduate
Some courses professionally accredited with:
Royal Society of Biology   https://www.rsb.org.uk/
Chartered Scientist

Microbiology: Undergraduate and Postgraduate
Some courses professionally accredited with:
Institute of Biomedical Science IBMS   https://www.ibms.org/

Microbiology: Undergraduate
Some courses professionally accredited with:
Royal Society of Biology   https://www.rsb.org.uk/
Chartered Scientist

Molecular and Cellular Biology: Undergraduate
Some courses professionally accredited with:
Royal Society of Biology   https://www.rsb.org.uk/
Chartered Scientist

Neuroscience: Undergraduate
Some courses professionally accredited with:
Royal Society of Biology   https://www.rsb.org.uk/

Neuroscience: Undergraduate and Postgraduate
Links to courses available at the
British Neuroscience Association   https://www.bna.org.uk/careers/courses/
Chartered Scientist

Pharmacology: Undergraduate and Postgraduate
Core curricula guidelines for courses with:
British Pharmacology Society
https://www.bps.ac.uk/education-careers/teaching-pharmacology/core-curricula

Pharmacology: Undergraduate
Some courses professionally accredited with:
Royal Society of Biology   https://www.rsb.org.uk/
Chartered Scientist

Physiology: Undergraduate and Postgraduate
Some courses professionally accredited with:
Registration Council for Clinical Physiologists   https://www.rccp.co.uk

Physiology: Undergraduate
Some courses professionally accredited with:
Royal Society of Biology   https://www.rsb.org.uk/
Chartered Scientist

Sports Science: Undergraduate
Some courses endorsed by
British Association of Sport and Exercise Science   http://www.bases.org.uk/Courses

Zoology: Undergraduate
Some courses professionally accredited with:
Royal Society of Biology   https://www.rsb.org.uk/

Physical Science
Biotechnology / Applied Molecular Biology: Undergraduate and Postgraduate
Some courses professionally accredited with:
Institute of Biomedical Science IBMS   https://www.ibms.org/

Materials Science: Undergraduate and Postgraduate
Some courses professionally accredited with:
Engineering Council   http://www.engc.org.uk/
Some courses professionally accredited with:
Institute of Materials, Minerals and Mining   http://www.iom3.org/

Medical Physics: Undergraduate and Postgraduate
Some courses professionally accredited with:
Engineering Council   http://www.engc.org.uk/
Institute for Physics and Engineering in Medicine   http://www.ipem.ac.uk/
Chartered Engineer

Nuclear Science: Undergraduate and Postgraduate
Some courses accredited with:
Institute of Physics   https://www.iop.org/

Physics: Undergraduate and Postgraduate
Some courses accredited with:
Institute of Physics   https://www.iop.org/

Healthcare Science:
Undergraduate NHS Practitioner Training Programme (PTP)
Postgraduate NHS Scientist Training Programme (STP)

Academy for Healthcare Science: Overarching body
for the whole of healthcare science   http://www.ahcs.ac.uk

Registration as a Clinical Scientist, Biomedical Scientist and Hearing Aid Dispenser is with:
Health and Care Professions Council HCPC   http://www.hcpc-uk.org

Registration as a Medical Physiologist, Medical Physical Scientist and Biomedical Engineer is with:
Academy for Healthcare Science: http://www.ahcs.ac.uk

There are separate healthcare science training schemes which accredit courses in England, Wales, Northern Ireland and Scotland

England and Wales
National School for Healthcare Science   http://www.nshcs.hee.nhs.uk/

Wales
NHS Wales   http://www.wales.nhs.uk/nhswalesaboutus

Northern Ireland
Northern Ireland Government   http://www.nidirect.gov.uk/healthcare-scientist

Scotland
NHS Education for Scotland   http://www.nes.scot.nhs.uk/education-and-training/

Healthcare Science:
Clinical Bioinformatics Postgraduate NHS Scientist Training Programme (STP)
Clinical Bioinformatics: Genomics: Postgraduate NHS Scientist Training Programme (STP)

Some courses professionally accredited with:
Institute of Biomedical Science IBMS   https://www.ibms.org/
Registration as a Clinical Scientist is with:
Health and Care Professions Council HCPC   http://www.hcpc-uk.org

Clinical Bioinformatics: Health Informatics: Postgraduate NHS Scientist Training Programme (STP)

Some courses professionally accredited with:
Institute of Biomedical Science IBMS   https://www.ibms.org/
Registration as a Clinical Scientist is with:
Health and Care Professions Council HCPC   http://www.hcpc-uk.org

Clinical Bioinformatics: Physical Sciences: Postgraduate NHS Scientist Training Programme (STP)

Some courses professionally accredited with:
Institute of Biomedical Science IBMS   https://www.ibms.org/
Registration as a Clinical Scientist is with:
Health and Care Professions Council HCPC   http://www.hcpc-uk.org

Healthcare Science:
Life Sciences / Biomedical Sciences: Undergraduate NHS Practitioner Training Programme (PTP)

Blood Science Undergraduate NHS Practitioner Training Programme (PTP)
Professional accreditation is a requirement with:
Institute of Biomedical Science IBMS   https://www.ibms.org/
Registration as a Biomedical Scientist is with:
Health and Care Professions Council HCPC   http://www.hcpc-uk.org

Cellular Science Undergraduate NHS Practitioner Training Programme (PTP)
Professional accreditation is a requirement with:
Institute of Biomedical Science IBMS   https://www.ibms.org/
Registration as a Biomedical Scientist is with:
Health and Care Professions Council HCPC   http://www.hcpc-uk.org

Genomics /Genetics Science / Technology Undergraduate NHS Practitioner Training Programme (PTP)
Professional accreditation is a requirement with:
Institute of Biomedical Science IBMS   https://www.ibms.org/
Registration as a Biomedical Scientist is with:
Health and Care Professions Council HCPC   http://www.hcpc-uk.org

Infection Science Undergraduate NHS Practitioner Training Programme (PTP)
Professional accreditation is a requirement with:
Institute of Biomedical Science IBMS   https://www.ibms.org/
Registration as a Biomedical Scientist is with:
Health and Care Professions Council HCPC   http://www.hcpc-uk.org

Life science (provides a broad base before specialising in one of the above areas Undergraduate NHS Practitioner Training Programme (PTP)
Professional accreditation is a requirement with:
Institute of Biomedical Science IBMS   https://www.ibms.org/
Registration as a Biomedical Scientist is with:
Health and Care Professions Council HCPC   http://www.hcpc-uk.org

Healthcare Science:
Life Sciences / Biomedical Sciences: Postgraduate NHS Scientist Training Programme (STP)

Clinical / Medical Microbiology: Postgraduate NHS Scientist Training Programme (STP)
Professional accreditation is a requirement with:
Institute of Biomedical Science IBMS   https://www.ibms.org/
Registration as a Biomedical Scientist is with:
Health and Care Professions Council HCPC   http://www.hcpc-uk.org

Clinical Biochemistry: Postgraduate NHS Scientist Training Programme (STP)
Professional accreditation is a requirement with:
Institute of Biomedical Science IBMS   https://www.ibms.org/
Registration as a Biomedical Scientist is with:
Health and Care Professions Council HCPC   http://www.hcpc-uk.org

Clinical Immunology: Postgraduate NHS Scientist Training Programme (STP)
Professional accreditation is a requirement with:
Institute of Biomedical Science IBMS   https://www.ibms.org/
Registration as a Biomedical Scientist is with:
Health and Care Professions Council HCPC   http://www.hcpc-uk.org

Clinical Microbiology: Postgraduate NHS Scientist Training Programme (STP)
Professional accreditation is a requirement with:
Institute of Biomedical Science IBMS   https://www.ibms.org/
Registration as a Biomedical Scientist is with:
Health and Care Professions Council HCPC   http://www.hcpc-uk.org

Cytopathology: Postgraduate NHS Scientist Training Programme (STP)
Professional accreditation is a requirement with:
Institute of Biomedical Science IBMS   https://www.ibms.org/
Registration as a Biomedical Scientist is with:
Health and Care Professions Council HCPC   http://www.hcpc-uk.org

Genomic Counselling (Formerly Genetic Counselling): Postgraduate NHS Scientist Training Programme (STP)
Professional accreditation is a requirement with:
Institute of Biomedical Science IBMS   https://www.ibms.org/
Registration as a Biomedical Scientist is with:
Health and Care Professions Council HCPC   http://www.hcpc-uk.org

Genomics /Genetics Science: Postgraduate NHS Scientist Training Programme (STP)
Professional accreditation is a requirement with:
Institute of Biomedical Science IBMS   https://www.ibms.org/
Registration as a Biomedical Scientist is with:
Health and Care Professions Council HCPC   http://www.hcpc-uk.org

Haematology and Transfusion Science: Postgraduate NHS Scientist Training Programme (STP)
Professional accreditation is a requirement with:
Institute of Biomedical Science IBMS   https://www.ibms.org/
Registration as a Biomedical Scientist is with:
Health and Care Professions Council HCPC   http://www.hcpc-uk.org

Histocompatibility and Immunogenetics: Postgraduate NHS Scientist Training Programme (STP)
Professional accreditation is a requirement with:
Institute of Biomedical Science IBMS   https://www.ibms.org/
Registration as a Biomedical Scientist is with:
Health and Care Professions Council HCPC   http://www.hcpc-uk.org

Histopathology: Postgraduate NHS Scientist Training Programme (STP)
Professional accreditation is a requirement with:
Institute of Biomedical Science IBMS   https://www.ibms.org/
Registration as a Biomedical Scientist is with:
Health and Care Professions Council HCPC   http://www.hcpc-uk.org
Reproductive Science: Postgraduate NHS Scientist Training Programme (STP)
Professional accreditation is a requirement with:
Institute of Biomedical Science IBMS   https://www.ibms.org/
Registration as a Biomedical Scientist is with:
Health and Care Professions Council HCPC   http://www.hcpc-uk.org

Healthcare Science:
Medical Physics Technology and Biomedical (Clinical) Engineering NHS Practitioner Training Programme (PTP)

Healthcare Science:
Biomedical (Clinical) Engineering NHS Practitioner Training Programme (PTP)
Biomedical / Clinical / Medical / Engineering Undergraduate NHS Practitioner Training Programme (PTP)
Professional accreditation is a requirement with:
Engineering Council   http://www.engc.org.uk/
Some courses professionally accredited with:
Institute of Physics and Engineering in Medicine IPEM http://www.ipem.ac.uk/
Registration as a Medical Physical Scientist / Biomedical Engineer is with:
Academy for Healthcare Science (AHCS)   http://www.ahcs.ac.uk/

Radiation Engineering: Undergraduate NHS Practitioner Training Programme (PTP)
Professional accreditation is a requirement with:
Engineering Council   http://www.engc.org.uk/
Some courses professionally accredited with:
Institute of Physics and Engineering in Medicine IPEM http://www.ipem.ac.uk/
Registration as a Medical Physical Scientist / Biomedical Engineer is with:
Academy for Healthcare Science (AHCS)   http://www.ahcs.ac.uk/

Rehabilitation Engineering: Undergraduate NHS Practitioner Training Programme (PTP)
Professional accreditation is a requirement with:
Engineering Council   http://www.engc.org.uk/
Some courses professionally accredited with:
Institute of Physics and Engineering in Medicine IPEM http://www.ipem.ac.uk/
Registration as a Medical Physical Scientist / Biomedical Engineer is with:
Academy for Healthcare Science (AHCS)   http://www.ahcs.ac.uk/

Healthcare Science:
Medical Physics Technology NHS Practitioner Training Programme (PTP)
Nuclear Medicine: Undergraduate NHS Practitioner Training Programme (PTP)
Professional accreditation is a requirement with:
Engineering Council   http://www.engc.org.uk/
Some courses professionally accredited with:
Institute of Physics and Engineering in Medicine IPEM http://www.ipem.ac.uk/
Registration as a Medical Physical Scientist / Biomedical Engineer is with:
Academy for Healthcare Science (AHCS)   http://www.ahcs.ac.uk/

Radiation Physics: Undergraduate NHS Practitioner Training Programme (PTP)
Professional accreditation is a requirement with:
Engineering Council   http://www.engc.org.uk/
Some courses professionally accredited with:
Institute of Physics and Engineering in Medicine IPEM http://www.ipem.ac.uk/
Registration as a Medical Physical Scientist / Biomedical Engineer is with:
Academy for Healthcare Science   http://www.ahcs.ac.uk/

Radiotherapy Physics: Undergraduate NHS Practitioner Training Programme (PTP)
Professional accreditation is a requirement with:
Engineering Council   http://www.engc.org.uk/
Some courses professionally accredited with:
Institute of Physics and Engineering in Medicine IPEM http://www.ipem.ac.uk/
Registration as a Medical Physical Scientist / Biomedical Engineer is with:
Academy for Healthcare Science   http://www.ahcs.ac.uk/

Healthcare Science:
Medical Physics Technology and Biomedical (Clinical) Engineering: Postgraduate NHS Scientist Training Programme (STP)
Biomedical / Clinical / Medical / Engineering: Postgraduate NHS Scientist Training Programme (STP)
Professional accreditation is a requirement with:
Engineering Council   http://www.engc.org.uk/
Some courses professionally accredited with:
Institute of Physics and Engineering in Medicine IPEM http://www.ipem.ac.uk/
Registration as a Medical Physical Scientist / Biomedical Engineer is with:
Academy for Healthcare Science (AHCS)   http://www.ahcs.ac.uk/

Clinical Pharmaceutical Science: Postgraduate NHS Scientist Training Programme (STP)
Professional accreditation is a requirement with:
Engineering Council   http://www.engc.org.uk/
Some courses professionally accredited with:
Institute of Physics and Engineering in Medicine IPEM http://www.ipem.ac.uk/
Registration as a Medical Physical Scientist / Biomedical Engineer is with:
Academy for Healthcare Science (AHCS)   http://www.ahcs.ac.uk/
Medical Physics: Postgraduate NHS Scientist Training Programme (STP)
Professional accreditation is a requirement with:
Engineering Council   http://www.engc.org.uk/
Some courses professionally accredited with:
Institute of Physics and Engineering in Medicine IPEM http://www.ipem.ac.uk/
Registration as a Medical Physical Scientist / Biomedical Engineer is with:
Academy for Healthcare Science (AHCS)   http://www.ahcs.ac.uk/

Healthcare Science:
Physiological Sciences (Clinical) NHS Practitioner Training Programme (PTP)

Healthcare Science:
Cardiovascular, Respiratory and Sleep Sciences
Audiology: Undergraduate NHS Practitioner Training Programme (PTP)
Professional accreditation is a requirement with:
Registration Council for Clinical Physiologists   https://www.rccp.co.uk
Registration as a Hearing Aid Dispenser is with:
Health and Care Professions Council HCPC   http://www.hcpc-uk.org

Neurophysiology: Undergraduate NHS Practitioner Training Programme (PTP)
Professional accreditation is a requirement with:
Registration Council for Clinical Physiologists   https://www.rccp.co.uk
Registration as a Medical Physiologist is with:
Academy for Healthcare Science: http://www.ahcs.ac.uk

Healthcare Science:
Neurosensory Sciences
Cardiac physiology: Undergraduate NHS Practitioner Training Programme (PTP)
Professional accreditation is a requirement with:
Registration Council for Clinical Physiologists   https://www.rccp.co.uk
Registration as a Medical Physiologist is with:
Academy for Healthcare Science   http://www.ahcs.ac.uk

Respiratory and sleep physiology: Undergraduate NHS Practitioner Training Programme (PTP)
Professional accreditation is a requirement with:
Registration Council for Clinical Physiologists   https://www.rccp.co.uk
Registration as a Medical Physiologist is with:
Academy for Healthcare Science   http://www.ahcs.ac.uk

Healthcare Science:
Physiological Sciences (Clinical): Postgraduate NHS Scientist Training Programme (STP)
Audiology: Postgraduate NHS Scientist Training Programme (STP)
Professional accreditation is a requirement with:
Registration Council for Clinical Physiologists   https://www.rccp.co.uk
Registration as a Hearing Aid Dispenser is with:
Health and Care Professions Council HCPC   http://www.hcpc-uk.org

Cardiac Science: Postgraduate NHS Scientist Training Programme (STP)
Professional accreditation is a requirement with:
Registration Council for Clinical Physiologists   https://www.rccp.co.uk
Registration as a Medical Physiologist is with:
Academy for Healthcare Science   http://www.ahcs.ac.uk

Critical Care Science: Postgraduate NHS Scientist Training Programme (STP)
Professional accreditation is a requirement with:
Registration Council for Clinical Physiologists   https://www.rccp.co.uk
Registration as a Medical Physiologist is with:
Academy for Healthcare Science   http://www.ahcs.ac.uk

Gastrointestinal Physiology: Postgraduate NHS Scientist Training Programme (STP)
Professional accreditation is a requirement with:
Registration Council for Clinical Physiologists   https://www.rccp.co.uk
Registration as a Medical Physiologist is with:
Academy for Healthcare Science   http://www.ahcs.ac.uk

Neurophysiology: Postgraduate NHS Scientist Training Programme (STP)
Professional accreditation is a requirement with:
Registration Council for Clinical Physiologists   https://www.rccp.co.uk
Registration as a Medical Physiologist is with:
Academy for Healthcare Science   http://www.ahcs.ac.uk

Ophthalmic and Vision Healthcare Science: Postgraduate NHS Scientist Training Programme (STP) (not always available)
Also see:
Ophthalmology (qualified medical doctor) see Healthcare sector: Medicine
Orthoptics: See Healthcare sector: Ophthalmic and Vision Science
Optometry: see Healthcare sector: Ophthalmic and Vision Science
Dispensing Optician see Healthcare sector: Ophthalmic and Vision Science
Registration as a Medical Physiologist is with:
Academy for Healthcare Science   http://www.ahcs.ac.uk
Professional accreditation is a requirement with:
Registration Council for Clinical Physiologists   https://www.rccp.co.uk
Registration as a Medical Physiologist is with:
Academy for Healthcare Science   http://www.ahcs.ac.uk

Urodynamic Science: Postgraduate NHS Scientist Training Programme (STP)
Professional accreditation is a requirement with:
Registration Council for Clinical Physiologists   https://www.rccp.co.uk
Registration as a Medical Physiologist is with:
Academy for Healthcare Science   http://www.ahcs.ac.uk

Vascular Science: Postgraduate NHS Scientist Training Programme (STP)
Professional accreditation is a requirement with:
Registration Council for Clinical Physiologists   https://www.rccp.co.uk
Registration as a Medical Physiologist is with:
Academy for Healthcare Science   http://www.ahcs.ac.uk

28.   Social Care
Careers Guidance / Careers Coaching: Postgraduate
Undergraduate training courses level 6;
Postgraduate certificate, diploma, master's degree
Approved courses required for professional eligibility to register with the:
Career Development Institute
http://www.thecdi.net/Getting-Qualified/Master's-and-other-courses
Registered Careers Adviser (voluntary)

Career Education, Information and Guidance in HE (CEIGH): Postgraduate
Postgraduate certificate, diploma, master's degree
Delivered by the University of Warwick   https://warwick.ac.uk/
in collaboration with the
Association of Graduate Careers Advisory Service (AGCAS) http://www.agcas.org.uk/
Optional courses

Play Therapy: Postgraduate
Master's degree
Professional accreditation is a requirement with:
British Association of Play Therapists   http://www.bapt.info
Registered Play Therapist (voluntary)

Professional Qualification in Probation (PQiP); Community Justice Learning (CJL): Undergraduate and Graduate
England and Wales
Professional accreditation is a requirement with:
National Probation Service   http://www.traintobeaprobationofficer.com/

England and Wales
National Probation Service
England and Wales https://www.gov.uk/government/organisations/national-probation-service

Northern Ireland
Social Work qualification
Northern Ireland Social Care Council
http://www.niscc.info/index.php/education-for-our-training-providers/degree-in-social-work-education

Scotland
Social Work qualification
Scottish Social Services Council: Social work   http://www.sssc.uk.com

Social Work: Undergraduate and Postgraduate
Professional accreditation is a requirement with:
England
Health and Care Professions Council regulates Social Workers in England:
Register of Courses   http://www.hcpc-uk.org/education/programmes/register/

Wales
Care Council for Wales:
Social Work Courses   http://www.ccwales.org.uk/social-work-degree/

Northern Ireland
Northern Ireland Social Care Council
http://www.niscc.info/index.php/education-for-our-training-providers/degree-in-social-work-education

Scotland
Scottish Social Services Council (SSSC) Social Workers http://www.sssc.uk.com
Registered Social Worker

Youth and Community Work: Undergraduate and Postgraduate
Professional accreditation is a requirement with:

England
National Youth Agency England   http://www.nya.org.uk
Recognised by the Joint Negotiating Committee for youth and community workers

Wales
Education and Training Standards Wales: Youth Work http://www.etswales.org.uk

Northern Ireland
Youth Council Northern Ireland   http://www.ycni.org

Scotland
The Standards Council: Community Learning and
Development for Scotland   http://www.cldstandardscouncil.org.uk
Registered Youth Worker

29. Social Arts, Science, Social Policy, Philosophy and Politics Sector
Philosophy: Undergraduate and Postgraduate
Links to some Philosophy courses with:
British Philosophy Association   http://www.bpa.ac.uk/

Sociology: Undergraduate and Postgraduate
Links to some Sociology courses with:
British Sociological Association   https://www.britsoc.co.uk/

30. Sport Sector
Sport and Exercise Psychology: Undergraduate and Postgraduate
Professional accreditation is a requirement with:
British Psychology Society   http://www.bps.org.uk/
Chartered Sport and Exercise Psychologist

Sport and Exercise Science: Postgraduate
Some courses endorsed with:
British Association of Sport and Exercise Sciences   http://www.bases.org.uk/Courses

Sports Coaching: Undergraduate and Postgraduate
Some courses endorsed with:
Chartered Institute for the Management of Sport and
Physical Activity (CIMSPA)   http://www.cimspa.co.uk
Chartered member
British Association of Sport and Exercise Sciences: http://www.bases.org.uk/Courses
Formal recognition of training courses
Sports Coach UK   http://www.sportscoachuk.org

Sports Development: Undergraduate and Postgraduate
Some courses endorsed with:
Chartered Institute for the Management of Sport and
Physical Activity (CIMSPA)   http://www.cimspa.co.uk
Chartered member

Sports Policy, Business and Management: Postgraduate
Some courses endorsed with:
British Association of Sport and Exercise Sciences   http://www.bases.org.uk/Courses

Sports Therapy: Undergraduate and Postgraduate
Professional accreditation is a requirement with:
The Society of Sports Therapists   http://www.society-of-sports-therapists.org

31.   Transport and Logistics Sector
Aviation Transport Management: Undergraduate and Postgraduate
Some courses professionally accredited with: (provides some exemption from the academic requirements for membership)
Chartered Institute of Logistics and Transport   http://www.ciltuk.org.uk/
Chartered Member

Logistics and Supply Chain Management: Undergraduate and Postgraduate
Some courses professionally accredited with:
Chartered Institute of Logistics and Transport CILT   http://www.ciltuk.org.uk
Chartered Member
Chartered Institute of Purchasing and Supply CIPS   http://www.cips.org
Chartered Purchasing and Supply Professional

Logistics / Transport Management: Undergraduate and Postgraduate
Some courses professionally accredited with: provides some exemption from the academic requirements for membership
Chartered Institute of Logistics and Transport   http://www.ciltuk.org.uk/
Chartered Member

Marine Operations / Management / Nautical Science: Undergraduate
Leading to the award of a UK Maritime and Coastguard Agency (MCA) Standards for Training Certification and Watch keeping (STCW) Deck Officer Certificate of Competency (CoC)
Professional accreditation is a requirement with:
Maritime and Coastguard Agency (MCA)
https://www.gov.uk/government/organisations/maritime-and-coastguard-agency
Merchant Navy Training Board (MNTB)   http://mntb.org.uk/

Chapter 6
Higher Education Course Modes of Study, Teaching and Assessment

6.1 Higher Education Course Modes of Study

There are many different ways you can study for a course in higher education and you can choose to study in a way that suits your needs. Courses may be available to study full time or part time as well as by flexible or distance learning.

If you study full time, you will complete your course more quickly. A small number of courses are available as accelerated courses, which will provide a quicker route, which may suit you although studying for these can be quite intensive.

Studying part time or by distance learning may enable you to fit your studying around your other commitments. Many universities and colleges offer the option of studying courses part time, although some courses are only available full time. Some universities offer only part time courses such as the Open University http://www.openuniversity.co.uk or Birkbeck, University of London http://www.bbk.ac.uk/

Financial implications are also an important consideration, so you will need to research what will be most appropriate for you.

Academic Year

The academic year for most higher education courses starts in September / October in England, Wales and Northern Ireland and in August in Scotland. Although some courses at some universities may start at different times of the year, with often more flexibility to start part time, flexible or distance learning courses.

The academic year may be divided into three terms, and referred to as autumn, winter and spring terms with the summer months, usually being the vacation, although some courses such as master's degree courses will have provision for you to undertake your dissertation throughout the summer period.

However, the academic year is usually divided into two parts called semesters for teaching and assessment purposes, with the first semester usually starting during September / October (or August in Scotland) through to January/ February; and the second semester from February through to June / July.

Study Options

Full Time Study Courses
A full time course in higher education is usually defined as lasting at least one academic year and would involve you attending for at least 24 weeks out of the year, with at least 21 hours of study, tuition or work experience per week during term time.

Most full time higher education courses will last between 30 - 40 weeks each academic year, varying according to the course and the university or college, and stop during the summer months, although, some courses, especially some professional or accelerated courses, last longer than this, such as nursing degrees which may last up to 45 weeks in duration.

Duration of full time higher education courses

A full time honours degree course usually lasts for three academic years in England, Wales and Northern Ireland; and for four academic years in Scotland, although some may last for longer. An integrated master's degree which combines an honours and a master's degree usually lasts for an additional year, being four years in England, Wales and Northern Ireland; and five years in Scotland.

A full-time master's degree usually lasts for one year although some may last for up to two years. A full-time doctoral degree usually lasts for three to four years. Other full time postgraduate courses such as graduate certificates / diplomas and postgraduate certificates/ diplomas may last between six months to one year.

A full-time PhD, DPhil or Professional Doctorate is usually a minimum of three years. There may be some Doctoral degrees which last for four years which incorporate some taught modules.

Part time study courses

A part time course is usually one which lasts less than 24 weeks in the academic year, or if lasting longer, the number of hours of study, tuition or work experience involved in the course lasts less than 21 hours of study per week during term time. The actual duration of the course will be dependent on the number of modules you choose to complete in a year and you will take longer to gain your qualification than if studying full-time. Higher education courses which can be studied part time may have teaching integrated with full time courses.

You can choose how many modules you want to take each year to suit your personal circumstances, although there may be a maximum number of years for you to complete your course. You should check if courses are available during the evenings, weekends or days and times that fit in with your commitments.

Part time day release study courses

Part time courses may provide teaching on 1 or 2 days per week. Courses may be available during the day and some employers may provide you with day release or a flexitime agreement where you make up the work time, which enables you to study whilst you are earning a salary. Some employers may not agree to day release and some part time courses may also be available in the evenings.

Part time block study courses

Some courses may be taught flexibly by condensing the teaching time for subject modules to a shorter intense period of time, such as one week blocks. This might suit you if it is easier to take separate weeks away if you are in work and your employer supports this, rather than 'day-release'. You would be expected to complete the required research and revision during your own time. Teaching may be within the campus of the university or lectures may be delivered elsewhere by arrangement.

Distance learning or e-learning study courses

There may be the option to study by distance / e-learning for some courses through a university or college or through a distance learning provider. This option will allow you to fit your studies around your work or other commitments without the need to attend face-to face tutorials or lectures.

Distance learning courses are those that don't involve regular face-to-face contact between students, and use technology to convey learning. They are also sometimes called e-learning courses and usually involve a mix of formal teaching and learning systems with course material provided which can be carried out remotely through electronic communication, on-line. This means you can study wherever you live and the course can be delivered by distance learning providers virtually anywhere in the world.

Some distance learning courses involve periods of teaching where students have contact time with each other and lecturers at a weekend or during a summer school, where practical. You may be required to attend a higher education institution or a specified centre to take examinations. If you live overseas, there may be training centres in the country you reside in where examinations may be sat. Video conferencing may also be available.

You would need to check teaching and learning methods with the relevant distance /e-learning provider. Many higher education institutions offer distance learning courses but check that the accreditation body is recognised in the UK.

Flexible learning study courses

Some courses may allow for flexible learning combining different delivery modes, such as a mix of part-time day, part-time block mode and part-time distance learning.

Duration of part time, flexible or distance learning higher education courses

Each university will have individual regulations therefore you should confirm the maximum amount of time to complete your course. Generally a part time, flexible or distance learning honours degree course usually lasts for between four - six academic years although some may be gained within eight years, depending on the university regulations, in England, Wales and Northern Ireland; in Scotland, depending on the university regulations, you may have a maximum of eight years to gain a general or ordinary degree and 10 years to gain an honours degree.

Part-time postgraduate graduate certificates / diplomas and postgraduate certificates/ diplomas may be studied for between one to two years. A part-time, flexible or distance learning master's taught or research degree usually lasts for two academic years although some may last for up to four years; a part-time MPhil may last four - six years, depending on the university regulations. A part-time doctoral degree usually lasts between four - eight years, depending on the university regulations.

Accelerated Study Courses

For some courses, you can fast track and these are called accelerated courses, which is a shortened version. These courses are condensed into a shorter period of time and may include extra teaching and study during the vacation weeks. Some accelerated courses are available at bachelor's honours degree level or graduate conversion courses for graduates who have a degree in another subject and wish to change careers can transfer their skills and knowledge, hence the course is shorter in length.

Duration of accelerated study courses

Accelerated / fast track honours degree courses if studied full time may be completed in 2 years instead of the usual 3 years, or for medicine or dentistry graduate entry degrees, may be completed in 4 years instead of 5 years in England, Wales or Northern Ireland; or in 3 years instead of 4 years in Scotland.

Courses Which Include Work Experience

Some courses include relevant work experience for a length of time as part of a higher education course, outside of the university or college, also known as 'sandwich' courses. This may be for one year or for periods less than this. Sandwich courses are usually undertaken on a full time basis, although part time options may be possible.

This can involve working in the UK or overseas. Some professional degree courses have work experience which is an essential part and will usually include this as part of the degree assessment. Other courses with work experience may include shorter periods which may be optional.

A sandwich course involves taught classes with periods of relevant work experience, also known as placements or internships. A 'thick' sandwich course involves a year in a work experience placement and a 'thin' sandwich course involves alternating a shorter period of work experience with university study throughout the course.

Degree courses may last longer to take account of the time spent in the work placement. There may be some opportunities to get paid by an employer during your time undertaking work experience, although not all placements are paid. Travel expenses for courses allied to health professions may be available to eligible students.

Also go to:
Chapter 9
Studying Abroad
The Erasmus programme
http://www.erasmusprogramme.com/ is for higher education students, studying any subject, in the UK who would like to study, undertake a work placement, or be a language assistant for between three months and one academic year as part of a degree in another European country. Go to
Chapter 9.3
Erasmus: Study and Work Experience Programme in another European Country
Chapter 12.6
Erasmus Funding Support for Undergraduate and Postgraduate Students

Sponsorship and Scholarships

A small number of usually larger companies may provide sponsorship for a small number of degrees mainly including construction, engineering and physical science degrees. If you intend to join the armed forces sponsorship for specialist degree courses may also be available for eligible applicants. Scholarships may also be available for some subjects through professional organisations or universities. Postgraduate sponsorship may be available from some larger law or accountancy firms; graduate training programmes also enable graduates to undertake paid work and professional training in a range of careers including accountancy, human resources and health management; graduate schemes may also provide some funding such as teaching through Schools Direct (salaried) or Teach First. Further information may be found at Get into Teaching: School-led Training https://getintoteaching.education.gov.uk/explore-my-options/teacher-training-routes/school-led-training/school-direct

Some organisations may employ school or college leavers and pay for you to study for an HND, honours degree or a professional qualification. Specified grades at 'A' level or equivalent and

GCSE or equivalent may be required and usually these options involve part time study or distance learning. Some employers may sponsor you whilst on your degree course, which may involve working for the employer during the vacation and for a set period of time after graduating. Employers may pay for costs such as tuition fees, accommodation during study schools, and travel, as well as a salary however, not all schemes cover such costs. You may also be required to work for the organisation for a set period of time or repay costs, so research this information carefully. These options tend to be extremely competitive to obtain and deadlines may apply. Usually there are specific courses at designated higher education institutions (HEIs) that have sponsorship options; information should be available on HEI websites.

Attend careers events and organisation information days to gain further information. Professional bodies may have company sponsorship and scholarship details on the relevant websites. University and college careers services will also have information about company sponsorship schemes as well as scholarships on their websites.

Intermitting

If you decide to intermit / suspend your studies, depending on the university regulations you may have a period of one or two years to return, providing you complete an official form available from your university, otherwise you will need to officially withdraw and reapply through the usual application process. You should obtain advice before you decide as your tuition fee liability may continue to accrue if you don't inform the university.

Transferring your Course and University

If you decide you wish to proceed with a transfer of study within your university, providing this has been agreed informally, you will need to complete the appropriate university form and have this approved by your current School / Department and if a different subject, also by the School / Department you wish to transfer to. If you wish to transfer to another university, you should obtain advice from the university you wish to transfer to and you will need to officially withdraw and apply again through the usual application process, which is usually UCAS for a full time course and directly to the university for a part time course. You should obtain advice before you decide as your tuition fee liability may continue to accrue if you don't inform your current the university.

6.2 Higher Education Teaching and Assessment

Higher Education Teaching

How you will study in higher education will be dependent on the course and the university or college. However, there are formal as well as informal teaching methods and you will be expected to take responsibility for your own personal study, learning and development. Many universities and colleges will expect you to study for 35 hours per week for a full time course and you may be required to attend a specified number of lectures unless you have a good reason for absence. It is also important to arrive on time to lectures and seminars for as well as being disruptive to other students; you may be marked absent if you arrive after a set time.

Teaching methods
When you start your higher education course, you will be taught your subject/s through a variety of methods such as lectures, seminars, practical sessions, personal tutorial sessions or supervisions. You will also need to carry out independent research. Some courses also include field trips, study visits, work experience as well as study or work abroad.

Lectures
Lectures cover a topic related to the subject you are studying and act as a starting point for you to carry out your own research. The duration of a lecture is usually for one or two hours. Lectures are usually delivered to larger numbers of students varying between 30 to several hundred students. Many lecturers are experts in their field and the lecture is an opportunity to find out about the latest research.

Seminars
Seminars provide the opportunity to explore a topic in more detail and in a more informal session. They are for smaller groups of students varying usually between 10 to 30 students and you may be put into smaller groups to discuss the topic in more detail or carry out activities. The duration of a seminar is usually one or two hours. They are led by lecturers but are more interactive and personal than a lecture. You will be expected to have prepared reading around the topic and contribute actively to the discussions.

Practical sessions

Practical sessions enable you to develop skills and techniques that you need to be able to apply your knowledge in subjects with a practical element. They may be laboratory classes or may involve carrying out field research. Practical work may be assessed and contribute towards your final marks for your course.

Personal tutorial sessions or supervisions

Personal tutorial sessions or supervisions are sessions provided by a lecturer for one to one support with a student, although there may be options for smaller group sessions. They are led by a member of teaching staff who is your personal tutor for the teaching period and usually last in duration for a shorter period of time, varying between 15 minutes to up to one hour.

They enable you to discuss your topic in greater depth or if you are having any difficulties with any aspect of the course. They help you to develop independent learning skills, discuss your work and receive constructive feedback. You may have a personal tutorial on a regular basis or periodically, depending on the course and higher education institution. You may be required to carry out some preparatory work which is discussed during a tutorial / supervision.

Independent research

Undergraduate courses involve you undertaking independent research and you will usually be required to submit one or more research projects or a dissertation which will be assessed.

Field trips, study visits, language courses

As part of your course, you may be required to carry out other activities which help you develop a greater understanding of the subject you are studying. These will depend on your course and there may be options to undertake field trips, study visits or language courses in the UK or in some situations, abroad.

Work experience

Some courses at some higher education institutions include a period of work experience or internship which will give you valuable experience, help you to explore career options, provide the opportunity to make contact with employers and may lead to a job opportunity after you graduate. Some professional courses require you to undertake work experience as an integral part of the course.

Some courses at some higher education institutions include the opportunity to study outside of the UK through exchange programmes. There may be linked with other higher education institutions or may be through the Erasmus Scheme. See the:
Chapter 9.3
Erasmus: Study and Work Experience Programme in another European Country
Chapter 12.6
Erasmus Funding Support for Undergraduate and Postgraduate Students

Higher Education Assessment

Learning in higher education involves being able to develop a range of skills. Assessment will take the form of a variety of methods to take account how you have developed these skills, helping you to develop a well-rounded set of abilities by the time you graduate. Some assessment methods will cover different skills and abilities and will vary between courses and higher education institutions
The following are the most commonly used

- Dissertations
- Examinations
- Essays
- Group work projects
- Individual presentations
- Research project
- Practical skills
- Practical work based competencies
- Reports

Assessment of skills and abilities
The following highlights the range of skills and abilities that you may need to demonstrate.

Thinking critically and making judgements
Being able to develop arguments and debates, reflect, evaluate, assess and judge theories.

Types of assessment may include:
Writing essays, reviews and articles, reports and journals

Solving problems and developing plans
Identifying and defining problems, analysing data, undertaking reviews, designing experiments, planning and applying information.

Types of assessment may include:
Group work; work based problem; researching; analysing articles and reports

Performing procedures and demonstrating techniques
Using technology to analyse data, using relevant equipment, producing artefacts or material relevant to the course, carrying out laboratory procedures, carrying out instructions

Types of assessment may include:
Individual presentations; group presentations; role play; production of a film, music, artwork, script; laboratory report; observation of professional practice

Self-management and organisation
Working and learning independently, working with others, managing your time effectively, managing tasks independently and with others, ability to reflect on your positive strengths and how to improve your weaknesses.

Types of assessment may include:
Group work; individual projects or reports; writing a journal; producing a portfolio

Accessing and managing information
Researching, investigating, interpreting, organising reviewing and paraphrasing information, collecting data, searching and managing information sources, observing and interpreting

Types of assessment may include:
Research projects; dissertations; undertaking applied tasks; producing annotated bibliographies

Demonstrating knowledge and understanding
Being able to recall, describe, report, recount, recognise, identify and interpret relevant information

Types of assessment may include:
Written examinations; oral examinations; essays; evaluative and reflective reports; reports; dissertations; multiple choice questions

Designing, creating, performing
Includes designing, visualising, producing, creating, showing innovation, performing.

Types of assessment may include:
Performances; portfolios; individual and group presentations; projects; production of a piece of work

Communication
Includes writing, speaking, listening, developing arguments and debates, describing, interviewing, negotiating, presenting.

Types of assessment may include:
Essays; evaluative and reflective reports; reports; individual presentation; group work; debates and role play; observation of professional practice

Qualification Size

As well as qualification levels, qualifications are also given a qualification size which is expressed as Total Qualification Time (TQT). This is a measure of how long it takes to complete a specific qualification, referring to the estimated total amount of time it typically takes to study and be assessed, which may be a matter of hours or several years of study, with some students taking different amounts of time to study the same qualification. The part of that time spent being taught or supervised rather than studying alone, is known as Guided Learning Hours (GLH). Qualifications may sit at different levels but require similar amounts of study and assessment time.

Higher Education Course Credit Structure

Your higher education subject will consist of a number of topics taught as units or elements known as modules. Each module is worth a set number of credits completed as part of the qualification with each unit having a credit value, developing into qualifications over time. Credit values may be different depending on the course and the higher education institution.

Higher education credits are part of a national scheme which allows you to work towards a nationally recognised award at most higher education institutions. Credits are recognition by your university or college when you have successfully completed a unit of study.

The credit value indicates how long it will usually take to complete a unit. One credit usually takes 10 hours of learning to complete. Credits are usually assigned to a unit of study in multiples of 10. They give an indication of the level at which you are working and the amount of work involved. Each module may usually be worth 10, 20 or 30 credits and will vary between courses and higher education institutions.

Modules are usually single awards but may also be offered as double or treble modules and are combined together to form the course.

Some modules consist of core (mandatory or compulsory) subjects which means you will have to study these subjects but others will be optional and you will have a choice of what subjects to choose.

The number of credits and combination of module subjects required for your course should be detailed in the regulation information supplied by your university or college such as a course handbook or fact sheets which should be given to you during the induction period, or available on the institution website.

Credit Accumulation and Transfer Scheme (CATS)

The Credit Accumulation and Transfer Scheme (CATS), adopted by the majority of higher education institutions (HEIs), is a method expressing a particular credit mark or weighting for each unit (module) of learning. The CAT scheme equates 1 credit (or credit point) with 10 hours of learning time, used as a measure.

The learning time is the number of hours expected that you as a learner, at a particular level, will spend, on average, to achieve the specified learning outcomes. This includes a range of teaching and learning activities including lectures, seminars, laboratory sessions and self-directed learning time, such as reading prior to classes, research for written assignments, and examination preparation. A module allocated 20 credits or CATS points, should require you to commit about 200 hours of work to achieve the learning outcomes for the module. Further information may be found at the:
Quality Assurance Agency: Credit Accumulation and Transfer Scheme (CATS),
http://www.qaa.ac.uk/assuring-standards-and-quality/academic-credit

The number of credits required to achieve a higher education course may vary between courses and universities or colleges. However, the nationally accepted amount of credits for a full-time undergraduate (UG) course is 120 credits for each higher education level (each year if studying full time).

You usually need to obtain up to 360 credits in total, sometimes more, at specified HE levels to be awarded an honours degree. However, the number of credits required may vary between courses as HEIs may have different requirements. It may be possible to obtain fewer than 360 credits to still be awarded an honours degree for some courses.

Credits for each HE level will need to be successfully passed before continuing on to the next level. Usually the credits passed for the first level of your degree don't count towards your final degree classification however you will need to successfully pass this level before you can progress to the second level. To achieve an honours degree, you will need to successfully pass the requirements of the assessment of your course at each designated level. Information about credits may be found on the:
Quality Assurance Agency for Higher Education (QAA): Academic Credit
http://www.qaa.ac.uk/assuring-standards-and-quality/the-quality-code/academic-credit

Undergraduate Course Credits

Undergraduate course credits are generally awarded for:
- Certificate of Higher Education: awarded:
  120 credits at level 4 (FHEQ) or level 7 (SCQF)
- Diploma of Higher Education awarded:
  240 credits with
  120 at level 4 (FHEQ) or level 7(SCQF) and
  120 at level 5 (FHEQ) or level 8 (SCQF)
- Bachelor's Honours Degree awarded:
  360 credits in total with
  120 credits at level 4 (FHEQ) or 7(SCQF), 120 credits at level 5 (FHEQ) or level 8 (SCQF) and
  120 credits at level 6 (FHEQ) or level 9 /10 (SCQF).

Some degrees may be worth more credits, especially if they include professional qualifications and some will last longer than three years. Integrated master's degree courses, which combine an honours and master's' degree are also worth more credits with usually 360 credits for the undergraduate course and 120 postgraduate credits.

Universities may also refer to the year of higher education study as: HE level 0 preparation course equal to level 3 RQF;

HE level 1 equal to level 4 FHEQ, HE level 2 equal to level 5 FHEQ; or HE level 3 equal to level 6 FHEQ. You will usually be required to pass each level before moving to the next level, dependent on your university regulations. If you study for a joint degree, you will usually be awarded 360 credits in total with 180 credits in each subject. If you study for a major/minor degree you will usually need 360 credits in total with 240 credits in the major subject and 120 credits in the minor subject. A bachelor's ordinary degree will usually be awarded with 300 credits, although you would need to have a set number of credits at HE levels 1, 2 and 3 (FEHQ 4, 5 and 6), dependent on your university regulations.

Foundation year and extended year courses are usually awarded:
 120 credits at HE level 0

These courses are not usually counted in the full degree award, although you would need to pass this type of course successfully before moving to a higher level. Many honours degree courses don't count the HE level 1 credits towards your final degree classification but you would need to successfully complete this level before moving into HE level 2.

Postgraduate Course Credits

Postgraduate course credits for modules may also vary but generally are awarded:

- Postgraduate Certificate awarded: 60 credits at level 7 (FEHQ) or level 11 (SCQF)
- Postgraduate Diploma awarded: 120 credits at level 7 (FEHQ) or level 11 (SCQF)

  Master's Degree awarded: 180 credits at level 7 (FEHQ) or level 11 (SCQF).

Not all universities allocate credits to research based courses such as MPhils or Doctorate Degrees, but those that do may allocate

- MPhil awarded: 360 credits at level 7 (FEHQ) or level 11 (SCQF)
- Doctorate Degree awarded: 540 credits at level 8 (FEHQ) or level 12 (SCQF).

European Credit Transfer Systems (ECTS)

Credits for higher education courses are recognised throughout Europe. The European Credit Transfer Systems (ECTS) system makes it easier for students to study in higher education in other parts of Europe. Further information may be found on Europa: European Credit Transfer Systems (ECTS) http://ec.europa.eu/education/ects/ects_en.htm

Chapter 7
Universities, Higher Education Colleges and Specialist Institutions

7.1 Types and Groups of Universities, Colleges of Higher Education and Specialist Institutions

Although each higher education institution (HEI) is unique, it may be helpful to understand the UK higher education sector by looking at the types of higher education providers and the groups and associations that define the different universities and colleges.

Universities and colleges may be referred to within a set type such as old university, new university, college of higher education, specialist institution (offering a small number of courses such as a conservatoire, art school or agricultural / horticultural college), distance learning provider, further education college (some also offer higher education courses) or the more recent university technical colleges.

A number of universities and colleges have also joined together to form groups and associations with common interests, although many remain unaffiliated. The groups include various regional associations and the 'mission groups'. Along with representing member institutions, these groups work to develop policy and lobby government on higher education issues.

University league tables, where you can compare data on a range of aspects, may refer to some of these groups of universities and rank them in order of achievement. The following information explains these different types and groups of higher education institutions in more detail.

Types of Higher Education Institutions

- Old Universities
- Ancient Universities
  - Collegiate Universities
- Redbrick Universities
- Plate-Glass Universities
- New Universities
- Colleges of Higher Education with University Status

- Conservatoires
- Art Schools
- Distance Learning
- Colleges of Further Education
- University Technical Colleges
- Private Higher Education Providers

Old Universities

'Old Universities' in the UK are those that were founded before the late 1960's and gained university status before 1992. They can be subdivided into three subcategories; ancient (collegiate), red brick and plate glass universities, although some 'old universities' don't fit into any category.

Ancient Universities

'Ancient' universities were the first universities to be founded before 19th century and are world leaders in research, offering traditional academic courses with usually very high entry requirements. Ancient universities may be made up of a number of colleges, and are known as collegiate universities, so although they may be large institutions, the colleges provide an environment with smaller numbers of students.

Collegiate Universities

The 'ancient' collegiate universities founded before 1800 include the following
See below for the university colleges

England
University of Oxford, founded in the 11th century   http://www.ox.ac.uk/
University of Cambridge, founded in 13th century   http://www.cam.ac.uk

Scotland
University of St Andrews, founded in 15th century   https://www.st-andrews.ac.uk/
University of Glasgow, founded in 15th century   http://www.gla.ac.uk/
University of Aberdeen, founded in 15th century   http://www.abdn.ac.uk
University of Edinburgh, founded in 16th century   http://www.ed.ac.uk/

Republic of Ireland (not part of the UK)
University of Dublin, now Trinity College Dublin, founded in 16th century
Trinity College Dublin   http://www.tcd.ie/

Universities founded in 19th century and often included with the 'Ancient' Universities
England
Durham University
http://www.durhamstudent.co.uk/
London University (which now has a number of separate institutions)
London University
http://www.london.ac.uk/
The Royal College of Art
https://www.rca.ac.uk/

Wales
University of Wales, (which now has a number of separate institutions)
University of Wales
http://www.wales.ac.uk

England: Collegiate Universities

University of Cambridge
http://www.cam.ac.uk/
The University of Cambridge is a collegiate system, consisting of 31 independent and self-governing colleges. For undergraduate courses, you would apply through UCAS to an individual College of the University of Cambridge.

Durham University
http://www.durham.ac.uk
Durham, England
Durham University consists of two campuses with colleges at both campuses:
Durham Campus has 14 colleges, with 13 undergraduate and 1 postgraduate only
Queen's campus has two colleges. If your course is based in Durham, you will be a member of a Durham-based college. If your course is based at Queen's Campus, Stockton, you will be a member of a Queen's-based college.
For undergraduate courses, you would apply through UCAS to Durham University and may be allocated a college.

Lancaster University
http://www.lancs.ac.uk
Lancashire, England
The University of Lancaster consists of nine colleges, eight for undergraduates and one for postgraduates. For undergraduate courses, you would apply through UCAS to the University of Lancaster and may be allocated a college.

University of London: Colleges and Institutes
http://www.london.ac.uk/
The University of London is a federal university, with teaching carried out by 18 self-governing colleges and 10 research institutes that comprise the University. Students belong to a particular College as well as the University of London, enabling access to a wide range of facilities and services. The Colleges are self-governing and are considered individual institutions, when it comes to making an application to study, however check types of courses on the individual College websites as each College may vary in provision, with some offering specialist subjects and some providing only postgraduate courses.

Each College sets their own entrance criteria and some have their own degree awarding powers.

Imperial College London
http://www3.imperial.ac.uk/
obtained independence from the University of London in 2007.
For undergraduate courses, you would apply through UCAS to an individual College / University of the University of London.

University of Oxford
http://www.ox.ac.uk/
Oxfordshire, England
The University of Oxford is a collegiate system consisting of 44 four independent and self-governing Colleges (38) and Halls (6). For undergraduate courses, you would apply through UCAS to an individual College of the University of Oxford

University of York
http://www.york.ac.uk
The University of York has nine Colleges

Scotland: Collegiate Universities

University of Aberdeen
http://www.abdn.ac.uk/
The university consists of three colleges with two campuses at Old Aberdeen and Foresterhill
For undergraduate courses, you would apply through UCAS to the University of Aberdeen and may be allocated a college.

University of Edinburgh
http://www.ed.ac.uk/home
Edinburgh, Midlothian, Scotland
The University of Edinburgh consists of three colleges containing twenty two schools
For undergraduate courses, you would apply through UCAS to the University of Edinburgh and may be allocated a college.

University of Glasgow
http://www.gla.ac.uk/
Glasgow, Lanarkshire, Scotland
The University of Glasgow consists of four colleges
For undergraduate courses, you would apply through UCAS to the University of Glasgow and may be allocated a college.

Wales: Universities

University of Wales
http://www.wales.ac.uk
Changes have happened with the University of Wales and it now consists of a number of separate institutions with the former constituent colleges leaving the University of Wales structure. The University of Wales, Swansea Metropolitan University and the University of Wales: Trinity St David merged in 2011.

A unified institution is now called the: University of Wales: Trinity Saint David
http://www.uwtsd.ac.uk/

For undergraduate courses, you would apply through UCAS to an individual University of the University of Wales.

Website links to collegiate colleges may be found in the chapters on Universities in alphabetical order and by region.

Redbrick Universities

The origin of the term 'red brick' was used to describe the first six 'civic' non-collegiate universities founded in the industrial cities of England which achieved university status in the early 19th century, after the distinctive colour of the red brick of the University of Liverpool. However, some universities have formed groups with other similar universities and the modern use of the term 'redbrick', is often used to refer to the group of universities termed the 'Russell Group', which includes the 'Ancient Universities'. Additional 'redbrick' universities were members of the 1994 Group of universities which has now disbanded. Further information on 'Higher Education groups' can be found below.

Russell Group 'Red Brick' Universities

The original six civic 'red brick' members of the Russell Group universities https://russellgroup.ac.uk/
University of Birmingham
http://www.birmingham.ac.uk/
University of Bristol
http://www.bristol.ac.uk/
University of Leeds
https://www.leeds.ac.uk/
University of Liverpool
http://www.liv.ac.uk/
University of Manchester
http://www.manchester.ac.uk/
University of Sheffield
http://www.sheffield.ac.uk/

Additional 'Red Brick' Members of the Russell Group
University of Cambridge
http://www.cam.ac.uk
Cardiff University
http://www.cardiff.ac.uk/
Durham University
http://www.durhamstudent.co.uk/
University of Edinburgh
http://www.ed.ac.uk/
University of Exeter
http://www.exeter.ac.uk/
University of Glasgow
http://www.gla.ac.uk/
Imperial College London
https://www.imperial.ac.uk/
King's College London
http://www.kcl.ac.uk/
University of Liverpool
http://www.liv.ac.uk/
London School of Economics & Political Science
http://www.lse.ac.uk/
Newcastle University
http://www.ncl.ac.uk/
University of Nottingham

http://www.nottingham.ac.uk/
Queen Mary, University of London
http://www.qmul.ac.uk/
Queen's University Belfast
http://www.qub.ac.uk/
University College London
http://www.ucl.ac.uk/
University of Oxford
http://www.ox.ac.uk/
University of Southampton
http://www.southampton.ac.uk/
University of Warwick
https://www2.warwick.ac.uk/
University of York
http://www.york.ac.uk/

Additional 'Redbrick' Universities: Not Members of the Russell Group
Birkbeck, University of London
http://www.bbk.ac.uk/
University of East Anglia (UEA)
http://www.uea.ac.uk
University of Essex
http://www.essex.ac.uk
Goldsmiths, University of London
http://www.gold.ac.uk
Institute of Education University of London
http://www.ioe.ac.uk/
Lancaster University
http://www.lancs.ac.uk
University of Leicester
http://www.le.ac.uk
Loughborough University
http://www.lboro.ac.uk/
Royal Holloway, University of London
http://www.rhul.ac.uk
School of Oriental and African Studies (SOAS)
http://www.soas.ac.uk
University of Sussex
http://www.sussex.ac.uk

Plate-Glass Universities

The term 'plate-glass' was a term used by Michael Beloff , to described universities that reflected a particular architectural design, which had a lot of plate glass in steel or concrete frames and mostly gained university status during the 1960's. This term is rarely used now.

Universities that may be referred to as Plate-glass

Aston University
http://www.aston.ac.uk/
University of Bath
http://www.bath.ac.uk/
University of Bradford
http://www.bradford.ac.uk/
Brunel University
http://www.brunel.ac.uk/
City University London
http://www.city.ac.uk/
University of East Anglia (UEA)
http://www.uea.ac.uk
University of Essex
http://www.essex.ac.uk
Heriot-Watt University
http://www.hw.ac.uk
Keele University
http://www.keele.ac.uk
University of Kent

http://www.kent.ac.uk
Lancaster University
http://www.lancs.ac.uk
Loughborough University
http://www.lboro.ac.uk/
University of Salford
http://www.salford.ac.uk
University of Stirling
http://www.stir.ac.uk/
University of Strathclyde Glasgow
http://www.strath.ac.uk
University of Surrey
http://www.surrey.ac.uk
University of Sussex
http://www.sussex.ac.uk
University of Ulster
http://www.ulster.ac.uk
University of Warwick
http://www2.warwick.ac.uk/
University of York
http://www.york.ac.uk

New Universities

'New universities' are those higher education institutions which were originally called 'Polytechnics' in England, Wales and Northern Ireland, and 'Central Institutions' in Scotland. They were mostly formed during the expansion of higher education in the 1960's. In 1992, these higher education institutions became independent and gained university status, often referred to as the 'New Universities'.

'New Universities' awarded university status in 1992

University of Abertay Dundee
http://www.abertay.ac.uk/
Anglia Ruskin University
http://www.anglia.ac.uk/
Bath Spa University
https://www.bathspa.ac.uk/
University of Bedfordshire
http://www.beds.ac.uk/
Birmingham City University
http://www.bcu.ac.uk/
University of Bolton
http://www.bolton.ac.uk/
Bournemouth University
http://home.bournemouth.ac.uk/
University of Brighton
http://www.brighton.ac.uk/
University of Central Lancashire
http://www.uclan.ac.uk/
Coventry University
http://www.coventry.ac.uk
De Montfort University
http://www.dmu.ac.uk
University of Derby
http://www.derby.ac.uk
University of East London
http://www.uel.ac.uk
Edge Hill University
http://www.edgehill.ac.uk
Edinburgh Napier University
http://www.napier.ac.uk
Glasgow Caledonian University
http://www.gcu.ac.uk
University of Gloucestershire
http://www.glos.ac.uk
University of Greenwich
http://www2.gre.ac.uk/
University of Hertfordshire
http://www.herts.ac.uk
University of Huddersfield
http://www.hud.ac.uk
Kingston University
http://www.kingston.ac.uk
Leeds Becket University
http://www.leedsbeckett.ac.uk/
University of Lincoln
http://www.lincoln.ac.uk
Liverpool Hope University

http://www.hope.ac.uk
Liverpool John Moores University
http://www.ljmu.ac.uk
London Metropolitan University
http://www.londonmet.ac.uk
London South Bank University
http://www.lsbu.ac.uk
Manchester Metropolitan University
http://www2.mmu.ac.uk/
Middlesex University
http://www.mdx.ac.uk
Northumbria University
http://www.northumbria.ac.uk
Nottingham Trent University
http://www.ntu.ac.uk
University of Northampton
http://www.northampton.ac.uk/
Oxford Brookes University
http://www.brookes.ac.uk
Plymouth University
https://www.plymouth.ac.uk/
University of Portsmouth
http://www.port.ac.uk
Robert Gordon University
http://www.rgu.ac.uk
University of Roehampton
http://www.roehampton.ac.uk
Southampton Solent University
http://www.solent.ac.uk
Staffordshire University
http://www.staffs.ac.uk/
University of Sunderland
http://www.sunderland.ac.uk
Southampton Solent University
http://www.solent.ac.uk/
Teesside University
http://www.tees.ac.uk
University of West London
http://www.uwl.ac.uk
University of the West of England
http://www.uwe.ac.uk/
University of the West of Scotland
http://www.uws.ac.uk
University of Westminster
http://www.westminster.ac.uk
University of Wolverhampton
http://www.wlv.ac.uk

Colleges of higher education originally provided courses in specialist areas such as subjects in the arts, agriculture or teacher training, and had degree awarding powers. Some Colleges of Higher Education were awarded university status in 2005 and others in 2012.

The UK government announced in 2012 that a higher education institution in England could be called a university if it had a minimum of 1,000 (reduced from 4,000), full time equivalent students of whom at least 750 are registered on degree courses, including foundation degree courses, and the number of full time equivalent (FTE) higher education students must exceed 55% of the total number of FTE students, in order to reduce the confusion over the nature of university colleges.

Some of these universities provide additional courses as well as the original specialist courses. Some Colleges of Higher Education have merged or joined a partnership with other Universities.

In Scotland and Northern Ireland, colleges applying for University Title (UT) are expected to have at least 300 FTE higher education students in five subject areas, with at least 4,000 FTE enrolled students including 3,000 FTE students on degree level courses, with at least 60 current research degree registrations and more than 30 registered on Doctor of Philosophy courses.

Further information may be found at Quality Assurance Agency for Higher Education (QAA): right to award degrees http://www.qaa.ac.uk/en/Publications/Documents/right-to-award-degrees.pdf

Colleges of Higher Education granted full university status since 2005:
These Universities may have had the title of university before 2005 but were granted full university status from 2005.
Canterbury Christ Church University
http://www.canterbury.ac.uk/
Queen Margaret University
http://www.qmu.ac.uk
University of Chester
http://www.chester.ac.uk/
University of Chichester
http://www.chi.ac.uk
University of Cumbria
http://www.cumbria.ac.uk
University of Winchester
http://www.winchester.ac.uk
University of Worcester
http://www.worcester.ac.uk
York St John University
http://www.yorksj.ac.uk

Colleges of Higher Education granted university status in 2012
Arts University Bournemouth
http://aub.ac.uk/
Bishop Grosseteste University College
http://www.bishopg.ac.uk/
Falmouth University
http://www.falmouth.ac.uk/
Harper Adams University
http://www.harper-adams.ac.uk
Leeds Trinity University
http://www.leedstrinity.ac.uk
Newman University
http://www.newman.ac.uk
Norwich University of the Arts
http://www.nua.ac.uk
Royal Agricultural University
http://www.rac.ac.uk
St Mary's University
http://www.smuc.ac.uk
University College Birmingham
http://www.ucb.ac.uk/
University St Mark and St John Plymouth
http://www.marjon.ac.uk/

Conservatoires

Conservatoires UK
http://www.conservatoiresuk.ac.uk/
Many Higher Education Institutions (HEIs) provide music, dance and drama courses, however Conservatoires are specialist institutions that provide only practice based music, dance or drama courses. Conservatoires UK (CUK) is the umbrella organisation which represents the collective views of music education and training across nine major UK conservatoires.

Conservatoires UK is a group of 9 specialist member institutions which offer undergraduate and postgraduate music courses with some also offering, drama and dance.

UCAS run a clearing house
https://www.ucas.com/ucas/conservatoires/ucas-conservatoires-apply-and-track for applications for selective courses, where you may have up to six course choices, although some conservatoire courses should be made through the standard UCAS applications route https://www.ucas.com/ where you may have up to five course choices.

For applications to the Guildhall School of Music and Drama, you would need to apply directly to the institution and not through UCAS.

Members of Conservatoires UK

Members of Conservatoires UK
Birmingham Conservatoire
http://www.bcu.ac.uk/pme/conservatoire
Guildhall School of Music and Drama:
http://www.gsmd.ac.uk/
Leeds College of Music
http://www.lcm.ac.uk/
Royal Academy of Music
http://www.ram.ac.uk/
Royal College of Music

http://www.rcm.ac.uk/
Royal Northern College of Music
http://www.rncm.ac.uk/
Royal Conservatoire of Scotland
http://www.rcs.ac.uk/
Royal Welsh College of Music and Drama
http://www.rwcmd.ac.uk/
Trinity Laban Conservatoire of Music and Dance
http://www.trinitylaban.ac.uk/

Art Schools

Whilst many Higher Education Institutions (HEIs) provide a range of courses, including Art subjects, some specialist institutions only provide visual Arts, which include drawing, painting, sculpture, graphic design, illustration, photography, commercial art, fashion, textiles or history of art subjects. In the UK, the term Art School is used to describe a specialist institution with undergraduate or postgraduate courses in the arts.

Distance Learning

Distance learning is a method of education you can study online without face to face contact with a teacher. This means you can study in your own time and at the place of your choice, at home, at work or in a centre that has access to technology. Distance Learning is also known as Supported Open Learning, Flexible Learning or Flexible Distributed Learning. Many higher education institutions offer the option of Distance Learning for some courses however the Open University http://www.open.ac.uk/ offers only Distance Learning courses.

Colleges of Further Education

Further education colleges (FECs) offer a range of academic, vocational and professional courses for post-school students who are 16 years and above. FECs tend to be influenced by the industry and commerce in the local community and the majority of full time students are usually aged 16-19 years with most part time students being over 19 years of age.

Qualification levels include, introductory through to advanced level and will be awarded by recognised awarding bodies. Some of these colleges may also offer some higher education level courses for students aged 18 years and above and may be known as colleges of further and higher education. These higher education (HE) qualifications need to be awarded by a recognised university or college in order for the college to meet the approval to receive funding by the Higher Education Funding Council (HEFCE).

Some FECs have a franchise arrangement whereby students will be registered with a higher education institution (HEI) but some or all of the teaching is delivered through a sub-contractual arrangement. Contacts for Further Education Colleges may be found in local directories, from your local Careers Service or through links on the Higher Education Funding Councils websites.

Further Education Course Search

Further education courses, including art foundation courses and access courses, may be found by searching further education colleges at:

England
Association of Colleges England
https://www.aoc.co.uk/

Wales
College Wales
http://www.collegeswales.ac.uk/

Northern Ireland
Colleges Northern Ireland
http://www.anic.ac.uk/

Scotland
Colleges Scotland
http://www.collegesscotland.ac.uk/

University Technical Colleges

University Technical Colleges (UTCs) http://www.utcolleges.org/utcs are recent education institutions, with the first opening in 2010, based around England. They provide technically oriented courses for students aged 14-18 and are sponsored by universities and businesses, providing progression routes into higher education or further work based learning. UTCs specialise in technical subjects, including engineering, product design, health sciences, construction, land and environmental services.

Private Higher Education Providers

Recently, there has been a growth in private higher education providers in the UK and worldwide. Subjects available in private HEIs may be specialist or limited, and entry requirements may vary so check with individual providers. Some privately funded HEIs have official degree awarding powers. Recognised privately funded HEIs that don't have degree awarding powers will have a partnership with other universities that are officially recognised to award degrees. The privately funded HEIs should have information about which universities provide accreditation of their courses on the websites

Selection of some private higher education providers

- BPP University
  http://www.bpp.com
- College of Estate Management
  http://www.cem.ac.uk
- Cranfield University
  http://www.cranfield.ac.uk/
- Hult International Business School
  http://www.hult.edu/
- IFS (Institute of Financial Studies) School of Finance
  http://www.ifslearning.ac.uk
- Kaplan
  http://www.kaplan.co.uk/
- Laureate Online Education
  http://www.laureate.net

Working in partnership with:
University of Liverpool: delivering online graduate and doctoral programs and
University of Roehampton: delivering online degrees.
- Pearson College
  http://www.pearsoncollege.com/
- Regents College
  http://www.regents.ac.uk
- The University of Buckingham
  http://www.buckingham.ac.uk
- University of Law (previously College of Law)
  http://www.law.ac.uk/

Groups, Associations and Affiliations of Higher Education Institution

Some universities and colleges are members of a mission group or association. The following groups may change members at times, so check on the given websites for up to date information. The 1994 group disbanded in November 2013.

- The Cathedrals Group
  http://www.cathedralsgroup.ac.uk/
- GuildHE
  http://guildhe.ac.uk/
  Associate and Sub Associate group of Guild HE:
- Consortium for Research Excellence, Support and Training (CREST)
  http://crest.ac.uk/
  Associate and Sub Associate group of Guild HE:

- United Kingdom Arts and Design Institutions Association (UKADIA)
  http://ukadia.ac.uk/
- Million Plus Group
  http://www.millionplus.ac.uk/
- The Russell Group
  http://www.russellgroup.ac.uk/
- University Alliance
  http://www.unialliance.ac.uk/
- Universities UK
  http://www.universitiesuk.ac.uk

Universities UK

Universities UK
http://www.universitiesuk.ac.uk
A large number of universities do not belong to any of the associations or mission groups but many do belong to 'Universities UK' which is a group of over one hundred member universities and some colleges of higher education in the UK which seek to influence and create higher education policy.

Members of the Universities UK: higher education institutions
Links to a group of over one hundred member universities and some colleges of higher education in the UK:
Universities UK
http://www.universitiesuk.ac.uk

The Cathedrals Group

The Cathedrals Group
http://www.cathedralsgroup.ac.uk/
This is not a mission group but an association of universities and colleges with Church foundations, supporting the

Churches' continuing role in Higher Education and has close links with the Anglican, Roman Catholic and Methodist Churches

Members of the Cathedrals Group: Higher Education Institutions

Bishop Grosseteste University College
http://www.bishopg.ac.uk/
Canterbury Christ Church University
http://www.canterbury.ac.uk/
Heythrop College, University of London
http://www.heythrop.ac.uk
Leeds Trinity University
http://www.leedstrinity.ac.uk
Liverpool Hope University
http://www.hope.ac.uk
Newman University
http://www.newman.ac.uk
St Mary's University
http://www.smuc.ac.uk
University of Chester
http://www.chester.ac.uk/

University of Chichester
http://www.chi.ac.uk
University of Cumbria
http://www.cumbria.ac.uk
University of Gloucestershire
http://www.glos.ac.uk
University of Roehampton
http://www.roehampton.ac.uk
University St Mark and St John Plymouth
http://www.marjon.ac.uk/
University of Wales Trinity Saint David
http://www.uwtsd.ac.uk/
University of Winchester
http://www.winchester.ac.uk
York St John University
http://www.yorksj.ac.uk

GuildHE

GuildHE

http://guildhe.ac.uk/

GuildHE is a representative body for higher education in the UK. It is a Company Limited by guarantee and a Charity, originally founded in 1967 as the Standing Conference of Principals. It registered as a company in 1992 and became GuildHE in 2006. This group of Higher Education Institutions (HEIs) represents institutions specialising in art and design, teacher training, agriculture, music and drama.

Members of GuildHE: Higher Education Institutions

Arts University Bournemouth
http://aub.ac.uk/
Ashridge Business School
http://ashridge.org.uk
University College Birmingham
http://www.ucb.ac.uk/
Bishop Grosseteste University College
http://www.bishopg.ac.uk/
Buckinghamshire New University
http://bucks.ac.uk/
University for the Creative Arts
http://www.ucreative.ac.uk
University of Chichester
http://www.chi.ac.uk
Falmouth University
http://www.falmouth.ac.uk
Glyndwr University
http://www.glyndwr.ac.uk
Harper Adams University
http://www.harper-adams.ac.uk
Leeds College of Art
http://www.leeds-art.ac.uk
Leeds Trinity University
http://www.leedstrinity.ac.uk
The Liverpool Institute for Performing Arts
http://www.lipa.ac.uk
Newman University
http://www.newman.ac.uk
Norwich University of the Arts
http://www.nua.ac.uk

Ravensbourne Higher Education College
http://www.ravensbourne.ac.uk/
Regent's University London
http://www.regents.ac.uk/
Rose Bruford College of Theatre and Performance
http://www.bruford.ac.uk
Royal Agricultural University
http://www.rac.ac.uk
Royal Central School of Speech and Drama
http://www.cssd.ac.uk/
Southampton Solent University
http://www.solent.ac.uk/
University of St Mark and St John Plymouth
http://www.marjon.ac.uk/
St Mary's University College Belfast
https://www.stmarys-belfast.ac.uk/
St Mary's University
http://www.smuc.ac.uk
University of Winchester
http://www.winchester.ac.uk
University of Worcester
http://www.worcester.ac.uk
Writtle College
http://www.writtle.ac.uk
York St John University
http://www.yorksj.ac.uk

Associate Members of GuildHE: Higher Education Institutions

Bradford College
https://www.bradfordcollege.ac.uk/
Cleveland College of Art and Design
http://www.ccad.ac.uk
Milton Keynes College
http://www.mkcollege.ac.uk
Plymouth College of Art
http://www.plymouthart.ac.uk
SAE Institute

http://uk.sae.edu/
Anglo European College of Chiropractic
http://www.aecc.ac.uk/
The British School of Osteopathy
http://www.bso.ac.uk/
The Tavistock and Portman NHS Trust
http://tavistockandportman.uk/
UCFB College of Football business Ltd
http://www.ucfb.com/

Consortium for Research Excellence, Support and Training (CREST) Sub-Association of GuildHE

Consortium for Research Excellence, Support and Training (CREST)
http://crest.ac.uk/

CREST provides an innovative model for how to further research excellence and promote institutional and interdisciplinary collaboration. It is a sub-association of GuildHE

Members of the Consortium for Research Excellence, Support and Training (CREST) Sub-Association of GuildHE: Higher Education Institutions

Bishop Grosseteste University College
http://www.bishopg.ac.uk/
Buckinghamshire New University
http://bucks.ac.uk/
Glyndwr University
http://www.glyndwr.ac.uk
Harper Adams University
http://www.harper-adams.ac.uk
Leeds College of Art
http://www.leeds-art.ac.uk:
Leeds Trinity University
http://www.leedstrinity.ac.uk
Newman University
http://www.newman.ac.uk
Norwich University of the Arts
http://www.nua.ac.uk
Plymouth College of Art
http://www.plymouthart.ac.uk
Ravensbourne Higher Education College
http://www.ravensbourne.ac.uk/
Regent's University London
http://www.regents.ac.uk/
Royal Agricultural University

http://www.rac.ac.uk
Southampton Solent University
http://www.solent.ac.uk
St Mary's University Twickenham
http://www.smuc.ac.uk
University for the Creative Arts
http://www.ucreative.ac.uk
University of Chichester
http://www.chi.ac.uk
University of Cumbria
http://www.cumbria.ac.uk
University of St Mark and St John Plymouth
http://www.marjon.ac.uk/
University of Winchester
http://www.winchester.ac.uk
University of Worcester
http://www.worcester.ac.uk
Writtle College
Writtle College
http://www.writtle.ac.uk
York St John University
http://www.yorksj.ac.uk

United Kingdom Arts and Design Institutions Association (UKADIA) Sub-Association of Guild HE

United Kingdom Arts and Design Institutions Association (UKADIA)
http://ukadia.ac.uk/

UKADIA, sub-association of GuildHE, is a group of some of the specialist arts and design institutions from across the UK's higher and further education

Members of the United Kingdom Arts and Design Institutions Association (UKADIA) sub-association of Guild HE: higher education institutions

University of the Arts London
http://www.arts.ac.uk
Arts University Bournemouth
http://aub.ac.uk/
University for the Creative Arts
http://www.ucreative.ac.uk
Falmouth University
http://www.falmouth.ac.uk
Hereford College of Arts
http://www.hca.ac.uk
Leeds College of Art
http://www.leeds-art.ac.uk:
Norwich University of the Arts
http://www.nua.ac.uk

Northern School of Art (previously Cleveland College of Art and Design)
https://northernart.ac.uk/
Plymouth College of Art
http://www.plymouthart.ac.uk
Ravensbourne Higher Education College
http://www.ravensbourne.ac.uk/
Rose Bruford College of Theatre and Performance
http://www.bruford.ac.uk
Royal Central School of Speech and Drama
http://www.cssd.ac.uk/
Royal College of Art
http://www.rca.ac.uk/

Million Plus Group

Million Plus Group
http://www.millionplus.ac.uk/
The Million+, formerly called Campaigning for Mainstream Universities (CMU), is a university think-tank which publishes research reports and policy papers to provide solutions to problems in higher education.

Members of the Million Plus Group: higher education institutions
Affiliates

University of Abertay
http://www.abertay.ac.uk/
Anglia Ruskin University
http://www.anglia.ac.uk/
Bath Spa University
https://www.bathspa.ac.uk/
University of Bedfordshire
http://www.beds.ac.uk/
University of Bolton
http://www.bolton.ac.uk/
Canterbury Christ Church University
http://www.canterbury.ac.uk/
University of Central Lancashire
http://www.uclan.ac.uk/
University of Central Lancashire
http://www.uclan.ac.uk/
University of Cumbria
http://www.cumbria.ac.uk

University of East London
http://www.uel.ac.uk
Edinburgh Napier University
http://www.napier.ac.uk
Middlesex University
http://www.mdx.ac.uk
Leeds Becket University
http://www.leedsbeckett.ac.uk/
London Metropolitan University
http://www.londonmet.ac.uk
University of the West of Scotland
http://www.uws.ac.uk
Staffordshire University
http://www.staffs.ac.uk/
University of Sunderland
http://www.sunderland.ac.uk
University of West London
http://www.uwl.ac.uk

The Russell Group

The Russell Group
http://www.russellgroup.ac.uk/
The Russell Group was established in 1994 and is an association of leading, major research-intensive universities, including the 'Ancient' universities.

Members of the Russell Group 'Red Brick' Universities: higher education institutions
The original six civic 'red brick' members of the Russell Group universities

University of Birmingham
http://www.birmingham.ac.uk/
University of Bristol
http://www.bristol.ac.uk/
University of Leeds
https://www.leeds.ac.uk/
University of Liverpool
http://www.liv.ac.uk/
University of Manchester
http://www.manchester.ac.uk/
University of Sheffield
http://www.sheffield.ac.uk/

Additional 'Red Brick' Members of the Russell Group

University of Cambridge
http://www.cam.ac.uk
Cardiff University
http://www.cardiff.ac.uk/

Durham University
http://www.durhamstudent.co.uk/
University of Edinburgh
http://www.ed.ac.uk/
University of Exeter
http://www.exeter.ac.uk/
University of Glasgow
http://www.gla.ac.uk/
Imperial College London
https://www.imperial.ac.uk/
King's College London
http://www.kcl.ac.uk/
University of Liverpool
http://www.liv.ac.uk/
London School of Economics & Political Science
http://www.lse.ac.uk/
Newcastle University
http://www.ncl.ac.uk/

University of Nottingham
http://www.nottingham.ac.uk/
Queen Mary, University of London
http://www.qmul.ac.uk/
Queen's University Belfast
http://www.qub.ac.uk/
University College London
http://www.ucl.ac.uk/

University of Oxford
http://www.ox.ac.uk/
University of Southampton
http://www.southampton.ac.uk/
University of Warwick
https://www2.warwick.ac.uk/
University of York
http://www.york.ac.uk/

University Alliance

University Alliance
http://www.unialliance.ac.uk/
The University Alliance was formed in
2006 and adopted the name in 2007. It is
a group of innovative and entrepreneurial
universities with a focus on science,
technology, design and the creative
industries.

Members of the University Alliance: higher education institutions

Bournemouth University
http://home.bournemouth.ac.uk/
University of Bradford
http://www.bradford.ac.uk/
Cardiff Metropolitan University
http://www3.cardiffmet.ac.uk/
Coventry University
http://www.coventry.ac.uk
Glasgow Caledonian University
http://www.gcu.ac.uk
University of Greenwich
http://www2.gre.ac.uk/
University of Hertfordshire
http://www.herts.ac.uk
University of Huddersfield
http://www.hud.ac.uk
Kingston University
http://www.kingston.ac.uk
University of Lincoln
http://www.lincoln.ac.uk
Liverpool John Moores University
http://www.ljmu.ac.uk

Manchester Metropolitan University
http://www2.mmu.ac.uk/
Northumbria University
http://www.northumbria.ac.uk
Nottingham Trent University
http://www.ntu.ac.uk
Oxford Brookes University
http://www.brookes.ac.uk
Plymouth University
https://www.plymouth.ac.uk/
University of Portsmouth
http://www.port.ac.uk
University of Salford
http://www.salford.ac.uk
Sheffield Hallam University
http://www.shu.ac.uk
University of South Wales / Prifysgol De
Cymru
http://www.southwales.ac.uk/
Teesside University
http://www.tees.ac.uk
University of the West of England
http://www.uwe.ac.uk/

Universities, Conservatoires, Art Schools, Higher Education Colleges and Other Specialist Institutions Which Have University Status in the UK By Region

England Regions
- North East England
- North West England
- Yorkshire and the Humber
- East Midlands
- West Midlands
- East of England
- London
- South East
- South West

Wales
Northern Ireland
Scotland

To find recognised universities in England, Wales, Northern Ireland or Scotland go to the UK Government:
UK Government: Check a University is Officially Recognised
https://www.gov.uk/check-a-university-is-officially-recognised/overview

England Regions

North East England
Counties: Durham; Northumberland; Tyne and Wear; Cleveland
Main Towns:
Durham: Bishop Aukland; Darlington; Durham; Hartlepool; Gateshead; Middlesbrough; Middleton-in-Teesdale; Sunderland; Stockton;
Northumberland: Alnwick; Amble; Ashington; Bedlington; Beal; Berwick-upon-Tweed; Blyth; Cramlington; Haltwhistle; Hexham; Lindisfarne; Morpeth; Prudhoe
Tyne and Wear: Gateshead; Houghton le Spring; Jarrow; Newburn; Newcastle-upon-Tyne; South Shields; Sunderland; Washington; Whitley Bay,

North East England: Universities, Conservatoires and Art Schools
Durham University   http://www.durham.ac.uk
Durham, England
Durham University consists of two campuses with colleges at both campuses:
Durham Campus has 14 colleges, with 13 undergraduate and 1 postgraduate only
Queen's campus has two colleges. If your course is based in Durham, you will be a member of a Durham-based college. If your course is based at Queen's Campus, Stockton, you will be a member of a Queen's-based college.
Northern School of Art   https://northernart.ac.uk/
(previously Cleveland College of Art and Design)
Middlesbrough and Hartlepool

Durham University: Colleges
Queen's Campus Colleges:
Stockton, England
- **John Snow College**   https://www.dur.ac.uk/johnsnow.college/
- **Stephenson College**   https://www.dur.ac.uk/stephenson/

Durham campus colleges:
Durham, England
- **Collingwood College**   https://www.dur.ac.uk/collingwood/
- **Grey College**   https://www.dur.ac.uk/grey.college/
- **Hatfield College**   https://www.dur.ac.uk/hatfield.college/
- **Josephine Butler College**   https://www.dur.ac.uk/butler.college/
- **St Aidans College**   https://www.dur.ac.uk/st-aidans.college/
- **St Chads College**   https://community.dur.ac.uk/StChads/
- **St Cuthberts College**   https://www.dur.ac.uk/st-cuthberts.society/
- **College of St Hild and St Bede**   https://www.dur.ac.uk/hild-bede/
- **St John's College**   https://www.dur.ac.uk/st-johns.college/
- **St John's College: Cranmer Hall:**
  Theological College   https://community.dur.ac.uk/cranmer.hall/
- **St Mary's College**   https://www.dur.ac.uk/st-marys.college/
- **Trevelyan College**   https://www.dur.ac.uk/trevelyan.college/
- **University College**   https://www.dur.ac.uk/university.college/
- **Van Mildert College**   https://www.dur.ac.uk/van-mildert.college/
- **Ustinov College (Postgraduate only)** https://www.dur.ac.uk/ustinov.college/

Newcastle University   http://www.ncl.ac.uk/
Newcastle upon Tyne, Tyne and Weir, England
- **School of Arts and Cultures**   http://www.ncl.ac.uk/sacs/
  Newcastle-upon-Tyne, England. Part of Newcastle University

Northumbria University   http://www.northumbria.ac.uk
Newcastle upon Tyne, Tyne and Weir, England

University of Sunderland   http://www.sunderland.ac.uk
Sunderland (part of Tyne and Weir), England

Teesside University   http://www.tees.ac.uk
Middlesborough, Tees Valley (Durham and North Yorkshire), England

North East England: Higher Education Colleges and other Specialist Institutions
Bishop Auckland College   http://www.bacoll.ac.uk/
County Durham, England

City of Sunderland College   http://www.sunderlandcollege.ac.uk
Sunderland, England

Derby College   http://www.derby-college.ac.uk
Derbyshire England

East Durham College   http://www.eastdurham.ac.uk/
Peterlee, Sunderland, England

Gateshead College   http://www.gateshead.ac.uk
Gateshead, Tyne and Weir England

Lindisfarne   http://lindisfarnertp.org/
North Shields, Northumberland, England
Church of England / Wales Recognised Theological Education Institution

New College Durham   http://www.newcollegedurham.ac.uk
Durham, England

Newcastle College   http://www.newcastlecollege.co.uk
Newcastle upon Tyne, Tyne and Weir, England

Northumberland College   https://www.northumberland.ac.uk/
Northumberland, England

South Tyneside College
Tyne and Weir, England

http://www.stc.ac.uk

Sunderland College
Sunderland (part of Tyne and Weir), England

http://www.sunderlandcollege.ac.uk

Tyne Metropolitan College
Tyne and Weir, England

http://www.tynemet.ac.uk

North West England

Counties: Cheshire; Cumbria; Lancashire; Greater Manchester; Merseyside; Isle of
Main Towns:
Cheshire: Chester; Crewe; Birkenhead; Ellesmere Port; Knutsford; Macclesfield; Nantwich,
Runcorn; Stockport; Wallasey; Warrington; Wilmslow
Cumbria: Ambleside; Barrow–in-Furness; Bowness; Carlisle; Cockermouth; Kendal;
Keswick; Maryport; Penrith; Whitehaven; Windermere
Workington
Lancashire: Blackburn; Blackpool; Burnley; Chorley; Lancaster; Ormskirk; Preston
Greater Manchester: Bolton; Bury; Manchester; Oldham; Rochdale; Stockport; Salford;
Tameside; Trafford; Wigan
Merseyside: Birkenhead; Bootle; Crosby; St Helens; Liverpool; Southport; Wallasey;
Warrington; Wirral
Isle of Man: Castletown; Douglas; Peel; Port Erin; Ramsey

North West England: Universities, Conservatoires and Art Schools

BPP University: Business and the Professions   http://www.bpp.com/
Centres in Abingdon, Birmingham, Bristol, Cambridge, Croydon, Leeds Park Row, Leeds
Whitehall Quay, Liverpool, London city, London Holborn, London King's Cross, London
Shepherds Bush, London waterloo, Manchester St James's Building, Newcastle, Swindon,
England

University of Bolton   http://www.bolton.ac.uk/
Bolton, Greater Manchester, England

University of Chester   http://www.chester.ac.uk/
Campuses in Chester and Warrington, Cheshire, England

University of Cumbria   http://www.cumbria.ac.uk
Sites and campuses in Cumbria, Penrith, London and Workington

Edge Hill University   http://www.edgehill.ac.uk
Ormskirk, Lancashire, England

University of Central Lancashire   http://www.uclan.ac.uk/
Lancashire, England

Lancaster University   http://www.lancs.ac.uk
Lancashire, England
The University of Lancaster consists of nine colleges, eight for undergraduates and one for
postgraduates

Lancaster University: Colleges (undergraduates)
- **Bowland College**   http://bowland.lusu.co.uk/
- **Cartmel College**   http://www.lancaster.ac.uk/colleges/cartmel/
- **The County College**   http://www.lancaster.ac.uk/colleges/county
- **Furness College**   http://furnesscollege.co.uk/
- **Fylde College**   http://fyldecollege.wordpress.com/
- **Grizedale College**   http://www.lancaster.ac.uk/colleges/grizedale/
- **Lonsdale College**   http://www.lancaster.ac.uk/colleges/lonsdale/
- **Pendle College**   http://www.lancaster.ac.uk/colleges/pendle/

Lancaster University: College (postgraduates)
- **Graduate College**   http://www.lancaster.ac.uk/colleges/graduate/

Laureate Online Education   http://www.laureate.net
Working in partnership with:
- The University of Liverpool, delivering online graduate and doctoral programs.
- The University of Roehampton, delivering online degrees.

The University of Law   https://www.law.ac.uk/
Locations in Birmingham, Bristol, Chester, Guildford, Leeds, London Bloomsbury, London
Moorgate, Manchester, Nottingham, University of Exeter, University of Liverpool, University
of Reading, England and Hong Kong

University of Liverpool   http://www.liv.ac.uk
Liverpool, Merseyside, England
Liverpool Hope University   http://www.hope.ac.uk
Liverpool, Merseyside, England
Liverpool John Moores University   http://www.ljmu.ac.uk
Liverpool, England
- **Liverpool School of Art and Design**   http://www.ljmu.ac.uk/LSA/
- **Maritime Knowledge Hub**
University of Manchester   http://www.manchester.ac.uk
Manchester, England
Manchester Business School, University of Manchester http://www.mbs.ac.uk/
Manchester, England
Manchester Metropolitan University   http://www2.mmu.ac.uk/
Manchester, England
- **Manchester School of Art**   http://www.artdes.mmu.ac.uk/
Manchester, England
University Campus Oldham   http://www.uco.oldham.ac.uk
Greater Manchester, England. Partnership between the University of Huddersfield and Oldham College
Royal Northern College of Music   http://www.rncm.ac.uk/
Manchester, England
University of Salford   http://www.salford.ac.uk
Manchester, England

North West England: Higher Education Colleges and other Specialist Institutions
Accrington & Rossendale College   https://www.accross.ac.uk/
Lancashire, England. The college has one main campus
Blackburn College   http://www.blackburn.ac.uk/
Lancashire, England
Blackpool and The Fylde College   http://www.blackpool.ac.uk/
Lancashire an Associate College of Lancaster University
Bolton College   http://www.boltoncollege.ac.uk/
Bolton, Greater Manchester, England
Burnley College Burnley   http://www.burnley.ac.uk/
Lancashire, England
Bury College   http://www.burycollege.ac.uk/
Bury, Manchester, England
Cheshire College, South and West   https://www.ccsw.ac.uk/
Cheshire, England
Cumbria Christian Learning   https://www.cumbriachristianlearning.org.uk/
Cumbria, England
Furness College   http://www.furness.ac.uk/
Barrow-in-Furness, Cumbria, England
Grampus Heritage and Training Ltd   http://www.grampusheritage.co.uk/
Cumbria, England
Holy Cross College   http://www.holycross.ac.uk/
Bury, Manchester
Hopwood Hall College   http://www.hopwood.ac.uk
Rochdale and Middleton, Manchester, England
Hugh Baird College   http://www.hughbaird.ac.uk
Bootle, Liverpool, England
Kendal College   http://www.kendal.ac.uk/
Kendal, Lancashire, England

Knowsley Community College http://www.knowsleycollege.ac.uk/
Roby, Liverpool, Kirby, Lancashire and Merseyside, England
Lakes College - West Cumbria http://www.lcwc.ac.uk
Cumbria, England
Liverpool Community College http://www.liv-coll.ac.uk
Liverpool, England
The Liverpool Institute for Performing Arts http://www.lipa.ac.uk
Liverpool, England
Macclesfield College http://www.macclesfield.ac.uk
Cheshire, England
The Manchester College http://www.themanchestercollege.ac.uk
Manchester, England
Mid Cheshire College http://www.midchesh.ac.uk
Cheshire, England
Myerscough College http://www.myerscough.ac.uk
Preston, Lancashire, England
Nazarene Theological College http://www.nazarene.ac.uk
Manchester, England
Newton Rigg College http://www.newtonrigg.ac.uk/
Cumbria, England
Oldham College http://www.oldham.ac.uk/
Greater Manchester, England
Preston College http://www.preston.ac.uk/
Preston, England
Reaseheath College http://www.reaseheath.ac.uk
Nantwich, Cheshire, England
Runshaw College http://www.runshaw.ac.uk/
Leyland, Lancashire, England
Salford City College http://www.salfordcc.ac.uk/
Salford, England
St Helens College http://www.sthelens.ac.uk
Merseyside, England
St Mary's College http://www.stmarysblackburn.ac.uk
Blackburn: Lancashire, England
Southport College http://www.southport-college.ac.uk
Southport, Sefton, Lancashire, England
Stockport College http://www.stockport.ac.uk
Greater Manchester, England
Tameside College http://www.tameside.ac.uk
Ashton-under-Lyne, Greater Manchester, England
Trafford College http://www.trafford.ac.uk/
Cheshire and Manchester, England
Warrington Collegiate http://www.warrington.ac.uk
Cheshire, England. Associate college of University of Chester
Wigan and Leigh College http://www.wigan-leigh.ac.uk
Wigan, England
Wirral Metropolitan College http://wmc.ac.uk/
Wirral, North West England

Yorkshire and the Humber
Counties: East Yorkshire; North Yorkshire; South Yorkshire; West Yorkshire
Main Towns:
East Yorkshire: Beverley; Bridlington; Cottingham; Driffield; Goole; Hessle; Hull; Pocklington;
North Yorkshire: Harrogate; Knaresborough; Redcar; Richmond, Ripon; Scarborough; Skipton; Whitby; York
South Yorkshire: Barnsley; Doncaster; Rotherham; Sheffield
West Yorkshire: Bradford; Calderdale; Halifax; Huddersfield; Kirklees; Leeds; Mirfield; Saltaire; Wakefield

Yorkshire and the Humber: Universities, Conservatoires and Art Schools

University of Bradford http://www.bradford.ac.uk/
Bradford, West Yorkshire, England
University of Huddersfield http://www.hud.ac.uk
Huddersfield, West Yorkshire, England
University of Hull http://www.hull.ac.uk
Hull, East Yorkshire, England
Hull York Medical School,
University of Hull and University of York http://www.hyms.ac.uk/
East Yorkshire and North Yorkshire, England
University of Leeds http://www.leeds.ac.uk
Leeds, West Yorkshire, England
Leeds Arts University http://www.leeds-art.ac.uk
Leeds, West Yorkshire, England
Leeds Becket University http://www.leedsbeckett.ac.uk/
(formally Leeds Metropolitan University): Leeds, West Yorkshire, England
Leeds College of Music: Conservatoire http://www.lcm.ac.uk
Leeds, West Yorkshire, England. A Music Conservatoire, partnered with the University of Hull
Leeds Trinity University http://www.leedstrinity.ac.uk
Leeds, West Yorkshire, England
Sheffield Hallam University http://www.shu.ac.uk
Sheffield, South Yorkshire, England
The University of Law https://www.law.ac.uk/
Locations in Birmingham, Bristol, Chester, Guildford, Leeds, London Bloomsbury, London Moorgate, Manchester, Nottingham, University of Exeter, University of Liverpool, University of Reading, England and Hong Kong
University of Sheffield http://www.sheffield.ac.uk
Sheffield, South Yorkshire, England
University of York http://www.york.ac.uk
The University of York has nine Colleges
University of York: Colleges
- **Alcuin College** http://www.york.ac.uk/colleges/alcuin/
- **Constantine College** http://www.york.ac.uk/colleges/constantine
- **Derwent College** http://www.york.ac.uk/colleges/derwent/
- **Goodricke College** http://www.york.ac.uk/colleges/goodricke/
- **Halifax College** http://www.york.ac.uk/colleges/halifax/
- **James College** http://www.york.ac.uk/colleges/james/
- **Langwith College** http://www.york.ac.uk/colleges/langwith/
- **Vanbrugh College** http://www.york.ac.uk/colleges/vanbrugh/
- **Wentworth College** http://www.york.ac.uk/colleges/wentworth/
York St John University http://www.yorksj.ac.uk
York, North Yorkshire, England

Yorkshire and the Humber: Higher Education Colleges and other Specialist Institutions

Askham Bryan College   http://www.askham-bryan.ac.uk/

York, Guisborough, Harrogate, Thirsk, Bradford, Scarborough, Wakefield, Newton Rigg, Newcastle, England. The college offers higher education courses in land based subjects. Centres are based in York, Guisborough, Halifax; Harrogate, Thirsk, Bradford, Scarborough, Wakefield, Newton Rigg, Newcastle, England

Barnsley College   http://www.barnsley.ac.uk/

Barnsley, South Yorkshire, England

Bishop Burton College   http://www.bishopburton.ac.uk/

East Yorkshire and Lincolnshire, England. Land Based subjects

Bradford College   http://www.bradfordcollege.ac.uk/

Bradford, West Yorkshire, England

Calderdale College   http://www.calderdale.ac.uk/

Halifax, West Yorkshire, England

Cliff College (Bible College)   http://www.cliffcollege.ac.uk

Hope Valley near Sheffield, South Yorkshire, England

College of the Resurrection   http://college.mirfield.org.uk/

Mirfield, West Yorkshire, England

Church of England / Wales Recognised Theological Education Institution

Craven College   http://www.craven-college.ac.uk

North Yorkshire, England

Dearne Valley College   http://www.dearne-coll.ac.uk

Rotherham, South Yorkshire, England

Doncaster College   http://www.don.ac.uk

Doncaster, South Yorkshire, England

East Riding College   http://www.eastridingcollege.ac.uk

East Yorkshire and Hull

Hull College   http://www.hull-college.ac.uk/

Kingston upon Hull, East Yorkshire, England

Kirklees College   http://www.kirkleescollege.ac.uk

Huddersfield, West Yorkshire, England

Leeds City College   http://www.leedscitycollege.ac.uk

West Yorkshire, England

Leeds College of Building   http://www.lcb.ac.uk

West Yorkshire, England

Rotherham College   http://www.rotherham.ac.uk/

Rotherham, South Yorkshire, England

Scarborough TEC   https://scarboroughtec.ac.uk/

Scarborough, North Yorkshire, England

Sheffield College   http://www.sheffcol.ac.uk

Sheffield, South Yorkshire, England

Shipley College   http://www.shipley.ac.uk/

Saltaire, West Yorkshire

Wakefield College   http://www.wakefield.ac.uk

Wakefield, West Yorkshire, England

York College   http://www.yorkcollege.ac.uk

York, North Yorkshire, England

West Midlands

Counties: Herefordshire; Shropshire; Staffordshire; Warwickshire; West Midlands; Worcestershire.

Main Towns:

Herefordshire: Bromyard; Glasbury; Hay-on-Wye; Hereford; Kington; Ledbury; Leominster; Ross-on-Wye; Symonds Yat; Wye Valley

Shropshire: Albrighton; Bridgnorth; Brosley; Ellesmere; Ironbridge; Ludlow; Madeley; Market Drayton; Much Wenlock; Newport; Oswestry; Shifnal; Shrewsbury; Telford; Wellington; Wem; Whitchurch;

Staffordshire: Burntwood; Burton-upon-Trent; Cannock; Great Wyrley; Kidsgrove; Leek; Lichfield; Rugesley; Stafford; Stoke-on-Trent; Tamworth; Uttoxeter

Warwickshire: Coventry; Halford; Hatton; Kenilworth; Leamington Spa; Market Bosworth; Nuneaton; Oxhill; Solihull; Stratford Upon Avon; Warwick;

West Midlands: Birmingham; Dudley; Solihul; Stourbridge; Walsall; West Bromwich; Wolverhampton

Worcestershire: Bewdley; Broadway; Bromsgrove; Droitwich Spa; Evesham; Kiddierminster; Malvern; Pershore; Redditch; Stourport-on-Severn; Tenbury Wells; Upton-upon-Severn; Worcester

West Midlands: Universities, Conservatoires and Art Schools

Arden University, Midland Management Centre http://www.rdi.co.uk/
Coventry, England. Online distance learning provider for Anglia Ruskin University, University of Bradford, University of Sunderland, Pearson Edexcel

Aston University   http://www.aston.ac.uk/
Birmingham, England

University of Birmingham   http://www.birmingham.ac.uk/
Birmingham, England

Birmingham City University   http://www.bcu.ac.uk/
Birmingham, England

Birmingham Conservatoire   http://www.bcu.ac.uk/pme/conservatoire
Birmingham, England. Part of Birmingham City University

Birmingham City University: School of Art   https://www.bcu.ac.uk/art
Birmingham, England. Part of Birmingham City University

University College Birmingham   http://www.ucb.ac.uk/
Birmingham, England

BPP University College of Professional Studies http://www.bpp.com/
Centres in Abingdon, Birmingham, Bristol, Cambridge, Croydon, Leeds Park Row, Leeds Whitehall Quay, Liverpool, London city, London Holborn, London King's Cross, London Shepherds Bush, London waterloo, Manchester St James's Building, Newcastle, Swindon, England

Coventry University College   http://www.coventry.ac.uk
Coventry, England

Harper Adams University   http://www.harper-adams.ac.uk
Newport, Shropshire, England

Keele University   http://www.keele.ac.uk
Staffordshire, England

Newman University Birmingham   http://www.newman.ac.uk/
Birmingham, England. A Catholic University

Staffordshire University   http://www.staffs.ac.uk/
Stoke on Trent, Staffordshire, England

The University of Law   https://www.law.ac.uk/
Locations in Birmingham, Bristol, Chester, Guildford, Leeds, London Bloomsbury, London Moorgate, Manchester, Nottingham, University of Exeter, University of Liverpool, University of Reading, England and Hong Kong

University of Warwick https://warwick.ac.uk/
Coventry, England
University of Wolverhampton http://www.wlv.ac.uk
Wolverhampton, England
University of Worcester http://www.worcester.ac.uk
Worcestershire, England

West Midlands: Higher Education Colleges and other Specialist Institutions

Access to Music http://www.accesstomusic.co.uk/
Birmingham, England
Independent music college with centres in Birmingham, Brighton, Bristol, Darlington, Lincoln, London, Manchester RNCM, Norwich, York
ACS Distance Education http://www.acsedu.co.uk/
Stourbridge, Staffordshire, England
Birmingham Metropolitan College http://www.bmetc.ac.uk/
Birmingham, England
Coventry College https://www.coventrycollege.ac.uk/
Coventry, England
City of Wolverhampton College http://www.wolvcoll.ac.uk/
Wolverhampton, England
College of Osteopaths http://www.collegeofosteopaths.ac.uk/
Locations in Hertfordshire and Stoke-on-Trent, Staffordshire
Derwen College http://www.derwen.ac.uk/
Oswestry, Shropshire
Dudley College of Technology http://www.dudleycol.ac.uk
Dudley, England
Heart of Worcestershire College http://www.howcollege.ac.uk/
North East Worcestershire, England
Hereford College of Arts http://www.hca.ac.uk
Hereford, England
Maryvale Institute
International Catholic College https://www.maryvale.ac.uk/
Birmingham, England
National Land Based College https://nlbc.uk/
City and Guilds Land Based Services
Courses throughout the UK; Warwickshire, England
North Shropshire College http://www.nsc.ac.uk/
Oswestry Campus; Walford Campus; Shipley Campus; Aspire Centre
Shropshire, England
North Warwickshire and South Leicester College https://www.nwslc.ac.uk/
- **North Warwickshire and Hinckley College**
  Warwickshire, England
- **South Leicester College**
  South Leicester, England
The Queen's Foundation http://www.queens.ac.uk/
Birmingham, England
Church of England / Wales Recognised Theological Education Institution
Sandwell College http://www.sandwell.ac.uk
West Bromwich, Birmingham, England
Solihull College http://www.solihull.ac.uk
Solihull, England
South & City College Birmingham http://www.sccb.ac.uk
Birmingham, England
South Staffordshire College http://www.southstaffs.ac.uk/
Staffordshire, England

Stratford-upon-Avon College
Warwickshire, England

http://www.stratford.ac.uk

Telford College
Shropshire, England

https://www.telfordcollege.ac.uk/

Walsall College
West Midlands, England

http://www.walsallcollege.ac.uk

Warwickshire College

http://www.warwickshire.ac.uk

Warwickshire, England. Six main centres: Leamington, Rugby, Moreton Morrell, Pershore College (Animal and Land Based courses), Henley-in-Arden, Trident Centre, Warwickshire, England

East Midlands

Counties: Derbyshire; Leicestershire; Lincolnshire; Northamptonshire; Nottinghamshire; Rutland

Main Towns:

Derbyshire: Alfreton; Belper; Bolsover; Buxton; Chesterfield; Derby; Glossop; Ilkeston; Long Eaton; Staveley; Swadlincote

Leicestershire: Ashby-de-la-Zouch; Leicester; Loughborough; Lutterworth; Hinckley; Coalville; Wigston; Melton Mowbray; Market Harborough

Lincolnshire: Boston; Cleethorpes; Gainsborough; Grantham; Grimsby; Lincoln; Louth; Scunthorpe; Skegness; Sleaford; Spalding; Stamford; Waltham; Woodhall spa

Northamptonshire: Brackley; Burton Latimer; Corby; Daventry; Higham Ferrers; Irthlingborough; Kettering; Northampton; Oundle; Rushden; Thrapston; Towcester; Wellinborough

Nottinghamshire: Beeston; Hucknall; Mansfield; Newark; Nottingham; Retford; Worksop

Rutland: Cottesmore; Oakham; Uppingham;

East Midlands: Universities, Conservatoires and Art Schools

De Montfort University   http://www.dmu.ac.uk
Leicestershire, England

Loughborough University   http://www.lboro.ac.uk/
Leicestershire, England

Nottingham Trent University   http://www.ntu.ac.uk
Nottingham, England

University of Derby   http://www.derby.ac.uk
Derbyshire, England

The University of Law   https://www.law.ac.uk/
Locations in Birmingham, Bristol, Chester, Guildford, Leeds, London Bloomsbury, London Moorgate, Manchester, Nottingham, University of Exeter, University of Liverpool, University of Reading, England and Hong Kong

University of Leicester   http://www.le.ac.uk
Leicestershire, England

University of Lincoln   http://www.lincoln.ac.uk
Lincolnshire, England

University of Nottingham   http://www.nottingham.ac.uk
Nottingham, England

East Midlands: Higher Education Colleges and other Specialist Institutions

Bishop Burton College   http://www.bishopburton.ac.uk/
East Yorkshire and Lincolnshire, England. Land Based subjects

Bishop Grosseteste University College   http://www.bishopg.ac.uk/
Lincolnshire, England

Brooksby Melton College   http://he.brooksbymelton.ac.uk/
Leicestershire, England

Central College Nottingham   http://www.centralnottingham.ac.uk/
Nottingham, England

Chapel Violins   http://www.chapelviolins.com/site/
Balderton, Newark, Nottinghamshire, England

Chesterfield College   http://www.chesterfield.ac.uk/
Derbyshire, England

Derby College   http://www.derby-college.ac.uk
Derbyshire, England

Grimsby Institute of Further and Higher Education http://www.grimsby.ac.uk
Lincolnshire, England

Leicester College   http://www.leicestercollege.ac.uk
Leicestershire, England

Lincoln College incorporating   http://www.lincolncollege.ac.uk
- **Newark College; Gainsborough College**

Sites in Lincoln and Gainsborough, Lincolnshire; Newark, Nottinghamshire, England

Lincoln School of Theology and Ministry   http://www.lincoln.anglican.org/

Lincoln, England

Church of England / Wales Recognised Theological Education Institution

Loughborough College   http://www.loucoll.ac.uk

Loughborough, Leicestershire, England

Markfield Institute of Higher Education,   http://www.mihe.org.uk/

linked with Newman University, Leicestershire, England. Islamic Studies

Northamptonshire, England

Newark School of Violin Making part of Lincoln College http://www.lincolncollege.ac.uk/

Newark, Nottinghamshire, England

North Lindsey College   http://www.northlindsey.ac.uk

North Lincolnshire, England

Nottingham College   https://www.nottinghamcollege.ac.uk/

Nottingham: Nottinghamshire, England

St John's College Nottingham   http://www.stjohns-nottm.ac.uk/

Nottingham, England

Church of England / Wales Recognised Theological Education Institution

Spalding Horticultural Training Group   http://www.shtg.co.uk/

Spalding, Lincolnshire, England

Stephenson College   http://www.stephensoncoll.ac.uk

Coalville, Leicestershire, England

East England
Counties: Bedfordshire; Cambridgeshire; Essex; Hertfordshire; Suffolk; Norfolk
Main Towns:
Bedfordshire: Bedford; Cranfield; Dunstable; Leighton Buzzard; Luton; Woburn
Cambridgeshire: Cambridge; Ely; Grantchester; Huntingdon; Peterborough; Ramsey; St Neot's; Wisbech;
Essex: Basildon; Braintree; Brentwood; Canvey Island; Chelmsford; Clacton; Colchester; Epping; Grays; Harlow; Harwich; Ilford; Rainham; Rayleigh; Southend; Stansted; Waltham Abbey; Walton-on-the-Naze; Wickford
Hertfordshire: Barnet; Berkhamsted; Bishop Stortford; Broxbourne; Cheshunt; Enfield; Hatfield; Hertford; Kings Langley; Knebworth; Potters Bar; St Albans; Stevenage; Tring; Waltham Cross; Watford; Welwyn;
Suffolk: Aldeburgh; Bury St Edmonds; Ely; Eye; Felixstowe; Ipswich; Lavenham; Newmarket; Orford; Otley; Southwold; Stowmarket; Woodbridge
Norfolk: Attleborough; Banham; Cromer; Diss; Great Yarmouth; Kings Lynn; Norwich; Wisbech

East of England: Universities, Conservatoires and Art Schools

Anglia Ruskin University   https://www.anglia.ac.uk/
Cambridgeshire and Essex, England
The university has main campuses at Cambridge and Chelmsford with two centres at Fulbourn, Cambridgeshire and Peterborough.
University of Bedfordshire   http://www.beds.ac.uk/
Bedfordshire, England
University of Cambridge   http://www.cam.ac.uk/
The University of Cambridge is a collegiate system, consisting of 31 independent and self-governing Colleges.
University of Cambridge: Colleges   http://www.cam.ac.uk/colleges-and-departments

- **Christ's College**   http://www.christs.cam.ac.uk/
- **Churchill College**   https://www.chu.cam.ac.uk/
- **Clare College**   http://www.clare.cam.ac.uk/Home/
- **Clare Hall (Graduate College)**   http://www.clarehall.cam.ac.uk/
- **Corpus Christi College**   http://www.corpus.cam.ac.uk/
- **Darwin College (Graduate College)**   http://www.darwin.cam.ac.uk/
- **Downing College**   http://www.dow.cam.ac.uk/
- **Emmanuel College**   http://www.emma.cam.ac.uk/
- **Fitzwilliam College**   http://www.fitz.cam.ac.uk/
- **Girton College**   http://www.girton.cam.ac.uk/
- **Gonville and Caius College**   http://www.cai.cam.ac.uk/
- **Homerton College**   http://www.homerton.cam.ac.uk/
- **Hughes Hall**   http://www.hughes.cam.ac.uk/
- **Jesus College**   http://www.jesus.cam.ac.uk/
- **King's College**   http://www.kings.cam.ac.uk/
- **Lucy Cavendish College**   http://www.lucy-cav.cam.ac.uk/
- **Magdalene College**   http://www.magd.cam.ac.uk/
- **Murray Edwards College**   http://www.murrayedwards.cam.ac.uk/
- **Newnham College**   http://www.newn.cam.ac.uk/
- **Pembroke College**   http://www.pem.cam.ac.uk/
- **Peterhouse**   http://www.pet.cam.ac.uk/
- **Queen's College**   http://www.queens.cam.ac.uk/
- **Robinson College**   http://www.robinson.cam.ac.uk/
- **Selwyn College**   http://www.sel.cam.ac.uk/
- **Sidney Sussex College**   http://www.sid.cam.ac.uk/

- **St Catharine's College**   http://www.caths.cam.ac.uk/home/
- **St Edmund's College**   http://www.st-edmunds.cam.ac.uk/
- **St John's College**   http://www.joh.cam.ac.uk/
- **Trinity College**   http://www.trin.cam.ac.uk/
- **Trinity Hall**   http://www.trinhall.cam.ac.uk/
- **Wolfson College**   http://www.wolfson.cam.ac.uk/

Cranfield University   http://www.cranfield.ac.uk/
Bedfordshire and Wiltshire, England. Cranford campus, Bedfordshire; Shrivenham campus, Swindon, Wiltshire Post graduate only Specialist university in research and teaching in science, engineering, technology and management

University of East Anglia   http://www.uea.ac.uk
Norwich, Norfolk, England

University of Essex   http://www.essex.ac.uk
Colchester, Essex, England

- **East 15 Acting School**   http://www.east15.ac.uk/
  Loughton, Essex, England

University of Hertfordshire   http://www.herts.ac.uk
Hertfordshire, England

Norwich University of the Arts   http://www.nua.ac.uk
(formerly Norwich University College of the Arts)
Norwich, England. An independent specialist arts, design and media University

University Centre Peterborough   http://www.anglia.ac.uk/ucp
Peterborough, England. A joint venture between Anglian Ruskin University and Peterborough Regional College

University of Suffolk   https://www.uos.ac.uk/
Suffolk, England.

East of England: Higher Education Colleges and other Specialist Institutions

Barnet and Southgate College   http://www.barnetsouthgate.ac.uk/
Hertfordshire, England

Barnfield College   https://www.barnfield.ac.uk/
Luton, England

Bedford College   http://www.bedford.ac.uk/
Bedfordshire, England

- **Shuttleworth College: Part of Bedford College** http://www.bedford.ac.uk/
  Land based Courses, Bedfordshire, England

Cambridge School of Visual & Performing Arts   http://www.csvpa.com/
Cambridge, England

Cambridge Theological Federation,
Eastern Region Ministry course   http://www.ermc.cam.ac.uk/
Cambridge, England
Church of England / Wales Recognised Theological Education Institution

City College Norwich   http://www.ccn.ac.uk/
Norwich, England

Colchester Institute   http://www.colchester.ac.uk
Essex, England

East Coast College   https://www.eastcoast.ac.uk/
Lowestoft, Suffolk, England

Easton and Otley College   http://www.eastonotley.ac.uk/
Easton Campus, Norfolk; Otley Campus, Suffolk, England

Edge Hotel School   http://www.edgehotelschool.ac.uk/
Colchester, Essex, England. Partnered with the University of Essex

Havering College of Further and Higher Education   http://www.havering-college.ac.uk
Essex, England

Hult International Business School http://www.hult.edu/
Commercial Road, East London
- **Ashridge Executive Education**
  Berkhampstead, Herfordhsire

Margaret Beaufort Institute of Theology http://www.margaretbeaufort.cam.ac.uk/
Cambridge, England. Catholic Connections

Performers College http://performerscollege.co.uk/
Corringham, Essex, England

Peterborough Regional College http://www.peterborough.ac.uk/
University Centre Peterborough
Peterborough, England

Ridley Hall http://www.ridley.cam.ac.uk/
Cambridge, England
Church of England / Wales Recognised Theological Education Institution

Ruskin College Oxford http://www.ruskin.ac.uk
Oxfordshire, England. An independent college specialising in providing educational
opportunities for adults with few or no qualifications.

South Essex College of Further & Higher Education http://www.southessex.ac.uk
Basildon, Essex, England

College of West Anglia https://www.cwa.ac.uk/
Campuses at: Kings Lynne, Norfolk; Isle, Wisbech, Cambridgeshire; Cambridge, Milton,
Cambridgeshire, England

Von Hugel Institute St Edmunds College http://www.vhi.st-edmunds.cam.ac.uk/
Cambridge, England. Catholic Connections

Westcott House http://www.westcott.cam.ac.uk/
Cambridge, England
Church of England / Wales Recognised Theological Education Institution

Writtle College http://www.writtle.ac.uk
Chelmsford, Essex, England
Subjects include: Agriculture; Animal Science and Animal Management, Conservation and
Environment; Design; Equine; Floristry; Horticulture; Sports and Exercise Performance;
Veterinary Physiotherapy. Degrees are validated by the University of EsseX

Greater London: Universities, Conservatoires and Art Schools

University of the Arts London   http://www.arts.ac.uk
England
The University of the Arts consists of six Arts, Design, Fashion and Media Colleges:
- **Camberwell College of Arts**   http://www.arts.ac.uk/camberwell/
  South East London, England
- **Central Saint Martins**   http://www.arts.ac.uk/csm/
  Kings Cross, North London, England
- **Chelsea College of Arts**   http://www.arts.ac.uk/chelsea/
  South West London, England
- **London College of Communication**   http://www.arts.ac.uk/lcc/
  Elephant and Castle, South East London, England
- **London College of Fashion**   http://www.arts.ac.uk/fashion/
  West London, England, London, England
- **Wimbledon College of Arts**   http://www.arts.ac.uk/wimbledon/
  South West London, England

BPP University: Business and the Professions   http://www.bpp.com/
Centres in Abingdon, Birmingham, Bristol, Cambridge, Croydon, Leeds Park Row, Leeds Whitehall Quay, Liverpool, London city, London Holborn, London King's Cross, London Shepherds Bush, London waterloo, Manchester St James's Building, Newcastle, Swindon, England

Brunel University   http://www.brunel.ac.uk/
Middlesex, England

Christie's Education   http://www.christies.com/
West London, England. Postgraduate Art courses

The Courtauld Institute of Art   http://courtauld.ac.uk/
West Central London, England

City University London   http://www.city.ac.uk/
London, England

The City Law School, City University   http://www.city.ac.uk/law
London

University of East London   http://www.uel.ac.uk
London, England

University of Greenwich   http://www2.gre.ac.uk/
London, England

GSM, London   http://www.gsm.org.uk/
Campuses Greenford, Greenwich and London Bridge, London, England Private University

Guildhall School of Music and Drama: Conservatoire http://www.gsmd.ac.uk/
London

Imperial College London   http://www3.imperial.ac.uk/
Berkshire, Kent, Middlesex; and West; South West; North West London, England
Main site is in South Kensington, London with campuses in London: South Kensington, Charing Cross, Hammersmith, Chelsea (Royal Brampton), Paddington (St Mary's), Middlesex (North West London Hospitals), Park Royal (Central Middlesex Hospital); and Silwood Park, Berkshire ; Wye, Kent

Institute of Financial Services – ifs University College http://www.ifslearning.ac.uk
London, England

Kingston University   http://www.kingston.ac.uk
Surrey, England

The University of Law   http://www.law.ac.uk/
Previously the College of Law
Locations in Birmingham, Bristol, Chester, Guildford, Leeds, London Bloomsbury, London Moorgate, Manchester, England

University of London http://www.london.ac.uk/
London, England
- **Birkbeck, University of London** http://www.bbk.ac.uk/
  West Central London, England
- **Courtauld Institute of Art, University of London** http://www.courtauld.ac.uk
  London, England
- **Goldsmiths, University of London** http://www.gold.ac.uk
  South East London, England
- **Heythrop College, University of London** http://www.heythrop.ac.uk/
- West London, England. Member of the Cathedrals Group. Catholic Connections
- **The Institute of Cancer Research** http://www.icr.ac.uk/
  A College of the University of London, Surrey, England
  Postgraduate courses only
- **King's College London, University of London** http://www.kcl.ac.uk
  West Central London, England
- **London Business School** http://www.london.edu/
  Part of University of London: Regents Park, North West London, England
  Postgraduate courses only
- **London School of Economics and Political Science** http://www.lse.ac.uk
  University of London: West Central London, England
- **London School of Hygiene and Tropical Medicine**https://www.lshtm.ac.uk/
  West Central London, England
- **Queen Mary, University of London** http://www.qmul.ac.uk
  East London, England
- **Royal Academy of Music** http://www.ram.ac.uk/
  North West London, England
- **Royal Central School of Speech and Drama** http://www.cssd.ac.uk/
  North West London, England
- **Royal Holloway, University of London** http://www.rhul.ac.uk
  Surrey, England
- **Royal Veterinary College, University of London** http://www.rvc.ac.uk
  Camden Campus, North West London and Hawkshead Campus, Hertfordshire:
  England
- **St George's, University of London** http://www.sgul.ac.uk
  South West London, England
- **School of Oriental and African Studies (SOAS)** http://www.soas.ac.uk
  University of London: West London, England
- **School of Advanced Study (Postgraduate courses** http://www.sas.ac.uk/
  Senate House, West London, England
- **University of London Institute in Paris** http://www.ulip.london.ac.uk
  Paris, France. Offers a BA in French Studies
- **University of London
  International Programmes** http://www.londoninternational.ac.uk/
- **(Distance Learning)**
  Russell Square, West London, England
- **University College London (UCL), University of London** http://www.ucl.ac.uk
  Gower Street, West Central London, England
- **University College London (UCL) merger with
  Institute of Education University of London** http://www.ucl.ac.uk/ioe
  Gower Street, West Central London, England
- **UCL Eastman Dental Institution** http://www.ucl.ac.uk/eastman/
  Part of University College London: West Central London, England.
  The Institution is a centre for research and postgraduate courses.

London Metropolitan University   http://www.londonmet.ac.uk
London, England
- **The Cass**   http://www.thecass.com/
  (Sir John Cass Faculty of Art, Architecture and Design):
  North London, England. Merged with London Metropolitan University

London South Bank University   http://www.lsbu.ac.uk
London. England

Middlesex University   http://www.mdx.ac.uk
North West London, England

Regent's University London   http://www.regents.ac.uk/
Regent's Park, North West London, England
Independent University with the following Schools:
- **European Business School London;**
- **Regent's American College London;**
- **Regent's Business School London;**
- **Regent's Institute of Languages and Culture;**
- **Regent's School of Psychotherapy and Psychology;**
- **Regent's School of Drama, Film and Media;**
- **Regent's School of Fashion and Design**

University of Roehampton   http://www.roehampton.ac.uk
South West London, England

Royal Academy of Arts   https://www.royalacademy.org.uk/
- **Royal Academy Schools**   http://www.royalacademy.org.uk/raschools/
Part of the Royal Academy of Arts: West London, England. Postgraduate only
A charity and privately funded institution founded in 1768

Royal Academy of Music: Conservatoire   http://www.ram.ac.uk/
North West London, England. Graduates of the Academy receive University of London degrees

Royal College of Art   http://www.rca.ac.uk/
Kensington, South West London, England. Postgraduate only.

St Mary's University Twickenham   http://www.smuc.ac.uk
Middlesex, England

Slade School of Fine Art: http://www.ucl.ac.uk/slade
West London, England

Sotherby's Institute of Art   http://www.sothebysinstitute.com/
West Central London, England Postgraduate only

University of West London   http://www.uwl.ac.uk
Middlesex; Reading and West London, England
Sites at Ealing, West London; Brentford, Middlesex; Hub in Reading, Berkshire, England
- **London College of Music,**
  University of West London   http://www.uwl.ac.uk/academic-schools/music
  Ealing, West London, England

University of Westminster   http://www.westminster.ac.uk
West London, England

Trinity Laban Conservatoire of Music and Dance: http://www.trinitylaban.ac.uk/
South East London, England

Greater London: Higher Education Colleges and Specialist Institutions

Associated Board of the Royal Schools of Music (ABRSM) http://gb.abrsm.org/
Music Performance Exam Board

British College of Osteopathic Medicine http://www.bcom.ac.uk/
North West London, England

British Institute of Technology & E-commerce (BITE) http://www.bite.ac.uk/
Campuses in Stratford, East London; Oxford Street, West London and Suffolk, England
Private College

Capel Manor College http://www.capel.ac.uk/
Enfield, Middlesex, England

City and Islington College http://www.candi.ac.uk/HE
London, England

City of Westminster College http://www.cwc.ac.uk
West London, England. Campuses: Paddington Green and Queens Park

College of Osteopaths http://www.collegeofosteopaths.ac.uk/
Locations in Hertfordshire and Stoke-on-Trent, Staffordshire

Croydon College http://www.croydon.ac.uk
Croydon, England

European School of Economics https://www.ese.ac.uk/
South West London, England. Private College of Higher Education

Hadlow College http://www.hadlow.ac.uk/
South East London and Kent, England

Hult International Business School http://www.hult.edu/
Commercial Road, East London
- **Ashridge Executive Education**
  Berkhampstead, Herfordhsire

The College of Haringey http://www.conel.ac.uk
Enfield and North East London: London, England

Harrow College http://www.harrow.ac.uk
Middlesex, England

Istituto Marangoni (The Fashion School) http://www.istitutomarangoni.co.uk
London, England

Islamic College for Advanced Studies http://www.islamic-college.ac.uk
London, England

John Ruskin College http://www.johnruskin.ac.uk
Croydon, England

Kaplan http://www.kaplan.co.uk/
London, England

Kaplan Open College https://opencollege.kaplan.com/
Distance learning

Kensington and Chelsea College http://www.kcc.ac.uk
London, England

Kensington College of Business http://www.kensingtoncoll.ac.uk
London, England

Leo Baeck College http://www.lbc.ac.uk/
North London, England. Jewish Education Institution

London Academy of Dramatic Art https://www.lamda.org.uk/
London

The London College, UCK http://www.lcuck.ac.uk
London, England

London College of Osteopathic Medicine http://www.lcom.org.uk/
(For medical doctors)
Marylebone, London

London School of Osteopathy http://lso.ac.uk/
South East London, England

LCA Business School http://lca.anglia.ac.uk/
London, England. Private institution
London Institute of Banking and Finance http://www.libf.ac.uk/
London, England (distance learning)
London School of Commerce http://www.lsclondon.co.uk
London, England. Associate college of Cardiff Metropolitan University
London School of Hygiene and Tropical Medicine https://www.lshtm.ac.uk/
London, England
London School of Jewish Studies http://www.lsjs.ac.uk/
North West London, England. Jewish Education Institution
London School of Science and Technology http://www.lsst.ac
Middlesex, England
London School of Marketing http://www.londonschoolofmarketing.com
London, England. An Associate College of Anglia Ruskin University
London Theological Seminary http://www.ltslondon.org/
North London, England
Evangelical Theological Education Institution
Merrist Wood College http://www.merristwood.ac.uk/
Guildford, Surrey
Met Film School http://www.metfilmschool.ac.uk/
Ealing, London
Montefiore College https://www.montefioreendowment.org.uk/
West London, England. Jewish Education Institution
Mountview Academy of Theatre Arts http://www.mountview.org.uk/
London, England
New City College https://www.ncclondon.ac.uk/
- **Attlee A Level Academy** https://www.ncclondon.ac.uk/a-level-academy
  East London, England
- **Epping Forest Campus** https://www.ncclondon.ac.uk/epping-forest
  Loughton, Essex, England
- **Hackney Campus** https://www.ncclondon.ac.uk/hackney
  North London, England
- **Redbridge Campus** https://www.ncclondon.ac.uk/redbridge
  Redbridge, Essex, England
- **Tower Hamlets Campus** https://www.ncclondon.ac.uk/tower-hamlets
  East London, England
Newham College of Further Education https://www.newham.ac.uk/
East London, England
Oak Hill Theological College http://www.oakhill.ac.uk/
Southgate, North London, England
Church of England / Wales Recognised Theological Education Institution
Oasis College of Higher Education http://www.oasiscollege.org/
London SE
Pearson College http://www.pearsoncollege.com
London, England
A private Business School, which is part of Pearson, a leading FTSE 100 company and awards degrees form validating partners also acquired Escape Studios, the Visual Effects Academy (computer graphics)
Pearson College Escape Studios http://www.escapestudios.com/
West London, England. Graphics design courses
Proclamation Trust: Cornhill Training Course https://www.proctrust.org.uk/
South London, England
Evangelical Theological Education Institution

Ravensbourne http://www.ravensbourne.ac.uk/
Greenwich Peninsula, South East London, England offers creative courses.
Richmond, The American International University in London http://www.richmond.ac.uk
South West London, England. Privately funded Charity
Richmond upon Thames College http://www.rutc.ac.uk
Twickenham, Middlesex, England
Royal Academy of Dance https://www.royalacademyofdance.org/
South West London, England
SAE Institute http://uk.sae.edu/en-gb/home/
Campuses in the UK: London, Liverpool, Oxford (also the world headquarters), England and
Glasgow, Scotland. SAE Institute is accredited by Middlesex University, England.
A practical creative media educator with 54 campuses in 26 countries
St Mellitus College http://www.stmellitus.org/
London
Church of England / Wales Recognised Theological Education Institution
St Patrick's http://www.st-patricks.ac.uk
West London, England
Salvation Army William
Booth College http://www.salvationarmy.org.uk/william-booth-college
South East London, England Salvation Army Education Institution
South Thames College http://www.south-thames.ac.uk/
Wandsworth, South West London, England
Trinity College London http://www.trinitycollege.com/
Performing Arts and English language Exam Board
Tottenham Hotspur Foundation http://www.tottenhamhotspur.com/foundationdegree
Tottenham, North London, England
University College of Osteopathy https://www.uco.ac.uk/
South East London, England
Uxbridge College http://www.uxbridgecollege.ac.uk
Middlesex, London
West Herts College http://www.westherts.ac.uk/
Watford, England
West London College http://www.wlc.ac.uk
West London, England
- **Ealing Green College**
- **Hammersmith and Fulham College**
- **Southall Community College**
- **West London Construction Academy**
West Thames College http://www.west-thames.ac.uk
Middlesex, England
Westminster Kingsway College http://www.westking.ac.uk
London England
Centres in: Kings Cross, West Central London; Soho, West London; Victoria, South West
London; and Regents Park, North West London
Working Men's College http://www.wmcollege.ac.uk
North West London, England. Oldest surviving adult education institute in Europe, serving
the whole community, accepting women as well as men
YMCA George Williams College http://www.ymca.ac.uk/
Canning Town London E16

South East England

Counties: Berkshire; Buckinghamshire; Hampshire; Isle of Wight; Kent; Oxfordshire; Surrey; East Sussex; West Sussex
Main Towns:
Berkshire: Ascot; Henley on Thames; Hungerford; Maidenhead; Newbury; Pangbourne; Reading; Slough; Twyford; Windsor; Wokingham
Buckinghamshire: Amersham; Aylesbury; Bedford; Bletchley; High Wycombe; Langley; Milton Keynes; Wendover; Wolverton
Hampshire: Alsdershot; Andover; Basingstoke; Fareham; Farnborough; Havant; Portsmouth; Southampton; Winchester
Isle of Wight: Cowes; Newport; Newton; Sandown; Shanklin; Ventor; Ryde; Yarmouth
Kent: Ashford; Canterbury; Chatham; Dover; Faversham; Gillingham; Gravesend; Herne Bay; Hever; Maidstone; Rainham; Rochester; Sevenoaks; Sittingbourne Tonbridge Wells; Whitstable
Oxfordshire: Banbury; Chalbury; Cholsey; Didcot; Kingham; Oxford
Surrey: Bagshot; Camberley; Croydon; Dorking; Farnham; Gatwick; Godalming; Guildford; Milford; Oxted; Reigate; Woking
East Sussex: Bexhill-on-Sea; Brighton; Eastbourne; Hastings; Lewes; Newhaven; Rye; Seaford; Uckfield
West Sussex: Arundel; Barnham; Bognor Regis; Chichester; Crawley; Horsham; Littlehampton; Southbourne; Westbourne; Worthing

South East England: Universities, Conservatoires and Art Schools

BPP University: Business and the Professions   http://www.bpp.com/
Centres in Abingdon, Birmingham, Bristol, Cambridge, Croydon, Leeds Park Row, Leeds Whitehall Quay, Liverpool, London city, London Holborn, London King's Cross, London Shepherds Bush, London Waterloo, Manchester St James's Building, Newcastle, Swindon, England
University of Brighton   http://www.brighton.ac.uk/
Brighton, East Sussex, England
Brighton and Sussex Medical School   http://www.bsms.ac.uk/
Sussex, England
A partnership between the Universities of Brighton and Sussex with the NHS
University of Buckingham   http://www.buckingham.ac.uk/
Buckinghamshire, England
Buckinghamshire New University   http://bucks.ac.uk/
Buckinghamshire, England
Canterbury Christ Church University   http://www.canterbury.ac.uk/
Kent, England
University of Chichester   http://www.chi.ac.uk
West Sussex, England
University for the Creative Arts   http://www.ucreative.ac.uk
Sites in Kent and Surrey, England
University of Kent   http://www.kent.ac.uk
Kent, England
Medway School of Pharmacy   http://www.msp.ac.uk/
Kent, England. A collaboration between the University of Greenwich and the University of Kent
The Open University   http://www.openuniversity.co.uk
Distance Learning. Academic faculties and research centres in: Milton Keynes, Buckinghamshire, England. Approximately 250,000 part time distance learning students supported by centres in the UK, Ireland and Europe together with worldwide partnerships

The University of Law　　　　　　　　https://www.law.ac.uk/
Locations in Birmingham, Bristol, Chester, Guildford, Leeds, London Bloomsbury, London Moorgate, Manchester, Nottingham, University of Exeter, University of Liverpool, University of Reading, England and Hong Kong

University of Oxford　　　　　　　　http://www.ox.ac.uk/
Oxfordshire, England. The University of Oxford is a collegiate system consisting of 44 independent and self-governing Colleges (38) and Halls (6)

University of Oxford: Colleges and Halls　　http://www.ox.ac.uk/

- **All Souls College**　　http://www.all-souls.ox.ac.uk/
- **Balliol College**　　http://www.balliol.ox.ac.uk/
- **Blackfriars Hall and Stadium**　　http://www.bfriars.ox.ac.uk/
- **Brasenose College**　　http://www.bnc.ox.ac.uk/
- **Campion Hall**　　http://www.campion.ox.ac.uk/
- **Christ Church**　　http://www.chch.ox.ac.uk/
- **Corpus Christi College**　　http://www.ccc.ox.ac.uk/
- **Exeter College**　　http://www.exeter.ox.ac.uk/
- **Green Templeton College**　　http://www.gtc.ox.ac.uk/
- **Harris Manchester College**　　http://www.hmc.ox.ac.uk/
- **Hertford College**　　http://www.hertford.ox.ac.uk/
- **Jesus College**　　http://www.jesus.ox.ac.uk/
- **Keble College**　　http://www.keble.ox.ac.uk/
- **Kellog College**　　http://www.kellogg.ox.ac.uk/
- **Lady Margaret Hall**　　http://www.lmh.ox.ac.uk/
- **Linacre College**　　http://www.linacre.ox.ac.uk/
- **Lincoln College**　　http://www.lincoln.ox.ac.uk/
- **Magdalen College**　　http://www.magd.ox.ac.uk/
- **Mansfield College**　　http://www.mansfield.ox.ac.uk/
- **Merton College**　　http://www.merton.ox.ac.uk/
- **New College**　　http://www.new.ox.ac.uk/
- **Nuffield College**　　http://www.nuffield.ox.ac.uk/
- **Oriel College**　　http://www.oriel.ox.ac.uk/
- **Pembroke College**　　http://www.pmb.ox.ac.uk/
- **The Queen's College**　　http://www.queens.ox.ac.uk/
- **Regent's Park College**　　http://www.rpc.ox.ac.uk/
- **St Anne's College**　　http://www.st-annes.ox.ac.uk/
- **St Antony's College**　　http://www.sant.ox.ac.uk/
- **St Benet's Hall**　　http://www.st-benets.ox.ac.uk/
- **St Catherine's College**　　http://www.stcatz.ox.ac.uk/
- **St Cross College**　　http://www.stx.ox.ac.uk/
- **St Edmund Hall**　　http://www.seh.ox.ac.uk/
- **St Hilda's College**　　http://www.sthildas.ox.ac.uk/
- **St Hugh's College**　　http://www.st-hughs.ox.ac.uk/
- **St John's College**　　http://www.sjc.ox.ac.uk/
- **St Peter's College**　　http://www.spc.ox.ac.uk/
- **St Stephen's House**　　https://www.ssho.ox.ac.uk/
- **Somerville College**　　http://www.some.ox.ac.uk/
- **Trinity College**　　http://www.trinity.ox.ac.uk/
- **University College**　　http://www.univ.ox.ac.uk/
- **Wadham College**　　http://www.wadham.ox.ac.uk/
- **Wolfson College (Graduate only)**　　https://www.wolfson.ox.ac.uk/
- **Worcester College**　　http://www.worc.ox.ac.uk/
- **Wycliffe Hall**　　http://www.wycliffe.ox.ac.uk/

Oxford University Permanent Private Halls
There are five Permanent Private Halls at Oxford University that admit undergraduate students:

- **Blackfriars Hall and Stadium** — http://www.bfriars.ox.ac.uk/
- **St Benet's Hall** — http://www.st-benets.ox.ac.uk/
- **St Edmund Hall**
- **St Stephen's House** — https://www.ssho.ox.ac.uk/
- **Wycliffe Hall** — http://www.wycliffe.ox.ac.uk/

Campion Hall is a Jesuit academic community with students including priests, clergy and other orders and congregations as well as some laymen. It doesn't usually cater for lay undergraduates, although some are admitted occasionally in exceptional circumstances

- **Campion Hall** — http://www.campion.ox.ac.uk/

University of Oxford University Art Department:
The Ruskin School of Art — http://www.rsa.ox.ac.uk/
Oxfordshire, England

University of Portsmouth — http://www.port.ac.uk
Hampshire, England

University of Reading — http://www.reading.ac.uk
Berkshire, England

Royal Holloway, University of London — http://www.rhul.ac.uk
Surrey, England

University of Southampton — http://www.southampton.ac.uk
Southampton, England

Southampton Solent University — http://www.solent.ac.uk
Southampton, England

University of Surrey — http://www.surrey.ac.uk
Surrey, England

University of Sussex — http://www.sussex.ac.uk
Brighton, Sussex, England

University of Winchester — http://www.winchester.ac.uk
Winchester, Hampshire, England

South East England: Higher Education Colleges and other Specialist Institutions

Abingdon and Witney College — http://www.abingdon-witney.ac.uk/
Abingdon, Oxford, England

Academy of Contemporary Music — https://www.acm.ac.uk/
Guildford, Surrey

Activate Learning — https://activatelearning.ac.uk/

- **Banbury and Bicester College**
  Banbury, Oxfordshire, England
- **Bracknell and Wokingham College**
  Bracknell, Berkshire
- **City of Oxford College**
  Oxford, England
- **Reading College**
  Reading, Berkshire, England

Anglo-European College of Chiropractic (AECC) — http://www.aecc.ac.uk/
Bournemouth, England

Arboventure — http://www.arborventure.co.uk/
Hampshire, England

Ashford College — https://www.ashford.ac.uk/
Ashford, Kent, England

Basingstoke College of Technology — http://www.bcot.ac.uk/
Hampshire, England

Berkshire College of Agriculture   http://www.bca.ac.uk/
Berkshire, England
Bespoke Education and Specialist Training
(BEST) in Horticulture Group   http://www.bestinhorticulture.co.uk/
Abingdon on Thames, Oxfordshire, England
Brighton Institute of Modern Music (BIMM)   http://www.bimm.co.uk/
London, Manchester, Brighton, Bristol and Dublin, England and the Republic of Ireland.
Music colleges are based in London, Manchester, Brighton, Bristol and Dublin
Brooklands College   http://www.brooklands.ac.uk/
Surrey, England
Bromley College of Further and Higher Education http://www.bromley.ac.uk/
Kent, England
Buckinghamshire College Group   https://www.buckscollegegroup.ac.uk/
- **Aylesbury Campus**
- **Amersham Campus**
- **Wycombe Campus**
  Buckinghamshire
Carshalton College   http://www.carshalton.ac.uk/
Surrey, England
Chichester College   http://www.chichester.ac.uk
West Sussex, England
Creative Academy   http://www.creativeacademy.org/
Slough, Berkshire
East Surrey College   http://www.esc.ac.uk
Surrey, England
East Sussex Coast Hastings   http://www.sussexcoast.ac.uk/
East Sussex, England
European School of Osteopathy   http://www.eso.ac.uk
Maidstone, Kent, England
Fareham College   http://www.fareham.ac.uk
Hampshire, England
Farnborough College of Technology   http://www.farn-ct.ac.uk
Hampshire, England
Greater Brighton Metropolitan College   https://www.gbmc.ac.uk/
- **Central Brighton Campus**
- Brighton, England
- **West Durrington Campus**
- Worthing, England
Guildford OLM Scheme   http://www.cofeguildford.org.uk/
Guildford, Surrey, England
Church of England / Wales Recognised Theological Education Institution
Havant and South Downs College   https://www.hsdc.ac.uk/
Hampshire, England
Institute of St Anselm   http://st.anselm.org.uk/
Kent, England. Catholic Connections
Institute of Financial Services   http://institute.ifslearning.ac.uk/
Canterbury, Kent, England The Professional Body of ifs University College
Institute of Groundsmanship   http://www.iog.org/
Milton Keynes, Buckinghamshire, England
Guildford College   http://www.guildford.ac.uk
Surrey, England
Highbury College   http://www.highbury.ac.uk
Hampshire, England

Kingston College
http://www.kingston-college.ac.uk
Surrey, England

The McTimoney College of Chiropractic
http://www.mctimoney-college.ac.uk/
Oxfordshire, England

Merrist Wood College
http://www.merristwood.ac.uk/
Guildford, Surrey

MidKent College
http://www.midkent.ac.uk
Kent, England

Milton Keynes College
http://www.mkcollege.ac.uk
Milton Keynes, **England**

NESCOT, Epsom's College of Further and Higher Education http://www.nescot.ac.uk/
Surrey, England

North Kent College of Further Education
http://www.northkent.ac.uk/
Dartford and Gravesend, Kent, England

Oxford OLM Scheme
http://www.oxford.anglican.org/
Oxford, England
Church of England / Wales Recognised Theological Education Institution

Plumpton College
http://www.plumpton.ac.uk
Sussex, England. Specialist Land Based courses

Ripon College
http://www.rcc.ac.uk/
Cuddesdon, Oxfordshire, England
Church of England / Wales Recognised Theological Education Institution

Royal Horticultural Society (RHS) Gardens Wisley https://www.rhs.org.uk/
Surrey, England

Royal School of Needlework
http://www.royal-needlework.org.uk/
Hampton Court Palace, Surrey, England. Degree validated by the University for the Creative Arts

Rose Bruford College of Theatre and Performance http://www.bruford.ac.uk
Kent, England

Institute of St Anselm
http://st.anselm.org.uk/
Kent, England. Catholic Connections

St Augustine's College of Theology
https://staugustinescollege.ac.uk/
West Malling, Kent, England. Centres in Canterbury Christchurch University, Kent and Southwark, South East London
Church of England / Wales Recognised Theological Education Institution

St Stephen's House
https://www.ssho.ox.ac.uk/
Oxford, England
Church of England / Wales Recognised Theological Education Institution

Swindon College
https://www.swindon.ac.uk/
Swindon, Wiltshire, England

Union School of Theology
https://www.ust.ac.uk/
Head-quarters, Oxford, England
Evangelical Theological Education Institution

University Centre Sparsholt
http://www.sparsholt.ac.uk
   • **Sparsholt College Hampshire**
Hampshire, England

University College of Estate Management
https://www.ucem.ac.uk/
Berkshire, England. UCEM provides distance learning for real estate and construction professionals at diploma, undergraduate and postgraduate level

Warsash Maritime Academy
http://www.warsashacademy.co.uk/
Warsash, Southampton, England

West Dean College
https://www.westdean.org.uk/
West Dean, Nr Chichester, West Sussex

West Kent College
https://www.westkent.ac.uk/
Tonbridge, Kent, England

Counties: Cornwall; Devon; Dorset; Gloucestershire; Somerset; Wiltshire;
Main Towns:
Cornwall: Bodmin; Falmouth; Looe; Newquay; Penzance; St Ives; Truro;
Devon: Barnstaple; Bideford; Brixham; Bude; Dartmouth; Dawlish; Exeter; Honiton;
Ilfracombe; Paignton; Plymouth; Sidmouth; Tiverton; Teignmouth; Totnes; Torquay
Dorset: Bournemouth; Dorchester; Lyme Regis; Poole; Shaftsbury; Weymouth
Gloucestershire: Cheltenham; Cirencester; Gloucester; Stroud; Tetbury; Tewkesbury;
Somerset: Bath; Bridgewater; Bristol; Cheddar; Frome; Glastonbury; Minehead; Shepton
Mallet; Taunton; Wells; Weston Super Mare; Wiltshire; Yeovil
Wiltshire: Bradford on Avon; Chippenham; Devizes; Malmesbury; Marlborough; Salisbury;
Swindon; Trowbridge; Warminster

South West England: Universities, Conservatoires and Art Schools

Cranford campus, Bedfordshire; Shrivenham campus, Swindon, Wiltshire
Post graduate only. Specialist university in research and teaching in science, engineering,
technology and management

University of Bath   http://www.bath.ac.uk/
Bath, England
Bath Spa University   https://www.bathspa.ac.uk/
Bath, England
  • **Bath School of Art and Design**   http://artdesign.bathspa.ac.uk/
     Bath, England. Part of Bath Spa university
Bournemouth University   http://home.bournemouth.ac.uk/
Bournemouth, Dorset, England
BPP University: Business and the Professions   http://www.bpp.com/
Centres in Abingdon, Birmingham, Bristol, Cambridge, Croydon, Leeds Park Row, Leeds
Whitehall Quay, Liverpool, London city, London Holborn, London King's Cross, London
Shepherds Bush, London waterloo, Manchester St James's Building, Newcastle, Swindon,
England
Cranfield University   http://www.cranfield.ac.uk/
Bedfordshire and Wiltshire, England
University of Bristol   http://www.bristol.ac.uk/
Bristol, England
University of Exeter   http://www.exeter.ac.uk
Exeter, Devon, England
Cambourne School of Mines, Exeter University   http://emps.exeter.ac.uk/csm/
Exeter, Devon, England a department in Engineering, Mathematics and physical Sciences
Falmouth University incorporating   http://www.falmouth.ac.uk/
  • **Dartington College of Arts:**   http://www.falmouth.ac.uk/art-at-falmouth
Cornwall, England
University of Gloucestershire   http://www.glos.ac.uk
Gloucestershire, England
Plymouth University   https://www.plymouth.ac.uk/
Plymouth, Devon, England
Royal Agricultural University   http://www.rac.ac.uk
Cirencester, Gloucestershire, England
The University of Law   https://www.law.ac.uk/
Locations in Birmingham, Bristol, Chester, Guildford, Leeds, London Bloomsbury, London
Moorgate, Manchester, Nottingham, University of Exeter, University of Liverpool, University
of Reading, England and Hong Kong
University of St Mark and St John Plymouth
(Plymouth Marjon University)   http://www.marjon.ac.uk/
Devon, England

University of the West of England http://www.uwe.ac.uk/
Bristol, England
University Centre Yeovil http://www.ucy.ac.uk
Somerset, England

South West England: Higher Education Colleges and other Specialist Institutions

Anglo European College of Chiropractic http://www.aecc.ac.uk/
Bournemouth, Dorset, England
The college provides specialist chiropractic undergraduate and postgraduate courses.
The Arts University College at Bournemouth http://aub.ac.uk/
Dorset, England
The university college offers specialist degree courses in art, design, media and performance across the creative industries with one campus.
Bicton College https://www.bicton.ac.uk/
Devon, England
Bournemouth and Poole College http://www.thecollege.co.uk/
Bournemouth and Poole, England
Bridgewater and Taunton College http://www.bridgwater.ac.uk/
Bridgewater Centre; Cannington Centre; Paignton Centre; Yeovil Centre, Somerset, England
- **University Centre Somerset** http://www.somerset.ac.uk
  Somerset, England
City of Bath College http://www.citybathcoll.ac.uk/
Bath, England
City of Bristol College http://cityofbristol.ac.uk/
Bristol, England
Cornwall College Group https://www.cornwall.ac.uk/
- **Cornwall College Group**
  Duchy University Hub https://www.duchy.ac.uk/duchy-university
  Cornwall, England. Bicton College Merger with the Cornwall College Group
- **Bicton College Campus** https://www.duchy.ac.uk/
  Budleigh Salterton, East Devon, England
- **Cornwall College: Cambourne Campus** https://www.duchy.ac.uk/
  Redruth, Cornwall, England
- **Cornwall College:**
  The Eden Project: Horticultural courses https://www.duchy.ac.uk/
  Boldeva, Cornwall, England
- **Cornwall College: Newquay Campus** https://www.duchy.ac.uk/
  Newquay, Cornwall, England
- **Cornwall College: Saltash Campus** https://www.duchy.ac.uk/
  Saltash, Cornwall, England
- **Cornwall College: St Austell Campus** https://www.duchy.ac.uk/
  St Austell, Cornwall, England
- **Cornwall College:**
  Plymouth Engineering Skills Centre https://www.duchy.ac.uk/
  Plymouth, Devon, England
- **Cornwall College Group:**
  The Centre for Housing and Support http://www.chs.ac.uk/
  Worcester, England
- **dBs Music: Bristol Campus** https://www.duchy.ac.uk/
  Bristol, England
- **dBS Music: Plymouth Campus** https://www.duchy.ac.uk/
  Plymouth, England
- **Duchy College: Rosewarne Campus** http://www.duchy.ac.uk
  Cambourne, Cornwall, England

- **Duchy College: Stoke Climsland Campus** http://www.duchy.ac.uk
  Stoke Climsland, Callington, Cornwall
- **Falmouth Marine School: Falmouth Campus:** https://www.duchy.ac.uk/
  Falmouth, Cornwall, England

Exeter College http://www.exe-coll.ac.uk
Exeter, Devon, England

Gloucestershire College http://www.gloscol.ac.uk
Gloucestershire, England

Horticultural Correspondence College http://www.hccollege.co.uk/
Holsworthy, Devon

Kingston Maurward College http://www.kmc.ac.uk
Dorset, England

Moorland Bible College http://www.moorlands.ac.uk/
Dorset, England
Evangelical Theological Education Institution

Norland College http://www.norland.co.uk/
Bath, England

Petroc College of Further and Higher Education http://www.petroc.ac.uk
Devon, England

Plymouth College of Art http://www.plymouthart.ac.uk
Plymouth, Devon, England

Sarum College http://www.sarum.ac.uk/
Salisbury, Wiltshire, England
Church of England / Wales Recognised Theological Education Institution

School of the Annunciation at Buckfast Abbey https://www.sota-edu.com/
Devon, England. Catholic Connections

Somerset College of Arts and Technology http://www.somerset.ac.uk
Somerset, England

South Devon College http://www.southdevon.ac.uk
Devon, England

South West Ministry Training Course http://swmtc.org.uk/
Exeter, Devon, England
Church of England / Wales Recognised Theological Education Institution

Trinity College https://www.trinitycollegebristol.ac.uk/
Bristol, Somerset, England
Church of England / Wales Recognised Theological Education Institution

Truro and Penwith College http://www.truro-penwith.ac.uk
Cornwall, England

Weston College http://www.weston.ac.uk
Weston-super-Mare, North Somerset, England

Weymouth College http://www.weymouth.ac.uk
Dorset, England

Wiltshire College http://www.wiltshire.ac.uk
Wiltshire, England

Wales

Counties:
North Wales: Conwy
North West Wales: Isle of Anglesey; Gwynedd
North East Wales: Denbighshire; Flintshire; Wrexham
West Wales: Carmarthenshire; Ceredigion; Pembrokeshire
Mid Wales: Monmouthshire; Powys
South Wales: Blaennau Gwent; Bridgeend; Caerphilly; Cardiff; Newport; Merthyr Tydfil; Neath Port Talbot; Rhondda Cynon Taf; Swansea; Torfaen; Vale of Glamorgan

Main Towns:
North Wales:
Conwy: Conwy; Betws-y-Coed; Colwyn Bay
North West Wales:
Isle of Anglesey: Holyhead;
Gwynedd: Barmouth; Porthmadog
North East Wales:
Denbighshire: Denbigh; Llangollen
Flintshire: Mold; Holywell;
Wrexham: Rhosllanerchrugog; Wrexham
West Wales:
Carmarthenshire: Carmarthen; Llandovery
Ceredigion: Cardigan; Aberystwyth
Pembrokeshire: Pembrokeshire; Swansea
Mid Wales:
Monmouthshire: Abergavenny; Monmouth; Chepstow
Powys: Brecon; Welshpool; Montgomery
South Wales:
Blaennau Gwent: Ebbw Vale; Tredegar
Bridgend: Bridgeend; Portcawl
Caerphilly: Blackwood; Caerphilly
Cardiff: Cardiff city; Llandaff
Newport: Newport; Caerleon
Merthyr Tydfil: Merthyr Tydfil; Treharris
Neath Port Talbot: Port Talbot; Neath
Rhondda Cynon Taf: Aberdare; Pontypridd
Swansea: Moriston; Swansea
Torfaen: Pontypool
Vale of Glamorgan: Barry; Cowbridge; Penarth

Wales Regions

Wales: Universities, Conservatoires and Art Schools

Aberystwyth University — http://www.aber.ac.uk/
Ceredigion, Mid Wales. The university has campuses at Penglais and Gogerddan as well as the Llanbadarn centre.
- **Aberystwyth University School of Art** — http://www.aber.ac.uk/en/art/
  Aberystwyth, Ceredigion, Wales

Bangor University — http://www.bangor.ac.uk/
Gwynedd, North Wales

Cardiff University — http://www.cardiff.ac.uk/
South Wales

Cardiff Metropolitan University — http://www3.cardiffmet.ac.uk/
South Wales

Open University: Wales http://www.open.ac.uk/wales/
Distance learning
Swansea University / Prifysgol Abertawe http://www.swansea.ac.uk/
Swansea, West Wales
University of South Wales http://www.southwales.ac.uk/
Pontypridd, Wales. A merger of the University of Glamorgan and the University of Wales, Newport; also includes the Royal Welsh College of Music and Drama
- **Royal Welsh College of Music and Drama: Conservatoire** http://www.rwcmd.ac.uk/
  Cardiff, South Wales. Part of University of South Wales
University of Wales http://www.wales.ac.uk/
Cardiff, South Wales
Changes have happened with the University of Wales and it now consists of a number of separate institutions with the former constituent colleges leaving the University of Wales structure
Merger between Swansea Metropolitan University and the University of Wales: Trinity Saint David. Carmarthen Campus, Camarthen; Lampeter Campus, Ceredigion, Wales
- **University of Wales Trinity Saint David** http://www.uwtsd.ac.uk/
  Cardiff, South Wales.
Wrexam Glyndwr University http://www.glyndwr.ac.uk
Campuses at Wrexham, North Wales and Elephant and Castle, London, England

Wales: Higher Education Colleges and other Specialist Institutions
Carmarthenshire College/ Coleg Sir Gar http://www.colegsirgar.ac.uk/
West Wales
Cliff College (Bible College) http://www.cliffcollege.ac.uk
Hope Valley near Sheffield, England
Wrexham, Wales
Coleg Cambria (previously Deeside and Yale Colleges) https://www.cambria.ac.uk/
Deeside Campus; Northtop Campus; Flintshire, Wales; Llysfasi Campus, Denbighshire, Wales;
Bersham Road Campus; Yale Campus, Wrexham, Wales
Gower College Swansea http://www.gowercollegeswansea.ac.uk
West Wales
Grwp Llandrillo Menai http://www.gllm.ac.uk/
Gwynedd, North Wales
Comprises Coleg Llandrillo, Coleg Menai and Coleg Meiroion-Dwyfor, Wales
- **Coleg Llandrillo** https://www.gllm.ac.uk/llandrillo/
- **Coleg Menai** https://www.gllm.ac.uk/menai/
- **Coleg Meiroion-Dwyfor** https://www.gllm.ac.uk/meirion-dwyfor/
Merthyr Tydfil College http://www.merthyr.ac.uk/
Merthyr Tydfil, South Wales. Part of University of South Wales Group
NPTC Group http://www.nptcgroup.ac.uk/
Wales. A merger of Neath Port Talbot College and Coleg Powys.
St Padarn's Institute https://www.stpadarns.ac.uk/
Cardiff, South Wales
Church of England / Wales Recognised Theological Education Institution

Northern Ireland Regions
Counties: Antrim; Armagh; Down; Fermanagh; Londonderry; Tyrone

Main Towns:
Antrim (largest part of Belfast); Carrickfergus; Ballymena
Armagh: Armagh
Down (smallest part of Belfast); Bangor
Fermanagh; Enniskillen
Londonderry: Londonderry
Tyrone: Omagh

Northern Ireland: Universities, Conservatoires and Art Schools
Open University: Ireland http://www.open.ac.uk/
Distance learning
Queen's University Belfast http://www.qub.ac.uk
Belfast, Co. Antrim, Northern Ireland
- **Saint Mary's University College Belfast:**
  College of Queen's University https://www.stmarys-belfast.ac.uk/
  Belfast, Co. Antrim, Northern Ireland
Stranmillis University College http://www.stran.ac.uk
Belfast, Northern Ireland. A College of Queen's University Belfast:
St Mary's University College Belfast http://www.stmarys-belfast.ac.uk/
Belfast, Co. Antrim, Northern Ireland
University of Ulster http://www.ulster.ac.uk
Belfast, Co. Antrim, Northern Ireland
Campuses in: Belfast city centre and Jordanstown in co. Antrim; Coleraine and Magee in Londonderry, Northern Ireland as well as two branch campuses in Birmingham and Holborn, London, England.

Northern Ireland: Institutes of Higher Education and other Specialist Institutions
College of Agriculture, Food and Rural Enterprise http://www.cafre.ac.uk/
Campuses in Co. Antrim; Co. Fermanagh; Co. Tyrone, Northern Ireland
Belfast Metropolitan College http://www.belfastmet.ac.uk/
Belfast, Co. Antrim, Northern Ireland
Irish Baptist College http://www.irishbaptistcollege.co.uk/
Co. Down, Northern Ireland
Evangelical Theological Education Institution
Northern Regional College http://www.nrc.ac.uk/
Campuses in Co.Antrim, Ballymena, Ballymoney, Coleraine, Larne, Magherafelt, Newtonabbey, Northern Ireland
North West Regional College http://www.nwrc.ac.uk/
Campuses in Co. Londonderry, Limavady, Strabane, Northern Ireland
South East Regional College (SERC) http://www.serc.ac.uk/
Campuses in Co. Antirim; County Down, Northern Ireland
South West College http://www.swc.ac.uk/
Co. Tyrone, Northern Ireland
Southern Regional College https://www.src.ac.uk/
Campuses in Co. Armagh, Banbridge, Kilkeel, Lurgan, Newry, Portadown, Northern Ireland

Scotland Regions

North Scotland, Highland and Northern Islands:
Highland; Orkney Islands; Shetland Islands;
Western Isles / Outer Hebrides: Isle of Harris; Isle of Lewis; The Uists; Isle of Barra; St Kilda
North East Scotland:
Aberdeen city; Aberdeenshire; Angus; Clackmannanshire; Dundee city; Fife; Moray; Perth and Kinross; Stirling
Mid Scotland:
Dunbartonshire; Falkirk; Glasgow city; Lanarkshire; Renfrewshire
Mid West Scotland:
Argyll; Ayrshire; Dumfries and Galloway; Inner Hebrides: Isle of Arran; Isle of Bute; Isle of Iona; Isle of Islay; Isle of Jura; Isle of Skye; Isle of Mull; Inverclyde
South East Scotland:
East Lothian; Edinburgh city; Midlothian; Scottish Borders; West Lothian

Main Towns:
North Scotland, Highland and Northern Islands:
Highland: Aviemore; Fort William; Glencoe; Inverness; Lock Ness
Orkney Islands: Kirkwell
Shetland Islands: Lerwick
Western Isles / Outer Hebrides: Isle of Harris: Tarbert; **Isle of Lewis:** Stornoway; **The Uists:** Lochmaddy; **Isle of Barra:** Castlebay;
Mid East Scotland:
Aberdeenshire: Aberdeen city
Angus: Dundee city
Clackmannanshire: Alloa
Fife: St Andrews
Moray: Elgin
Perth and Kinross: Perth; Pitlochry
Stirling: Stirling
Mid Scotland:
Dunbartonshire: Clydebank; Dunbarton
Falkirk: Falkirk
Lanarkshire: Glasgow city
Renfrewshire: Renfrew
Mid West Scotland:
Argyll: Oban
Ayrshire: Irvine
Dumfries and Galloway: Dumfries; Stranraer
Inner Hebrides: Isle of Arran: Brodick; **Isle of Bute:** Rothesay; **Isle of Iona:** Baile Mor; **Isle of Islay:** Bowmore; **Isle of Jura:** Craighouse; **Isle of Skye:** Portree; Sleat; **Isle of Mull:** Tobermory
Inverclyde: Greenock
South East Scotland:
East Lothian: Haddington
Midlothian: Edinburgh city
Scottish Borders: Galashiels; Hawick; Peebles
West Lothian: Livingston

Scotland: Universities, Conservatoires and Art Schools

University of Aberdeen http://www.abdn.ac.uk/

The university consists of three colleges with two campuses at Old Aberdeen and Foresterhill

University of Aberdeen: Colleges

- **College of Arts and Social Sciences** http://www.abdn.ac.uk/cass/
- **College of Life Sciences and Medicine** http://www.abdn.ac.uk/clsm/
- **College of Physical Sciences** http://www.abdn.ac.uk/cops/

Abertay University http://www.abertay.ac.uk/

Dundee, Angus, Scotland

The university is located on a city centre campus, with all of its buildings within a quarter of a mile of each other.

University of Dundee http://www.dundee.ac.uk

Dundee, Angus, Scotland

- **Duncan of Jordanstone College of Art and Design**
  http://www.dundee.ac.uk/djcad/
  Dundee, Angus, Scotland

University of Edinburgh http://www.ed.ac.uk/home

Edinburgh, Midlothian, Scotland

The University of Edinburgh consists of three colleges containing twenty two schools

University of Edinburgh: Colleges

- **College of Humanities and Social Science**
  http://www.ed.ac.uk/schools-departments/humanities-soc-sci
- **College of Medicine and Veterinary Medicine**
  http://www.ed.ac.uk/schools-departments/medicine-vet-medicine/
- **College of Science and Engineering**
  http://www.ed.ac.uk/schools-departments/science-engineering
- **Edinburgh College of Art (ECA)** http://www.eca.ed.ac.uk/
  Edinburgh, Scotland. Part of Edinburgh University

Edinburgh Napier University http://www.napier.ac.uk

Edinburgh, Midlothian, Scotland

University of Glasgow http://www.gla.ac.uk/

Glasgow, Lanarkshire, Scotland

The University of Glasgow consists of four colleges

University of Glasgow: Colleges

- **College of Arts** http://www.gla.ac.uk/colleges/arts/
- **College of Medical, Veterinary and Life Sciences**
  http://www.gla.ac.uk/colleges/mvls/
- **College of Science and Engineering**
  http://www.gla.ac.uk/colleges/scienceengineering/
- **College of Social Sciences**
  http://www.gla.ac.uk/colleges/socialsciences/

Glasgow Caledonian University http://www.gcu.ac.uk

Glasgow, Lanarkshire, Scotland

Glasgow School of Art http://www.gsa.ac.uk

Glasgow, Lanarkshire, Scotland

Heriot-Watt University http://www.hw.ac.uk

Edinburgh, Midlothian, Scotland

University of the Highlands and Islands   https://www.uhi.ac.uk/

Scotland   13 College campuses:

- **Argyll College**   https://www.argyll.uhi.ac.uk/
  East Mainland, Islands of Argyll, Scotland
- **Lews Castle College**   https://www.lews.uhi.ac.uk/
  Stornaway, Isle of Lewis, Scotland
- **NAFC Marine Centre**   https://www.nafc.uhi.ac.uk/
  Scalloway, Shetland Islands, Scotland
- **Orkney College**   https://www.orkney.uhi.ac.uk/
  Kirkwell and Stromnes, Orkney Islands
- **Highland Theological College**   https://www.htc.uhi.ac.uk/
  Dingwall, Ross-shire, Scotland
- **Inverness College**   https://www.inverness.uhi.ac.uk/
  Inverness, Inverness-shire, Scotland
- **Moray College**   https://www.moray.uhi.ac.uk/
  Moray Street, Elgin, Inverness-shire, Scotland
- **North Highland College**   https://www.northhighland.uhi.ac.uk/
  Thurso, Caithness, Scotland
- **Perth College**   https://www.perth.uhi.ac.uk/
  Perth, Perthshire, Scotland
- **Sabhal Mor Ostaig**   http://www.smo.uhi.ac.uk/en/
  Sleat, Isle of Sky, Scotland
- **Scottish Marine Institute**   http://www.sams.ac.uk/
  Scottish Association for Marine Science (SAMS)
  Oban, Argyll, Scotland
- **Shetland College**   https://www.shetland.uhi.ac.uk/
  Lerwick, Shetland, Scotland
- **West Highland College**   https://www.whc.uhi.ac.uk/
  Fort William, Scotland

Leith School of Art   http://www.leithschoolofart.co.uk/

Edinburgh, Midlothian, Scotland

An independent institution, registered as a charity. Not a higher education institution but offers a Foundation Art course.

Open University in Scotland   http://www.open.ac.uk/scotland/

Distance Learning, Scotland

Queen Margaret University   http://www.qmu.ac.uk

Edinburgh, Midlothian, Scotland

Robert Gordon University   http://www.rgu.ac.uk

Aberdeen, Aberdeenshire, Scotland

- **Gray's School of Art**   http://www.rgu.ac.uk/
  Aberdeen, Aberdeenshire, Scotland

Royal Conservatoire of Scotland   https://www.rcs.ac.uk/

Glasgow, Lanarkshire, Scotland

University of St Andrews   http://www.st-andrews.ac.uk

Fife, Scotland

University of Stirling   http://www.stir.ac.uk

Inverness and Stornoway, Scotland

University of Strathclyde Glasgow   http://www.strath.ac.uk

Glasgow, Lanarkshire, Scotland

University of the West of Scotland   http://www.uws.ac.uk

Campuses in: Ayr, Dumfries, Hamilton, Paisley, Scotland; London borough of Southwark, England

Scotland: Higher Education Colleges and other Specialist Institutions

Dundee and Angus College   https://dundeeandangus.ac.uk/
Dundee, Angus, Scotland

City of Glasgow College   http://www.cityofglasgowcollege.ac.uk/
Glasgow, Lanarkshire, Scotland

Glasgow Clyde College   http://www.glasgowclyde.ac.uk/
Glasgow, Lanarkshire, Scotland

Glasgow Kelvin College   https://www.glasgowkelvin.ac.uk/
Glasgow, Lanarkshire, Scotland

Interactive Design Institute   http://idesigni.co.uk/
East Lothian, Scotland. Online art and design courses accredited by University of Hertfordshire

**National Trust for Scotland: School of
Heritage Gardening**   http://www.nts.org.uk/Site/Heritage-gardening/Training-Careers/
Edinburgh, Midlothian, Scotland

North East Scotland College   http://www.nescol.ac.uk/
incorporating Scottish Maritime Academy
Aberdeen, Scotland

Royal Botanic Garden Edinburgh   http://www.rbge.org.uk/education/home
Edinburgh, Midlothian, Scotland

Scottish Agricultural College   http://www.sac.ac.uk
Campuses in Aberdeen, Ayr, Broxburn, Cupar, Dumfries and Edinburgh, Scotland

Scotland's Rural College   http://www.sruc.ac.uk/
Aberdeen Campus, Aberdeen; Ayr Campus, Ayr; Barony Campus, Dumfries and Galloway; Edinburgh Campus, Edinburgh; Elmwood Campus, North East Fife; Oatridge Campus, West Lothian, Scotland

Specialist Institutions by Region

Art Schools by Region
North East England
Newcastle University School of Arts and Cultures http://www.ncl.ac.uk/sacs/
Newcastle-upon-Tyne, England
Northern School of Art https://northernart.ac.uk/
(previously Cleveland College of Art and Design)
Middlesbrough and Hartlepool

North West England
Liverpool School of Art and Design http://www.ljmu.ac.uk/LSA/
Liverpool, England. Part of Liverpool John Moores University
Manchester School of Art http://www.artdes.mmu.ac.uk/
Manchester, England. Part of Manchester Metropolitan University

Yorkshire and the Humber
Leeds Arts University http://www.leeds-art.ac.uk
Leeds, West Yorkshire, England
University of Leeds, School of Fine Art http://www.fine-art.leeds.ac.uk/
Leeds, England

West Midlands
Birmingham Institute for Art and Design (BIAD) http://www.bcu.ac.uk/biad
Birmingham, England

London
Undergraduate and Postgraduate Courses
University of the Arts http://www.arts.ac.uk
London, England
The University of the Arts consists of six Arts, Design, Fashion and Media Colleges:
- **Camberwell College of Arts:** http://www.arts.ac.uk/camberwell/
  South East London, England
- **Central Saint Martins:** http://www.arts.ac.uk/csm/
  Kings Cross, North London, England
- **Chelsea College of Arts:** http://www.arts.ac.uk/chelsea/
  South West London, England
- **London College of Communication:** http://www.arts.ac.uk/lcc/
  Elephant and Castle, South East London, England
- **London College of Fashion:** http://www.arts.ac.uk/fashion/
  West London, England
- **Wimbledon College of Arts:** http://www.arts.ac.uk/wimbledon/
  South West London, England

The Cass
(Sir John Cass Faculty of Art,
Architecture and Design) https://www.londonmet.ac.uk/schools/the-cass/
North London, England. Merged with London Metropolitan University
The Courtauld Institute of Art http://courtauld.ac.uk/
West Central London, England
Goldsmiths, University of London: http://www.gold.ac.uk/art/
London, England
Slade School of Fine Art: http://www.ucl.ac.uk/slade
West London, England

London
Postgraduate Courses:
Christie's Education   http://www.christies.com/
West London, England
Royal Academy of Arts   https://www.royalacademy.org.uk/
  • **Royal Academy Schools**   http://www.royalacademy.org.uk/raschools/
West London, England
Part of the Royal Academy of Arts: Postgraduate only
A charity and privately funded institution founded in 1768
Sotheby's Institute of Art   http://www.sothebysinstitute.com/
West Central London, England. Postgraduate only

South East England
University of Brighton – Faculty of Arts and Architecturehttp://arts.brighton.ac.uk/
Brighton, England
University of Oxford University Art Department:
The Ruskin School of Art   http://www.rsa.ox.ac.uk/
Oxfordshire, England
The Ruskin School of Drawing and Fine Art   http://www.ruskin-sch.ox.ac.uk/
Oxford University: Oxford, England

South West England
Bath School of Art and Design   http://artdesign.bathspa.ac.uk/
Bath, England. Part of Bath Spa university
Falmouth University   http://www.falmouth.ac.uk/art-at-falmouth
Incorporating Dartington College of Arts: Cornwall, England

Wales:
Aberystwyth University School of Art   http://www.aber.ac.uk/en/art/
Aberystwyth, Ceredigion, Wales
Cardiff School of Art and Design   http://cardiff-school-of-art-and-design.org/
Cardiff, Wales
Wrexam Glyndwr University:
School of Art and Design   http://www.glyndwr.ac.uk
Wrexham, North Wales

Scotland:
University of Dundee:
Duncan of Jordanstone College of Art and Design http://www.dundee.ac.uk/djcad/
Dundee, Angus, Scotland
Edinburgh College of Art (ECA)   http://www.eca.ed.ac.uk/
Edinburgh, Midlothian, Scotland. Part of Edinburgh University
Glasgow School of Art   http://www.gsa.ac.uk/
Glasgow, Lanarkshire, Scotland
Leith School of Art   http://www.leithschoolofart.co.uk/
Edinburgh, Midlothian, Scotland
An independent institution, registered as a charity. Not a higher education institution but offers a Foundation Art course.
Robert Gordon University: Gray's School of Art http://www.rgu.ac.uk/
Aberdeen, Aberdeenshire, Scotland

Chiropractic Higher Education Institutions by Region

South East England
Anglo-European College of Chiropractic (AECC) http://www.aecc.ac.uk/
Bournemouth, England
The McTimoney College of Chiropractic http://www.mctimoney-college.ac.uk/
Oxfordshire, England

Wales
University of Wales, Welsh Institute of Chiropractic http://www.southwales.ac.uk/
Pontypridd, Wales

Conservatoires: Music; Dance; Drama by Region
The following are members of Conservatoires UK http://www.conservatoiresuk.ac.uk/

North West England
Royal Northern College of Music: http://www.rncm.ac.uk/
Manchester, England

Yorkshire and the Humber
Leeds College of Music: http://www.lcm.ac.uk/
Leeds, England. Degrees are validated by the University of Hull

West Midlands
Birmingham Conservatoire: http://www.bcu.ac.uk/pme/conservatoire
Birmingham, England. Part of Birmingham City University

London
Guildhall School of Music and Drama http://www.gsmd.ac.uk/
Barbican, East Central London. Applications need to be made directly to this Conservatoire.
Royal Academy of Music: http://www.ram.ac.uk/
North West London, England. Graduates of the Academy receive University of London degrees
Royal College of Music: http://www.rcm.ac.uk/
South West London, England
Trinity Laban Conservatoire of Music and Dance: http://www.trinitylaban.ac.uk/
South East London, England

Wales
Royal Welsh College of Music and Drama: http://www.rwcmd.ac.uk/
Cardiff, Wales. Part of the University of South Wales Group

Scotland
Royal Conservatoire of Scotland: http://www.rcs.ac.uk/
Glasgow, Scotland

343

Land Based Colleges: Agriculture and Horticulture; some Animal Courses by Region

North West England

Grampus Heritage and Training Ltd
Cumbria, England

http://www.grampusheritage.co.uk/

Myerscough College
Preston, England

http://www.myerscough.ac.uk

Newton Rigg College
Cumbria, England

http://www.newtonrigg.ac.uk/

Reaseheath College
Nantwich, Cheshire

http://www.reaseheath.ac.uk

Yorkshire and the Humber

Askham Bryan College
York, North Yorkshire, England

http://www.askham-bryan.ac.uk/

Bishop Burton College
Bishop Burton, East Yorkshire

https://www.bishopburton.ac.uk/

West Midlands

ACS Distance Education
Stourbridge, Staffordshire, England

http://www.acsedu.co.uk/

NPTC City and Guilds Land Based Services
Courses throughout the UK; Warwickshire, England

http://www.nptc.org.uk/

South Staffordshire College
Staffordshire, England

http://www.southstaffs.ac.uk/

Warwickshire College
Pershore College (Animal and Land Based courses), Henley-in-Arden, Trident Centre, Warwickshire, England

http://www.warwickshire.ac.uk

East Midlands

Brooksby Melton College
Leicestershire, England

http://www.brooksbymelton.ac.uk/

Moulton College
Northamptonshire, England

http://www.moulton.ac.uk

Spalding Horticultural Training Group
Spalding, Lincolnshire, England

http://www.shtg.co.uk/

East of England

Easton and Otley College
Norfolk and Suffolk, England

http://www.eastonotley.ac.uk/

Shuttleworth College
Part of Bedford College
Bedfordshire, England

http://www.bedford.ac.uk/

Greater London

Capel Manor College
Enfield, Middlesex, England

http://www.capel.ac.uk/

Hadlow College
South East London and Kent, England

http://www.hadlow.ac.uk/

344

South East England

Arboventure
http://www.arborventure.co.uk/
Hampshire, England
Berkshire College of Agriculture
https://www.bca.ac.uk/
Maidenhead, Berkshire, England
Bespoke Education and Specialist Training
(BEST) in Horticulture Group
http://www.bestinhorticulture.co.uk/
Abingdon on Thames, Oxfordshire, England
Chichester College
https://chichester.ac.uk/
West Sussex, England
Institute of Groundsmanship
http://www.iog.org/
Milton Keynes, Buckinghamshire, England
Merrist Wood College
http://www.merristwood.ac.uk/
Guildford, Surrey
Plumpton College
http://www.plumpton.ac.uk
Sussex, England. Specialist Land Based courses
Royal Botanic Gardens
Kew
http://www.kew.org/learn/specialist-training/horticulture-courses
Richmond, Surrey
Royal Horticultural Society (RHS) Gardens Wisley https://www.rhs.org.uk/
Surrey, England
Sparsholt College Hampshire
http://www.sparsholt.ac.uk
Hampshire, England

South West England

Cornwall College Group
https://www.cornwall.ac.uk/
- **Cornwall College: The Eden Project**
  Boldeva, Cornwall, England
- **Cornwall College Group**
  Duchy University Hub
  https://www.duchy.ac.uk/duchy-university
  Cornwall, England. Bicton College Merger with the Cornwall College Group

Horticultural Correspondence College
http://www.hccollege.co.uk/
Holsworthy, Devon, England
Kingston Maurward College
http://www.kmc.ac.uk/
Dorset, England

Northern Ireland

College of Agriculture, Food and Rural Enterprise http://www.cafre.ac.uk/
County Antrim; County Fermanagh; County Tyrone, Northern Ireland

Scotland

National Trust for Scotland: School of
Heritage Gardening
http://www.nts.org.uk/Site/Heritage-gardening/Training-Careers/
Edinburgh, Midlothian, Scotland
Royal Botanic Garden Edinburgh
http://www.rbge.org.uk/education/home
Edinburgh, Midlothian, Scotland
Scotland's Rural College
http://www.sruc.ac.uk/
Aberdeen Campus, Aberdeen; Ayr Campus, Ayr; Barony Campus, Dumfries and Galloway; Edinburgh Campus, Edinburgh; Elmwood Campus, North East Fife; Oatridge Campus, West Lothian, Scotland

Music Instrument Building and Repair Colleges by Region

East Midlands
Chapel Violins http://www.chapelviolins.com/site/
Balderton, Newark, Nottinghamshire, England
Newark School of Violin Making part of Lincoln College http://www.lincolncollege.ac.uk/
Newark, Nottinghamshire, England

Greater London
South Thames College http://www.south-thames.ac.uk/
Wandsworth, South West London, England

South East England
West Dean College https://www.westdean.org.uk/
West Dean, Nr Chichester, West Sussex

Scotland
Glasgow Clyde College http://www.glasgowclyde.ac.uk/
Glasgow, Lanarkshire, Scotland

Nautical Colleges and Universities by Region
Links to nautical colleges and universities may be found at the
Merchant Navy Training Board
http://mntb.org.uk/education-training/nautical-colleges-universities/

North East England
South Tyneside College http://www.stc.ac.uk/
South Shields and Jarrow, Tyne and Weir, England

North West England
Blackpool and the Fylde College: Fleetwood Nautical Campus
http://www.blackpool.ac.uk/
Fleetwood, Lancashire, England
Liverpool John Moores University: Maritime Knowledge Hub https://www.ljmu.ac.uk/
Liverpool, Merseyside, England

East England
Counties: Bedfordshire; Cambridgeshire; Essex; Hertfordshire; Suffolk; Norfolk
Lowestoft College https://www.lowestoft.ac.uk/
Lowestoft, Suffolk, England

South East England
North Kent College of Further Education http://www.northkent.ac.uk/
Dartford and Gravesend, Kent, England
Warsash Maritime Academy http://www.warsashacademy.co.uk/
Warsash, Southampton, England

South West England
Plymouth University https://www.plymouth.ac.uk/
Plymouth, England

Scotland

City of Glasgow College   http://www.cityofglasgowcollege.ac.uk/
Glasgow, Lanarkshire, Scotland
University of the Highlands and Islands
- **Lews Castle College**   https://www.lews.uhi.ac.uk/
  Western Isles, Scotland
- **NAFC Marine Centre**   https://www.nafc.uhi.ac.uk/
  Scalloway, Shetland Islands, Scotland
- **Orkney College**   https://www.orkney.uhi.ac.uk/
  Kirkwell and Stromnes, Orkney Islands

North East Scotland College: Scottish Maritime Academy http://www.nescol.ac.uk/
Aberdeenshire, Scotland

Ireland

National Maritime College of Ireland   http://www.nmci.ie/
Co. Cork, Ireland

Osteopathy Higher Education Institutions by Region

West Midlands

College of Osteopaths   http://www.collegeofosteopaths.ac.uk/
Locations in Hertfordshire and Stoke-on-Trent, Staffordshire

Greater London

British College of Osteopathic Medicine   http://www.bcom.ac.uk/
North West London, England
British School of Osteopathy   http://www.bso.ac.uk/
South East London, England
College of Osteopaths   http://www.collegeofosteopaths.ac.uk/
Locations in Hertfordshire and Stoke-on-Trent, Staffordshire
London College of Osteopathic Medicine   http://www.lcom.org.uk/
(For medical doctors)
Marylebone, London
London School of Osteopathy   http://lso.ac.uk/
South East London, England

South East England

European School of Osteopathy   https://www.eso.ac.uk/
Maidstone, Kent
NESCOT, Epsom's College of Further and Higher Education:
Surrey Institute of Osteopathic Medicine   http://www.nescot.ac.uk/
Surrey, England

South West England

University of St Mark and St John Plymouth
(Plymouth Marjon University)   http://www.marjon.ac.uk/
Devon, England

Wales

Swansea University / Prifysgol Abertawe   http://www.swansea.ac.uk
Swansea, Wales

Religion / Theology Education Institutions by Region

Many universities and colleges provide courses in religion / theology however the following education institutions provide specialist courses in religion / theology.

North East England

Counties: Durham; Northumberland; Tyne and Wear; Cleveland
Durham University,
Centre for Catholic Studies   https://www.dur.ac.uk/theology.religion/ccs/
Durham, England. Catholic Connections
University of Durham: St John's College: https://www.dur.ac.uk/
Cranmer Hall: Theological College   https://community.dur.ac.uk/cranmer.hall/
Durham, England
Church of England / Wales Recognised Theological Education Institution
Lindisfarne   http://lindisfarnertp.org/
North Shields, Northumberland, England
Church of England / Wales Recognised Theological Education Institution

North West England

Counties: Cheshire; Cumbria; Lancashire; Greater Manchester; Merseyside; Isle of
University of Chester,
All Saints' Centre for Mission and Ministry   http://allsaintscentre.org/
Warrington, England
University of Chester   http://www.chester.ac.uk/
Campuses in Chester and Warrington, England. Member of the Cathedrals Group
Church of England / Wales Recognised Theological Education Institution
University of Cumbria   http://www.cumbria.ac.uk
Sites and campuses in Cumbria, Penrith, London and Workington, England member of the Cathedrals Group
Cumbria Christian Learning   https://www.cumbriachristianlearning.org.uk/
Cumbria, England
Lancashire and Cumbria Theological Partnership http://lctp.co.uk/
Lancashire and Cumbria, England
Church of England / Wales Recognised Theological Education Institution
Liverpool Hope University   http://www.hope.ac.uk
Liverpool, England. Member of the Cathedrals Group. Catholic Connections

Yorkshire and the Humber

Counties: East Yorkshire; North Yorkshire; South Yorkshire; West Yorkshire
College of the Resurrection   http://college.mirfield.org.uk/
Mirfield, West Yorkshire, England
Church of England / Wales Recognised Theological Education Institution
Leeds Trinity University   http://www.leedstrinity.ac.uk
Leeds, West Yorkshire, England. Member of the Cathedrals Group. Catholic Connections
York St John University   http://www.yorksj.ac.uk
Yorkshire, England. Member of the Cathedrals Group
Yorkshire Ministry Course   http://www.ymc.org.uk/
Mirfield, West Yorkshire, England
Church of England / Wales Recognised Theological Education Institution

West Midlands

Counties: Herefordshire; Shropshire; Staffordshire; Warwickshire; West Midlands; Worcestershire.

Maryvale Institute
International Catholic College   http://www.maryvale.ac.uk/
Birmingham, England. Catholic Connections
Newman University   http://www.newman.ac.uk
Birmingham, England. Member of the Cathedrals Group. Catholic Connections
The Queen's Foundation   http://www.queens.ac.uk/
Birmingham, England
Church of England / Wales Recognised Theological Education Institution

East Midlands

Counties: Derbyshire; Leicestershire; Lincolnshire; Northamptonshire; Nottinghamshire; Rutland

Bishop Grosseteste University College   http://www.bishopg.ac.uk/
Lincolnshire, England. Member of the Cathedrals Group
Lincoln School of Theology and Ministry   http://www.lincoln.anglican.org/
Lincoln, England
Church of England / Wales Recognised Theological Education Institution
Markfield Institute of Higher Education,   http://www.mihe.org.uk/
linked with Newman University, Leicestershire, England. Islamic Studies
St Johns School of Mission   http://www.stjohns-nottm.ac.uk/
Nottingham, England
Church of England / Wales Recognised Theological Education Institution

East England

Counties: Bedfordshire; Cambridgeshire; Essex; Hertfordshire; Suffolk; Norfolk

Cambridge Theological Federation,
Eastern Region Ministry course   http://www.ermc.cam.ac.uk/
Cambridge, England
Church of England / Wales Recognised Theological Education Institution
Margaret Beaufort Institute of Theology   http://www.margaretbeaufort.cam.ac.uk/
Cambridge, England. Catholic Connections
Ridley Hall   http://www.ridley.cam.ac.uk/
Cambridge, England
Church of England / Wales Recognised Theological Education Institution
Von Hugel Institute St Edmunds College   http://www.vhi.st-edmunds.cam.ac.uk/
Cambridge, England. Catholic Connections
Westcott House   http://www.westcott.cam.ac.uk/
Cambridge, England
Church of England / Wales Recognised Theological Education Institution

Greater London

Counties: London and surrounding areas: East London; Central London; North London; South London; West London; Middlesex; parts of Surrey

Heythrop College, University of London   http://www.heythrop.ac.uk/
West London, England. Member of the Cathedrals Group. Catholic Connections
Leo Baeck College   http://www.lbc.ac.uk/
North London, England. Jewish Education Institution
London School of Jewish Studies   http://www.lsjs.ac.uk/
North West London, England. Jewish Education Institution

London Theological Seminary   http://www.ltslondon.org/
North London, England
Evangelical Theological Education Institution

Montefiore College   https://www.montefioreendowment.org.uk/
West London, England. Jewish Education Institution

Oak Hill Theological College   http://www.oakhill.ac.uk/
Southgate, North London, England
Church of England / Wales Recognised Theological Education Institution

Proclamation Trust: Cornhill Training Course   https://www.proctrust.org.uk/
South London, England
Evangelical Theological Education Institution

University of Roehampton   http://www.roehampton.ac.uk
London: South West London, England. Member of the Cathedrals Group. Catholic Connections

St Mary's University, Twickenham   http://www.stmarys.ac.uk/
Twickenham, London, England. Member of the Cathedrals Group. Catholic Connections

St Mellitus College   http://www.stmellitus.org/
London
Church of England / Wales Recognised Theological Education Institution

Salvation Army
William Booth College   http://www.salvationarmy.org.uk/william-booth-college
South East London, England. Salvation Army Education Institution

South East England

Counties: Berkshire; Buckinghamshire; Hampshire; Isle of Wight; Kent; Oxfordshire; Surrey; East Sussex; West Sussex

Canterbury Christ Church University   http://www.canterbury.ac.uk/
Kent, England. Member of the Cathedrals Group

University of Chichester   http://www.chi.ac.uk
West Sussex, England. Member of the Cathedrals Group

Franciscan International Study Centre   http://www.franciscans.ac.uk/
Canterbury, Kent, England. Catholic Connections

Guildford OLM Scheme   http://www.cofeguildford.org.uk/
Guildford, Surrey, England
Church of England / Wales Recognised Theological Education Institution

University of Oxford, Blackfriars Stadium   http://www.bfriars.ox.ac.uk/
Oxford, England. Catholic Connections

University of Oxford, Campion Hall   http://www.campion.ox.ac.uk/
Oxford, England. Catholic Connections

University of Oxford, St Benet's Hall   http://www.st-benets.ox.ac.uk/
Oxford, England. Catholic Connections

University of Oxford, Wycliffe Hall   http://www.wycliffehall.org.uk/
Oxford, England
Church of England / Wales Recognised Theological Education Institution

Oxford OLM Scheme   http://www.oxford.anglican.org/
Oxford, England
Church of England / Wales Recognised Theological Education Institution

Ripon College   http://www.rcc.ac.uk/
Cuddesdon, Oxfordshire, England
Church of England / Wales Recognised Theological Education Institution

Institute of St Anselm   http://st.anselm.org.uk/
Kent, England. Catholic Connections

St Augustine's College of Theology https://staugustinescollege.ac.uk/
West Malling, Kent, England. Centres in Canterbury Christchurch University, Kent and
Southwark, South East London
Church of England / Wales Recognised Theological Education Institution
St Stephen's House https://www.ssho.ox.ac.uk/
Oxford, England
Church of England / Wales Recognised Theological Education Institution
South East Institute for Theological Education http://www.seite.co.uk/
Canterbury Christchurch University, Kent
Union School of Theology https://www.ust.ac.uk/
Head-quarters, Oxford, England
Evangelical Theological Education Institution
University of Winchester http://www.winchester.ac.uk
Winchester, Hampshire, England. Member of the Cathedrals Group

South West England
Counties: Cornwall; Devon; Dorset; Gloucestershire; Somerset; Wiltshire;
University of Gloucestershire http://www.glos.ac.uk
Gloucestershire, England. Member of the Cathedrals Group. Salvation Army Officer
Training: validated diploma of higher education
Moorland Bible college http://www.moorlands.ac.uk/
Dorset, England
Evangelical Theological Education Institution
Sarum College http://www.sarum.ac.uk/
Salisbury, Wiltshire, England
Church of England / Wales Recognised Theological Education Institution
University of St Mark and St John Plymouth http://www.marjon.ac.uk/
Devon, England. Member of the Cathedrals Group
School of the Annunciation at Buckfast Abbey http://www.maryvale.ac.uk/
Devon, England. Catholic Connections
South West Ministry Training course http://swmtc.org.uk/
Exeter, Devon, England
Church of England / Wales Recognised Theological Education Institution
Trinity College https://www.trinitycollegebristol.ac.uk/
Bristol, Somerset, England
Church of England / Wales Recognised Theological Education Institution

Wales
North Wales; North West Wales; North East Wales; West Wales; Mid Wales; South Wales
St Padarn's Institute https://www.stpadarns.ac.uk/
Cardiff, South Wales
Church of England / Wales Recognised Theological Education Institution
University of Wales Trinity Saint David http://www.uwtsd.ac.uk/
Cardiff, South Wales. Member of the Cathedrals Group

Northern Ireland
Counties: Antrim (largest part of Belfast); **Armagh; Down** (smallest part of Belfast);
Fermanagh; Londonderry; Tyrone
Irish Baptist College http://www.irishbaptistcollege.co.uk/
Co. Down, Northern Ireland
Evangelical Theological Education Institution

Chapter 8
Applying for Higher Education Courses

8.1   Applying for a Course through the University and College Admissions Service (UCAS)

Once you have decided which subject, course and university or college to apply to, you will need to make an application which should be completed ensuring you meet the advised application deadline, which are different for some universities and courses. Most full time undergraduate and some postgraduate courses are applied for through the Universities and Colleges Admission Service (UCAS) https://www.ucas.com/

About the University and College Admission Service (UCAS)

The Universities and Colleges Admission Service (UCAS) https://www.ucas.com/ is the organisation which most of the UK universities and higher education colleges are members. UCAS is responsible for managing undergraduate applications to higher education as well as running specialist application services for courses in conservatoires, UCAS Conservatoire https://www.ucas.com/ucas/conservatoires postgraduate teacher training courses, UCAS Teacher Training https://www.ucas.com/ucas/teacher-training (previously known as the Graduate Teacher Training Registry GTTR); and some postgraduate courses through the UCAS online postgraduate application service UCAS: UK Postgraduate Application and Statistical Service (UKPASS) https://www.ucas.com/ucas/postgraduate/postgraduate-study

For most full-time degrees or other undergraduate courses which start at the beginning of the academic year you would need to apply through UCAS. Most undergraduate and postgraduate courses usually start at the beginning of the academic year in September or October in England, Wales and Northern Ireland or in August in Scotland, although there may be some variations. Some full-time undergraduate courses have starting dates at other times of the year and you may be required to apply directly to the higher education institution for these.

You would also usually apply directly to a university or college if you are thinking of studying for a part-time undergraduate course or part-time distance learning course. If you are considering postgraduate study, many full-time and part - time postgraduate courses require you to apply directly to the higher education institution. However, postgraduate courses in social work, nursing, medicine and LLB law accelerated courses are applied for through the UCAS undergraduate application service and some additional postgraduate courses will require an application through UCAS Postgraduate.

Many postgraduate teaching courses require you to apply through UCAS Teacher Training, although for courses in Scotland, the application is through the undergraduate UCAS system. Some postgraduate school centred teacher training available in England and Wales will require an application directly through the relevant organisation. Some professional postgraduate courses such as law and clinical psychology need to be applied to through a clearing house. Information about making applications will be on the higher education institution's website as well as the UCAS website.

The Republic of Ireland (Southern Ireland) is not part of the UK and admissions to universities and colleges are made through the Central Applications Office (CAO) in Ireland https://www.cao.ie/ .
University admissions tests

For certain courses, you will need to take a special entrance exam / test. You will need to firstly register to take the relevant test and registration deadlines may be before you submit your UCAS application form. Some tests are sat before you apply for a university course through UCAS and others may be sat after but the tests form part of the admissions process and if you have registered too late to sit a test, your application may not be considered. See the chapter on University Admissions Tests.

Higher Education Course UCAS Application Process

Applying for full time undergraduate courses starting at the beginning of the academic year

Applications for UK full time degrees and other undergraduate courses, starting at the beginning of the academic year, are usually made through the University and College Admission Service (UCAS) https://www.ucas.com/. In England, Wales and Northern Ireland, courses usually start in September/October and in Scotland, courses usually start in August. Some foundation year / extended year courses may require an application through UCAS but some may require a direct application, therefore you should confirm this with the relevant university or college.

Applying for full time undergraduate courses starting later in the year

Some higher education courses start at other times in the year and if you are applying for a full-time degree or other full-time undergraduate course starting at a date after September / October you would usually need to apply directly to universities or colleges using their own application form.

Applying for part time undergraduate courses

If you are applying for a part-time degree or other part-time undergraduate course starting at any time during the academic year, you would usually need to apply directly to universities or colleges using their own application form. If you are unsure about the application process, check with the relevant university or college and information is usually available on their websites.

Applying for distance learning courses

If you want to study for a degree or other undergraduate course through a distance learning provider, these courses are classed as part time and you would usually apply directly to the organisation, university or college managing the course you are interested in. Postgraduate distance learning courses are also applied for directly with the distance learning provider.

Applying for postgraduate courses

If you want to apply for a full-time or part-time postgraduate course you would usually apply direct to the university or college, although for some courses at specified universities, applications can be through UCAS Postgraduate https://www.ucas.com/ucas/postgraduate . Universities and colleges using UCAS postgraduate can be found on this website.

However postgraduate courses in social work, nursing, medicine, LLB law accelerated and teacher training in Scotland are applied for through the UCAS undergraduate application service. Some undergraduate courses can also lead to an integrated master's qualification and such courses are also applied for though the UCAS undergraduate applications process.

Applying for teacher training courses

If you want to apply for postgraduate teacher training courses, applications for the Post / Professional Graduate Certificate of Education (PGCE) in England and Wales are made through UCAS Teacher Training https://www.ucas.com/ucas/teacher-training , or for the Post Graduate Diploma of Education (PGDE) in Scotland through the undergraduate UCAS route. However for Northern Ireland PGCE applications, you should apply directly to universities and colleges.

Applying for courses at Conservatoires

Conservatoires UK are a group of nine specialist member institutions which offer undergraduate and postgraduate music courses with some also offering, drama and dance courses. Some specialist music full time undergraduate and postgraduate courses available in Conservatoires will require an application to made through UCAS Conservatoires https://www.ucas.com/ucas/conservatoires , meeting the required application deadline of beginning of October (the date may vary slightly) where you may have up to six course choices.

Some specialist postgraduate Conservatoire courses may also be made directly with the Conservatoire. For other full time undergraduate courses available in Conservatoires such as drama, dance, musical theatre or music technology, you should apply through the standard UCAS applications route https://www.ucas.com/ meeting the deadline of 15th January where you may have up to five course choices.

It is important to check on the relevant Conservatoire website for information to check which application you will need to use and any additional information required well in advance of the application deadline requirements. You may make applications for courses using both UCAS Conservatoires or the standard UCAS applications, choosing up to 11 courses, however if you accept an offer through each application system, you will be required to just select one as a firm offer.

For applications to the Guildhall School of Music and Drama https://www.gsmd.ac.uk/ you would need to apply directly to the institution and not through UCAS

There are some exceptions for certain audition locations, international applicants or postgraduate courses therefore you should check the conservatoire websites for full application details. If you miss the deadline, you may still apply for some courses until towards the end of August if there are still vacancies, therefore you should contact the conservatoire before submitting a late application and check if they will consider you. Many courses taught in conservatoires will require you to attend an interview and audition for which you will need to pay a fee.

Undergraduate Course Choices

Applying through UCAS https://www.ucas.com/, you can choose to apply for up to five courses for most subjects. The exception is for Medicine, Dentistry or Veterinary Medicine / Veterinary Science where you can only apply for up to four courses, a fifth choice may be another subject.

If applying to Conservatoires https://www.ucas.com/ucas/conservatoires you may choose up to six courses, and if you wish may also apply through the standard UCAS applications route choosing an additional five courses. On the UCAS application process, there is no preference order and courses should be listed in the alphabetical order in which they appear in the UCAS directory. You will need to list the course codes and higher education institution codes which should be on the higher education institution website or the UCAS website.

The universities or colleges won't be able to see where else you have applied to until after you have replied to any offers you are made.

If you choose to, you can usually select more than one course at the same university or college, although each course will count towards the maximum of five.

The exception is for the Universities of Cambridge and Oxford, where you can only select one course at each university and you will need to select to apply to either the University of Cambridge or the University of Oxford as you can't apply to both of the universities.

If you are unsuccessful for your chosen course, the university or college may offer you a place on an alternative course that you haven't listed, although there is no guarantee this will happen.

Therefore making more than one application for a related course at the same university or college may need to be considered carefully. It is important to check out the courses you want to apply for thoroughly in advance of your application. You can if you choose just apply for one course but in order to guarantee a successful offer, you are advised to apply for more than one course.

Medicine, dentistry, veterinary medicine course applications

You are only allowed a maximum of four courses in any one of the medicine, dentistry or veterinary medicine subjects on your UCAS application. Your fifth choice should be another subject that you would also be interested in studying should you not be successful in getting offers for you main choices.

Course choices at the University of Cambridge and University of Oxford

You can only apply to one course at either the University of Cambridge or the University of Oxford.

Deferred entry applications

Some universities and colleges may give you an offer if you choose to defer the start date of your course to the following academic year, however you should confirm with the higher education institution as this may not be an option. Making a successful application for deferred entry is seen as slightly more competitive since the university or college is effectively committing to a decision on your application before they have seen other students applying the following year.

Key Dates for the UCAS Application Process

The following information includes key application deadline dates, however you should check the UCAS website for up to date information on key dates https://www.ucas.com/ucas/undergraduate /apply-and-track/key-dates

It is important to meet the set deadlines for highly competitive courses. However if you apply after the deadline for some courses your application may still be considered, although there is no guarantee. A number of courses may still have spaces in the 'clearing' period later in the summer period.

The following are the main UCAS deadlines and your application needs to be with UCAS by 18.00 on the relevant day

- 1st October deadline for some music courses at Conservatoires
- 15th October deadline for Medicine, Dentistry, Veterinary Medicine and all courses at the University of Cambridge and University of Oxford
- 15th January deadline for the majority of courses
- 24th March deadline for some Art and Design courses

Have your application ready in advance
Although the above dates are the UCAS set deadlines to apply for courses, you can apply before these dates as soon as the application process opens, which is usually in the middle of September for most courses; except for some music courses at conservatoires for which you can start applying for courses from mid-July the year before a conservatoire course starts.

For students who are still at school or college, it is usual to have your application ready by an earlier date in order for teachers and lecturers to supply references for you well in advance of the deadline. If you are not in education, you will need to leave enough time to get your references.

You won't be able to submit your UCAS form until the reference section is completed. To check individual course application deadline dates, you will need to search the course information on the UCAS web site.

Main Steps to Applying Through UCAS

Before you can apply, you will need to register by entering your personal details. If you are applying through a school, college, careers centre or any other organisations you will be asked to use the 'buzzword' provided by them.
Alternatively, you can apply as an individual. Once you have registered, a username will be automatically generated and you will be asked to create a password.
For further information, see the chapter:
Chapter 8.3
Writing your Application for an Undergraduate Course

Choosing courses and higher education providers
Firstly, consider what course you want to study and at which university or college. Check out the chapters on Choosing Higher Education Subjects, Types of Courses and Universities Colleges of Higher Education or Specialist Institutions; Undergraduate Course Types and University Entry Requirements; and Professional Organisations and Accredited Undergraduate and Postgraduate Courses, to help you carry out research and decide on what is best for you. You can 'save' courses you are interested in on your unique favourites' page for further consideration when you are ready to apply on the UCAS website.

Completing the UCAS application form
You can complete the UCAS application form with up to five course choices. You will need to complete an application with your personal details, course choices and a personal statement. As you only send in one application for all your choices, you will have just one personal statement which will need to relate to all the subject/s you have chosen. Go to:
Chapter 8.3
Writing your Application for an Undergraduate Course

The UCAS, university and college application forms should be completed on line. Although it is preferred for you to apply on line, if for any reason this isn't possible, UCAS may send out a paper based form if you telephone and request one. If you are applying directly to a university or college, many use an online application form but it may be possible to download an application form as a word document and either return it as an attachment or in the post. You should confirm with the university or college if you are unable to submit an online form, and check on alternative methods. It is important your application meets the required deadlines and completing an online form may be advisable but if you are posting an application, you would need to allow plenty of time for it to be received and sending by recorded or registered post may be advisable

UCAS administration fee

An administration fee is charged by UCAS and you will need to pay this when you submit your application, although you may pay through your school or college. If only one course is applied for, the administration fee is slightly less but the full administration fee is charged for two to five course choices. However, if you only apply for one course and this application is declined, the full administration fee is charged for any additional courses applied for at a later date.

If you are applying for a course directly to universities or colleges, there is usually no limit on how many courses you can apply for and there is usually no administration fee charged (although some universities do charge for postgraduate applications), however, you can't apply directly to a university or college if you are required to apply through UCAS.

Once you have submitted your UCAS application form, you won't be able to amend your course choice, so check carefully before you submit.
You will need to pay an application fee to UCAS at the time when you are ready to submit your application. If undertaking an audition, you may need to pay an additional fee which will need to be paid before your application form is submitted by the required deadline

Completing your UCAS profile

You can register on UCAS and start to complete your profile. It is useful to do this well in advance as you can complete the application in stages, saving your progress and signing back in at any time. There are five sections you will need to complete. The reference section will need to be completed by your referee/s.
1. Personal details
2. Course choices
3. Education
4. Employment
5. Personal Statement
All five sections will need to be completed before you can submit your application

References for your UCAS application

You will need to obtain a reference and then pay the required amount before you submit your form to UCAS. Remember that the dates set for the UCAS deadlines for completed applications, will include receiving references for you by your teacher or lecturer, so make sure your referee/s are aware that you are applying.

Your application can't be sent to UCAS until your reference/s section has been completed. You will need to arrange for your teacher or lecturer to write an academic reference; and for performance courses you may also need a practical reference. If you are in school or college, UCAS will automatically send an online link which can be accessed by your referee, available in Adviser Track. If you are no longer studying in a school or college at the time of applying for a course you would usually need to obtain a reference from a previous teacher or lecturer and UCAS will send an email link to your named referee

Track and offers

When you have completed your application and UCAS has registered you, you can use the online tracking system 'Track' to keep up-to-date with the progress of your application and reply to your offers. You can also make amendments if needed if your details have change such as changing your email address or telephone number. For postgraduate courses, Apply is combined with Track

The universities and colleges will inform you of their decision by email and will give you one of the following offers.
- Unconditional offer, when you have met all the entry requirements and offered a definite place.
- Conditional offer, when your offer is based on you obtaining specified grades for your exams.
- No offer, when your application hasn't been accepted.

You may get invited for an interview or audition before a decision is made so you will need to respond to agree to attend.

Conditional offers: firm and insurance acceptance

Many offers will be conditional and this may be on the basis of your exam results. You can select a firm acceptance for your preferred choice and an insurance acceptance for your second preferred choice, in case you don't meet the conditions for your firm choice. Therefore, it is usual to have as your insurance choice, a lower conditional offer than for your firm choice. You need to decline any other offers.

Conditional offer met

When you get your results, if you have met the conditional offer requirements you will be offered a place. If you haven't quite got the required grades, you should check with the university or college as they may still offer you a place. If you have met and exceeded your conditional offer, you may be able to check for an alternative course in the UCAS Adjustment service, while still holding your original confirmed place in case you don't obtain another offer.

Conditional offer not met

If you were given a conditional offer but didn't meet the conditions, during the 'clearing' period you can search for courses that still have vacancies.

Reply to your offers

When you have all the decisions from the universities and colleges you have applied to, you will need to reply to your offers by a specified deadline.

No offer or you decline

If you haven't been offered a place on a course, or if you decide to decline the offer, you can still find other courses by adding more choices one at a time in UCAS Extra service. You need to add one course at a time and wait to be informed of a decision by the university or college before you can add another course if you have no offer.

UCAS Extra

Extra usually starts on 25th February and usually ends at the beginning of July. Receiving a response from universities or colleges may vary depending when you submitted your application form but there are key dates when you need to reply to any offers. However, if you have applied through UCAS using all five choices on your application, received decisions from all these choices and had no offers, or declined any offers received, therefore you are not holding any offers, UCAS Extra enables you to add another course that still has vacancies.

You are only allowed to apply for one additional course at a time, so it may be advisable to check with the university or college to make sure they can consider your application and make sure the place is still available before you add it.

If you are offered a place, you can choose to accept it or decline. If you accept, you are committed which means you can't apply anywhere else. The date for when you need to reply for your offer is shown in Track. If you don't get an offer, if you decline or if you haven't received a decision within the required period of time, you can apply for a different choice through Extra if time permits. If you don't get an offer during the Extra period, you can still apply during the Clearing period.

Firm acceptance

If you have an unconditional offer for the course that you want, you can accept the offer. This is your firm acceptance as you will have a definite place on a course.

Exam results

If you are waiting for your exam results, schools and colleges will send some exam results directly to the universities and colleges as the results will be available for restricted release the day before results are available to students, therefore you may check track to see if you are accepted on your chosen course. If you are taking additional exams independently from school or college, you may need to send additional exam results directly yourself.

Published exam results

Check with your school or college if you are unsure.

- International Baccalaureate results for the November exam session, the results are usually published in the first week in January; and for the May exam sessions, the results are usually published in the first week in July. Check with the IBO: Getting Results http://www.ibo.org/programmes/diploma-programme/assessment-and-exams/getting-results/
- The GCE 'A' levels, 'AS' levels, BTEC Nationals and the Advanced Diploma results are usually published on the third Thursday in August in England, Wales and Northern Ireland. Check with UCAS: Undergraduate Results https://www.ucas.com/ucas/undergraduate/apply-and-track/ucas-undergraduate-results
- The Scottish Higher and Advanced Higher results in Scotland are usually published on the first Tuesday in August. Check with Scottish Qualifications Agency (SQA): Results Day https://www.sqa.org.uk/

Next steps

If you are accepted on a course you will receive confirmation by the university or college. You will need to confirm your accommodation and student finance, Go to: Student Accommodation and Student Finance for more information. You will need to have the official student finance letter for when you attend your university or college enrolment before the start of your course. You may also need books and equipment required for the start of your course, your university or college should confirm requirements.

The adjustment process

The adjustment process is for undergraduate courses if you pass your exams with better results than expected, and you have exceeded the exam conditions of your conditional firm choice. UCAS have introduced adjustment so if you choose to, you can reconsider where and what to study in a university that asks for the higher grades, if you change your mind while still holding your original confirmed place.

The adjustment period lasts for five days from the day you receive your 'A' level exam results. Some universities hold 'open days' during these five days for you to speak to university staff and see the university, so you can make an informed choice.

If you decide to change universities, it is important to ask questions about available accommodation as you will need to apply if you are living away from home.

Clearing period July to September

If you just miss out on the required grades or UCAS tariff points you should contact the university to confirm as you may still be accepted. However, if you don't obtain the required grades for your course, or you have no offers, you may apply for a course during the clearing period.

Applications received after 30th June will be entered into the 'clearing' period which starts on 1st July and finishes in September when entry to higher education courses process are closed. The busiest time is after the 'A' level exam results are published in August.

If you don't achieve the qualifications and grades required by your chosen course, you will be able to check other suitable vacancies available for other higher education courses. There are usually spaces for a range of courses at this time, except for those that are usually very competitive to enter.

You may be able to apply directly to a university or college, instead of going through UCAS, during this period. If you have been given an offer of a place on a course in clearing, universities and colleges may have their own procedures for notifying UCAS but check with the higher education institution first.

If you haven't applied through UCAS and aren't already in the UCAS system, applying to just one university which offers you an unconditional place in clearing, you may be able to complete a Record of Prior Acceptance form for UCAS available from the university for which there is usually no fee charged.

When the UCAS clearing period is closed, you should contact universities and colleges directly to check on vacancies. Some universities and colleges will not accept new students after the course has started, therefore you should always contact universities and colleges directly as there are different start dates for courses in different institutions.

Changing your mind
You may have until 28th July to change your mind about your decision for your Firm choice of university or course. You may choose from your Insurance or one of your Declined university courses if you change your mind about your Firm choice of university or course, if involving your original five applications made through UCAS.

You would need to contact the university which you want to change to confirm you will be accepted before contacting your original Firm choice university to let them know about your change, before informing UCAS.

It may be possible to transfer to another course, university or college during your course in the first few weeks of your first year or between years if the course is similar. This isn't an easy decision but if you feel this is the right decision for you, there are actions you will need to take, although procedures may be different at different universities, so get advice from a student adviser first. Go to:
Chapter 8.6
What Options you Have if your Plans Don't Work Out

8.2   Applying to the University of Cambridge or the University of Oxford

About the University of Cambridge and the University of Oxford

The University of Cambridge and the University of Oxford often referred to as 'Oxbridge', are very popular and the most competitive universities to apply to.
University of Cambridge
http://www.cam.ac.uk/
University of Oxford
http://www.ox.ac.uk/

The following are brief guidelines and you should check full information on the relevant website. The University of Cambridge and the University of Oxford offer a broad range of courses and have world class teaching facilities.

Both universities have a collegiate structure, with each College like a mini campus and having its own entry requirements. The University of Oxford collegiate system consists of thirty eight independent and self-governing Colleges

and there are also five Permanent Private Halls at Oxford University that admit undergraduate students. The University of Cambridge collegiate system consists of thirty one autonomous Colleges.

The Colleges provide lectures, small group teaching with tutorials (at the University of Oxford) and supervisions (at the University of Cambridge), providing academic and pastoral support, a wide range of extra-curricular options and accommodation. There are excellent graduate opportunities, irrespective of degree discipline.

Financial support combined with subsidised living is also available, with a number of bursaries available, offering eligible lower income students' higher financial support.

Application Process for the University of Cambridge and University of Oxford Quick Guide

- Research the university websites, prospectus and attend open days and higher education fairs in the first year of your 'A' levels or equivalent qualifications.

- Choose your course, not all courses are offered at both universities

- Choose your College or decide to leave an open application

- Check if a university admissions test is required and the date when you need to register by. Also check the date when you need to sit the test, which may be before or after you apply through UCAS. Check if you need to provide additional written work

- Apply to UCAS by 15th October, leave time for your references to be added

- Supplementary Application Questions (SAQs) required for the University of

Cambridge are usually required in addition to the UCAS form by 22nd October (confirm date)

- Written work samples in addition to the UCAS form are required for the University of Oxford by early in November (confirm date).

- Interviews for selected applicants are usually in December; the University of Oxford will interview around 60-65% of applicants; the University of Cambridge will interview around 80% of applicants.

- A decision will be made whether to offer you a place and you will be informed in January if you have been successful or unsuccessful.

- 1 in 5 applicants are made an offer, on average

University Admissions Aptitude Tests
For some courses at some of the Colleges of both the University of Cambridge and

the University of Oxford, university admissions aptitude tests are also used as part of the admissions process for applicants and there are usually required deadlines when to register to apply to take these tests. The Colleges will publish what tests they require for applications to which courses on their websites.

Sitting of tests may be required prior to you submitting your UCAS form, so you need to check well in advance about registration and deadlines. Practice tests are available on the relevant admission test administration websites. It is useful to sit past tests as it is important to familiarise yourself with what will be required in the actual test and practice writing tests within the set times as poor time management may affect your results.

Further information may be found in the:
Chapter 8.4
University Admissions Tests

Completing your UCAS application form for the University of Cambridge or the University of Oxford

The deadline for online UCAS applications for undergraduate courses at the University of Cambridge and the University of Oxford is 15th October.

Schools and colleges will usually set an earlier deadline to allow for academic references to be produced. There may be earlier application deadlines for applicants wishing to be interviewed overseas. Registration for university admissions tests will be required in addition to your UCAS application and deadlines will apply for registration and sitting of tests.

On the UCAS application form, you are only allowed to apply for one undergraduate course at either the University of Cambridge or the University of Oxford, you can't apply to both universities and you can't apply for more than one course.
In your UCAS application form you will need to list either the University of Cambridge or University of Oxford as one of your options in the 'Choices' section. You will also need to enter the appropriate College (campus) code however you will need to find out which Colleges offer your chosen course but can only select one College.

When selecting a College, you can either choose a particular College to receive your application or if you have no particular preference, you can make an 'open' application and leave it for the university to assign you a college, which is done by computer. You may be allocated a College you haven't applied to if the university believe you will be better suited. All applications are dealt with through a central applications system first before allocated to the Colleges. The selected College will assess your application and making an open application or specifying a preference makes no difference of your chances of being made an offer providing you meet the required entry qualifications. No College is any easier to enter.

If you receive an offer from your department, you will also receive an offer from a College or Hall, although this might not be the College stated as your preference if you indicated one. Very good students who are not offered a place by their College of choice may be placed in a 'winter pool' for other Colleges who have places to consider.

Each College or Halls has rooms where students live, as well as clubs and societies to join, dining room and other student facilities as well as a college library. Some teaching may be undertaken in a College but usually all students on the same course, regardless of your College, attend the same lectures, seminars and practical sessions together, and sit the same exams.

When considering which College or Halls to select you will need to check that the course you want to study is available. Halls are similar to Colleges except they are smaller and were founded by particular Christian denominations, offering fewer courses than most Colleges.

Some Colleges are exclusively for students aged 21 years or over and some are only for female students. There may be variations in the number of students, so some Colleges have more students than others; in addition facilities and accommodation may differ. Therefore check the College websites and visit where possible.

If you have a disability, this should be mentioned on the UCAS application as this will assist the university in supporting you with additional needs you may have.

Each application is considered on individual merit and both Universities consider the application process as a whole: checking your academic record such as GCSE grades and predicted 'A' level grades; and your personal statement, which should consist of 80% content relevant to the academic aims and abilities.

The University of Oxford will usually require 'A' levels ranging between A*A*A* and AAA depending on the course https://www.ox.ac.uk/admissions/undergraduate/courses/entrance-requirements/level-offers

The University of Cambridge will usually require 'A' levels ranging between A*A*A* and A*AA depending on the course

http://www.undergraduate.study.cam.ac.uk/applying/entrance-requirements

Tutors then shortlist applicants based on the UCAS application, any additional written work and performance in the pre-interview or at interview test. Everyone who has a realistic chance of being offered a place on a course at the University of Cambridge or University of Oxford is offered an interview.

You will be assessed on the basis of choosing the right course for you; obtaining the required results for 'A' level or equivalent exams; demonstrating being an active learner being proactive in engaging with your chosen subject; and how you perform in tests and interview/s.

Therefore it is important to choose a course subject based on your interest, motivation and suitability, demonstrating your enthusiasm. Your application will also be assessed on teachers academic references; performance in admission tests; content of any required additional written work; consideration of contextual data such as how you performed compared with other students in your peer group; and how you performed at interview.

The admissions process also takes into positive consideration applicants who have a home postcode or socio-economic background with fewer students at either university however the universities are interested in the best students.

University of Cambridge: Supplementary Application Questionnaire (SAQ)

When your UCAS application has been received by the University of Cambridge it will be acknowledged and you will be emailed a link and asked to complete the online Supplementary Application Questionnaire (SAQ). There is a deadline for the SAQ so check with the course and College details on the website, but it is usually within a week after the deadline for submitting the UCAS form.

There are eight sections on the SAQ: Application Type; Photograph; Personal Details; Course Details; Education; Qualifications; Additional Information; Submit. Before submitting, check the University of Cambridge: Guide to Completing the SAQ http://www.undergraduate.study.cam.ac.uk/applying/saq

University of Oxford Application Written Work

For many courses, although not all, you will need to send in written work as part of your application. You should send in something you have produced as part of your normal school or college work which has been marked by a teacher. It should demonstrate your analytical, reasoning, language and writing skills as appropriate for your chosen degree course.

There is a limit on the number of words expected and a deadline in November when it needs to be received by. After you have submitted your UCAS application, the College or Halls considering your application, will contact you about how you should submit your written work.

You may be able to send in a paper copy or you may be asked for it electronically. Before submitting, check the University of Oxford: Guide to Completing Written Work https://www.ox.ac.uk/admissions/undergra duate/applying-to-oxford/written-work

Additional applications
You may need to submit another application in addition to your UCAS application if you are:
- Attending a school, college, university outside the EU at the time of your application
- Living in a country outside the EU at the time of application
- Applying for the graduate medicine course
- Applying for an organ scholarship

You will also need to attend an interview if your application is successful and depending on the course and college you apply to, you may need to submit school or college essays which will then be discussed at your interview. You may also need to undertake a specific admissions test for certain courses when you attend for an interview or beforehand.

Applications for Medicine at the University of Cambridge

The following is a guide only and you will need to confirm details on the University of Cambridge website. There are two medicine courses at the University of Cambridge, the standard course, which lasts for six years, and the graduate course, which is a four year accelerated course for applicants who already possess a degree. All colleges require Standard Medicine Course and Graduate Medicine Course applicants to take the Bio-Medical Admissions Test (BMAT), confirm dates on the university website or the Cambridge Assessment Admissions Testing Service http://www.admissionstestingservice.org/fo r-test-takers/bmat/about-bmat/

Both courses require an application through UCAS. You can only apply for one Medicine degree course at the University

of Cambridge, with the exception for applicants who already possess a degree in another subject who are applying for the Graduate Medicine course, who can also apply for the Standard Medicine Course. However, if you choose to apply for both courses, you will need to apply to the same College for both courses (Lucy Cavendish or Wolfson College). Further information may be found at University of Cambridge: Medicine https://www.undergraduate.study.cam.ac. uk/courses/medicine . Applicants for the Graduate Course in Medicine are required to submit an additional form to the University of Cambridge the deadline for the receipt of both forms in 15th October. Check the University of Cambridge Medical School website for more details. http://www.medschl.cam.ac.uk/education/c ourses/cgc/

Applications for the Accelerated Medicine Course at the University of Oxford

If you have a science degree and are applying for the four year Accelerated Medicine course you must complete a supplementary application form which also needs to be submitted by 15th October, in addition to the UCAS application. In addition you must register for the BMAT entrance test, confirm dates on the university website or the Cambridge Assessment Admissions Testing Service: BMAT http://www.admissionstestingservice.org/for-test-takers/bmat/about-bmat/

Choral or Organ Award at the University of Oxford

If you want to apply for a choral or organ award you must complete an additional online application form usually by 1st September before applying through UCAS, but confirm the date on the university website. You will also need to attend an interview if your application is successful and depending on the course and College you apply to, you may need to submit school or college essays which will then be discussed at your interview. You may also need to undertake a specific test for certain courses when you attend for an interview or beforehand. Further information may be found at the University of Oxford Choral and Organ Awards https://www.ox.ac.uk/admissions/undergraduate/applying-to-oxford/choral-and-organ-awards.

Teacher References

The teacher reference should be weighted with around 80% focusing on the academic achievements or merits of the student. Outlining how able the student is in comparison with other students is also considered useful. Wider educational activities and social development highlighted in context may also be useful to mention. If there are any personal extenuating situations which may affect the student's achievements, this should also be highlighted with agreement from the student

Writing your Personal Statement for the University of Oxford or University of Cambridge

Competition for places on all courses at the universities of Oxbridge and Cambridge is fierce. Academic requirements and ability is considered most important and should consist of 80% of the personal statement. You therefore need to submit an excellent personal statement also check the chapter:
Chapter 8.3
Writing your Application for an Undergraduate Course

Applying to the university of Oxford or Cambridge is a challenging process and requires you to demonstrate your ability, motivation, determination and passion about your subject. Your personal statement needs to be original and written by you showing your ability to think logically and laterally about your subject, to analyse challenging new ideas and be confident to demonstrate your personality and desire to study for the subject.

The course you want to study is the most important aspect, so you need to demonstrate your personal interests and research the course thoroughly. You need to be proactive in your learning, demonstrating your engagement and exploration of current studies and interests relevant to your intended degree subject. Your exam results will be very important therefore, you will need to also demonstrate your ability to work hard and do well in your studies.

In the academic section, you should also highlight what reading and projects you have done in addition to your 'A' level subjects' (or equivalent qualifications) syllabuses, which are relevant to the subject you want to study.

Outline reasons why you have engaged with an aspect of the course you are interested in studying for and use your reading as examples to back this up. Be selective in what reading you write about as you will usually be asked further information about this during your interview, therefore focusing on a selection will mean you can focus your preparation more closely.

Highlight any relevant super curricula activities which you have undertaken outside of school or college. You may have attended field trips, listened to debates or additional talks, visited relevant places such as museums, galleries or talked to people working in a relevant career and kept up to date with current information.

Relevant extra-curricular activities such as work experience, community work or voluntary work may be highlighted and the universities admissions staff will be looking at your additional qualities and experiences with your ability to reflect on what you have learned.

Additional extra-curricular activities may be mentioned but may not be taken into consideration by the University of Oxford or University of Cambridge unless relevant to the course however the additional four universities you have also applied to in your UCAS application may consider these important.

It is useful to identify additional experience or skills and it is important to consider what other universities will be interested in as you will only write one personal statement for all the universities you have applied for.

Further information about University admissions aptitude tests for the University of Cambridge or the University of Oxford may be found in the:
Chapter 8.4
University Admissions Tests

Interviews at the University of Cambridge or University of Oxford

You will receive an email or letter indicating if you have been invited for an interview which will usually take place in December. You may not receive this until a week before the interviews are due to take place.

You may have one, two or three interviews, each lasting between 25 and 45 minutes which are mainly academic and subject related. These are academic discussion based and you will be asked questions relevant to the course you have applied for as well as about the information you have provided in your application.

The interview provides an opportunity to assess your academic potential and suitability for your chosen course, to study at a very high level, engage with new ideas and think conceptually as well as how you will respond to the teaching methods used, treating the interview like a conversation about your chosen subject.

Interview questions may be about why you have chosen the subject and why you want to study at the university. You may be asked technical or general questions related to your chosen course and may be given a course specific task such as a piece of reading or a problem to solve just prior to the interview.

You will also have the opportunity to expand on the written elements of your application and show what you think of your chosen subject, demonstrating passion and commitment as well as your ability to think critically and independently. It is helpful to read a range of material around your chosen subject including newspaper articles, websites, journals, magazines and other publications.

Check out the bibliographies or the journals and articles referenced in the books you have mentioned in your personal statement and re-read these prior to your interview.

This will provide you with a wealth of reading material to refer to when answering questions using examples; and will help you to show your interests and wider reading as well as demonstrating your ability to prove your opinion and back up your ideas.

Consider a critical view and think about all sides of any debate. You should have some background knowledge if you are applying for a course not normally studied at school or college such as medicine, law, biochemistry or oriental studies. However, you won't be expected to have a detailed understanding of specific or technical topics.

Tutors will be looking for your self-motivation and enthusiasm for your subject with the ability to think independently and engage with new ideas. Make sure you are confident in your subject knowledge, show sufficient analytical ability and clarity of thought.

It is important to show your understanding of a subject and be able to back up your ideas with evidence and what you have read but also to show willingness to re-think ideas in the face of contrary evidence and be able to see arguments for both sides.

Practice by discussing your academic interest with teachers, family and friends as well as having practice interviews with questions you may be asked.

Where to Find Undergraduate Courses

Undergraduate courses may be found on individual university and college websites, as well as on the University and College Admission Service UCAS website https://www.ucas.com/. There are also search engines on websites that highlight undergraduate courses which may be useful to use to find specialist subjects, however you should confirm up to date information on the relevant university website.

Professional organisations that accredit higher education courses will also have links to relevant universities and colleges on the websites. Go to: 4 Higher Education Qualifications, Subjects and Courses and Professional Organisations which Professionally Accredited Undergraduate and Postgraduate Courses

Undergraduate course websites
- University and College Admission Service UCAS https://www.ucas.com/
- UCAS conservatoires https://www.ucas.com/ucas/conservatoires/
- UK Course Finder http://www.ukcoursefinder.com/
- HEAP University Degree Course Offers http://www.heaponline.co.uk/

Your school or college will need to buy a licence for you to access this online; alternatively it is published as a book and may be found in education or public libraries.

Applying for Undergraduate Courses

What you write on your application form will determine if you are given an offer for the course or not, or shortlisted for those courses requiring an interview or audition, so you need to consider carefully that the information you provide matches with the course requirements. Although the whole application is important, the most persuasive parts of your application is the section for your qualification grades or predicted grades for exams in the subjects you have studied or are currently studying; what you write in the personal statement section and what your referee/s write about you in the reference section.

Before you start to complete the application, check with the university and college websites to make sure you will have the necessary qualifications, grades/predicted grades and you know what competencies the course requires such as relevant qualities and skills.

University and College Application Forms
The sections will be similar to the UCAS application form however there is usually no application fee, although there may be some exceptions. Although the following information relates to the UCAS undergraduate application, if you are applying directly to a university or college, much of this information will also be relevant.

Firstly you will need to register and complete some personal details, create a password and set your security questions. You will then be able to start writing the application, which is divided into sections.

UCAS application sections

Personal details
Complete your name and address, contact details include a telephone number and email address (use an appropriate email address), date of birth, country of birth and nationality.
Complete details about your residential and nationality status.
Complete details if you have any special needs or disabilities if relevant.

Student finance arrangements
You will need to include details about financial arrangements if you are a UK applicant. You will also need to apply separately for student finance.

Course choices
You can choose up to five courses (up to six if applying to Conservatoires) and there is no preference order. The universities or colleges won't be able to see where else you have applied to until after you have replied to any offers you are made. You will need the course and higher education institution codes which should be on the higher education institution website or the UCAS website.

Course choices for medicine, dentistry or veterinary medicine courses
You are only allowed a maximum of four courses in any one of these subjects, a fifth choice should be an additional course that you are interested in.

Course choices for the University of Cambridge and University of Oxford courses
You can only apply to one course at either the University of Cambridge or the University of Oxford.

Education
You need to provide details of qualifications you have taken with results and qualifications you are currently studying or waiting for results. You also need to provide details of the school, college or university where you are currently studying or where you have studied.

Employment
This section is for any paid full time or part time jobs you have had or are currently doing. You can provide information on up to five employers or if you have had more, highlight the most relevant. Unpaid or voluntary work should be included in your personal statement.

Personal statement
This is the section where you write why you are interested in the course you are applying for and why you would be an excellent student.

Reference section and fee payment
Your referee should be a teacher or lecturer, if you are still at school or college, or if you have left school or college, you may chose a previous teacher, lecturer or a professional person who knows you well (but not related to you).

Give your referee plenty of time to write your reference. Your reference needs to be done online as UCAS can't accept paper or email references. Ensure you let your referee know about your achievements, especially those achieved outside of education.

Your reference needs to be written in English (or Welsh if you are only applying to Welsh universities or colleges).

The content should include information relating to how you are suitable for the course:

- What you have achieved in your current or previous courses
- What your predicted grades will be for current qualifications
- Information about your personal qualities and circumstances
- Information about your career ambitions and any supporting work experience

If applying through a school or college centre

If you are applying through a school or college centre your teacher or lecturer will write your reference. You may pay through the school or college (your teachers / lecturers will let you know when to pay). Alternatively you may pay directly online to UCAS with a debit / credit card, before your reference is added but check arrangements with your school or college before you do this. The reference and application will be sent to UCAS by your school or college.

If applying as an individual

If you have left school or college and are applying as an individual, your reference should be from a teacher, lecturer or a professional person who knows you well (but not related to you). Firstly ask the person if they would be willing to write a reference for you and then add their email and telephone number to the reference page and click on the 'Ask referee to complete reference' section.

UCAS will email your referee with a link and password to the reference page of your application, and then ask them to confirm their identity before they write your reference.

Alternatively, you can contact a previous teacher or lecturer at a registered school, college or centre to write your reference and if they are acceptable, you can add their details and buzzword. You then need to pay your application fee and send your application to UCAS

1. View all details page

Check to see if you need to amend anything on your application, then mark it as complete and agree the declaration which allows UCAS to process your information and send to the universities or colleges you are applying to.

2. Pay and send

When your application is ready to send you will need to pay the application fee before sending in your form.

Writing Your Personal Statement for Undergraduate Courses

The personal statement is the most important part of your application so it is important to give yourself time to plan what you want to write.

An impressive personal statement may be the deciding factor in being offered a place on the course you want to study. There will be competition for many popular courses and you want to make sure you receive an offer. Your personal statement needs to contain important information about you to ensure your application is successful and you achieve offers for your chosen course at your preferred university.

If you are applying through UCAS, you will only have the one application and one personal statement which can't be changed after your application has been sent. You won't need to mention the universities or colleges by name in your personal statement as this information will already be on the application form.

Many higher education courses are very competitive with too many applications for available spaces on courses and, as many universities and colleges don't interview applicants, the only information they have about you is what you have written in your application.

You can only submit one personal statement for all the courses you have selected. You may have just one subject in mind but some courses offer combined subjects and if applying to up to five courses, you should ideally choose similar subjects although you may have selected slightly different courses. If the courses are varied, then make sure you include information that is relevant to all of them.

Admission staff and university selection criteria

Admissions staff will offer you a place based on selection criteria:

- Clear communication skills, including good grammar and spelling
- Information relevant to the course you are applying for
- Your interest in the course, demonstrated with explanation and evidence
- If relevant for the course, your work and life experiences.

Admissions staff will be reading thousands of applications and you want your personal statement to stand out so you need to make sure it is original, impelling and carefully written. They will make the decision on giving you an offer or not so they need to have an idea about your potential as a student on their course. You need to show you are motivated, enthusiastic and will work to the best of your ability.

Your personal statement will give you the opportunity to 'sell' your passion for the subject and best assets, showing that you have the ability and suitability to study the course. You need to provide the admissions staff with information which will help them consider you to be an appropriate potential student at their university or college.

You should have researched the entry requirements for the course and will either already have or be predicted, the required grades for subjects which will be on your application form. The admissions staff will be efficiently scanning your application to check you meet the required entry criteria and your references are appropriate before determining if your personal statement meets the expected standard to ensure an offer being made. Therefore you need to make sure your personal statement is written to a high standard and is all your own work.

Plagiarism, which means copying other people's work, is completely unacceptable and any copied personal statements will not be considered. UCAS uses sophisticated software to screen applications and personal statements. Your personal statement is your opportunity to show your individual personal qualities, skills, abilities, enthusiasm and motivation which are unique to you.

Offers

Offers for courses will be based on you having the right grades, good references and an excellent personal statement. Admissions staff will have huge numbers of applications to read so, to ensure your application is successful you need to write your personal statement using appropriate words, correct grammar and spelling, as well as conveying your enthusiasm for your chosen course to make you stand out in the crowd.

Personal Statement Content

Layout

The UCAS personal statement has a limit of 4,000 characters on 47 lines therefore as you are restricted on how much you can write, you need to provide a summary of your attributes, abilities and key skills in relation to the course you want to study. If you are applying directly, using the university or college application form, there may also be advised word limits and your personal statement needs to be presented in a clear and concise way, with excellent grammar, spelling and punctuation.

You should highlight your positive qualities in a concise and engaging format in order to make a good impression with the admission staff. Your personal statement should be written in a precise and organised way with defined sections, including a clear beginning, informed middle and comprehensive ending.

The structure should involve paragraphs which run smoothly and don't include repetition, include information on your academic background and non-academic interests, showing you as a capable person who would be an asset at your chosen university or college.

Preparation

1. Research the courses and the higher education institutions. Check for:
   - Entry requirements: grades and any specified subjects at 'A' level or equivalent qualifications
   - The skills and qualities highlighted
   - Deadlines for course applications
   - If Admissions Tests are required and deadlines for applying and sitting
2. Register with UCAS and check out the application form.
3. Start to write down bullet points using the guide for writing the Personal Statement below.

Writing your personal statement preparation guide

Key points

- The personal statement is a key part of your application
- Helps to distinguish you from other applicants with similar grades
- Gives you a chance to highlight your talents, achievements and your writing style
- There is a limited amount of space so keep it concise
- Use positive language
- Emphasise your interest and enthusiasm for the subject

Consider

- What makes you unique
- Why you want to study for the subject

- Why you chose to study particular subjects at 'A' level or equivalent qualification
- Why should the university or college choose you
- What career aspirations you have
- What you hope to gain from the course

Preparation

Make a list of all your achievements to include:
- Work experience to include paid and voluntary experience
- Interests and hobbies in school and outside of school
- Awards you have such as Duke of Edinburgh
- Your involvement in any clubs, societies or groups involving teamwork
- Make a list of the skills you have gained.
- Highlight responsibilities you have had with examples of duties undertaken
- Be reflective and give explanations
- Mention briefly relevant authors and artists when undertaking related background reading and writing about specific research
- Carry out a spelling and grammar check and have someone else read it through
- Be clear and concise as admissions staff will have many applications to check
- Don't mention a specific institution as this will be on your application form
- Attend university open days.

Research

- Give yourself enough time to write your statement. You will probably need to read it and revise your ideas several times before you are happy with it over a period of a few weeks.
- Research the course information you are applying for on the university and college websites. You should be able to access a list of modules (subject units that together make up the complete course).
  You won't have space to list everything so just highlight aspects of the course that interest you such as a few specific modules.

- Research the relevant websites and find out about career opportunities and talk to professionals and students about their career ideas and experiences.
- List competencies and skills for the course required by the university or college.
- Research your career options as it helps to have an idea about what career you would like to work in.

Structure

Make a list of:

- Reasons why you want to study the course you are applying for, why that subject interests you and what ambitions you have for your future career.
- Subjects you are currently studying or have studied that you enjoy and have achieved high marks. Consider why you like these subjects.
- Your interests, hobbies and social activities you enjoy such as sport, music, drama, art or any other interests.
- Any work experience you have had, voluntary or paid.
- Your personal qualities, skills, knowledge, achievements and experience you have gained in education and outside of education and consider your suitability for the course. Ask your friends or family what makes you unique to them. It is important to show your abilities to make you stand out.
- The skills, competencies and qualities that the university or college values as most important for the courses applying for and then structure your information in an order that is most relevant to these.
- Your life skills and experience to highlight, if you are a mature applicant, and select the relevant and most recent aspects.
- Make a list of key aspects before arranging in order. Then prepare paragraphs in the following sections.

- ➢ Your interest in the subject/s you want to study
- ➢ Your interest in the subjects you are studying or have studied
- ➢ Your suitability for the course/s
- ➢ Your work experience (paid or voluntary)
- ➢ Your personal experiences which may be relevant to your decision to study the subject/s.
- ➢ Your interests or hobbies
- ➢ Your career ambitions

- Highlight examples of how your skills have been gained.
- If applying through UCAS, your statement will go to all universities so you need to keep it general and don't include specific university information.

Style

- It is important to write the personal statement yourself using your own words as it needs to be personal to you so don't copy other people's personal statements. UCAS screen all personal statements across the Copycatch similarity detection system and if you have copied (plagiarised) another personal statement, this could have serious consequences for your application
- Use appropriate language which makes you sound enthusiastic and motivated about your chosen subject/s. Write in English (or in Welsh if only applying to Welsh universities or colleges).
- Spelling, grammar and punctuation needs to be accurate
- Write in the first person and use 'I' as your statement is personal about you
- Write a first draft, adding any further appropriate information and remove anything you don't think is relevant.
- Ask for constructive feedback from one or two other people such as a teacher, lecturer, your parents, a relevant professional person you know or a careers adviser to read and give you feedback.

Format

- Keep within the word/character count and remember you have a limit of 4,000 characters and 47 lines on the UCAS personal statement.
- It is advisable to produce a Word document which you can copy and paste into your application when you are confident you are happy with the content. Not all word packages are the same, so check your settings to make sure your completed statement fits into the space provided.
- Avoid italics, bold or underlining.
- Paragraphs should be of a reasonable length, not too long or too short, and are used to break up the content into relevant sections.
- Sentences need to be of a reasonable length, not too long or too short.
- Ensure your statement flows easily and fluently.

The content of your personal statement

The admissions and subject tutors will be checking the following information you have supplied in your personal statement:

Have you demonstrated the following information:

- Why you want to study the course that you are applying for, including subject interests
- What has inspired you to apply
- Do you have the necessary qualifications, skills and qualities for the course
- Your personal commitment to this course and have researched it well
- You have a genuine interest in the subject and a desire to learn more about it
- What relevant subjects and qualifications you are studying or have studied
- You are conscientious, hardworking and determined to complete the course
- You will work to your best ability and are able cope with the demands of the course
- You have the required skills such as communication, team work and organisation

- Details of any work experience, community work or positions of responsibility, paid or voluntary, you have undertaken
- Details of your interests or hobbies and if these are relevant to your chosen course

Think of the word **CHARACTER** as an acronym to remind you about the content of your personal statement:

Course Have you demonstrated why you want to study your chosen course?

Hardworking: Have you demonstrated your motivation and commitment to study for the course?

Abilities: Have you highlighted your qualities and abilities in relation to the course?

Research: Have you researched the entry criteria and the content of the course?

Activities: Have you highlighted any work experience or interests that you have?

Career: Do you have a career in mind and if the course relates to this?

Transferable Skills: Have you highlighted any relevant skills you have developed?

Enjoyment: Have you demonstrated a passion for the subject?

Relevant: Is your personal statement structured in a clear and relevant way?

Suggested paragraphs

Your interest in the subject/s

Start your statement with a strong opening sentence which is relevant and personal to you and will engage the admissions tutor reading your application. You need to provide evidence of why you have chosen the course, your ability to study the subject and how enthusiastic you are.

It is important to demonstrate why you are very interested in your chosen subject. It may be useful to highlight what reading and projects you have done in addition to your 'A' level (or equivalent qualifications) syllabus, which are relevant to the subject you want to study.

Outline reasons why you have engaged with an aspect of the course you are interested in studying for and use your reading as examples to back this up. At least 50% of your statement should be about your academic interests, with Russell group universities preferring at least 75%.

Your academic background

You need to highlight the reasons for why you want to study your chosen subject. State how interested you are in the subjects you are currently studying or have studied and how they relate to your chosen higher education course.

Information that shows how you are suitable for the course/s

Key competencies or skills may be required for specific courses, so check these on the university or college website. These may include transferable skills such as communication skills, teamwork and organisation. Or you may be required to have specific ability, for example in languages, music or sports. Give examples or where you have gained these skills.

Highlight any work experience (paid or voluntary)

Do you have any experience outside of education that is relevant to your chosen course? What paid or unpaid work experience have you had and what skills have you developed? Are you involved in any music, sport, drama, volunteering or other activities that show you have commitment and able to work in a team? Consider how you can show determination to succeed.

Interests or hobbies

Demonstrate how you work under pressure and teamwork with examples such as activities or performances in sport, music or drama or other activities and that show you are able to combine your interests with study. If you have any awards and achievements such as the Duke of Edinburgh award, or have you taken part in competitions or events, mention these.

Personal experiences relevant to your decision to study the subject/s

Demonstrate experiences which have helped you to make a decision about the course you want to study and your ambitions for the future.

Career ambitions

Highlight what ambitions you have for when you finish the course and how will the course you want to study help you in your future career.

What not to write

Don't exaggerate
Don't waffle
Don't plagiarise
Don't cram too much in
Don't repeat yourself
Don't just list the subjects you are taking, without expanding on the reasons for your interest
Don't start with a quotation
Don't make grammar, punctuation or spelling errors

High-Powered Words

High-powered words can be used to highlight motivation and enthusiasm. Think of your own words to use or use an appropriate selection of these words in context and make sure you use the correct tense.

A
Ability
Accuracy
Achievement
Active
Ambition
Analysis
Appreciation
Arrangement
Articulate
Aspiration
B
Beneficial
Build
C
Challenge
Confident
Convince
Created
Creative
Curious
D
Dedication
Demanding
Demonstration
Desire
Determination
Developed
Devised
Discover
Drive
Dynamic
E
Eagerness
Effective
Efficient
Encourage
Enhancing
Enjoyment
Enormously

Enrich
Enthusiasm
Equip
Essential
Evidence
Excel
Excitement
Experience
Experiment
Explore
F
Fascination
I
Illustrate
Impact
Impress
Importance
Improve
Incentive
Increase
Individual
In-depth
Influence
Ingenuity
Initiative
Involved
Innovate
Insight
Inspire
Intention
Interacting
Interesting
Intriguing
Involvement
K
Keen
Knowledge
L
Leadership

M
Meticulous
Motivation
O
Objective
Organising
P
Participate
Passion
Perfect
Planned
Pleasure
Positive
Prepared
Q
Quality
Quantity

R
Reason
Regard
Reliable
Research
Respect
Responsible
Rewarding
S
Significant
Strengths
Success
Supervised
T
Talent
Transferable skills
U
Understanding
Unique
V
Valuable
Versatile

Full-time undergraduate art and design courses are applied for through UCAS undergraduate and can be found at

- UCAS undergraduate
  https://www.ucas.com/

A list of Art Schools may be found at:

- The United Kingdom Arts and Design Institutions Association (UKADIA)
  http://ukadia.ac.uk/

Foundation diploma in art

Applications for the foundation diploma in art courses should be made directly to the School, 6th Form Centre or Further Education College you want to apply to. Deadlines for applications may vary, therefore check with the relevant education provider, but direct applications are likely to have deadlines by the end of January, preceding the start of the course.

You can apply to as many education providers that you want but if one provides more than one foundation art diploma, it is likely you can only apply to one course per provider. Applications for full time foundation diploma in art courses in universities or colleges of higher education will usually need to be applied for through UCAS https://www.ucas.com/

Undergraduate courses

You will need to apply for full time undergraduate art courses through UCAS http://www.ucas.com, meeting the required application deadline, although some private art higher education institutions may accept direct applications. The universities of Oxford and Cambridge have a deadline of 15th October; other universities will usually have a deadline of 15th January, but for some art and design courses, the deadline is 24th March. If you apply after this date you may be accepted by some universities if places are available.

You are advised to check application and any additional information required by the universities and colleges on the relevant website before you make an application.

Course choices

On the UCAS form, you are allowed to choose a maximum of five undergraduate art courses.

You can only apply to one course at either the University of Cambridge or the University of Oxford.

Postgraduate courses

You will need to apply for full time or part time postgraduate art courses directly to the university or college. Some art master's degrees are also integrated as part of a four year undergraduate bachelor's degree course and for these courses, you would apply through UCAS.

Portfolios of your art work
Portfolio Submission

When you apply for a creative art degree, you will usually be required to submit a portfolio of relevant art work as part of the entry requirements. You may need to pay a portfolio handling fee to the relevant higher education institutions.

There may be an option at some universities or colleges to deliver your art portfolio consisting of your original work in person if you live near to the higher education institution (HEI), however this is not an option with all HEIs. If this is possible, there are deadlines and dates you will need to meet with delivering and collecting your portfolio, so check instructions carefully with the relevant HEI.

Many universities or colleges will require you to submit an electronic portfolio of copies of your art work. There are usually deadlines to upload your portfolio, so check these with relevant higher education institutions. Details of how to upload your portfolio are usually emailed to you after you have submitted your UCAS application.

There are usually requirements of a set number of items which represent a variety of your art / design work and your approaches.

Digital portfolios will need to be submitted in appropriate formats which may include slides, files limited to a specified size, PDF or PowerPoint or audio compositions / moving image work which may be embedded within PowerPoint, mp3 or QuickTime files limited to a specified size.

Electronic images may need to be .jpg image files or .mp3 audio files. You may also need to upload additional work from your level 3 (RQF) art course such as an essay from your 'A' level, BTEC national, foundation diploma or equivalent qualification course. If selected for interview, you may also be required to bring along an additional portfolio containing the originals of your recent art or design work.

If you live outside the UK, check with the institution information about how you can submit your portfolio. You may be able to submit it on a CDRom (CD-R) or DVD with a set number of images as a PowerPoint presentation, but there is likely to be specific requirements and you are likely to be advised to have duplicates of the material you send as it might not be returnable.

Make sure all your submitted material is properly documented, citing materials used and where appropriate, explaining the processes used. Very importantly, make sure your name and email is on each piece of original work in your portfolio and on each file attachment on an electronic portfolio.

Always check the requirements for portfolios on the relevant institution website. Carefully follow the instructions on specified formats and check on specified deadline dates for submission. If portfolios aren't submitted in the specified format, your application may be rejected.

Each art and design course will have different requirements regarding your portfolio, therefore you will need to undertake research on each university or college website, ask questions at Open Days or contact the relevant art department to enquire if you are unsure.

Content of the portfolio

As a general guide, the portfolio should contain a selection of your current and recent work which may include drawings, photographs, paintings, sketchbooks and notebooks. Larger paintings may be required to be shown as photographic prints.

Videos or films may be asked for in QuickTime on a DVD for a specified duration. There may also be specified measurements and maximum weights for the portfolio. If not required in electronic form, you should also make sure that your work is packaged in a durable portfolio.

General guide to producing your portfolio

- Carry out early preparation and work constantly on your portfolio before applying as you may get an early interview.

- Include relevant work which is related to the subject you are interested in and check the course details. Show how your ideas have developed or been experimented with. Within your portfolio, consider if you have demonstrated the knowledge of the subject discipline and which practitioners have inspired you. Include work that demonstrates your ability and which you are proud of.

- Consider the basic elements and show examples of relevant work such as paintings, drawings, photographs, three-dimensional work, time-base work and other examples related to the subject you are interested in. Include a variety of relevant work such as drawings, collages, prints, stitching or paintings in a variety of styles and a variety of large, medium and small scale work.

- Tell a story, try to show one full project from start to finish with the preparatory drawings included. Annotations are helpful to show how you researched and reflected on the development of your work.

- Include a number of final pieces that you are able to talk about. Depending on your chosen subject, this may include paintings, sketches, 3D models or photographs.

- Include sketchbooks as this will give an understanding of how you think and demonstrates the development of your drawing. If the portfolio is digital, you may photograph or scan some of the best pages.

- With presentation of your portfolio, use thick black or white card to mount your work and keep it the same throughout. Try to avoid plastic wallets as tutors like to have a clear look at your work.

Your portfolio might be viewed when you aren't present, therefore you should make it easy to use. It may be helpful to think of it as a book, placing your name and a title on the outside at the front. A physical portfolio may be any size but you should be able to carry it, therefore a maximum of 20 sheets may be acceptable, but check requirements with the university or college.

Consider what the first piece of work will be seen in your portfolio, as this should grab the attention of the course admissions tutor, what will be the mid-point highlight and what you will end with, finishing with a page that will leave the reviewer with a positive final impression.

Enjoy putting the portfolio together and think about how the portfolio flows to keep viewers interested. Have a tutor to check through your portfolio before submitting.

8.4   University Admissions Aptitude Tests

About University Admissions Aptitude Tests

Some universities use tests as part of the admissions process for specified courses. Some admissions tests may be taken at the university you have applied to, usually on the day of the interview for your course, referred to as 'at-interview tests'.

Other admissions tests are taken pre-interview and usually happen at the beginning of the University and Colleges Admissions Service (UCAS) application cycle, with some being required to be taken before the earlier 15th October deadline for the UCAS applications.

Tests include assessments in thinking skills; admissions tests for medicine, dentistry and healthcare as well as some additional subject specific aptitude tests; and behavioural styles assessment. Some tests are computer based with others involving pen and paper.

The University of Cambridge requires applicants for most undergraduate courses in all Colleges to take a written assessment either pre-interview or at-interview. The University of Oxford requires applicants for most of its courses to take a test pre-interview as part of the application process; tutors then shortlist applicants based on the UCAS application, any additional written work and performance in the pre-interview test.

Other universities will use admission tests for specific course subjects such as medicine and dentistry courses. Some universities will also require admissions tests for additional subjects, including some veterinary medicine, some biomedical science, some mathematics, some law, some graduate business as well as some additional course subjects.

The following information as a guide only and you will need to confirm up to date information on the relevant websites.

Registration for Admissions Aptitude Tests

For pre-interview tests, there are set deadlines to register and often registration must be from mid-September by 15th October, however deadlines for registration for some tests may vary depending on the course and university applying to and there may be earlier deadlines therefore confirm with the relevant university early on in the application process.

Registration may be required to be made for you through an authorised test centre which may be your school, college or by the university you have applied to but if you are no longer at school or college, or if you are required to sit the test at a private authorised test centre, you may need to register yourself independently. The tests are sat on set dates and form part of the admissions process; if you have registered too late to sit a test, your application may

not be considered. If registration is by you, your school or college, or a recognised test centre, you may need an early registration before you have sent in your UCAS application form and you will need to be registered for the test separately in addition to submitting the UCAS application form.

Many of the courses that use admissions tests also have the UCAS 15th October application deadline, which include courses at the University of Cambridge, University of Oxford, medicine, dentistry or veterinary courses, although there are additional course subjects with UCAS 15th January application deadline that may require you to sit an admissions test. Therefore you will need to research information well in advance to make sure you meet the requirements for any deadlines.

Some tests are free but for others, test administration centres will require you to pay an entry fee and, and although there are strict deadlines for registration, some may allow for a late entry but will usually charge a higher fee.

The following information provides a useful guide, although universities may change the test requirements annually therefore you should check the relevant university or admission test centre websites for further details about tests used, registration, key dates for sitting of tests and payment where needed.

Different test arrangements may apply to applicants interviewed overseas therefore you should confirm these with the relevant university. If you have a disability or a special educational need such as dyslexia, you should check with the test centres and universities about special arrangements or reasonable adjustments.

Preparation and practice
Practice tests are usually available on the relevant university or admissions test administration centre websites. It is a good idea to prepare for the actual test by becoming familiar with the type of questions and timing yourself by carrying out some practice tests in advance of taking the actual test.

Assessment Admission Testing Services

Australian Council for Educational Research (ACER) Testing Service

The Australian Council for Educational Research (ACER) https://www.acer.org/ in conjunction with the Consortium of Graduate Medical Schools provides a testing service to assist in the selection of students to participate in the graduate entry medicine programmes in the UK, Ireland and Australia. This test is the Graduate Medical School Admissions Test GAMSAT https://gamsat.acer.org/

Pre-interview assessments administered by the Australian Council for Educational Research (ACER)
- Graduate Medical School Admissions Test GAMSAT
- Health Professions Admission Test HPAT (University of Ulster)

Pearson Vue Testing Service

Pearson Vue https://www.pearsonvue.co.uk/ part of Pearsons is a testing service and administers the Graduate Management Admission Test (GMAT) https://www.mba.com/global GMAT which is required for some postgraduate business courses at many business schools.

Person Vue also administers the UK Clinical Aptitude Test (UKCAT) https://www.ukcat.ac.uk/ which is required for medicine and dentistry courses at some universities.

Pearson Vue also administers some professional qualification tests.

Pre-interview assessments administered by Pearson Vue
- Bar Course Aptitude Test (BCAT), Bar Standards Board
- Graduate Management Admission Test (GMAT)
- National Admissions Test for Law (LNAT)
- UK Clinical Aptitude Test (UKCAT)

Cambridge Assessment Admissions Testing Service

Some universities use their own admission tests, whilst others use the services of an independent admissions test service provider. The Cambridge Assessment Admissions Testing Service http://www.admissionstestingservice.org/ is a part of Cambridge Assessment, a not-for-profit department of English language assessment at the University of Cambridge. The testing service offers a range of pre-interview and at-interview assessment tests, administered in partnership with the Universities of Cambridge and Oxford, as well as additional universities requiring some admissions tests for some courses, including the Biomedical Admissions Test (BMAT) http://www.admissionstesting.org/for-test-takers/bmat/about-bmat/ used for applications to medicine and dentistry courses at some universities.

University Admissions Aptitude Tests for the University of Cambridge or the University of Oxford

For some courses at some of the Colleges of both the University of Cambridge and the University of Oxford (commonly referred to as Oxbridge), university admissions aptitude tests are also used as part of the admissions process for applicants and there are usually required deadlines when to register to apply to take these tests. The Colleges will publish what tests they require for applications to which courses on their websites.

Sitting of tests may be required prior to you submitting your UCAS form, so you need to check well in advance about registration and deadlines. Practice tests are available on the relevant admission test administration websites (see below). It is useful to sit past tests as it is important to familiarise yourself with what will be required in the actual test and practice writing tests within the set times as poor time management may affect your results.

University of Cambridge Admissions Aptitude Tests

The University of Cambridge requires applicants for most undergraduate courses in all Colleges to take a written assessment either pre-interview or, if short listed, at-interview. In addition some Colleges will require applicants for courses mainly in the arts and social sciences to submit examples of your written work as one or two school or college essays which may be discussed at your interview. Each course will have information about requirements which you should confirm on the University of Cambridge website.

Tutors then shortlist applicants based on the UCAS application, any additional written work and performance in the pre-interview test. Everyone who has a realistic chance of being offered a place on a course at the University of Cambridge is offered an interview. If English is not your first language, a good level of spoken English will be required

(check English language requirements). Most pre-interview tests are administered by the Cambridge Assessment Admissions Testing Service. Each course will have information about test and entry requirements which you should confirm on the University of Cambridge website. Admissions tests are administered by the Cambridge Assessment Admissions Testing Service in partnership with the University of Cambridge. These tests are used for some courses at the University of Cambridge and other universities may also use some of the tests. Details should be on the university websites.

The following is a brief guide to courses and test requirements therefore you should confirm up to date information by checking with the University of Cambridge and the Cambridge Assessment Admissions Testing Service websites. Also check the information in the: Chapter 8.2

Applying to the University of Cambridge or the University of Oxford

Further information can be found at:

University of Cambridge: courses

- University of Cambridge: Undergraduate Study; Courses
http://www.undergraduate.study.cam.ac.uk/link/courses

University of Cambridge: course listing pre-interview and at-interview tests

- University of Cambridge: Undergraduate Study; Admission Assessments
http://www.undergraduate.study.cam.ac.uk/applying/admission-assessments

- University of Cambridge: Undergraduate Study; Admissions Tests
http://www.undergraduate.study.cam.ac.uk/applying/admissions-tests

- University of Cambridge: Undergraduate Study, Pre-Interview
http://www.undergraduate.study.cam.ac.uk/applying/admissions-assessments/pre-interview

- Cambridge Law Test
http://ba.law.cam.ac.uk/applying/cambridge_law_test/

University of Cambridge: undergraduate written work

- University of Cambridge: Admission Assessments; Submitted Work
https://www.undergraduate.study.cam.ac.uk/applying/admission-assessments/submitted-work

Cambridge Assessment Admissions Testing Service: University of Cambridge

- Cambridge Assessment Admissions Testing Service
http://www.admissionstestingservice.org/

- Cambridge Assessment Admissions Testing Service: Cambridge Pre-Interview Assessments
http://www.admissionstestingservice.org/for-test-takers/cambridge-pre-interview-assessments/

- Cambridge Assessment Admissions Testing Service: Pre-Interview Assessments for Test Takers
http://www.admissionstestingservice.org/for-test-takers/

University of Cambridge: Courses with Pre-Interview Written Assessments Administered by the Cambridge Admissions Testing Service

Pre-interview tests will need to be registered for usually from mid-September to early / mid-October by a set deadline, separately to applying through UCAS and you may sit them in your school, college or a test centre near to your home address. Registration for most pre-interview admissions tests are usually made through an authorised test centre. Most pre-interview tests are administered by the:
Cambridge Admissions Testing Service
http://www.admissionstestingservice.org/for-test-takers/

In addition the Cambridge Law Test which is designed by the University of Cambridge is used by most Cambridge Colleges. Some subject based tests are organised by individual Colleges when you attend for an interview, check requirements with each College.

The following is a brief guide to courses and test requirements therefore you should confirm up to date information by checking with the University of Cambridge and the Cambridge Assessment Admissions Testing Service websites.

University of Cambridge pre-interview tests administered by the Cambridge Assessment Admissions Testing Service

- Anglo-Saxon, Norse and Celtic Admissions Assessment (ASNCAA)
- Asian and Middle Eastern Studies Admissions Assessment (AMESAA)
- Biomedical Admissions Test (BMAT)
- Economics Admissions Assessment (ECAA)
- Engineering Admissions Assessment (ENGAA)
- Natural Sciences Admissions Assessment (NSAA)
- English Literature Admissions Test (ELAT)
- Geography Admissions Assessment (GAA)
- History Admissions Assessment (HAA)
- Modern and Medieval Languages (MML) at interview
- History Admissions Assessment (HAA)
- Human, Social and Political Sciences Admissions Assessment (HSPSAA)
- Sixth Term Examination Paper STEP (taken in June in year 13)
- Biomedical Admissions Test BMAT
- Natural Sciences Admissions Assessment (NSAA)
- Psychological and Behavioural Sciences Admissions Assessment (PBSAA)
- Natural Sciences Admissions Assessment (NSAA)

Course subjects with pre-interview written assessments

Course subjects with pre-interview written assessments include the following subjects. Some courses may also require a written test at-interview. Confirm up-to-date information on the University of Cambridge website.

Anglo-Saxon, Norse and Celtic:
Anglo-Saxon, Norse and Celtic Admissions Assessment (ASNCAA)

Asian and Middle Eastern Studies:
Asian and Middle Eastern Studies Admissions Assessment (AMESAA)

Economics:
Economics Admissions Assessment (ECAA)

Engineering:
Engineering Admissions Assessment (ENGAA)
Sixth Term Examination Paper Mathematics STEP (for some Colleges)

Chemical Engineering:
Engineering Admissions Assessment (ENGAA) or
Natural Sciences Admissions Assessment (NSAA)

English:
English Literature Admissions Test (ELAT)

Geography:
Geography Admissions Assessment (GAA)
History:
History Admissions Assessment (HAA)

History and Modern Languages:
History Admissions Assessment (HAA) and Modern and Medieval Languages (MML) at interview

History and Politics:
History Admissions Assessment (HAA)

Human, Social and Political Sciences:
Human, Social and Political Sciences Admissions Assessment (HSPSAA)

Mathematics:
Sixth Term Examination Paper Mathematics STEP (taken in year 13)

Medicine:
Biomedical Admissions Test BMAT

Natural Sciences:
Natural Sciences Admissions Assessment (NSAA)

Psychological and Behavioural Sciences:
Psychological and Behavioural Sciences Admissions Assessment (PBSAA)
Veterinary Medicine:
Natural Sciences Admissions Assessment (NSAA)

At-interview tests are taken at the University College you have applied to, usually on the day of the interview for your course, after you have been short-listed.

Course subjects with at-interview written assessments include the following subjects (confirm up-to-date information on the University of Cambridge website).

Archaeology:
At-interview written assessment

Architecture:
At-interview written assessments

Classics:
At-interview written assessments

Computer Science:
Computer Science Admissions Test CSAT (at interview)

Education:
At-interview written assessments

Engineering:
At-interview written assessments (for some Colleges)
At-interview written assessments

History and Modern Languages:
At-interview written assessments

History of Art:
At-interview written assessments

Land Economy:
Thinking Skills Assessment (TSA) (at interview)

Law:
Cambridge Law Test (at interview)
Linguistics:
At-interview written assessments

Modern and Medieval Languages:
At-interview written assessments

Music:
Short tasks at interview

Philosophy:
At-interview written assessments

Theology, Religion and Philosophy of Religion:
At-interview written assessments

The University of Oxford requires applicants for most undergraduate courses in all Colleges to take a pre-interview assessment test as part of the application process. Applicants are shortlisted based on the application and performance in the test.

In addition some Colleges will require applicants for courses to submit examples of written work as one or two school or college essays, marked by a teacher / lecturer, which may be discussed at your interview which should be submitted with a written work cover sheet to arrive by a set date in early November.

Tutors then shortlist applicants based on the UCAS application, any additional written work and performance in the pre-interview test. Everyone who has a realistic chance of being offered a place on a course at the University of Oxford is offered an interview. If English is not your first language, a good level of spoken English will be required (check English language requirements). Most pre-interview tests are administered by the Cambridge Assessment Admissions Testing Service.

Each course will have information about test and entry requirements which you should confirm on the University of Oxford website.

Admissions tests are administered by the Cambridge Assessment Admissions Testing Service in partnership with the University of Oxford. These tests are used for some courses at the University of Oxford and other universities may also use some of the tests. Details should be on the university websites.

The following is a brief guide to courses and test requirements therefore you should confirm up to date information by checking with the University of Oxford and the Cambridge Assessment Admissions Testing Service websites.

Also check the information in the chapter 7.2 Applying to the University of Cambridge or University of Oxford.

Further information can be found at:
University of Oxford: courses
- University of Oxford: Undergraduate Courses
https://www.ox.ac.uk/admissions/under graduate/courses-listing

University of Oxford: course listing pre-interview and at-interview tests
- University of Oxford: Undergraduate; Tests
https://www.ox.ac.uk/admissions/under graduate/applying-to-oxford/tests

University of Oxford: undergraduate written work
- University of Oxford: Undergraduate Written Work
https://www.ox.ac.uk/admissions/under graduate/applying-to-oxford/written-work

Cambridge Assessment Admissions Testing Service: University of Oxford
- Cambridge Assessment Admissions Testing Service
http://www.admissionstestingservice.org/

- Cambridge Assessment Admissions Testing Service: Oxford pre-interview assessments
http://www.admissionstesting.org/for-test-takers/oxford-tests/

- Cambridge Assessment Admissions Testing Service: Pre-Interview Assessments
http://www.admissionstestingservice.org/for-test-takers/

University of Oxford: Courses with pre-interview written assessments administered by the Cambridge Admissions Testing Service

Pre-interview tests will need to be registered for usually from mid-September to early / mid-October by a set deadline, separately to applying through UCAS and you may sit them in your school, college or a test centre near to your home address. Registration for most pre-interview admissions tests are usually made through an authorised test centre. Most pre-interview tests are administered by the:
Cambridge Admissions Testing Service
http://www.admissionstestingservice.org/for-test-takers/

Further information may be found at:
Cambridge Admissions Testing Service
http://www.admissionstestingservice.org/for-test-takers/

The following is a brief guide to courses and test requirements therefore you should confirm up to date information by checking with the University of Oxford and the Cambridge Assessment Admissions Testing Service websites.

University of Oxford pre-Interview tests administered by the Cambridge Assessment Admissions Testing Service
- Biomedical Admissions Test (BMAT)
- Classics Admissions Test (CAT)
- English Literature Admissions Test (ELAT)
- History Aptitude Test (HAT)
- Mathematics Admissions Test (MAT)
- Test of Mathematics for University Admission
- Modern Languages Admissions Tests (MLAT)
- Oriental Languages Aptitude Test (OLAT)
- Physics Aptitude Test (PAT)
- University of Oxford Philosophy Test
- STEP Sixth Term Examination Paper Mathematics
- Thinking Skills Assessment (TSA)

Course subjects with pre-interview written assessments
Course subjects with pre-interview written assessments include the following subjects; confirm up-to-date information on the University of Oxford website.

Biomedical sciences:
Biomedical Admissions Test BMAT

Chemistry:
Thinking Skills Assessment (TSA)

Classics:
Classics Admissions Test (CAT)
Classics Language Test (if not studied Latin or Greek at 'A' level)

Classics and English:
Classics Admissions Test (CAT) and English Literature Admissions Test (ELAT)

Classics and Modern Languages:
Classics Admissions Test (CAT) and Modern Language Admissions Test (MLAT)

Classics and Oriental Studies:
Classics Admissions Test (CAT) and if studying:
Arabic, Turkish, Hebrew, Persian:
Oriental Language Aptitude Test (OLAT)

Computer Science:
Mathematics Admissions Test (MAT)

Computer Science and Philosophy:
Mathematics Admissions Test (MAT)

Economics and Management:
Thinking Skills Assessment (TSA)

Engineering Science:
Physics Aptitude Test (PAT)

English and Modern Languages:
Modern Language Admissions Test (MLAT)

English Language and Literature:
English Literature Admissions Test (ELAT)

European and Middle Eastern Languages (EMEL):
Modern Language Admissions Test (MLAT) and
Oriental Language Aptitude Test (OLAT)

Fine Art:
Practical test at interview

Geography:
Thinking Skills Assessment (TSA)

History:
History Aptitude Test (HAT)

History, Ancient and Modern:
History Aptitude Test (HAT)

History and Economics
History Aptitude Test (HAT)

History and English:
History Aptitude Test (HAT)

History and Modern Languages:
History Aptitude Test (HAT) and Modern Languages Admission Test (MLAT)

History and Politics:
History Aptitude Test (HAT)

Human Sciences:
Thinking Skills Assessment (TSA)

Law (Jurisprudence):
Law National Admissions Test (LNAT)

Law with Law Studies in Europe,
Law National Admissions Test (LNAT)

Law with Law Studies in Europe with French, German, Italian or Spanish Law options
Law National Admissions Test (LNAT) and may have an oral test in the relevant language in December

Materials Science:
Physics Aptitude Test (PAT)

Mathematics:
Mathematics Aptitude Test (MAT)

Mathematics and Computer Science:
Mathematics Aptitude Test (MAT)

Medicine:
Biomedical Admissions Test BMAT

Modern Languages:
Modern Languages Admission Test (MLAT)

Modern Languages and Linguistics:
Modern Languages Admission Test (MLAT)

Music:
Practical test in December

Oriental Studies:
Oriental Languages Admission Test (OLAT)

Philosophy and Modern Languages:
Modern Languages Admission Test (MLAT) and a philosophy paper

Philosophy and Theology:
Philosophy Test

Philosophy, Politics and Economics (PPE):
Thinking Skills Assessment (TSA)

Physics:
Physics Aptitude Test (PAT)

Physics and Philosophy:
Physics Aptitude Test (PAT)

Psychology, Experimental:
Thinking Skills Assessment (TSA)

Psychology, Philosophy and Linguistics:
Thinking Skills Assessment (TSA)

Religion and Oriental Studies; applying to the Judaism and Islam strands intending to study Hebrew, Arabic Persian or Turkish
Oriental Language Aptitude test (OLAT)

At-interview tests are taken at the College you have applied to, usually on the day of the interview for your course, after you have been short-listed.

Course subject with at-interview written assessments include the following subject (confirm up-to-date information on the University of Oxford website).

Fine Art:
Practical Tests

Further information can be found at:
- University of Oxford: Undergraduate, Tests
https://www.ox.ac.uk/admissions/undergraduate/applying-to-oxford/tests

Course Subjects and Admission Aptitude Test Requirements

Medicine; Dentistry; Veterinary Medicine (some courses); Biomedical Science (some courses) Courses

- **Pre-interview admission tests**

Undergraduate and some graduate courses

All universities which offer medicine, dentistry, some veterinary medicine and some biomedical science courses will require you to sit one of the following pre-interview admissions tests, depending on the university and course.

Biomedical Admissions Test (BMAT)

The Biomedical Admissions Test (BMAT) is administered by the Cambridge Assessment Admissions Testing Service http://www.admissionstestingservice.org/

The BMAT is for applicants to medicine, veterinary medicine and related courses at certain universities. Universities using the BMAT will include this information on their websites.

The BMAT test is a 2 hour pen and paper test divided into three sections: Aptitude and Skills; Scientific Knowledge and Applications; Writing Task.

You cannot register for BMAT yourself and you will need to be registered by a BMAT test centre.

You can sit the test at an authorised test centre. Details of authorised centres can be found on the Cambridge Admissions Testing Service website. Check the Cambridge Admissions Testing Service website for information on how to register, deadline key dates and costs.

UK Clinical Aptitude Test (UKCAT)

The UK Clinical Aptitude Test (UKCAT) https://www.ukcat.ac.uk/ has been produced by a consortium of universities (UKCAT Consortium) which offer medicine and dentistry courses; the test is administered by Pearson Vue https://www.pearsonvue.co.uk/ and is delivered worldwide through Pearson VUE's centres.

The Clinical Aptitude Test (UKCAT) is a pre-admission test that helps universities to make more informed choices about applicants to some university medical and dental degree courses.

UKCAT helps to ensure candidates selected have the right cognitive abilities, attitudes and professional behaviour required by doctors and dentists. It is used in collaboration with other admissions processes, including the UCAS application and academic qualifications.

You will need to register yourself independently on-line on the UKCAT website. You will need to sit the test at an authorised private test centre usually between 1st July and the beginning of October, and as these dates can get very busy, you are advised to book early. If you fail to take the test in time and apply to a course for which the test is required, your application will be rejected unless you have been exempt from the test.

You can check further details and a list which universities and courses use UKCAT, are on the UKCAT website.

You should always check the entry requirements for each course on individual university websites before booking a test. Check the UKCAT website for information on how to register, deadline key dates and costs.

Graduate Medical School Admissions Test (GAMSAT)

The Graduate Medical School Admissions Test (GAMSAT) https://gamsat.acer.org/ is for graduate entry to medicine courses, which has been developed by the Australian Council for Educational Research (ACER) in conjunction with the Consortium of Graduate Medical Schools.

This admission test assists in the selection of students to participate in the graduate-entry medicine programmes in the UK, Ireland and Australia.

The following information is for guidance only and you will need to confirm which universities require which admissions tests for which courses, as changes may occur. GAMSAT is designed to assess applicants, who have already obtained a degree in another subject, with the capacity to undertake high level intellectual studies in the medical and health professional programmes.

Graduate applications for Medical degrees are considered on the basis of possessing an honours degree, GAMSAT results and an interview. Individual Medical schools may also apply additional criteria, so check details on relevant university websites.

GAMSAT is divided into three sections designed to assess performance in the areas of:
Reasoning in Humanities and Social Sciences; Written Communications; Reasoning in Biological and Physical Sciences.

You will need to register yourself for the GAMSAT UK test on-line on the GAMSAT website.

The GAMSAT test is offered twice a year, in March and September. Registration opens in early November to the beginning of February for the March test and early June to the beginning of August for the September test. Late registrations may be accepted up to a week later with an additional fee.

Natural Sciences Admissions Assessment (NSAA)

The Natural Sciences Admissions Assessment (NSAA) is a pre-interview admissions test for Veterinary Medicine managed by the Cambridge Assessment Admissions Testing Service with the University of Cambridge and you will need to be registered by an authorised test centre that administers the NSAA.

Dentistry Courses

Biomedical Admissions Test BMAT
- **Pre-interview admission test**

University requiring the BMAT

Undergraduate and graduate courses
- University of Leeds: Dentistry: Dentistry undergraduate courses Dentistry graduate entry courses

Further information can be found at: Cambridge Admissions Testing Service: Biomedical Admissions Test BMAT http://www.admissiontestingservice.org/for-test-takers/bmat/about-bmat/
Check for up to date information

Graduate Medical School Admissions Test GAMSAT
- **Pre-interview admission test**

University requiring the GAMSAT
Graduate courses
- Plymouth University Peninsula School of Medicine and Dentistry: Dentistry graduate entry

Further information can be found at: Graduate Medical School Admissions Test GAMSAT: https://gamsat.acer.org/ Graduate Medical School Admissions Test: Register https://gamsat.acer.org/register Check for up to date information

UK Clinical Aptitude Test UKCAT
- **Pre-interview admission test**

Universities requiring the UKCAT
Undergraduate and graduate courses
- University of Aberdeen: Dentistry
- University of Birmingham: Dentistry
- Cardiff University: Dentistry
- University of Dundee: Dentistry
- University of Glasgow: Dentistry
- Kings College London: Dentistry
- University of Liverpool: Dentistry
- University of Manchester: Dentistry

Oral health science
- University of Newcastle: Dentistry
- Plymouth University: Dentistry
- Queen's University Belfast: Dentistry
- University of Sheffield: Dentistry

Further information can be found at: UK Clinical Aptitude Test UKCAT: http://www.ukcat.ac.uk/ UK Clinical Aptitude Test UKCAT: registration http://www.ukcat.ac.uk/registration Check for up to date information

Medicine and some Biomedical Science Courses
Biomedical Admissions Test BMAT
- **Pre-interview admission test**

Universities requiring the BMAT
Undergraduate and graduate courses
- Brighton and Sussex Medical School:
  Medicine undergraduate and graduate entry
- Imperial College London:
  Medicine undergraduate and graduate entry
  Biomedical science;
  Biomedical science with management
- Lancaster University:
  Medicine undergraduate and graduate entry
- University College London:
  Medicine undergraduate and graduate entry
- University of Cambridge:
  Medicine undergraduate and graduate entry

- University of Leeds:
  Medicine undergraduate and graduate entry
- University of Oxford :
  Medicine courses undergraduate and graduate entry;
  Biomedical science

Further information can be found at:
Cambridge Assessment Admissions Testing Service
http://www.admissionstestingservice.org/
Cambridge Assessment Admissions Testing Service: Biomedical Admissions Test BMAT
http://www.admissionstestingservice.org/for-test-takers/bmat/about-bmat/
Check for up to date information

Graduate Medical School Admissions Test GAMSAT
- **Pre-interview admission test**

Universities requiring the GAMSAT
Graduate courses
- Cardiff University
  Medicine graduate entry
- University of Exeter
  Medicine graduate entry
- University of Liverpool Graduate entry
  Medicine graduate entry
- Nottingham University Graduate entry
  Medicine graduate entry
- Plymouth University Peninsula School of Medicine and Dentistry:
  Medicine graduate entry

- St George's University of London
  Medicine graduate entry
- Swansea University
  Medicine graduate entry

Further information can be found at:
Graduate Medical School Admissions Test GAMSAT https://gamsat.acer.org/
Graduate Medical School Admissions Test: register
https://gamsat.acer.org/register
Check for up to date information

394

UK Clinical Aptitude Test UKCAT

- **Pre-interview admission test**

Universities requiring the UKCAT

Undergraduate courses

- University of Aberdeen: Medicine undergraduate
- University of Birmingham: Medicine undergraduate
- Cardiff University: Medicine undergraduate
- University of Central Lancashire: Medicine undergraduate
- University of Dundee: Medicine undergraduate
- Durham University: Medicine undergraduate
- University of East Anglia: Medicine undergraduate
- University of Edinburgh: Medicine undergraduate
- University of Exeter: Medicine undergraduate
- University of Glasgow: Medicine undergraduate
- Hull York Medical School: Medicine undergraduate
- Keele University: Medicine undergraduate
- Kings College London: Medicine undergraduate
- University of Leicester: Medicine undergraduate
- University of Liverpool: Medicine undergraduate
- University of Manchester: Medicine undergraduate

Check for up to date information

- University of Newcastle: Medicine undergraduate
- University of Nottingham: Medicine undergraduate
- Plymouth University: Medicine undergraduate
- Queen Mary, University of London: Medicine undergraduate
- Queen's University Belfast: Medicine undergraduate
- University of Sheffield: Medicine undergraduate
- University of Southampton: Medicine undergraduate
- University of St Andrews: Medicine undergraduate Biomedical science
- St George's University of London: Medicine undergraduate
- University of Warwick: Medicine undergraduate

Further information can be found at:
UK Clinical Aptitude Test UKCAT:
http://www.ukcat.ac.uk/
UK Clinical Aptitude Test UKCAT: registration
http://www.ukcat.ac.uk/registration
It is advisable to undertake practice tests which may be available on the relevant website as well as the Medic Portal
https://www.themedicportal.com/

Veterinary Medicine Courses

Natural Sciences Admissions Assessment (NSAA)
- **Pre-interview admission test**

University requiring the NSAA
Undergraduate courses
- University of Cambridge:
  Veterinary medicine

Further information can be found at:
Cambridge Assessment Admissions
Testing Service: Cambridge Pre-Interview
Assessments
http://www.admissionstestingservice.org/fo
r-test-takers/cambridge-pre-interview-
assessments/
Check for up to date information

Biomedical Admissions Test BMAT
- **Pre-interview admission tests**

University requiring the BMAT
Undergraduate courses
- Royal Veterinary College:
  Veterinary medicine

Further information can be found at:
Cambridge Assessment Admissions
Testing Service
http://www.admissionstestingservice.org/

Cambridge Assessment Admissions
Testing Service: Biomedical Admissions
Test BMAT
http://www.admissionstestingservice.org/fo
r-test-takers/bmat/about-bmat/

Check for up to date information

Economics, Management and Psychology
Psychology and Linguistics
Philosophy, Politics and Economics (PPE)

Thinking Skills Assessment (TSA)
- **Pre-interview admission test**

Universities requiring the TSA
Undergraduate courses
- University of Cambridge:
  Land Economy
- University of Oxford:
  Economics and Management
  Philosophy and Linguistics
  Philosophy, Politics and Economics
  (PPE)
  Experimental Psychology
  Human Sciences
  Psychology and Linguistics
  Psychology and Philosophy
- University College London:
  European social and Political Studies

Further information can be found at:
Cambridge Admissions Testing Service
http://www.admissionstestingservice.org/
Cambridge Admissions Testing Service:
Thinking Skills Assessment
http://www.admissionstestingservice.org/fo
r-test-takers/thinking-skills-assessment/
Check for up to date information

Law Courses

Cambridge Law Test
- **At-interview admission test**

University requiring the Cambridge Law Test
Undergraduate course
- University of Cambridge
  Law: (at interview)

Further information can be found at:
University of Cambridge: Admission Assessments
http://www.undergraduate.study.cam.ac.uk/applying/admission-assessments
University of Cambridge: Cambridge Law Test
http://ba.law.cam.ac.uk/applying/cambridge_law_test/
Check for up to date information

Law LLB Courses

National Admissions Test for Law (LNAT)
- **Pre-interview admission test**

The LNAT testing system is managed by Pearson VUE and you will need to register using the Pearson VUE online registration system. The LNAT is written and calibrated by Edexcel for Pearson VUE. The test is in two parts as a multiple choice question based on passages of text and an essay.

The National Admissions Test for Law (LNAT) is used by some universities to choose applicants by testing aptitude for the skills required for a law course and is used as a part of the undergraduate law admissions process.

Universities requiring the LNAT:
Undergraduate law courses
- University of Birmingham:
  Law
- University of Bristol:
  Law
- Durham University:
  Law
- University of Glasgow:
  Law
- Kings College London:
  Law
- University of Nottingham:
  Law
- University of Oxford:
  Law

- School of Oriental and African Studies (SOAS)
  Law
- University College London
  Law

Further information can be found at:
National Admissions Test for Law (LNAT)
http://www.lnat.ac.uk/

Pearson VUE Pearson VUE
https://www.pearsonvue.co.uk/

Check for up to date information

Barrister Training Courses: England and Wales

Bar Course Aptitude Test (BCAT) Postgraduate courses
- **Pre-interview admission test**

On successful completion of an LLB law degree (or equivalent), all applicants for the Bar Professional Training Course (BPTC) in England and Wales need to pass the Bar Course Aptitude Test (BCAT) and all BPTC providers will require this test which forms part of the Bar Professional Training course (BPTC) application. You won't be able to start a BPTC without the BCAT.

The registration centre for the BCAT is the Bar Standards Board Certification Testing. The BCAT testing system is managed by Pearson VUE and you will need to register yourself using the Pearson VUE BSB online registration system. You can sit the BCAT test through a Pearson VUE Test centre in the UK and in other countries. You will be asked to select a test centre when you register.

Appointments to sit the test may be made between November and early September prior to the start of the bar professional training course (BPTC). You can take a practice test prior to the actual test through the Talentlens website

The BCAT is a form of a psychometric test which measures your critical thinking ability, being able to look at a situation and clearly understand it from multiple perspectives whilst separating facts from opinions and assumptions. It tests your ability to think logically with clarity and precision, using an approach that is objective and accurate to evaluate arguments and your ability to focus on information that is relevant to draw a conclusion.

All universities providing barrister training in England and Wales require BCAT Postgraduate courses

Further information can be found at:
Bar Standards Board (BSB) Certificate Testing: Bar Course Aptitude Test (BCAT)
https://www.barstandardsboard.org.uk/qualifying-as-a-barrister/current-requirements/bar-professional-training-course/bar-course-aptitude-test/

Pearson VUE
https://www.pearsonvue.co.uk/

Pearson VUE: Test Taker
https://www.pearsonvue.co.uk/test-taker.aspx

Pearson VUE Bar Standards Board (BSB) Certificate Testing (BCAT) Online Registration System
http://www.pearsonvue.com/bsb/

Practice Bar Course Aptitude Test (BCAT):
Talentlens: Practice Bar Course Aptitude Test
http://www.talentlens.co.uk/BCAT

Links to test centres are available on the Pearson Vue website:
Pearson VUE BSB
http://www.pearsonvue.com/bsb/

Check for up to date information

Solicitor and Barrister Training Courses: Northern Ireland

- **Pre-interview admission test**

Law Admissions Test

As part of the application process for the solicitor or barrister course in Northern Ireland you will need to sit the law admissions test which is usually held in December at Queens University, Belfast: Institute of Professional Legal Studies

University requiring the Law Admissions Test (Northern Ireland)

Postgraduate courses

- Queens University, Belfast: Solicitor and Barrister Training: Northern Ireland

Further information can be found at: Queens University, Belfast: Institute of Professional Legal Studies; Law Admissions Test https://www.qub.ac.uk/schools/InstituteofProfessionalLegalStudies/Admissions/

Check for up to date information

Management Courses

- **Pre-interview admission test**

Graduate Management Admissions Test (GMAT)

The Graduate Management Admissions Test GMAT was created by the Graduate Management Admission Council (GMAC) for use by some Graduate Business and Management Schools worldwide. A list of some UK business schools and universities are available on the GMAC approved website MBA global.

You will need to register with the Graduate Management Admissions Council GMAC. A GMAT score may be a requirement as part of the admissions process for some postgraduate business courses and you should check individual business schools and universities to confirm. You should check with the test centres about payment for the test.

The GMAT is a computerised test which is available year round at testing centres globally, although test centres operate on individual schedules. There are test centres available in major towns and cities in the UK and these can be found using the GMAC website http://www.gmac.com/

Business Schools requiring Graduate Management Admissions Test GMAT

Postgraduate courses

- Some universities: business schools MBA Global: graduate entry courses

Links to Business Schools: MBA Global http://www.mba.com/global

Further information can be found at: MBA Global: Graduate Management Admissions Test GMAT: http://www.mba.com/global

Graduate Management Admission Council (GMAC) http://www.gmac.com/
Graduate Management Admissions Council GMAC: register https://accounts.gmac.com/Account/Register
Check for up to date information

Mathematics Courses

Mathematics Admissions Test MAT:
- **Pre-interview admission test**

The Mathematics Admissions Test MAT is managed by the Cambridge Assessment Admissions Testing Service.

You cannot register yourself and will need to be registered by a MAT centre. The

MAT is a paper based test lasting for 2 hours and 30 mns. You can sit the test at an authorised test centre. Details of authorised centres can be found on the Cambridge Admissions Testing Service website.

Universities requiring the MAT
Undergraduate courses
- University of Oxford: Mathematics, mathematics and computer science
- Imperial College London: All mathematics courses

Further information can be found at: Cambridge Assessment Admissions Testing Service
http://www.admissionstestingservice.org/
Cambridge Assessment Admissions Testing Service: Mathematics Admissions Test MAT
http://www.admissionstestingservice.org/for-test-takers/mat/about-mat/

Check for up to date information

Sixth Term Examination Paper for Mathematics (STEP)
- **Pre-interview admission test**

The Sixth Term Examination Paper (STEP) for Mathematics is managed by the Cambridge Admissions Testing Service, you cannot register for STEP yourself and you will need to be registered by a STEP centre.

The Sixth Term Examination Paper Mathematic STEP is a well-established mathematics examination taken in year 13, designed to test candidates on questions that are similar in style with the content of undergraduate mathematics courses. STEP is used by the University of Cambridge and the University of Warwick as the basis for conditional offers for mathematics courses.

Other universities sometimes ask candidates to take STEP as part of their offer for mathematics courses and will advise you on which papers to take. It is also possible to take STEP even if it isn't a requirement by a university.

The STEP test consists of up to three 3 hour paper based examinations involving Pure Mathematics, Mechanics, Probability and Statistics based on Mathematics of Further Mathematics 'A' level content: STEP 1, STEP 2 and STEP 3. You are usually required to sit either one or two of the examinations, depending on the university requirements.

Universities requiring the STEP

Undergraduate courses
- University of Cambridge:
  Mathematics
  Computer Science
  Economics
  Engineering
  Natural Science
- University of Warwick:
  may be required for
  Mathematics

The following universities encourage mathematics applicants to take the STEP
- University of Bristol
  Mathematics
- University of Bath
  Mathematics
- University of East Anglia
  Mathematics
- University of Oxford
  Mathematics
- Imperial College London
  Mathematics

Further information can be found at:
Cambridge Assessment Admissions
Testing Service
http://www.admissionstestingservice.org/

Cambridge Assessment Admissions
Testing Service: Sixth Term Examination
Paper STEP: Mathematics
http://www.admissionstestingservice.org/for-test-takers/step/about-step/

Check for up to date information

Test of Mathematics for University Admission

- **Pre-interview admission test**

The Test of Mathematics for University Admission testing system is managed by the Cambridge Assessment Admissions Testing Service and you will need to be registered by a test centre.

Universities accepting the Test of Mathematics for University Admission:

Undergraduate courses
- Durham University:
  Mathematics
- Lancaster University:
  Mathematics
- University of Warwick:
  Mathematics
- London School of Economics and
  Political Science (LSE):
  Mathematics and Economics

If you are applying to study mathematics courses at Durham University, Lancaster University or University of Warwick you are encouraged to take the Test of Mathematics for University Admission test as part of your application and although it is not compulsory, a good performance in this test may result in a reduced offer.

Candidates will also be able to share their results with the London School of Economics and Political Science (LSE) if planning to study mathematics and economics.

Further information can be found at:
Cambridge Assessment Admissions
Testing Service
http://www.admissionstestingservice.org/
Cambridge Assessment Admissions
Testing Service: Test of Mathematics for
University Admission
http://www.admissionstestingservice.org/for-test-takers/test-of-mathematics-for-university-admission/about-the-test-of-mathematics-for-university-admission/

Check for up to date information

You may get an offer for a course on the basis of your application form, personal statement and predicted grades and many universities won't require you to attend an interview for your chosen course. However the Universities of Cambridge and University of Oxford (Oxbridge) will require you to attend an interview for all courses and other universities such as Imperial College London and University College of London may interview you for some courses.

You will also be required to attend an interview for professional degrees such as medicine, dentistry, nursing, social work and teacher training. You may also be required to attend an interview for some course subjects that are creative such as architecture, art and design, drama or music and for performance based courses, you may also be asked to attend an audition.

Some universities may interview for some science, engineering or computing courses. For architecture and art and design courses you may be required to bring additional work in a portfolio, which you will be asked about.

Although it is natural to feel nervous, being asked to attend an interview or audition means that the admissions tutors are impressed with your application and they will want you to do well. Interviews may be in the form of an informal discussion designed to encourage you to express your views on why you have chosen the course or may be like an oral examination such as those conducted for Oxbridge interviews.

Some interviews may also vary depending on the subject, for example, you may be asked about why you are applying for your chosen course subject; why you are applying for the course at a particular university; what you have written in your application; about your understanding of what the relevant course will involve; your career aspirations; to discuss an author in relation to your chosen subject; about what you have learned from any relevant work experience you have undertaken; to discuss a research topic in relation to your chosen subject; your knowledge about a particular aspect of your chosen subject such as for a science based course, being asked about a chemical compound; or you may be asked to solve a subject related logic problem.

Remember that the interview is a two way interaction and give full answers to the questions. Try to relax and see the interview as an opportunity to discuss a subject that you really enjoy. There are no perfect answers and the interviewer is trying to find out how you think and respond to the question as well as how enthusiastic you are. It is the process of reaching your answer that is most important.

Answer questions in your own way as interviewers want to hear what you have to say about your subject from your own perspective as they want to assess your potential as well as how you think and apply your knowledge.

Have some questions ready to ask the interviewer about the course at the end of the interview. It is useful to undertake a practice interview before you attend. Useful information may be found on individual university and college websites and at UCAS: Undergraduate Interview Invitations https://www.ucas.com/ucas/undergraduate/apply-and-track/track-your-application/undergraduate-interview-invitations

Further information may be found in the relevant job sector book: A Careers Advice Guide: Choosing a Career, Working In Series: 1-16

Types of Interviews and Preparation

The different types of interviews include:
- Traditional interviews where you will be interviewed by one person or by a panel of two or three people
- Interviews which consist of practical assessments involving a scenario with questions asked by an interviewer about your opinion.
- Group tasks where you will need to work in a group on an activity or discuss a set topic.
- Oxbridge interviews (see applying to the University of Cambridge or Oxford).

Preparation
- Check the time and the date and check travel arrangements so you arrive in plenty of time.
- Check any requirements for requests for examples of your work such as portfolios or essays.
- Wear smart clothing and something you feel comfortable in.
- Prepare answers to questions about what you have written in your application as well as your interest and knowledge about the subject you want to study.
- Keep up to date with any recent issues, articles or news reports in relation to your chosen subject.
- Stay positive and interested, with good eye contact with the interviewer/s.
- Prepare questions you want to ask at the end of the interview.
- Smile and thank the interviewer/s before you leave.

After the interview
- After the interview, make notes when you get home as this will help for additional interviews.
- Reflect on what went well and how you might improve for the next interview

Interview Questions

The following are a selection of possible questions and suggestions on how you may answer but it is important to answer in your own way.

1. **To expand on the information you wrote in your personal statement, (keep a copy for reference before your interview). If you are required to have a portfolio, you will be asked questions about your work.**

Highlight a few key points which you can expand on in a positive and enthusiastic way.

Show your motivation, passion, enthusiasm and commitment for wanting to study for your chosen subject; what you have done to learn about the subject; and your suitability to studying for the course.

Expand on what relevant personal qualities, abilities and key skills you have, providing evidence of how and where you have gained these.

2. **Why you chose the particular subjects for 'A' level or equivalent qualification**

Explain how the subjects complement each other and are relevant to the course you want to study.

Highlight subjects you genuinely enjoy; identify aspects of the course and give your reasons for why you enjoy them.

3. **Why you are interested in the subject you have applied for; or what you hope to achieve from the course and your career ambitions. You may be asked technical, general or problem solving questions related to your chosen course to test your knowledge and how you would find a solution.**

Research the course and highlight what interests you about the modules.

Explain how your chosen subject fits in with your career plans.
If you are applying for a subject such as medicine, engineering or other professional subject, you should have some background knowledge of the field and what it involves.

If you are applying for an arts or performance based subject, it may be useful to identify any prominent people in the field who has influenced you.

4. **Why you want to study at the relevant university or college**

Aspects to mention may include the excellent facilities; reputation for research; you like the approach the university takes with the course or good employment prospects on completion of the course.

Check published work by the lecturers in the department and emphasise how you are impressed with the reputation for the subject.

5. **What work experience you have had and what you have learnt**

Highlight any relevant work experience and explain what you enjoyed and learnt.

Give an example of how you dealt with any challenges or difficult situations in a positive way.

Emphasise any skills you have gained.

6. **What achievement you are most proud of**

Highlight any events you have been involved with or organised. If you have volunteered or undertaken community work experience, highlight your involvement.

Highlight any competitions or performances you have entered or taken part in; or any awards you have won.

7. **Why the university should offer you a place**

Emphasise your positive skills and strengths.
If you haven't already discussed your career aims, this may be a good opportunity to expand on how the university course will help you to achieve your ambitions.

8. **What you have read in relation to your chosen course**

Provide examples of books or articles you have read which are relevant to your chosen subject.

Provide some examples of up to date developments in your subject such as topics that are current in the media.

9. **Current issues related to your chosen subject**

Expand on information you have read in relevant articles published in newspapers, magazines and on websites to keep up to date with current issues; as well as information you have gained by talking to professionals working in the relevant field.

10. **Examples of how you have used a particular skill or core quality relevant to your chosen subject such as problem solving, team work, organisation or communication skills.**

Highlight examples of positive experiences you have had where you have used your skills to gain positive outcomes.

Have some questions ready to ask the interviewer/s, possible questions may include:

- How the course is structured
- How you will be assessed, how much of the degree is assessed by examination and how much by course work
- What you can specialise in
- What careers support there is
- What options are there for work experience or mentoring
- What is the ratio of lecturers and students for tutorials and seminars

Auditions

You may be required to attend an audition if you have applied for a music, drama or dance course. The purpose of an audition is to determine if you are able learn to the required standard on the course you have applied for.

You may have one or more people auditioning you. They aren't looking for perfection but look for students who will work well with others and show the potential to develop. It is important to practice and with the right preparation in advance, you will make a good impression.

Research what the audition requirements are. This may be on the university or college website or be sent to you in a letter or email. If you are unsure about anything, contact the relevant department before your audition. It may be helpful to practice in front of family or friends before the real audition. Keep positive and prepare a list of questions to ask at the end of the audition about the course.

Auditions can be a difficult process but it is important to keep things in perspective if you don't get selected. You can learn from the experience and use this to do better at the next audition.

Dance auditions
Dance institutions will send you correspondence about the requirements but usually you will be required to present a short dance solo. When choreographing

your performance, ask for feedback from a friend or teacher.

If using music, make sure the recording is at the start for the audition and it may be advisable to take a back-up copy with you. You may be asked why you chose the particular piece of music. You may also be asked to perform an improvisation. Before you dance, make sure you spend some time warming up and to prepare yourself. Try to connect with the audience and project yourself throughout your solo, demonstrating energy and intention.

Drama auditions
Check with the information sent to you as you may be required to bring particular clothes.

It is advisable to wear something comfortable for movement classes. If you have prepared a speech, bring it with you for reference while you are waiting to be seen. Make sure you know your speech well.

You may also be asked to improvise. Don't overstretch or force you voice. Try to visualise what your character is thinking and feeling to bring meaning to the lines. Stay calm if you forget your lines, take some deep breaths and start again. The audition staff will be looking for your understanding of the text and character.

Music auditions

You will be required to demonstrate good tone quality, intonation and practical ability with your chosen instrument or for a vocal audition. You may be asked to perform scales in a range of styles and speed.

Practice modal scales at different tempos in a variety of styles and volumes. Practice your technique and your posture while playing. You will usually be required to perform a piece of music that you know well and may be asked to sight read a piece of music you haven't seen before.

Practice sight reading, take note of the time signature, recommended tempo and key signature before you start playing. Choose some expressive pieces of music at your skill level that you enjoy playing and which show your music strengths and demonstrates your versatility as a performer.

It is great when all your plans work out just right, but sometimes you may have to revise your ideas. If you are given a conditional offer for the course you want to study and you don't get the required grades for your 'A' levels /equivalent qualifications; you are declined for your chosen course; or if you change your mind about what you want to do, you will need to think through your options carefully to make the right decision for you.

It can be very disappointing when your plans don't initially work out, especially when your friends seem to be sorted. However, everyone at some stage will experience disappointment and it is more important how you deal with it that counts. You will have a range of options to consider, so think through what will be best for you.

Options if you don't Get Offered a Place on the Course you Want to Study

Your options:
Apply in clearing to another university or college for the same course.
Universities and colleges may have vacancies for courses in clearing, which starts at the end of June, although not all courses will be available, especially those with competitive entry requirements. You may want to check out other universities or colleges which are offering courses in clearing which you are interested in, consider where they are located and if you aren't familiar with the area, try to visit before you make a decision to make sure the university or college is the right one for you.

Apply in clearing for another course that will accept your grades
You may be interested in other related subjects and sometimes the university or college you applied to may offer an alternative course if you are unsuccessful with your first choice, or there may be other degree courses with lower entry requirements.
Some higher education subjects are also available as a Certificate (Cert HE) or

Diploma of Higher Education (DipHE), Higher National Certificate (HNC), Higher National Diploma (HND) or a two year Foundation degree with lower entry requirements. You can usually top up to an honours degree after successfully completing the Foundation degree, Dip HE or HND, however check with the university or college about progression routes before you make a decision.

Retake 'A' level subjects / equivalent qualification subjects
This may be an option and you may be able to gain additional experience whilst studying for another year. If you are reapplying for the following year for a competitive degree course, admissions tutors may require a valid explanation why you didn't achieve the grades at the first sitting, so you will need to write a positive personal statement, highlighting what you are doing in the additional year. Maybe undertaking additional relevant work experience will help to boost your skills and abilities.

You may want to remain at your school or college, or you may wish to study in a new environment. You should be entitled to free education up to the age of 19 years during the academic year if you are studying at a publicly funded school or college, so you shouldn't have to pay tuition fees if you are eligible.

There are some private colleges that provide fast track 'A' levels, although you will have to pay for tuition at these institutions. You may also be able to study by distance learning, although you would have to pay for tuition and some people prefer to study in a classroom with other students. Therefore, make sure you choose what will be the best option for you.

Take a university preparation course such as a Foundation course or Extended year of a degree course
Some degree subjects provide the option for students to take 'A' level 3 (QCF) or HE level 0 Foundation or Extended year course which usually last for one academic year and, providing you successfully pass, you may be able to move onto the first level of the degree. Some universities and colleges may have higher education preparation courses which last for a shorter time period.

If you study on one of these courses, you may have to reapply through UCAS for the degree subject you want to study, although some Foundation / Extended year courses may lead directly onto the degree course at the same institution. Only some universities or colleges will offer these preparation courses and they may not be relevant for some degree subjects, therefore check out progression routes before you decide on this option.

If you are studying in higher education for a preparation level course, you are usually charged tuition fee costs at higher education rates, although you should, if eligible, be able to access student funding from Student Finance. You should consider the financial implications and your other options before making a decision. Foundation / Extended year courses should be listed on individual university and websites as well as on the website of University and College Admissions Service (UCAS) https://www.ucas.com/

Take an Access to Higher Education course
If you are a mature student, you may want to study for the one year Access to Higher Education (HE) course https://www.accesstohe.ac.uk/ . Tuition fees may be less than for a university preparation Foundation or Extended year course.

Access to HE courses may be available in a range of subjects and are accepted for many higher education courses, providing the required level is achieved. However,

there are a small number of competitive entry degree courses that may not accept the Access to HE as an entry qualification so you should confirm degree entry requirements before you decide on this route.

Your options:
Apply for a job, apprenticeship, voluntary work, or take a gap year
You may decide that studying isn't for you at this time. You may want to find a job or an apprenticeship which may be an opportunity to enter the type of work you are interested in through another route.

If you decide to take a year out as a gap year, admissions tutors will be interested to know how you spend the year. If you can't find paid work, volunteering will also give you additional skills and experience, or you may decide to travel.

There are a number of volunteering schemes which involve going abroad, although you may need to pay costs. If you decide last minute to take a gap year, you should check with the university or college if they will offer you deferred entry for the following year. If not, you will need to reapply through UCAS again, meeting the required deadlines.

Options if you don't Pass the Required Subjects / Modules on Your Undergraduate or Postgraduate Course

Your options:
Retake modules
If you miss the deadline for submission of your work, your marks may be capped at a set percentage mark. If you don't get the required marks to pass a module, you may get the opportunity to retake the module or you may be able to transfer to another related module, so check the requirements and regulations for your course.

Leaving with a lower qualification
If you haven't quite reached the standard for an honours degree, you may be awarded a pass or ordinary degree. Alternatively, you may leave with a lower qualification such as a Certificate or Diploma of Higher Education or a Higher National Certificate / Diploma, if you have enough credits.

It may be possible to top up to another degree course in a similar subject with these qualifications at a later time but check time limits with the university or college regulations as well as the financial costs involved and eligibility with Student Finance.

If you haven't reached the required standard on a postgraduate master's degree you may be awarded a lower qualification such as a postgraduate certificate or diploma. Universities will have different policies, and some may not allow for this, however, you may be able to use the credits you have gained and transfer to a university that will allow you to top up to a master's degree in a similar subject by undertaking additional modules.

Options if you are Unhappy With Your Course or University / College

Your options:
Intermitting or transferring to another course within the same higher education institution
If you give careful consideration about the course you want to study and which university or college you want to study at, you are more likely to be happy with your choice, however, whilst not an easy decision, you may decide that it would be best for you to change to a different subject, course or university.

If you aren't happy with your course or university or college, it is a good idea to discuss your options with a student adviser or a lecturer before you make a decision about leaving or transferring to another higher education institution. Sometimes it may be possible to resolve the problem quite easily.

However, if you decide that you want to leave your university or college, check out your options for transferring to another course, or university. Each university and college will have individual requirements. If you stop your course before completing an HE level; decide to change to a different subject; or if you leave some time before deciding to resume your studies, it may be the case that you will be expected to start a new course from the beginning again.

If you wish to transfer to another university, you should obtain advice from the university you wish to transfer to and you will need to officially withdraw and apply again through the usual application process. You should obtain advice before you decide as your tuition fee liability may continue to accrue if you don't inform your current the university and you will usually be required to complete an appropriate form supplied by your university or college.

Intermitting your course
If you decide to intermit / suspend your studies, depending on the university regulations you may have a period of one or two years to return to the same course, providing you complete an official form available from your university, otherwise you will need to officially withdraw and reapply through the usual application process. You should obtain advice before you decide as your tuition fee liability may continue to accrue if you don't inform the university. Each university and college may have different regulations in relation to the amount of time considered therefore discuss your options with a student adviser.

Transferring to another course within the same higher education institution
If you decide you wish to proceed with a transfer of study to a different course within your university, providing this has been agreed informally, you will need to complete the appropriate university form and have this approved by your current School / Department and the School / Department you wish to transfer to.

Transferring to another higher education institution

It may be possible in some situations to change to a different university or college mid-course. You will need to contact the university you want to transfer to in order to check that they would accept you onto the course and you would need to provide your exam results. If you want to transfer within the first few weeks of starting a course, it may be possible if the course is similar, otherwise it may be difficult to catch up with the work already taught.

If you want to transfer between years to a similar course at another university, you would need to contact the admissions staff of the university where you want to transfer to find out if you would be accepted. They would need to check that you have studied relevant modules to the level required. Your full academic history will be considered although greater weight will be placed on your current studies as these are most recent at a higher level.

You will need to get confirmation from the new university to show to your current university and will need to apply to the new university through UCAS, using the option on the form to select which year of the course you want to start. If offered a place at a new university, you will need to talk to your tutor about when you will be leaving. You will also need to notify Student Finance.

You would usually need to complete a higher education course at HE level 1 or level 2 before being able to transfer. However, some universities will consider applications from students studying at another university but won't accept transfers and you would need to start the course from the beginning. You should contact the relevant university or college admissions office to get advice and check if you would be accepted, although you may need to submit an application first before a decision is made. You would usually need to apply again through UCAS for a full time course.

Each university and college will usually have regulations regarding a minimum and maximum time period that you will need to complete an undergraduate or postgraduate qualification. Some will allow you to have up to 1 or 2 years to take a break (intermit) before having to withdraw and reapply for a new course. Some will accept transfers but you may only be given exemptions from some modules. Some universities will allow you to transfer certain courses but not for other courses although some universities may have more flexibility over some subjects. Some won't accept postgraduate transfers.

If you have successfully completed some higher education study at a recognised higher education institution (HEI), you may be eligible to transfer your credits if you decide to study a related subject elsewhere. You would usually be required to have completed a course to a minimum of higher education level 1 (level 4 RQF/FHEQ, level 7 SCQF). Your study should have been credit rated by the higher education institution where you studied. The Credit Accumulation and Transfer Scheme (CATS) http://www.qaa.ac.uk/assuring-standards-and-quality/academic-credit is used by many universities and colleges, allowing for credits for courses to be transferred.

Higher education institutions don't usually consider credit transfer if you stopped your course more than a specified number of years previously, the cut-off point is commonly 4 or 5 years for most HEIs but is dependent on the policy for the HEI. However, distance/e-learning courses such as through the Open University may offer more flexibility and may consider credit transfer for completed courses further back in time than this. However, the Open University won't accept any credit older than 16 years. Further information may be found at the Open University: Credit Transfer http://www.open.ac.uk/study/credit-transfer/

If you decide to leave your course instead of transferring, you may decide to apply to university at a later date. You should talk to your tutor or a student adviser about your options.

Depending on your university, you may need to complete a form and a student adviser will help you with this. You can reapply through UCAS for another full time course when you are ready.

You will also need to inform your country's Student Finance organisation that you have transferred or left university and check on the financial situation as you may end up with less money and be required to pay some of your own tuition fees. If you were studying in London but transfer to a university in a different location, you may need to return some of the loan as you would be provided with a higher amount of student finance to cover the higher amount of living costs in London.

Some older qualifications don't have a credit rating and the HEI will need to provide confirmation that the study was credit bearing which means the course was assessed to the same standard as a degree or other relevant course. You will need a minimum number of credits of study and these may differ between HEIs and courses.

When you apply to transfer to an HEI, you will need to provide a formal academic transcript, which may be obtained from your awarding HE institution. An academic transcript will show all the modules (elements or units of subjects) you completed with the marks awarded and how many credits each module was worth. You may also need to provide syllabus information.

Changing to a different course

If you decide that the course isn't what you had expected, it may be possible to change to a different course but it is important to consider your options before making a decision. Firstly consider your current course as you may have encountered one module that you aren't happy with but the rest of the course will have different modules that you may like. If you are having problems with the course and not doing as well as expected, find out if you can get any additional support.

If you decide you definitely want to change to a different course, you will need to research the course that you want change to and check this is the right course for you. You may be able to transfer to this course at the same university or you may want to transfer to a different university.

You should check with a student adviser about the process at your university for changing courses as you may need to complete a form. You will also need to talk to your current tutor about why you want to change to another course and contact the admissions staff for the course you want to study to check they would accept a transfer to as they will want to make sure you are making the right decision before you change. They will want to know why you want to change course and will need to check your exam results.

If you are part way through a year, you may need to start the new course at the start of the next academic year and this may affect your Student Finance entitlement, as you are eligible to receive support for a certain number of years, therefore it is important to check this before making a decision. If you transfer to another course at the same university, you may need to complete a transfer form but if you transfer to another university you would need to apply though UCAS again.

Chapter 9
Studying Abroad

9.1 About Studying Abroad

Studying abroad is becoming an increasingly popular option. You may want to study your entire undergraduate or postgraduate course overseas. Alternatively, you may wish to study mainly in the UK with the option of studying or working abroad as part of your UK course.

The following information identifies a variety schemes which include being enrolled in a UK university and studying abroad; funding and scholarships to support with enrolling and studying in a university abroad; and issues to consider. If you want to study abroad, useful information about studying may be found on the websites of the relevant country government and the embassy, consulate or high commission where you want to study as this will provide you with a strong grasp of that country's politics, society and culture as well as important travel information.

Embassies are diplomatic missions in non-Commonwealth countries and High Commissions are diplomatic missions in Commonwealth countries. Links to embassies and consulates may be found at UK Government: World Organisations https://www.gov.uk/government/world/orga nisations .

Official country immigration departments' websites also contain useful information. Links to overseas countries with information including passports, visa requirements and travel advice may be found on UK Government: World https://www.gov.uk/government/world

Education Systems and Qualifications in Other Countries

Information about European and some non-European countries' education systems including links to recognised higher education institutions, university education and qualification frameworks may be found at European Network of Information Centres (ENIC) and the National Academic Recognition Information Centres (NARIC) ENIC-NARIC http://www.enic-naric.net/
Further information may be found in:
Chapter 5.2
Undergraduate Courses and University Entry Requirements
European Network of Information Centres (ENIC)

Qualification Comparisons

UK NARIC https://www.naric.org.uk/ is the designated United Kingdom national agency for the recognition and comparison of international qualifications and skills, providing a service to compare UK qualifications with overseas qualifications. You may be charged for using this service however universities and colleges may subscribe to NARIC and may be able to check your qualifications on your behalf at no cost. For further information, check the European Network of Information Centres (ENIC) and the National Academic Recognition Information Centres (NARIC): ENIC-NARIC http://www.enic-naric.net/ . http://www.ecctis.co.uk/naric/

Further information about NARIC may be found in the:
Chapter 5.2
Undergraduate Courses and University Entry Requirements
National Academic Recognition Information Centre (NARIC)
European Network of Information Centres (ENIC)

Countries Listed on the ENIC-NARIC Website:

Austria	Georgia	Moldova	Spain
Azerbaijan	Germany	Monaco	Sweden
Belarus	Greece	Montenegro	Switzerland
Belgium	Holy See	Netherlands	The former
Bosnia and	Hungary	New Zealand	Yugoslav
Herzegovina	Iceland	Norway	Republic of
Bulgaria	Ireland	Poland	Macedonia
Canada	Israel	Portugal	Turkey
Croatia	Italy	Romania	Ukraine
Cyprus	Kazakhstan	Russian	United Kingdom
Czech Republic	Latvia	Federation	United States of
Denmark	Liechtenstein	San Marino	America
Estonia	Lithuania	Servia	
Finland	Luxembourg	Slovak Republic	
France	Malta	Slovenia	

Study and Work Abroad Funding Support and Schemes

If you are enrolled in a UK university but study part of your course or a work placement related to your course of study overseas, providing you meet the eligibility criteria you should be eligible for student loans from one of the UK student finance companies.

If you are on an Erasmus study placement https://www.erasmusplus.org.uk/study-abroad or Erasmus work placement abroad https://www.erasmusplus.org.uk/work-abroad , you may be able to access a travel grant. Further information about Erasmus may be found in the:
Chapter 9.3
Erasmus: Study and Work Experience Programme in another European Country
Chapter 12.6
Erasmus Funding Support for Undergraduate and Postgraduate Students

If you are a medical or dental student studying abroad or studying an approved health related course attending a clinical placement in the UK you may be able to access a travel grant. Each UK country has a different process. Information about eligibility for funding and travel grants may be found at the Student Finance companies where you are resident. .

UK Government: England
https://www.gov.uk/student-finance
UK Government:
England Travel Grants for Students
https://www.gov.uk/travel-grants-students-england
Student Finance Wales
http://www.studentfinancewales.co.uk/
Student Finance Northern Ireland
http://www.studentfinanceni.co.uk/
Student Awards Agency Scotland
http://www.saas.gov.uk/

The British Council has information on a number of schemes for students wishing to study abroad and financial support. Further information may be found at British Council: Study Abroad
https://www.britishcouncil.org/study-work-create/opportunity/study-abroad

British Council: Funding Studies
https://www.britishcouncil.org/study-work-create/practicalities/funding-studies

If you study for your full degree abroad you won't be eligible to get UK student finance. A number of EU countries don't charge tuition fees for undergraduate courses to resident students or students from the EU/EEA or Switzerland. A small number of EU countries also don't charge tuition fees for postgraduate courses to eligible students from the EU/EEA or Switzerland. However you will need finance to cover living costs and other expenses. Changes may occur when the UK leaves the EU in 2019.

Enrolling for an Undergraduate or Postgraduate Course in a University Abroad

With higher education costs an important factor, many overseas courses offer competitive rates, although there will also be some overseas courses that cost more than in the UK. Many overseas courses are also taught in English including countries where English isn't the first language, so a knowledge of another language may not be essential.

There are options to study undergraduate or postgraduate courses and some professional organisations in the UK recognise relevant professional qualifications gained overseas, however you should always confirm with the relevant professional body before making an application.

You may need to apply directly to a university abroad rather than going through a clearing house such as UCAS in the UK. Funding support may be dependent on you being offered a place on a course first, therefore you will need to research what your finance options are and if there are any scholarships or grants available.

There will be deadlines for when to apply for courses and funding support so ensure you give yourself plenty of time to carry out the research. Funding information will be highlighted on a university website and there are a range of useful study abroad websites listed in the 'studying in specific countries' section below.

Considering your Options When Studying Abroad

Whilst gaining valuable life experiences, studying outside of your home country isn't always an easy option so it is important to consider the pros and cons. The following are some aspects that you may like to consider before making a decision if overseas study is for you.

Personal experiences

You will have the opportunity to meet and make friends with other students from different countries and cultures. You will develop skills and confidence living in a country with different cultures and lifestyles. If studying in a non-English speaking country, you may already need a grasp of the relevant language but you will get the opportunity to develop your language skills further, however a number of courses abroad may be taught in English.

Travelling on your own and adjusting to a new lifestyle can help you to develop independence and grow in confidence. You will become more adaptable and gain a global awareness, having interesting aspects to include on your CV which should help to impress employers when competing for jobs. The scenery and climate may be attractive, including universities near a beach, overlooking mountains or in another town or city.

However, you will be further away from your family and friends so it won't be as easy to pop back to see people. If you haven't travelled to the country before, it may take some time to adjust to a different culture, lifestyle and education system. Some countries will expect you to already have knowledge of the relevant language before applying for a course.

Financial Implications

When you factor in the cost of fees and student loans, there are many overseas courses that will cost less than in the UK and you may be able to obtain a scholarship or bursary to cover full or partial costs.

You will also need to consider costs for fares for travelling, visa costs, living expenses for accommodation, food, utility bills, travel and medical / health insurance and insurance for valuable items such as musical instruments, lap tops, cameras or any other equipment or possessions that are valuable as it is advisable to pay for insurance to protect against theft or damage. If you want to travel back to the UK regularly, this may be expensive.

You won't be eligible to get UK student finance if you study for your full degree abroad. Most EU countries have schemes which provide loans and financial support, although these may not be available to students from other member states. The EU rules ensure that students from other member states are entitled to access universities for the same tuition fees as domestic students but individual countries don't need to provide financial support on the same basis unless a student has been living in the country for at least 5 years prior to starting studying for a higher education course. Some EU countries however do provide financial support to students from other EU member states. Changes may occur when the UK leaves the EU.

A number of overseas universities, governments and other recognised organisations may also offer scholarship schemes, bursaries or grants to students who meet the eligibility criteria. Some universities may have student international exchange programmes or links with other organisations which provide scholarships for students studying abroad. Details should be on the university and college websites.

It may be possible to fund your studies by undertaking part-time work during the course or in the vacations if studying in an EU / EEA country, although you will need a good understanding of the relevant language although you may not be entitled to work in a non-EU country, depending on the regulations. Taking a loan from a UK bank may be an option but you would need to consider this carefully as you will need to repay the loan in full with interest as soon as you access the loan, therefore it may be advisable to consider other financial options if possible.

Academic conditions
In some countries, the entry requirements for courses may be lower than in the UK, although the demands of the course will be of a similar standard. You may develop new or improve your language skills. If you choose to study for a postgraduate course, this may help you gain more from your chosen career, by broadening your knowledge and helping you to effectively compete for jobs.

An individual recognised as a professional in one EU Member State could also be recognised as such in another, providing the profession concerned was regulated in both Member States. If you want to work in another EU country, further information about professional qualification requirement may be found at Europa: Recognition of Professional Qualifications http://europa.eu/youreurope/citizens/work/professional-qualifications/recognition-of-professional-qualifications/index_en.htm

If the profession you want to study for, or are already qualified for, is regulated in the UK, you can search for it in English to find out the EU countries where it is regulated on the Europa: EU Regulated Professions Database http://ec.europa.eu/growth/tools-databases/regprof/index.cfm?action=homepage .

If the country doesn't appear it may mean that the profession is not regulated there, however if you don't find the profession on the database you can contact the EU national contact points for professional qualifications http://ec.europa.eu/growth/single-market/services/free-movement-professionals/#contacts in the country where you want to work. They can help you to identify the competent authority and which documents you need to submit.

If you choose to study for a professional qualification abroad, you will need to check that the course is recognised by the relevant UK professional registration body if you wish to return to work in the UK, such as for medicine degrees, check with the General Medical Council (GMC) http://www.gmc-uk.org ; for dentistry degrees, check with the General Dental Council http://www.gdc-uk.org ; for veterinary medicine, check with the Royal College of Veterinary Surgeons (RCVS) http://www.rcvs.org.uk/ .

For further information on professional organisations check the chapter:
Chapter 5.4
Professional Organisations: Accredited Undergraduate and Postgraduate Courses

Some courses may last longer than in the UK, with full time degrees often lasting 4 years, instead of the usual 3 years in the UK, except in Scotland, which is usually 4 years, and some full time master's degrees often last for two years (instead on the usual one year in the UK).

Some subjects aren't available to be taught in the English language and you will need to have a high level of ability in the required language. Even if your course is taught in English, you will need to get by in a non-English speaking country so you may need to learn a new language.

You may be advised to check on the student contact hours with academic staff as some full time courses may be limited to between just 6 – 18 hours per week, although others will be more than this, whereas in the UK this is 21 hours per week.

Choosing a country where you want to study
Where in the world do you want to study?
- Africa
- Americas : North America: Canada and the USA; Central America and the Caribbean; South America
- Asia
- Australia; New Zealand
- Europe: Eastern Europe; Western Europe; Southern Europe; Northern Europe.

You may have in mind a country where you want to study and may be considering an English speaking country, such as a commonwealth country or the USA, so you won't need to learn a new language; a number of non-English speaking countries also provide some university courses which are taught in English.

Alternatively, you may have studied another language and want to study in a country where you can use and improve this language.

You may be familiar with a particular country and may have relatives overseas, or you may have travelled to a country on a holiday, being aware of the culture, lifestyle and education system, wanting to continue your studies somewhere you are familiar with. Or you may want to try out a completely new experience and see studying abroad as a great adventure which will provide you with many new skills.

Choosing a course to study
You may have decided on the course you want to study and there may be financial considerations with recognised courses overseas being a cheaper option. Professionally accredited courses such as medicine, dentistry and veterinary science degree courses are all highly competitive in the UK and take longer to complete than other degrees.

Professionally recognised courses overseas may offer a less expensive route, however it is important to check with the relevant UK professional organisation that overseas courses are recognised in the UK. Some courses may offer scholarships or bursaries where all or part of your study costs will be paid by the university.

You may not have the required grades for entry into a UK course but some courses overseas may accept your grades. The course may be taught in English, even in a non-English speaking country, alternatively, you may want to study in another language to develop you current language ability

There are many universities world-wide and the following are websites for some counties. You can also do a search using your preferred search engine for studying in higher education in your chosen country.

Australia
Studying in Australia
http://www.studying-in-australia.org/
Australian Government International Education: Endeavour Scholarship and Fellowship
https://internationaleducation.gov.au/Pages/default.aspx.
Australia Government Awards: International Postgraduate Research Scholarships (IPRS)
http://education.gov.au/international-postgraduate-research-scholarships

Austria
Study in Austria
http://www.studyinaustria.at/

Belgium
Study in Belgium
http://www.studyinbelgium.be/en

Brazil
Study in Brazil
http://studyinbrazil.com.br/en/

Canada
Study in Canada
http://www.studyincanada.com/
University Canada
http://www.university-canada.net/

China
British Council: Study Abroad China
https://www.britishcouncil.org/study-work-create/opportunity/study-abroad/china
China Scholarship Council
http://www.csc.edu.cn/studyinchina/
Campus China
http://www.campuschina.org/

Denmark
Study in Denmark
http://studyindenmark.dk/

Europe
Europa: European Union
http://europa.eu/youreurope/citizens/education/university/index_en.htm
Study in Europe
http://www.studyineurope.eu/

Finland
Study in Finland
http://www.studyinfinland.fi/

France
Studying in France
http://www.studying-in-france.org/
And Campus France
http://www.campusfrance.org/en/

Germany
Studying in Germany
http://www.studying-in-germany.org/

Hong Kong
Hong Kong
http://studyinhongkong.edu.hk/en/

Iceland
Study in Iceland
http://www.studyiceland.is/

Ireland
Education Ireland
http://www.educationinireland.com/en/

Italy
Study in Italy
http://www.study-in-italy.it/

Japan
Study in Japan
http://www.studyjapan.go.jp/en/
Gateway to study in Japan
http://www.g-studyinjapan.jasso.go.jp/en/

The Netherlands
Study in Holland
http://www.studyinholland.co.uk/

Norway
Study in Norway
http://www.studyinnorway.no/

Sweden
Study in Sweden
https://studyinsweden.se/

New Zealand
Education New Zealand
http://www.education-newzealand.org/
New Zealand Education
https://www.studyinnewzealand.govt.nz/

South Africa
South Africa: Universities
http://www.southafrica.info/about/education/universities.htm

United States of America
Education USA
https://www.educationusa.info/
Studying in the US
http://www.studying-in-us.org/
The US-UK Fulbright Commission
http://www.fulbright.org.uk/
USA government: study in US
https://www.usa.gov/study-in-us

The following websites may also be useful:
Study Abroad
http://www.studyabroad.com/

Prospects: Graduate Careers
https://www.prospects.ac.uk/postgraduate-study/study-abroad
Prospects has study information on a range of different countries

The UK Council for International Affairs (UKCISA)
http://www.ukcisa.org.uk/

HE Global Integrated Advisory Service
http://heglobal.international.ac.uk/home.aspx
HE Global aims to bring together the UK government, national agencies and Higher Education sector expertise and experience. There is a section on countries which includes information on universities.

Worldwide Ranking of Universities

Using the links from the ranking websites, you can search for universities. It may be important for you to study a course that is ranked highly in the world ranking league tables. Although there are many worldwide rankings of universities, there are three main ones:
The Times Higher Education World Rankings (THE)
http://www.timeshighereducation.co.uk/world-university-rankings/
The Academic Ranking of World Universities (ARWU)
http://www.shanghairanking.com/index.html
The QS World Ranking (QS)
http://www.topuniversities.com/university-rankings/world-university-rankings

However, many institutions may not be listed on these rankings but still offer high quality education so it is important to carry out your research carefully and consider what is right for you. Whilst league tables

may be helpful it is important to consider what course and university is going to be appropriate for your needs. You can use your preferred search engine to search for universities in the country of your choice.

What to research
- The type and size of the university
- Academic pass rates
- Costs of tuition fees for courses
- Cost of living expenses including accommodation, food and travel
- Financial implications in comparison with UK costs
- Graduate destinations
- Language requirements
- Research quality
- Scholarships or bursaries provided
- Student satisfaction
- Student support
- Teaching quality
- UK recognition, especially with professional courses

Student Visas

To study abroad, you may need a valid student visa for the country where you wish to study. Student visas are temporary visas that allow people to come to the particular country for a specified period to study at an educational institution. You would usually need an offer of acceptance to study in a particular university or college first. You will need to contact the official government immigration visa office in the country where you wish to study.

It may take some time to have your visa application processed so you may need to apply well in advance of the start of your course. You will need to be prepared to pay a fee to have your student visa application processed. Some overseas universities may provide support with organising a student visa.

Countries in the EU and EEA

The European Union (EU) is an economic and political union of 28 countries, until 2019 when the UK will leave the EU. People resident in the member states are allowed free movement between the countries. Students resident in the EEA and Switzerland don't require a student visa if studying in one of these countries.

EU Countries
Austria, Belgium, Bulgaria, Croatia, Republic of Cyprus, Czech Republic, Denmark, Estonia, Finland, France, Germany, Greece, Hungary, Irish Republic, Italy, Latvia, Lithuania, Luxembourg, Malta, Netherlands, Poland, Portugal, Romania, Slovakia, Slovenia, Spain, Sweden and the UK (until 2019).

The European Economic Area (EEA)
The EEA includes EU countries and also Iceland, Liechtenstein and Norway. Switzerland is neither an EU nor EEA member but is part of the single market which means Swiss nationals have the same rights to live, study and work in the UK as other EEA nationals.

Vaccinations

Depending what country you want to study in you may be required to have specified vaccinations before being able to enter that country. You would need to arrange these with your GP and you may be required to pay.

You can get further information from NHS Travel Vaccinations https://www.nhs.uk/conditions/travel-vaccinations/

9.2   Studying in a Commonwealth Country and Funding Schemes

Commonwealth Scholarships and Fellowships for UK Citizens
The Commonwealth Scholarship and Fellowship Plan (CSFP), provide scholarships and fellowships which are offered to citizens of the UK to study in other Commonwealth countries through a specific scheme.

Applying for a commonwealth scholarship and fellowship plan (CSFP)
To apply for a Commonwealth Scholarship and Fellowship Plan (CSFP), you would need to apply through the Commonwealth Scholarship Commission in the UK website http://cscuk.dfid.gov.uk/apply/scholarships-uk-citizens/ .

Further information may be found at Commonwealth Scholarship Commission in the UK http://cscuk.dfid.gov.uk/

Studying in Australia

Australia has 43 universities as well as additional institutions which offer higher education courses. The length of a full time degree course in Australia is 2 years for an Associate degree; 3 years for a bachelor degree; 4 years for a bachelor honours degree (although specialist courses such as medicine may be longer; 1 or 2 years for a master's degree; and typically 3 years for a doctoral degree.

The academic year usually starts in March and finishes in November, consisting of two semesters although there may be some variation between universities and some have three semesters. For most courses you would start in semester 1 in March, although for some courses it may be possible to start at the beginning of semester 2 at the end of July. International students are eligible to work part-time during their course. The Skilled Migration Programme is aimed at international students and others who meet the requirements of a certain skillset but who aren't already sponsored by an employer. Further information may be found at the Australian Government Department of Border and Control http://www.border.gov.au/Trav/Work

Applying for an undergraduate course in Australia

Applications for undergraduate and postgraduate university courses in Australia are usually made directly to each individual university by international students and you can choose to apply to as many courses as you want.

For eligible resident Australian students, there is also a centralised application system, the University Admissions Centre (UAC) http://www.uac.edu.au/ which processes applications for admission at participating institutions mainly located in New South Wales (NSW) and the Australian Capital Territory (ACT) providing the option to choose up to 9 courses to apply for. Applications for undergraduate university courses should be made by mid-November to late December for those starting in March semester 1 depending, on the university;

and should be made by mid to late May for those starting in July semester 2, depending on the university (check advised dates on university websites).

Costs

Tuition fees for higher education in Australia for international students will vary depending on the university which set their own fees. Tuition fees may range from around £9,500 to £18,500 plus per year for a bachelor degree, with some courses such as veterinary or medicine costing more. Living costs for accommodation, food and additional costs will vary depending on where you are studying.

Eligible resident Australian students may be able to access a government loan that allows you to repay your tuition fees once you start earning above an annual salary. Further information may be found at Study in Australia https://www.studyinaustralia.gov.au/

Scholarships

Scholarships, grants and bursaries are offered by the Australian Government, education institutions and other public and private organisations. Further information may be found at Study in Australia: Scholarships http://www.studyinaustralia.gov.au/global/australian-education/scholarships The Association of Commonwealth Universities https://www.acu.ac.uk/

Australia Government awards: endeavour scholarships and fellowships

The Australia Government Awards: Endeavour Scholarships and Fellowships https://internationaleducation.gov.au/Pages/default.aspx are the Australian Government's competitive merit-based schemes providing opportunities for Australians to undertake study, research or professional development overseas and for overseas citizens to do the same in Australia. Funding support ranges from short-term fellowships or research placements to full postgraduate degrees.

Applying for an endeavour scholarship or fellowship

To apply for an Endeavour Scholarship or Fellowship, applications must be made on the Australian Government International Education Awards: Endeavour Scholarship and Fellowship https://internationaleducation.gov.au/Pages/default.aspx meeting advised deadlines.

Australia Government awards: international postgraduate research scholarships

The Australia Government Awards: International Postgraduate Research Scholarships (IPRS) http://education.gov.au/international-postgraduate-research-scholarships are for eligible international postgraduate students of all countries (except New Zealand) for a period of two years for a research master's degree or three years for a research doctorate degree.

Applying for IPRS funding

To apply for IPRS funding, IPRS is administered by individual universities on behalf of the Department of Education and each university has its own application and selection process, therefore you will need to contact your chosen university directly to discuss how to apply for the IPRS scheme

Study in Canada

Canada has over 100 universities and colleges which offer higher education courses. It may be possible to choose one, two or three subjects to specialise. The length of a full time degree course in Canada is 3 or 4 years for a bachelor degree, 1or 2 years for a master's degree and 4 or 5 years for a PhD. The academic year usually starts in September and finishes in April.

Many universities encourage students to undertake relevant work experience which may provide credits towards the degree course and may lead to job offers on completion of the course. International students are eligible to work part-time during their course and may apply for an open 3 year work permit on completion of their course.

Applying for an undergraduate course in Canada

Applications for undergraduate and postgraduate university courses in Canada are usually made directly to each individual university but as education is the responsibility of individual Provinces, the process may vary.

Some exceptions involve some Provinces having a centralised application system for undergraduate courses which involves applying to multiple universities on one single application, however not all universities in that Province may use this system therefore you should check application requirements with each university.

Centralised applications are available for some higher education institutions in Alberta, Apply Alberta https://www.applyalberta.ca/ ; British Columbia, Apply Education Planner BC https://apply.educationplannerbc.ca/;

Ontario, Ontario Universities Application Centre (OUAC) https://www.ouac.on.ca/

Quebec, Service Regional d'admission au Collegial de Quebec (SRACQ) https://www.sracq.qc.ca/ ,

Service Regional d'admission du Montreal Metropolitan (SRAM) https://www.sram.qc.ca/ and

Service Regional de la admission des cegepes du Saguenay-Lac-Saint-Jean (SRASL) https://www.srasl.qc.ca/

Applications for undergraduate university courses should be made between October to December/January prior to the course starting the following September, although some universities will have a rolling application system, offering places to those who apply first, and some universities will accept later applications.

Costs

Tuition fees for higher education in Canada for international students will vary depending on the university and college which set their own fees. Tuition fees for undergraduate courses may range from around £8,500 to £25,000 plus per year. Living costs for accommodation, food and additional costs will vary depending on where you are studying.

Eligible resident Canadian students may access a student loans programme provided by banks which set their own conditions for repayment. Further information may be found at the Canadian Government: Edu Canada http://educanada.ca/

Scholarships
Scholarships may be available from universities or colleges, or by external organisations
Information on scholarships may be found at the Canadian Government Scholarships:
Scholarships-Bourses
http://www.scholarships-bourses.gc.ca/ and Scholarship Canada
http://www.scholarshipscanada.com/

Further information may be found at:
Canadian Government: Edu Canada
http://educanada.ca/
Canadian Government Scholarships:
Scholarships-Bourses
http://www.scholarships-bourses.gc.ca/
Canadian Information Centre for International Credits https://www.cicic.ca/
Canada Immigration and Citizenship
http://www.cic.gc.ca/
You Tube: Education Canada Channel
Study in Canada
http://www.studyincanada.com/
Scholarship Canada
http://www.scholarshipscanada.com/
Association of Commonwealth Universities
https://www.acu.ac.uk/

Studying in New Zealand
New Zealand has eight universities which offer higher education courses. The length of a full time degree course in New Zealand is 3 or 4 years for a bachelor degree, 2 years for a master's degree and 3 years for a PhD.

The academic year usually starts in March and finishes in October or November, consisting of two or three semesters

although there may be some variation between universities. International students may be eligible to work part-time during their course

Applying for an undergraduate course in New Zealand
Applications for undergraduate and postgraduate university courses in New Zealand are usually made directly to each individual university.

Applications for undergraduate university courses should be made by January for those starting in March, semester 1, depending on the university; and by June for those starting in July, semester 2, depending on the university (check advised dates on university websites).

Costs
Tuition fees for higher education in New Zealand for international students will vary depending on the university and college which set their own fees. Tuition fees for undergraduate courses may range from around £10,500 to £14,500 plus per year. International students will need to pay tuition fees payable before starting your course.

Eligible resident New Zealand students may be able to access a government loan that allows you to repay your tuition fees in full.

Further information may be found at Universities New Zealand http://www.universitiesnz.ac.nz/ and Study in New Zealand https://www.studyinnewzealand.govt.nz/

Scholarships
Information about scholarships may be found at Universities New Zealand http://www.universitiesnz.ac.nz/studying-in-nz
Study in New Zealand https://www.studyinnewzealand.govt.nz/
The Association of Commonwealth Universities https://www.acu.ac.uk/

New Zealand international doctoral research scholarship (NZIDRS)
The New Zealand International Doctoral Research Scholarship (NZIDRS) https://enz.govt.nz/support/funding/scholarships/new-zealand-international-doctoral-research-scholarships/ is a government funded scholarship administered by Education New Zealand for up to 3 years to eligible applicants undertaking a PhD, aiming to attract and retain the best international researchers to New Zealand.

Applying for a New Zealand international doctoral research scholarship (NZIDRS)
To apply for a New Zealand International Doctoral Research Scholarship (NZIDRS) you will firstly need to apply to an individual New Zealand university. Information about applying for the NZIDRS may be found on the New Zealand International Doctoral Research Scholarship (NZIDRS) https://enz.govt.nz/support/funding/scholarships/new-zealand-international-doctoral-research-scholarships/

Further information may be found at New Zealand Education https://www.studyinnewzealand.govt.nz/

9.3   Studying in a European Country and Funding Schemes

Information about studying in a European country may be found at
Europa: European Union http://europa.eu/youreurope/citizens/education/university/index_en.htm
Study in Europe http://www.studyineurope.eu/

The following information provides general advice however when the UK leaves the EU in 2019, there may be changes in relation to costs and UK students studying in the EU / EEA, therefore you should confirm details on relevant university and college websites.

Studying in Austria
Austria has public and private universities, universities of applied sciences (UAS) (Fachhochschule) http://www.fachhochschulen.ac.at/en/all_universities (offering science, technology and engineering courses) and university colleges of teacher education. The length of a full time degree course in Austria is 3 or 4 years for a bachelor degree, 1or 2 years for a master's degree and 4 or 5 years for a PhD. The academic year usually starts in the beginning of October and finishes in June with 2 semesters, semester 1 from October to end of January and semester 2, lasting from the beginning of March to June.

Applying for an undergraduate course in Austria
Applications for undergraduate and postgraduate university courses in Austria are usually made directly to each individual university. Applications for full time undergraduate university courses should be made by the deadline set by the university, which may vary between universities, but may be by the end of March for courses starting in October although there may be some variation and extension periods for some courses), therefore confirm dates on university websites.

Some courses may start in semester 2, beginning of March, and some universities may accept applications by the beginning of February. Some courses have entrance examinations such as for medical universities, universities of the arts and UAS degree programmes, and deadlines for the application for entrance exams may be up to 6 months before the beginning of the semester.

Costs
Tuition fees for undergraduate higher education in Austria are free for students from the EU/EEA providing you don't exceed the minimum duration of the study programme plus two semesters, however private universities, university colleges of

teacher training and universities of applied sciences (around £600 plus per year) and are able to set their own tuition fees and you would need to confirm these with the individual institution. Further information may be found at Study in Austria http://www.studyinaustria.at/
Austrian Foreign Ministry https://www.bmeia.gv.at/en/embassy/otta wa/bilateral-relations/youth-education-science/studies-universities.html

Scholarships
Scholarships are offered by a wide variety of institutions and further information may be found at Study in Austria: Scholarships http://www.studyinaustria.at/scholarships/ and Austria: Grants http://www.grants.at/

Studying in Belgium
Belgium is divided into the Flemish community and French community and has public and private universities and university colleges offering professional and academic courses, schools of art / arts colleges and, in the Flemish community, a higher maritime institute offering nautical sciences

Applying for an undergraduate course in Belgium
Applications for undergraduate and postgraduate university courses in Belgium are usually made directly to each individual university. Applications for full time undergraduate university courses should be made by the deadline set by the university, which may vary between universities, but may be by the end of April or May for European Economic Area (EEA) students or by the end of February / May for students outside of the EEA, although there may be some variation for some courses, therefore confirm dates on university websites. Some courses may start in semester 2, beginning of March, and some universities may accept applications by the beginning of February. Some courses have entrance examinations such as for medical universities, universities of the arts and UAS degree programmes, and deadlines for the application for entrance exams may be up to 6 months before the beginning of the semester.

Tuition fees for higher education in Belgium for students from the EU/EEA are very reasonable and much lower than comparable with UK tuition fees, with much of the real cost of higher education borne by the authorities. Further information may be found at Study in Belgium http://www.studyinbelgium.be/en

Scholarships and grants may be available for eligible students with further information at
Study in Belgium: Financing your studies http://www.studyinbelgium.be/en/program mes-de-bourses

Studying in Denmark
Tuition fees for higher education in Denmark are free for students from the EU/EEA and Switzerland as well as for students participating in an exchange programme. A number of scholarships and grants are available from the institutions and from public funded schemes.
Further information may be found at Study in Denmark http://studyindenmark.dk/
Information about scholarships may be found at: Study in Denmark: Tuition fees and Scholarships http://studyindenmark.dk/study-options/tuition-fees-scholarships

The Anglo-Danish society scholarships
The Anglo-Danish Society administers scholarships http://www.anglo-danishsociety.org.uk/scholarships awarded to eligible Danish students at postgraduate level studying at a recognised UK university or other higher education institution and eligible British students at postgraduate level studying at a recognised Danish university or other higher education institution in any subjects.

Applying for an Anglo-Danish society scholarship
To apply for an Anglo-Danish Society scholarship you will need to complete an application form available on: Anglo-Danish Society http://www.anglo-danishsociety.org.uk/scholarships Meeting advised deadlines.

The Anglo-Danish society special scholarship together with the Ove Arup Foundation

The Anglo-Danish Society administers a special scholarship together with the Ove Arup Foundation http://www.anglo-danishsociety.org.uk/ove-arup-foundation-scholarship awarded to eligible Danish students at postgraduate level studying at a recognised UK university or other higher education institution and eligible British students at postgraduate level studying at a recognised Danish university or other higher education institution in subjects relating to the 'Built Environment'

Applying for an Ove Arup Foundation award

To apply for an Ove Arup Foundation Award you will need to complete an application form available on:
Anglo-Danish Society http://www.anglo-danishsociety.org.uk/guidance-for-applicants
Meeting advised deadlines.

Studying in Finland

Tuition fees for higher education in Finland are free for students from the EU/EEA and Switzerland taught in English, although not for PhD studies or bachelor's and master's degree studies in Finnish of Swedish.

Further information may be found at
Study in Finland
http://www.studyinfinland.fi/
Further information about tuition fees and scholarships may be found at Study in Finland Tuition Fees and Scholarships http://www.studyinfinland.fi/tuition_fees_and_scholarships/tuition_fee_information_listed_by_institution

Studying in France

Tuition fees for higher education in France are the same cost charged to French students as for international students, although less expensive than costs for higher education in the UK, however private institutions may charge higher fees.

Further information may be found at Studying in France http://www.studying-in-france.org/
And Campus France http://www.campusfrance.org/en/

Individual universities may offer scholarships, check information on the university website. The French Ministry of Foreign and European Affairs may offer grants to eligible international students.

Further information may be found at:
France Diplomatie http://www.diplomatie.gouv.fr/en/coming-to-france/studying-in-france/
Information about finance and funding support may be found at Campus France http://www.campusfrance.org/en/rubrique/etudier-en-france

Studying in Germany

Tuition fees for public undergraduate higher education in Germany are free for all students from the EU/EEA and non-EU countries.

However tuition fees are charged for postgraduate courses and private universities will also charge fees. Further information may be found at Studying in Germany http://www.studying-in-germany.org/

Scholarships are available and further information may be found at Studying in Germany: Scholarships http://www.studying-in-germany.org/scholarships/

Studying in Iceland

Tuition fees for higher education in Iceland varies between universities and whether it is state funded or a private institution. Scholarships are available to eligible students from Reykjavik University http://en.ru.is/services/student-services/scholarships-and-awards/ and the University of Iceland http://sjodir.hi.is/english

The Icelandic Ministry of Education, Science and Culture awards annually a number of scholarships http://www.arnastofnun.is/page/studentast yrkir_menntamalaraduneytis_en to foreign students of language and literature for the study of Icelandic language, literature and history at the University of Iceland, Reykjavik.

Further information may be found at Study in Iceland http://www.studyiniceland.is/

Studying in the Irish Republic
Tuition fees are free for undergraduate higher education courses in Ireland for eligible students from the EU / EEA and Switzerland, although you will need to pay a registration fee. Tuition fees are charged for postgraduate courses. Further information may be found at Education Ireland http://www.educationinireland.com/en/

Further information about scholarships may be found at Education Ireland: Scholarships http://www.educationinireland.com/en/How -Do-I-Apply-/Tuition-Costs- Scholarships/Scholarships/

Studying in Italy
Tuition fees for higher education in Italy varies between universities and whether it is state funded or a private institution. Tuition fees for publicly funded higher education are much lower than tuition fees charged in the UK, although private universities tuition fees may be higher. Further information may be found at Study in Italy http://www.study-in-italy.it/

Further information on financial information may be found at Study in Italy: Fees and Costs http://www.study-in-italy.it/studying/fees- costs.html The Diritto allo Studio Universitario (DSU Office) provides information on Scholarships and Financial Aid http://www.dsu.toscana.it/servizi/benefici- agli-studenti/borsa-di-studio-e-posto- alloggio/

Studying in the Netherlands
Tuition fees for higher education in the Netherlands are standard for publicly funded universities but are lower than tuition fees charged in the UK, although private universities tuition fees may be higher.

The Netherlands enable EU students from another member country to be eligible for a tuition fee loan from the Dutch government called Collegegeldkrediet if you don't have the finance to pay for fees up front. This is paid in monthly instalments. However, some universities may require the tuition fees to be paid in full for the whole year or semester before you receive your loan and you will need to have the finances to pay in advance. You may also be eligible for support towards living costs.

You will need to repay the loan with interest within a set amount of time. Further information may be found at Study in Holland http://www.studyinholland.co.uk/ Further information on loans and grants may be found at Study in Holland: Loans and Grants http://www.studyinholland.co.uk/loans_and _grants.html and Study in Holland: Find a Scholarship https://www.studyinholland.nl/scholarships /find-a-scholarship

Studying in Norway
Tuition fees for the majority of Norwegian universities and state university colleges in Norway are free for foreign students studying at all levels including undergraduate, master's degrees and PhDs, although a small number of specialist courses mayo have tuition fees.

However, students will need to pay a semester fee in order to take any exams, which also provide additional benefits. Most privately funded higher education institutions have tuition fees for all courses which may be lower than in other countries. Further information may be found at Study in Norway http://www.studyinnorway.no/

427

Some national courses offer scholarships and other types of funding for international students wishing to study in Norway. Further information may be found at Study in Norway: Scholarships http://www.studyinnorway.no/study-in-norway/Scholarships

Studying in Sweden

Tuition fees for higher education in Sweden are free for students from the EU/EEA and Switzerland. Further information may be found at
Study in Sweden
https://studyinsweden.se/

Information about Scholarships for students wishing to study in Sweden may be found at University Admissions Sweden
https://www.universityadmissions.se/en/All-you-need-to-know1/Applying-for-studies/Fees-and-scholarships/Scholarships/

Traineeships / Stages Programme in Europe

Traineeships / stages are available in Europe with the European Commission. These are temporary placements that may be paid or unpaid, available for students and university graduates within a range of job areas. Further information may be found at the European Commission: Stages http://ec.europa.eu/stages/ .

Erasmus: Study and Work Experience Programme in another European Country

The European Region Action Scheme for the Mobility of University Students, known as the Erasmus programme http://www.erasmusprogramme.com/ is a programme that is available for undergraduate and postgraduate students following a course of higher education in any subject in one participating European country, who wish to spend part of their course studying or working in another participating European country.

The Erasmus programme involves an exchange of students organised by the universities concerned and approved by the European Commission under the Erasmus scheme.
You may undertake an Erasmus study placement
https://www.erasmusplus.org.uk/study-abroad or an Erasmus work placement abroad
https://www.erasmusplus.org.uk/work-abroad

If you are enrolled as a student in higher education at a university or college in the UK and wish to study, undertake a work placement or be a language assistant for between three to 12 months in an EU, EEA or a candidate country, you may be

eligible to participate in the Erasmus Programme.

As well as accessing UK student finance, you should be eligible for an Erasmus grant, which is not means-tested, but you must be enrolled / registered at a participating UK Higher Education institution which holds an Erasmus University Charter (EUC) and the study or work experience must relate to your degree, so check out if your university and course provides the option for studying or working abroad with Erasmus,

Although students from all subject areas are eligible, not all institutions offer the Erasmus programme for all subjects, so check with your institution's Erasmus co-ordinator first. To participate in a study mobility programme, you can only attend partner institutions.

For work mobility placements, you must attend eligible work experience placements. If you are applying for higher education, you would need to check that your chosen university or college offers the Erasmus programme with the course you want to study.

During your time in higher education, you can receive one Erasmus grant for study or work experience. It may be possible to combine a period of study with a work placement as a single period if there are no gaps between the two activities, although you will need to check with your institution's Erasmus co-ordinator for further details. The Erasmus scheme is for undergraduate students, however postgraduate students may also take part, provided your grant quota hasn't been exceeded.

Funding for Erasmus students
The European Commission usually provides a grant to UK Erasmus students, which contributes towards the extra costs arising from studying abroad. The Erasmus grants are paid through your institution in the UK and are paid in addition to the standard grants or loans to which you are entitled.

During your Erasmus period, you will continue to receive any student loan or other funding to which you are entitled and the Erasmus grant is a supplementary, non-repayable grant which is intended to help with any additional expenses you may have while you are abroad.
The grant varies depending on the country you visit as some are more expensive

than others and some students may be eligible for additional funding. You will need to be prepared to pay for accommodation and general living costs. In many countries this may be lower than in the UK whilst other countries may be more expensive.

Applications for the Erasmus scheme
Applications should be made through the higher education institution where you are studying as they will set their own application deadlines. Check with the institution's Erasmus Co-ordinator regarding how and when to apply, contact the university or college to obtain the details. For full details and further information, check the
British Council, Erasmus website
https://www.britishcouncil.org/study-work-create/opportunity/study-abroad/erasmus
Erasmus study placement
https://www.erasmusplus.org.uk/study-abroad
Erasmus work placement abroad
https://www.erasmusplus.org.uk/work-abroad
For further information about funding see Chapter 12.6
Erasmus Funding Support for Undergraduate and Postgraduate Students

9.4   Studying in the United States of America and Funding Schemes

The United States of America (USA) has over 2,400 universities and colleges which offer four year degree level courses, in public, private, technical and liberal arts universities and colleges. You may study a range of subjects in year one, declaring a major subject at the end of year two, which may be different from the subject you had originally planned to study.

The length of a full time degree course in the USA is usually 4 years for a bachelor degree, with some professions requiring a bachelor degree before continuing with additional study such as for medicine or law; 1, 2 or 3 years for a master's degree and around 5 years for a PhD.

International students are usually eligible to work part-time up to 20 hours per week during their course and some universities may offer student employment on campus. Every university will set individual dates for the academic year and vacations which may vary between universities.

The academic year is divided into Fall (Autumn), Spring and Summer semesters and usually starts in the middle to the end of August/ beginning of September in Fall and finishes at the beginning of May, at the end of the Spring semester. Some students may also opt to take classes over the summer term lasting from the middle to the end of May to the beginning of August if they wish to get ahead or catch up, if the universities provide this option.

Applying for an undergraduate course in the USA

Applications for university courses in the USA are made directly to each individual university or through a centralised applications body, the Common Application https://www.commonapp.org/ which is an undergraduate admissions application used by over 600 universities.

You will need to submit your academic record, test scores (SAT or ACT), essays for each university applying to (most universities will request supplemental essays tailored to the individual university), extracurricular activities and teacher recommendations. You may have an interview conducted over the phone or online such as through skype.

Applications for university courses may be made between August and 31st December, although some courses may have an earlier deadline in October / November. Some regular applications may be accepted in January and some up to March, preceding the start of the course the following August / September, therefore you will need to check deadlines for applications on the university websites. You can apply to as many universities as you want however it is usual to apply for six to eight.

You will need to check with each university or college regarding entry requirements however it is a requirement by many universities and colleges, in addition to academic requirements, that you would usually be required to sit a university entrance test, either SAT or ACT before applying. The SAT tests your ability in mathematics and English and the ACT tests your ability in mathematics, English and science. All universities accept both tests. There are also SAT subject tests for some specified subjects required by more competitive universities. The SAT needs to be registered through the College Board https://www.collegeboard.org/ . The ACT needs to be registered through the ACT http://www.act.org/ .

You would need to pay a fee to sit the test/s. There are a number of test centres around the UK where you can sit these tests which are held several times a year. It may be advisable to sit your admission test/s in the spring of year 12 (lower 6th form) to allow for time to re-sit the tests if needed but may be taken up to October or November (confirm dates with centres). If you are also sitting the SAT subject tests you may need to plan for two SAT testing dates. You can take practice tests on the College Board and ACT websites. There are organisations in the UK that may help with admission test preparation however there is usually a charge for this.

Costs

Tuition fees for higher education in the United States of America (USA) for international students will vary depending on the university and college, which set their own admission requirements, application deadline and fees. However, tuition fees are generally higher than tuition fees charged at UK universities, ranging from around £15,000 to £30,000 plus per year.

Living costs for accommodation, food and additional expenses will vary depending on where studying. Resident eligible USA students may access federal and state student aid. Further information about studying in the USA may be found at USA government: study in US https://www.usa.gov/study-in-us

Scholarships

Scholarships may be available from universities or colleges, or by external organisations and may be awarded dependent on those students who are in financial need; achieve high academic standards; excel in a sport; or have other required abilities. Information on scholarships may be found on university and college websites; the US government's free online scholarships search tool Career One Stop: Scholarships https://www.careeronestop.org/toolkit/training/find-scholarships.aspx and the US-UK Fulbright Commission http://www.fulbright.org.uk/

The United States – United Kingdom US-UK Fulbright Commission is responsible for education exchange programmes, and aims to foster cultural understanding between the UK and US. The Fulbright Awards Programme offers opportunities for studying for an undergraduate or postgraduate course; short term study for a summer, semester or academic year available at all levels from school to post-doctoral level; lecturing or pursuing research in any academic field. For people who are UK citizens, there are various grants and places on special programmes to the United States of America (USA). Fulbright also supports students, parents and advisers on the application process to US universities and is endorsed by the US Department of State as the official source of information on US higher education in the UK.

If you are interested in studying for an undergraduate or postgraduate course in the US, the US-UK Fulbright Commission provides an advising team which operates as the US Government's official source of information on the application process for studying in higher education in the US. Information about choosing universities, funding, admissions tests, applying to universities as well as additional information can be found on the US-UK Fulbright commission website. Events are organised at various places in the UK and you can find more details about seminars where advisers will provide a comprehensive guide to applying to US universities; USA College Day where you can meet representatives from US universities; and webinars which are live online presentations and webchats.

There is also a monthly E-Newsletter as well as online communities. These can also provide advice on the implications of studying abroad in terms of career aspirations, employment prospects, student finance and student support. Students interested in a Fulbright programme, will need to complete an application and interview process and if successful you will receive a high level of support ranging from visa processing and health insurance as well as a pre-departure orientation and re-entry advice. The Fulbright Commission also supports US citizens coming to the UK on exchange programmes and support throughout the year including an arrival orientation in September and an annual Fulbright Forum on current political, social and cultural issues. Fulbright also offers a variety of UK based and US based academic Summer Institutes for high school students and undergraduates.

Funding for students on Fulbright schemes

For people who are UK citizens, there are various grants and places on special programmes to the US. Fulbright provides sources of information about undergraduate funding and the Fulbright Commission also offers some funding awards for study and research at postgraduate and postdoctoral level. For further information on pre-university / high school exchange programmes, Internships and Summer Work / Travel see:
Fulbright: short term study
http://www.fulbright.org.uk/study-in-the-usa/short-term-study
Education USA
https://educationusa.state.gov/
Education USA: short term
https://educationusa.state.gov/your-5-steps-us-study/research-your-options/short-term . For further information on the US-UK Fulbright Commission about studying for an undergraduate or postgraduate course in the USA see:
The US-UK Fulbright Commission
http://www.fulbright.org.uk/
Education USA
https://educationusa.state.gov/

Applying to Fulbright

To apply for postgraduate funding you will need to make an application at Fulbright: Postgraduates
http://www.fulbright.org.uk/fulbright-awards/exchanges-to-the-usa/postgraduates

Studying in Brazil

Tuition fees for higher education in Brazil for students may very between universities but you are not usually charged for public universities although you will need to pay a registration fee. Tuition fees at private universities will vary so check with individual institutions. Further information may be found at Study in Brazil http://studyinbrazil.com.br/en/

Studying in China

Tuition fees for higher education in Canada for foreign students will vary depending on the university but are generally less than those charged at UK, Australian or USA universities.
Further information may be found at China Scholarship Council http://www.csc.edu.cn/studyinchina/

Generation UK China scholarships

Generation UK China Scholarships provide funding for between five to 11 months of study, starting in February or September, at a Chinese university enabling you to learn Mandarin and get a deeper understanding of China. Scholarships cover tuition fees, accommodation and a basic monthly living allowance. You would need to fund costs for return flights, travel and medical insurance and visa costs. You can decide which location and subject to study (which is at non-degree level). You will need to meet the eligibility criteria and be a full time student enrolled at a UK university or a recent graduate applying within one year of your graduation date.

Applying for a Generation UK China scholarship

To apply for a Generation UK China Scholarship, you will need to meet the application deadlines. For further information and application details check: British Council study abroad China https://www.britishcouncil.org/study-work-create/opportunity/study-abroad/china

Chinese Government scholarships

Chinese Government Scholarships may be available through the China

Scholarship Council http://www.csc.edu.cn/Laihua/ and Campus China http://www.campuschina.org/ and are for students on undergraduate or postgraduate courses. Some Chinese universities provide undergraduate and postgraduate courses that are conducted in the English language which have no requirements of Chinese language.

Applying for a Chinese Government scholarship

To apply for a Chinese Government Scholarship you will need to make an application with the China Scholarship Council http://www.csc.edu.cn/Laihua/ or Campus China http://www.campuschina.org/

Studying in Japan

Tuition fees for higher education in Japan for foreign students will vary depending on the university but are generally less than those charged at UK, Australian or USA universities.
Further information may be found at Study in Japan http://www.studyjapan.go.jp/en/ . Further information on finance and scholarships may be found at Gateway to study in Japan http://www.g-studyinjapan.jasso.go.jp/en/

Japanese MEXT scholarship programme

The Japanese Ministry of Education, Culture, Sports, Science and Technology (MEXT) Scholarship Programme provides funding to outstanding British graduates who wish to study at Japanese universities. The scholarship programme is for a period of 18 months to 2 years and awarded to UK graduates who wish to pursue independent research or enrol on a postgraduate course at a Japanese university. For eligibility criteria, application details and further information check the Embassy of Japan in the UK: Study http://www.uk.emb-japan.go.jp/itpr_en/study.html

The Japan Society for the Promotion of Science (JSPS) postdoctoral fellowship programme

The Japan Society for the Promotion of Science (JSPS) Postdoctoral Fellowship Programme http://www.britac.ac.uk/jsps-postdoctoral-fellowship-programme-overseas-researchers funds overseas researchers who are early career postdoctoral researchers wishing to conduct research in Japan with leading research groups in Japanese universities and other institutions under the guidance of a host. The British Academy is an overseas nomination authority or this scheme and nominates a designated number of candidates each year. Applications for the JSPS Postdoctoral Fellowship Programme must be submitted online using the British Academy's electronic Grant Application and Processing (eGAP) system https://egap.britac.ac.uk/Login.aspx , meeting the advised deadlines.

Applications may also be made independently of the British Academy by an open recruitment route through host researchers in Japan.

The Daiwa Anglo-Japanese Foundation

The Daiwa Anglo-Japanese Foundation http://www.dajf.org.uk/ is a UK charity which supports closer links between Britain and Japan, providing grants to promote links and scholarships to British graduates to study Japan and its language.

Further information on Daiwa Scholarships and the application procedure may be found at the Daiwa Anglo-Japanese Foundation http://www.dajf.org.uk/scholarships/daiwa-scholarship and Daiwa Anglo-Japanese Foundation http://www.dajf.org.uk/scholarships/japanese-studies

9.6   Studying Worldwide Funding Schemes and Scholarships

International Association for the Exchange of Students for Technical Experience (IASTE)

The International Association for the exchange of Students for Technical Experience (IASTE) https://iaeste.org/ provides work experience placements for students on technical courses in over 80 countries worldwide giving you the opportunity to gain experiences of other cultures and create links with other countries. Placements usually last between 8-12 weeks usually during the summer but longer term placements are available throughout the year. Working overseas may help you to stand out from others when competing for jobs. English is the standard language required and other languages are mostly optional but check on the job specifications.

Costs

You will need to pay for an initial fee to IAESTE; your flights or other travel to and from the country; visa and vaccination costs; as well as additional spending money. You will earn a salary while you are on your placement which should cover

your accommodation and living costs. IAESTE students undertaking a placement in the EU may also be eligible for an Erasmus grant Go to: 9.3

Erasmus: Study and Work Experience Programme in another European Country

Chapter 12.6 Erasmus Funding Support for Undergraduate and Postgraduate Students

Engineering students being nominated for a work placement in the automotive industry can apply for a student travel Bursary from FISITA (Federation Internationale des Societes d'Ingenieurs des Techniques de L'Automobile) FISITA http://www.fisita.com/yfia/academia-industry/travelbursary . IASTE is open to degree level students over the age of 19 years studying science, engineering, technology and applied arts students in the second year of study and above. The majority of traineeships take place in the summer months, although longer periods are available.

For students applying from the UK, you need to be a UK resident (an EEA national or a non-EU national with British Citizenship verification).
Overseas students will need to visit the IAESTE global site for further information IAESTE http://www.iaeste.org/students/

Applying for the UK IASTE scheme
You will need to complete an online application form on the British Council IASTE website http://www.britishcouncil.org/iaeste and applications open in September. You will need to apply by the advised deadline and include a 300 word personal statement as well as a CV.

BUTEX Scholarships
BUTEX works with a number of UK universities, colleges and other higher education institutions who have a shared interest in learning abroad, awarding a number of £500 scholarships to students studying abroad for either a semester or for one academic year at a BUTEX affiliated institution. The scholarship is paid to students who are selected once they have arrived and registered at their host university. The scholarship is open to all undergraduate students who are affiliated to a BUTEX full member institution and may be affiliated as an incoming or outgoing study abroad student providing you meet the eligibility criteria. A list of full member institutions may be found at BUTEX list of members http://www.butex.ac.uk/members/list-of-members/
Further information may be found at BUTEX http://www.butex.ac.uk/scholarships/are-you-eligible/

International Student Exchange Programme (ISEP)
The International Student Exchange Programme (ISEP) works in partnership with more than 300 universities in 56 countries. You may be eligible for an ISEP Community Scholarship if you are attending an ISEP member university and meet the eligibility criteria. For further information see ISEP https://www.isepstudyabroad.org/

Leverhulme Trust
The Leverhulme Trust https://www.leverhulme.ac.uk/ provides funding to cover maintenance and research expenses for eligible applicants who hold an undergraduate degree or a further degree, to spend a period of 12 to 24 months on advanced study or research at a centre of learning in any overseas country (excluding the USA). Further information about studentships may be found at:
The Leverhulme Trust: Studentships https://www.leverhulme.ac.uk/funding/grant-schemes/study-abroad-studentships

Universities Partnered with Santander
A number of UK universities have funding to support students with educational international opportunities abroad. Santander is working with certain UK universities with mobility funding packages. Further information and a list of participating universities may be found at Santander http://www.santander.co.uk/uk/santander-universities/about-us/our-partner-universities

UNESCO Fellowships Bank Schemes
The United Nations Educational, Scientific and Cultural Organisation (UNESCO) is a global scholarship scheme which provides the UNESCO Co-Sponsored Fellowship Scheme programmes to give qualified people practicing or intending to practice a profession in the field of the UNESCO programme priorities an opportunity to receive additional and practical training abroad. UNESCO has partnerships with governments, higher education institutions and foundations so as to increase training in other Member States. Under the scheme, Member States, foundations, institutions and Private donors may offer fellowships in field within UNESCO's competence. Fellowship programmes on Education; Natural Sciences; Social and Human Sciences; Culture; Communication and Information. Applications must be made through and endorsed by the National Commission for UNESCO of the candidate's country http://www.unesco.org/new/en/fellowships/programmes/how-to-apply/

Chapter 10
International Student Advice

10.1 Information and Advice for International Students

UK universities and colleges have a long tradition of welcoming students from all over the world. This diversity has helped to create a dynamic environment, culturally, socially and academically, and there are many positive reasons why international students want to study in the UK.

As an international student, there are lots of aspects that you will need to consider before you come to the UK and this chapter highlights the key issues for international students and where you can find further information from a number of sources, details of which can be found at the end of this chapter.

In the UK, there are different regulations for students who are resident in the UK (home), EU and those who are resident from outside the EU (Overseas / International).

If you are resident in a country outside of the UK that isn't in the European Economic Area or Switzerland, and you want to come to study in the UK, you will need to apply for a Student Visa. You will usually need to apply online. When the UK leaves the EU in 2019, there may be changes in relation to conditions for students resident in the EU / EEA.

The UK Council for International Student Affairs (UKCISA) is the UK's national advisory body serving the interests of international students and the people who work with them.

You can find information about preparation and planning your studies, when you arrive, fees and finance, study and work. If you are unsure about your student status and need to confirm, you should consult the UK Council for International Student Affairs UKCISA website http://www.ukcisa.org.uk/

There may be a set number of places for international students for some courses at publicly funded universities and colleges, although the situation may be different at privately funded education institutions.

Some nursing and health related courses require you to meet eligibility criteria in order to be accepted on the course and you may not be eligible for these types of courses as an international student.

Therefore, it is always advisable to check your eligibility for specific courses if you are unsure with individual universities and colleges before you make an application.

To help you decide where to study, every university and college publishes information on their websites and in their prospectuses. Information includes entry requirements, English language requirements, course details, university or college facilities, tuition fees, student accommodation and student support services as well as additional information. Usually a copy of the prospectus may be downloaded from the individual website or may be requested and sent to you.

The British Council Education UK is the official website for international students who are interested in studying in the UK. This website contains lots of useful information about all aspects of studying in the UK, including studying in higher education
The British Council Education UK
http://www.educationuk.org/global/

If you are applying for undergraduate courses or for some foundation courses, as a full time student, you will need to apply through the University and College Central Admissions Service UCAS which is the central organisation that processes applications for UK Universities and Colleges. You can find a list of universities and colleges on the University and College Admissions Service UCAS website https://www.ucas.com/ , as well as in this book in the chapter:
Chapter 5:
Higher Education Qualification Subjects and Courses

It will take time to exchange essential papers, validate qualifications and to obtain, where appropriate, visas and other travel documents, so it is important to apply well in advance of when the course starts. You should get your application in for the deadline of 15th January for most courses, except for the University of Cambridge or the University of Oxford and for certain universities if you are applying for medicine, dentistry or veterinary courses, where the application must be in by 15th October.

You would be advised to meet the UCAS deadlines but you may still be able to apply after 15th January for some courses, except those with the 15th October deadline, although competitive entry courses will usually be filled early on.

There may also be earlier application deadlines for applicants wishing to be interviewed overseas, although many courses may not require you to have an interview, details will be on the relevant university or college websites. You will usually be able to choose up to 5 course choices, except for medicine, dentistry and veterinary medicine for which you may only choose 4 courses with a 5th in a different subject. For further information check the chapter:
Chapter 8
Applying for Higher Education Courses

You will need to complete your application and write a 'personal statement' therefore you should check the chapter:
Chapter 8.3
Writing your Application for an Undergraduate Course

When applying to universities or colleges, you may wish to consider financial factors such as living expenses, tuition fees and the cost of accommodation as these will vary between the education institutions and where you will be based in the UK.

If you are an international student, you will need to have achieved qualifications which are equivalent to the UK qualifications required for entry to the higher education course you want to apply for, and these will need to be checked by your chosen university or college to make sure they meet the required standard for entry for the course of your choice.

Many overseas certificates and diplomas will be recognised for higher education courses, although entry requirements will vary between courses and universities and colleges. Information about entry requirements, as well as in some cases country specific information about qualifications for international students, will be available on each higher education institution website and in their prospectus.

Each university or college will set their own entry requirements for higher education courses and if you are unsure you should contact the international office or admissions department to confirm. Many higher education institutions (HEIs) websites will have a department especially for international students.

10.4 Validating your Qualifications

If you need advice on the validity of your qualifications it is always advisable that you contact the HEI admissions department for further information first but you may need confirmation from the National Academic Recognition Information Centre (NARIC) https://www.naric.org.uk/ .

NARIC is the National UK Agency responsible for providing information, advice and expert opinion on qualifications worldwide and will provide you with information about how your qualifications compare with equivalent UK qualifications. NARIC usually charge a fee for the service for sending you official documentation with equivalency statements. However, most HEIs will be registered with NARIC or have their own institution guidelines and may be able to advise you accordingly, so check with the university or college first.

For further information about the National Academic Recognition Information Centres (NARIC) http://www.enic-naric.net/ or http://www.ecctis.co.uk/naric/ see:
Chapter 5.2
Undergraduate Courses and University Entry Requirements
National Academic Recognition Information Centre (NARIC)

10.5 English Language Requirements

If your first language is not English, you will be required to produce evidence of your English language proficiency in addition to the academic entry requirements for higher education courses in the UK.

For students from the EU, a high grade in English taken as part of a leaving examination such as the European / French Baccalaureate or Abitur, may be accepted.

For international students, you will need to meet both the Home Office rules and the English language requirements set by universities and colleges in the UK, requirements will vary between courses and HEIs, so check this information on the relevant HEI website in advance of applying.

The Home Office regulations require all students entering into the UK with a Tier 4 visa, to reach a minimum standard in English.

If you need a Tier 4 visa, you will need to meet both the Home Office requirements and the specific entry requirements of the course you have applied to study.

Further information about Tier 4 visas may be found on the:
UK Government website
https://www.gov.uk/tier-4-general-visa
The Home Office regulations state that if you are applying to study at degree level, you must have achieved the required standard of B2 level in speaking, reading, writing and listening.

For information about the levels, which are set by the Common European Framework of Reference for Languages: Learning, Teaching, Assessment (CEFR), check the Council of Europe: CEFR Languages:
https://www.coe.int/en/web/common-european-framework-reference-languages/

The CEFR describes foreign language proficiency at six levels: A1 and A2 (elementary); B1 and B2; C1 and C2 (mastery). It also defines three plus levels A2+, B1+, B2+. These levels make it possible to compare tests and examinations across languages and national boundaries.

The Home Office has set requirements for English language tests and you will need to undertake a Secure English Language Test (SELT) for a Tier 4 student visa.

A PDF list of the SELT tests approved by UK Visas and Immigration may be found at UK Government: Approved English Language Tests https://www.gov.uk/government/publications/guidance-on-applying-for-uk-visa-approved-english-language-tests

Some universities and colleges may provide pre-sessional English language courses for students who need to improve their English language skills and some provide International Foundation courses, which also include English language teaching.

These courses will be prior to your undergraduate or postgraduate studies and will enable you to develop your English language skills to the required standard. Some courses last for one academic year and others are for shorter periods. Your university or college will be able to advise you about these courses.

The Secure English Language Tests include Integrated Skills in English and the International English Language Testing System (IELTS) http://www.ielts.org/ . IELTS is recognised worldwide by many organisations including higher education institutions, employers, professional bodies and government agencies.

IELTS Scores

The IELTS Test Report Form reports a score for your performance for each of the four skills: listening, reading, writing and speaking, as well as an Overall Band Score. Half band scores may also be awarded which indicates a strong performance within a particular band.

IELTS is designed to assess English language skills at all levels with band scores from 1 (the lowest) to 9 (the highest) and half scores may also be used e.g. 6.5. The IELTS score requirement varies between courses and higher education institutions with ranges from 4.0 to 7.0, although for entry to degrees and postgraduate courses, generally many HEIs require levels of 6.0, to 7.5. HEIs will publish the English language level requirements on their websites. IELTS scores are valid for two years and organisations won't usually accept a Test Report Form that is more than two years old unless you are able to provide evidence that you have actively maintained or improved your English since taking the test.

IELTS Scores Chart

1	2	3	4	5	6	7	8	9
Non user	Intermittent user	Extremely limited user	Limited user	Modest user	Competent user	Good user	Very good user	Expert user

For many courses, you won't need an interview but if admission for your course is by interview, as an international student you may be required to speak to an academic adviser over the telephone to discuss your application. You may then receive a conditional offer which will convert to an unconditional offer when your qualifications have been verified. Further information may be found in the chapter on
Chapter 8.5
Interviews and Auditions

10.7 Student Visas

International students studying in the UK

If you are resident in a country outside of the UK that isn't in the European Economic Area or Switzerland, and you want to come to study in the UK you will need to apply for a Student Visa before coming to the UK to study and there are a number of conditions which you must satisfy the UK Government with. Changes are likely to take place in 2019 when the UK leaves the European Union. Depending on the course, you may need to apply for a Student Visitor Visa or a General Visa. You will usually need to apply online. You will also need to satisfy the English language requirements. The UK government Home Office provides further information about student visas at on the website https://www.gov.uk/government/organisations/uk-visas-and-immigration

You must have an unconditional offer of a full-time place on a course at your chosen higher education institution. UK immigration requires that courses for foreign students should have a minimum of 15 contact hours each week, and classed as a full-time course. You should try to ensure that you obtain a visa which covers the full period that you intend to stay in the UK otherwise you may need to pay an additional fee if you need to extend the period of time later. If you intend to travel to the UK via an airport in a third country, you may also need a Transit Visa. Everyone who arrives in the UK has to pass through Immigration Control and the rules of entry are strictly enforced therefore you will need to have obtained all the necessary information prior to leaving your home country. You may be allowed to work during your studies but not usually full-time, and you will need to demonstrate that you are financially able to meet the costs of your course which includes tuition fees, study costs for books and equipment as well as accommodation throughout your studies. You must also be able to prove your knowledge of the English language when you apply and this usually means passing a Secure English language Test (SELT), which is recognised by the UK Government. For a General Student Visa, you will need to satisfy the eligibility and required conditions as well as having been offered a place on a course. Check the UK Government: Tier-4 General Visa Requirements https://www.gov.uk/tier-4-general-visa . If you are applying do a short course in the UK, you will need a short term study visa. As these courses should provide English language tuition, your English language ability shouldn't need to be tested. Further information may be found at Student Visitor Visa: Short Term Study https://www.gov.uk/study-visit-visa

Documents you will need when applying for a student visa are:

- A valid passport
- Evidence of your educational qualifications
- A letter of acceptance and other documentation from the training establishment confirming tuition fees paid and (if applicable) the balance of fees due
- Documentation showing that you have sufficient funds to support your living expenses for the period of study/stay in the UK

Tuition fee costs will vary depending on what type of course you wish to study and which university or college where you want to study. All higher education institutions charge two different rates of tuition fees; Home / EU student rates and Overseas' student rates which is higher, as there are no Government subsidies given to universities for international students' education costs. If your course lasts more than one year, the fees you are charged in your second and later years will usually increase each year in line with inflation. Tuition fee rates for students who resident in the EU / EEA may change when the UK leaves the EU in 2019.

You may intend to study a foundation course before continuing on to top up to a full degree course. Foundation courses may vary in length, although many usually last for one academic year, with costs differing according to what type of course and university or college you want to attend.

Undergraduate tuition fees will vary, and likely to be higher at competitive entry universities and for competitive courses. Courses such as medicine are likely to be most expensive. Postgraduate tuition fees for international students will also vary with postgraduate certificates and diplomas usually costing less than a master's degree and with PhDs costing more.

Some universities and colleges may require you to pay your tuition fees in full at the start of your course each year and some may offer discounts if you pay the tuition fees in full before or during enrolment. There may also be options to pay in instalments, to spread your costs. Check with the relevant university or college regarding up to date information on fees.

To help you consider what you will need to budget for, the Brightside website provides international students with an interactive guide to living costs, as well as useful information and student profiles. Brightside is an independent education charity which aims to help students prepare for the financial side of UK higher education. Brightside International Student Calculator http://international.studentcalculator.org/

If you are resident in a country outside of the UK that isn't in the European Economic Area or Switzerland, and you want to come to work in the UK you will need to apply for a work permit. Changes are likely to take place in 2019 when the UK leaves the European Union. There are strict rules and therefore you should check the UK Government website for information

UK Government Work Visas
https://www.gov.uk/browse/visas-immigration/work-visas
The UK Visas and Immigration Service: Home Office
https://www.gov.uk/government/organisations/uk-visas-and-immigration
You should also check information and advice with the UK Council for International Student Affairs UKCISA
http://www.ukcisa.org.uk/

10.10 Scholarships and Bursaries

Scholarships may be available for some international students which will help to pay some or possibly all of your costs. Check on the British Council web site http://www.britishcouncil.org/ for more details. You may also be able to obtain funding from your country's Government Education Department. Individual universities and colleges may also provide funding initiatives for international students. Information should be available on the relevant university or college website. The following websites have information about scholarships for international students.

British Council
http://www.britishcouncil.org/
Chevening: UK Government Global Scholarship Programme
http://www.chevening.org/
Commonwealth Scholarship and Fellowship Plan (CSFP)
http://www.csfp-online.org/
Marshalls Scholarship: for US students in the UK
http://www.marshallscholarship.org/
Fulbright Commission: for US students in the UK
http://www.fulbright.org.uk/

10.11 International Student Advice

Banking
You will need to open a bank account in the UK and it is essential that you discuss in advance with your bank how you will transfer funds to your UK bank account. In order to open an account in the UK you will need your passport, confirmation of your local address and the original copy of the university or college letter accepting you as a student. You should also check on how much you will be able to bring with you in travellers' cheques and / or cash to cover your expenses for the start of your stay. Whilst there is no restriction on the amount of money that you can bring into the UK, you should check how much local currency you are allowed to take out of your own country as regulations may apply. If you intend to use a credit card, you may need to organise this with your own bank before your travel to the UK.

Accommodation for International Students
The university or college where you are studying should provide information about student accommodation. International undergraduate students who are studying for at least one full academic year are usually guaranteed accommodation organised by many universities providing your application is received sufficiently in advance. There may also be provision available to postgraduate international students. Always check the accommodation details on the relevant university or college website or by phone to confirm the details well in advance.

Experienced staff will be able to assist you and accommodation is generally available to you about a week before your course will start to allow you time to settle in. Most universities offer a free welcome service where you can make a reservation for someone to meet you at the airport and take you to your accommodation.
Be aware that if you are an international student and if you have paid your deposit and accepted the accommodation agreement you may be committed to the tenancy regardless of any visa issues which may arise, therefore check and confirm all the details well in advance. Courses will usually have an induction week at the start of a new course, so you will need to be prepared to be in the UK in time to attend.

Healthcare for International Students
You must make a payment for the healthcare surcharge, unless you are exempt, before you submit or send your visa or immigration application. Details are at the UK Government: Healthcare Immigration Application https://www.gov.uk/healthcare-immigration-application/pay .

It is also essential that you register with a Doctor (General Practitioner) in your local area as soon as possible after you arrive in the UK. Dental treatment may be expensive and it is advisable to have a check-up before you leave your own country and ensure you have adequate insurance to cover any treatment you might need during your stay in the UK.

Vaccinations
You may be required to have specified vaccinations before being able to enter the UK. You would need to arrange these with your medical practitioner before leaving your country.

Social Activities
Universities and colleges will usually arrange events which are designed to welcome new students from overseas, usually through the induction period. In addition during your studies, your university or college student union usually has a social and welfare role and will provide a range of social and sporting activities and events. Each university or college will usually have its own chaplaincy and will welcome students of all religions and none, providing a pastoral support for the student community. There will also be local facilities in the community for students to attend to practice their religion. HOST http://www.hostuk.org/ is a national organisation which arranges hospitality for overseas students and promotes international friendship and understanding by arranging for international students at British universities to meet UK residents in their houses.

Driving
Before you can drive in the UK, you must have a valid driving licence and evidence that you and your vehicle are roadworthy. In the UK, we drive on the left and you must observe 'the Highway Code' https://www.gov.uk/browse/driving/highway-code . If you need to take a driving test, a driving instructor will help you apply for your test date. Every car on the public road must display a tax disc as evidence that car tax has been paid, even if it is not driven, and this can be obtained from the post office on presentation of a current MOT certificate and valid insurance documents.

Further information can be found on the UK Government: Driver and Vehicle Licensing Agency https://www.gov.uk/government/organisations/driver-and-vehicle-licensing-agency

Public Transport
In London, the 'Oyster' card is used as a payment method for travelling on buses, tube trains, the docklands light railway (DLR), London over-ground and most national rail services in London. Oyster is a plastic smartcard which can hold pay as you go credit, travel-cards and transport season tickets. Other towns may have a similar payment system but will call the card by a different name. It may also be possible to use a 'contactless' debit bank card to pay for travel. You can purchase train tickets at stations, although a ticket for the underground may cost more in London if you don't use an Oyster card.

You can obtain an Oyster card from a range of places including London Travel Information Centres, Oyster Ticket Stops and Stations. If you live in the UK you may also obtain one from Oyster online.
For further information, check: Transport for London http://www.tfl.gov.uk/fares-and-payments/

Television Licence
It is also a legal requirement that if you own or rent a television, you must purchase a television licence. Further information may be found at TV licensing http://www.tvlicensing.co.uk/

International Student Advice and Status Regulations

British Council
http://www.britishcouncil.org/
The British Council Education UK
http://www.educationuk.org/global/
UK Council for International Student Affairs UKCISA http://www.ukcisa.org.uk/

Visa Information

The UK Visas and Immigration Service is part of the
UK's Home Office
https://www.gov.uk/government/organisati
ons/uk-visas-and-immigration
Student Visitor Visa: short term study
https://www.gov.uk/study-visit-visa
General Student Visa Tier 4 General Visa
https://www.gov.uk/tier-4-general-visa

International Student Scholarships and Bursaries

British Council
http://www.britishcouncil.org/
Chevening: UK Government Global Scholarship Programme
http://www.chevening.org/
Commonwealth Scholarship and Fellowship Plan (CSFP)
http://www.csfp-online.org/
Marshalls Scholarship: for US students in the UK
http://www.marshallscholarship.org/
Fulbright Commission: for US students in the UK
http://www.fulbright.org.uk/

University and College Admissions Service UCAS

University and College Admissions Service UCAS
https://www.ucas.com/

Qualification Information

National Academic Recognition Information Centre (NARIC)
https://www.naric.org.uk/ .

Council of Europe Common European Framework of Reference for Languages: Learning, Teaching, Assessment (CEFR)
http://www.coe.int/t/dg4/linguistic/cadre1_
en.asp

English Language Tests

International English Language Testing System (IELTS) http://www.ielts.org/
Secure English Language Test (SELT) for a Tier 4 student visa.
PDF list of the SELT tests approved by UK Visas and Immigration
https://www.gov.uk/government/publicatio
ns/guidance-on-applying-for-uk-visa-
approved-english-language-tests

International Student Finance Calculator

Brightside: International Student Calculator
http://international.studentcalculator.org/

International Student Healthcare

UK Government website
https://www.gov.uk/healthcare-
immigration-application/pay

Hospitality Information

HOST hospitality for overseas students
http://www.hostuk.org/

Driving

Highway Code
https://www.gov.uk/browse/driving/highwa
y-code
Driver and Vehicle Licensing Agency
https://www.gov.uk/government/organisati
ons/driver-and-vehicle-licensing-agency

Public Transport

Transport for London
http://www.tfl.gov.uk/fares-and-payments/

TV Licence

TV licensing
http://www.tvlicensing.co.uk/

Chapter 11
Student Accommodation

11.1. Student Accommodation

Settling Into Your Student Accommodation

Moving into your student accommodation is an exciting time and it may take a little while to feel settled but everyone will have similar feelings. Meeting and getting to know your hall, flat or house mates will give you the opportunity to make new friends; you may be able to share housing items such as saucepans and crockery. Attending the freshers' fair and joining clubs or societies will also give you the opportunity to meet like-minded people.

What to Bring With you

As well as your personal belongings and technology devices, you will need to have bedding to include a duvet, pillows, two or three sets of sheets, pillow cases and duvet covers; towels; clothes hangers; crockery; cutlery; mugs and glasses; and cooking equipment to include one or more saucepans, a frying pan, baking tray, casserole dish and sandwich toaster may also be useful, as well as cooking utensils. A laundry bag may also be helpful and you may wish to buy a clothes horse once you settle in, if not supplied. A smaller suitcase is useful in addition for when you travel home for the weekend or visit friends. You should have access to a kettle and toaster, but should confirm this. You will also need some food and basic cleaning products until you can go shopping as you won't know what shopping facilities will be until you explore the area. If you are travelling to your university by car you may have more room for your belongings than if you travel by train, but don't over-pack as you may not always have access to a car. You may want to bring stationery including an academic diary, paper and folders although you will be able to buy these from the student shop. One or more extension leads may be useful. Electronic devices and electronic chargers; USBs or external hard drive may be needed.

Consider that it may be possible for your computer or the university computers to 'crash' unexpectedly so always back up your work with an external hard drive, or sign up to online storage sites such as Cloud http://www.thecloud.net/ , Dropbox https://www.dropbox.com/ or Onedrive https://onedrive.live.com/about/en-gb/

Important documents you will need include ID such as your passport, a driving licence if you have passed your test, National Insurance card, NHS number or medical insurance and insurance documents for insured items such as electrical or musical instruments. Remember to bring financial documents relating to your student loan and it is also useful to have confirmation letters if you have been awarded a scholarship or bursary, as well as your bank card. It may be worth you getting a travel discount card such as a 16-25 railcard, an Oyster card for travelling in London or other city travel card when you arrive although you can also use a contactless bank card. You may want to bring some posters to go on the wall, although check the conditions regarding blue tack as when removed it may leave a mark on the wall which you may be charged for painting over from your deposit, white tack may leave less of a stain. Some photos of family and friends will help if you are missing them. Some board games and a pack of cards will help you break the ice with your flat or house mates and will be good when entertaining friends.

Click2Campus http://www.click2campus.com/index.html offers a facility for you to purchase a pack of essential items that include bedding and kitchen items which can be delivered to your university accommodation or a student reception area.

After applying for your higher education course and once you have contacted the student accommodation office, you will usually be categorised depending on the type of offer you hold for your course with the university or college (conditional or unconditional offer), eligibility criteria and the availability.

Universities and colleges may have different requirements, so check with the relevant institution about this and make sure you have information sent to you as an email or in writing.

Always check the accommodation details on the relevant university or college website or by phone to confirm the details well in advance of you starting your course.

If you meet the eligibility criteria and hold a conditional firm or unconditional firm offer, when you are eligible to apply for a place in student halls, the university accommodation office should send you an email containing the details of how to apply.

Some universities ask you to apply as soon as you have read this information, not waiting until your course offer is unconditional, although will only allocate a room once your offer becomes unconditional; other universities may only accept your application when you have met all the conditions for a conditional offer and after accepting your offer of a course on UCAS Track.

If you have an unconditional offer and accept your place, you should be able to apply for student accommodation immediately the application for student accommodation opens.

You will need to complete an application which is usually made on line and returned by the required deadline to ensure you get your desired place.

There may be a last date for applications to arrive which may be before your exam results come out therefore you should check all the information carefully well in advance of advised deadlines which will be advertised on the university website.

You may be asked to put your accommodation choice in order of preference, although there is no guarantee you will get your first choice. There may also be more applications than places, meaning you should apply as soon as possible.

International students: how to apply for university student accommodation
If you are an international student you should make sure you meet all the visa entry requirements as once you have paid your deposit and accepted the accommodation agreement you may be committed to the tenancy regardless of any visa issues which may arise afterwards.

If you are arriving in the country before the date shown on your agreement contract you will usually need to find alternative accommodation until your contract start date, but should confirm with the university accommodation office.

11.3 Deciding Where to Live Whilst Studying

Starting a higher education course is an exciting time and deciding on where you are going to live is a big decision, so you want to make sure of all your options. If your university is near to your family home, you may decide to continue living at home, but if your university is further away or if you want to move away from home, you may decide to move into student accommodation which may be part of the university or you may decide to rent in the private rented sector.

If moving away from home, it is important to be aware of your options, rights and responsibilities before making any decisions. Accommodation costs can be expensive and rental costs will vary depending on what part of the UK you are studying. Living away from home, you will also need to manage a budget for costs for rents, bills and food.

University Priority for Student Accommodation

Each university or college will have their own eligibility conditions but in many cases, priority for university student accommodation in halls of residence, abbreviated to 'halls' is given to students in the first year of their studies and students with disabilities.

Postgraduate students may also be considered as well as international students who meet the specified conditions. However some universities may not have enough accommodation for all first year students and will allocate rooms to those who are eligible and apply first.

It may be possible for students in other years to rent rooms in halls if there are sufficient rooms with vacancies, and some universities provide the option of student accommodation for all undergraduates for at least three years, although most undergraduates starting the second year of their courses will need to find student accommodation in the private rented sector.

If you aren't allocated a place in halls by your university, check if they will provide help with finding private accommodation and if they have property lists or information about accredited landlords and letting agents in the area.

Living at Home with your Family

If you decide to live at your family home whilst studying in higher education, this will be a cheaper option than renting university or private student accommodation, although you may be expected to pay a contribution to the family household expenses. It will also mean that you don't have to search for accommodation, pack up your belongings and relocate, and may not need to think so much about rent and money issues, cooking, cleaning and laundry.

You will also get the opportunity to socialise with other students on your course or through student union activities, although may need to make more effort. However, being under your parents' roof may mean that you have less independence than moving away.

Living in University or College Student Accommodation

Student accommodation may be owned and managed by a university or college; owned and managed in partnership with a private company; or solely owned and managed by a private company. University student accommodation is commonly known as halls of residence, abbreviated to 'halls'. If you live in student accommodation provided by a university or college, you will be an' Occupier with Basic Protection'. Universities that provide halls of residence must belong to a government approved code or be licensed by the local authority.

The codes ensure you have safe and good quality accommodation and provide a way of dealing with issues if something isn't right in your accommodation.

The codes set out the standards to measure the good management practice of student accommodation for repairs and maintenance, fire gas and electrical safety, security, management of your tenancy/licence and complaints.

For halls of residence managed by universities or colleges, your university will have signed up for a code of practice with either of the following:

- Universities UK / Guild HE Code of Practice for the Management of Student Housing often known as the Student Accommodation Code http://www.universitiesuk.ac.uk/

- Accreditation Network UK (ANUK) / Unipol code of Standards for Larger Residential Developments for student accommodation managed and controlled by education establishments. http://www.nationalcode.org/

For halls of residence owned and managed by private companies, the company will have signed up for a code of practice with:
- ANUK / Unipol Code of Standards for Larger Developments not managed and controlled by educational establishments. http://www.nationalcode.org/

University Run Halls of Residence

Many universities will have student accommodation based on the university campus or nearby which means you will be within easy walking or cycling distance of the university departments and facilities. Universities will have information about student housing on their website which you should check when you decide to apply for a course.

If you will be living away from home for the first time, living in halls will give you the opportunity to make new friends and you won't need to travel far to attend lectures or social events in the university. Your student accommodation rent also usually includes costs for utilities such as gas and electricity use so you won't need to think about budgeting for bills and any repairs will be carried out through the accommodation department. You will also be able to get extra support from your university should you need it.

University student accommodation facilities
University student accommodation will usually consist of a series of flats or houses with your own bedroom, although a small number have shared room

options, and have access to a shared kitchen/ living / laundry area and bathroom, with some rooms having en-suite facilities. The size of the flat or house may vary but usually there are options for between three to eight students per residence. Some universities also provide studio flats. Accommodation costs will vary depending on the size of the flat or house and types of facilities, with en-suite rooms costing more than standard rooms and studio flats usually costing more than flats housing more students. Usually you will be expected to supply your own bed linen and towels as well as cooking utensils, crockery and cutlery.

Although you can request your preferred type of accommodation, there is no guarantee you will be offered your first choice. Some university accommodation staff may try to match you with compatible flat or roommates based on your course subject or with people who live near to where you normally live. However many university accommodation staff will allocate students to rooms randomly and this will be a good opportunity to meet new people.

University student accommodation catering facilities

University student accommodation may provide the option of being 'catered', 'part-catered' or 'self-catered'. Self-catered provides you with the option to cater for yourself with access to a shared kitchen and you can choose to buy cafeteria style meals in cafes or restaurants based in the university. Catered student accommodation gives you the option of being half-board or full-board with breakfast, lunch or dinner being provided in the cost of the accommodation.

Students with disabilities

Universities and colleges may have rooms that are designed especially for students with disabilities or special needs. It is important to inform the accommodation organisation about the kind of disability or special need you have so that your application can be prioritised.

Rental costs

You will usually be charged rent for the weeks of the academic year you are enrolled as a student which may not include the summer vacation (unlike most privately rented student accommodation), therefore for those courses which are of a shorter duration, the accommodation costs may be lower.

Living in Private Rented Student Accommodation

The main types of privately rented accommodation for students are private halls of residence; flats or houses, usually shared with others, let by a private landlord or a lettings agent; or a room in the same property as the landlord. Sometimes a university accommodation office may manage private flats and houses and would be seen as your landlord.

You may prefer to live in privately rented student accommodation and it may be the case for students entering the second year of their studies, aren't guaranteed university halls and need look elsewhere to live. Living in privately rented accommodation may give you the option to choose who you share with and what area you want to live.

Living in privately run student halls of residence

Some universities have access to privately run student halls of residence which is similar to university halls but owned by a private company.

Private halls of residence may not be linked to a specific university but some are purpose built as student accommodation and run as commercial enterprises whereas others are run as charitable

trusts and will have specific eligibility requirements. You may be further away from the university facilities but you may be better situated near to shops and entertainment venues.

Universities will have an approved list of such accommodation which should abide by a voluntary code relating to health and safety, maintenance and repair and the relationship between managers and student tenants.

Further information may be found about privately run halls of residence on the National Code http://www.nationalcode.org/

Rental costs

Usually you will have an assured shorthold tenancy if you are a student in private halls of residence, fixed for 50 or 51 weeks, although some may be for shorter periods.

Your accommodation rent usually includes utility bills, but you should confirm this. Most facilities include a self-catering option but you should check this as well as confirming what communal areas are on site such as shared kitchens and laundry facilities.

Renting a Privately Owned Flat or House With Landlords and Letting Agents

Private rented student accommodation properties may be let by agencies, which help to find tenants for properties, or directly with the landlord. Some universities may also manage flats and houses owned by private landlords.

Universities and colleges should have lists of accredited properties offered by private landlords or agencies and can give you advice on private tenancy agreements. Although voluntary, private landlords may sign up to an accreditation scheme which means being certified to meet an agreed standard. Different schemes exist in the UK countries. Some schemes allow for either the properties or the landlord to be accredited therefore you should confirm that properties have been inspected. It is advisable to rent properties which are advertised through the university accommodation department.

For competitive rental areas, you may need to start looking for a flat or house to rent from January onwards for moving in the following September. Spend some time deciding on who you want to share with and what area you will be looking in.

Rental costs

As well as rental costs, you will need to pay for utility bills as additional costs every month in addition. Depending on the tenancy agreement, you may have to pay for rent for a full calendar year, even if you decide not to live there during the university vacations.

Letting Agents and Landlords Accreditation Scheme

Letting agents and landlords aren't regulated which means that anyone can trade as a letting agent or a landlord without any qualifications or a licence. Therefore it is advisable to use a lettings agent or landlord that has signed up to a voluntary accreditation scheme, agreeing to defined standards, such as the National Approved Letting Scheme (NALS) http://www.nalscheme.co.uk/ . The national approved letting scheme is an independent licensing scheme for lettings and management agents. Members of NALS have agreed to meet defined standards of customer service, are part of a client money protection scheme and have a customer complaints procedure offering independent redress.

Some lettings agents are members of a self-regulating body. Lettings agents and landlords that are part of one of these schemes or organisations have agreed to meet certain standards and signed up to a private rented sector code of practice, which sets out legal requirements of agents. A copy of the code of practice is available at the Royal Institution of Chartered Surveyors http://www.rics.org/uk/ .

Lettings agents that have the Safe Agent registered mark indicate that they protect your money through a client money protection scheme. Landlords or lettings agents may display the schemes logo on their websites, on property adverts or in their offices and you can check the websites for a list of members.

Self-regulating organisations include:
- Association of Residential Lettings Agents
  http://www.arla.co.uk/
- National Approved Letting Scheme, (NALS) https://www.nalscheme.co.uk/
- National Landlords Association
  http://www.landlords.org.uk/
- Residential Landlords Associationhttp://www.rla.org.uk/
- Royal Institution of Chartered Surveyors
  http://www.rics.org/uk/
- UK Association of Letting Agents
  http://www.ukala.org.uk/

There are many different local and national accreditation schemes that may also be run by:
- Universities or student unions
- Local councils
  https://www.gov.uk/find-your-local-council
- Unipol: the student housing charity
  https://www.unipol.org.uk/

Unipol provides accommodation to students in Leeds, Nottingham and Bradford with properties either owned by Unipol directly or leased under a number of partnerships with local housing associations, local authorities and private companies, with properties meeting the Unipol code of the National Code for larger developments. In England, Wales and Scotland, letting agents are also legally required to be a member of one of three government approved redress schemes for dealing with complaints about letting private rented accommodation. If you have a complaint which hasn't been resolved using the agent's own complaints procedure, you can complain to the scheme that the agent belongs to.

Letting agency redress schemes:
The Property Ombudsman
https://www.tpos.co.uk/
The Property Redress Scheme
https://www.theprs.co.uk/
The Ombudsman Services
http://www.ombudsman-services.org/

If a property is let to several tenants who aren't members of the same family it may be a House in Multiple Occupation (HMO) and landlords will need an HMO licence https://www.gov.uk/house-in-multiple-occupation-licence . A household consists of either a single person or members of the same family who live together. A property may be an HMO if both of the following apply: at least 3 tenants live there forming more than one household and the toilet, bathroom or kitchen facilities are shared.

Lodging in your Landlords' Home

If you decide to rent a room in your landlords' home, sharing some rooms such as a kitchen and bathroom, you would be known as a lodger. A lodger doesn't have exclusive possession of a room and the landlord can enter the room without the lodger's permission. A lodger may also receive other services as part of the accommodation such as meals and cleaning.

Your landlord might own the property or may be a tenant themselves, renting a room to you. In either case, you would be known as an excluded occupier provided you share some of the accommodation with your landlord; and your landlord is occupying the accommodation as their only or principal home at the time your agreement begins and at the time it ends.

Landlords Housing Responsibilities, Maintenance and Repairs

Landlords are required to keep rented properties safe, in good condition and free from health hazards; ensure that all gas and electrical equipment is safely installed and maintained, provide an energy performance certificate for the property and protect tenants' deposits in a government approved scheme. Landlords are responsible for repairs to the structure of the property; basins, sinks, baths and other sanitary fittings; heating and hot water systems. They are also responsible for fitting and testing smoke alarms and carbon monoxide alarms; following fire safety regulations for properties in blocks of flats or houses adapted into flats. You should also have an annual gas check and you should confirm with the landlord about arranging this. The accommodation should

be cleaned before you move in and all the tenants also have responsibilities to ensure the property is cleaned whilst you are living there. The Housing, Health and Safety Rating System (HHSRS) https://www.gov.uk/government/publications/housing-health-and-safety-rating-system-guidance-for-landlords-and-property-related-professionals is used by councils to ensure that properties are safe for people who live there and may inspect a property if needed. If your landlord doesn't make repairs to remove hazards, you can ask the council to inspect the property under the HHSRS and the council will take any action that is necessary. If serious hazards are found, the council must take enforcement action to ensure the hazard is removed.

When you sign a tenancy or licence agreement you enter a legal contract which is ended properly when you move out. If you live in university student residential halls, you will usually be given a hall licence for the duration of the time you are resident. If you are renting privately shared accommodation you will usually be on a tenancy. The tenancy arrangements will vary and you should check the type of tenancy you have before you agree and sign a contract. Your rights and responsibilities will vary depending on whether you have joint or sole tenancy or whether you have a tenant as your resident landlord.

If you have joint tenancy, this a tenancy agreement which each student in the property signs; with sole tenancy, each student in the property has their own tenancy agreement; or with sole tenancy, it may be possible, if it is allowed, for the one student to have sole tenancy and then sub-let rooms separately to other students as sub-tenants or as lodgers.

The information given to you about your licence or tenancy should include the date it began, the date of when the rent is due and when it must be paid, how and when the rent can be changed and the length of any fixed term. It should also contain information relating to returning of your deposit at the end of the tenancy and you should check what the terms and conditions are.

You must be given a copy of the licence or tenancy agreement before you move in and always read the details, checking it carefully before signing. In England and Wales, your landlord must provide a name and address where you can contact them. If it doesn't include all of the required information you should ask for it in writing

as your landlord must respond within 28 days.

Licence agreement for students in university halls of residence

If you are in university or college accommodation, you may be on a 'license' instead of a tenancy, so check the details of the agreement with the institution regarding the terms relating to your deposit. By paying your accommodation deposit and prepayment as well as accepting the agreement, you may be committed to the tenancy.

Most students in halls of residence will have a fixed term agreement, which means you have agreed to rent your accommodation for a certain period of time which is usually the academic year, although there may be shorter periods for courses lasting fewer weeks. In halls of residence you would usually move out on the day that the fixed term agreement ends without having to give notice to your landlord.

You can only end the agreement early if there is a term in your agreement known as a break clause or your landlord agrees to you ending the agreement early called surrender. If you leave before the end of the fixed term without your landlord's consent you are liable to pay the rent until the fixed term ends even if you aren't living there.

Although not common, you may have a periodic agreement, for example month to month, whereby you will be expected to give notice to end the periodic agreement in writing, keeping a copy, for the required period of time. The codes that universities sign up to say that deposits should returned within 28 days of your agreement ending.

Rental costs will vary according to the type of accommodation provided and where about in the country you will be living, with London being the most expensive area. You will usually be charged for a full calendar year for privately rented accommodation whereas the cost of university halls of residence may vary depending on how many weeks you are charged for with some requiring rent for 51 weeks and other charging rental costs for an academic year for the duration of your course. Therefore in some cases university halls of residence may be a cheaper option than private rented accommodation.

University halls of residence rental costs

The costs for university halls of residence accommodation will vary depending on what is available. A standard room will be the cheapest option, en-suite rooms may cost more, with studio flats for one or two people likely to cost more than shared accommodation for more students. Some universities rent out houses and will charge for the cost of the house with students sharing the rent. If you opt for catered or part-catered facilities, you will be charged a higher rate to cover the cost of food.

If you live in student accommodation organised through your university or college, you may be charged rent for the deemed number of weeks for an academic year for the duration of the course, although some will charge you for a full calendar year or 51 weeks to allow for cleaning. The undergraduate course duration for the academic year will vary depending on the course and university, with some lasting for 30 weeks and others lasting up to 40 weeks. Nursing courses may last for 48 weeks and postgraduate courses may last up to 50 weeks. Therefore courses that last for 30 weeks may allow for cheaper annual rent compared with courses that last for longer. You may need to pay a higher amount of rent for professional nursing courses and postgraduate courses which have a longer

academic year than undergraduate courses. Students in halls of residence don't usually have to pay for utility bills for gas and electricity for heating, lighting, and use of electrical items, Wi-Fi and water or council tax; with costs usually included in the price of the accommodation rent. Universities that provide halls of residence are required to belong to a 'code of standards' (see above).

Private accommodation rental costs

If you rent student accommodation from the private sector, you will usually be charged for up to a full calendar year, even if you won't be living there during the vacation period. You will also have to pay in addition for utility bills for heating, lighting and water, as well as council tax. Therefore you may find you will be paying more for private accommodation than you would in university halls of residence.

Using a guarantor

Most private landlords will require a third party, such as a parent or close relative, to act as a guarantor for the rent payments if you don't pay them, before they will agree to let a property to a student. A guarantee agreement may also extend to other conditions under the tenancy such as any damage caused to the property. There is a legal requirement for a guarantee agreement to be in writing and sets out the guarantor's legal obligation, therefore it is important that the guarantor checks the tenancy agreement to see what obligations they are guaranteeing and when the guarantor's liability ends, for as soon as it is signed, the guarantor is bound by its terms and conditions. Your landlord can take legal action to recover any unpaid rent from your guarantor. If you share accommodation with other tenants under one tenancy agreement, a joint tenancy, it is usual for one guarantee to apply to all of the rent and not just your share, although it may be possible to negotiate a variation and provide additional guarantor/s.

When to pay your rent for university halls of residence

Universities will advertise accommodation rental costs on the website and may provide information on what it will cost you for one week, one calendar month, termly and/ or annually. Rental fees for accommodation in a university or private halls of residence is often due at the start of each term to coincide with your student loan instalments, however there may be other options to pay and it may be the case if you pay for the full amount for the annual rental fees at the start of your course, some universities may offer you a discount.

When to pay your rent for privately rented accommodation

Rent for privately owned flats or houses may usually be paid monthly, although your contract may state that you will need to pay monthly for the property for a full calendar year, even if you won't be there during the vacations. It may be usual for rental costs to be paid from one person's bank account and therefore it is important that all the flat/house mates have an agreement to pay the correct proportion of the costs. It is helpful to have a written agreement, even if you are all the best of friends.

11.6 Moving in to Your Student Accommodation

Security Deposits and Advance Rent Payments Costs

Your contract will begin on the date shown on your accommodation agreement and you will be unlikely to move in before to this date. Before you move into your accommodation, you will need to be prepared to pay an amount of money for a security deposit usually equivalent to one month's rent as well as an additional month's rent in advance. If using a lettings agent you may need to pay a room or property booking fee which is non-refundable. Always get a written receipt which should include the landlord's name and address for the money you have paid for your deposit, rent pre-payment and booking fee.

In privately rented accommodation, when a deposit is taken for an assured shorthold tenancy the money must be paid into a deposit scheme approved by the UK government https://www.gov.uk/deposit-protection-schemes-and-landlords/overview . You must be provided with details of the scheme and this allows you to be paid back as much of your deposit as you are entitled to at the end of the tenancy, or provides an alternative dispute resolution service that can be used if there is a disagreement about the deposit. You will also usually be required to pay one month's rent in advance in addition to the security deposit but should

confirm in advance when the next rent payment will be due.

Accommodation places will only be secured after the university / college, lettings agent or landlord, receive this amount of money. The security deposit should be returned to you at the end of your licence or tenancy when you vacate your room / flat / house, providing the property is left in a clean and undamaged state and there is no outstanding rent for the property when you leave.

Agencies and landlords may prefer a deposit in the name of one of the tenants, if sharing with others. If this is the case, make sure your flat / house mates pay the correct proportion into the relevant person's bank account. Again it is helpful to have a written agreement, even if you are all the best of friends.

Always read the details of the tenancy agreement before you sign it. If you are moving into private rented accommodation, hopefully you won't encounter any problems with your landlord but it is usual to agree an inventory with your landlord when you move in so they can't claim for any damage that might have been done before you moved in.

Inform them to any outstanding repairs or damage by the previous tenants by marking the inventory and sending information in a letter or by email (always keep a copy). If you make changes to the inventory, ensure you and the landlord signs and dates that they agree with these changes. Hopefully you won't incur any problems but it is always useful to be prepared.

It is a good idea to take photographs of your room / flat / house as you move in as evidence of the condition of the property for when you move in and the time when you leave. Label the photographs with dates and explanations. Take utility meter readings and give these to the supplier to ensure you aren't charged for tenant's bills.

It is important that all the tenants take care of the property during the tenancy and report any damage if it happens. Always keep a copy of records of correspondence with your landlord about repairs, if you discuss anything on the telephone back it up with an email which you should keep.

Usually the amount you will be required to pay for a deposit is the equivalent of one month's rent for security against damage or getting into rent arrears. You would get your deposit back when you vacate your room/flat/house, at the end of the licence or tenancy. Some universities provide the option to deduct the cost of the deposit from your rent in term 2 and 3, so you will be paying less towards rent in this period.

University and letting agency room or property booking fee costs
Some universities and lettings agents will also charge you a booking or administration fee to cover the costs of booking a room which is usually non-refundable. This fee covers drawing up tenancy agreements, inventories and checking references.

You may also be charged a holding deposit if you agree to take a property but haven't yet signed a tenancy agreement, but should obtain information about the conditions for returning your deposit such as you passing credit checks, if you change your mind about the tenancy, if the landlord decides not to go ahead with the tenancy, if the tenancy doesn't happen and if your deposit transfers to another property. If you do pay a holding deposit, this is usually deducted from the security deposit you pay when you move in. You can register with more than one agent at a time and they can't charge you for registering with them or providing a list of properties.

11.7 Moving out of Your Student Accommodation

Check your tenancy agreement before you move out so that you are aware of what you need to do to get your deposit back and avoid any charges that may apply. Ensure the property is cleaned and the rubbish removed.

Remember to fully take away all of your belongings. Take final metre readings as proof that you have paid your final bills before your landlord will release your deposit.

Take photos of the property when you move out. If your deposit isn't returned at the end of your tenancy within 2-4 weeks, check there isn't any unpaid rent.

Most landlords and agencies are decent and fair but if you do have difficulties getting your deposit refunded, the photographs will be useful to have.

Agencies/landlords may refuse to refund a deposit, or reduce the refund, if there is any damage to the property that they consider has been caused by you or your flat/house mates.

Returning your deposit at the end of your licence or tenancy

If your deposit is not returned at the end or within 2-4 weeks after your licence or tenancy finishes, check for clauses in the tenancy agreement that allows the landlord to deduct charges from the deposit such as:

- Unpaid rent, including rent arrears owed by other joint tenants
- Damage to the property, but not if this was caused by normal usage
- Replacement of missing items from the inventory
- Cleaning if the property has been left in a dirty condition
- Additional charges which you should check and negotiate if needed at the time of signing the contract.

There will be a check to make sure the property is left in a clean and undamaged state and if it is deemed that the room or property isn't left in a fit state or if you owe money for rent you may forfeit some or all of your deposit. Agencies/landlords may refuse to refund a deposit, or reduce the refund, if there is any damage to the property that they consider has been caused by you or your flat/house mates

Encountering problems with having your deposit returned

If you don't agree with some or all of the deductions you should put this in writing to your landlord keeping a copy, and refer to your tenancy agreement, any photos that were taken and other emails or correspondence you have.

If you can't resolve the dispute with your landlord, you can notify your tenancy deposit protection scheme, but will need to raise a dispute within three months of the end of the tenancy. If you encounter any problems for having your deposit returned in full you may be able to contact the local authority Trading Standards Officer, Tenancy Relations Officer or a housing specialist. Your student union may also be able to advise you.

11.8 What to do if you want to Change Your Student Accommodation

Hopefully all will go well with your accommodation and your course, however should you want to leave your course early, if you aren't happy with the standard of student accommodation or if things don't work out with your room / flat mates and you want to change your accommodation, it is a good idea to discuss your options with a student adviser before you make a decision.

Once you sign a tenancy or licence agreement for your student accommodation, you enter into a legal contract which must be ended properly when you move out. Providing you get appropriate advice before taking action you will reduce any problems you may encounter.

Leaving university halls of residence early

If you are in a halls of residence you will usually have a fixed term agreement which means you have agreed to rent your accommodation for a certain period of time, commonly for the length of the academic year your course lasts for, moving out of your halls on the day that the fixed term agreement runs out without having to give notice to your landlord.

If you want to move out earlier you can only end the agreement if there is a break clause term in your signed license agreement, which allows you to end the agreement early and states how much notice you will need to give.

Alternatively your landlord may agree to end the agreement early which is called surrender. If you leave before the end of the fixed term you should discuss this with your landlord as without your landlord's consent you are liable to pay the rent until the fixed term ends, even if you aren't living there.

Leaving privately rented accommodation early

If you want to leave during the course of a fixed term tenancy, and the other tenants want to stay, you or the other tenants could find a replacement tenant who is acceptable to the remaining tenants and the landlord; or not find a replacement tenant and either you would continue to pay your share of the rent or the remaining tenants make up the shortfall.

Whatever is decided, you will need to speak to your landlord first as they will need to agree which change can go ahead, ending the existing tenancy and creating a new one or amending the existing tenancy and everyone signing and dating the variation to the agreement on the relevant date.

Notice by one tenant will not end the tenancy. If you have a periodic tenancy, such as monthly tenancy, you can give the appropriate notice to the landlord without the other tenants' knowledge and consent.

If you have sole tenancy and want to leave early you will need to raise it with your landlord. Your landlord is likely to want to get a new tenant to replace you and the other tenants may have no control over who that person will be, unless your landlord asks for their input.

If you landlord is the sole tenant, with you as a sub-tenant or lodger, and the tenancy with the head landlord ends this will affect your right to remain in the property, you may be able to negotiate with the head landlord but you may need to get specialist housing advice.

11.9 Watch out for Student Rental Scams

Providing you use accredited private landlords or agencies from university or college lists, you will limit student housing problems. However, the National Fraud and Cyber Crime Reporting Centre http://www.actionfraud.police.uk/ provides advice about the potential for fraudsters targeting students who are looking for accommodation.

The scams work by offering to let property in prime areas at below market rents and asking for deposits or full payment up front to secure the property prior to visiting it. Prospective tenants are convinced to part with either credit card details, cheques or cash before seeing the property which then turns out not to exist.

Payments are then not returned and the student can't get in contact with the supposed 'landlord'. There have been occasions whereby fraudsters gain access to properties to take prospective tenants around, portraying the property to be vacant and under their control.

How to protect yourself
- Do not send money upfront.
Make sure you are certain the person and property exists and that the person has

control of the property. Deposits are standard in renting but paying money up front to secure a room is not.

- Protect your deposit
When a deposit is taken the money must be paid into a deposit scheme approved by the UK government https://www.gov.uk/deposit-protection-schemes-and-landlords/overview

- Visit the house you intend to rent.
Make sure you visit the property with the landlord to confirm if the house share is bona fide, be suspicious of anyone who refuses to let you visit the property.

- Ask for ID from the Landlord.
Check the landlord's driving licence and/or passport to establish if they are who they say they are. Check that the landlord is a member of the National Landlords Association via the NLA landlord accreditation.

- Check that the owner is on an approved accommodation list.

Check with your university or college accommodation office or student union as most will have an approved housing list. Also look for accreditation membership with a self-regulating organisation such as:

Self-regulating organisations include:
- Association of Residential Lettings Agents
  http://www.arla.co.uk/
- National Approved Letting Scheme, (NALS) https://www.nalscheme.co.uk/
- National Landlords Association
  http://www.landlords.org.uk/
- Residential Landlords Association
  http://www.rla.org.uk/
- Royal Institution of Chartered Surveyors
  http://www.rics.org/uk/
- UK Association of Letting Agents
  http://www.ukala.org.uk/

- Ask for copies of tenancy agreements and safety certificates

Safety certificates should be available for utilities such as gas and electricity or if the property is included as a house in multiple occupation (HMO), the landlord will need a licence.

- Be aware of adverts with no telephone numbers and just an email address

Look for telephone numbers that are based in the UK but be wary of phone numbers beginning with 070 or+ 4470 which are non-geographic business numbers. Check the numbers work and are not fax numbers.

- Check the legitimacy of any adverts Avoid adverts with no photographs or where multiple adverts have the same photograph.

- Be cautious on how you send money The safest way to make a payment is by a credit card in person at the letting agent's office.

A formal contract should also be signed before any money has changed hands. Be sceptical if you are asked to transfer money via money transfer agents. Only use these money transfers to send money to people that you know and trust.

Don't respond to 'proof of funds' scam whereby you are asked to send money to a friend and then send the details of the transaction to the 'landlord'. The funds can be withdrawn using forged identification and allows scammers to access the funds.

11.10 Additional Costs for Utility Bills and Television Licence

Paying bills in shared accommodation
When paying bills in shared accommodation, it may be best to have an account set up using the names of everyone who lives in the property so the supplier can chase anyone for any outstanding debts even if you have already paid your share.

If only your name is on the utility bill, you are legally responsible for the whole of the bill until you end the contract, therefore if someone else who lives with you doesn't pay their share, you will usually have to pay the bill and take legal action against them for the money.

If you can only set up an account in one person's name, get a signed written agreement with your flat or house mates, even if you are all the best of friends.

Utility bills
As well as the rent, you will need to consider additional costs such as utility bills for gas, electricity, water, Wi-Fi, phone charges and council tax. Some accommodation rental costs may include the utility bills and most universities/colleges include this if you live in halls, although always confirm this with the relevant university/college.

Television licence
Television licensing
http://www.tvlicensing.co.uk/
If you move away from home and you have your own TV or watch 'live' TV shows via the internet, it is essential to pay for a TV licence. If you live in halls, there will probably be a licence covering communal areas but you will also need to be covered for your room.

If you have a separate tenancy agreement for your own room and live in self-contained accommodation in a separate flat or annex you will need to pay for a TV licence on top of your accommodation rental costs.

If you have a joint tenancy agreement, living in privately rented accommodation with others, you may need a TV licence for the whole property and you can share the costs with your flat/house-mates. However, there may be other reasons why you need your own TV licence so if unsure, check with the TV licensing company.

If you fail to pay for a TV licence when you need one, you risk getting a fine of £1,000.

You can usually pay one yearly instalment (which may be a slightly cheaper option), monthly or quarterly. Check the above website for further information.

Insurance
Insurance isn't essential but if you have valuable items such as a musical instrument, lap top, camera or any other equipment or possessions that are valuable, it is advisable to pay for insurance to protect against theft or damage.

Housing benefit
Full time students aren't usually eligible for housing benefit unless you have children or have a disability. Further information may be found at UK Government: Housing Benefit
https://www.gov.uk/housing-benefit/further-information

You may need to apply through your local council for Housing Benefit in England and Wales
UK Government: Apply Housing Benefit from Council
https://www.gov.uk/apply-housing-benefit-from-council

11.11 Student Housing Information

The following organisations have useful information about accommodation.

Citizens Advice Bureaux
http://www.adviceguide.org.uk

The Citizens Advice Bureaux offers free, confidential, impartial and independent advice in many locations including high street offices and many other different types of community centres. Advice is available on debt and a range of other issues. Advice is usually face-to-face or by phone, although some provide email advice.

National Union of Students (NUS)
http://www.nus.org.uk
The National Union of Students (NUS) has a range of lots of useful information, including student accommodation.

- Shelter
  http://www.shelter.org.uk/
- Shelter England:
  http://england.shelter.org.uk/
- Shelter Wales:
  http://www.sheltercymru.org.uk/
- Shelter Northern Ireland
  http://www.shelterni.org/
- Shelter Scotland:
  http://scotland.shelter.org.uk/

Shelter is the housing and homelessness charity and proves information on private renting, tenancy deposits, housing benefit, council housing, eviction, repairs, energy costs and homelessness.

Estate agents may also offer a lettings agency. Find an Estate Agent:
National Association of Estate Agents
http://www.naea.co.uk/

Chapter 12
Student Finance

12.1 Student Loans Company (SLC)

- UK Student Loans Company (SLC)
  http://www.slc.co.uk

The Student Loans Company (SLC) is a non-profit government organisation working with:
- UK Government Department for Education (DfE)
  https://www.gov.uk/government/organisations/department-for-education

- Department for Education and Skills (DfES), Wales
  https://gov.wales/topics/educationandskills

- Department for the Economy (DfEcon), Northern Ireland;
  https://www.economy-ni.gov.uk/

- Scottish Government: Department for Education and Training)
  https://www.gov.scot/Topics/Education

- Student Awards Agency for Scotland (SAAS)
  http://www.saas.gov.uk/

As well as with higher and further education providers and other education delivery partners.

The SLC acts as an agent to provide tuition fee loans to eligible English, Welsh, Northern Irish, Scottish students who meet the residence requirements or for EU students studying in the UK; as well as maintenance loans for living costs and studying expenses to eligible English, Welsh, Northern Irish and Scottish students studying courses at universities and colleges in the UK. These loans need to be repaid.

The SLC also administers some grants, bursaries and scholarships on behalf of universities and colleges which don't need to be repaid.

If you take out a loan, depending on where you are ordinarily resident, your contract is with the relevant government Student Finance Company in that country. You will need to apply for loans and grants to the relevant Student Finance Company for the country where you are eligible and meet the residence requirements. There are different processes in each UK country.

The SLC is responsible for paying out the loans and grants, keeping details of your account, adding interest and sending you a statement each year.

The tuition fee loans (England, Wales and Northern Ireland or tuition fee grants (Scotland) are paid directly to universities and colleges where you are studying. The maintenance loans (England, Wales, Northern Ireland and Scotland) and maintenance grants (Wales, Northern Ireland and Scotland), for eligible students, are paid into your bank or building society account once you start your course.

You will be charged interest on your tuition fee loan and maintenance loan from the first day the money is paid to your university or college, and interest is added until the loan is paid off in full.

Some students who meet certain conditions may also be eligible for additional bursaries, scholarships or grants. These may be applied for directly with the university or college where you are studying or through the relevant finance organisation administrating the funding. The Student Loans Company provides useful resources on Student Finance which can be accessed at:
- Student Loans Company: Practitioners: Resources
  http://www.practitioners.slc.co.uk/resources/

12.2 Student Finance Companies

You will need to apply for student funding by completing on line form/s through the Student Finance Company where you are eligible and meet the residence requirements or for EU students, the country where you are studying.

You will need to apply every year of your course. Changes may occur for EU students when the UK leaves the EU. There is a different process in England, Wales, Northern Ireland or Scotland.

Student Finance Companies

England
Student Finance England
https://www.gov.uk/student-finance

Wales
Student Finance Wales
http://www.studentfinancewales.co.uk

Northern Ireland
Student Finance Northern Ireland
http://www.studentfinanceni.co.uk

Scotland
Student Awards Agency Scotland
http://www.saas.gov.uk

Further information about student finance is available at:
UK Government: Student Finance
https://www.gov.uk/browse/education/student-finance
Student Loans Company
http://www.slc.co.uk

12.3 Residence Requirements for Student Funding

Student fees may be charged as home or overseas rate. The student fee rate you are charged, according to Government regulations, depends on your nationality, your immigration status in the UK, where you have been living and what you have been doing in the three years prior to the start of your course.

For home fees, to meet the residence eligibility conditions, you must have been 'ordinarily resident' in the United Kingdom (UK), the Channel Islands or the Isle of Man for three years immediately before the relevant date, being the first day of the first academic year of the course. You must also be ordinarily resident in the relevant UK country where you are applying for Student Finance. By 'ordinarily resident' this means that you, your parents or your husband, wife or civil partner live in a country year after year by choice.

Non-EU nationals are charged overseas tuition fees unless settled in the UK (as set out in the Immigration Act 1971) on the relevant date.

Further information on residence requirements and fee status

- UK Government: Student Finance Who Qualifies
  https://www.gov.uk/student-finance/who-qualifies

- UK Government: Right to Reside
  https://www.gov.uk/right-to-reside
- UK Government: Home Office: UK Visas and Immigration
  https://www.gov.uk/government/organisations/uk-visas-and-immigration

- UK Council for International Affairs: Home or Overseas Fees the basics
  https://www.ukcisa.org.uk/Information--Advice/Fees-and-Money/Home-or-Overseas-fees-the-basics

- UK Council for International Affairs: England Fee Status
  https://www.ukcisa.org.uk/Information--Advice/Fees-and-Money/England-fee-status

- UK Council for International Affairs: Wales Fee Status
https://www.ukcisa.org.uk/Information--Advice/Fees-and-Money/Wales-fee-status

- UK Council for International Affairs: Northern Ireland Fee Status
https://www.ukcisa.org.uk/Information--Advice/Fees-and-Money/Northern-Ireland-fee-status

- UK Council for International Affairs: Scotland Fee Status
https://www.ukcisa.org.uk/Information--Advice/Fees-and-Money/Scotland-fee-status

12.4 European Union (EU) Student Funding in the UK

European Union (EU) national students who are studying for full-time or part-time courses in the UK can apply for a tuition fee loan if studying in England, Wales or Northern Ireland. If studying in Scotland, EU students can apply for a tuition fee grant. You should be eligible for tuition fee finance support on a similar basis as students who meet the residence requirements in these countries.

However, EU students can't apply for a maintenance loan or maintenance grant, unless you meet the residence eligibility conditions. Changes may occur when the UK exits the EU.

You will need to apply for funding through the relevant Student Finance Company in the UK country where you are studying and will need to apply every year of your course. You will also need to post any additional required documents with your application form to ensure your application isn't delayed. You should check details for EU students with the Student Finance

Company in the country where you want to study.

Funding is different for students studying in England, Wales, Northern Ireland and Scotland. Further information for EU students can be found on the Student Finance websites:

Some EU national students in the UK may be eligible for additional help providing you meet specified conditions and the following applies to you (check on Student Finance websites).
- You are an EU national, or the family member of someone who is and
- You have lived in the UK for at least three years before your course starts and
- You will be living in the UK on the first day of the academic year in which you start your course and
- Your main reason for living in the UK was not to receive full time education.

Eligible students aged between 16-18/19 years in the academic year of studying for qualifications in secondary schools, further education colleges or other approved learning providers in the public education sector don't need to pay tuition fees for these courses. However in the private sector, colleges which also offer GCSEs, AS and 'A' levels or equivalent qualifications will usually charge tuition fees.

If you are aged over 19 years you may study for further education academic or vocational qualifications lower than higher education qualifications with a recognised learning provider, however tuition fees may be charged, so contact the relevant college or learning provider for details as costs will vary depending on the learning provider. You may be eligible for funding support and each UK country, England, Wales, Northern Ireland and Scotland have different funding criteria.

The types of further education learning providers for students over the age of 16 years include secondary schools; further education colleges; some higher education institutions; training organisations; some distance learning providers; local authorities and some employers who receive funding through an approved loans facility or loans bursary fund agreement to deliver education and training.

England: Secondary and Further Education Students Funding Support

Eligible students who meet the residence requirements in England aged 19 years and over and considering studying for a further education course with an approved training organisation may be eligible for funding with an Advanced Learning Loan. Education Maintenance Allowance (EMA) is now closed in England.

Advanced Learning Loans are provided by the Education and Skills Funding Agency (ESFA) in England and are available through the Student Loans Company (SLC), administered by Student Finance England. Links to a register of approved training organisations in England may be found at:

- UK Government: Register of Training Organisations
  https://www.gov.uk/government/publica
  tions/register-of-training-organisations

- Advanced Learning Loans for FE students 19 years and over

Apply to Student Finance England: Advanced Learning Loans for FE students 19 years and over
Student Finance England
https://www.gov.uk/student-finance

Further information about applications may be found at
UK Government: Advanced Learning Loans: How to Apply
https://www.gov.uk/advanced-learner-loan/how-to-apply

Wales: Secondary and Further Education Students Funding Support

Eligible students who meet the residence requirements in Wales aged between 16 and 18 years who want to continue their education after school leaving age are able to apply for an Education Maintenance Allowance (EMA) which is income assessed. Students who are aged 19 years and over and considering studying for an approved course in further education (FE) may be eligible for funding with a Welsh Learning Grant (WLG) (FE).

- Education Maintenance Allowance (EMA)
- Welsh Learning Grant (WLG) (FE): Wales

Apply to Student Finance Wales: Education Maintenance Allowance (EMA); Welsh Learning Grant (WLG) (FE)
Student Finance Wales: EMA; Welsh Learning Grant (WLG) (FE)
https://www.studentfinancewales.co.uk/

Further information may be found at
Student Finance Wales: FE
http://www.studentfinancewales.co.uk/fe/

Northern Ireland: Secondary and Further Education Students Funding Support

Eligible students who meet the residence criteria in Northern Ireland aged between 16 and 19 years who want to continue their education or taking part in the Training for Success Programme are able to apply for an Education Maintenance Allowance (EMA) which is income assessed, through Northern Ireland Direct https://www.nidirect.gov.uk/

Eligible students who meet the residence criteria in Northern Ireland aged up to 25 years studying for a course which leads to your first level 2 or 3 (RQF) qualification, may be able to get free tuition. Other courses may provide free tuition for eligible students. You will need to contact your college or training provider.

- Education Maintenance Allowance (EMA)
- Eligible students aged up to 25 years studying for a course which leads to your first level 2 or 3 (RQF) qualification may be able to get free tuition
- Other courses may provide free tuition for eligible students

Apply to Northern Ireland Direct: Education Maintenance Allowance (EMA)
Northern Ireland Direct
https://www.nidirect.gov.uk/articles/how-apply-money-learn-education-maintenance-allowance

Apply to your further education college or other training provider: free tuition if studying for a course which leads to your first level 2 or 3 (RQF) qualification

Further information may be found at
Northern Ireland Direct: Education Maintenance Allowance
https://www.nidirect.gov.uk/information-and-services/education-maintenance-allowance/money-learn-education-maintenance-allowance

Northern Ireland Direct: 14-19 Education Employment and Training Options: Education Maintenance Allowance
https://www.nidirect.gov.uk/information-and-services/14-19-education-employment-and-training-options/education-maintenance-allowance

Northern Ireland Direct: Financial Help for Adult Learners
https://www.nidirect.gov.uk/information-and-services/adult-learning/financial-help-adult-learners

Scotland: Secondary and Further Education Students Funding Support

Eligible students who meet the residence criteria in Scotland aged between 16 and 19 years who want to continue their education after school leaving age are able to apply for an Education Maintenance Allowance (EMA) which is usually income assessed, however if you aged below 18 years and eligible for EMA, your study allowance may not be income assessed. Eligible students who meet the residence criteria in Scotland aged between 18 and 25 years, and some over 25 years who want to study full time in further education do not usually have to pay tuition fees and may get a bursary which is income assessed dependent on your age and family circumstances.

- Education Maintenance Allowance (EMA)
- Eligible students aged between 18 and 25 years, and some over 25 years who want to study full time in further education do not usually have to pay tuition fees and may get a bursary which is income assessed

Apply through your school or college: Education Maintenance Allowance (EMA);
Apply to your further education college or other training provider: free tuition; bursary funding

Further information may be found at:
My World of Work: Funding
https://www.myworldofwork.co.uk/learn-and-train/funding

My Gov Scotland: EMA
https://www.mygov.scot/ema/

12.6 Higher Education Students Funding Support

Higher Education Funding Support Available in the UK for New Students Starting From the Academic Year 2018-2019

The following information is for guidance only. It is important, however, to check on the relevant Student Finance Company or NHS / Department of Health (DoH) student bursary organisation websites for the relevant country for more detailed information and to check if there are any changes that may take place after the publication of this book. Each UK country, England, Wales, Northern Ireland and Scotland have different funding criteria. Changes in funding may occur each year.

Funding for undergraduate courses
The main expense for studying for an undergraduate course at a university or college will be the cost of your course tuition fees and your living costs. Living costs include rent and utility bills for your accommodation, food, clothing, books, other course necessities and travel expenses. Living costs and payment of tuition fees will vary depending on where you live in the UK, which course you

study, and the university or college you attend. Living in London is more expensive than living in other parts of the UK. Financial support is available to eligible undergraduate students who meet the residence requirements in England, Wales and Northern Ireland for tuition fee loans, which are non-income assessed and maintenance loans for living costs which are income assessed, with some students in Wales and Northern Ireland eligible for maintenance grants which are income assessed. Financial support is available to eligible undergraduate students who meet the residence requirements in Scotland for tuition fee grants, which are non-income assessed and maintenance loans for living costs, with some students eligible for maintenance bursaries / grants which are income assessed. Loans need to be repaid whereas grants / bursaries don't need to be repaid.

Undergraduate Courses which are Recognised for Student Funding

To be eligible for undergraduate financial support your course must be a higher education course at a publicly funded UK university or college or a specifically designated course at a privately funded university or college leading to an approved course:

England, Wales, Northern Ireland, Scotland Undergraduate student funding courses

- BA / BSc or other recognised titled degree with or without honours
- Foundation degree (Fd)
- Diploma of Higher Education (DipHE) or Higher National Diploma (HND)
- Certificate of Higher Education (CertHE) or Higher National Certificate (HNC)
- Foundation course if the foundation year is an integral part of a higher education course when students enrol for the full length of the extended course
- Integrated master's degree
- Postgraduate Initial Teacher Training (ITT) course: Post / Professional Graduate Certificate of Education (PGCE) (England, Wales, Northern Ireland) / Post / Professional Graduate Diploma of Education (Scotland) (funded as an undergraduate course)
- Architecture degree (RIBA part I); placement year and postgraduate diploma (RIBA part II); part II is seen as a continuation of the undergraduate part I

- For other higher education qualifications, confirm with the relevant Student Finance organisation

England

- Pre-registration postgraduate nursing, midwifery and some allied health courses (England), eligible students who have a degree in a different subject may also access undergraduate student finance

Additional undergraduate funding

- Students on nursing and midwifery or some allied health courses may be awarded a National Health Service (NHS) / Department of Health (DoH) bursary (Wales, Northern Ireland, Scotland)
- Students on medicine and dentistry courses for specified years may be awarded a National Health Service (NHS) / Department of Health (DoH) bursary / Student Finance grant (England, Wales, Northern Ireland, Scotland)
- Students on some social work courses may be awarded a bursary (England, Wales, Northern Ireland, Scotland)

Tuition Fees for Undergraduate Higher Education Courses

The following information is about student finance support as loans and grants available for students who are ordinarily resident in England, Wales, Northern Ireland and Scotland.

England, Wales, Northern Ireland and Scotland have different tuition fee regulations which affect students who meet the residence requirements in each country.

Students who are ordinarily resident in the European Union studying in one of the UK countries may currently access student finance for tuition fees the country where you are studying. Changes may occur when the UK leaves the EU.

If you are a UK or EU resident and meet the eligibility criteria, planning to study in higher education as an undergraduate full time student or a part time student, you will be eligible to apply to the Student Finance Company in England, Wales or Northern Ireland for finance support as a tuition fee loan; or to apply to the Student Awards Agency for Scotland in Scotland for a tuition fee grant if studying in Scotland to meet the cost of your course.

There are different amounts of tuition fee support available, depending if you are studying at a publicly funded or privately funded university or college and you will need to apply each year you are studying.

Tuition fees for undergraduate courses academic year 2018-2019
Universities and colleges in the UK are able to set their own costs for undergraduate and postgraduate courses. However currently there is a maximum amount public higher education institutions can charge, which varies depending on the UK country.

There are different systems in place for universities and colleges in England, Wales, Northern Ireland and Scotland, with tuition fee processes dependent on which country you meet the residence requirements.

Tuition fees for undergraduate courses and some postgraduate courses such as Initial Teacher Training (ITT) courses will vary depending on the course and the university or college where you are studying. However, publicly funded universities and colleges can currently charge home students and EU students up to a maximum of £9,250 per year (academic year 2018-2019) for a full time undergraduate course, although some courses will cost less than this.

Tuition fees for part-time higher education courses may be charged pro-rata per year. Tuition fees for overseas students will be higher. Tuition fee costs may increase each year. Some graduate entry courses are assessed at undergraduate level, such as the teacher training and graduate entry medicine courses, with tuition fees charged at the same rate as undergraduate level courses.
Privately funded universities and colleges may charge more than this amount. Postgraduate tuition fees vary considerably, although highly competitive and private universities may charge higher fees.

England: Tuition Fees for Undergraduate Courses Academic Year 2018-2019

Eligible students who meet the residence requirements in England, Wales, Northern Ireland or Scotland as well as EU students studying in England, the maximum tuition fee cost in a publicly funded university or college in England for an undergraduate full time course is:

- £9,250 per year

In England, the government has introduced the Teaching Excellence and Outcomes Framework (TEF) https://www.officeforstudents.org.uk/advice-and-guidance/teaching/what-is-the-tef/ managed by the Office for Students https://www.officeforstudents.org.uk/ Those universities and colleges with a TEF Award may charge up to the maximum £9,250 per year and those without a TEF Award may charge up to a maximum of £9,000 per year.

Part time undergraduate tuition fees are usually charged as a proportion depending on course intensity. Privately funded universities and colleges may charge higher fees.

Wales: Tuition Fees for Undergraduate Courses Academic Year 2018-2019

Eligible students who meet the residence requirements in Wales, England, Northern Ireland or Scotland as well as EU students studying in Wales, the maximum tuition fee cost in a publicly funded university or college in Wales for an undergraduate full time course is:

- £9,000 per year

Part time undergraduate tuition fees are usually charged as a proportion depending on course intensity. Privately funded universities and colleges may charge higher fees.

Northern Ireland: Tuition Fees for Undergraduate Courses Academic Year 2018-2019

Eligible students who meet the residence requirements in Northern Ireland or Republic of Ireland as well as EU students studying in Northern Ireland, the maximum tuition fee cost in a publicly funded university or college in Northern Ireland for an undergraduate full time course is:

- £4,160 per year

Eligible students who meet the residence requirements in England, Wales or Scotland studying in Northern Ireland, the maximum tuition fee cost in a publicly funded university or college in Northern Ireland for an undergraduate full time course is:

- £9,250 per year.

Part time undergraduate tuition fees are usually charged as a proportion depending on course intensity. Privately funded universities and colleges may charge higher fees.

Scotland: Tuition Fees for Undergraduate Courses Academic Year 2018-2019

Eligible students who meet the residence requirements in Scotland as well as EU students studying in Scotland, the maximum tuition fee cost in a publicly funded university or college in Scotland for an undergraduate full time course is usually:

- £1,820 per year for a degree and
- £1,285 per year for an HNC, HND or other sub degree (although there may be some variation).

Eligible students who meet the residence requirements in Scotland studying in England, Wales or Northern Ireland will be eligible to apply for a tuition fee loan from the Student Awards Agency for Scotland. Eligible students who meet the residence requirements in England, Wales or Northern Ireland studying in Scotland the maximum tuition fee cost in a publicly funded university or college in Scotland for an undergraduate full time course is:

- £9,250 per year

Part time undergraduate tuition fees are usually charged as a proportion depending on course intensity. Privately funded universities and colleges may charge higher fees.

Tuition Fee Loans and Grants for Undergraduate Higher Education Students

England, Wales, Northern Ireland and Scotland have different tuition fee regulations which affect students who meet the residence requirements in each country. Eligible students who meet the residence requirements in England, Wales and Northern Ireland can get a tuition fee loan which is available for full time and part time students pro-rata (studying at least 25% of a full time equivalent course) and can be taken out to cover the cost of the fees for your course, paid directly to your university or college. Eligible students who meet the residence requirements in Scotland and studying in Scotland can get a tuition fee grant, or if studying in England, Wales or Northern Ireland, a tuition fee loan which are non-income assessed.

Depending on where you are ordinarily resident, you may be able to borrow up to the maximum amount of £9,250 per year for a course at a publicly funded university or college but if your course fees are less than the maximum tuition fee loan allowed, you will only be entitled to the cost of the course. If studying a course at a privately funded university or college, the maximum amount you can borrow may be less and if the course fees are higher, you will need to be able to pay the difference yourself.

You will need to apply for funding support each year you are studying. The tuition fees are paid directly to the university or college where you are studying and for loans, you will need to repay this money. A tuition fee loan or grant isn't based on your household income and you can apply for a loan to cover all or part of your higher education course.

Chart: Undergraduate Courses Tuition Fee Loans and Grants at Publicly and Privately Funded Universities and Colleges

Undergraduate courses tuition fee loans and grants at publicly funded universities and colleges: England, Wales, Northern Ireland, Scotland Academic year 2018-2019

Students who meet the residence requirements	Studying in England Up to	Studying in Wales Up to	Studying in Northern Ireland Up to	Studying in Scotland Up to
England Residence	£9,250 /£9,000ft £6,935 pt Tuition fee loan	£9,000 ft £6,935 pt Tuition fee loan	£9,250 ft £6,935 pt Tuition fee loan	£9,250 ft £6,935 pt Tuition fee loan
Wales Residence	£9,250 /£9,000ft £6,165 pt Tuition fee loan	£9,000 £6,165 pt Tuition fee loan	£9,250 £6,165 pt Tuition fee loan	£9,250 loan £6,165 pt Tuition fee loan
Northern Ireland Residence	£9,250 /£9,000ft £3,120 pt Tuition fee loan £1,230 pt Tuition fee grant	£9,000 ft £3,120 pt Tuition fee loan £1,230 pt Tuition fee grant	£4,160 ft £3,120 pt Tuition fee loan £1,230 pt Tuition fee grant	£9,250 ft £3,120 pt Tuition fee loan £1,230 pt Tuition fee grant
Scotland Residence	£9,250 /£9,000ft Tuition fee loan	£9,000 ft Tuition fee loan	£9,250 ft Tuition fee loan	£1,820 ft degree, PGDE £1,285 ft HNC, HND £1,805 pt degree £1,274 pt HNC, HND Tuition fee grant

Undergraduate courses tuition fee loans and grants at privately funded universities and colleges: England, Wales, Northern Ireland, Scotland Academic year 2018-2019

Students who meet the residence requirements	Studying in England Up to	Studying in Wales Up to	Studying in Northern Ireland Up to	Studying in Scotland Up to
England Residence	£6,165 Tuition fee loan	£6,165 Tuition fee loan	£6,165 Tuition fee loan	£6,165 Tuition fee loan
Wales Residence	£6,165 Tuition fee loan	£6,165 Tuition fee loan	£6,165 Tuition fee loan	£6,165 Tuition fee loan
Northern Ireland Residence	£3,575 Tuition fee loan	£3,575 Tuition fee loan	£3,575 Tuition fee loan	£3,575 Tuition fee loan
Scotland Residence	Tuition fee loan	Tuition fee loan	Tuition fee loan	£1,195 Tuition fee grant

England, Wales, Northern Ireland and Scotland have different maintenance loan and grant regulations which affect students who meet the residence requirements in each country.

Eligible students who meet the residence requirements in England, Wales and Northern Ireland or Scotland may get a maintenance loan for living costs and some students may also get a maintenance grant / bursary if resident in Wales, Northern Ireland or Scotland. Maintenance loans and grants are income assessed. Loans have to be repaid, and interest is also charged from the time of your first payment.

However, if you are eligible to be awarded a student maintenance grant, other grant, bursary, scholarship or award, these don't need to be repaid. If you decide to take out a loan from any other organisation this will need to be repaid and you should make sure you check all the conditions and understand any interest you will be charged in addition, as well as when the loan needs to be repaid before you commit.

A maintenance loan, and if eligible a maintenance grant, is available for full time and part time students pro-rata (studying at least 25% of a full time equivalent course) for eligible students who meet the residence requirements in England, Wales, Northern Ireland or Scotland. The maintenance loan / maintenance grant is for living costs for undergraduate students, those on initial teacher training courses and other eligible courses and the amount you can get depends on your household income. There are different regulations for students who started a course before 1st August 2016. Check the Student Finance companies for eligibility.

The amount of maintenance loan or maintenance grant you are entitled to will depend on a range of factors and is dependent on where you live whilst a student during term time; if you live at home with your parents, if you live away from your parental home, if you live in London or if you live in another part of the UK, the year of your course and your entitlement to other financial support, such as NHS bursaries. If you are in the final year of your course, you will get less.

The maintenance loan or grant is available from the Student Loans Company and you should apply to the Student Finance Company where you meet the residence requirements. The main proportion of a maintenance loan is independent of your household income and is available to all students. However, part of the maintenance loan and grant is income assessed, so that some students on lower household incomes may be eligible for a higher amount.

The maintenance loan / maintenance grant is paid directly to you in three instalments and paid directly into your bank account at the start of each academic term. A maintenance loan will need to be repaid once you meet specified criteria. You need to apply for a maintenance loan / maintenance grant each year you are a student. You become liable for each instalment once it is paid. You will be charged interest on your maintenance loan from the first day the money is paid into your bank account until the loan is repaid in full or written off.

Further information
Student Loans Company: Practitioners: Maintenance Loan Eligibility
http://www.practitioners.slc.co.uk/products/full-time-undergraduate-education/full-time-maintenance-loan/eligibility/

Students on some postgraduate courses may be able to access a student loan which are non-income assessed however each UK country, England, Wales, Northern Ireland and Scotland have different funding criteria.

Students studying for a graduate entry / postgraduate course in teacher training are eligible for the same student finance support as undergraduate students in the relevant country. Students studying for an architecture degree are eligible for the same support as undergraduate students which includes RIBA part I, placement year and postgraduate diploma, RIBA part II, as part II is seen as a continuation of the undergraduate part I.

Other graduate entry or postgraduate courses which lead to accelerated nursing, midwifery, some allied health and some additional health related professional qualifications at honours degree or postgraduate level may also qualify for student finance or NHS bursary funding. For some postgraduate courses, there may be additional funding support in the form of grants or bursaries, such as some teacher training courses and social work courses.

To be eligible for postgraduate financial support your course must be a higher education course at a publicly funded UK university or college or a specifically designated course at a privately funded university or college leading to a recognised course: There is a different process in England, Wales, Northern Ireland or Scotland.

England
Eligible students who meet the residence requirements in England may apply for a postgraduate loan if studying in England, Wales, Northern Ireland or Scotland for a full time or part time postgraduate master's degree course or doctoral degree course.

Wales
Eligible students who meet the residence requirements in Wales may apply for a postgraduate loan if studying in England, Wales, Northern Ireland or Scotland for a full time or part time postgraduate master's degree course or doctoral degree course.

Northern Ireland
Eligible students who meet the residence requirements in Northern Ireland may apply for a postgraduate loan if studying in England, Wales, Northern Ireland or Scotland for a full time or part time postgraduate certificate, diploma or master's degree course taught or research

Scotland
Eligible students who meet the residence requirements in Scotland may apply for a postgraduate loan if studying in England, Wales, Northern Ireland or Scotland for a full time or part time postgraduate diploma or master's degree course.

Additional Funding Support for Eligible Students

There may be additional funding support for eligible students depending on your circumstances and if you meet specified criteria such as for students on low incomes, students leaving care, students who have dependent children or adults, and students with disabilities. In addition, universities and colleges as well as some other funding organisations may provide bursaries, scholarships and grants to eligible students.

The following grants are available for undergraduate students who meet specified conditions. Check the regulations with the relevant Student Finance Company. Relevant forms will be available on each of the websites for the different countries in the UK. Additional funding support for some students who are receiving NHS / DoH bursary finance who meet certain conditions may be available from the NHS bursary organisation for the country where you meet the residence requirements.

NHS Bursary Funding for Eligible Students on Some Courses

Eligible students who meet the residency requirements may be able to access bursary funding for some courses for some years. There are different funding regulations in England, Wales, Northern Ireland and Scotland therefore you should check out further information on the relevant bursary organisation website. You should confirm details with the relevant funding authority as regulations and allowances may be subject to review and may change as well as individual circumstances may vary.

Some students on some of the following courses for some years may be eligible to receive a bursary from the NHS England; NHS Wales; Department of Health (DoH) Northern Ireland; or Scottish Health and Social Care bursary administration organisations
- Allied health and additional health specified undergraduate and postgraduate courses
- Medicine and dentistry undergraduate and graduate courses
- Nursing and midwifery undergraduate and postgraduate courses

NHS England; NHS Wales; Department of Health (DoH) Northern Ireland; Scottish Health and Social Care bursary administration organisations
England
NHS Business Service Authority
https://www.nhsbsa.nhs.uk/nhs-bursary-students
Wales
NHS Student Awards Services
http://www.nwssp.wales.nhs.uk/student-awards
Northern Ireland
Student Finance Northern Ireland
http://www.studentfinanceni.co.uk/
Scotland
Students Awards Agency Scotland (SAAS)
http://www.saas.gov.uk/

Further information NHS / health bursaries
England
UK Government: NHS Bursaries
https://www.gov.uk/nhs-bursaries
Additional bursary, scholarships or grant funding for the following courses may be available for some eligible students from various funding organisations.
- Paramedic science undergraduate courses
- Physician associate postgraduate courses
- Social work undergraduate and postgraduate courses
- Teacher initial teacher training (ITT) postgraduate courses

Bursaries, Scholarships, Awards and Grants

Bursaries, scholarships, awards and grants may be available directly from your university or college in addition to any other student funding and won't need to be repaid. Other funding organisations may also provide funding. Research councils may also provide funding for eligible postgraduate students.

Some universities and colleges may offer bursaries, scholarships and awards which are dependent on your household income, the course you study, the tuition fee charged or if you meet specified conditions. You should check the university or college websites regarding available bursaries and scholarships and application details, including deadlines for when to apply. Further information about bursaries, scholarships and awards should be available on individual university and college websites.

Apply to Universities, Colleges or Funding Organisations: Grants, Bursaries and Scholarships

Disabled Students' Allowances (DSAs)

If you have a physical disability, learning difficulty, mental health problem or long term health condition you can apply for Disabled Students' Allowances (DSAs) to cover some of the extra costs.

You would need to be studying for a full or part time undergraduate or postgraduate course that lasts at least a year, including the Open University or by distance learning and qualify for funding with the Student Finance Company for the relevant UK country. If you are a part time student your course intensity can affect how much you get.

How much funding support you get is dependent on your individual needs, not your household income. The DSA may pay for:
- Specialist equipment such as a computer if needed due to your disability
- Non-medical helpers
- Extra travel due to your disability
- Other disability related costs of studying

Once your eligibility for DSA is confirmed, the Student Finance Company may ask you to have a needs assessment with a contact assessment centre to identify what help you need. After the assessment you will get a report listing the equipment and other support you can get for your course.

The funding is either paid directly into your bank account or directly to the organisation supplying the equipment. You will need to meet the eligibility criteria.

Apply to Student Finance: Disabled Students Allowances
Student Finance England
https://www.gov.uk/student-finance
Student Finance Wales
http://www.studentfinancewales.co.uk/
Student Finance Northern Ireland
http://www.studentfinanceni.co.uk
Student Awards Agency Scotland
http://www.saas.gov.uk

If you are receiving bursary funding for a course through the NHS England; NHS Wales; Department of Health (DoH); Scottish Department of Health and Social Care you may need to apply the bursary organisation for DSA funding support. See NHS bursary funding above.

Further information
You may qualify for additional disability related benefits, with further information at:
UK Government: Financial Help Disabled:
https://www.gov.uk/financial-help-disabled

DSA information and assessment centres
Disabled Student Allowances Quality Assurance Group https://dsa-qag.org.uk/

England and general advice

UK Government: Disabled Students Allowances
https://www.gov.uk/disabled-students-allowances-dsas
UK Government Student Finance Forms
https://www.gov.uk/student-finance-forms
UK Government: Disabled Students Allowances; How to Claim
https://www.gov.uk/disabled-students-allowances-dsas/how-to-claim

Wales

Student Finance Wales: Disabled Students Allowances
http://www.studentfinancewales.co.uk/practitioners/undergraduate-students/full-time/disabled-students-allowances.aspx

Northern Ireland

Student Finance Northern Ireland: Disabled Students Allowances
https://www.studentfinanceni.co.uk/types-of-finance/postgraduate/northern-ireland-student/extra-help/disabled-students-allowances/what-are-they/

Scotland

Student Awards Agency for Scotland: Disabled Students Allowances
http://www.saas.gov.uk/full_time/ug/independent/funding_available.htm

Students on Low Incomes

If you are on a low income you may contact your university of college to check if you are eligible for extra funding support. Your university of college will decide how much funding support you can get and it may be paid as a lump sum or by instalments. If you are eligible for a grant you won't need to repay this money.

However if you get a loan, you will need to repay this money. You will need to contact the student services department at your university of college as they will decide if you are eligible for funding support.

Eligibility may be based on if you are a:
- Student with dependent children, especially a single parent
- Mature student with existing financial commitments
- Student from a low income family
- Student who has a disability
- Student who is a care leaver
- Student who is homeless or living in a foyer

Apply to your university or college student services department: financial hardship funding

Students with Children or Dependant Adults

If you are a student with children or adult dependents and on a low income you may apply for the following extra financial support with the Student Finance Company in the country where you meet the residence requirements in England, Wales, Northern Ireland or Scotland. If receiving an NHS / health bursary you can apply for the following extra funding support with the NHS / Health bursary funding organisation in the relevant country in England, Wales, Northern Ireland or Scotland.

Eligible students in England, Wales or Northern Ireland with children or adult dependents may apply for the following financial support.
- Childcare Grant (CCG)
- Parents' Learning Allowance (PLA)
- Adult Dependents Grant (ADG)

Eligible students in Scotland with children or adult dependents may apply for the following financial support.
- Dependants Grant
- Lone Parents Grant

Childcare Grant (CCG): England; Wales; Northern Ireland

The Childcare Grant (CCG) may be available for eligible students who meet the residence requirements in England, Wales or Northern Ireland depending on your circumstances to provide extra help towards the cost of registered or approved childcare.

Apply to Student Finance: Childcare Grant: England; Wales; Northern Ireland
Student Finance England
https://www.gov.uk/student-finance
Student Finance Wales
http://www.studentfinancewales.co.uk/
Student Finance Northern Ireland
http://www.studentfinanceni.co.uk

Lone Parents' Grant: Scotland

The lone parents grant may be available for eligible students who meet the residence requirements in Scotland if you are single, widowed, divorced, separated or your civil partnership has dissolved and you are bringing up children on your own.

Apply to Student Finance: Lone Parents' Grant: Scotland
Student Awards Agency Scotland
http://www.saas.gov.uk

Childcare Fund

The childcare fund may be available depending on your circumstances to provide extra help towards the cost of registered or approved childcare.

Apply to your university or college student services department

Parents' Learning Allowance (PLA): England, Wales, Northern Ireland

The Parents' Learning Allowance (PLA) is extra help intended to cover some of the additional costs incurred if you have one or more children that are financially dependent on you. This funding doesn't need to be paid back. The amount available is dependent on your income, that of your partner, children and any other dependents.

Apply to Student Finance: Parents' Learning Allowance (PLA): England; Wales; Northern Ireland
Student Finance England
https://www.gov.uk/student-finance
Student Finance Wales
http://www.studentfinancewales.co.uk/
Student Finance Northern Ireland
http://www.studentfinanceni.co.uk

Adult Dependants' Grant (ADG) / Dependants Grant: England, Wales, Northern Ireland, Scotland

The Adult Dependants' Grant (ADG) / Dependants' Grant is available if you have a partner or another adult who is financially dependent on you for eligible students who meet the residence requirements in England, Wales, Northern Ireland or Scotland. The Adult Dependents' Grant / Dependants' Grant is income assessed on your income and that of your partner and any other dependents. Part time students will get a percentage based on course intensity.

Apply to Student Finance: Adult Dependants Grant (ADG): Wales; Northern Ireland
Student Finance England
https://www.gov.uk/student-finance
Student Finance Wales
http://www.studentfinancewales.co.uk/
Student Finance Northern Ireland
http://www.studentfinanceni.co.uk

Apply to Student Finance: Dependants Grant (ADG): Scotland
Student Awards Agency Scotland
http://www.saas.gov.uk

Special Support Grant

If you qualify for certain benefits, you may be able to receive the Special Support Grant (SSG) which is intended to help with costs such as books, course equipment and travel for eligible students who meet the residence requirements in Wales or Northern Ireland.

Apply to Student Finance: Special Support Grant (SSG): Wales; Northern Ireland
Student Finance Wales
http://www.studentfinancewales.co.uk
Student Finance Northern Ireland
http://www.studentfinanceni.co.uk

Further information
Student Finance Wales: Special Support Grant (SSG)
https://www.studentfinancewales.co.uk/undergraduate-students/new-students/what-financial-support-is-available/help-with-living-costs.aspx#SpecialSupportGrant
Student Finance Northern Ireland: Special Support Grant (SSG)
https://www.studentfinanceni.co.uk/types-of-finance/undergraduate/full-time/northern-ireland-student/help-with-the-costs-of-living/special-support-grant/what-is-it/#main

Child Tax Credit

If eligible you may be able to claim child tax credit.

Further information:
UK Government: Child Tax Credit
https://www.gov.uk/child-tax-credit
UK Government: Tax Credits Enquiries
https://www.gov.uk/contact/hm-revenue-customs/tax-credits-enquiries

Apply to UK Government: Child Tax Credit
UK Government: Child Tax Credit: How to Claim
https://www.gov.uk/child-tax-credit/how-to-claim

Income Support

If you meet the eligibility criteria you may apply for income support.

Further information
UK Government: Income Support Eligibility
https://www.gov.uk/income-support/eligibility

Students Leaving Care

If you are leaving local authority care, or are estranged from you parents, as well as applying for student finance, you may be able to apply for a bursary from your local authority and a bursary from your university or college.

The following organisations provide information and support. In Scotland if you are under 26 years of age you may apply for a grant to help with accommodation costs during the summer vacation.

- Stand Alone
  http://standalone.org.uk/
- Propel
  http://propel.org.uk/UK/

- National Network for the Education of Care Leavers
  http://www.nnecl.org/
- Who Cares Scotland
  https://www.whocaresscotland.org/

Apply to your Local Authority; University or College: Care Leaver Funding

Apply to Student Finance: Care Experienced Accommodation Grant: Scotland
Student Awards Agency Scotland
http://www.saas.gov.uk

Travel Grant for Clinical Placements

Students on medicine, dentistry and some health professional courses who attend clinical training as part of UK institutions' courses can claim reimbursement of their travel costs.

Apply to NHS England; NHS Wales; Department of Health (DoH) Northern Ireland; Scottish Department of Health and Social Care bursary administration organisations: travel grant for clinical placements. See NHS bursaries above

Travel Grant for Students Studying Abroad

If you are studying abroad as part of your course or on an Erasmus study or work placement, you may be eligible for travel expense grants.

Apply to Student Finance: Travel Grant for Students Studying Abroad. See Student Finance Companies above

Other Sources of Funding

Other organisations, such as charitable trusts, may provide some finance support in the form of grants, scholarships and bursaries to eligible students. A list of websites can be found in the further information section below.

Erasmus Funding Support for Undergraduate and Postgraduate Students

The European Region Action Scheme for the Mobility of University Students (Erasmus) is a study or work experience programme that is available for undergraduate and postgraduate students following a course of higher education in one participating European country who wish to spend part of their course studying or working in another participating European country. Go to: on 'Study Abroad' for more information. You may undertake an:
Erasmus study placement
https://www.erasmusplus.org.uk/study-abroad or an
Erasmus work placement abroad
https://www.erasmusplus.org.uk/work-abroad

Funding for Erasmus students

The European Commission usually provides a grant to UK Erasmus students, which contributes towards the extra costs arising from studying abroad. The Erasmus grants are paid through your institution in the UK and are paid in addition to the standard grants or loans to which you are entitled. During your Erasmus period, you will continue to receive any student loan or other funding to which you are entitled and the Erasmus grant is a supplementary, non-repayable grant which is intended to help with any additional expenses you may have while you are abroad. The grant varies depending on the country you visit as some are more expensive than others and some students may be eligible for additional funding. You will need to be prepared to pay for accommodation and general living costs. In some countries this may be lower than in the UK whilst other countries may be more expensive.

Apply through the university or college where you are studying: Erasmus scheme
Applications should be made through the higher education institution where you are studying as they will set their own application deadlines. Check with the institution's Erasmus Co-ordinator regarding how and when to apply and for further details.

Further information and for full details check:
British Council, Erasmus website
https://www.britishcouncil.org/study-work-create/opportunity/study-abroad/erasmus
Erasmus study abroad placement
https://www.erasmusplus.org.uk/study-abroad
Erasmus work abroad placement
https://www.erasmusplus.org.uk/work-abroad
Chapter 9.3
Erasmus: Study and Work Experience Programme in another European Country

Professional and Career Development Loans (PCDL)

A Professional and Career Development Loan (PCDL) https://www.gov.uk/career-development-loans may be an option if you are unable to fund your course through other means, although there are certain conditions attached to eligibility. A PCDL will only be considered if you have spoken to a Careers Adviser and you have already sought financial support from the institution where you want to study for the course.

PCDLs are managed in partnership by the UK Government and two high street banks, the Co-operative bank and Barclays bank. PCDLs can support courses in a wide range of vocational areas. If you are 18 years or over and plan to train in the UK you may be eligible to apply for between £300 and £10,000 to cover the cost of course fees and other costs such as books and travel. A PCDL can support any the of full time, part time or distance learning course if it is related to a job, although not necessarily to a current job.

Eligibility for a professional and career development loan (PCDL)

PCDLs can support courses in a wide range of vocational subjects, which can be studied full-time, part-time or by distance learning as long as it will help with your career.

- The learning organisation needs to be on the Professional and Career Development Loan Register in the UK.
- The course should last no more than 2 years, or 3 years if they include 1 year of work experience.
- You will need to be aged 18 years or over.
- You have been living in the UK for at least 3 years before your course starts.
- You plan to work in the UK, European Union or Economic Area (EEA) after completing the course.
- You can't get a PCDL for first-full time degrees.

You will need to complete an application form with the bank and the bank will make a decision if you qualify for a loan. You should apply 3 months before the start of your course in order for your application to be processed.

You will need to repay the loan but won't make any repayments while you are studying for your course, or for up to 17 months if you are unemployed when the repayments are due to start. However after one month after completion of your course you will be responsible to make the loan repayments and any additional interest.

If you are claiming or intend to claim for social security benefits, you will need to contact your local Jobcentre Plus or Department for Works and Pension (DWP) Office to find out how a PCDL will affect your benefits.

UK Government: Contact Jobcentre Plus https://www.gov.uk/contact-jobcentre-plus
UK Government: Department for Works and Pension (DWP) https://www.gov.uk/government/organisations/department-for-work-pensions
Apply to the Co-operative bank or Barclays bank: Professional and Career Development Loan (PCDL) after speaking with a careers adviser

National Careers Websites in the UK and Ireland
England
National Careers Service
https://nationalcareersservice.direct.gov.uk/
Wales
Careers Wales
http://www.careerswales.com/en/
Northern Ireland
Northern Ireland Direct Careers
https://www.nidirect.gov.uk/campaigns/careers
Scotland
Skills Development Scotland:
Careers
https://www.skillsdevelopmentscotland.co.uk/
Further information
Professional and Career Development Loan (PCDL)
https://www.gov.uk/career-development-loans

Further education courses student funding: full and part time students: England	
Finance available	**Where to apply**
Advanced learner loan	**Apply to Student Finance England: Advanced learner loan** Student Finance England https://www.gov.uk/student-finance

Undergraduate course student funding: full time and part time students (pro-rata) who meet the residency requirements in England academic year 2018-2019

Finance available	Tuition fee loan Full time and part time (pro-rata) Non-income assessed	Maintenance loan Full time and part time (pro-rata) Income assessed	Additional funding support for eligible undergraduate students	Where to apply
Studying in England, Wales, Northern Ireland or Scotland	*Tuition fee loan: publicly funded university or college up to £9,250 *Tuition fee loan: privately funded university or college up to £6,165	*Maintenance loan: living away from home, in London *Maintenance loan: living away from home, outside London *Maintenance loan: living at parental home	*Disabled Student Allowance *Childcare Grant; *Adult Dependents Grant; *Parents Learning Allowance *Travel grant for students studying part of a course abroad or on clinical work placements *Care leaver funding (also local authority funding)	Apply to Student Finance England: tuition fee loan; maintenance loan; additional funding Student Finance England https://www.gov.uk/student-finance

Postgraduate courses student funding: full time and part time (pro-rata) students who meet the residency requirements in England academic year 2018-2019

Finance available	Postgraduate loan: non-income assessed:	Additional funding support for eligible postgraduate students	Where to apply
Studying in England, Wales, Northern Ireland or Scotland	*Postgraduate master's degree loan: full time and part time (pro-rata) up to £10,609 Non-income assessed *Postgraduate doctoral degree loan: full time and part time (pro-rata) up to £25,000 Non-income assessed	*Postgraduate Disabled Student Allowance	Apply to Student Finance England: postgraduate master's loan; postgraduate doctoral loan; additional funding Student Finance England https://www.gov.uk/student-finance

Wales: Students who meet the Residency Requirements in Wales

Further education courses student funding: full and part time students who meet the residency requirements in Wales	
Finance available	**Where to apply**
*Education Maintenance Allowance (EMA)

*Welsh Learning Grant (WLG) (FE) | **Apply to Student Finance Wales: EMA; Welsh Learning Grant (WLG) (FE)**
Student Finance Wales: EMA; WLG FE
https://www.studentfinancewales.co.uk/ |

Undergraduate course student funding: full time and part time (pro-rata) students who meet the residency requirements in Wales academic year 2018-2019					
Finance available	**Tuition fee loan Non-income assessed**	**Maintenance loan Income assessed**	**Welsh Government Learning Grants (WGLG) Income assessed**	**Additional funding support for eligible undergraduate students**	**Where to apply**
Studying in England, Wales, Northern Ireland or Scotland	*Tuition fee loan: publicly funded university or college in Wales up to £9,000

*Tuition fee loan: publicly funded university or college in England, Northern Ireland or Scotland up to £9,250

*Tuition fee loan: privately funded university or college in England, Northern Ireland or Scotland up to £6,165 | *Maintenance loan: living away from home, in London

*Maintenance loan: living away from home, outside London

*Maintenance loan: living at parental home | *WGLG maintenance grant: living at parental home

*WGLG maintenance grant: living away from home, outside London

*WGLG maintenance grant: living away from home, in London | *Disabled Student Allowance
*Childcare Grant;
*Adult Dependents Grant;
*Parents Learning Allowance
*Travel grant for students studying part of a course abroad or on clinical work placements
*Care leaver funding (also local authority funding) | Apply to Student Finance Wales: tuition fee loan; maintenance loan; WGLG; additional funding support

Student Finance Wales https://www.studentfinancewales.co.uk/ |

Postgraduate courses student funding: full time and part time (pro-rata) students who meet the residency requirements in Wales academic year 2018-2019			
Finance available	**Postgraduate loan Non-income assessed**	**Additional funding support for eligible postgraduate students**	**Where to apply**
Studying in England, Wales, Northern Ireland or Scotland	*Postgraduate master's degree loan: full time and part time (pro-rata) up to £13,000 *Postgraduate doctoral degree loan: full time and part time (pro-rata) up to £25,000	*Postgraduate Disabled Student Allowance	Apply to Student Finance Wales: postgraduate master's loan; postgraduate doctoral loan; additional funding support Student Finance Wales https://www.studentfinancewales.co.uk/

Further education courses student funding: full and part time students who meet the residency requirements in Northern Ireland	
Finance available	**Where to apply**
* Education Maintenance Allowance (EMA): income assessed *Students aged up to 25 years studying a course leading to a first level 2 or 3 (RQF) qualification may be able to get free tuition *Other courses may provide free tuition for eligible students	Apply to Student Finance Northern Ireland: EMA Student Finance Northern Ireland https://www.studentfinanceni.co.uk/ Apply to colleges: courses leading to a first level 2 or 3 (RQF) qualification

Undergraduate course student funding: full time and part time (pro-rata) students who meet the residency requirements in Northern Ireland academic year 2018-2019					
Finance available	**Tuition fee loan full and part time (pro-rata) students Non-income assessed**	**Maintenance loan full-time students Income assessed**	**Maintenance grant Special Support Grant Income assessed**	**Additional funding support for eligible undergraduate students**	**Where to apply**
Studying in England, Wales, Northern Ireland or Scotland	*Tuition fee loan: publicly funded university or college in Northern Ireland up to £4,160 *Tuition fee loan: publicly funded university or college in Wales up to £9,000 *Tuition fee loan: publicly funded university or college in England or Scotland tuition fee loan: up to £9,250 *Tuition fee loan: privately funded university or college in Northern Ireland, England, Wales, or Scotland up to £3,575	* Maintenance loan: living at parental home * Maintenance loan: living away from home outside London *Maintenance loan: living away from home, in London *Maintenance loan studying overseas *If your course is longer than 30 term time weeks, plus short holidays, you can get an extra amount of loan to cover living costs.	*Maintenance grant or *Special support grant	*Disabled Student Allowance *Childcare Grant; *Adult Dependents Grant; *Parents Learning Allowance *Travel grant for students studying part of a course abroad or on clinical work placements *Care leaver funding (also local authority funding)	Apply to Student Finance Northern Ireland: tuition fee loan; maintenance loan; maintenance grant; additional funding support Student Finance Northern Ireland http://www.studentfinanceni.co.uk

Postgraduate courses student funding: full time and part time (pro-rata) students who meet the residency requirements in Northern Ireland academic year 2018-2019			
Studying for a full time or part time postgraduate certificate, diploma or master's degree course taught or research			
Finance available	Postgraduate loan Non-income assessed:	Additional funding support for eligible postgraduate students	Where to apply
Studying in England, Wales, Northern Ireland or Scotland	* Postgraduate certificate, diploma, master's degree loan: non-income assessed Full time and part time (pro-rata) up to £5,500	• Postgraduate Disabled Student Allowance	Apply to Student Finance Northern Ireland: postgraduate certificate, diploma, master's degree loan; additional funding support Student Finance Northern Ireland http://www.studentfinanceni.co.uk

Further education courses student funding: full and part time students who meet the residency requirements in Scotland	
Finance available	**Where to apply**
* Education Maintenance Allowance (EMA) *Eligible students aged between 18 and 25 years, and some over 25 years who want to study full time in further education do not usually have to pay tuition fees and may get a bursary which is income assessed	Apply through your school or college: Education Maintenance Allowance (EMA); Bursary funding

Undergraduate course student funding: full time and part time (pro-rata) students who meet the residency requirements in Scotland academic year 2018-2019				
Finance available	**Tuition fee loan full and part time (pro-rata) students Non-income assessed**	**Maintenance loan full-time students Income assessed**	**Additional funding support for eligible undergraduate students**	**Where to apply**
Studying in England, Wales, Northern Ireland or Scotland	*Tuition fee grant: HNC; HND; other sub-degree course: Publicly funded university or college in Scotland £1,285 *Tuition fee grant: First degree; Initial Teacher Education PGDE Publicly funded university or college in Scotland £1,820 *Tuition fee grant: Undergraduate course Privately funded university or college in Scotland £1,205 * Studying in England, Wales or Northern Ireland academic year 2018-2019 Tuition fee grant: full time students: non-income assessed: academic year 2018-2019 Scotland *Tuition fee loan: undergraduate course publicly funded university or college in England, Wales or Northern Ireland up to £9,250	*Maintenance bursary income assessed *Maintenance loan income assessed *The funding available to the following groups of students may be different from the standard funding available: Students studying medicine at St Andrews University Students who are studying abroad Students on a practical placement / sandwich course	*Disabled Student Allowance *Lone Parents Grant; Dependents Grant *Travel grant for students studying part of a course abroad or on clinical work placements *Care leaver funding (also local authority funding)	Apply to the Student Awards Agency for Scotland: full time tuition fee grant or tuition fee loan; maintenance bursary and loan Student Awards Agency for Scotland http://www.saas.gov.uk

485

Postgraduate courses student funding: full time and part time (pro-rata) students who meet the residency requirements in Scotland academic year 2018-2019				
Studying for a full time or part time postgraduate diploma or master's degree course at a publicly funded or privately funded university or college with specific designation in Scotland:				
Finance available	**Postgraduate loan: non-income assessed:**	**Postgraduate living cost loan: Income assessed**	**Additional funding support for eligible postgraduate students**	**Where to apply**
Studying in England, Wales, Northern Ireland or Scotland	*Tuition fee loan: Postgraduate diploma or master's degree loan full time students up to £5,500 *Tuition fee loan: Postgraduate diploma or master's degree loan part time students split across each year of the course up to £5,500	*Postgraduate living cost loan: full time students:	*Postgraduate Disabled Student Allowance	Apply to Student Awards Agency for Scotland: postgraduate loan Student Awards Agency for Scotland http://www.saas.gov.uk

12.7 Applying for and Repaying Student Finance

How to Apply for Student Finance

There are different processes for funding support for students who meet the residence requirements in England, Wales, Northern Ireland and Scotland therefore you should make an application for the tuition fee loan (England, Wales and Northern Ireland) / tuition fee grant (Scotland), maintenance loan, maintenance grant and other grants with the relevant Student Finance Company in the UK country where you meet the residence requirements. It is important that you read the full information and application details provided on the relevant Student Finance web site.

You will need to make an application each year for student funding, using the online application form. If you are unable to use the online application form it may be possible to download and complete a paper application form, which you will need to post to the relevant address available on the Student Finance website however you should confirm the process. You must include your National Insurance Number on the application. Make sure you submit all the required information and follow instructions.

When to Apply for Student Finance

You can apply for your student finance support from the relevant Student Finance Company as soon as the applications are open. Applications for student finance opens in advance of when your course is starting and opens at different times for the Student Finance Company in England, Wales, Northern Ireland and Scotland.

It is important to apply as soon as possible but by the advised deadlines, in order to obtain your student funding in time for when you start your course. You should apply as soon as you know you want to study a course in higher education. You don't need to have applied for a course, or if you have applied for a course, you don't need a confirmed place and you don't need to wait until you obtain your exam results before applying for student finance.

If you don't get accepted for the course you want, you can change or cancel your application. However, you will only receive funding when your place is officially confirmed by your university or college. You will need to take your payment schedule letter, which will be required to initiate payment, at the time of registration to the university or college which has offered you a place on a course.

It can take up to six weeks to process your application to when you will get a loan or

grant declaration in the post, which you will need to sign and return. You need to make sure you have supplied the required information as soon as possible which will ensure there are no delays while your application is being processed.

You will then be sent a Student Finance letter which you will need when you enrol at your university or college. Your money for maintenance costs will be paid into your bank account after you register on your course. You need to apply for student finance every year you are studying for your course.

Once you have submitted your application, you may be asked to supply supporting financial evidence and you should usually send photocopies, not original documents (unless specifically asked for). You should include your customer reference on all the supporting information. Don't forget that if you apply online, you must sign, date and return a declaration form to the Student Finance Company.

When your application has been assessed you will be sent a Student Finance entitlement letter which shows how much student finance you are entitled to. Make sure you keep this in a safe place as you will need to take it to registration when you start your higher education course.

Make sure you meet the required deadlines to apply for Student Finance to ensure your loans and grants / bursary payments are available at the start of your academic year. Late applications may sometimes be accepted although there is usually a cut-off date, so check details before you apply.

After your course starts, if you decide that you want to apply for financial help, you may usually still apply for student finance for up to a set period of time after the first date of the academic year relevant to your course. Some Student Finance companies allow for up to nine months after your academic year starts, in Scotland the time is less, therefore confirm regulations with the relevant Student Finance Company. This is the same if you are a full time or part time student. You will need to check with your university or college when your academic year starts as this date isn't always the same as the first day of your course.

In England, Wales and Northern Ireland, the usual academic year starts from 1st September, although course start dates will vary and decided by the higher education providers however some courses may have different start dates throughout the year. You should confirm deadlines and further information on the Student Finance website in case of changes.

In Scotland, the usual academic year starts from 1st August, although course start dates will vary and decided by the higher education providers. You should confirm deadlines and further information on the Student Finance website in case of changes.

If you apply late you aren't guaranteed to have money paid into your bank account for the start of term, therefore you are advised to apply as soon as possible.

Academic year dates
Usual academic year starts:
- England, the academic year usually starts on 1st September
- Wales, the academic year usually starts on 1st September
- Northern Ireland, the academic year usually starts on 1st September
- Scotland, the academic year usually starts on 1st August

Some courses will start at different dates throughout the year, decided by the higher education providers and the academic year period will change accordingly, there may be different deadlines to apply for student finance depending on when in the academic year your course starts from.

Courses starting:
1stSeptember- 31st December
Academic year period starts from
1st September

Courses starting:
1st January- 31st March
Academic year period starts from
1st January

Courses starting:
1st April -30th June
Academic year period starts from
1st April

Courses starting:
1st July - 31st August
Academic year period starts from
1st July

NHS England; NHS Wales; Department of Health (DoH) Northern Ireland; Scottish Department of Health and Social Care bursary administration organisations funding deadline

Your application for NHS / DoH / Scottish Department of Health and Social Care bursary funding deadline may be before your course starts, although there may be some flexibility and there are different application deadline dates for medicine and dentistry courses and non-medicine and dentistry courses.

If you are eligible to apply for an NHS / DoH / Dept of Health and Social care bursary, you must apply each academic year for your course tuition fees to be paid.

If you don't apply, you will be responsible for paying for your own tuition fees. You should confirm deadlines and further information on the NHS / DoH health bursary administration organisation.

Further information about application deadlines for student finance may be found at:

England
Student Finance England: Apply for Student Finance
https://www.gov.uk/apply-for-student-finance/when

Wales
Student Finance Wales: When to Apply
http://www.studentfinancewales.co.uk/undergraduate-students/new-students/how-and-when-to-apply.aspx

Northern Ireland
Student Finance Northern Ireland: Applications
http://www.studentfinanceni.co.uk/

Scotland
Student Awards Agency Scotland: Forms; Funding Guide http://www.saas.gov.uk/

Further information about application deadlines for student NHS / DoH health bursaries may be found at: NHS England; NHS Wales; Department of Health (DoH) Northern Ireland; Scottish Department of Health and Social Care bursary administration organisations

England
NHS Business Service Authority
https://www.nhsbsa.nhs.uk/nhs-bursary-students

Wales
NHS Student Awards Services
http://www.nwssp.wales.nhs.uk/student-awards

Northern Ireland
Student Finance Northern Ireland
http://www.studentfinanceni.co.uk/

Scotland
Students Awards Agency Scotland (SAAS)
http://www.saas.gov.uk/

Further information NHS health bursaries
England
UK Government: NHS Bursaries
https://www.gov.uk/nhs-bursaries

Information you will Need to Provide When Applying for Student Finance

Check the requirements carefully on the relevant Student Finance website. You will need to supply the following information and you may be asked for additional information.
- UK Passport number
- Bank account details
- National Insurance number
- University or college course details. You should use the details of the course you are most likely to start as you can update any information at a later date if needed.

Bank or Building Society Requirements
You will need to have a bank or building society account in the UK, registered in your name. If you don't know your term time address when you apply, you should use your home address on your application and update the information on your online account when you have these details. Providing you submit your application with the correct information and evidence, it should be processed between four to six weeks.

What you need to do to make sure you get your student finance on time

- You need to have a bank or building society account and provide these details on your application form.
- You will need to provide your National Insurance number if you are applying for a tuition fee loan (England, Wales or Northern Ireland) tuition fee grant (Scotland), maintenance loan (England, Wales, Northern Ireland or Scotland) and maintenance grant (Wales, Northern Ireland or Scotland).
- Make sure you give your full name, as it appears on your birth certificate or passport, on all the documents.

- Make sure you include any additional information asked for and follow the guidelines.
- Make sure you sign and return your declaration form.

- When you attend enrolment for your course at your university or college, make sure you bring all the required documents. These are issued together in your pack from the Student Loans company and should include the student finance letter, notice of support and the payment schedule letter.

Be Aware of Scam Emails

Student Finance will never send you an email to ask for your login, user name or bank account details. If you do get such an email, this is fraudulent and known as 'phishing' and will connect you to a fake website. It is important not to disclose any personal or bank details in response to email requests which appear to be from Student Finance or the Student Loans Company.

If you get such an email, check advice with the Student Loans Company: Counter Fraud
https://www.slc.co.uk/about-us/what-we-do/counter-fraud.aspx

For further advice about phishing check UK Government: report suspicious emails websites
phishing https://www.gov.uk/report-suspicious-emails-websites-phishing

Repaying of Your Student Loan

You start repaying your student finance tuition fee loan and / or maintenance loan once you are in employment and earn over a certain amount with the amount of the monthly repayments dependent on what you earn.

You will be charged interest on the loan from the day you take it out from the day your first payment is made until it is repaid in full or cancelled and the terms and conditions may change. Other student finance as grants, bursaries and scholarships don't need to be paid back.

The Student Loans Company (SLC) http://www.slc.co.uk and Her Majesty's Revenue and Customs (HMRC) http://www.hmrc.gov.uk/ have a shared responsibility for the repayment of student loans. The Student Loans Company , a non-profit government organisation, is

acting as an agent on behalf of the Government.
Loans for tuition fees and maintenance support are repayable through Income Contingent Repayment (ICR), which means your repayments are based on how much you earn and not how much you borrowed.

You won't start paying back your loan until you are earning a set amount each year and the amount of the monthly repayments is dependent on what you earn although interest is added to your loan from the time you start to receive it.

You will usually only start to repay your loan once you have left university or college and your income is above the minimum threshold as set by the government.

The interest rate you will be charged will depend on which repayment plan your loan falls under.

You will need to confirm arrangements with the relevant Student Finance Company for when the loan may be cancelled as this varies depending when you took out the loan and which UK country you are resident; the terms and conditions may change. There are different payment plans your loan falls under depending on where you are resident and when you took out the loan.

If you come under plan 1 you will start to pay back your loan when you earn over the UK threshold which is a lower amount.

If you come under plan 2 you will start to pay back your loan when you earn over the UK threshold which is a higher amount. Further information may be found at Student Loan Repayment http://www.studentloanrepayment.co.uk/

You can pay back some or all of your student loan at any time and you won't be charged any extra. If you are working for an employer, they will work out your repayments and deduct the money along with your tax. If you are self-employed you will need to repay through self-assessment when you complete your tax returns.

If you decide to leave your course early, you will still have to repay any loan you have been allocated. If you travel abroad for more than 3 months, you will be required to complete an overseas income assessment form. Student Finance will then work out your repayments.

Interest Rates on Student Loans

Income contingent student loans were issued from 1st September 1998 but there are different rules on interest rates charged and minimum income thresholds on student loans for people who started studying for a course before 1st September 2012 and for people who started studying after this date, with separate regulations for students resident in England, Wales, Northern Ireland or Scotland.

The following information is relevant in 2018 however student finance may change each year and repayment of loans and interest rates may change and you should confirm up to date information.

You are on plan 1 if you are an English or Welsh student who started an undergraduate course before 1st September 2012; or a Northern Irish or Scottish student. You start repaying your student loan when you are earning over £18,330. This amount changes beginning of April every year.

You are on plan 2 if you are an English or Welsh student who started an undergraduate course on or after 1st September 2012. You start repaying your student loan when you are earning over £25,000.
A different repayment plan applies to postgraduate loans.
Further information may be found at:
UK Government: Student Finance Repayments
https://www.gov.uk/student-finance/repayments

You will be paying interest from the time of your first payment until you pay your loan back in full. Plan 1 interest repayments are 9% of anything you earn over £18,330. Plan 2 interest repayments are charged the rate of inflation, known as the Retail Price Index (RPI) (3.1%) plus 3%.

Repayment of loans and interest rates may change however and to obtain up to date information, you should go to:
Student Loans Company: Student Loan Repayment
http://www.studentloanrepayment.co.uk/

Further information:
Student Loans Company: Student Loan
Repayment
http://www.studentloanrepayment.co.uk/
UK Government: Student Finance
Repayments
https://www.gov.uk/student-
finance/repayments

England
UK Government:
Student Finance England: Repaying your
Student Loan
https://www.gov.uk/repaying-your-student-
loan
Student Finance England: Master's Loan
Repayment
https://www.gov.uk/master's-
loan/repayment

Student Finance England: Doctoral Loan
Repayment
https://www.gov.uk/doctoral-
loan/repayment

Wales
Student Finance Wales: Repayment of
Undergraduate Course Loans
https://www.studentfinancewales.co.uk/
Student Finance Wales: Repayment of
Postgraduate Course Loans
https://www.studentfinancewales.co.uk/

Northern Ireland
Student Finance Northern Ireland: Terms
and Conditions Guide; Repayment
https://www.studentfinanceni.co.uk/

Scotland
Student Awards Agency for Scotland:
Loan Repayments
http://www.saas.gov.uk/my_money/loan_r
epayments.htm

Changing Your Undergraduate Higher Education Course and Student Finance

If you decide to change your higher education course or university, before you make any decisions you should discuss your plans with an adviser at your university or college. If you have started your course you will need to discuss this with your course personal tutor. However, you will also need to notify the Student Finance Company at the earliest opportunity about any changes to your course or university.

If you decide to change your course before you start, or decide to transfer to a new university or college before the start of term one, you should be eligible to obtain student finance support and your full tuition fee loan if you normally live in England, Wales or Northern Ireland, tuition fee grant if you normally live in Scotland and studying in Scotland or tuition fee loan if you normally live in Scotland and studying in England, Wales or Northern Ireland, which will be paid to your new university or college.

If you transfer to a new university or college during your first year a proportion of your tuition fee will be paid to the university or college you have transferred from and the university or college you have transferred to. If the tuition fee is higher at your new university or college, you will need to confirm payment with the Student Finance organisation. If you have already started on a course and decide to change to a different course before the start of the second year, you will be reassessed for student finance support but only if you have not changed courses before.

If you decide to change your course after the start of the second year or are changing course for the second or more times, you may have to pay your own tuition fees for part of the new course. This will depend on the duration of your new course and the number of years of previous study you have been supported for.

It is important to check with the Student Finance Company where you are normally resident to confirm your situation before you make a decision. The general rule is that you are eligible for funding support for the length of your higher education course plus one year where a qualification is not achieved.

However the funding support will be reduced by the number of years you have previously studied and you will need to self-fund for the year/s not eligible for. You will need to pay back any loans for tuition fees and maintenance and, dependent on the year you are in, the Student Finance Company will assess your financial situation and inform you about the loan amounts available and how much you need to pay back.

If you have Studied in Higher Education Previously

If you decide to leave your course and university and plan to return at a later date, you may have a set amount of time to transfer any credits you have achieved, if studying for the same or similar course. You would need to confirm with the university if you can continue your course or if you would need to start at the beginning of a new course, as well as confirming with Student Finance what funding support you may get.

If you have studied in higher education previously you will usually only get student finance if you are studying for your first higher education qualification, even if your previous course was self-funded as your course would still have received public funding. You may be eligible for limited funding in certain circumstances.

If you don't already have a degree you may get limited funding if:
- You change your course
- You leave your course but decide to start again.

If you already have a degree you may get funding for the following courses:

England, Wales, Northern Ireland or Scotland
- You are 'topping up' a higher education qualification such as if you have completed an HNC, HND or Foundation degree and want to top up to an honours degree.

Medicine or dentistry course as a second degree
England, Wales, Northern Ireland or Scotland
- You are studying a medicine or dentistry course as a second degree for students with a degree in another subject, for years 1-4 you will need to fund the tuition fees for the first four years yourself, but may apply for a maintenance loan which is income assessed. Year 5 and where relevant year 6 tuition fees are funded through the National Health Service (NHS) / health bursary as a tuition fee bursary which is non-income assessed, a grant which is non-means tested and a maintenance bursary which is income assessed, administered through the bursary administration organisation in the relevant country.

Medicine or dentistry course as a graduate entry second degree
England and Wales
- You are studying a medicine or dentistry course as a graduate entry fast track four year courses as a second degree for students with a degree in another subject, for years 1-4 you will be eligible for a tuition fee part self-funded / part tuition fee loan: non-income assessed and a maintenance loan: income assessed: Student Finance: England; Wales

Northern Ireland and Scotland
- You are studying a medicine or dentistry course as a graduate entry fast track four year courses as a second degree for students with a degree in another subject, for years 1-4 you will need to self-fund the tuition fees but may apply for a maintenance loan which is income assessed Student Finance Northern Ireland; Students Awards Agency Scotland (SAAS)

Engineering, technology or computer science part-time honours degree
England
- You are studying for a part-time honours degree in engineering, technology or computer science (or a joint honours degree in 2 of these subjects) and you hold an honours degree or higher level qualification in another subject; for eligible students' who meet the resident requirements in England.

Nursing, midwifery or specified allied health undergraduate, graduate or postgraduate course as a second degree
England
- Studying a nursing, midwifery or specified allied health undergraduate, graduate or postgraduate course as a second degree for students with a degree in another subject funded through Student Finance England from academic year 2018-2019, you will be able to access the undergraduate loans system as a tuition fee loan and maintenance loan (not a postgraduate loan).

Wales, Northern Ireland or Scotland
- Studying a nursing midwifery course as a second degree for students with a degree in another subject you are funded through the National Health Service (NHS) / Department of Health (DoH) NI / Scottish Department of Health and Social Care bursary as a tuition fee bursary which is non-income assessed and a maintenance bursary which is income assessed, administered through the health bursary administration organisation in Wales, Northern Ireland or Scotland.

Wales, Northern Ireland or Scotland
- Studying a specified allied health course as a second degree for students with a degree in another subject you are funded through the National Health Service (NHS) / Department of Health (DoH) NI/ Scottish Department of Health and Social Care bursary as a tuition fee bursary which is non-income assessed and a maintenance bursary which is income assessed, administered through the NHS bursary administration organisation in Wales, Northern Ireland or Scotland.

Teacher training Initial Teacher Education (ITE)
England, Wales, Northern Ireland or Scotland
- Studying a teacher training Initial Teacher Education (ITE) graduate or postgraduate course as a second degree for students funded through Student Finance will be able to access the undergraduate loans system as a tuition fee loan (England, Wales and Northern Ireland), a tuition fee grant (Scotland) and maintenance loan (not a postgraduate loan).

Social work
England, Wales, Northern Ireland or Scotland
- Studying a social work undergraduate or postgraduate qualification some eligible students may get some funding towards tuition fees and a bursary available from the social work funding organisation in the UK country where you are ordinarily resident, for some students but not all.

Further information if you have studied before:
If you have studied before
https://www.gov.uk/student-finance/who-qualifies

England
UK Government Student Finance England: Who Qualifies
https://www.gov.uk/student-finance/who-qualifies

Wales
Student Finance Wales: Previous Study Rules
https://www.studentfinancewales.co.uk/undergraduate-students/new-students/previous-study-rules.aspx

Northern Ireland

Northern Ireland Direct: Qualifying Student Finance
https://www.nidirect.gov.uk/articles/qualifying-student-finance

Scotland

Student Awards Agency for Scotland: Previous Study
http://www.saas.gov.uk/full_time/ug/young/eligibility_previous_study.htm

Nursing, Midwifery and Allied Health Professions

The Funding Clinic: Studying in England
https://thefundingclinic.org.uk/
The Funding Clinic: Studying in Wales, Northern Ireland and Scotland
https://thefundingclinic.org.uk/

Gap Year Students

If you apply to study in the UK but subsequently decide to take a gap year, you will need to inform your chosen university or college as soon as possible that you want to defer your place for a year.

You should receive written confirmation of your course place from them and you will need this when you re-apply for student finance the following year.

You will also need to notify the Student Finance Company regarding your situation. Universities and colleges will have their own requirements regarding offering you a deferred place and for some courses, you may be required to put in a new application for the following year. Check this information with the relevant university or college.

If you get into Financial Problems

It is important to keep to a budget but if managing your finances is a problem and you find yourself getting into financial difficulties, seek advice and guidance as soon as possible. It is usually easier to rectify financial problems the sooner you deal with them.

Your university will have student money advisers who can talk through your problems and provide advice and guidance. If you want more general help to develop your money management skills, there are lots of resources you can use.

The following are a selection of financial support contacts that have useful information on their web sites, with some organisations able to provide free advice and support. The law concerning debt varies depending on where you live in England, Wales, Northern Ireland or Scotland, so if seeking advice, make sure you let the adviser know what part of the UK you live.

Citizens Advice Bureaux

Citizens Advice Bureaux
http://www.adviceguide.org.uk
The Citizens Advice Bureaux offers free, confidential, impartial and independent advice in many locations including high street offices and many other different types of community centres. Advice is available on debt and a range of other issues. Advice is usually face-to-face or by phone, although some provide email advice.

Money Advice Service

Money Advice Service
https://www.moneyadviceservice.org.uk/
The Money Advice Service, set up by the UK government, provides free and impartial money advice to help improve your finances; tools and calculators to help you keep track and plan ahead; as well as support in person, over the phone and online.

National Association of Student Money Advisers (NASMA)
National Association of Student Money Advisers (NASMA)
http://www.nasma.org.uk/
The National Association of Student Money Advisers (NASMA) has student money advisers in universities and colleges throughout the UK. You can find your nearest adviser online

NASMA members are recognised as the leading authority on matters relating to student advice and funding. The website contains useful information for people who are considering attending university or college, have already applied, currently studying for a course or have graduated, including for full-time, part-time, undergraduate and postgraduate students.

National Debtline
National Debtline
http://www.nationaldebtline.co.uk/

Free phone number: 0808 808 4000
The National Debtline is a helpline that provides free confidential and independent advice on how to deal with debt problems.

National Union of Students (NUS)
National Union of Students (NUS)
http://www.nus.org.uk
The National Union of Students (NUS) has a range of lots of useful information, including financial advice, on their website with links to useful contacts.

Personal Finance Education Group (PFEG)
Personal Finance Education Group (PFEG)
http://www.pfeg.org/
The Personal Finance Education Group (PFEG) is part of Young Enterprise, a UK charity that empowers young people to harness their personal business skills and helps those who are teaching them about money.

Chapter 13
Student Bursary Funding

13.1 Bursary Funding for Eligible Students on Specified Courses

Eligible students who meet the residency requirements may be able to access bursary funding for some courses for some years. The following information is for guidance only and you should confirm details with the relevant funding authority as regulations and allowances may be subject to review and may change as well as individual circumstances may vary. There are different funding regulations in England, Wales, Northern Ireland and Scotland therefore you should check out further information on the relevant bursary organisation website.

Additional funding as grants for eligible students are available from the Student Finance Company or the Bursary Funding Organisation in England, Wales, Northern Ireland and Scotland.

Additional funding for eligible students: England, Wales and Northern Ireland
- Disabled Student Allowance
- Childcare Grant; Adult Dependents Grant; Parents Learning Allowance

Additional funding support for eligible students: Scotland
- Disabled Student Allowance
- Lone Parents Grant; Dependents Grant

Healthcare Bursary Administration Organisations

NHS England; NHS Wales; Department of Health (DoH) Northern Ireland; Scottish Health and Social Care bursary administration organisations

- Allied health and additional health specified courses
- Medicine and dentistry
- Nursing and midwifery

England
NHS Business Service Authority
https://www.nhsbsa.nhs.uk/nhs-bursary-students
Administers funding from the: NHS England   https://www.england.nhs.uk/

Wales
NHS Student Awards Services
http://www.nwssp.wales.nhs.uk/student-awards
Administers funding from the: NHS Wales
http://www.wales.nhs.uk/

Northern Ireland
Student Finance Northern Ireland
http://www.studentfinanceni.co.uk/
Administers funding from the:
Department of Health Northern Ireland
https://www.health-ni.gov.uk/

Scotland
Students Awards Agency Scotland (SAAS)
http://www.saas.gov.uk/
Administers funding from the:
Scottish Government Health and Social Care Directorateshttp://www.sehd.scot.nhs.uk/

13.2 Allied Health Undergraduate and Postgraduate Courses Student Funding

England:
Allied Health Undergraduate and Some Postgraduate Courses Student Funding:

Funding support for undergraduate and some postgraduate allied health courses student funding are available is the same as undergraduate student finance. The NHS Learning Support Fund funding support may be available for some eligible undergraduate and postgraduate students for the following pre-registration courses

A list of specified undergraduate and postgraduate pre-registration allied health courses which are approved for undergraduate student finance and for NHS England learning support fund support may be available from:

NHS Business Services Authority
http://www.nhsbsa.nhs.uk/students

- Dietetics
- Occupational therapy
- Operating department practitioner
- Orthoptics
- Orthotics and prosthetics
- Physiotherapy
- Podiatry
- Radiography (diagnostic and therapeutic)
- Speech and language therapy

Eligible students who meet the residence requirements in England, studying in England, Wales, Northern Ireland or Scotland

All years undergraduate and some postgraduate allied health courses Undergraduate student finance
- Tuition fee loan: non-income assessed; maintenance loan income assessed: Student Finance: England NHS Learning Support Fund funding support may be available for some students NHS England grant

Apply to Student Finance England: tuition fee loan; maintenance loan
Student Finance England
https://www.gov.uk/student-finance

Apply to NHS England Business Services Authority: Learning support fund NHS Business Services Authority
http://www.nhsbsa.nhs.uk/students

Wales:
Allied Health and Some Additional Health Undergraduate and Postgraduate Courses Student Funding

Funding support for undergraduate and some postgraduate allied health and some additional health courses student funding are available as NHS Wales bursaries. NHS Wales bursary funding support for eligible undergraduate and some postgraduate students for the following pre-registration courses available from: NHS Wales Student Awards Services: Student Awards
http://www.nwssp.wales.nhs.uk/student-awards

- Dental Hygiene / Dental Therapy
- Dietetics
- Healthcare Science: Audiology
- Healthcare Science: Biomedical Science - Blood, Infection; Cellular And Genetics
- Healthcare Science: Cardiac Physiology
- Healthcare Science: Neurophysiology
- Healthcare Science: Nuclear Medicine And Radiotherapy Physics
- Healthcare Science: Respiratory And Sleep Science
- Occupational Therapy
- Operational Department Practice
- Paramedic Science
- Physicians Associate Studies

- Physiotherapy
- Podiatry
- Radiography (Therapeutic and Diagnostic)
- Speech And Language Therapy

Eligible students who meet the residence requirements in Wales studying in Wales
All years undergraduate and some postgraduate allied health courses
- Tuition fee grant: non-income assessed; maintenance bursary: income assessed: NHS / DoH bursary
- Maintenance loan: income assessed for first degree students: Student Finance Wales

Students who already have a first degree and undertaking a pre-registration course at postgraduate diploma or master's degree level will have access to the NHS bursary but no access to the student maintenance loan.

Apply to NHS Wales Student Awards Services: Student Bursaries
NHS Wales Student Awards Services: Bursary Scheme Terms and Conditions
http://www.nwssp.wales.nhs.uk/student-awards

Northern Ireland:
Allied Health Undergraduate Courses Student Funding

Funding support for specified undergraduate allied health courses are available as Department of Health Northern Ireland bursaries.
Department of Health Northern Ireland bursary funding support for eligible undergraduate students for the following pre-registration courses available from: Department of Health (DoH) Northern Ireland https://www.health-ni.gov.uk/

- Dietetics
- Occupational therapy
- Physiotherapy
- Podiatry
- Radiography; diagnostic and therapeutic

- Speech and language therapy

Eligible students who meet the residence requirements in Northern Ireland studying in Northern Ireland

All years' undergraduate specified allied health courses
- Tuition fee grant: non-income assessed; maintenance bursary: income assessed: DoH bursary

Apply to Student Finance Northern Ireland: tuition fee bursary and maintenance bursary with the Department of Health (DoH)
Student Finance Northern Ireland
http://www.studentfinanceni.co.uk/

Scotland:
Allied Health Undergraduate Courses Student Funding

Funding support for specified undergraduate allied health courses are available as the usual undergraduate support package with Student Awards Agency for Scotland

List of specified allied health courses available from the
Student Awards Agency for Scotland
http://www.saas.gov.uk/

- Diagnostic imaging degree only
- Diagnostic radiography
- Dietetics
- Nutrition and dietetics
- Occupational therapy
- Orthoptics
- Orthotics
- Paramedics
- Physiotherapy
- Podiatry
- Prosthetics and orthotics

- Radiography
- Radiography and oncology
- Speech and language therapy
- Speech and language pathology
- Therapeutic radiography

Eligible students who meet the residence requirements in Scotland studying Scotland

All years' undergraduate allied health courses
- Tuition fee grant: non-income assessed; maintenance bursary: income assessed: DoH bursary

Apply to Student Awards Agency for Scotland: tuition fee grant, maintenance loan, maintenance bursary
Student Awards Agency for Scotland
http://www.saas.gov.uk

Scotland:
Allied Health Graduate and Postgraduate Courses Student Funding

Eligible students who meet the residence requirements in Scotland studying an allied health undergraduate, graduate or postgraduate course as a second degree for students with a degree in another subject are able to get funding for the first two years of the course. Students can't obtain this finance support if you already hold a first degree in one of the allied health professions.
Year 1 and 2
- Tuition fee grant: non-income assessed; maintenance loan and a maintenance bursary: income assessed Student Awards Agency Scotland

Years 3 and 4
- Maintenance loan: income assessed Student Awards Agency Scotland

If you wish to study in England, Wales or Northern Ireland you will need to contact Student Awards Agency Scotland for advice on funding.

Apply to Student Awards Agency for Scotland: tuition fee grant, maintenance loan, maintenance bursary
Student Awards Agency for Scotland
http://www.saas.gov.uk

13.3 Medicine and Dentistry Course Student Funding

England: Medicine and Dentistry Undergraduate Standard Degree Course Lasting Five / Six Years Student Funding

Eligible students who meet the residence requirements in England, studying in England, Wales, Northern Ireland or Scotland

Years 1,2,3,4 including intercalation year

- Tuition fee loan: non-income assessed; maintenance loan income assessed: Student Finance: England
- Clinical placement travel expenses Student Finance: England; Wales

Year 5 and year 6 including intercalation year
NHS England bursary

- Tuition fee grant: non-income assessed; maintenance bursary: income assessed: NHS England bursary
- Maintenance loan: income assessed: Student Finance England
- Clinical placement travel expenses NHS England
- NHS grant of £1,000 per year to help with living costs NHS England

England: Medicine and Dentistry Undergraduate Standard Second Degree Course (for Students With A Degree In Another Subject) Lasting Five / Six Years Student Funding

Eligible students who meet the residence requirements in England, studying in England, Wales, Northern Ireland or Scotland

Years 1,2,3,4 including intercalation year

- Tuition fee self-funded
- Maintenance loan: income assessed Student Finance: England;
- Clinical placement travel expenses Student Finance: England

Year 5 and year 6 including intercalation year
NHS England bursary

- Tuition fee grant: non-income assessed: NHS England bursary
- Maintenance bursary: income assessed: NHS England bursary
- Maintenance loan: income assessed: Student Finance England
- Clinical placement travel expenses NHS England grant
- NHS grant of £1,000 per year to help with living costs NHS England

501

England:
Medicine and Dentistry Graduate Entry Accelerated Degree Course (for Students with Another Degree) Lasting Four Years Student Funding

Eligible students who meet the residence requirements in England, studying in England, Wales, Northern Ireland or Scotland

Year 1

- Tuition fee part self-funded / part tuition fee loan: non-income assessed Student Finance: England
- Maintenance loan: income assessed: Student Finance England
- Clinical placement travel expenses Student Finance England

Years 2, 3 and 4
NHS England bursary

- Tuition fee part NHS bursary / part tuition fee loan: non-income assessed NHS England bursary / Student Finance England

- Maintenance bursary: income assessed: NHS England
- Maintenance loan: income assessed: Student Finance England
- Clinical placement travel expenses NHS England grant
- NHS grant of £1,000 per year to help with living costs NHS England

Apply to Student Finance England: tuition fee loan; maintenance loan
Student Finance England
https://www.gov.uk/student-finance

Apply to Business Services Authority: medicine and dentistry bursary
NHS Business Services Authority
http://www.nhsbsa.nhs.uk/students

Wales
Medicine and Dentistry Undergraduate Standard Degree Course Lasting Five / Six Years Student Funding

Eligible Students who meet the residence requirements in Wales studying in England, Wales, Northern Ireland or Scotland
Years 1,2,3,4 including intercalation year

- Tuition fee loan: non-income assessed; maintenance loan income assessed; maintenance grant: income assessed Student Finance Wales
- Clinical placement travel expenses Student Finance Wales

Year 5 and year 6 including intercalation year
NHS Wales bursary

- Tuition fee grant: non-income assessed; maintenance bursary: income assessed: NHS Wales bursary
- Maintenance loan: income assessed: Student Finance Wales
- Clinical placement travel expenses NHS Wales grant
- NHS grant of £1,000 per year to help with living costs NHS Wales grant

Wales:
Medicine and Dentistry Undergraduate Standard Second Degree Course (for Students with a Degree in Another Subject) Lasting Five / Six Years Student Funding

Eligible students who meet the residence requirements in Wales, studying in England, Wales, Northern Ireland or Scotland

Years 1,2,3,4 including intercalation year

- Tuition fee self-funded
- Maintenance loan: income assessed; maintenance grant: income assessed Student Finance Wales
- Clinical placement travel expenses Student Finance Wales

Year 5 and year 6 including intercalation year
NHS Wales bursary

- Tuition fee grant: non-income assessed; maintenance bursary: income assessed: NHS bursary
- Maintenance loan: income assessed: Student Finance Wales
- Clinical placement travel expenses NHS Wales grant
- NHS grant of £1,000 per year to help with living costs NHS Wales grant

Wales:
Medicine and Dentistry Graduate Entry Accelerated Degree Course (for Students With Another Degree) Lasting Four Years Student Funding

Eligible students who meet the residence requirements in Wales, studying in England, Wales, Northern Ireland or Scotland

Year 1
- Tuition fee part self-funded / part tuition fee loan: non-income assessed Student Finance Wales
- Maintenance loan: income assessed: Student Finance Wales
- Clinical placement travel expenses Student Finance Wales

Years 2, 3 and 4
NHS Wales bursary
- Tuition fee part NHS bursary / part tuition fee loan: non-income assessed NHS Wales bursary / Student Finance Wales

- Maintenance bursary: income assessed: NHS Wales bursary
- Maintenance loan: income assessed: Student Finance: Wales
- Clinical placement travel expenses NHS Wales grant
- NHS grant of £1,000 per year to help with living costs NHS Wales

Apply to Student Finance Wales: tuition fee loan; maintenance loan
Student Finance Wales
https://www.studentfinancewales.co.uk/

Apply to NHS Wales Student Awards Services: Bursary
NHS Wales Student Awards Services: Bursary
http://www.nwssp.wales.nhs.uk/student-awards

Northern Ireland:
Medicine and Dentistry Undergraduate Standard Degree Course Lasting Five / Six Years Student Funding

Eligible students who meet the residence requirements in Northern Ireland, studying in England, Wales, Northern Ireland or Scotland

Years 1,2,3,4 including intercalation year
- Tuition fee loan: non-income assessed; maintenance loan income assessed; maintenance grant: income assessed Student Finance Northern Ireland

Year 5 and year 6 including intercalation year
Department of Health (DoH) Northern Ireland bursary
- Tuition fee grant: non-income assessed; maintenance bursary: income assessed: DoH bursary
- Maintenance loan: income assessed: Student Finance Northern Ireland
- Clinical placement travel expenses for students receiving a maintenance grant Department of Economy Northern Ireland

Northern Ireland:
Medicine and Dentistry Undergraduate Standard Second Degree Course (for Students With a Degree in Another Subject) Lasting Five / Six Years Student Funding

Eligible students who meet the residence requirements in England, Wales or Northern Ireland, studying in England, Wales, Northern Ireland or Scotland

Years 1,2,3,4, 5 / 6 including intercalation year
Undergraduate student
- Tuition fee self-funded
- Maintenance loan: income assessed; Student Finance Northern Ireland

Northern Ireland:
Medicine and Dentistry Graduate Entry Accelerated Degree Course (for Students With Another Degree) Lasting Four Years Student Funding

Eligible students who meet the residence requirements in Northern Ireland, studying in England, Wales, Northern Ireland or Scotland

All years 1,2,3,4

- Tuition fee self-funded
- Maintenance loan: income assessed; income assessed Student Finance Northern Ireland

Apply to Student Finance Northern Ireland: tuition fee loan, maintenance loan, maintenance grant
Student Finance Northern Ireland
http://www.studentfinanceni.co.uk/

Apply to Student Finance Northern Ireland: tuition fee bursary and maintenance bursary with the Department of Health (DoH)
Student Finance Northern Ireland
http://www.studentfinanceni.co.uk/

England, Wales Northern Ireland: Medicine and Dentistry Intercalation Year

If you are intercalating your medicine or dentistry course to study for a bachelor or master's' degree, but not a PhD, the intercalating years can be counted towards the qualifying period for NHS

Bursary support and may be eligible for funding from your 5th year of study onwards, regardless of when your intercalation year occurs.

Scotland:
Medicine and Dentistry Undergraduate Standard Degree Course Lasting Five / Six Years' Student Funding

Eligible students who meet the resident requirements in Scotland, studying in Scotland

Years 1,2,3,4,5 / 6 including intercalation year

- Tuition fee grant: non-income assessed; maintenance loan: income assessed: maintenance bursary: income assessed: Students Awards Agency Scotland

Studying in Scotland: dentistry course (additional funding support)
Also available for students from England, Wales or Northern Ireland studying in Scotland

Years 1-4

- Dental Student Support Grant (DSSG)

Eligible students who meet the resident requirements in Scotland, studying in England, Wales or Northern Ireland

Years 1-4 including intercalation year

- Tuition fee loan: non-income assessed; maintenance loan: income assessed; maintenance bursary: income assessed: Students Awards Agency Scotland

Year 5 and year 6 including intercalation year
Scottish Government Health and Social Care bursary

- Tuition fee grant health bursary: non-income assessed; maintenance loan: income assessed; maintenance bursary: income assessed: Students Awards Agency Scotland

Scotland:
Medicine and Dentistry Undergraduate Standard Degree Course Lasting Five / Six Years' Student Funding St Andrews University Plus Additional University

BSc honours medicine degree:
Studying in Scotland: St Andrews University
Years 1-3

- Tuition fee grant: non-income assessed; maintenance loan: income assessed: maintenance bursary: income assessed: Students Awards Agency Scotland

Transferring in Scotland: medicine degree course (MBChB / MBBS)
Years 4

- Tuition fee grant: non-income assessed; maintenance loan: income assessed: maintenance bursary: income assessed: Students Awards Agency Scotland

Transferring to England, Wales or Northern Ireland: medicine course MBChB / MBBS
Years 4

- Tuition fee loan: non-income assessed; maintenance loan: income assessed; maintenance bursary: income assessed: Students Awards Agency Scotland

Years 5 and 6 studying in England, Wales, Northern Ireland or Scotland
Scottish Government Health and Social Care bursary

- Tuition fee health grant: non-income assessed; maintenance loan: income assessed; maintenance bursary: income assessed Students Awards Agency Scotland

Scotland:
Medicine and Dentistry Undergraduate Standard Second Degree Course (for Students With a Degree in Another Subject) Lasting Five / Six Years Student Funding

Eligible students who meet the residence requirements in Scotland, studying in England, Wales, Northern Ireland or Scotland
Years 1,2,3,4 including intercalation year

- Tuition fees self-funded
- Maintenance loan: income assessed; maintenance grant: income assessed Students Awards Agency Scotland

Year 5 and year 6 including intercalation year
Scottish Government Health and Social Care bursary

- Tuition fee grant health bursary: non-income assessed; maintenance loan; maintenance health bursary: income assessed: Students Awards Agency Scotland

Scotland:
Medicine and Dentistry Graduate Entry Accelerated Degree Course (for Students With Another Degree) Lasting Four Years Student Funding

Eligible students who meet the residence requirements in Scotland, studying in England, Wales, Northern Ireland or Scotland
Years 1-4
Undergraduate student finance

- Tuition fee self-funded
- Maintenance loan: income assessed; maintenance grant: income assessed Students Awards Agency Scotland

Apply to Students Awards Agency Scotland (SAAS): Tuition fee grant, tuition fee loan, maintenance loan, maintenance bursary
Students Awards Agency Scotland (SAAS) http://www.saas.gov.uk/

Apply to your university after completing the application for the Dental Student Grant available at:
My Gov Scotland: Dental Student Grant https://www.mygov.scot/dental-student-grant/

13.4 Nursing and Midwifery Courses Student Funding

England:
Nursing and Midwifery Undergraduate and Postgraduate Courses Student Funding

Funding support for undergraduate and postgraduate nursing and midwifery is the same as undergraduate student finance. The NHS Learning Support Fund funding support may be available for some eligible undergraduate and postgraduate students pre-registration nursing and midwifery courses.

Eligible students who meet the residence requirements in England, studying in England, Wales, Northern Ireland or Scotland

All years: undergraduate and postgraduate nursing and midwifery Undergraduate student finance

- Tuition fee loan: non-income assessed; maintenance loan income assessed: Student Finance: England
- NHS Learning Support Fund funding support may be available for some students NHS England grant

Apply to Student Finance England: tuition fee loan; maintenance loan
Student Finance England
https://www.gov.uk/student-finance

Apply to NHS England Business Services Authority: Learning support fund NHS Business Services Authority
http://www.nhsbsa.nhs.uk/students

Wales:
Nursing and Midwifery Undergraduate and Postgraduate Courses Student Funding

Funding support for undergraduate and postgraduate nursing and midwifery courses are available as NHS Wales bursaries.

**Eligible students who meet the residence requirements in Wales studying in Wales
All years' undergraduate and postgraduate nursing and midwifery courses**

- Tuition fee grant: non-income assessed; maintenance bursary: income assessed: NHS Wales bursary
- Maintenance loan: income assessed for first degree students: Student Finance Wales

Students who already have a first degree and undertaking a pre-registration course at postgraduate diploma or master's degree level will have access to the NHS bursary but no access to the student maintenance loan.

Apply to NHS Wales Student Awards Services: Student Bursaries
NHS Wales Student Awards Services: Bursary Scheme Terms and Conditions
http://www.nwssp.wales.nhs.uk/student-awards

Northern Ireland: Nursing and Midwifery Undergraduate Courses Student Funding

Funding support for undergraduate nursing and midwifery courses are available as Northern Ireland Department of Health (DoH) bursaries. Students who are studying nursing as a second degree are also eligible for bursary funding support.

Eligible students who meet the residence requirements in Northern Ireland studying in Northern Ireland

All years: undergraduate nursing and midwifery courses

- Tuition fee grant: non-income assessed; maintenance bursary: income assessed: DoH bursary

Apply to HSC Business Services Organisation: tuition fee bursary and maintenance bursary with the Department of Health (DoH)

HSC Business Services Organisation
http://www.hscbusiness.hscni.net/services/2662.htm

Scotland: Nursing and Midwifery Undergraduate and Postgraduate Courses Student Funding

Funding support for undergraduate and postgraduate nursing and midwifery courses are available as Scotland Department of Health and Social Care bursaries.

Eligible students who meet the residence requirements in Scotland studying in Scotland

All years: undergraduate and postgraduate nursing and midwifery courses

- Tuition fee grant; maintenance bursary: non-income assessed Student Awards Agency for Scotland
- Initial expenses bursary Student Awards Agency for Scotland
- Clinical placements expenses allowance Student Awards Agency for Scotland

If you wish to study in England, Wales or Northern Ireland you will need to contact Student Awards Agency Scotland for advice on funding.

Apply to Student Awards Agency for Scotland: nursing and midwifery bursary

Student Awards Agency for Scotland
http://www.saas.gov.uk

13.5 Paramedic Science Courses Student Funding

Paramedic science course student funding is different in England, Wales, Northern Ireland and Scotland.

England:
Paramedic Science Undergraduate Courses Student Funding

Eligible students who meet the residence requirements in England studying an undergraduate paramedic science qualification in a university can get undergraduate student funding from Student Finance England funded with a tuition fee loan and maintenance loan. Some courses may be funded with tuition fees paid for by a local Health Education Trust, details should be available on the relevant university website. Some ambulance services employ student paramedics who train in-service whilst in employment and fund the training.

All years: paramedic science course in a university

- Tuition fee loan, undergraduate; maintenance loan, undergraduate: income assessed Student Finance England

Some courses may be funded with tuition fees paid and a bursary by a local Health Education Trust

- Tuition fee grant: non-income assessed; maintenance bursary Health Education Trust
- Reduced maintenance loan, undergraduate: income assessed Student Finance England

Paramedic in-service training

- Some ambulance services pay for training and employ student paramedics who train whilst in employment

Apply to Student Finance England: tuition fee loan; maintenance loan
Student Finance England
https://www.gov.uk/student-finance

Apply to Ambulance Service Trusts: In-service training
List of Ambulance Trusts in the UK
College of Paramedics: Ambulance Trusts
https://www.collegeofparamedics.co.uk/how_to_become_a_paramedic/ambulance_trusts

Eligible students who meet the residence requirements in Wales studying an undergraduate paramedic science qualification in a university can get undergraduate student funding as an NHS Wales bursary funded with a tuition fee grant which is non-income assessed and maintenance bursary, providing you commit to working in Wales for a two year period after completing your course.

Otherwise you can apply for undergraduate funding from Student Finance Wales funded with a tuition fee loan which is income assessed, a maintenance loan and maintenance grant which in income assessed. Some ambulance services employ student paramedics who train in-service whilst in employment and fund the training.

A list of specified allied health courses eligible for NHS Wales bursary is available from:
NHS Wales Student Awards Services: Student Awards
http://www.nwssp.wales.nhs.uk/student-awards

All years: paramedic science course in a university student NHS Wales bursary
- Tuition fee grant: non-income assessed; maintenance loan, undergraduate: income assessed NHS Wales bursary

Paramedic science in a university Student Finance funding
- Tuition fee loan, undergraduate: non-income assessed; maintenance loan, undergraduate: income assessed; maintenance grant, undergraduate: income assessed Student Finance Wales

Paramedic in-service training
- Some ambulance services pay for training and employ student paramedics who train whilst in employment

Apply to NHS Wales Student Awards Services: Student Bursaries
NHS Wales Student Awards Services: Bursary Scheme Terms and Conditions
http://www.nwssp.wales.nhs.uk/student-awards

Apply to Student Finance Wales: tuition fee loan; maintenance loan
Student Finance Wales
https://www.studentfinancewales.co.uk/

Apply to Ambulance Service Trusts: In-service training
List of Ambulance Trusts in the UK
College of Paramedics: Ambulance Trusts
https://www.collegeofparamedics.co.uk/how_to_become_a_paramedic/ambulance_trusts

Northern Ireland: Paramedic Science Undergraduate Courses Student Funding

By 2020 a paramedic science will be an honours degree qualification requirement Currently Ambulance Trusts train paramedics in-service and pay a trainee salary. This will be changing and the honours degree in paramedic science will be available only in universities. No decision has been made currently and the Department of Health (DoH) Northern Ireland https://www.health-ni.gov.uk/ may provide student bursary funding in the future, check for up to date information.

All years: paramedic science course in a university

- Tuition fee loan, undergraduate: non-income assessed; maintenance loan, undergraduate: income assessed; maintenance grant, undergraduate: income assessed Student Finance Northern Ireland

Courses may be funded with tuition fees paid and a bursary by the Department of Health DoH) Northern Ireland (in consultation)

- Tuition fee grant: non-income assessed; maintenance bursary DoH bursary

Paramedic in-service training (being phased on in Northern Ireland)

- Some ambulance services pay for training and employ student paramedics who train whilst in employment

Apply to Student Finance Northern Ireland: tuition fee loan, maintenance loan, maintenance grant
Student Finance Northern Ireland http://www.studentfinanceni.co.uk/

Apply to Student Finance Northern Ireland: tuition fee bursary and maintenance bursary with the Department of Health (DoH)
Student Finance Northern Ireland http://www.studentfinanceni.co.uk/

Apply to Ambulance Service Trusts: In-service training (being phased out in Northern Ireland)
List of Ambulance Trusts in the UK
College of Paramedics: Ambulance Trusts https://www.collegeofparamedics.co.uk/how_to_become_a_paramedic/ambulance_trusts

Scotland: Paramedic Science Undergraduate Courses Student Funding

Paramedic training in Scotland is undertaken with the Scottish Ambulance Service in-service, firstly training as an ambulance technician and once qualified you may apply for a paramedic position an undertake further training. In-service training is funded by the Scottish Ambulance Service

Paramedic in-service training: Scotland
The Scottish Ambulance Service employs student ambulance technicians who train in-service whilst in employment; and then may undertake in-service training to become a paramedic.

Ambulance technician and paramedic courses student funding

- Scottish Ambulance Service pay for training and employ student ambulance technicians and paramedics who train whilst in employment

Apply to Scottish Ambulance Service: In-service training
Scottish Ambulance Service http://www.scottishambulance.com/

13.6 Physician Associate Courses Student Funding

New students starting academic year 2018- 2019:
Eligible students who meet the residence requirements in England, Wales, Northern Ireland or Scotland studying a physician associate postgraduate course may get some funding. Physician associate postgraduate course student funding is different in England, Wales, Northern Ireland and Scotland.

Some students may get funding for full or partial tuition fees, or sponsorship, paid through
Health Education England;

local NHS trusts, Clinical Commissioning Groups (CCGs), Health Education Boards or other health employers. As funding is not nationalised, this is down to local agreements and students may be required to self-fund all or part of the tuition fees. Some universities may have a limited number of funded places; some may also offer scholarships or bursaries for some students. Some courses offer a period of paid work experience. Funding options should be highlighted on each university course website. You may be able to get some funding as a postgraduate loan from the Student Finance Company in the relevant UK country.

England:
Physician Associate Postgraduate Courses Student Funding

New students starting academic year 2018-2019
Eligible students who meet the residence requirements in England, studying for a postgraduate diploma or master's degree physician associate qualification, Health Education England (HEE) will provide a bursary spread over two years and how this is managed / paid may vary depending on local agreements in place. For some courses in certain regions the funding is to support travel to required clinical placements; other regions the funding is to support students on placements and also for when newly qualified physician associates start a period of transition, being supported by a preceptor. Some regions may pay funding to students in one sum, split over two years, or when completing preceptorship. The bursary amount may not cover the full cost of tuition fees and students may need to self-fund tuition fees.

If studying for a master's degree physician associate qualification, you may be able to get a postgraduate master's degree loan from Student Finance England, which is in addition to any student funding from HEE. The postgraduate diploma (PGDip) does not qualify for a government funded postgraduate loan, however some universities are only offering the master's degree.

Funding details should be available on the relevant university website. A list of local offices of Health Education England (HEE) is available from Health Education England (HEE) https://hee.nhs.uk/ . Some universities may have scholarships and bursaries available for some students.

Physician associate postgraduate diploma; master's degree student funding: England
- Tuition fees self-funded
- Grant towards tuition fees and additional costs for some students or for clinical placement expenses: local office of Health Education England (HEE)
- University scholarships and bursaries for some eligible students

Physician associate master's degree additional student funding
- Postgraduate master's degree loan Student Finance England

Students eligible for a grant will be nominated by the university
Apply to the university: Physician associate postgraduate diploma; master's degree: HEE grant

Apply to Student Finance England: Postgraduate master's degree loan
Student Finance England
https://www.gov.uk/student-finance

Wales:
Physician Associate Postgraduate Courses Student Funding

New students starting academic year 2018-2019
Eligible students who meet the residence requirements in Wales, studying for a postgraduate diploma or master's degree physician associate qualification may be able to get a bursary provided by NHS Wales providing you are able to commit to work in Wales for a minimum of 18 months on completion of the course. Students who have a first degree and undertaking a pre-registration programme at postgraduate diploma or master's degree level will have access to the NHS bursary package but no access to the reduced student maintenance loan.

Further information may be found at:
List of specified bursary funded health courses available from
NHS Wales Student Awards Services: Student Awards: New Students: Terms and Conditions
http://www.nwssp.wales.nhs.uk/student-awards

Physician associate postgraduate diploma; master's degree student funding: Wales
- Tuition fee grant; maintenance grant: NHS Wales bursary

Apply to NHS Wales Student Awards Services: NHS Wales bursary
NHS Wales Student Awards Services
http://www.nwssp.wales.nhs.uk/student-awards

Northern Ireland:
Physician Associate Postgraduate Courses Student Funding

New students starting academic year 2018-2019
Eligible students who meet the residence requirements in Northern Ireland, studying for a postgraduate diploma or master's degree physician associate qualification may have funding for tuition fees to be paid for as a grant by a local health trust, contact details are available at Health and Social Care Northern Ireland
http://online.hscni.net/hospitals/health-and-social-care-trusts/ . Funding may also be provided for GPs and health trusts for student clinical placements. If studying for a postgraduate diploma or master's degree physician associate qualification, you may be able to get a postgraduate tuition fee loan from Student Finance Northern Ireland, however you would need to confirm if receiving bursary funding.

Physician associate postgraduate diploma; master's degree student funding: Northern Ireland
- Tuition fees grant; funding for clinical placements: Department of Health (DoH) bursary
- University scholarships and bursaries for some eligible students

Physician associate postgraduate diploma or master's degree additional student funding
- Postgraduate tuition fee loan: Student Finance Northern Ireland.

Students eligible for a grant will be nominated by the university
Apply to the university: Physician associate postgraduate diploma; master's degree: health trust grant
Apply to Student Finance Northern Ireland: Postgraduate tuition fee loan:
Student Finance Northern Ireland
http://www.studentfinanceni.co.uk/

Scotland:
Physician Associate Postgraduate Courses Student Funding

New students starting academic year 2018- 2019:Scotland

Eligible students who meet the residence requirements in Scotland, studying for a postgraduate diploma or master's degree physician associate qualification may be able to get a postgraduate tuition fee loan and maintenance loan from Student Awards Agency for Scotland

Physician associate postgraduate diploma; master's degree student funding: Scotland

- Tuition fees self-funded
- University scholarships and bursaries for some eligible students

Physician associate postgraduate diploma or master's degree additional student funding

- Postgraduate tuition fee loan: non-income assessed; postgraduate living cost loan: income assessed Student Awards Agency for Scotland

Apply to Student Awards Agency for Scotland: Postgraduate loan

Student Awards Agency for Scotland
http://www.saas.gov.uk

13.7 Social Work Courses Student Funding

New students starting academic year 2018- 2019

Some social work students on undergraduate and postgraduate courses in England, Wales, Northern Ireland and Scotland may be eligible for a bursary for tuition fees and maintenance costs.

Social work bursary administration organisations
England

NHS Business Service Authority (NHSBSA) https://www.nhsbsa.nhs.uk/

Wales

Social Care Wales
https://socialcare.wales/careers/social-work-bursary-funding

Northern Ireland

Department of Health Northern Ireland: Office of Social Services
https://www.health-ni.gov.uk/contact

Scotland

Scottish Social Services Council
http://www.sssc.uk.com/

You must be studying or intending to study on a university or college based social work course approved by the following professional care profession regulators:

Professional care profession regulators

England: Health and Care Professions Council http://www.hcpc-uk.org/
Wales: Social Care Council for Wales https://socialcare.wales/
Northern Ireland: Northern Ireland Social Care Council http://www.niscc.info/
Scotland: Scottish Social Services Council http://www.sssc.uk.com/

England:
Social Work Undergraduate Course Student Funding

New students starting academic year 2018- 2019
Eligible students who meet the residence requirements in England studying a social work honours degree course

NHS Business Services Authority
http://www.nhsbsa.nhs.uk/students
NHS England bursary
Years 2 and 3

- Tuition fee contribution bursary: some eligible students; Maintenance bursary: some eligible students: NHS England bursary

Student Finance England:
All years

- Tuition fee loan: non-income assessed; maintenance loan: income assessed: Student Finance England

England:
Social Work Postgraduate Course Student Funding

Eligible students who meet the residence requirements in England studying a social work master's degree course
Years 1 and 2
NHS England bursary

- Tuition fee contribution bursary: non-income assessed; maintenance bursary: income assessed: some eligible students: NHS England bursary
- Grant, including placement travel allowance for non-bursary recipients: non-income assessed: NHS England grant

Student Finance England:
Years 1 and 2

- Postgraduate master's degree loan: non-income assessed: Student Finance England

Apply to the NHS Business Service Authority (NHSBSA): Social Work Students; Apply Undergraduate Bursary
NHS Business Service Authority (NHSBSA)
https://www.nhsbsa.nhs.uk/social-work-students/apply-undergraduate-bursary
Your university or college will nominate named students on approved honours degree and master's degree social work courses for a bursary and will notify you on how to apply. Nominated students should also complete an application by the advised deadline on the NHS Business Authority Services website.

Apply to Student Finance England: undergraduate finance; postgraduate master's degree loan
Student Finance England
https://www.gov.uk/student-finance

Wales:
Social Work Undergraduate Course Student Funding

Eligible students who meet the residence requirements in Wales studying a social work honours degree course
Social Care Wales: Social Work Bursary Funding
https://socialcare.wales/careers/social-work-bursary-funding
Years 1, 2 and 3

- Tuition fee contribution bursary: some eligible students; maintenance bursary:

some eligible students: Social Care Wales

Student Finance England:
All years

- Tuition fee loan: non-income assessed; maintenance loan; maintenance grant income assessed: Student Finance Wales

Wales:
Social Work Postgraduate Course Student Funding

Eligible students who meet the residence requirements in Wales studying a social work master's degree course

Social Care Wales: Social Work Bursary Funding

https://socialcare.wales/careers/social-work-bursary-funding

Years 1 and 2

- Tuition fee contribution bursary: non-income assessed some eligible students; maintenance bursary: income assessed: some eligible students: Social Care Wales

Student Finance Wales
Years 1 and 2

- Postgraduate master's degree loan: non-income assessed: Student Finance Wales

Apply to the Social Care Wales: Social Work Bursary Funding

Social Care Wales: Social Work Bursary Funding

https://socialcare.wales/careers/social-work-bursary-funding

Your university or college will nominate named students on approved honours degree and master's degree social work courses for a bursary and will notify you on how to apply.

Northern Ireland:
Social Work Undergraduate Course Student Funding

(Currently under review)

Eligible students who meet the residence requirements in Northern Ireland studying a social work honours degree course Northern Ireland the Department of Health Northern Ireland Office of Social Services

https://www.health-ni.gov.uk/contact

Years 1, 2 and 3

- Tuition fee contribution bursary: non-income assessed; maintenance bursary: some eligible students: non-income assessed: some eligible students: Student Incentive Scheme Bursary

Student Finance England:
All years

- Tuition fee loan: non-income assessed; maintenance loan; maintenance grant: income assessed: Student Finance Northern Ireland

Northern Ireland:
Social Work Graduate Two Year Accelerated Course Student Funding

Eligible students who meet the residence requirements in Northern Ireland studying a social graduate two year accelerated degree course
Northern Ireland the Department of Health Northern Ireland Office of Social Services
https://www.health-ni.gov.uk/contact

Years 1 and 2

* Tuition fee contribution bursary: non-income assessed; maintenance bursary: some eligible students: non-income assessed: some eligible students: Student Incentive Scheme Bursary

Apply to the Department of Health Northern Ireland Office of Social Services: Student Incentive Scheme for Students Entering a Social Work degree

Department of Health Northern Ireland: Office of Social Services
https://www.health-ni.gov.uk/contact
You must be accepted on one of the approved social work courses in Northern Ireland. Your chosen course will send you an application form and Notes of Guidance for the Incentive Scheme together with your course enrolment instructions. You will need to complete the application and return it to the Office of Social Services (OSS). You are usually awarded the funding after your course has started therefore students should also contact your local Northern Ireland Education Authority
http://www.eani.org.uk/ at an early stage regarding student support finance arrangements

Scotland:
Social Work Undergraduate Course Student Funding

Eligible students who meet the residence requirements in Scotland studying a social work honours degree course

All years

* Tuition fee grant: non-income assessed; maintenance loan; maintenance grant: income assessed: Student Awards Agency for Scotland

Scotland:
Social Work Postgraduate Course Student Funding

Eligible students who meet the residence requirements in Scotland studying a social work postgraduate diploma or master's degree course
Scottish Social Services Council (SSSC)
http://www.sssc.uk.com/

Years 1 and 2

* Tuition fee contribution bursary: non-income assessed; maintenance bursary: income assessed: some eligible students: Scottish Social Services Council

Apply to the Student Awards Agency for Scotland (SAAS): Undergraduate Funding
Student Awards Agency for Scotland (SAAS): Undergraduate
http://www.saas.gov.uk/

Apply to the Scotland the Scottish Social Services Council (SSSC): Postgraduate Social Work Bursary Funding
Eligible students are nominated by the course education provider to:
Scotland the Scottish Social Services Council (SSSC)
http://www.sssc.uk.com/registration/what-qualifications-do-i-need/funding-for-training

13.8 Teaching: Initial Teacher Training (ITT) Course Student Funding

Funding support for postgraduate initial teacher training (ITT) courses is the same as undergraduate student finance and tuition fee costs are the same as for undergraduate courses. Bursaries and scholarships are available for some subjects

England:
Initial Teacher Training (ITT) Postgraduate Courses Student Funding

Eligible students who meet the residence requirements in England studying a postgraduate initial teacher training (ITT) course is able to apply for undergraduate student finance

- Tuition fee loan non-income assessed; maintenance loan income assessed Student Finance England

Apply to Student Finance England: postgraduate ITT funding same as undergraduate: tuition fee loan; maintenance loan
Student Finance England
https://www.gov.uk/student-finance
Students studying a graduate entry master's degree with early years' teacher status (EYTS) full time and part time employment based can get tuition fees student funding through the Department for Education (DfE) and may be eligible for an early years ITT bursary.

- Tuition fee grant; maintenance bursary for some students: DfE

Apply to the university as will nominate students for the EYTS bursary

England:
Bursaries and Scholarships Available for Specified Subjects

Mathematics
Bursary for teacher trainees with an honours degree 1st class, 2:1, 2:2; master's degree or PhD
Early career payments

Physics, Chemistry, Languages, Computing, Geography
Scholarships and bursaries for teacher trainees with an honours degree 1st class, 2:1, 2:2; master's degree or PhD

Classics, Biology,
Bursaries for teacher trainees with an honours degree 1st class, 2:1, 2:2; master's degree or PhD

Design and Technology, English, History, Music, Religious Education, Primary Mathematics
Bursaries for teacher trainees with an honours degree 1st class, 2:1, 2:2; master's degree or PhD

Applying for a bursary
You don't need to apply for a bursary as all eligible students will begin to receive monthly payments from your chosen teacher training provider when you start your course.
Further information:
Get into Teaching: Scholarships
https://getintoteaching.education.gov.uk/funding-and-salary/overview/scholarships

England:
Scholarships for Specified Subjects

Scholarships may be awarded in place of a bursary to the most gifted teacher trainees in physics, mathematics, chemistry, computing, languages or geography in partnership with professional subject associations. You will need to want to teach chemistry, computing, geography, languages, mathematics or physics.
To be eligible for a scholarship you will need a minimum of a 2:1 honours degree; you may apply if you have a 2:2 but you will need to provide evidence of significant relevant experience.

Chemistry
You will need a minimum of an honours degree class 2:2 in chemistry or a combined subject with chemistry of at least 50%; or undertake a Subject Knowledge Enhancement (SKE) chemistry course.

Apply to Royal Society of Chemistry: teacher training scholarships
Royal Society of Chemistry: teacher training scholarships
http://www.rsc.org/awards-funding/funding/teacher-training-scholarships/#eligibility

Computing
You will need a minimum of an honours degree class 2:2 preferably in computer science or mathematics; or a subject with extensive computing content such as with a Science, Technology, Engineering or Mathematics (STEM); or have a degree and significant professional experience as part of the computing industry; or undertake a subject knowledge enhancement (SKE) computing course.

Apply to BCS the Chartered Institute of Computing: BCS Scholarship
BCS the Chartered Institute of Computing: BCS Scholarship
http://www.computingatschool.org.uk/bcs-scholarship

Geography
You will need a minimum of a 2:1 honours degree in Geography or related subject; you may apply if you have a 2:2 but you will need to provide evidence of significant relevant experience; or have a relevant master's degree or PhD

Apply to Royal Geographical Society: Teacher Training Scholarships
Royal Geographical Society: Teacher Training Scholarships
https://www.rgs.org/schools/teacher-training-scholarships/

Languages
You will need to be on a teacher training course for French, German or Spanish.

You will need a minimum of a 2:1 honours degree in a French, German or Spanish subject; you may apply if you have a 2:2 but you will need to provide evidence of significant relevant experience; or have a relevant master's degree or PhD

Apply to British Council: Languages Teacher Training Scholarships
British Council: Languages Teacher Training Scholarships
https://www.britishcouncil.org/study-work-create/opportunity/uk/languages-teacher-training-scholarships

Mathematics
You will need a minimum of a 2:1 honours degree in mathematics or a subject with strong mathematical content; you may apply if you have a 2:2 but you will need to provide evidence of significant relevant experience; or have a relevant master's degree or PhD; or undertake a subject knowledge enhancement (SKE) mathematics course.

Apply to Institute of Mathematics and its Applications (IPA): Mathematics Training Scholarships
Institute of Mathematics and its Applications (IPA): Mathematics Training Scholarships
http://teachingmathematicsscholars.org/home

Physics
You will need a minimum of a 2:1 honours degree in physics or related subject with strong physics content such as engineering or astronomy; you may apply if you have a 2:2 but you will need to provide evidence of significant relevant experience; or have a relevant master's degree or PhD; or undertake a subject knowledge enhancement (SKE) mathematics course.

**Apply to Institute of Physics: Teach:
IOP Teacher Training Scholarships**
Institute of Physics: Teach: IOP Teacher
Training Scholarships
http://www.iop.org/education/teach/

Further information
UK Government: Get into Teaching;
Funding and Salary; Overview
https://getintoteaching.education.gov.uk/fu
nding-and-salary/overview
UK Government: Get into Teaching;
Funding and Salary; Scholarships
https://getintoteaching.education.gov.uk/fu
nding-and-salary/overview/scholarships
UK Government: Teacher Training
Funding https://www.gov.uk/teacher-
training-funding

England: Postgraduate School Centred Salaried Primary and Secondary Teacher Training Courses

School centred teacher training
programmes which involve being
employed by your school as an unqualified
teacher while you train being paid a
salary. Your teacher training course fees
may be paid for by your training provider
however you will need to confirm this with
your training provider. If you do need to
pay fees to cover the cost of your course
yourself, eligible students may be able to
apply for a tuition fee loan.

**Researcher in Schools Programme
(England) Postgraduate ITET Route:
Salaried**
**Apply to Researcher in Schools
Programme (England) Postgraduate
ITET Route: Salaried**
Researcher in Schools website
http://www.researchersinschools.org/

School Direct (salaried)
Get into Teaching: School Direct
https://getintoteaching.education.gov.uk/e
xplore-my-options/teacher-training-
routes/school-led-training/school-direct

Teach First (salaried)
Apply to Teach First (salaried)
Teach First https://www.teachfirst.org.uk/

Troops to Teachers
Apply to Troops to Teachers
UCAS https://www.ucas.com/

Further information
Get into Teaching: Troops to Teachers
https://getintoteaching.education.gov.uk/e
xplore-my-options/teacher-training-
routes/specialist-training-options/troops-to-
teachers
University of Brighton
https://www.brighton.ac.uk/programmes/st
udy/troops-to-teachers-non-graduate-
programme.aspx

**Assessment Only (AO) leading to
Qualified Teacher Status (QTS)**
If you have a degree and experience of
teaching but don't have qualified teacher
status (QTS), you may not be required to
undertake further training. This route may
also be an option for overseas trained
teachers. You will need to follow the
Assessment Only (AO) route which will
last around 3 months with an accredited
learning provider and leads to QTS.

**Apply to Assessment Only Approved
Provider**
Get into Teaching: Assessment Only
https://getintoteaching.education.gov.uk/e
xplore-my-options/teacher-training-
routes/specialist-training-
options/assessment-only

Wales:
Initial Teacher Training (ITT) Postgraduate Courses Student Funding

Eligible students who meet the residence requirements in Wales studying a postgraduate initial teacher training (ITT) course is able to apply for undergraduate student finance

- Tuition fee loan non-income assessed; maintenance loan income assessed; maintenance grant income assessed Student Finance Wales

Apply to Student Finance Wales: postgraduate ITT funding same as undergraduate: tuition fee loan; maintenance loan
Student Finance Wales
https://www.studentfinancewales.co.uk/

Further information
Discover Teaching Wales: Routes into Teaching
http://discoverteaching.wales/routes-into-teaching/

Welsh Government: Learning: Teacher Training Incentives in Wales
http://learning.gov.wales/

Wales:
Bursaries and Scholarships for Specified Subjects

Postgraduate secondary ITT Mathematics
Bursary for teacher trainees with an honours degree 1st class, 2:1, 2:2; master's degree or PhD

Physics, Chemistry, Welsh, Computer Science
Scholarships and bursaries for teacher trainees with an honours degree 1st class, 2:1, 2:2; master's degree or PhD

Art, Biology, Business Studies, Design and Technology, Drama, English, General Science, Geography, History, Music, Physical Education, Religious Education, Outdoor Studies
Bursaries for teacher trainees with an honours degree 1st class and or master's degree or PhD

Design and Technology, English, History, Music, Religious Education, Primary Mathematics
Bursaries for teacher trainees with an honours degree 1st class, 2:1, 2:2; master's degree or PhD

Modern Foreign Languages
Bursaries for teacher trainees with an honours degree 1st class, 2:1; and or master's degree or PhD

Postgraduate Primary
With a degree subject specialism of English, Welsh, Mathematics, of Core Science
Bursaries for teacher trainees with an honours degree 1st class and or master's degree or PhD
Applying for a bursary
You don't need to apply for a bursary as all eligible students will begin to receive monthly payments from your chosen teacher training provider when you start your course.

Further information:
Welsh Government: Learning Teacher Training Incentives
http://learning.gov.wales/

Wales:
Postgraduate School Centred Salaried Primary and Secondary Teacher Training Courses

School centred teacher training programmes which involve being employed by your school as an unqualified teacher while you train being paid a salary. Your teacher training course fees may be paid for by your training provider however you will need to confirm this with your training provider. If you do need to pay fees to cover the cost of your course yourself, eligible students may be able to apply for a tuition fee loan.

Graduate Teacher Programme (GTP) (Wales) Postgraduate ITET Route (Salaried)
GTP Teacher Training Wales: Discover Teaching Wales:
Links for GTP
http://discoverteaching.wales/
The GTP is offered by the Welsh Government and pays all training costs.

Teach First (Salaried)
Teach First
https://www.teachfirst.org.uk/

Further information
Discover Teaching Wales:
Routes into Teaching
http://discoverteaching.wales/routes-into-teaching/

Northern Ireland:
Initial Teacher Training (ITT) Postgraduate Courses Student Funding

Eligible students who meet the residence requirements in Northern Ireland studying a postgraduate initial teacher training (ITT) course is able to apply for undergraduate student finance

- Tuition fee loan non-income assessed; maintenance loan income assessed; maintenance grant income assessed Student Finance Northern Ireland

Apply to Student Finance Northern Ireland: postgraduate ITT funding same as undergraduate: tuition fee loan; maintenance loan; maintenance grant
Student Finance Northern Ireland: Undergraduate Students
https://www.studentfinanceni.co.uk/

Scotland:
Initial Teacher Training (ITT) Postgraduate Courses Student Funding

Eligible students who meet the residence requirements in Scotland studying a postgraduate initial teacher training (ITT) course in Scotland is able to apply for undergraduate student finance
- Tuition fee grant non-income assessed; maintenance loan income assessed; maintenance grant income assessed Student Awards Agency for Scotland

Apply to Student Awards Agency Scotland: postgraduate ITT funding same as undergraduate: tuition fee loan; maintenance loan
Student Awards Agency Scotland
http://www.saas.gov.uk/

521

Scotland: Bursaries and Scholarships for Certain Subjects

Eligible students ordinarily resident in Scotland studying for a postgraduate initial teacher training (ITT) course for primary and secondary teaching who have been employed for at least three of the last five years and have a degree in:

- Mathematics, computing, technical education or physics may be eligible for a bursary.

Scotland: Postgraduate Courses Teacher Training ITT Bursaries

How much funding you can get can be found at:
Teach in Scotland: Portfolio; STEM Teacher Education Bursaries
http://teachinscotland.scot/portfolio/stem-teacher-education-bursaries/

Further information
Teach in Scotland: How to Apply; New to Teaching
http://teachinscotland.scot/how-to-apply/new-to-teaching/

Chapter 14
Website References

14.1 Website References for Chapters 12 and 13
Student Finance and Student Bursary Funding:
Sources of Funding, Information and Advice

Secondary and Further Education Students Funding Support

England: Secondary and Further Education Students Funding Support
Links to a register of approved training organisations in England may be found at:
UK Government: Register of Training Organisations
https://www.gov.uk/government/publications/register-of-training-organisations
Advanced Learning Loans for FE students 19 years and over
Student Finance England https://www.gov.uk/student-finance
Further information about applications may be found at
UK Government: Advanced Learning Loans: How to Apply
https://www.gov.uk/advanced-learner-loan/how-to-apply

Wales: Secondary and Further Education Students Funding Support
Education Maintenance Allowance (EMA); Welsh Learning Grant (WLG) (FE)
Student Finance Wales: EMA; Welsh Learning Grant (WLG) (FE)
https://www.studentfinancewales.co.uk/
Further information may be found at
Student Finance Wales: FE http://www.studentfinancewales.co.uk/fe/

Northern Ireland: Secondary and Further Education Students Funding Support
Northern Ireland Direct https://www.nidirect.gov.uk/
Education Maintenance Allowance (EMA)
Northern Ireland Direct
https://www.nidirect.gov.uk/articles/how-apply-money-learn-education-maintenance-allowance
Further information may be found at
Northern Ireland Direct: Education Maintenance Allowance
https://www.nidirect.gov.uk/information-and-services/education-maintenance-allowance/money-learn-education-maintenance-allowance
Northern Ireland Direct: 14-19 Education Employment and Training Options: Education Maintenance Allowance
https://www.nidirect.gov.uk/information-and-services/14-19-education-employment-and-training-options/education-maintenance-allowance
Northern Ireland Direct: Financial Help for Adult Learners
https://www.nidirect.gov.uk/information-and-services/adult-learning/financial-help-adult-learners

Scotland: Secondary and Further Education Students Funding Support
Education Maintenance Allowance (EMA);
Further information may be found at:
My World of Work: Funding https://www.myworldofwork.co.uk/learn-and-train/funding
My Gov Scotland: EMA https://www.mygov.scot/ema/

Higher Education Students Funding Support

UK Student Loans Company (SLC)
UK Student Loans Company (SLC) http://www.slc.co.uk
The Student Loans Company (SLC) is a non-profit government organisation working with:
UK Government Department for Education (DfE)
https://www.gov.uk/government/organisations/department-for-education
Department for Education and Skills (DfES), Wales
https://gov.wales/topics/educationandskills
Department for the Economy (DfEcon), Northern Ireland https://www.economy-ni.gov.uk/
Scottish Government: Department for Education and Training)
https://www.gov.scot/Topics/Education
Student Awards Agency for Scotland (SAAS) http://www.saas.gov.uk/
Student Loans Company: Practitioners: Resources
http://www.practitioners.slc.co.uk/resources/
Student Loans Company: Practitioners: Maintenance Loan Eligibility
http://www.practitioners.slc.co.uk/products/full-time-undergraduate-education/full-time-maintenance-loan/eligibility/

Student Finance Companies
England
Student Finance England   https://www.gov.uk/student-finance
Wales
Student Finance Wales   http://www.studentfinancewales.co.uk
Northern Ireland
Student Finance Northern Ireland   http://www.studentfinanceni.co.uk
Scotland
Student Awards Agency Scotland   http://www.saas.gov.uk

Further information student finance
UK Government: Student Finance https://www.gov.uk/browse/education/student-finance ,
UK Government:
England Travel Grants for Students   https://www.gov.uk/travel-grants-students-england
England, Teaching Excellence and Outcomes Framework (TEF)
https://www.officeforstudents.org.uk/advice-and-guidance/teaching/what-is-the-tef/
Office for Students   https://www.officeforstudents.org.uk/
Student Loans Company   http://www.slc.co.uk
Northern Ireland
Northern Ireland Government Department for the Economy: Higher Education Finance
https://www.economy-ni.gov.uk/topics/higher-education

Health Courses Student Bursary Administration Organisations
Applications for Health courses student bursaries
England
NHS England Business Service Authority https://www.nhsbsa.nhs.uk/nhs-bursary-students
Wales
NHS Wales Student Awards Services   http://www.nwssp.wales.nhs.uk/student-awards
Northern Ireland
Student Finance Northern Ireland   http://www.studentfinanceni.co.uk/
Scotland
Students Awards Agency Scotland (SAAS)   http://www.saas.gov.uk/

NHS England; NHS Wales; Department of Health (DoH) Northern Ireland; Scottish Government Health and Social Care Scotland: Health Courses Student Bursaries
England
NHS England Business Service Authority https://www.nhsbsa.nhs.uk/nhs-bursary-students
Administers funding for the:
Department of Health and Social Care (DHSC)
https://www.gov.uk/government/organisations/department-of-health-and-social-care
Further information NHS / health bursaries
England
UK Government: NHS Bursaries   https://www.gov.uk/nhs-bursaries
Wales
NHS Wales Student Awards Services   http://www.nwssp.wales.nhs.uk/student-awards
Administers funding for the:
Department of Health and Social Care (DHSC)
https://www.gov.uk/government/organisations/department-of-health-and-social-care
Northern Ireland
Student Finance Northern Ireland   http://www.studentfinanceni.co.uk/
Administers funding for the:
Department of Health Northern Ireland   https://www.health-ni.gov.uk/
Scotland
Students Awards Agency Scotland (SAAS)   http://www.saas.gov.uk/
Administers funding for the:
Scottish Government Health and Social Care Directorates http://www.sehd.scot.nhs.uk/
National Health Services
NHS England   https://www.england.nhs.uk/
NHS Wales   http://www.wales.nhs.uk/
Department of Health (DoH) Northern Ireland   https://www.health-ni.gov.uk/
NHS Scotland   http://www.scot.nhs.uk/
Further information NHS bursaries
England
UK Government: NHS Bursaries   https://www.gov.uk/nhs-bursaries

Disabled Students Allowances
Apply to Student Finance: Disabled Students Allowances
England and General Advice
UK Government: Disabled Students Allowances
https://www.gov.uk/disabled-students-allowances-dsas
Wales
Student Finance Wales: Disabled Students Allowances
http://www.studentfinancewales.co.uk/practitioners/undergraduate-students/full-
time/disabled-students-allowances.aspx
Northern Ireland
Student Finance Northern Ireland: Disabled Students Allowances
https://www.studentfinanceni.co.uk/types-of-finance/postgraduate/northern-ireland-
student/extra-help/disabled-students-allowances/what-are-they/
Scotland
Student Awards Agency for Scotland: Disabled Students Allowances
http://www.saas.gov.uk/full_time/ug/independent/funding_available.htm
Further information at:
UK Government: Financial Help Disabled: https://www.gov.uk/financial-help-disabled
DSA Information and Assessment Centres
Disabled Student Allowances Quality Assurance Group https://dsa-qag.org.uk/

If you have Studied in Higher Education Previously
Further information if you have studied before:
If you have studied before https://www.gov.uk/student-finance/who-qualifies
England
UK Government Student Finance England: Who Qualifies
https://www.gov.uk/student-finance/who-qualifies
Wales
Student Finance Wales: Previous Study Rules
https://www.studentfinancewales.co.uk/undergraduate-students/new-students/previous-study-rules.aspx
Northern Ireland
Northern Ireland Direct: Qualifying Student Finance
https://www.nidirect.gov.uk/articles/qualifying-student-finance
Scotland
Student Awards Agency for Scotland: Previous Study
http://www.saas.gov.uk/full_time/ug/young/eligibility_previous_study.htm
Nursing, Midwifery and Allied Health Professions
The Funding Clinic: Studying in England https://thefundingclinic.org.uk/
The Funding Clinic: Studying in Wales, Northern Ireland and Scotland
https://thefundingclinic.org.uk/

Repaying Your Student Loan
Student Loans Company (SLC)   http://www.slc.co.uk
Her Majesty's Revenue and Customs (HMRC) http://www.hmrc.gov.uk/
Student Loans Company: Student Loan Repayment http://www.studentloanrepayment.co.uk/
UK Government:
Student Finance Repayments   https://www.gov.uk/student-finance/repayments
England
UK Government:
Student Finance England:
Repaying your Student Loan   https://www.gov.uk/repaying-your-student-loan
Student Finance England:
Master's Loan Repayment   https://www.gov.uk/master's-loan/repayment
Student Finance England:
Doctoral Loan Repayment   https://www.gov.uk/doctoral-loan/repayment
Wales
Student Finance Wales:
Repayment of Undergraduate Course Loans https://www.studentfinancewales.co.uk/
Student Finance Wales:
Repayment of Postgraduate Course Loans   https://www.studentfinancewales.co.uk/
Northern Ireland
Student Finance Northern Ireland:
Terms and Conditions Guide; Repayment   https://www.studentfinanceni.co.uk/
Scotland
Student Awards Agency for Scotland:
Loan Repayments   http://www.saas.gov.uk/my_money/loan_repayments.htm

Interest Rates on Student Loans
UK Government:
Student Finance Repayments   https://www.gov.uk/student-finance/repayments

Be Aware of Scam Emails

If you get such an email, check advice with the
Student Loans Company:
Counter Fraud   https://www.slc.co.uk/about-us/what-we-do/counter-fraud.aspx
For further advice about phishing check
UK Government: Report Suspicious
Emails Websites Phishing   https://www.gov.uk/report-suspicious-emails-websites-phishing

If you get into Financial Problems

Citizens Advice Bureaux

Citizens Advice Bureaux   http://www.adviceguide.org.uk
Money Advice Service

Money Advice Service   https://www.moneyadviceservice.org.uk/
National Association of Student Money Advisers (NASMA)

National Association of Student Money Advisers (NASMA) http://www.nasma.org.uk/
National Debtline

National Debtline   http://www.nationaldebtline.co.uk/
National Union of Students (NUS)

National Union of Students (NUS)   http://www.nus.org.uk
Personal Finance Education Group (PFEG)

Personal Finance Education Group (PFEG)   http://www.pfeg.org/

Residence Requirements

Further information on residence requirements and fee status

UK Government: Student Finance Who Qualifies
https://www.gov.uk/student-finance/who-qualifies
UK Government: Right to Reside https://www.gov.uk/right-to-reside
UK Government: Home Office: UK Visas and Immigration
https://www.gov.uk/government/organisations/uk-visas-and-immigration
UK Council for International Affairs: Home or Overseas Fees the basics
https://www.ukcisa.org.uk/Information--Advice/Fees-and-Money/Home-or-Overseas-fees-the-basics
UK Council for International Affairs: England Fee Status
https://www.ukcisa.org.uk/Information--Advice/Fees-and-Money/England-fee-status
UK Council for International Affairs: Wales Fee Status
https://www.ukcisa.org.uk/Information--Advice/Fees-and-Money/Wales-fee-status
UK Council for International Affairs: Northern Ireland Fee Status
https://www.ukcisa.org.uk/Information--Advice/Fees-and-Money/Northern-Ireland-fee-status
UK Council for International Affairs: Scotland Fee Status
https://www.ukcisa.org.uk/Information--Advice/Fees-and-Money/Scotland-fee-status

Funding Information

Army Education Grant

If you are considering a career in the army after your degree you may qualify for an
education grant provided by the armed services. The scheme is open to UK passport
holders who have studied or plan to study at an educational establishment in the UK,
Channel Islands, Isle of Man or at any British forces School overseas. To confirm if you
qualify you will need to check with the Armed forces
Further information may be found at:

Army: Officer Bursary
https://apply.army.mod.uk/how-to-join/entryoptions/officer-bursary
Royal Airforce: Sponsorship Education
https://www.raf.mod.uk/recruitment/how-to-apply/sponsorship-education/

Royal Navy: Funding and Scholarships
https://www.royalnavy.mod.uk/careers/joining/funding-and-scholarships
Defence Academy of the UK: Defence Technical Undergraduate Scheme
https://www.da.mod.uk/colleges-and-schools/defence-sixth-form-defence-technical-undergraduate-scheme/dtus
UK Government: Defence Engineering Sponsorship Scheme
https://www.gov.uk/government/collections/desg-sponsorship-scheme
UK Government: Defence Engineering and Science Group
https://www.gov.uk/government/collections/desg-graduate-scheme

Child Tax Credit
Further information:
UK Government: Child Tax Credit   https://www.gov.uk/child-tax-credit
UK Government: Tax Credits Enquiries
https://www.gov.uk/contact/hm-revenue-customs/tax-credits-enquiries
Apply to UK Government: Child Tax Credit
UK Government: Child Tax Credit:
How to Claim   https://www.gov.uk/child-tax-credit/how-to-claim

Income Support
Further information
UK Government: Income Support Eligibility https://www.gov.uk/income-support/eligibility

Students Leaving Care
Stand Alone   http://standalone.org.uk/
Propel   http://propel.org.uk/UK/
National Network for the Education of Care Leavers http://www.nnecl.org/
Who Cares Scotland   https://www.whocaresscotland.org/
Student Awards Agency Scotland   http://www.saas.gov.uk

Professional and Career Development Loans (PCDL)
Professional and Career
Development Loan (PCDL)   https://www.gov.uk/career-development-loans
UK Government:
Contact Jobcentre Plus   https://www.gov.uk/contact-jobcentre-plus
UK Government: Department for Works and Pension (DWP)
https://www.gov.uk/government/organisations/department-for-work-pensions
Apply to the Co-operative bank or Barclays bank: Professional and Career Development Loan (PCDL) after speaking with a careers adviser
National Careers Websites in the UK and Ireland
England
National Careers Service https://nationalcareersservice.direct.gov.uk/
Wales
Careers Wales http://www.careerswales.com/en/
Northern Ireland
Northern Ireland Direct Careers https://www.nidirect.gov.uk/campaigns/careers
Scotland
Skills Development Scotland:
Careers https://www.skillsdevelopmentscotland.co.uk/

Further information
Professional and Career Development Loan (PCDL)
https://www.gov.uk/career-development-loans

Bursaries, Scholarships, Awards and Grants

Bursaries, scholarships, awards and grants may be available directly from your university or college details will be listed on the university or college websites.

General Funding Sources

Bank of England: African Caribbean Scholarship
https://www.bankofenglandearlycareers.co.uk/our-programmes/african-caribbean-scholarship/
The Bank of England: African Caribbean Scholarship offers financial support to students from Black or Mixed African and Caribbean background who will be starting their undergraduate degree courses at UK universities.

British Council: Site search funding   http://www.britishcouncil.org
The British Council has information about sources of funding for students, teachers, young people and adult learners.

Directory of Social Change (DSC)   https://www.dsc.org.uk/
Directory of Social Change has a link to funding websites

Family Action: Grants   https://www.family-action.org.uk/what-we-do/grants/
Family Action distributes grants to help people and families in need.

NHS Health Careers: Funding through NHS
https://www.healthcareers.nhs.uk/career-planning/study-and-training/considering-or-university/financial-support-university/funding-through-nhs

Professional and Career Development Loans
https://www.gov.uk/career-development-loans
Professional and Carer Development Loans are bank loans to pay for courses and training that help with your career or help get you into work.

Prospects: funding postgraduate study
https://www.prospects.ac.uk/postgraduate-study/funding-postgraduate-study
Prospects has a guide to funding postgraduate study: scholarships, grants and postgraduate loans.

Scholarship Search   http://www.scholarship-search.org.uk/
Scholarship Search has a database of undergraduate and postgraduate scholarship awards

Scots Care   https://www.scotscare.com/

The Princes Trust   http://www.princes-trust.org.uk
The Princes Trust offers support for people trying to get into a job, training or education and need some financial support.

The Student Room   https://www.thestudentroom.co.uk/student-finance/
The Student Room has a range of tools and guidance on grants loans and bursaries

Turn 2 Us   https://www.turn2us.org.uk/
Turn 2 Us helps people in financial need gain access to welfare benefits, charitable grants and other financial help.

University and College Admissions Service (UCAS) http://www.ucas.com/
University and College Admissions Service (UCAS) has information on student finance.

UK Government: Grant and
Bursary Adult Learners   https://www.gov.uk/grant-bursary-adult-learners
Links to some grants and bursaries

UK Government: Dance and Drama Awards   https://www.gov.uk/dance-drama-awards
Information about dance a drama awards for some students

Scotland

My World of Work Individual Training Accounts
https://www.myworldofwork.co.uk/learn-and-train/sds-individual-training-accounts-ita

Educational Trusts

The following handbooks on educational trusts are usually available in larger public libraries but may also be available in college or university libraries.

Charities Digest published by WLR store, Wilmington Publishing and Information Services http://www.wlrstore.com/charity-choice/charities-digest.aspx

Directory of Grant Making Trusts published by the
Directory of Social Change (DSC) https://www.dsc.org.uk/publications/

Grants for Individuals part of
Directory of Social Change (DSC) http://www.grantsforindividuals.org.uk/

Subscription required and may be accessed through subscribing universities and local authorities.

Guide to Educational Grants
http://www.dsc.org.uk/Publications/Fundraisingsources/@161205

Register of Educational Endowments (Scottish Trusts) available with the
Student Awards Agency for Scotland http://www.saas.gov.uk/

The Grants Register published by Palgrave Macmillan http://www.palgrave.com/

Erasmus

British Council, Erasmus website
https://www.britishcouncil.org/study-work-create/opportunity/study-abroad/erasmus

Erasmus study abroad placement https://www.erasmusplus.org.uk/study-abroad

Erasmus work abroad placement https://www.erasmusplus.org.uk/work-abroad

Financial Advice Support

Citizens Advice Bureau https://www.citizensadvice.org.uk/

The Citizens Advice Bureau provides free, confidential and impartial advice including debt problems, benefit entitlement, housing and employment issues.

Money Advice Service https://www.moneyadviceservice.org.uk/

National Association of Student Money Advisors (NASMA) http://www.nasma.org.uk/

NASMA produces a magazine on student money matters.

National Debtline http://www.nationaldebtline.co.uk/

National Union of Students http://www.nus.org.uk/

The National Union of Students provides information on money and funding.

Personal Finance Education Group (PFEG) http://www.pfeg.org/

International Student Finance Support and Information

UK scholarships for international students are mainly available at postgraduate level. However, universities, higher education colleges and specialist institutions may provide bursaries, grants or other financial support for exceptional undergraduate international students.

The British Council

The British Council has information for international students on the
Education UK websiteshttp://www.educationuk.org/global/main/living-and-studying/

Council for International Education http://www.ukcosa.org.uk

Provides help and advice to prospective students from overseas. The site includes details of charitable trusts which give support to international students.

Chevening Scholarships http://www.chevening.org/

Chevening Scholarships are the UK government's global scholarship programme funded by the Foreign and Commonwealth Office (FCO) and partner organisations. The programme makes awards to outstanding scholars with leadership potential around the world to study postgraduate courses in the UK, providing full or part funding for full-time courses in any subject at any university in the UK.

Marshall Scholarships http://www.marshallscholarship.org/

Marshall Scholarships finance young Americans of high ability to study for a degree in any subject at any higher education institution in the UK

The Commonwealth Scholarship
Commission   http://cscuk.dfid.gov.uk/about-us/roles-and-functions/
The Commonwealth Scholarship Commission (CSC) in the UK is responsible for managing Britain's contribution to the Commonwealth Scholarship and fellowship Plan (CSFP). The CSC supports over 900 scholarships and fellowships for postgraduate study and professional development each year.

Medical, Dental and Veterinary Students Finance

British Medical Association (BMA)   http://bma.org.uk/
The British Medical Association (BMA) is the trade union and professional body for doctors in the UK
British Medical Association (BMA)
Charities   https://www.bma.org.uk/about-us/who-we-are/bma-charities
Information about the BMA Charities Trust Fund and the Dain Fund
British Medical Association (BMA): Medical Student Finance
https://www.bma.org.uk/advice/work-life-support/your-finances-and-protection/medical-student-finance
British Medical and Dental Students Trust:
Royal Society of Medicine: Student Elective Awards https://www.rsm.ac.uk/student-electives
For medicine or dentistry students planning an elective abroad and are in need of funding
Royal Veterinary College; University of London:
Funding Options   https://www.rvc.ac.uk/study/fees-and-funding/funding-options
Royal Medical Benevolent Fund: Medical Students   https://rmbf.org/medical-students/

Research Councils

Research councils may provide funding for eligible postgraduate students.
Research Councils UK   http://www.rcuk.ac.uk/
UK Research and Innovation   https://www.ukri.org/
Arts and Humanities Research Council (AHRC)   http://www.ahrc.ac.uk
Biotechnology and Biological science Research Council (BBSRC)http://www.bbsrc.ac.uk/
Economic and Social Research Council (ESRC)   http://www.esrc.ac.uk
Engineering and Physical Sciences Research Council (EPSRC) http://www.epsrc.ac.uk
Medical Research Council (MRC)   http://www.mrc.ac.uk
National Environment Research Council (NERC) http://www.nerc.ac.uk
Science and Technology Facilities Council (STFC) http://www.stfc.ac.uk/

Sponsorship and Scholarships

Some industrial organisations and some government departments have schemes for supporting students however this funding support is highly competitive. You should be able to get further information from the university or college you are applying to.

Student Bursary Funding

Allied Health and Additional Health Specified Courses Student Funding

Medicine and Dentistry Student Funding

Nursing and Midwifery Student Funding
England
NHS Business Service Authority https://www.nhsbsa.nhs.uk/nhs-bursary-students
Administers funding from the: NHS England   https://www.england.nhs.uk/
Wales
NHS Student Awards Services   http://www.nwssp.wales.nhs.uk/student-awards
Administers funding from the: NHS Wales   http://www.wales.nhs.uk/
Northern Ireland
Student Finance Northern Ireland   http://www.studentfinanceni.co.uk/
Administers funding from the:
Department of Health Northern Ireland   https://www.health-ni.gov.uk/
Scotland
Students Awards Agency Scotland (SAAS)   http://www.saas.gov.uk/
Administers funding from the:
Scottish Government Health and Social Care Directorates http://www.sehd.scot.nhs.uk/

Paramedic Science Courses Student Funding
Paramedic science course student funding is different in England, Wales, Northern Ireland and Scotland.
England:
Paramedic Science Undergraduate Courses Student Funding
Apply to Ambulance Service Trusts: In-service training
List of Ambulance Trusts in the UK
College of Paramedics: Ambulance Trusts
https://www.collegeofparamedics.co.uk/how_to_become_a_paramedic/ambulance_trusts
Wales:
Paramedic Science Undergraduate Courses Student Funding
Apply to NHS Wales Student Awards Services: Student Bursaries
NHS Wales Student Awards Services:
Bursary Scheme Terms and Conditions http://www.nwssp.wales.nhs.uk/student-awards
Apply to Student Finance Wales: tuition fee loan; maintenance loan
Student Finance Wales   https://www.studentfinancewales.co.uk/
Apply to Ambulance Service Trusts: In-service training
List of Ambulance Trusts in the UK
College of Paramedics: Ambulance Trusts
https://www.collegeofparamedics.co.uk/how_to_become_a_paramedic/ambulance_trusts
Northern Ireland:
Paramedic Science Undergraduate Courses Student Funding
Apply to Student Finance Northern Ireland: tuition fee loan, maintenance loan, maintenance grant
Student Finance Northern Ireland   http://www.studentfinanceni.co.uk/
Apply to Student Finance Northern Ireland: tuition fee bursary and maintenance bursary with the Department of Health (DoH)
Student Finance Northern Ireland   http://www.studentfinanceni.co.uk/
Apply to Ambulance Service Trusts: In-service training (being phased out in Northern Ireland)
List of Ambulance Trusts in the UK
College of Paramedics: Ambulance Trusts
https://www.collegeofparamedics.co.uk/how_to_become_a_paramedic/ambulance_trusts

Scotland:
Paramedic Science Undergraduate Courses Student Funding
Apply to Scottish Ambulance Service: In-service training
Scottish Ambulance Service
http://www.scottishambulance.com/

Physician Associate Courses Student Funding
England:
Physician Associate Postgraduate Courses Student Funding
Funding details should be available on the relevant university website. A list of local offices of Health Education England (HEE) is available from
Health Education England (HEE)   https://hee.nhs.uk/
Apply to Student Finance England: Postgraduate master's degree loan
Student Finance England   https://www.gov.uk/student-finance
Wales:
Physician associate postgraduate courses student funding
List of specified bursary funded health courses available from
NHS Wales Student Awards Services: Student Awards:
New Students: Terms and Conditions   http://www.nwssp.wales.nhs.uk/student-awards
Physician associate postgraduate diploma; master's degree student funding: Wales
Apply to NHS Wales Student Awards Services: NHS Wales bursary
NHS Wales Student Awards Services   http://www.nwssp.wales.nhs.uk/student-awards
Northern Ireland:
Physician associate postgraduate courses student funding
Health and Social Care
Northern Ireland   http://online.hscni.net/hospitals/health-and-social-care-trusts/
Apply to the university: Physician associate postgraduate diploma; master's degree: health trust grant
Apply to Student Finance Northern Ireland: Postgraduate tuition fee loan:
Student Finance Northern Ireland   http://www.studentfinanceni.co.uk/
Scotland:
Physician associate postgraduate courses student funding
Apply to Student Awards Agency for Scotland: Postgraduate loan
Student Awards Agency for Scotland   http://www.saas.gov.uk

Social Work Courses Student Funding
Social work bursary administration organisations
England
NHS Business Service Authority (NHSBSA)   https://www.nhsbsa.nhs.uk/
Wales
Social Care Wales   https://socialcare.wales/careers/social-work-bursary-funding
Northern Ireland
Department of Health Northern Ireland:
Office of Social Services   https://www.health-ni.gov.uk/contact
Scotland
Scottish Social Services Council   http://www.sssc.uk.com/
You must be studying or intending to study on a university or college based social work course approved by the following professional care profession regulators:
Professional care profession regulators
England: Health and Care Professions Council http://www.hcpc-uk.org/
Wales: Social Care Council for Wales   https://socialcare.wales/
Northern Ireland: Northern Ireland Social Care Council http://www.niscc.info/
Scotland: Scottish Social Services Council   http://www.sssc.uk.com/

Teaching: Initial Teacher Training (ITT) Course Student Funding
England:
Initial Teacher Training (ITT) Postgraduate Courses Student Funding
Apply to Student Finance England: postgraduate ITT funding same as undergraduate: tuition fee loan; maintenance loan
Student Finance England   https://www.gov.uk/student-finance
England:
Bursaries and Scholarships Available for Specified Subjects
Chemistry
Apply to Royal Society of Chemistry: teacher training scholarships
Royal Society of Chemistry: teacher training scholarships
http://www.rsc.org/awards-funding/funding/teacher-training-scholarships/#eligibility

Computing
Apply to BCS the Chartered Institute of Computing: BCS Scholarship
BCS the Chartered Institute of Computing: BCS Scholarship
http://www.computingatschool.org.uk/bcs-scholarship

Geography
Apply to Royal Geographical Society: Teacher Training Scholarships
Royal Geographical Society: Teacher Training Scholarships
https://www.rgs.org/schools/teacher-training-scholarships/

Languages
Apply to British Council: Languages Teacher Training Scholarships
British Council: Languages Teacher Training Scholarships
https://www.britishcouncil.org/study-work-create/opportunity/uk/languages-teacher-training-scholarships

Mathematics
Apply to Institute of Mathematics and its Applications (IPA): Mathematics Training Scholarships
Institute of Mathematics and its Applications (IPA): Mathematics Training Scholarships
http://teachingmathematicsscholars.org/home

Physics
Apply to Institute of Physics: Teach: IOP Teacher Training Scholarships
Institute of Physics: Teach: IOP Teacher Training Scholarships
http://www.iop.org/education/teach/
Further information
UK Government: Get into Teaching; Funding and Salary; Overview
https://getintoteaching.education.gov.uk/funding-and-salary/overview
UK Government: Get into Teaching; Funding and Salary; Scholarships
https://getintoteaching.education.gov.uk/funding-and-salary/overview/scholarships
UK Government: Teacher Training Funding https://www.gov.uk/teacher-training-funding

England:
Postgraduate School Centred Salaried Primary and Secondary Teacher Training Courses
Researcher in Schools Programme (England) Postgraduate ITET Route: Salaried
Apply to Researcher in Schools Programme (England) Postgraduate ITET Route: Salaried
Researcher in Schools website   http://www.researchersinschools.org/

School Direct (salaried)
Get into Teaching: School Direct
https://getintoteaching.education.gov.uk/explore-my-options/teacher-training-routes/school-led-training/school-direct

Teach First (salaried)
Apply to Teach First (salaried)
Teach First   https://www.teachfirst.org.uk/

Troops to Teachers
Apply to Troops to Teachers
UCAS   https://www.ucas.com/

Further information
Get into Teaching: Troops to Teachers https://getintoteaching.education.gov.uk/explore-my-options/teacher-training-routes/specialist-training-options/troops-to-teachers
University of Brighton
https://www.brighton.ac.uk/programmes/study/troops-to-teachers-non-graduate-programme.aspx

Assessment Only (AO) leading to Qualified Teacher Status (QTS)
Apply to Assessment Only Approved Provider
Get into Teaching: Assessment Only
https://getintoteaching.education.gov.uk/explore-my-options/teacher-training-routes/specialist-training-options/assessment-only

Wales:
Initial Teacher Training (ITT) Postgraduate Courses Student Funding
Apply to Student Finance Wales: postgraduate ITT funding same as undergraduate: tuition fee loan; maintenance loan
Student Finance Wales   https://www.studentfinancewales.co.uk/

Further information
Discover Teaching Wales:
Routes into Teaching   http://discoverteaching.wales/routes-into-teaching/

Welsh Government: Learning:
Teacher Training Incentives in Wales   http://learning.gov.wales/

Wales:
Bursaries and Scholarships for Specified Subjects
Further information:
Welsh Government: Learning Teacher Training Incentives http://learning.gov.wales/

Wales:

Postgraduate School Centred Salaried Primary and Secondary Teacher Training Courses

GTP Teacher Training Wales: Discover Teaching Wales:

Links for GTP   http://discoverteaching.wales/

The GTP is offered by the Welsh Government and pays all training costs.

Teach First (Salaried)

Teach First   https://www.teachfirst.org.uk/

Further information

Discover Teaching Wales:

Routes into Teaching   http://discoverteaching.wales/routes-into-teaching/

Northern Ireland:

Initial Teacher Training (ITT) Postgraduate Courses Student Funding

Apply to Student Finance Northern Ireland: postgraduate ITT funding same as undergraduate: tuition fee loan; maintenance loan; maintenance grant

Student Finance Northern Ireland:

Undergraduate Students   https://www.studentfinanceni.co.uk/

Scotland:

Initial Teacher Training (ITT) Postgraduate Courses Student Funding

Apply to Student Awards Agency Scotland: postgraduate ITT funding same as undergraduate: tuition fee loan; maintenance loan

Student Awards Agency Scotland   http://www.saas.gov.uk/

Scotland:

Funding Available for Postgraduate Teacher Training ITT Bursaries

How much funding you can get can be found at:

Teach in Scotland: Portfolio; STEM Teacher Education Bursaries

http://teachinscotland.scot/portfolio/stem-teacher-education-bursaries/

Further information

Teach in Scotland: How to Apply;

New to Teaching   http://teachinscotland.scot/how-to-apply/new-to-teaching/

Admissions Tests

Assessment Admission Testing Services
Australian Council for Educational Research (ACER) https://www.acer.org/
Pearson Vue   https://www.pearsonvue.co.uk/
Pearson VUE: Test Taker   https://www.pearsonvue.co.uk/test-taker.aspx
Cambridge Assessment Admissions
Testing Service   http://www.admissionstestingservice.org/
Cambridge Assessment Admissions Testing Service: Pre-Interview Assessments for
Test Takers   http://www.admissionstestingservice.org/for-test-takers/

Tests for Some Law Courses
National Admissions Test for Law (LNAT)   http://www.lnat.ac.uk/
Queens University, Belfast: Institute of Professional Legal Studies; Law Admissions Test
https://www.qub.ac.uk/schools/InstituteofProfessionalLegalStudies/Admissions/

Tests for Barrister Training in England and Wales
Bar Standards Board (BSB) Certificate Testing: Bar Course Aptitude Test (BCAT)
https://www.barstandardsboard.org.uk/qualifying-as-a-barrister/current-requirements/bar-professional-training-course/bar-course-aptitude-test/
Pearson VUE Bar Standards Board (BSB) Certificate Testing (BCAT)
Online Registration System   http://www.pearsonvue.com/bsb/
Practice Bar Course Aptitude Test (BCAT):
Talentlens: Practice Bar Course Aptitude Test http://www.talentlens.co.uk/BCAT
Links to test centres are available on the Pearson Vue website:
Pearson VUE BSB   http://www.pearsonvue.com/bsb/

Tests for some Medicine; Biomedical Science; Dentistry; Veterinary Medicine Courses
Cambridge Assessment Admissions Testing Service Admissions Testing Service
Biomedical Admissions Test (BMAT)
http://www.admissionstestingservice.org/for-test-takers/bmat/about-bmat/
UK Clinical Aptitude Test (UKCAT)   https://www.ukcat.ac.uk/
Graduate Medical School Admissions Test GAMSAT https://gamsat.acer.org/
Graduate Medical School Admissions Test: Register https://gamsat.acer.org/register

Tests for Some Management Courses
Graduate Management Admission Test (GMAT) https://www.mba.com/global
Links to Business Schools: MBA Global   http://www.mba.com/global
MBA Global: Graduate Management Admissions Test GMAT: http://www.mba.com/global
Graduate Management Admission Council (GMAC) http://www.gmac.com/
Graduate Management Admissions
Council GMAC: register   https://accounts.gmac.com/Account/Register

Thinking Skills Assessment Test
Cambridge Admissions Testing Service: Thinking Skills Assessment
http://www.admissionstestingservice.org/for-test-takers/thinking-skills-assessment/

Tests for some Mathematics Courses
Cambridge Assessment Admissions Testing Service: Mathematics Admissions Test MAT
http://www.admissionstestingservice.org/for-test-takers/mat/about-mat/
Cambridge Assessment Admissions Testing Service: Sixth Term Examination Paper STEP: Mathematics
http://www.admissionstestingservice.org/for-test-takers/step/about-step/
Cambridge Assessment Admissions Testing Service: Test of Mathematics for University Admission
http://www.admissionstestingservice.org/for-test-takers/test-of-mathematics-for-university-admission/about-the-test-of-mathematics-for-university-admission/

University of Cambridge Admissions Tests
University of Cambridge: Undergraduate Study; Admissions Tests
http://www.undergraduate.study.cam.ac.uk/applying/admissions-tests
University of Cambridge: Undergraduate Study, Pre-Interview
http://www.undergraduate.study.cam.ac.uk/applying/admissions-assessments/pre-interview
Cambridge Law Test http://ba.law.cam.ac.uk/applying/cambridge_law_test/

University of Oxford Admissions Tests
University of Oxford: Undergraduate; Tests
https://www.ox.ac.uk/admissions/undergraduate/applying-to-oxford/tests
Cambridge Assessment Admissions Testing Service: Oxford pre-interview assessments
http://www.admissionstesting.org/for-test-takers/oxford-tests/

Applications for Full Time Undergraduate and Some Postgraduate Courses

University and College Admissions Service (UCAS) UK
University and College Admissions Service (UCAS) https://www.ucas.com/
UCAS Conservatoire   https://www.ucas.com/ucas/conservatoires
UCAS Teacher Training   https://www.ucas.com/ucas/teacher-training
UCAS Key Dates
https://www.ucas.com/ucas/undergraduate/apply-and-track/key-dates
UCAS: Undergraduate Interview Invitations
https://www.ucas.com/ucas/undergraduate/apply-and-track/track-your-application/undergraduate-interview-invitations
UCAS: Undergraduate Results
https://www.ucas.com/ucas/undergraduate/apply-and-track/ucas-undergraduate-results

For applications to the Guildhall School of Music and Drama you would need to apply directly to the institution and not through UCAS
Guildhall School of Music and Drama   https://www.gsmd.ac.uk/

Republic of Ireland University Applications
Central Applications Office (CAO) in Ireland   https://www.cao.ie/ .

UCAS Entry Requirements and Tariff points
UCAS: Entry Requirements
https://www.ucas.com/ucas/undergraduate/getting-started/entry-requirements
UCAS: Tariff Calculator
https://www.ucas.com/ucas/undergraduate/getting-started/entry-requirements/tariff/calculator
Universities and Colleges Admission Service (UCAS) Tariff points.
https://www.ucas.com/ucas/ucas-Tariff-points

Course Search: Further Education, Undergraduate and Postgraduate Courses

Undergraduate Course and Subject Search in the UK
University and College Admission Service UCAS http://www.ucas.com
UCAS Conservatoires   https://www.ucas.com/
HEAP University Degree Course Offers   http://www.heaponline.co.uk/
Hot Courses   http://www.hotcourses.com/
UK Course Finder   http://www.ukcoursefinder.com/

Undergraduate Course and Subject Search in Ireland
Central Applications Office (CAO) in Ireland   https://www.cao.ie/

Higher National Certificate / Diploma Courses and Subject Search
Check availability with the relevant university or college.
Pearson Edexcel   http://qualifications.pearson.com/en/qualifications.html
Scottish Qualification Authority   http://www.sqa.org.uk/

Postgraduate Course and Subject Search
Find a master's   http://www.findamaster's.com/
Find a PhD   http://www.findaphd.com/
Master's portal   http://www.master'sportal.eu/
Postgrad.com   http://www.postgrad.com/
Prospects: Postgraduate Study http://www.prospects.ac.uk/postgraduate_study.htm
Target postgrad   http://targetpostgrad.com/
UCAS postgraduate   http://www.ucas.com
UCAS Teacher Training   http://www.ucas.com

Further Education Colleges Lnks
England
Association of Colleges England   https://www.aoc.co.uk/
Wales
College Wales   http://www.collegeswales.ac.uk/
Northern Ireland
Colleges Northern Ireland   http://www.anic.ac.uk/
Scotland
Colleges Scotland   http://www.collegesscotland.ac.uk/
Additional Further Education College links
Association of Employment and Learning Providers http://www.aelp.org.uk
Access to Higher Education   https://www.accesstohe.ac.uk/
University Technical Colleges (UTCs)   http://www.utcolleges.org/

Credit Accumulation and Transfer Scheme (CATS)
Quality Assurance Agency: Credit Accumulation and Transfer Scheme (CATS),
http://www.qaa.ac.uk/assuring-standards-and-quality/academic-credit
Europa: European Credit Transfer Systems (ECTS)
http://ec.europa.eu/education/ects/ects_en.htm

Regulation of Academic and Vocational Qualifications Below Higher Education Level and Awarding Bodies in the UK

England and Northern Ireland
Office of Qualifications and
Examinations Regulation (Ofqual) https://www.gov.uk/government/organisations/ofqual

Ofqual works in partnership with
Council for the Curriculum Examinations and Assessment (CCEA) in
Northern Ireland   http://ccea.org.uk/
Welsh Government   http://wales.gov.uk
Northern Ireland
Council for the Curriculum Examinations and Assessment (CCEA) in
Northern Ireland   http://ccea.org.uk/
Wales
Qualification Wales   http://qualificationswales.org/
Scotland
Scottish Qualifications Authority (SQA)   http://www.sqa.org.uk/

Vocational Qualifications Regulation
Vocational qualifications are regulated by:
England and Northern Ireland
Office of Qualifications and
Examinations Regulation (Qfqual) https://www.gov.uk/government/organisations/ofqual
Wales
Qualification Wales   http://qualificationswales.org/
Scotland
Scottish Qualifications Authority (SQA)   http://www.sqa.org.uk/

European Qualifications
European Qualifications Framework at:
Europa: Ploteus   https://ec.europa.eu/ploteus/en

International Qualifications
UCAS: EU and International Guides
https://www.ucas.com/ucas/undergraduate/getting-started/international-and-eu-students/international-guides

Secondary and Further Education (FE) Qualifications and Awarding Organisations
England, Wales and Northern Ireland
Regulated qualifications and courses that are found in the Regulated Qualification
Framework (RQF) may be found at:
UK Government: Ofqual
https://www.gov.uk/government/news/ofqual-to-introduce-new-regulated-qualifications-framework
UK Government:
Find a Regulated Qualification   https://www.gov.uk/find-a-regulated-qualification
You can search for recognised non-higher education academic and vocational qualifications
and awarding organisations in England, Wales and Northern Ireland that are regulated by
Ofqual, including GCSEs and 'A' levels, on the
Ofqual Register   http://register.ofqual.gov.uk/

Scotland
Scottish Qualifications Authority (SQA)   http://www.sqa.org.uk/

General Certificates of Secondary Education (GCSEs) level 1 and 2 (RQF)
England
UK Government: GCSE, AS and 'A' level reform
https://www.gov.uk/government/publications/get-the-facts-gcse-and-a-level-reform
Wales
Qualifications Wales   http://qualificationswales.org/
Northern Ireland
Northern Ireland Direct   http://www.nidirect.gov.uk/guide-to-qualifications

Awarding Organisations: GCSEs
England: Awarding Organisations: GCSEs (grades 9 - 1)
AQA   http://www.aqa.org.uk/
Pearson Qualifications   https://qualifications.pearson.com/
Oxford and Cambridge and RSA (OCR)   http://www.ocr.org.uk/

Northern Ireland Awarding Organisation; GCSEs (grades A*-G; by summer 2020 the remaining 9 - 1 graded GCSE subjects will be introduced).
The Council for Curriculum Examinations and Assessment (CCEA)
(Northern Ireland)   http://www.ccea.org.uk/

Wales: Awarding Organisation: GCSEs (grades A* - G)
Welsh Joint Education Committee (WJEC)   http://www.wjec.co.uk/

Wales: Awarding Organisation: GCSEs (grades 9 - 1)
Welsh Joint Education Committee (WJEC) subsidiary company:
Eduqas   http://www.eduqas.co.uk/

Scottish National Courses Level 4 and 5 (SCQF)
Awarding Organisation: Scottish National Courses 4 and 5 (SCQF)
Scottish Qualifications Authority (SQA)   http://www.sqa.org.uk/scqf

'A' Levels and 'AS' Levels Level 3 (RQF)
Further information about secondary and further education qualifications may be found at:
England
UK Government: GCSE, AS and 'A' level reform
https://www.gov.uk/government/publications/get-the-facts-gcse-and-a-level-reform
Wales
Qualifications Wales   http://qualificationswales.org/
Northern Ireland
Northern Ireland Direct   http://www.nidirect.gov.uk/guide-to-qualifications

Awarding organisations for GCSEs, 'AS' levels and 'A' levels in England, Wales and Northern Ireland
England: Awarding organisation:
'AS' Levels and 'A' Levels
AQA   http://www.aqa.org.uk/
Pearson Edexcel   http://www.edexcel.com/
Oxford and Cambridge and RSA (OCR)   http://www.ocr.org.uk/

Wales: Awarding organisation:
'AS' Levels and 'A' Levels
Welsh Joint Education Committee (WJEC)   http://www.wjec.co.uk/
Welsh Joint Education Committee (WJEC) subsidiary company:
Eduqas   http://www.eduqas.co.uk/

Northern Ireland: Awarding organisation: 'AS' levels and 'A' levels
The Council for Curriculum Examinations and
Assessment (Northern Ireland) (CCEA)   http://www.ccea.org.uk/

Northern Ireland: Additional Awarding Organisation: 'AS' levels and 'A' levels
AQA   http://www.aqa.org.uk/
Pearson qualifications   http://qualifications.pearson.com/
Oxford and Cambridge and RSA (OCR)   http://www.ocr.org.uk/

Access to Higher Education Diploma
England and Wales
Access to Higher Education (HE) Diploma   http://www.accesstohe.ac.uk/
Access to HE validating agencies are licensed by the
Quality Assurance Agency for Higher Education (QAA) http://www.qaa.ac.uk/en
Validation Agencies (AVAs) may be found at Access to HE: AVA Profiles
http://www.accesstohe.ac.uk/HowCourses/AVA-profiles/Pages/Default.aspx
Northern Ireland
Northern Ireland Direct: Routes to Higher Education
https://www.nidirect.gov.uk/articles/routes-higher-education
Scotland
Scottish Wider Access Programme   http://www.scottishwideraccess.org/

Baccalaureates

AQA Baccalaureate
Awarding Organisation: AQA Baccalaureate
AQA   https://www.aqa.org.uk/

European Baccalaureate Diploma (EB)
UK Government: European Baccalaureate
https://www.gov.uk/government/publications/information-on-the-european-baccalaureate
Awarding Organisation: European Baccalaureate Diploma (EB)
European Schools   http://www.eursc.eu/
European Schools: European Baccalaureate
https://www.eursc.eu/en/European-Schools/studies-certificates/European-Baccalaureate

International Baccalaureate (IB) Diploma Programme (DP) Level 3 (RQF)
International Baccalaureate Organisation (IBO) in Switzerland http://www.ibo.org/
Awarding and Overseeing Organisation: International Baccalaureate (IB) Diploma Programme
International Baccalaureate Organisation (IBO) in Switzerland http://www.ibo.org/

Welsh Baccalaureate Advanced Diploma
Welsh Baccalaureate   http://www.welshbaccalaureate.org.uk/
Awarding organisation: Welsh Baccalaureate
WJEC   http://www.wjec.co.uk/

BTEC Nationals level 3 (RQF)
Awarding Organisation: BTEC National
Pearson qualifications   http://qualifications.pearson.com/

Cambridge International Pre-U Certificate / Diploma
Cambridge International Exams   http://www.cie.org.uk/
Awarding Organisation: Cambridge International Pre-U
Cambridge International Exams   http://www.cie.org.uk/

542

Foundation Diploma in Art (FDA) (Level 3 and Level 4 QCF)
Awarding Organisations: Foundation Diploma in Art
The following are the Awarding Bodies that offer the Foundation Diploma / Studies in Art and Design (FDA). Universities may also be awarding bodies for higher education studied FDAs For further details, check on the relevant website.
ABC Level 3 and level 4 Diploma in Foundation Studies in Art and Design
ABC level 3 Foundation Diploma in Art, Design and Media
ABC Awards   http://www.abcawards.co.uk/
Pearson Edexcel Level 3 BTEC Foundation Diploma in Art and Design
Pearson Qualifications   http://qualifications.pearson.com/
University of the Arts (UAL): Foundation Diploma in
Art and Design   http://www.arts.ac.uk/about-ual/awarding-Organisation/qualifications/
WJEC Diploma in Foundation Studies in Art, Design and Media
WJEC   http://www.wjec.co.uk/

Scottish Qualifications: National Certificates level 6; Highers; Advanced Highers and Baccalaureate Levels 6/7 SCQF
Scottish Qualifications Authority (SQA)   http://www.sqa.org.uk/scqf
Awarding Organisation: Scottish Highers
Scottish Qualifications Authority (SQA)   http://www.sqa.org.uk/scqf

Replacement Exam Certificates
Information may be found at:
UK Government:
Replacement Exam Certificate   https://www.gov.uk/replacement-exam-certificate

Regulation of Higher Education in the UK

Regulation of Public Sector Higher Education Qualifications
England, Wales and Northern Ireland: Public sector higher education qualifications regulation
Quality Assurance Agency for Higher Education (QAA) http://www.qaa.ac.uk
QAA: Right to Award Degrees   http://www.qaa.ac.uk/en/Publications/
Scotland: Public sector higher education qualifications regulation
Scottish Office of the Quality Assurance Agency for
Higher Education (QAA Scotland)   http://www.qaa.ac.uk/about-us/scotland
Which works in partnership with other higher education organisations:
Scottish Qualifications Authority (SQA)   http://www.sqa.org.uk , the
Scottish Credit and Qualifications Framework (SCQF) http://www.scqf.org.uk
Colleges Scotland   http://www.collegesscotland.ac.uk/
Universities Scotland   http://www.universities-scotland.ac.uk/

Regulation of Private Sector Further and Higher Education Qualifications
British Accreditation Council (BAC)   http://www.the-bac.org/

Higher National Certificates and Higher National Diplomas Awarding Bodies
England, Wales and Northern Ireland are awarded by
Pearson qualifications   http://qualifications.pearson.com/ and in
Scotland are awarded by
Scottish Qualifications Authority (SQA)   http://www.sqa.org.uk/

English Language Centres in the UK and English Language Requirements

English Language Centres in the UK

English UK   https://www.englishuk.com/

English Language Requirements

Further information may be found at English language requirements:
UK Government tier 4 general visa
https://www.gov.uk/tier-4-general-visa/knowledge-of-english

Higher and Further Education Public Funding Bodies

From August 2019, the authority to grant degree awarding powers in England will transfer from the Privy Council to the
The Office for Students
https://www.officeforstudents.org.uk/advice-and-guidance/the-register/
Privy Council https://privycouncil.independent.gov.uk/
Quality Assurance Agency for Higher Education (QAA) http://www.qaa.ac.uk

England

Teaching funding

The Office for Students   https://www.officeforstudents.org.uk/
from March 2018 has replaced the
Higher Education Funding Council for England http://www.hefce.ac.uk/

Research funding

Research England   https://re.ukri.org/
is the new council within the
UK Research and Innovation   https://www.ukri.org/

Wales

Higher Education Funding Council for Wales   http://www.hefcw.org.uk/

Northern Ireland

Department for the Economy:
Higher Education   https://www.economy-ni.gov.uk/topics/higher-education

Scotland

Scottish Funding Council: Further and Higher Education http://www.sfc.ac.uk/

Higher Education Course Subjects and Professional Body Accreditation

Agriculture and Plants Sector

Chartered Institute of Horticulture   https://www.horticulture.org.uk/
Grow Careers   http://www.growcareers.info/
Institute of Agricultural Engineers   http://www.iagre.org/
Institute of Chartered Foresters   http://www.charteredforesters.org
International Federation of Landscape Architects http://iflaonline.org/
Royal Institution of Chartered Surveyors   http://www.rics.org/uk/
The Landscape Institute   http://www.landscapeinstitute.org

Animals and Conservation Sector

Association for Nutrition: Nutrition   http://www.associationfornutrition.org
British Society of Animal Science   http://bsas.org.uk/accreditation
Chartered Institute of Ecology and
Environmental Management (CIEEM)   http://www.cieem.net
Royal College of Veterinary Surgeons   http://www.rcvs.org.uk/
Royal Society of Biology   https://www.rsb.org.uk/

Art and Design Sector
Chartered Society of Designers   http://www.csd.org.uk
Drama UK   http://www.dramauk.co.uk
The Gemmological Association of Great Britain http://www.gem-a.com

Medical Illustration; Medical Photography: Postgraduate
Registration with
Academy for Healthcare Science   https://www.ahcs.ac.uk/

Product Design: Undergraduate
Chartered Society of Designers   http://www.csd.org.uk

Building Design, Planning, Surveying and Construction Sector
Architects Registration Board (ARB)   http://www.arb.org.uk
Association for Project Management APM   http://www.apm.org.uk
Chartered Institute of Architectural Technologists http://www.ciat.org.uk
Chartered Institute of Building   http://www.ciob.org/
Chartered Institution of Civil Engineering Surveyors https://www.cices.org/
International Federation of Landscape Architects http://iflaonline.org/
Landscape Institute   http://www.landscapeinstitute.co.uk/
Project Management Institute   http://www.pmi.org/
Royal Institute of British Architecture   http://www.architecture.com
Royal Institution of Chartered Surveyors (RICS) http://www.rics.org
Royal Town Planning Institute (RTPI)   http://www.rtpi.org.uk

Building Property Management and Housing Sector
Chartered Institute of Housing (CIH)   http://www.cih.org
Royal Institution of Chartered Surveyors (RICS) http://www.rics.org

Business Finance; Economics; Mathematics; Statistics Sector
Association of Chartered Certified Accountants ACCA http://www.accaglobal.com
Chartered Accountants England and Wales ICAEW http://www.icaew.com
Chartered Accountants Ireland CAI   http://www.charteredaccountants.ie
Chartered Banker Institute   http://www.charteredbanker.com
Chartered Institute of Management Accountants CIMA http://www.cimaglobal.com
Chartered Institute of Public Finance Accountancy CIPFA http://www.cipfa.org/
Chartered Institute of Taxation   http://www.tax.org.uk
Institute of Chartered Accountants Scotland ICAS http://icas.org.uk
Institute of Faculty of Actuaries http://www.actuaries.org.uk
Institute of Mathematics and its Applications   http://www.ima.org.uk
Mathematics and its Applications   http://www.ima.org.uk
Royal Statistical Society (RSS)   http://www.rss.org.uk

Business Management and Administration; Human Resources and Recruitment Sector
Association of MBAs   http://www.mbaworld.com
Association for Project Management APM   http://www.apm.org.uk
Chartered Institute of Personnel and Development http://www.cipd.co.uk
Chartered Management Institute   http://www.managers.org.uk/

Education and Teacher Training Sector

Teaching English as a Foreign Language (TEFL); Teaching English as a Second or Other Language (TESOL)

Cambridge English Language Assessment http://www.cambridgeenglish.org
Trinity College London http://www.trinitycollege.co.uk/

Primary and Secondary Teaching QTS: Undergraduate and Postgraduate
UK Teaching Registration Councils
England:
Department for Education and Teaching Regulation Agency
https://www.gov.uk/government/organisations/department-for-education
Wales
General Teaching Council Wales http://www.gtcw.org.uk
Northern Ireland
General Teaching Council Northern Ireland http://www.gtcni.org.uk
Scotland
General Teaching Council Scotland http://www.gtcs.org.uk

Further and Adult Education Teacher Training
FE Advice https://www.feadvice.org.uk/
England
Society for Education and Training (SET) https://set.et-foundation.co.uk/
Wales
Education Workforce Council (EWC): Wales http://www.ewc.wales/
Northern Ireland
Government, Northern Ireland: Department for the Economy
https://www.economy-ni.gov.uk/topics/further-education/qualifications-required-teach-further-education
Scotland
Scotland: General Teaching Council Scotland http://www.gtcs.org.uk

Higher Education Lecturing; Further Education Lecturing: Postgraduate
The Higher Education Academy https://www.heacademy.ac.uk/

Engineering and Technology Sector
Chartered Association of Building Engineers CBUILDE http://www.cbuilde.com
Chartered Institution of Water and
Environmental Management CIWEM http://www.ciwem.org.uk
Energy Institute EI https://www.energyinst.org/
Engineering Council http://www.engc.org.uk/
Institute of Physics and Engineering in Medicine IPEM http://www.ipem.ac.uk/
Institute of Materials, Minerals and Mining IOM3 http://www.iom3.org/
Institution Agricultural Engineers IAgrE http://www.iagre.org
Institution of Chemical Engineers IChmeE http://www.icheme.org/
Institution of Civil Engineers http://www.ice.org.uk
Institution of Engineering Designers IED http://www.ied.org.uk
Institution of Mechanical Engineers IMECHE http://www.imeche.org
Institution of Structural Engineers ISTRUCTE http://www.istructe.org
Institute of Physics and Engineering in Medicine IPEM http://www.ipem.ac.uk/
Nuclear Institute http://www.nuclearinst.com
Project Management Institute http://www.pmi.org/
Royal Institution of Chartered Surveyors (RICS) http://www.rics.org

Transport Engineering: Automotive; Aviation; Marine; Railway; Road
Engineering Council   http://www.engc.org.uk/
Institute of Marine Engineering, Science and Technology IMarEST http://www.imarest.org/
Institution of Mechanical Engineers IMECHE   http://www.imeche.org
Royal Aeronautical Society AEROSOCIETY   http://www.aerosociety.com

Environment Sector
Chartered Institute of Civil Engineering Surveyors https://www.cices.org/
Chartered Institution of Civil Engineering Surveyorshttps://www.cices.org/
Chartered Institution of Water and
Environmental Management CIWEM   http://www.ciwem.org
Geological Society   http://www.geolsoc.org.uk
Institute of Marine Engineering, Science and Technology http://www.imarest.org/
Institution of Environmental Science   https://www.the-ies.org
Royal Geographical Society   http://www.rgs.org/
Royal Institution for Chartered Surveyors   http://www.rics.org/uk/
Royal Institution of Chartered Surveyors   http://www.rics.org/uk/
Royal Meteorological Society   https://www.rmets.org/
Royal Society of Biology   https://www.rsb.org.uk/

Healthcare Sector
Allied Health Professions
Allied Health Profession Federation   http://www.ahpf.org.uk
Association of UK Dieticians   https://www.bda.uk.com
British and Irish Orthoptic society   http://www.orthoptics.org.uk
British Association and College of Occupational Therapists http://www.cot.co.uk
British Association of Art Therapists   http://www.baat.org
British Association of Drama Therapists   https://badth.org.uk
British Association of Prosthetists and Orthotists http://www.bapo.com
Chartered Society of Physiotherapy   http://www.csp.org.uk/
College of Paramedics   https://www.collegeofparamedics.co.uk
College of Podiatry   http://www.scpod.org
Royal College of Speech and Language Therapists http://www.rcslt.org
Society and College of Radiographers Diagnostic and Therapeutic https://www.sor.org/
Registration is a requirement with
Health and Care Professions Council   http://www.hcpc-uk.org

Alternative Health, Complementary and Creative Therapy
Association for Dance Movement Psychotherapy UKhttp://www.admt.org.uk
Association for Nutrition   http://www.associationfornutrition.org
British Acupuncture Accreditation Board (BAAB) http://www.baab.co.uk
Complementary and Natural Healthcare Council (CNHC) http://www.cnhc.org.uk/

Complementary Medicine
General Chiropractic Council   http://www.gcc-uk.org
General Osteopathic Council   http://www.osteopathy.org.uk

Medicine; Dentistry; Nursing and Midwifery; Operating Department; Optometry; Pharmacy

British Dental Association — https://www.bda.org
Consortium for the Accreditation of Sonographic Education http://www.case-uk.org/
General Medical Council (GMC) — http://www.gmc-uk.org
Nursing and Midwifery Council — http://www.nmc-uk.org
Health Care Professions Council — http://www.hcpc-uk.org
General Optical Council (GOC) — https://www.optical.org
General Pharmaceutical Council (GPhC) — http://www.pharmacyregulation.org

Public Health; Environmental Health; Health Promotion; Occupational Health

Chartered Institute of Environmental Health (CIEH) http://www.cieh.org
Chartered Institute of Ergonomics and Human Factors http://www.ergonomics.org.uk
Chartered Institution of Occupational Safety and Health (IOSH) https://www.iosh.co.uk/
NEBOSH — https://www.nebosh.org.uk/

History, Anthropology and Archaeology Sector

Institute of Conservation — http://www.icon.org.uk
Institute of Historic Building Conservation (IHBC) http://www.ihbc.org.uk
Museums Association — http://www.museumsassociation.org/

Hospitality, Culinary and Events Management Sector

Chartered Institute of Library and Information Professionals CILIP http://www.cilip.org.uk
Institute of Hospitality — https://www.instituteofhospitality.org/

Information and Library Studies Sector

Archives and Records Association (ARA) — http://www.archives.org.uk
Chartered Institute of Library and Information Professionals CILIP http://www.cilip.org.uk

Information / Computer Technology Sector

Chartered Institute of IT (BCS) — http://www.bcs.org/
Engineering Council — http://www.engc.org.uk/

Languages Sector

British Sign Language; Translation and Interpreting

Chartered Institute for Linguistics — https://www.ciol.org.uk/
Deafblind People (NRCPD) — http://www.nrcpd.org.uk
Institute of Translating and Interpreting — http://www.iti.org.uk/

Law Enforcement: Armed Forces Sector

Armed Forces: Education and Training — http://www.army.mod.uk/

Law Enforcement: Protection and Security Services Sector

College of Policing — http://www.college.police.uk/

Law

Chartered Institute of Legal Executives (CILEx) http://www.cilexcareers.org.uk/
Solicitors Regulation Authority (SRA) — http://www.sra.org.uk
Bar Standards Board — https://www.barstandardsboard.org.uk
The Bar of Northern Ireland — http://www.barofni.com
The Faculty of Advocates Scotland — http://www.advocates.org.uk

Graduate Diploma in Law: Graduate Conversion course

Lawcabs: Central applications Board — http://www.lawcabs.ac.uk/

Leisure and Tourism Sector
Institute of Hospitality	https://www.instituteofhospitality.org/
Institute of Travel and Tourism	http://www.itt.co.uk/

Media: Advertising, Communications, Marketing and Public Relations Sector

Advertising, Media Communications, Marketing, Public Relations
Chartered Institute of Marketing	http://www.cim.co.uk
Chartered Institute of Public Relations	http://www.cipr.co.uk

Journalism and Publishing
British Journalism Training Council BJTC	http://www.bjtc.org.uk
Professional Publishers Association: Journalism and Publishing http://www.ppa.co.uk

Media: Film, Radio, Television and Theatre Sector
BKSTS: Craft Skills and Technology: Film Industry	https://www.bksts.com/
Joint Audio Media Educational Support (James) http://www.jamesonline.org.uk/

Performing Arts Sector

Dance
Council for Dance Education and Training	http://www.cdet.org.uk

Drama
Drama UK	http://www.dramauk.co.uk
Grade and Certificate Examinations professionally accredited with:
Trinity College London	http://www.trinitycollege.com

Music
Music performance examinations awarded by
Associated Board of the Royal Schools of Music http://gb.abrsm.org/en/
Royal Academy of Music	https://www.ram.ac.uk/
Trinity College London	http://www.trinitycollege.com

Psychology, Counselling and Psychotherapy Sector

Counselling
Counselling and Psychotherapy: Some Undergraduate mostly Postgraduate
Professional accreditation is a requirement with an organisation registered with:
Professional Standards Authority
https://www.professionalstandards.org.uk/what-we-do/accredited-registers/find-a-register

Behavioural and Cognitive Psychotherapy
British Association for Behavioural and Cognitive Psychotherapies http://www.babcp.com

British Association for Behavioural and Cognitive Psychotherapies (BABCP)
British Association for Behavioural and
Cognitive Psychotherapies (BABCP)	http://www.babcp.com

British Association of Counselling and Psychotherapy
British Association of Counselling and Psychotherapy http://www.bacp.co.uk

British Psychoanalytic Council
British Psychoanalytic Council (Training Centres) http://www.bpc.org.uk

British Psychological Society (BPS)
British Psychological Society (BPS)   http://beta.bps.org.uk/

Child Psychotherapy
Association of Child Psychotherapists   http://www.childpsychotherapy.org.uk/

Christian Counselling
Association of Christian Counsellors   https://www.acc-uk.org/

Cognitive Analytic Therapy
Association for Cognitive Analytic Therapy (CAT) http://www.acat.me.uk/

Counselling and Psychotherapy in Scotland
Counselling and Psychotherapy in Scotland   http://www.cosca.org.uk/

Counselling and Psychotherapy Central Awarding Body (CPCAB)
Counselling and Psychotherapy Central Awarding Body (CPCAB) http://www.cpcab.co.uk/

Federation of Drug and Alcohol Professionals
Federation of Drug and Alcohol Professionals http://www.fdap.org.uk

Human Givens
Human Givens Institute   http://www.hgi.org.uk/

Humanistic Psychology Practitioners
UK Association for Humanistic Psychology Practitioners http://www.ahpp.org

Irish Association for Counselling and Psychotherapy
Irish Association for Counselling and Psychotherapy http://www.irish-counselling.ie

National Counselling Society
National Counselling Society   http://www.nationalcounsellingsociety.org

Play Therapy
British Association of Play Therapists (BAPT) http://www.bapt.info/
British Council for Therapeutic Interventions with Children http://www.bctiwc.org/
Play Therapy UK   http://www.playtherapy.org.uk/
Register of Play and Creative Arts Therapists http://www.playtherapyregister.org.uk/

Psychoanalysis
Institute of Psychoanalysis   http://www.psychoanalysis.org.uk

Sexual and Relationship Therapy
College of Sexual and Relationship Therapists (COSRT) http://www.cosrt.org.uk/

UK Council for Psychotherapy
UK Council for Psychotherapy   http://www.psychotherapy.org.uk
Registered Counsellor
Registered Psychotherapist

Genomic / Genetic Counselling: Postgraduate
Professional accreditation is a requirement with:
Professional registration with:
Genetic Counselling Registration Board (GCRB) http://www.gcrb.org.uk/
Registered Genomic / Genetic Counsellor

High Intensity Therapy
Professional accreditation is a requirement with:
British Association of Behavioural and Cognitive Psychotherapies
(BABCP)   http://www.babcp.com/
Registered High Intensity Therapist

Psychology
The British Psychological Society (BPS)   http://www.bps.org.uk
Practitioner and Registered Psychologist Registration is a requirement with
Health and Care Professions Council   http://www.hcpc-uk.org
Association of Educational Psychologists   http://www.aep.org.uk/

Religion and Theology Sector
Chaplaincy
Hospital Chaplaincies Council   http://www.nhs-chaplaincy-spiritualcare.org.uk/
Baptist
Baptist colleges   http://www.baptist.org.uk/Groups/220658/Colleges.aspx
Church of England
Church of England:
Recognised Theological Training Institutions   https://www.churchofengland.org/
Church of Scotland
Church of Scotland: Ministries
http://www.churchofscotland.org.uk/serve/ministries_council/ministries_in_the_church
Church of Wales
St Michaels College   http://stmichaels.ac.uk/
Evangelical Church
Fellowship of Independent
Evangelical Churches   https://fiec.org.uk/what-we-do/article/equipping-individuals
Rabbinical Training: Jewish Education: Postgraduate
Leo Baeck College   http://www.lbc.ac.uk/
Montefiore College   https://www.montefioreendowment.org.uk/
London School of Jewish Studies   http://www.lsjs.ac.uk/
Roman Catholic Church
National Office for Vocation   http://www.ukvocation.org/
Salvation Army
Salvation Army   http://www.salvationarmy.org.uk/

Retail Sector
Chartered Institute of Purchasing and Supply CIPS http://www.cips.org

Science Sector
Science Council   http://www.sciencecouncil.org

Biology, Chemistry and Healthcare Science
Association for Nutrition: Nutrition http://www.associationfornutrition.org
British Association of Sport and Exercise Science http://www.bases.org.uk/Courses
British Blood Transfusion Society   https://www.bbts.org.uk
British Pharmacology Society
https://www.bps.ac.uk/education-careers/teaching-pharmacology/core-curricula
Chartered Society for Forensic Sciences
http://www.charteredsocietyofforensicsciences.org/
Health Education England: Genomic Medicine
https://www.genomicseducation.hee.nhs.uk/taught-courses/courses/master's-in-genomic-medicine/
Institute of Biomedical Science IBMS https://www.ibms.org/go/qualifications/ibms-courses

Institute of Brewing and Distilling https://www.ibd.org.uk/
Institute of Food Science and Technology IFST http://www.ifst.org/
International Centre for Brewing and Distilling http://www.icbd.hw.ac.uk/courses.html
National Skills Academy: Food and Drink http://foodanddrink.nsacademy.co.uk/
Neuroscience Association https://www.bna.org.uk/careers/courses
Registration Council for Clinical Physiologists https://www.rccp.co.uk
Royal Anthropological Institute of
Great Britain and Ireland https://www.therai.org.uk/forensic-anthropology/
Royal Society of Biology https://www.rsb.org.uk/
Royal Society of Chemistry RSC http://www.rsc.org/

Physical Science
Engineering Council http://www.engc.org.uk/
Institute for Physics and Engineering in Medicine http://www.ipem.ac.uk/
Institute of Biomedical Science IBMS https://www.ibms.org/
Institute of Materials, Minerals and Mining http://www.iom3.org/
Institute of Physics https://www.iop.org/

Healthcare Science Undergraduate NHS Practitioner Training Programme (PTP
Overarching body for the whole of healthcare science
Academy for Healthcare Science: http://www.ahcs.ac.uk
Registration as a Clinical Scientist, Biomedical Scientist and Hearing Aid Dispenser is with:
Health and Care Professions Council HCPC http://www.hcpc-uk.org
Registration as a Medical Physiologist, Medical Physical Scientist and Biomedical Engineer is with:
Academy for Healthcare Science: http://www.ahcs.ac.uk
There are separate healthcare science training schemes which accredit courses in England, Wales, Northern Ireland and Scotland
England and Wales
National School for Healthcare Science http://www.nshcs.hee.nhs.uk/
Wales
NHS Wales http://www.wales.nhs.uk/nhswalesaboutus
Northern Ireland
Northern Ireland Government http://www.nidirect.gov.uk/healthcare-scientist
Scotland
NHS Education for Scotland http://www.nes.scot.nhs.uk/education-and-training/

Life Sciences / Biomedical Sciences NHS Practitioner Training Programme (PTP)
Institute of Biomedical Science IBMS https://www.ibms.org/

Medical Physics Technology and Biomedical (Clinical) Engineering NHS Practitioner Training Programme (PTP)
Engineering Council http://www.engc.org.uk/
Institute of Physics and Engineering in Medicine IPEM http://www.ipem.ac.uk/

Physiological Sciences (Clinical) NHS Practitioner Training Programme (PTP)
Registration Council for Clinical Physiologists https://www.rccp.co.uk

Social Care

Careers Guidance / Careers Coaching: Postgraduate
Approved courses required for professional eligibility to register with the:
Career Development Institute
http://www.thecdi.net/Getting-Qualified/Master's-and-other-courses

Career Education, Information and Guidance in HE (CEIGH): Postgraduate
Postgraduate certificate, diploma, master's degree
Delivered by the University of Warwick   https://warwick.ac.uk/
in collaboration with the Association of
Graduate Careers Advisory Service (AGCAS) http://www.agcas.org.uk/
Play Therapy: Postgraduate
British Association of Play Therapists   http://www.bapt.info

Probation Service
Train to be a Probation Officer: University Providers
http://www.traintobeaprobationofficer.com/
Professional Qualification in Probation (PQiP); Community Justice Learning (CJL): Undergraduate and Graduate
England and Wales
Professional accreditation is a requirement with:
National Probation Service   http://www.traintobeaprobationofficer.com/
England and Wales
National Probation Service
England and Wales https://www.gov.uk/government/organisations/national-probation-service
Northern Ireland
Social Work qualification
Northern Ireland Social Care Council
http://www.niscc.info/index.php/education-for-our-training-providers/degree-in-social-work-education
Scotland
Social Work qualification
Scottish Social Services Council: Social work http://www.sssc.uk.com

Social Work
Professional accreditation is a requirement with:
England
Health and Care Professions Council regulates Social Workers in England: register of courses http://www.hcpc-uk.org/education/programmes/register/
Wales
Care Council for Wales: Social Work courses http://www.ccwales.org.uk/social-work-degree/
Northern Ireland
Northern Ireland Social Care Council
http://www.niscc.info/index.php/education-for-our-training-providers/degree-in-social-work-education
Scotland
Scottish Social Services Council (SSSC) Social Workers http://www.sssc.uk.com

Youth and Community Work
Professional accreditation is a requirement with:
England
National Youth Agency England   http://www.nya.org.uk
Wales
Education and Training Standards Wales: Youth Work http://www.etswales.org.uk
Northern Ireland
Youth Council Northern Ireland   http://www.ycni.org
Scotland
The Standards Council: Community Learning and Development for Scotland
http://www.cldstandardscouncil.org.uk

Social Science, Social Arts, Social Policy, Philosophy and Politics Sector
British Philosophy Association   http://www.bpa.ac.uk/
British Sociological Association   https://www.britsoc.co.uk/

Sport Sector
British Association of Sport and Exercise Sciences BASES http://www.bases.org.uk/
British Psychology Society   http://www.bps.org.uk/
British Association of Sport and Exercise Sciences http://www.bases.org.uk/Courses
Chartered Institute for the Management of Sport and
Physical Activity (CIMSPA): Endorsed degrees http://www.cimspa.co.uk
Society of Sports Therapists   http://www.society-of-sports-therapists.org
Sports Coach UK   http://www.sportscoachuk.org

Transport and Logistics Sector
Chartered Institute of Logistics and Transport http://www.ciltuk.org.uk/
Chartered Institute of Purchasing and Supply CIPS: http://www.cips.org

Marine Operations / Management / Nautical Science
Maritime and Coastguard Agency (MCA)
https://www.gov.uk/government/organisations/maritime-and-coastguard-agency
Merchant Navy Training Board (MNTB)   http://mntb.org.uk/
Honourable Company of Master Mariners   http://www.hcmm.org.uk/

Higher Education Institutions: Groups, Associations and Affiliations
Cathedrals Group   http://www.cathedralsgroup.ac.uk/
GuildHE   http://guildhe.ac.uk/
Associate and Sub Associate groups of Guild HE:
   Consortium for Research Excellence, Support and Training (CREST) http://crest.ac.uk/
   United Kingdom Arts and Design Institutions Association (UKADIA) http://ukadia.ac.uk/
Million Plus Group   http://www.millionplus.ac.uk/
Russell Group   http://www.russellgroup.ac.uk/
Russell Group Informed Choices   http://www.russellgroup.org/InformedChoices-latest.pdf
Universities UK   http://www.universitiesuk.ac.uk
University Alliance   http://www.unialliance.ac.uk/

Conservatoires
Conservatoires UK   http://www.conservatoiresuk.ac.uk/

Collegiate Universities
England
University of Oxford, founded in the 11th century   http://www.ox.ac.uk/
University of Cambridge, founded in 13th century   http://www.cam.ac.uk
Universities founded in 19th century and often included with the 'Ancient' Universities
England
Durham University http://www.durhamstudent.co.uk/
London University (which now has a number of separate institutions)
London University http://www.london.ac.uk/
The Royal College of Art https://www.rca.ac.uk/
Lancaster University http://www.lancs.ac.uk

Wales
University of Wales, (which now has a number of separate institutions)
University of Wales http://www.wales.ac.uk

Scotland
University of St Andrews, founded in 15th century   https://www.st-andrews.ac.uk/
University of Glasgow, founded in 15th century   http://www.gla.ac.uk/
University of Aberdeen, founded in 15th century   http://www.abdn.ac.uk
University of Edinburgh, founded in 16th century   http://www.ed.ac.uk/

Republic of Ireland (not part of the UK)
University of Dublin, now Trinity College Dublin, founded in 16th century
Trinity College Dublin   http://www.tcd.ie/

Higher Education Fairs and Open Days

Dates for open days and events can be found advertised on the university websites as well as with
UCAS http://www.ucas.com/how-it-all-works/explore-your-options/events-and-open-days
UCAS has virtual tours for a number universities and colleges.
UCAS: Virtual Tours https://www.ucas.com/events/exploring-university/virtual-tours

Higher Education Policy

England
UK Government: Department for
Education https://www.gov.uk/government/organisations/department-for-education
Wales
Welsh Government:
Department for Education and Skills   http://gov.wales/topics/educationandskills/
Northern Ireland
Department for the Economy:
Higher Education   https://www.economy-ni.gov.uk/topics/higher-education
Scotland
Scottish Government   http://www.gov.scot/

Higher Education Statistics and Information

Higher Education Statistics Agency (HESA)   https://www.hesa.ac.uk/
Prospects (the graduate careers website)   https://www.prospects.ac.uk/
Association of Graduate Careers Advisory Service (AGCAS) https://www.agcas.org.uk/
Higher Education Careers Service Unit (HECSU) 'What do graduates do?'
https://www.hecsu.ac.uk/current_projects_what_do_graduates_do.htm

Destinations of Leavers from Higher Education survey (DELHE)

Higher Education Statistics Agency (HESA)   https://www.hesa.ac.uk/stats-dlhe

The National Student Survey (NSS) and Unistats

The NSS is commissioned by the Higher Education Funding bodies for the four UK countries and
Health Education England   https://hee.nhs.uk/
The NSS is conducted independently by Ipsos MORI and the data is published annually at:
Unistats website https://unistats.direct.gov.uk/
To find out more about the NSS and for current eligible students completing the NSS, the survey is available at
The Student Survey   http://www.thestudentsurvey.com/
Ipsos MORI   https://www.ipsos-mori.com/
Quality Assurance Agency for Higher Education (QAA) http://www.qaa.ac.uk
Scottish Qualifications Authority (SQA)   http://www.sqa.org.uk/

Higher Education League Tables

UK Universities League Tables
The Times and Sunday Times Good University Guide
http://www.thesundaytimes.co.uk/sto/University_Guide/
The Complete University Guide   http://www.thecompleteuniversityguide.co.uk/
The Guardian University Guide   http://www.theguardian.com/education/universityguide

The Main Three Worldwide Universities League Tables
The Times Higher Education World Rankings (THE)
http://www.timeshighereducation.co.uk/world-university-rankings/
The Academic Ranking of World Universities (ARWU) http://www.shanghairanking.com/
The Q5 World University Ranking (QS)   http://www.topuniversities.com/university-rankings

International Student Advice

International Student Advice and Status Regulations
British Council   http://www.britishcouncil.org/
The British Council Education UK   http://www.educationuk.org/global/
UK Council for International Student Affairs UKCISA http://www.ukcisa.org.uk/
UK Government: Healthcare
Immigration Application   https://www.gov.uk/healthcare-immigration-application/pay

Visa Information
UK Government Work Visas   https://www.gov.uk/browse/visas-immigration/work-visas
The UK Visas and Immigration Service is part of the
UK's Home Office https://www.gov.uk/government/organisations/uk-visas-and-immigration
Student Visitor Visa: short term study   https://www.gov.uk/study-visit-visa
UK Government: Tier-4 General Visa Requirements https://www.gov.uk/tier-4-general-visa
You should also check information and advice with the
UK Council for International Student Affairs UKCISA http://www.ukcisa.org.uk/

International Student Scholarships and Bursaries
British Council http://www.britishcouncil.org/
Chevening: UK Government Global Scholarship Programme http://www.chevening.org/
Commonwealth Scholarship and Fellowship Plan (CSFP) http://www.csfp-online.org/
Marhalls Scholarship: for US students in the UK http://www.marshallscholarship.org/
Fulbright Commission: for US students in the UK http://www.fulbright.org.uk/

University and College Admissions Service UCAS
University and College Admissions Service UCAS https://www.ucas.com/

Qualification Information
National Academic Recognition Information Centre (NARIC) https://www.naric.org.uk/ .
Council of Europe Common European Framework of Reference for Languages: Learning,
Teaching, Assessment (CEFR) http://www.coe.int/t/dg4/linguistic/cadre1_en.asp
Common European Framework of Reference for Languages: Learning, Teaching,
Assessment (CEFR), check the
Council of Europe: CEFR Languages:
https://www.coe.int/en/web/common-european-framework-reference-languages/

English Language Tests
International English Language Testing System (IELTS) http://www.ielts.org/
UK Government: Approved English Language Tests
Secure English Language Test (SELT) for a Tier 4 student visa.
PDF list of the SELT tests approved by UK Visas and Immigration
https://www.gov.uk/government/publications/guidance-on-applying-for-uk-visa-approved-english-language-tests

International Student Finance Calculator
Brightside: International Student Calculator http://international.studentcalculator.org/

International Student Healthcare
UK Government website https://www.gov.uk/healthcare-immigration-application/pay

International Student Finance
Brightside is an independent education charity which aims to help students prepare for the financial side of UK higher education.
Brightside International Student Calculator   http://international.studentcalculator.org/

Social and Hospitality Information
HOST hospitality for overseas students   http://www.hostuk.org/

Driving
Highway Code   https://www.gov.uk/browse/driving/highway-code
Driver and Vehicle Licensing Agency
https://www.gov.uk/government/organisations/driver-and-vehicle-licensing-agency

Public Transport
Transport for London   http://www.tfl.gov.uk/fares-and-payments/

TV Licence
TV licensing   http://www.tvlicensing.co.uk/

National Academic Recognition Information Centre (NARIC)
National Academic Recognition Information Centre (NARIC) http://www.ecctis.co.uk/naric/

European Network of Information Centres (ENIC)
European Network of Information Centres (ENIC) and the National Academic Recognition Information Centres (NARIC) ENIC-NARIC   http://www.enic-naric.net/

National Occupational Standards (NOS)
National Occupational Standards (NOS)   http://www.ukstandards.org.uk/
NOS UK Standards:
Links to Sector Skills Councils   http://www.ukstandards.org.uk/Pages/Contacts.aspx
The National Occupational Standards (NOS) are defined by the relevant Sector Skills Councils (SSCs) and Standard Setting Organisations (SSOs). SSCs and SSOs with links found at the:
Federation for Industry
Sector Skills Standards   http://fisss.org/sector-skills-council-body/directory-of-sscs/
Further information about National Occupational Standards (NOS) may be found at
UK Government Commission for Employment and Skills (UKCES): National Occupational Standards (NOS)
https://www.gov.uk/government/publications/national-occupational-standards

National Union of Students

| National Union of Students | http://www.nus.org.uk/ |
| National Union of Students NUS Scotland | http://www.nus.org.uk/en/nus-scotland/ |

Officially Recognised Universities, Colleges of Higher Education or Specialist Institutions in the UK

To find recognised universities go to the:
UK Government: Check a University is Officially Recognised
https://www.gov.uk/check-a-university-is-officially-recognised/overview

Further information may also be found at:
UK Government: Recognised Degrees and Bodies
https://www.gov.uk/guidance/recognised-uk-degrees#recognised-bodies
and
Information about recognised bodies and listed bodies:
UK Government: recognised UK degrees https://www.gov.uk/recognised-uk-degrees

Links to universities and colleges may be found at:
Register of English Higher Education Providers:
The Office for Students: The Register
https://www.officeforstudents.org.uk/advice-and-guidance/the-register/

University of Cambridge and University of Oxford

University of Oxford

| University of Oxford | http://www.ox.ac.uk/ |
| University of Oxford: Colleges | http://www.ox.ac.uk/about/colleges |

University of Oxford:
Undergraduate Courses   https://www.ox.ac.uk/admissions/undergraduate/courses-listing
University of Oxford: Entrance Requirements
https://www.ox.ac.uk/admissions/undergraduate/courses/entrance-requirements/level-offers
University of Oxford: Undergraduate Written Work
https://www.ox.ac.uk/admissions/undergraduate/applying-to-oxford/written-work
University of Oxford Choral and Organ Awards
https://www.ox.ac.uk/admissions/undergraduate/applying-to-oxford/choral-and-organ-awards

University of Cambridge

| University of Cambridge | http://www.cam.ac.uk/ |
| University of Cambridge: Colleges | http://map.cam.ac.uk/colleges |

University of Cambridge: Undergraduate Study; Courses
http://www.undergraduate.study.cam.ac.uk/link/courses
University of Cambridge: Undergraduate Study; Admission Assessments
http://www.undergraduate.study.cam.ac.uk/applying/admission-assessments
University of Cambridge: Entrance Requirements
http://www.undergraduate.study.cam.ac.uk/applying/entrance-requirements
University of Cambridge: Admission Assessments; Submitted Work
https://www.undergraduate.study.cam.ac.uk/applying/admission-assessments/submitted-work
Cambridge Assessment Admissions Testing Service: Cambridge Pre-Interview Assessments
http://www.admissionstestingservice.org/for-test-takers/cambridge-pre-interview-assessments/
University of Cambridge: Guide to Completing the SAQ
http://www.undergraduate.study.cam.ac.uk/applying/saq
University of Cambridge: Medicine
https://www.undergraduate.study.cam.ac.uk/courses/medicine

University of Cambridge Medical School
http://www.medschl.cam.ac.uk/education/courses/cgc/
University of Cambridge: Graduation: Cambridge MA
http://www.cambridgestudents.cam.ac.uk/your-course/graduation-and-what-next/cambridge-ma

Universities Offering Mainly Part Time Higher Education Courses
Open University   http://www.openuniversity.co.uk
Birkbeck, University of London   http://www.bbk.ac.uk/

Salary Rates
Office of National Statistics (ONS) Average Weekly Earnings
https://www.ons.gov.uk/employmentandlabourmarket/peopleinwork/employmentandemployeetypes/bulletins/uklabourmarket/latest#average-weekly-earnings
UK Government:
National Minimum Wage Rates   https://www.gov.uk/national-minimum-wage-rates
UK Government:
apprenticeships   https://www.gov.uk/apprenticeships-guide/pay-and-conditions4
Wage Foundation   http://www.livingwage.org.uk/
UK government:
pay and work rights helpline   https://www.gov.uk/pay-and-work-rights-helpline

Salary Ranges for Graduate Careers
Central Careers Hub: Longtiudinal Education Outcomes Data
https://www.centralcareershub.co.uk/longitudinal-education-outcomes-data/
Glass Door: Salaries   https://www.glassdoor.co.uk/Salaries/
Prospects: Graduate Careers: Job Profiles   https://www.prospects.ac.uk/
Target Jobs:
Choosing an Employer   https://targetjobs.co.uk/careers-advice/choosing-an-employer
UK Government: Graduate Employment and Earnings
https://www.gov.uk/government/collections/statistics-higher-education-graduate-employment-and-earnings
UK Government: Office for National Statistics
https://www.ons.gov.uk/employmentandlabourmarket/peopleinwork/earningsandworkinghours

Student Accommodation
Online storage sites such as
Cloud   http://www.thecloud.net/ ,
Dropbox   https://www.dropbox.com/
Onedrive   https://onedrive.live.com/about/en-gb/

Pre-purchasing essential packs
Click2Campus   http://www.click2campus.com/index.html

Accommodation Code of practice
Universities UK / Guild HE Code of Practice for the Management of Student Housing often known as the
Student Accommodation Code   http://www.universitiesuk.ac.uk/
Accreditation Network UK (ANUK) / Unipol code of Standards for Larger Residential Developments for student accommodation managed and controlled by education establishments.   http://www.nationalcode.org/

For halls of residence owned and managed by private companies, the company will have signed up for a code of practice with:
ANUK / Unipol Code of Standards for Larger Developments not managed and controlled by educational establishments:
National Code   http://www.nationalcode.org/

Self-regulating organisations include:
Association of Residential Lettings Agents   http://www.arla.co.uk/
National Approved Letting Scheme, (NALS)   https://www.nalscheme.co.uk/
National Landlords Association   http://www.landlords.org.uk/
Residential Landlords Association   http://www.rla.org.uk/
Royal Institution of Chartered Surveyors   http://www.rics.org/uk/
UK Association of Letting Agents   http://www.ukala.org.uk/

Local and national accreditation schemes
There are many different local and national accreditation schemes that may also be run by:
Universities or student unions
Local councils   https://www.gov.uk/find-your-local-council
Unipol: the student housing charity   https://www.unipol.org.uk/
The Property Ombudsman   https://www.tpos.co.uk/
The Property Redress Scheme   https://www.theprs.co.uk/
The Ombudsman Services   http://www.ombudsman-services.org/
UK Government: House in Multiple Occupation (HMO) Licence
https://www.gov.uk/house-in-multiple-occupation-licence
UK Government: The Housing, Health and Safety Rating System (HHSRS)
https://www.gov.uk/government/publications/housing-health-and-safety-rating-system-guidance-for-landlords-and-property-related-professionals
UK government: Deposit Protections Scheme
https://www.gov.uk/deposit-protection-schemes-and-landlords/overview

Additional housing information
Television licensing   http://www.tvlicensing.co.uk/
UK Government: Housing Benefit https://www.gov.uk/housing-benefit/further-information
National Union of Students (NUS)   http://www.nus.org.uk
Citizens Advice Bureaux   http://www.adviceguide.org.uk
Shelter   http://www.shelter.org.uk/
Shelter England: http://england.shelter.org.uk/
Shelter Wales: http://www.sheltercymru.org.uk/
Shelter Northern Ireland   http://www.shelterni.org/
Shelter Scotland: http://scotland.shelter.org.uk/
Find an Estate Agent:
National Association of Estate Agents   http://www.naea.co.uk/
Housing Benefit
UK Government:
Apply Housing Benefit from Council https://www.gov.uk/apply-housing-benefit-from-council

Studying Abroad
Links to overseas countries with information including passports, visa requirements and travel advice may be found on
UK Government: World   https://www.gov.uk/government/world
British Council: Study Abroad
https://www.britishcouncil.org/study-work-create/opportunity/study-abroad
British Council: Funding Studies
https://www.britishcouncil.org/study-work-create/practicalities/funding-studies
NHS Travel Vaccinations   https://www.nhs.uk/conditions/travel-vaccinations/

Useful Study Abroad Websites

The following websites may also be useful:

Study Abroad http://www.studyabroad.com/

Prospects: Graduate Careers https://www.prospects.ac.uk/postgraduate-study/study-abroad

Prospects has study information on a range of different countries

The UK Council for International Affairs (UKCISA) http://www.ukcisa.org.uk/

HE Global Integrated Advisory Service http://heglobal.international.ac.uk/home.aspx

Education Systems and Qualifications in Other Countries

European Network of Information Centres (ENIC) and the National Academic Recognition Information Centres (NARIC) ENIC-NARIC http://www.enic-naric.net/

Europa: EU Regulated Professions Database

http://ec.europa.eu/growth/tools-databases/regprof/index.cfm?action=homepage

EU national contact points for professional qualifications

http://ec.europa.eu/growth/single-market/services/free-movement-professionals/#contacts

General Medical Council (GMC) http://www.gmc-uk.org

General Dental Council http://www.gdc-uk.org

Royal College of Veterinary Surgeons (RCVS) http://www.rcvs.org.uk/

Studying in a Commonwealth Country

Commonwealth Scholarship Commission in the UK website

http://cscuk.dfid.gov.uk/apply/scholarships-uk-citizens/

Commonwealth Scholarship Commission in the UK http://cscuk.dfid.gov.uk/

Studying in Australia

Australia Government Awards: International Postgraduate Research Scholarships (IPRS)

http://education.gov.au/international-postgraduate-research-scholarships

Australian Government International Education Awards: Endeavour Scholarship and Fellowship https://internationaleducation.gov.au/Pages/default.aspx

Study in Australia https://www.studyinaustralia.gov.au/

Studying in Canada

Alberta, Apply Alberta https://www.applyalberta.ca/

Association of Commonwealth Universities https://www.acu.ac.uk/

British Columbia, Apply Education Planner BC https://apply.educationplannerbc.ca/;

Further information may be found at:

Canadian Government: Edu Canada http://educanada.ca/

Canadian Government Scholarships:

Scholarships-Bourses http://www.scholarships-bourses.gc.ca/

Canada Immigration and Citizenship http://www.cic.gc.ca/

Canadian Information Centre for International Credits https://www.cicic.ca/

Ontario, Ontario Universities Application Centre (OUAC) https://www.ouac.on.ca/

Quebec, Service Regional d'admission au

Collegial de Quebec (SRACQ) https://www.sracq.qc.ca/

Scholarship Canada http://www.scholarshipscanada.com/

Service Regional d'admission du Montreal Metropolitan (SRAM) https://www.sram.qc.ca/

Service Regional de la admission des cegepes du

Saguenay-Lac-Saint-Jean (SRASL) https://www.srasl.qc.ca/

Study in Canada http://www.studyincanada.com/

University Canada http://www.university-canada.net/

You Tube: Education Canada Channel Study in Canada http://www.studyincanada.com/

Studying in New Zealand

Further information may be found at

Education New Zealand · http://www.education-newzealand.org/

New Zealand Education · https://www.studyinnewzealand.govt.nz/

New Zealand International Doctoral Research Scholarship (NZIDRS)
https://enz.govt.nz/support/funding/scholarships/new-zealand-international-doctoral-research-scholarships/

Study in New Zealand · https://www.studyinnewzealand.govt.nz/

The Association of Commonwealth Universities https://www.acu.ac.uk/

The New Zealand International Doctoral Research Scholarship (NZIDRS)
https://enz.govt.nz/support/funding/scholarships/new-zealand-international-doctoral-research-scholarships/

Universities New Zealand · http://www.universitiesnz.ac.nz/ and

Studying in Europe

Europa: European Union
http://europa.eu/youreurope/citizens/education/university/index_en.htm

Study in Europe · http://www.studyineurope.eu/

Studying in Austria

Study in Austria · http://www.studyinaustria.at/

Studying in Belgium

Study in Belgium · http://www.studyinbelgium.be/en

Studying in Denmark

Study in Denmark · http://studyindenmark.dk/

Studying in Finland

Study in Finland · http://www.studyinfinland.fi/

Studying in France

Studying in France · http://www.studying-in-france.org/

And Campus France · http://www.campusfrance.org/en/

Studying in Germany

Studying in Germany · http://www.studying-in-germany.org/

Studying in Iceland

Study in Iceland · http://www.studyiniceland.is/

Studying in Ireland

Education Ireland · http://www.educationinireland.com/en/

Studying in Italy

Study in Italy · http://www.study-in-italy.it/

Studying in the Netherlands

Study in Holland · http://www.studyinholland.co.uk/

Studying in Norway

Study in Norway · http://www.studyinnorway.no/

Studying in Sweden

Study in Sweden · https://studyinsweden.se/

Erasmus Programme

Erasmus Programme · http://www.erasmusprogramme.com/

British Council · https://www.britishcouncil.org/

British Council, Erasmus website
https://www.britishcouncil.org/study-work-create/opportunity/study-abroad/erasmus

Erasmus study abroad placement · https://www.erasmusplus.org.uk/study-abroad

Erasmus work placement abroad · https://www.erasmusplus.org.uk/work-abroad

562

Studying in the United States of America

Education USA	https://www.educationusa.info/
Studying in the US	http://www.studying-in-us.org/
The US-UK Fulbright Commission	http://www.fulbright.org.uk/
USA government: study in US	https://www.usa.gov/study-in-us

Studying outside of the EU and USA

Studying in Brazil
Study in Brazil   http://studyinbrazil.com.br/en/

Studying in China
British Council: Study Abroad China
https://www.britishcouncil.org/study-work-create/opportunity/study-abroad/china
China Scholarship Council   http://www.csc.edu.cn/studyinchina/
Campus China   http://www.campuschina.org/

Studying in Hong Kong
Hong Kong   http://studyinhongkong.edu.hk/en/

Studying in Japan
Study in Japan   http://www.studyjapan.go.jp/en/
Gateway to study in Japan   http://www.g-studyinjapan.jasso.go.jp/en/
The Japan Society for the Promotion of Science (JSPS) Postdoctoral Fellowship Programme
http://www.britac.ac.uk/jsps-postdoctoral-fellowship-programme-overseas-researchers
British Academy's electronic Grant Application and
Processing (eGAP) system   https://egap.britac.ac.uk/Login.aspx
Daiwa Anglo-Japanese Foundation   http://www.dajf.org.uk/
Daiwa Anglo-Japanese Foundation http://www.dajf.org.uk/scholarships/daiwa-scholarship
Daiwa Anglo-Japanese Foundation http://www.dajf.org.uk/scholarships/japanese-studies

Studying in South Africa
South Africa: Universities   http://www.southafrica.info/about/education/universities.htm

Studying Worldwide Funding Schemes and Scholarships
BUTEX list of members   http://www.butex.ac.uk/members/list-of-members/
BUTEX   http://www.butex.ac.uk/scholarships/are-you-eligible/
Federation Internationale des Societes d'Ingenieurs des Techniques de L'Automobile
(FISITA)   http://www.fisita.com/yfia/academia-industry/travelbursary
International Association for the exchange of Students for
Technical Experience (IASTE)   https://iaeste.org/
IAESTE   http://www.iaeste.org/students/
Leverhulme Trust   https://www.leverhulme.ac.uk/
Leverhulme Trust: Studentships
https://www.leverhulme.ac.uk/funding/grant-schemes/study-abroad-studentships
National Commission for UNESCO of the candidate's country
http://www.unesco.org/new/en/fellowships/programmes/how-to-apply/
Santander
http://www.santander.co.uk/uk/santander-universities/about-us/our-partner-universities

Printed in Great Britain
by Amazon

79213310R00337